# Microsoft®
# Windows XP
# UNLEASHED

**Paul McFedries**

 800 East 96th Street, Indianapolis, Indiana 46240

# Microsoft Windows XP Unleashed

International Standard Book Number: 0-672-32833-X

Library of Congress Catalog Card Number: 2005928896

Printed in the United States of America

First Printing: September 2005

08   07   06   05          4   3   2   1

## Trademarks

All terms mentioned in this book that are known to be trademarks or service marks have been appropriately capitalized. Sams Publishing cannot attest to the accuracy of this information. Use of a term in this book should not be regarded as affecting the validity of any trademark or service mark.

## Warning and Disclaimer

Every effort has been made to make this book as complete and as accurate as possible, but no warranty or fitness is implied. The information provided is on an "as is" basis. The author and the publisher shall have neither liability nor responsibility to any person or entity with respect to any loss or damages arising from the information contained in this book.

## Bulk Sales

Sams Publishing offers excellent discounts on this book when ordered in quantity for bulk purchases or special sales. For more information, please contact

**U.S. Corporate and Government Sales**
**1-800-382-3419**
**corpsales@pearsontechgroup.com**

For sales outside of the U.S., please contact

**International Sales**
**international@pearsoned.com**

**Publisher**
Paul Boger

**Acquisitions Editor**
Loretta Yates

**Development Editor**
Songlin Qiu

**Managing Editor**
Charlotte Clapp

**Project Editor**
Andy Beaster

**Copy Editor**
Mike Henry

**Indexer**
Heather McNeill

**Proofreader**
Juli Cook

**Technical Editor**
Greg Perry

**Publishing Coordinator**
Cindy Teeters

**Interior Designer**
Gary Adair

**Cover Designer**
Alan Clements

**Page Layout**
Toi Davis

# Contents at a Glance

# Table of Contents

# About the Author

**Paul McFedries** is a computer consultant, programmer, and freelance writer. He has worked with computers in one form or another since 1975, he has a degree in mathematics, and he can swap out a hard drive in seconds flat, yet still, inexplicably, he has a life. He is the author or coauthor of more than forty computer books that have sold over three million copies worldwide. His recent titles include the Que Publishing books *Formulas and Functions with Microsoft Excel 2003*, *Tricks of the Microsoft Office Gurus*, and *Microsoft Access 2003 Forms, Reports, and Queries*.

# Dedication

*To my wife (yes!), Karen*

# Acknowledgments, Kudos, Plaudits, and Assorted Pats on the Back

Being an author is the most wonderful vocation (I don't think of it as a job) I can imagine. I get to play with words, I get to talk about things I'm intensely interested in, and I get some big-time warm, fuzzy feelings when people write to me to tell me that, in some small way, something I've written has helped them.

However, just because my name is the only one that appears on the cover, don't think that this book is solely my creation. Any book, but especially a project as massive as this one, is the result of the efforts of many hard-working people. The Sams editorial staff, in particular, never fails to impress me with its dedication, work ethic, and commitment to quality. You'll find a list of all the people who worked on this book near the front, but there are a few I'd like to thank personally: Acquisitions Editor Loretta Yates, Development Editor Songlin Qiu, Project Editor Andy Beaster, Copy Editor Mike Henry, and Technical Editor Greg Perry.

# We Want to Hear from You!

As the reader of this book, *you* are our most important critic and commentator. We value your opinion and want to know what we're doing right, what we could do better, what areas you'd like to see us publish in, and any other words of wisdom you're willing to pass our way.

As a publisher for Sams, I welcome your comments. You can email or write me directly to let me know what you did or didn't like about this book—as well as what we can do to make our books better.

*Please note that I cannot help you with technical problems related to the topic of this book. We do have a User Services group, however, where I will forward specific technical questions related to the book.*

When you write, please be sure to include this book's title and author as well as your name, email address, and phone number. I will carefully review your comments and share them with the author and editors who worked on the book.

**Email:**   feedback@samspublishing.com

**Mail:**   Paul Boger
Publisher
Sams
800 East 96th Street
Indianapolis, IN 46240 USA

For more information about this book or another Sams title, visit our website at www.samspublishing.com. Type the ISBN (excluding hyphens) or the title of a book in the Search field to find the page you're looking for.

# Introduction

*We shall not cease from exploration*

*And the end of all our exploring*

*Will be to arrive where we started*

*And know the place for the first time.*

*—T. S. Eliot*

My goal in writing *Microsoft Windows XP Unleashed, Second Edition* is to cover the good, the bad, and, yes, even the ugly of Windows XP. In particular, I give you complete coverage of the intermediate-to-advanced features of Windows XP. This means that I bypass basic topics, such as wielding the mouse, in favor of more complex operations, such as working with the Registry, maintaining and troubleshooting your system, networking, and getting around the Internet.

I've tried to keep the chapters focused on the topic at hand and unburdened with long-winded theoretical discussions. However, there are plenty of situations in which you won't be able to unleash the full power of Windows XP and truly understand what's going on unless you have a solid base on which to stand. In these cases, I'll give you whatever theory and background you need to get up to speed. From there, I'll get right down to brass tacks without any further fuss and bother.

## Who Should Read This Book

To keep the chapters uncluttered, I've made a few assumptions about what you know and what you don't know:

- I assume that you have knowledge of rudimentary computer concepts such as files and folders.

- I assume that you're familiar with the basic Windows skills: mouse maneuvering, dialog box negotiation, pull-down menu jockeying, and so on.

- I assume that you can operate peripherals attached to your computer, such as the keyboard and printer.

- I assume that you've used Windows for a while and are comfortable with concepts such as toolbars, scrollbars, and, of course, windows.

- I assume that you have a brain that you're willing to use and a good supply of innate curiosity.

# How This Book Is Organized

To help you find the information you need, this book is divided into seven parts that group related tasks. The next few sections offer a summary of each part.

## Part I: Unleashing Day-to-Day Windows XP

Part I examines your basic workaday Windows chores and reveals their inner mysteries, allowing you to become more productive. Topics include the myriad ways to get Windows XP off the ground (Chapter 1), how to use Windows XP to work with files and folders (Chapter 2), getting the most out of file types (Chapter 3), dealing with digital media (Chapter 4), installing and running applications (Chapter 5), and working with user accounts (Chapter 6).

## Part II: Unleashing Essential Windows XP Power Tools

The chapters in Part II get your advanced Windows XP education off to a flying start by covering the ins and outs of five important Windows XP power tools: Control Panel, group policies, and Tweak UI (Chapter 7), the Registry (Chapter 8), and the Windows Script Host (Chapter 9).

## Part III: Unleashing Windows XP Customization and Optimization

In Part III you dive into the deep end of advanced Windows work: customizing the interface (Chapter 10), performance tuning (Chapter 11), maintaining Windows XP (Chapter 12), troubleshooting problems (Chapter 13), and working with devices (Chapter 14).

## Part IV: Unleashing Windows XP Modem Communications

Part IV takes a good, hard look at the modem and shows you the theory behind modem communications (Chapter 15) and Windows XP features—such as Phone Dialer, HyperTerminal, Microsoft Fax, and NetMeeting—that use the modem (Chapter 16).

## Part V: Unleashing Windows XP for the Internet

Part V shows you how to work with Windows XP's Internet features. You start by getting the details behind TCP/IP, the language of the Internet (Chapter 17). From there, you learn how to get the most out of a number of Internet services, including the World Wide Web (Chapter 18), email (Chapter 19), and newsgroups (Chapter 20). This part ends with an extensive look at the Internet security and privacy features that come with Windows XP (Chapter 21).

## Part VI: Unleashing Windows XP Networking

To close out the main part of this book, Part VI takes an in-depth look at Windows XP's networking features. You learn some useful networking theory, how to set up a small network, and how to administer that network (all in Chapter 22), how to access your network from remote locations (Chapter 23), and how to troubleshoot network problems (Chapter 24).

## Part VII: Appendixes

To further your Windows XP education, Part VII presents a few appendixes that contain extra goodies. You'll find a complete list of Windows XP shortcut keys (Appendix A), a detailed look at using the Windows XP Command Prompt (Appendix B), a batch file primer (Appendix C), and a glossary of terms (Appendix D).

# Conventions Used in This Book

To make your life easier, this book includes various features and conventions that help you get the most out of this book and Windows XP itself:

| | |
|---|---|
| Steps | Throughout the book, I've broken many Windows XP tasks into easy-to-follow step-by-step procedures. |
| Things you type | Whenever I suggest that you type something, what you type appears in a **bold monospace** font. |
| Filenames, folder names, and code | These things appear in a `monospace` font. |
| Commands | Commands and their syntax use the `monospace` font as well. Command placeholders (which stand for what you actually type) appear in an *`italic monospace`* font. |
| Pull-down menu commands | I use the following style for all application menu commands—*Menu, Command*, where *Menu* is the name of the menu that you pull down and *Command* is the name of the command you select. Here's an example: File, Open. This means that you pull down the File menu and select the Open command. |
| Code continuation character | When a line of code is too long to fit on only one line of this book, it is broken at a convenient place and continued to the next line. The continuation of the line is preceded by a code continuation character (➥). You should type a line of code that has this character as one long line without breaking it. |

This book also uses the following boxes to draw your attention to important (or merely interesting) information:

---
**NOTE**

The Note box presents asides that give you more information about the current topic. These tidbits provide extra insights that give you a better understanding of the task at hand. In many cases, they refer you to other sections of the book for more information.

---

**TIP**

The Tip box tells you about Windows XP methods that are easier, faster, or more efficient than the standard methods.

**CAUTION**

The all-important Caution box tells you about potential accidents waiting to happen. There are always ways to mess things up when you're working with computers. These boxes help you avoid at least some of the pitfalls.

# PART I

# Unleashing Day-to-Day Windows XP

## IN THIS PART

# CHAPTER 1

# Customizing and Troubleshooting the Windows XP Startup

Assuming that you have Windows XP is safely installed on your computer, you can begin your journey, appropriately enough, at the beginning: the startup process. At first blush, this might seem like a surprising topic for an entire chapter. After all, the Windows XP startup procedure gives new meaning to the term no-brainer: You turn on your system, and a short while later, Windows XP reports for duty. What's to write about?

You'd be surprised. The progress of a typical boot appears uneventful only because Windows XP uses a whole host of default options for startup. By changing these defaults, you can take control of the startup process and make Windows XP start your way. This chapter takes you through the entire startup process, from go to whoa, and shows you the options you can use to customize it.

## The Boot Process, from Power Up to Startup

To better help you understand your Windows XP startup options, let's take a closer look at what happens each time you fire up your machine. Although a computer performs dozens of actions during the boot process, most of them appeal only to wireheads and other hardware hackers. (A **wirehead** is, broadly speaking, an expert in the hardware aspects of PCs.) For our purposes, we can reduce the entire journey to the following 12-step program:

1. When you flip the switch on your computer (or press the Restart button, if the machine is already

running), the system performs various hardware checks. The system's microprocessor executes the ROM BIOS code, which, among other things, performs the Power-On Self Test (POST). The POST detects and tests memory, ports, and basic devices such as the video adapter, keyboard, and disk drives. (You hear your floppy disk motors kick in briefly and the drive lights come on.) If the system has a Plug and Play BIOS, the BIOS also enumerates and tests the PnP-compliant devices in the system. If the POST goes well, you hear a single beep.

2. Now the BIOS code locates the **Master Boot Record (MBR)**, which is the first 512-byte sector on your system's hard disk. The MBR consists of a small program (the boot code) that locates and runs the core operating system files, as well as a partition table that contains data about the various partitions on your system. At this point, the BIOS code gives way to the MBR's boot code.

3. The boot code looks for a boot sector on drive A (the drive light illuminates once more). If a bootable disk is in the drive, the system will boot to the A:\ prompt; if a nonbootable disk is in the drive, the boot code displays the following message:

```
Non-system disk or disk error
Replace and press any key when ready
```

If no disk is in the drive, most modern systems will then check for a bootable disc in the CD-ROM or DVD-ROM drive. If there's still no joy, the boot code turns its attention to the hard disk and uses the partition table to find the active (that is, bootable) partition and its boot sector (the first sector in the partition).

> **NOTE**
>
> This explains why the Windows XP Automated System Recovery (ASR) floppy disk lets you regain control of your system in the event of a hard-drive crash. The BIOS first looks for a bootable disk in drive A. If it finds one, it bypasses the hard drive altogether. In Chapter 13, "Troubleshooting and Recovering from Problems," see "Recovering Using Automated System Recovery" for more about the ASR disk.

4. With the boot sector located, the MBR code runs the boot sector as a program. The Windows XP boot sector runs a program called NTLDR.

> **NOTE**
>
> Your system's bootable partition (usually drive C) might contain a file named BOOTSECT.DOS. This is a copy of the boot sector that's compatible with DOS, Windows 9x, and Windows Me. You'll see a bit later that Windows XP uses this copy to enable you to boot to your old operating system if you didn't upgrade it to Windows XP.

5. NTLDR switches from **real mode** (a single-tasking mode in which the processor can access only the first 640KB of memory) to **protected mode** (a multitasking mode in which the processor can access all memory locations).

6. NTLDR reads the BOOT.INI file and displays the OS Choices menu (assuming that your system can boot to two or more operating systems; see "Custom Startups with BOOT.INI," next). Note, too, that at this point you can invoke the Advanced Options Menu for custom startups; see "Custom Startups with the Advanced Options Menu," later in this chapter.

7. NTLDR runs NTDETECT.COM, which queries the BIOS for information about the system hardware, including the system buses, the disk drives, the ports, and more. This data is passed back to NTLDR, which eventually stores the data in the Windows XP Registry (in the HKEY_LOCAL_MACHINE\HARDWARE key).

> **NOTE**
>
> I mention the Windows XP Registry in several places throughout this chapter. If you're not familiar with the Registry, please see Chapter 8, "Getting to Know the Windows XP Registry."

8. The Starting Windows message and the progress bar appear. The progress bar tracks the loading of the device drivers that XP needs at startup. The bar advances each time a driver is loaded.

9. NTLDR loads the Windows kernel—NTOSKRNL.EXE—which handles the loading of the rest of the operating system.

10. The kernel launches the Session Manager—SMSS.EXE—which initializes the system environment variables and starts the Windows logon process by running WINLOGON.EXE.

11. Windows XP Professional displays the Press Ctrl-Alt-Delete prompt and then prompts you for a password. If your system has multiple user accounts, Windows XP Home Edition will display the Welcome screen to prompt you to pick a user.

12. New Plug and Play devices are detected and the contents of the Run Registry key and the Startup folder are processed.

Windows XP also provides several routes for personalizing your startup:

- Invoke the Windows XP Startup menu when the POST is complete
- Edit the BOOT.INI file to change the default startup options
- Add programs or documents to the Windows XP Run Registry key
- Add programs or documents to the Windows XP Startup folder

The next few sections cover these techniques.

## Custom Startups with BOOT.INI

If your system can boot to one or more operating systems other than Windows XP, you'll see a menu similar to the following during startup:

```
Please select the operating system to start:

    Microsoft Windows XP Professional
    Microsoft Windows

Use the up and down arrow keys to move the highlight to your choice.
Press ENTER to choose.
Seconds until highlighted choice will be started automatically: 30
```

If you do nothing at this point, Windows XP will boot automatically after 30 seconds. Otherwise, you highlight the operating system you want and then press Enter to boot it. The specifics of this menu are determined by a hidden text file named BOOT.INI, which resides in the root folder of your system's bootable partition (usually drive C).

Before you work with this file, you need to turn off the read-only attribute via the following steps:

1. Use My Computer to open C:\.

2. If you see a screen that says These files are hidden, click the Show the Contents of This Folder link to see the files.

> **TIP**
>
> If you don't see BOOT.INI, Windows XP probably isn't set up to show hidden files. To fix that, select Tools, Folder Options. In the Folder Options dialog box, display the View tab, deactivate the Hide Protected Operating System files check box, and then click Yes when XP asks you to confirm. You also need to activate the Show Hidden Files and Folders option, and then click OK.

3. Right-click BOOT.INI and then click Properties. The file's property sheet appears.

4. Deactivate the Read-Only check box.

5. Click OK.

Double-click the BOOT.INI icon to open the file. (Alternatively, select Start, Run, type **c:\boot.ini** and click OK.) Windows XP loads the file into Notepad and you see text similar to the following:

```
[boot loader]
timeout=30
default=multi(0)disk(0)rdisk(0)partition(1)\WINDOWS
[operating systems]
multi(0)disk(0)rdisk(0)partition(1)\WINDOWS="Microsoft Windows XP Professional"
➥/fastdetect
C:\="Microsoft Windows"
```

There are two sections in BOOT.INI: [boot loader] and [operating systems]. The [boot loader] section always has two values:

| | |
|---|---|
| timeout | This value determines the number of seconds after which NTLDR will boot the operating system that's highlighted in the menu by default. |
| default | This value determines which item listed in the [operating systems] section is highlighted in the menu by default at startup. |

The [operating systems] section lists the operating system to which the system can boot. The first line is almost always a reference to Windows XP, and subsequent lines reference the other bootable operating systems. The Windows XP line has a strange configuration, to say the least. The part up to the equal sign (=) is called an Advanced RISC Computer (ARC) pathname, and its purpose is to let NTLDR know how to find the kernel (NTOSKRNL.EXE). This syntax is also used to reference Windows NT and Windows 2000 operating systems.

Let's run through the various parts so that you understand what you're seeing:

| | |
|---|---|
| multi(n) | This is a reference to the drive controller that's used to access the Windows XP installation. The value n is 0 for the first controller, 1 for the second, and so on. On systems that use a SCSI controller, you might see scsi(n) instead of multi(n) (the exception is on systems that have the SCSI BIOS disabled). |
| disk(n) | This is a reference to the SCSI ID of the device on which Windows XP is installed. For multi devices, the value of n is always 0. |
| rdisk(n) | This is a reference to the hard disk on which Windows XP is installed. This disk is attached to the controller specified by multi(n). The value of n is 0 for the first hard disk, 1 for the second hard disk, and so on. |
| partition(n) | This is a reference to the partition on which Windows XP is installed. This partition is part of the disk specified by rdisk(n). |
| WINDOWS | This is the name of the folder into which Windows XP was installed. |
| Microsoft Windows XP Professional | This is the text that appears on the menu. |
| /fastdetect | The entry closes with one or more switches that determine how the operating system boots. See "Using the BOOT.INI Switches," later in this chapter. |

## Changing the Default Startup Operating System

To change which operating system is chosen by default at startup, you need to modify the default value in the [boot loader] section. To do that, find the operating system in the [operating systems] section, copy all the text to the left of the equal sign, and then paste it as the new default value. For example, suppose that the [operating systems] section includes the following entry:

```
C:\="Microsoft Windows"
```

In that case, you'd copy just the C:\ text and use that as the new default value:

```
default=C:\
```

If you always want your system to boot immediately to Windows XP and bypass the BOOT.INI menu, you have two choices:

- Change the timeout value to 0
- Delete all other operating systems listed in the [operating systems] section

## Using the BOOT.INI Switches

The ARC pathname syntax supports more than 30 different switches that enable you to control various aspects of the Windows XP startup. Here's a summary of the switches that are most useful:

| | |
|---|---|
| /3GB | Configures Windows XP to allocate 3GB of virtual memory to User mode processes (programs) and 1GB to Kernel mode (system) processes. (Normally, Windows XP allocates 2GB to each mode.) Use this switch if you have one or more programs that can take advantage of the extra virtual memory. To fine-tune the amount of virtual memory allocated to programs, see the /userva switch. |
| /basevideo | Boots XP using the standard VGA mode: 640×480 with 256 colors. This is useful for troubleshooting video display driver problems. Use this switch if Windows XP fails to start using any of the safe mode options, if you recently installed a new video card device driver and the screen is garbled or the driver is balking at a resolution or color depth setting that's too high, or if you can't load the Windows XP GUI. After Windows XP has loaded, you can reinstall or roll back the driver, or you can adjust the display settings to values that the driver can handle. |
| /bootlog | Boots XP and logs the boot process to a text file named NTBTLOG.TXT that resides in the %SystemRoot% folder. Move to the end of the file and you might see a message telling you which device driver failed. You probably need to reinstall or roll back the driver. Use this switch if the Windows XP startup hangs, if you need a detailed record of the startup process, or if you suspect (after using one of the other Startup menu options) that a driver is causing Windows XP startup to fail. |

**NOTE**

%SystemRoot% refers to the folder into which Windows XP was installed. This is usually either C:\WINNT or C:\WINDOWS.

| | |
|---|---|
| /burnmemory=*MB* | Specifies the amount of physical memory that Windows XP cannot use. For example, if you set this value to 256, the memory available to Windows XP is reduced by 256MB. Use this switch to simulate a low-RAM situation if you suspect that RAM depletion is causing problems. |
| /debug | Enables remote debugging of the Windows XP kernel. This sends debugging information to a remote computer via one of your computer's serial ports. If you use this switch, you can specify the serial port by also using the \debugport=*port* switch, where *port* is one of com1, com2, com3, com4, or 1394. If you use a COM port, you can specify the transmission speed of the debugging information by also using the \baudrate=*speed* switch, where *speed* is one of the following: 300, 1200, 2400, 4800, 9600, 19200, 38400, 57600, or 115200. If you use an IEEE 1394 (FireWire) connection, you can also add the /channel=*number* switch, where *number* is a channel value between 1 and 62. |
| /fastdetect | Tells Windows XP to not enumerate the system's serial and parallel ports during startup. These ports aren't needed during the boot process, so this reduces the system startup time. |
| /maxmem=*MB* | Specifies the maximum amount of memory, in megabytes, that Windows XP can use. Use this value when you suspect a faulty memory chip might be causing problems. |
| /noexecute=*level* (Service Pack 2 only) | Sets the Data Execution Prevention (DEP) policy level. DEP prevents malicious code from executing in protected memory locations. There are four levels: |

- OptIn—Windows system programs are protected by DEP, as well as any applications that have been programmed to take advantage of (opt into) DEP protection.

- OptOut—Provides DEP protection for the entire system, except for programs that have been specified to not use (opt out of) DEP.

|  |  |
|---|---|
|  | • `AlwaysOn`—Provides DEP protection for the entire system. |
|  | • `AlwaysOff`—Provides no DEP protection for the system. |
| `/noguiboot` | Tells Windows XP not to load the VGA display driver that is normally used to display the progress bar during startup. Use this switch if Windows XP hangs while switching video modes for the progress bar, or if the display of the progress bar is garbled. |
| `/numproc=n` | In a multiprocessor system, specifies the maximum of processors that Windows XP can use. Use this switch if you suspect that using multiple processors is causing a program to hang. |
| `/pcilock` | Tells Windows XP not to dynamically assign hardware resources for PCI devices during startup. The resources assigned by the BIOS during the POST are locked in place. Use this switch if installing a PCI device causes the system to hang during startup. |
| `/safeboot:minimal` | Boots Windows XP in **safe mode**, which uses only a minimal set of device drivers. Use this switch if Windows XP won't start, if a device or program is causing Windows XP to crash, or if you can't uninstall a program while Windows XP is running normally. |
| `/safeboot:minimal(alternateshell)` | Boots Windows XP in safe mode but also bypasses the Windows XP GUI and boots to the command prompt instead. Use this switch if the programs you need to repair a problem can be run from the command prompt or if you can't load the Windows XP GUI. |

**NOTE**

The shell loaded by the `/safeboot:minimal(alternateshell)` switch is determined by the value in the following Registry key:

`HKEY_LOCAL_MACHINE\SYSTEM\CurrentControlSet\SafeBoot\AlternateShell`

The default value is `CMD.EXE` (the command prompt).

|  |  |
|---|---|
| `/safeboot:network` | Boots Windows XP in safe mode but also includes networking drivers. Use this switch if the drivers or programs you need to repair a problem exist on a shared network resource, if you need access to email or other network-based communications for technical support, or |

|  |  |
|---|---|
|  | if your computer is running a shared Windows XP installation. |
| /safeboot:dsrepair | Boots Windows XP in safe mode and also restores a backup of the Active Directory directory service (this option applies only to domain controllers). |
| /sos | Displays the path and location of each device driver (using the ARC pathname syntax) as it is loaded, as well as the operating system version and build number and the number of processors. |
| /userva=*MB* | Specifies the amount of virtual memory allocated to programs when you also include the /3GB switch. Set the value to a number between 2,048 (2GB) and 3,072 (3GB). The difference between the value you specify and 3GB is allocated to the Kernel mode. |

## Using the System Configuration Editor to Modify BOOT.INI

Rather than edit the BOOT.INI file directly, you can modify the file indirectly by using the System Configuration Editor. To start this program, select File, Run, type **msconfig** in the Run dialog box, and then click OK. When the System Configuration Window appears, select the BOOT.INI tab, shown in Figure 1.1.

**NOTE**

To change any options in the System Configuration Utility, you must be logged on to Windows XP with Administrator-level permissions.

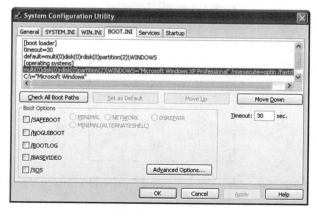

**FIGURE 1.1**   In the System Configuration Utility, use the BOOT.INI tab to modify the BOOT.INI startup file.

The large box near the top of the tab displays the current BOOT.INI text. You can't edit this text directly, however. All you can do is highlight one of the items in the [operating systems] section and then click one of the following buttons:

| | |
|---|---|
| Check All Boot Paths | Click this button to check the paths of each operating system to ensure they're valid. |
| Set as Default | Click this button to set the highlighted operating system as the default for the BOOT.INI menu. |
| Move Up | Click this button to move the highlighted operating system higher in the menu. |
| Move Down | Click this button to move the highlighted operating system lower in the menu. |

You can also use the Timeout text box to adjust the timeout value of BOOT.INI.

Use the check boxes in the Boot Options group to set the switches used with the currently highlighted operating system (assuming that operating system is Windows XP, 2000, or NT). You can add other switches (such as /maxmem and /debug) by clicking the Advanced Options button, which takes you to the BOOT.INI Advanced Options dialog box shown in Figure 1.2.

---

**TIP**

If you modify BOOT.INI using the System Configuration Utility, Windows XP maintains a copy of the original BOOT.INI. If you want to revert to that copy, display the General tab in the System Configuration Utility and activate the Use Original BOOT.INI option. If you need to use the edited version of BOOT.INI again, activate the Use Modified BOOT.INI option instead.

---

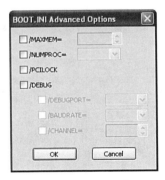

**FIGURE 1.2**    In the BOOT.INI tab, click Advanced Options to display the dialog box shown here.

# Custom Startups with the Advanced Options Menu

When the BOOT.INI menu appears at startup, you see the following message at the bottom of the screen:

```
For troubleshooting and advanced startup options for Windows, press F8.
```

This message remains on the screen while the progress bar that tracks the loading of startup devices is displayed. If you press F8, you get to the Advanced Options menu, which looks like this:

---

**TIP**

If your system doesn't automatically display the OS Choices menu at startup, you can display it manually. After you start your computer, wait until the POST is complete, and then press F8 to display the OS Choices menu. If your computer is set up to "fast boot," it might not be obvious when the POST ends. In that case, just turn on your computer and press F8 repeatedly until you see the OS Choices menu. Note, however, that if your system picks up two separate F8 presses, you might end up directly in the Advanced Options menu.

---

```
Microsoft Advanced Options Menu
Please select an option:

    Safe Mode
    Safe Mode with Networking
    Safe Mode with Command Prompt

    Enable Boot Logging
    Enable VGA Mode
    Last Known Good Configuration (your most recent settings that worked)
    Directory Services Restore Mode (Windows domain controllers only)
    Debugging Mode
    Disable automatic restart on system failure

    Boot Normally
    Reboot
    Return to OS Choices Menu

Use the up and down arrow keys to move the highlight to your choice.
```

The Boot Normally option loads Windows XP in the usual fashion. You can use the other options to control the rest of the startup procedure:

Safe Mode                          If you're having trouble with Windows XP—for example, if a corrupt or incorrect video driver is mangling your display, or if Windows XP won't start—you can use the Safe Mode option to run a stripped-down version of Windows XP that includes only the minimal set of device drivers that XP requires to load. You could reinstall or roll back the offending device driver and then load XP normally. When Windows XP finally loads, the desktop reminds you that you're in safe mode by displaying `Safe Mode` in each corner. (Also, the Help and Support Center appears with the Safe Mode Troubleshooter loaded.) Choosing the Safe Mode option is the same as using the following `BOOT.INI` switches:

```
/safeboot:minimal /bootlog /noguiboot /sos
```

> **NOTE**
>
> If you're curious to know which drivers are loaded during a safe mode boot, see the subkeys in the following Registry key:
>
> `HKEY_LOCAL_MACHINE\SYSTEM\CurrentControlSet\Control\SafeBoot\Minimal\`

| | |
|---|---|
| Safe Mode with Networking | This option is identical to plain safe mode, except that Windows XP's networking drivers are also loaded at startup. This enables you to log on to your network, which is handy if you need to access the network to load a device driver, run a troubleshooting utility, or send a tech support request. Choosing this option is the same as using the following `BOOT.INI` switches:<br><br>`/safeboot:network /bootlog /noguiboot /sos` |
| Safe Mode with Command Prompt | This option is the same as plain safe mode, except that it doesn't load the Windows XP GUI. Instead, it runs `CMD.EXE` to load a command prompt session. Choosing this option is the same as using the following `BOOT.INI` switches:<br><br>`/safeboot:minimal(alternateshell) /bootlog /noguiboot /sos` |
| Enable Boot Logging | This option is the same as the Boot Normally option, except that Windows XP logs the boot process in a text file named `NTBTLOG.TXT` that resides in the system root. Choosing this option is the same as using the following `BOOT.INI` switch:<br><br>`/bootlog` |
| Enable VGA Mode | This option loads Windows XP with the video display set to 640×480 and 256 colors. Choosing this option is the same as using the following `BOOT.INI` switch:<br><br>`/basevideo` |

| | |
|---|---|
| Last Known Good Configuration | This option boots Windows XP using the last hardware configuration that produced a successful boot. |
| Directory Services Restore Mode | This option is the same as using the following BOOT.INI switch:<br><br>`/safeboot:dsrepair` |
| Debugging Mode | This option is the same as using the following BOOT.INI switch:<br><br>`/debug` |
| Disable Automatic Restart on System Failure | This option (which is new with Service Pack 2) prevents Windows XP from restarting automatically when the system crashes. Choose this option if you want to prevent your system from restarting so that you can troubleshoot the problem. |
| Boot Normally | This options loads Windows XP normally. |
| Reboot | This option reboots the computer. |
| Return to OS Choices Menu | This option displays the BOOT.INI menu. |

> **TIP**
>
> For those advanced options that have equivalent BOOT.INI switches, you can use those switches to place individual advanced options on the OS Choices menu. You do this by adding an item to BOOT.INI's [operating systems] section that starts Windows XP with the appropriate switches. For example, to add an option to the OS Choices menu to start Windows XP in safe mode, you'd add the following to BOOT.INI's [operating systems] section:
>
> ```
> multi(0)disk(0)rdisk(0)partition(1)\WINDOWS="Safe Mode"
> ➥/safeboot:minimal /bootlog /noguiboot /sos
> ```

For more information about these options, see the section titled "When to Use the Various Advanced Startup Options," later in this chapter.

## Useful Windows XP Logon Strategies

When you install Windows XP, the setup program asks you to enter usernames for one or more people who will be accessing the computer. How you initially log on to Windows XP depends on what you did at that point of the install:

- If you entered only a single username and your computer is not part of a network domain, Windows XP logs on that username automatically.

- If you entered multiple usernames and your computer is not part of a domain, Windows XP displays the Welcome screen, which lists the users (Figure 1.3 shows an example). Click the username that you want to log on.

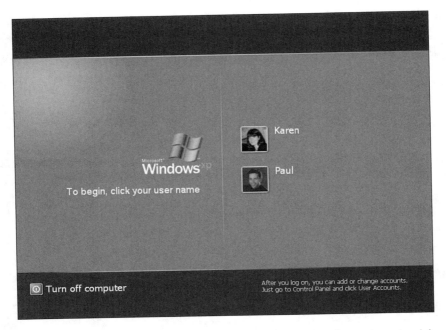

**FIGURE 1.3**    You see the Windows XP Welcome screen if your workgroup or standalone computer is set up with multiple users.

- If your computer is part of a domain, Windows XP first displays the Welcome to Windows dialog box, which prompts you to press Ctrl+Alt+Delete. When you do that, you see the Log On to Windows dialog box, shown in Figure 1.4. (Windows XP refers to this process as the *Classic* logon.) Change the username, if necessary, enter the password, and click OK.

**FIGURE 1.4**    You see the Log On to Windows dialog box if your computer is part of a network domain.

## Customizing the Logon

The default logon is fine for most users, but there are many ways to change Windows XP's logon behavior. The rest of this section looks at a few tips and techniques for altering the way you log on to Windows XP.

### Switching Between the Welcome Screen and the Classic Logon

Many people prefer the Classic Windows XP logon because the initial step of pressing Ctrl+Alt+Delete adds an extra level of security. It prevents automatic logons and it thwarts any malicious program—such as a password-stealing program—that might have been activated at startup. If your computer uses the Welcome screen logon, you switch to the Classic logon by using any of the following techniques:

- Launch the Control Panel's User Accounts icon, click Change the Way Users Log On or Off, and then deactivate the Use Welcome Screen check box.

- In the Group Policy editor (see Chapter 7, "Using Control Panel, Group Policies, and Tweak UI"), open Computer Configuration, Administrative Templates, System, Logon, and then enable the Always Use Classic Logon policy.

- In the Registry (see Chapter 8), set the following value to 1 (reset this to 0 to revert to the Welcome screen):

    HKLM\Software\Microsoft\Windows NT\CurrentVersion\Winlogon\LogonType

> **CAUTION**
>
> If your computer is part of a domain, you can't change the logon from the Classic method to the Welcome screen.

### Accessing the Administrator Account

Another chore you performed during the Windows XP setup routine was to specify an Administrator password. One of the confusing aspects about Windows XP is that, after the setup is complete, the Administrator account seems to disappear. The secret is that Administrator is actually a hidden account that appears only in a limited set of circumstances, such as when you boot Windows XP in Safe mode or when there are no other administrative-level accounts defined on your system. Outside of these scenarios, there are several ways to log on to Windows XP using the Administrator account:

- If you're using the Welcome screen, press Ctrl+Alt+Delete twice.

- If you're using the classic logon, type **Administrator** in the User Name text box.

- Set up an automatic logon using the Administrator (see the next section).

- Tweak Windows XP to make the Administrator account visible in the Welcome screen. To do this, open the Registry Editor and navigate to the following key:

    HKLM\Software\Microsoft\Windows NT\CurrentVersion\Winlogon\
    ➥SpecialAccounts\UserList

Add a new `DWORD` value named `Administrator` and set its value to 1. (To hide Administrator in the Welcome screen, set this value to `0`.)

---

**TIP**

The `UserList` Registry key is also useful for hiding accounts. If you have a user account defined but you don't want other users to see that name in the Welcome screen, add a `DWORD` value to the `UserList` key, give it the same name as the user, and set its value to `0`. You can access this account using the same methods that I outlined in this section for the Administrator account.

---

### Setting Up an Automatic Logon

If you're using a standalone computer that no one else has access to (or that will be used by people you trust), you can save some time at startup by not having to type a username and password. In this scenario, the easiest way to do this is to set up Windows XP with just a single user account, which means Windows XP will log on that user automatically at startup. If you have multiple user accounts (for testing purposes, for example) or if you want the Administrator account to be logged on automatically, you need to set up Windows XP for automatic logons.

---

**CAUTION**

Setting up an automatic logon is generally not a good idea for notebook computers because they're easily lost or stolen. By leaving the logon prompt in place, the person who finds or steals your notebook will at least be unlikely to get past the logon, so your data won't be compromised.

---

If you have Tweak UI (see Chapter 7), open the Logon, Autologon setting and activate the Log On Automatically at System Startup check box. Type the username and click Set Password to enter the account password. When you click OK, Tweak UI makes some changes in the following Registry key:

`HKLM\Software\Microsoft\Windows NT\CurrentVersion\Winlogon\`

The `AutoAdminLogon` value is set to 1, your username appears in the `DefaultUserName` setting, and your password appears in the `DefaultPassword` setting. Note that your password appears as plain text, so anyone can read it or even change it.

---

**TIP**

You can temporarily suspend the automatic logon by holding down the Shift key while Windows XP starts up.

---

If you only want the automatic logon to occur a set number of times, open the following Registry key:

`HKLM\Software\Microsoft\Windows NT\CurrentVersion\Winlogon\`

Create a new string setting named `AutoLogonCount` and set its value to the number of times you want the automatic logon to occur. With each logon, Windows XP decrements this setting until it reaches zero, at which point Windows XP sets `AutoAdminLogon` to `0` to disable the automatic logon.

## Setting Logon Policies

Windows XP Professional defines a number of security policies related to the logon process. (See Chapter 7 to learn how to use Windows XP's policy editors.) You can get to these policies in two ways:

- In the Group Policy editor, select Computer Configuration, Windows Settings, Security Settings, Local Policies, Security Options.

- In the Local Security Settings editor, select Security Settings, Local Policies, Security Options.

Most of the logon options are listed in the Interactive Logon grouping. Here's a list of the most useful options (note that all of these options apply to the Classic logon):

Do Not Display Last User Name
Enable this option to clear the User Name text box each time the Log On to Windows dialog box appears. Although it adds a bit of inconvenience to the logon, this is a good security feature because it denies an intruder an important piece of information: a legitimate system username. This policy modifies the following Registry key (0 = disable; 1 = enable):

```
HKLM\Software\Microsoft\Windows\
CurrentVersion\policies\system\
dontdisplaylastusername
```

Do Not Require CTRL+ALT+DEL
Enable this policy to bypass the initial Welcome to Windows dialog box (the one that prompts you to press Ctrl+Alt+Delete) and go directly to the Log On to Windows dialog box. This can save you a startup step, but it decreases the security of the logon. The main concern here is that your system might get infected with a virus or Trojan horse program that displays a fake Log On to Windows dialog box as a ruse to capture your username and password. If you decide to enable this policy, make sure that you have a good anti-virus program and that you use it often. This policy modifies the following Registry key (0 = disable; 1 = enable):

```
HKLM\Software\Microsoft\Windows\
CurrentVersion\policies\system\
DisableCAD
```

| | |
|---|---|
| Message Text for User Attempting to Log On | Use this option to specify a text message that appears in a dialog box after any user presses Ctrl+Alt+Delete (but before the Log On to Windows dialog box appears). This policy modifies the following Registry setting:<br><br>`HKLM\Software\Microsoft\Windows\CurrentVersion\`<br>`policies\system\legalnoticetext` |
| Message Title for Users Attempting to Log On | Use this option to set the title of the dialog box that contains the message to the user that you specified in the previous setting. This policy modifies the following Registry setting:<br><br>`HKLM\Software\Microsoft\Windows\CurrentVersion\`<br>`policies\system\legalnoticecaption` |
| Number of Previous Logons to Cache (In Case Domain Controller Is Not Available) | Use this option to set the number of previous domain logons (username, password, and domain) that Windows XP will retain.<br>By retaining a logon, Windows XP enables that user to log on to Windows XP even if a domain controller isn't present (for example, on a notebook that isn't always connected to the network at startup). This policy modifies the following Registry setting:<br><br>`HKLM\Software\Microsoft\Windows NT\`<br>`CurrentVersion\Winlogon\cachedlogonscount` |
| Prompt User to Change Password Before Expiration | Use this option to set the number of days before which a user's password expires that a warning message to that effect is displayed. (I'll show you how to set an expiration date for a password later in this chapter.) This policy modifies the following Registry setting:<br><br>`HKLM\Software\Microsoft\Windows NT\`<br>`CurrentVersion\Winlogon\passwordexpirywarning` |

## More Logon Registry Tweaks

As you saw in the previous section, the logon security policies are stored in the Registry. Windows XP has a number of other Registry-related logon settings that you'll learn about in this section:

- Controlling the Shift Key Override of an Automatic Logon—Use the following string value to determine whether the user can override an automatic logon by holding down the Shift key during startup ($0$ = enable Shift override; $1$ = disable Shift override):

```
HKLM\Software\Microsoft\Windows NT\CurrentVersion\Winlogon\
IgnoreShiftOverride
```

- Forcing an Automatic Logon—This is similar to overriding the Shift key at startup. That is, the following string setting determines whether the user can bypass an automatic logon (0 = bypass possible; 1 = bypass not possible):

```
HKLM\Software\Microsoft\Windows NT\CurrentVersion\Winlogon\
ForceAutoLogon
```

- Disabling Logon Options—The Log On to Windows dialog box (Classic logon) has an Options button that toggles on and off the Log On To list, the Log On Using Dial-Up Connection check box, and the Shut Down button. Use the following DWORD value to control whether these options appear (0 = disable; 1 = enable):

```
HKLM\Software\Microsoft\Windows NT\CurrentVersion\Winlogon\
ShowLogonOptions
```

- Adding Text to the Logon Dialog Box—Specify text in the following string setting to display a message in the Log On to Windows dialog box above the User Name text box:

```
HKLM\Software\Microsoft\Windows NT\CurrentVersion\Winlogon\
LogonPrompt
```

- Disabling the Dial-Up Logon—If you don't want users to attempt a dial-up connection to log on, use the following string setting to disable the Log On Using Dial-Up Connection check box in the Log On to Windows dialog box (0 = disable; 1 = enable):

```
HKLM\Software\Microsoft\Windows NT\CurrentVersion\Winlogon\
RASDisable
```

# Troubleshooting Windows XP Startup

Computers are often frustrating beasts, but few things in computerdom are as hair-pullingly, teeth-gnashingly frustrating as an operating system that won't operate. To help save some wear and tear on your hair and teeth, this section outlines a few common startup difficulties and their solutions.

## When to Use the Various Advanced Startup Options

You saw earlier that Windows XP has some useful options on its Advanced Options menu. But under what circumstances should you use each option? Well, because there is some overlap in what each option brings to the table, there are no hard and fast rules. It is possible, however, to lay down some general guidelines.

You should use the Safe Mode option if one of the following conditions occurs:

- Windows XP doesn't start after the POST ends.

- Windows XP seems to stall for an extended period.

- Windows XP doesn't work correctly or produces unexpected results.

- You can't print to a local printer.

- Your video display is distorted and possibly unreadable.

- Your computer stalls repeatedly.

- Your computer suddenly slows down.

- You need to test an intermittent error condition.

You should use the Safe Mode with Networking option if one of the following situations occurs:

- Windows XP fails to start using any of the other safe mode options.

- The drivers or programs you need to repair a problem exist on a shared network resource.

- You need access to email or other network-based communications for technical support.

- Your computer is running a shared Windows XP installation.

You should use the Safe Mode with Command Prompt option if one of the following situations occurs:

- Windows XP fails to start using any of the other safe mode options.

- The programs you need to repair a problem can be run from the command prompt.

- You can't load the Windows XP GUI.

You should use the Enable Boot Logging option in the following situations:

- The Windows XP startup hangs after switching to Protected mode.

- You need a detailed record of the startup process.

- You suspect (after using one of the other Startup menu options) that a protected-mode driver is causing Windows XP startup to fail.

After starting (or attempting to start) Windows XP with this option, you end up with a file named NTBTLOG.TXT in the %SystemRoot% folder. This is a text file, so you can examine it with any text editor. For example, you could boot to the command prompt (using the Save Mode with Command Prompt option) and then use EDIT.COM to examine the file.

Move to the end of the file and you might see a message telling you which device driver failed. You probably need to reinstall or roll back the driver.

You should use the Enable VGA Mode option in the following situations:

- Windows XP fails to start using any of the safe mode options.

- You recently installed a new video card device driver and the screen is garbled or the driver is balking at a resolution or color depth setting that's too high.

- You can't load the Windows XP GUI.

After Windows XP has loaded, you can either reinstall or roll back the driver, or you can adjust the display settings to values that the driver can handle.

Use the Last Known Good Configuration option under the following circumstances:

- You suspect the problem is hardware-related, but you can't figure out the driver that's causing the problem.

- You don't have time to try out the other more detailed inspections.

The Directory Services Restore Mode option is only for domain controllers, so you should never need to use it.

Use the Debugging Mode option if you receive a stop error during startup and a remote technical support professional has asked you to send debugging data.

## What to Do If Windows XP Won't Start in Safe Mode

If Windows XP is so intractable that it won't even start in Safe mode, your system is likely afflicted with one of the following problems:

- Your system is infected with a virus. You need to run an anti-virus program to cleanse your system.

- Your system has incorrect CMOS settings. Run the machine's CMOS setup program to see whether any of these settings needs to be changed or whether the CMOS battery needs to be replaced.

- Your system has a hardware conflict. See Chapter 14, "Getting the Most Out of Device Manager," for hardware troubleshooting procedures.

- There is a problem with a SCSI device. In this case, your system may hang during the SCSI BIOS initialization process. Try removing devices from the SCSI chain until your system starts normally.

## Troubleshooting Startup Using the System Configuration Utility

If Windows XP won't start, troubleshooting the problem usually involves trying various advanced startup options. It's almost always a time-consuming and tedious business.

However, what if Windows XP *will* start, but you encounter problems along the way? Or what if you want to try a few different configurations to see whether you can eliminate startup items or improve Windows XP's overall performance? For these scenarios, don't bother trying out different startup configurations by hand. Instead, take advantage of Windows XP's System Configuration Utility which, as you saw earlier in this chapter, gives you a graphical front-end that offers precise control over how Windows XP starts.

Launch the System Configuration Utility (select Start, Run, type **msconfig**, and click OK) and display the General tab, which has three startup options:

> **NOTE**
>
> Remember that the System Configuration Utility requires Administrator-level permissions.

| | |
|---|---|
| Normal Startup | This option loads Windows XP normally. |
| Diagnostic Startup | This option loads only those device drivers and system services that are necessary for XP to boot. This is equivalent to deactivating all the check boxes associated with the Selective Startup option, discussed next. |
| Selective Startup | When you activate this option, the check boxes below become available, as shown in Figure 1.5. Use these check boxes to select which portions of the startup should be processed. |

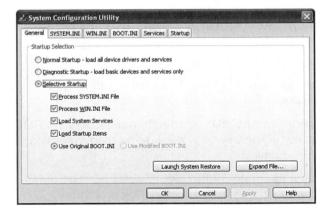

**FIGURE 1.5**    Use the System Configuration Utility to select different startup configurations.

For a selective startup, you control how Windows XP processes items using four categories:

| | |
|---|---|
| Process SYSTEM.INI File | This file contains system-specific information about your computer's hardware and device drivers. Most hardware data is stored in the Registry, but SYSTEM.INI retains a few settings that are needed for backward compatibility with older (16-bit) programs. The specific items loaded by SYSTEM.INI are listed in the SYSTEM.INI tab. |
| Process WIN.INI File | This file contains configuration settings relating to Windows XP and to installed Windows applications. Again, the bulk of this data is stored in the Registry, but WIN.INI is kept around for compatibility. The specific items loaded by WIN.INI are listed in the WIN.INI tab. |
| Load System Services | This category refers to the system services that Windows XP loads at startup. The specific services loaded by Windows XP are listed in the Services tab. |

**NOTE**

If you're coming to Windows XP from the consumer Windows world (Windows 9x or Me), this might be the first you've heard of services. Put simply, a **service** is a program or process that performs a specific, low-level support function for the operating system or for an installed program. For example, Windows XP's Automatic Updates feature is a service.

**NOTE**

The Services tab has an Essential column. Only those services that have Yes in this column are loaded when you choose the Selective Startup option.

| | |
|---|---|
| Load Startup Items | This category refers to the items in your Windows XP Startup group and to the startup items listed in the Registry. For the latter, the settings are stored in one of the following keys: |

```
HKEY_CURRENT_USER\SOFTWARE\Microsoft\
Windows\CurrentVersion\Run
HKEY_LOCAL_MACHINE\SOFTWARE\Microsoft\
Windows\CurrentVersion\Run
```

The specific items loaded from the Startup group or the Registry are listed in the Startup tab.

To control these startup items, the System Configuration utility gives you two choices:

- To prevent Windows XP from loading every item in a particular category, activate Selective Startup in the General tab and then deactivate the check box for the category you want. For example, to disable all items in WIN.INI, deactivate the Process WIN.INI File check box.

- To prevent Windows XP from loading only specific items in a category, display the category's tab and then deactivate the check box beside the item or items you want to bypass at startup.

Here's a basic procedure you can follow to use the System Configuration Utility to troubleshoot a startup problem (assuming that you can start Windows XP by using some kind of safe mode boot, as described earlier):

1. In the System Configuration Utility, activate the Diagnostic Startup option and then reboot the computer. If the problem did not occur during the restart, you know the cause lies in SYSTEM.INI, WIN.INI, the system services, or the startup items.

2. Activate the Selective Startup option.

3. Activate one of the four check boxes and then reboot the computer.

4. Repeat step 3 for each of the other check boxes until the problem reoccurs. When this happens, then you know that whatever item you activated just before rebooting is the source of the problem.

5. Display the tab of the item that is causing the problem. For example, if the problem reoccurred after you activated the Load Startup Items check box, display the Startup tab.

6. Click Disable All to clear all the check boxes.

7. Activate one of the check boxes to enable an item and then reboot the computer.

8. Repeat step 7 for each of the other check boxes until the problem reoccurs. When this happens, you know that whatever item you activated just before rebooting is the source of the problem.

---

**Troubleshooting by Halves**

If you have a large number of check boxes to test (such as in the Services tab), activating one check box at a time and rebooting can become very tedious very fast. A faster method is to begin by activating the first half of the check boxes and reboot. One of two things will happen:

- The problem doesn't reoccur—This means that one of the items represented by the deactivated check boxes is the culprit. Clear all the check boxes, activate half of the other check boxes, and then reboot.
- The problem reoccurs—This means that one of the activated check boxes is the problem. Activate only half of those check boxes and reboot.

Keep halving the number of activated check boxes until you isolate the offending item.

---

9. In the System Configuration Utility's General tab, activate the Normal Startup option.

10. Fix or work around the problem:

- If the problem is an item in SYSTEM.INI or WIN.INI, display the appropriate tab, highlight the problem item, and then click Disable.

---

**TIP**

Another way to edit SYSTEM.INI or WIN.INI is by using the System Configuration Editor. To load this program, select Start, Run, type **sysedit** in the Run dialog box, and then click OK.

---

- If the problem is a system service, you can disable the service. In Control Panel, open Administrative Tools and then Services. Double-click the problematic service to open its property sheet. In the Startup Type list, select Disabled and then click OK.

- If the problem is a Startup item, either delete the item from the Startup group or delete the item from the appropriate Run key in the Registry. If the item is a program, consider uninstalling or reinstalling the program.

### What to Do If Windows XP Still Won't Start

If Windows XP won't start no matter what you try, you're not out of luck just yet. You still have another couple of things to try:

| | |
|---|---|
| System Restore | This feature enables you to restore your system to a previous (and, presumably, operational) setup. To learn how to use System Restore, see the section in Chapter 13 titled "Recovering Using System Restore." |
| Automated System Recovery | This feature (which is available only with Windows XP Professional) enables you to boot to a floppy disk and then restore your entire system from a backup copy. For the details, see the section in Chapter 13 titled "Recovering Using Automated System Recovery." |

# From Here

Here are some other places in the book where you'll find information related to startup:

- In Chapter 5, see the section titled "Launching Applications and Scripts at Startup."

- In Chapter 6, see the section titled "Requiring Ctrl+Alt+Delete at Startup."

- In Chapter 11, see the section titled "Optimizing Startup."

- In Chapter 13, see the section titled "Booting Using the Last Known Good Configuration."

# Exploring Expert File and Folder Techniques

Whether you're looking to master Windows XP or just get your work done quickly and efficiently, a thorough knowledge of the techniques available for working with files and folders is essential. Or perhaps I should say that a thorough knowledge of **certain** techniques is essential. That's because, like the rest of Windows XP, Windows Explorer (the file management accessory) offers a handful of methods for accomplishing most tasks. Not all of these techniques are particularly efficient, however. Therefore, my goal in this chapter is to not only tell you **how** to do file management chores, but also to tell you the **best** ways to do those chores.

## Basic File and Folder Chores: The Techniques Used by the Pros

The most efficient way to work with Windows Explorer is to display the Folders explorer bar. However, if you simply click the Start menu's My Computer icon, the window that appears displays the Task Pane, instead, as shown in Figure 2.1.

The Task Pane is designed for novice users, so your first chore should be to replace it with the Folders explorer bar. You do that by clicking the Folders button in the toolbar (or by selecting View, Explorer Bar, Folders). Figure 2.2 shows Windows Explorer with the Folders explorer bar displayed.

Task Pane

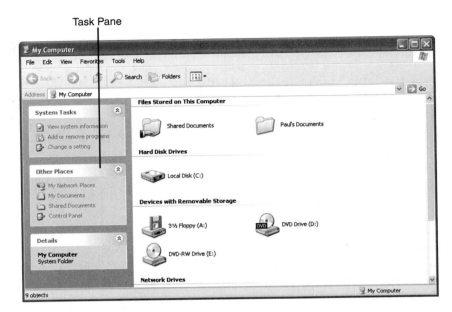

**FIGURE 2.1**    Windows Explorer displays the novice-oriented Task Pane by default.

Folders explorer bar                    Contents list

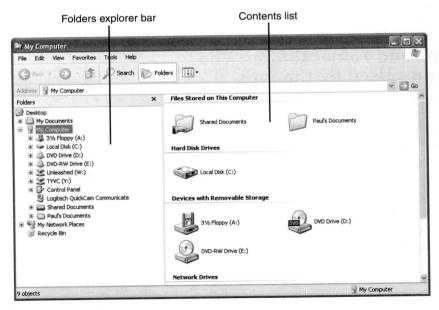

**FIGURE 2.2**    Windows Explorer with the Folders explorer bar displayed instead of the Task Pane.

With Windows Explorer ready for action, it's time to put it through a workout. The next few sections take you through a few basic file and folder chores: selecting, moving and copying, and renaming.

## Selecting Files and Folders

Before you can do anything in Windows Explorer—whether it's copying a file, renaming a folder, or deleting a shortcut—you have to **select** the object or objects you want to work with. For simplicity's sake, I use the generic term **object** to refer to any file or folder.

### Selecting a Single Object

Selecting a single object with the mouse is straightforward: click the object's name.

From the keyboard, follow this two-step procedure:

1. Pressing Tab cycles you through the Folders bar, the Contents list (which displays the files and other objects that reside in the currently selected folder), the Address bar, and the Folders bar's Close button. Therefore, press Tab to move the highlight into the area you want.

2. Use the Up Arrow and Down Arrow keys to move the highlight to the object you want to select.

Here are some notes to keep in mind when using the keyboard to select an object in the Contents list:

- If the Contents list shows objects displayed in two or more columns, use the left and right arrow keys to move between columns.

- If the current folder contains a large number of items, use the Page Up and Page Down keys to jump through the list quickly.

- Press the Home key to select the first object in the list; press the End key to select the last object in the list.

- If you press a letter, Windows Explorer will jump down to the first object that has a name that begins with that letter. Press that letter again to move to the next object that begins with the letter.

### Selecting Multiple Objects

To select two or more objects, click the first object, and then hold down Ctrl and click the rest of the objects. If the objects are contiguous, click the first object, and then hold down Shift and click the last object.

From the keyboard, use the following techniques:

- To select objects individually, use the navigation keys (the arrow keys, Page Up and Page Down, and so on) to select the first object. Now hold down the Ctrl key. For each of the other objects you want to select, use the navigation keys to move the selector to the object, and then press the spacebar.

- To select multiple contiguous objects, use the navigation keys to select the first object, hold down the Shift key, and then use the navigation keys to select the last object.

- To select every object in the current folder, run the Edit, Select All command, or press Ctrl+A.

- To reverse the current selection—that is, to deselect everything that's currently highlighted and to select everything that's not currently highlighted—run the Edit, Invert Selection command.

---

**Understanding Size on Disk**

The Windows Explorer status bar shows you how many objects you've selected and the total size of the selected objects. However, it doesn't take into account any objects that might be inside a selected subfolder. To allow for subfolders, right-click the selection and then click Properties. Windows XP counts all the files, calculates the total size as well as the total size on the disk, and then displays this data in the property sheet that appears.

What's the difference between the Size and Size on Disk values? Windows XP stores files in discrete chunks of hard disk space called **clusters**, which have a fixed size. This size depends on the file system and the size of the partition, but 4KB is typical. The important thing to remember is that Windows XP always uses full clusters to store all or part of a file. Suppose, for example, that you have two files, one that's 2KB and another that's 5KB. The 2KB file will be stored in an entire 4KB cluster. For the 5KB file, the first 4KB of the file will take up a whole cluster, and the remaining 1KB will be stored in its own 4KB cluster. So, the total size of these files is 7KB, but they take up 12KB on the hard disk.

---

## Making Sense of Windows XP's Rules for Moving and Copying

If you've used Windows before, you know that you can move text from one part of a document to another by cutting it and then pasting it in the new location. Windows also brings this cut-and-paste metaphor to file and folder copying and moving:

- If you want to copy an object, select it and then run the Edit, Copy command, or press Ctrl+C. If you want to move an object instead, select it and then run Edit, Cut, or press Ctrl+X.

- To perform the move or copy, go to the destination folder and then select Edit, Paste, or press Ctrl+V.

---

**TIP**

A quick way to make a backup copy of a file or folder is to highlight it, press Ctrl+C, and then Ctrl+V. This makes a copy of the object with `Copy of` appended to the filename in the same location as the original file.

---

An alternative—and often faster—method for moving and copying objects is to drag and drop them. This means that you use your mouse to drag the object to a specific destination and then drop it there.

You can use this drag-and-drop technique to move or copy files. Unfortunately, Windows XP uses a fairly arcane set of rules for how this works:

- If you drag an object to a destination on the **same** drive, Windows XP will move the object.

- If you drag an object to a destination on a **different** drive, Windows XP will copy the object. While you're dragging, the mouse pointer sprouts a small plus sign (+) as a visual indicator that you're copying the object.

- If you drag an executable file, Windows XP will create a shortcut for the object. While you're dragging, the mouse pointer displays a small arrow to indicate that you're creating a shortcut for the object.

To work around the last rule, and to avoid trying to remember the first two rules, use the following techniques:

| | |
|---|---|
| To move an object | Hold down the Shift key while you drag-and-drop. |
| To copy an object | Hold down the Ctrl key while you drag-and-drop. |
| Right-drag an object | **Right-drag** means that you drag the object while holding down the *right* mouse button. In this case, when you drop the object Windows XP displays a shortcut menu similar to the one shown in Figure 2.3. Click the command you want to run. |

> **TIP**
>
> If you have one of those awkward notebook pointing devices, or if your right mouse button doesn't work, you can simulate a right-drag by holding down both Ctrl and Shift while you drag-and-drop using the left mouse button.

## Choosing "No to All" When Copying or Moving

When you copy or move a file, if the destination folder has a file with the same name as a file in the original folder, the Confirm File Replace dialog box appears and asks whether you want to replace the file in the destination folder with the one being copied or moved. If you're moving multiple files and there are multiple potential file replacements in the destination folder, the dialog box will have a Yes to All button that you can click to avoid being prompted about each file. That's fine if you want to replace every file, but what if you don't want to replace any files? Rather than clicking No for each prompt, hold down Shift and click No. This tells Explorer not to replace any files, so it's the next best thing to having a No to All button.

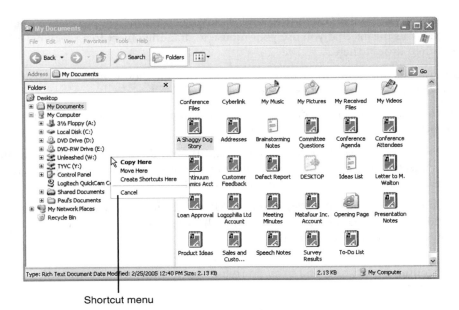

Shortcut menu

**FIGURE 2.3**    When you right-drag an object and then drop it, Windows XP displays this shortcut menu.

## Expert Drag-and-Drop Techniques

You'll use the drag-and-drop technique throughout your Windows career. To make drag and drop even easier and more powerful, here are a few pointers to bear in mind:

| | |
|---|---|
| Lassoing multiple files | If the objects you want to select are displayed in a block within the Contents list, you can select them by dragging a box around the objects, as shown in Figure 2.4. This is known as **lassoing** the objects. |
| Drag-and-scroll | Most drag-and-drop operations involve dragging an object from the Contents list and dropping it on a folder in the Folders bar. If you can't see the destination in the Folders bar, drag the pointer to the bottom of the Folders bar. Windows Explorer will scroll the list up. To scroll the list down, drag the object to the top of the Folders bar. |
| Drag-and-open | If the destination is a subfolder within an unopened folder branch, drag the object and hover the pointer over the unopened folder. After a second or two, Windows Explorer opens the folder branch. |
| Inter-window dragging | You can drag an object outside of the window and then drop it on a different location, such as the desktop. |

You can't drop an object on a running program's taskbar icon, but you can do the next best thing. Drag the mouse over the appropriate taskbar button and wait a second or two. Windows will then bring that application's window to the foreground, and you can then drop the object within the window.

Drag between Explorers

Windows XP lets you open two or more copies of Windows Explorer. If you have to use several drag-and-drop operations to get some objects to a particular destination, open a second copy of Windows Explorer and display the destination in this new window. You can then drag from the first window and drop into the second window.

Canceling drag-and-drop

To cancel a drag-and-drop operation, either press Esc or click the right mouse button. If you're right-dragging, click the left mouse button to cancel.

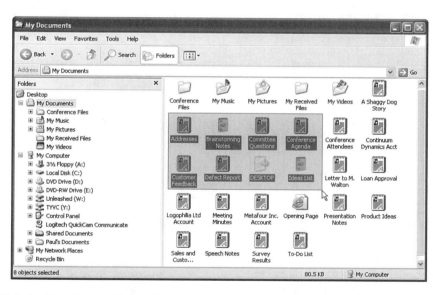

**FIGURE 2.4**    To select multiple objects, drag a box around the objects to lasso them.

## Taking Advantage of the Send To Command

For certain destinations, Windows XP offers an easier method for copying or moving files or folders: the Send To command. To use this command, select the objects you want to work with and then run one of the following techniques:

- Select File, Send To

- Right-click the selection and then click Send To in the shortcut menu

Either way, you see a submenu of potential destinations, as shown in Figure 2.5. Note that the items in this menu are taken from the %USERPROFILE%\SendTo folder that contains shortcut files for each item. This means that you can customize the Send To menu by adding, renaming, and deleting the shortcut files in your SendTo folder.

---

**NOTE**

The user profile folder for a user is the following:

    C:\Documents and Settings\User

Here, User is the person's username. Windows XP stores the user profile folder for the current user in the %USERPROFILE% environment variable.

---

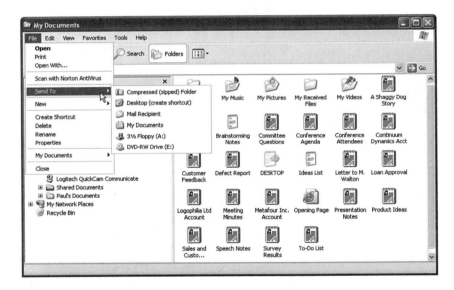

**FIGURE 2.5**    The Send To command offers a menu of possible destinations.

Click the destination you want and Windows XP will send the object there. What do I mean by **send**? I suppose **drop** would be a better word because the Send To command acts like the drop part of drag-and-drop. Therefore, Send To follows the same rules as drag-and-drop:

- If the Send To destination is on a different disk drive, the object is copied.

- If the Send To destination is on the same disk drive, the object is moved.

> **TIP**
>
> As with a drag-and-drop operation, you can force the Send To command to copy or move an object. To force a move, hold down Shift when you select the Send To command. To force a copy, hold down Ctrl when you select the Send To command.

## The Recycle Bin: Deleting and Recovering Files and Folders

In my conversations with Windows users, I've noticed an interesting trend that has become more prominent in recent years: People don't delete files as often as they used to. I'm sure that the reason for this is the absolutely huge hard disks that are offered these days. Even entry-level systems come equipped with double-digit gigabyte (10GB and up) disks, and hard disks with capacities of more than 100GB are no longer a big deal. Unless someone's working with digital video files, even a power user isn't going to put a dent in these massive disks any time soon. So, why bother deleting anything?

Although it's always a good idea to remove files and folders you don't need (it makes your system easier to navigate, it speeds up defragmenting, and so on), avoiding deletions does have one advantage: You can never delete something important by accident.

Just in case you do, however, Windows XP's Recycle Bin can bail you out. The Recycle Bin icon on the Windows XP desktop is actually a front-end for a collection of hidden folders named Recycled that exist on each hard disk partition. The idea is that when you delete a file or folder, Windows XP doesn't actually remove the object from your system. Instead, the object is just moved to the Recycled folder on the same drive. If you delete an object by accident, you can go to the Recycle Bin and return the object to its original spot. Note, however, that the Recycle Bin can hold only so much data. When it gets full, it permanently deletes its oldest objects to make room for newer ones.

> **TIP**
>
> If you're absolutely sure that you don't need an object, you can permanently delete it from your system (that is, bypass the Recycle Bin) by highlighting it and pressing Shift+Delete.

It's important to note that Windows XP bypasses the Recycle Bin and permanently deletes an object under the following circumstances:

- You delete the object from a floppy disk or any removable drive.
- You delete the object from the DOS prompt.
- You delete the object from a network drive.

### Setting Some Recycle Bin Options

The Recycle Bin has a few properties you can set to control how it works. To view these properties, right-click the desktop's Recycle Bin icon and then click Properties. Windows XP displays the property sheet shown in Figure 2.6.

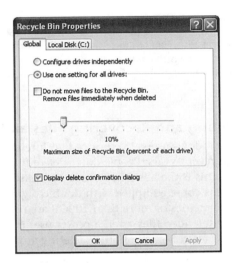

**FIGURE 2.6**   Use this property sheet to configure the Recycle Bin to your liking.

Here's a rundown of the various controls:

Configure Drives Independently

By default, the Recycle Bin uses the same settings on all your partitions (drives). To set up separate configurations for each partition, activate this option and then click the other tabs to configure the partitions.

Use One Setting for All Drives

This is the default setting for the Recycle Bin. It means that, for the next two controls, the configuration that you select is used for all your drives.

Do Not Move Files to the Recycle Bin. Remove Files Immediately When Deleted—If you activate this option, all deletions are permanent.

Maximum Size of Recycle Bin (Percent of Each Drive)—Use this slider to set the maximum size of the Recycle Bin, as a percentage of the total capacity of the drive. The higher the percentage, the more deleted files the Recycle Bin can hold, but the less disk space you'll have available. Unless you work with very large files, a maximum size of 3%–5% is more than adequate.

**TIP**

You can clean out your Recycle Bin at any time by right-clicking the desktop's Recycle Bin icon and then clicking Empty Recycle Bin. The Recycle Bin contents can also be purged using Windows XP's Disk Cleanup utility.

| Display Delete Confirmation Dialog | If you don't want Windows XP to ask for confirmation when you delete an object, deactivate this check box. |
|---|---|

Click OK to put the new settings into effect.

### Recovering a File or Folder

If you accidentally delete the wrong file or folder, you can return it to its rightful place by using the following method:

1. Open the desktop's Recycle Bin icon, or open any Recycled folder in Windows Explorer.

2. Select the object.

3. Select File, Restore. (You can also right-click the file and then click Restore.)

> **NOTE**
>
> If deleting the file or folder was the last action you performed in Windows Explorer, you can recover the object by selecting the Edit, Undo Delete command. Note, too, that Windows XP enables you to undo the 10 most recent actions.

## File Maintenance Using the Open and Save As Dialog Boxes

One of the best-kept secrets of Windows XP is the fact that you can perform many of these file maintenance operations within two of Windows XP's standard dialog boxes:

| Open | In most applications, you display this dialog box by selecting the File, Open command, or by pressing Ctrl+O. |
|---|---|
| Save As | You usually display this dialog box by selecting File, Save As. Or, if you're working with a new, unsaved file, by selecting File, Save, or by pressing Ctrl+S. |

There are three techniques you can use within these dialog boxes:

- To perform maintenance on a particular file or folder, right-click the object to display a shortcut menu like the one shown in Figure 2.7.

- To create a new object, right-click an empty section of the file list, and then click New to get the New menu.

- To create a new folder within the current folder, click the Create New Folder button.

Create New Folder

**FIGURE 2.7**    You can perform most basic file and folder maintenance from the Open and Save As dialog boxes.

# Powerful Search Techniques for Finding Files

I mentioned earlier that hard disks are getting huge, so people don't delete as much as they used to. Another consequence of these large disk capacities is that users don't move files to archival storage as much as they used to. Why bother when a multigigabyte drive can store tens of thousands of files? Keeping the file on disk is much more convenient, but **only** if you can find the file you want, and there's the rub.

Fortunately, Windows XP comes with a revamped Search utility that offers some reasonably powerful search options for tracking down files. Here's how to get started:

- To search within a specific folder, open the folder in Windows Explorer, and then click the Search toolbar button, or press Ctrl+E. (You can also select View, Explorer Bar, Search.)

- Select Start, Search.

---

**TIP**

If you have a keyboard with the Windows logo key, you can start Search by pressing Windows logo key+F (for *find*). Also, if you're in Windows Explorer or if you click the desktop, you can start Search by pressing F3.

---

## Reconfiguring the Search Behavior

The Search feature is set up initially with the Search Companion, a user-friendly front-end designed to appeal to novices. Depending on your level of experience with computers and your capacity to handle cute, animated characters, your opinion of the Search Companion probably runs from mild annoyance to outright loathing. In any case, the Search Companion is certainly inefficient, so it has to go. Follow these steps to change Windows XP's Search behavior:

1. Click the Change Preferences link.

2. Click Without an Animated Screen Character.

3. Click the Change Preferences link again.

4. Click Change Files and Folders Search Behavior.

5. Click the Advanced option.

6. Click OK.

Figure 2.8 shows the resulting Search bar.

**FIGURE 2.8**     Use the Search bar to find files on your system.

## Performing a Search

Here are the steps to follow to run a search:

1. Use the All or Part of the File Name text box to enter the name of the file you want to locate (this is optional). If you're not sure of the exact name, you can enter a **file specification**, which uses a partial name or a wildcard character or two. Here are some pointers for using this text box:

- Search doesn't differentiate between uppercase and lowercase letters (although, as you'll see later, Search has a Case Sensitive option that you can activate).

- Search always looks for filenames that **contain** the text you enter. Therefore, if you're not sure about a filename, enter just part of the name.

- Another way to broaden your search is to use wildcard characters. Use the question mark (?) to substitute for a single character (for example, `budget200?.doc`); use an asterisk (*) to substitute for a group of characters (for example, `*.txt`).

- To search for multiple file specifications, separate each one with a comma or semicolon.

2. Use the A Word or Phrase in the File text box to enter a word or phrase contained within the file (this is optional). Note that if you enter multiple words, Search will match only documents that contain the exact phrase you enter.

3. Use the Look In combo box to either type the drive and/or folder you want to check or select one of the predefined locations. To specify multiple locations, separate each path with a semicolon.

4. To narrow down your search even more, click the following items:

| | |
|---|---|
| When Was It Modified | Click this item to search using the file date and time stamps. You can choose a predefine criterion (such as Within the Last Week) or you can specify your own dates. |
| What Size Is It | Click this item to search by file size. Again, you can choose either a predefined criterion (such as Small or Medium) or specify a size. |
| More Advanced Options | Click this item to display several more search criteria. For example, you can search by file type, search Windows XP's system folders, search hidden files and folders, search the subfolders of the current folder, and search a tape backup. You can also activate the Case Sensitive check box if you want Search to exactly match the uppercase and lowercase letters you specify in the A Word or Phrase in the File text box. |

5. Click the Search button to begin the search. If Search locates any matching files, they appear in a list in the Contents area.

---

**NOTE**

If you entered a complex set of criteria that you think you might use again, you can save your search by selecting File, Save Search. Find gathers the search criteria and then prompts you to save them to a file. Open this file to display the Search bar with your saved criteria.

---

## Searching Faster with the Indexing Service

You've seen that Windows XP's Search feature enables you to search for files based on the name, modification date, and size. But its most powerful feature is its capability to search based on the contents of files. Enter a search term in the A Word or Phrase in the File text box, and Search will match those files that contain the text. This approach works well if you're searching only a few documents, but if you have hundreds or even thousands of documents, the search can be very slow. To speed things up considerably, use the Indexing Service, which indexes the file contents so that the search needs to examine only the index instead of the files themselves.

To use the Indexing Service, follow these steps:

> **CAUTION**
>
> If you don't have a particularly powerful computer (or if you have a system that's a couple of years old and is starting to show its age), you might find that the Indexing Service slows your machine even more. Indexing files is resource-intensive work, and it can cause noticeable slow-downs on computers that lack horsepower. If you notice system lags after turning on the Indexing Service, you might want to turn it off to improve performance.

1. Display the Search bar.
2. Click Change Preferences.
3. Click With Indexing Service.
4. Activate the Yes, Enable Indexing Service option.
5. Click OK.

# Customizing Windows Explorer

I close this chapter by examining various ways to customize the Windows Explorer interface. You'll likely be spending a lot of time with Windows Explorer over the years, so customizing it to your liking will make you more productive.

## Changing the View

The icons in Windows Explorer's Contents list can be viewed in five or six different ways, depending on the type of folder. To see a list of these views, either pull down the View menu or pull down the Views button in the toolbar. Here are your choices:

| | |
|---|---|
| Thumbnails | Displays the contents of each file instead of just its name. This works for many graphics formats—including BMP, GIF, JPG, and TIF—as well as for web pages (HTML files). |
| Tiles | Decreases the size of the icons and displays them in columns that you must scroll vertically. |

| | |
|---|---|
| Icons | Increases the size of the Contents list icons and displays those icons in rows across the list pane. |
| List | Icons are the same size as in the Small Icons view, but the icons are arranged in columns that you must scroll horizontally. |
| Details | Displays a vertical list of icons, where each icon has four columns: Name, Size, Type, and Modified. |
| Filmstrip | In a picture folder, displays thumbnails of each image along the bottom of the Contents list, and displays a larger version of the currently selected image above the thumbnails. |

---

**NOTE**

To change the folder type, right-click the folder, click Properties, and then display the Customize tab. In the Use This Folder Type as a Template list, choose the type you want: pictures, music, videos, and so on.

---

## Viewing Extra Details

Explorer's Details view (activate the View, Details command) is the preferred choice for power users because it gives you a great deal of flexibility. For example, here are some techniques you can use when working with the Details view:

- You can change the order of the columns by dragging the column headings to the left or right.

- You can sort on a column by clicking the column heading.

- You can adjust the width of a column by pointing the mouse at the right edge of the column's heading (the pointer changes to a two-headed arrow) and dragging the pointer left or right.

- You can adjust the width of a column so that it's as wide as its widest data by double-clicking the right-edge of the column's heading.

---

**TIP**

To adjust all the columns so that they're exactly as wide as their widest data, press Ctrl+plus sign (+), where the plus sign is the one on your keyboard's numeric keypad.

---

Also, the Details view is informative because it shows you not only the name of each file, but also its size, type, and the date it was last modified. These are useful, to be sure, but Explorer can display many more file tidbits, depending on the file type:

- Music files—Explorer can show the duration, the bit rate at which the song was recorded, and sometimes even the artist and album name.

- Images—Explorer can show the image dimensions and, for digital camera images, the date the picture was taken and the camera model used.

- Microsoft Office files—Explorer can show the author name, as well as the document title, subject, comments, and number of pages.

To see these and other extra details, select View, Choose Details. The Choose Details dialog box that appears (see Figure 2.9) enables you to activate the check boxes for the details you want to see, as well as rearrange the column order. Note, too, that you can also choose details by right-clicking any column header in Details view.

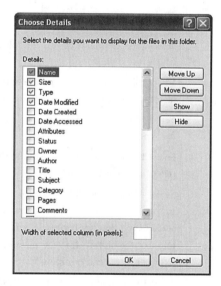

**FIGURE 2.9**   Use the Choose Details dialog box to add or remove columns in Windows Explorer's Details view.

## Running Explorer in Full-Screen Mode

If you want the largest possible screen area for the contents of each folder, you can place Windows Explorer in full-screen mode by pressing F11. (You can also hold down Ctrl and click the Maximize button; if Explorer is already maximized, you first have to click the Restore button.) This mode takes over the entire screen, removes the text from the toolbar buttons, turns off the title bar, menu bar, status bar, and address bar, and hides the Folders list. To choose a menu command, hold down Alt and press the menu's accelerator key, such as Alt+F for the File menu; to see the Folders list, move the mouse pointer to the left edge of the screen. To restore the window, click the Restore button.

**NOTE**

You can customize the Windows Explorer toolbar to display a Full Screen button. Right-click the toolbar and then click Customize to display the Customize Toolbar dialog box. In the Available Toolbar Buttons list, click Full Screen and then click Add.

## Sorting Files and Folders

The icons in the Contents list are sorted alphabetically by name, with folders displayed before files. You can change this sort order by selecting View, Arrange Icons (or right-clicking the Contents list and clicking Arrange Icons), and then selecting one of the following commands:

| | |
|---|---|
| Name | Select this command to sort the folder alphabetically by name (this is the default). |
| Size | Select this command to sort the folder numerically according to file size, with the smallest sizes at the top. |
| Type | Select this command to sort the folder alphabetically according to file type. |
| Date | Select this command to sort the folder by date, with the most recent dates at the top. |
| Show in Groups | Select this command to organize the files and folders into groups that are based on the current sort order. For example, if you have sorted the folder by name, Explorer displays a grouping for each letter of the alphabet; if you have sorted the folder by file type, Explorer displays a grouping for each type. |
| Auto Arrange | Activate this command to have Windows Explorer sort the folder automatically whenever you move icons or change the size of the window. Note that this command works only with the Large Icons and Small Icons views. |
| Align to Grid | In Thumbnails, Tiles, or Icons view, select this command to arrange the icons according to the invisible grid that determines the rows and columns in the view. |

**TIP**

An easier way to sort a folder is to click the column headers in Details view. For example, click the Size column to sort the folder by file size. Clicking the same column header toggles the sort order between ascending and descending.

## Exploring the View Options

Windows Explorer boasts a large number of customization options that you need to be familiar with. To see these options, you have two choices:

- In Windows Explorer, select the Tools, Folder Options command.

- Select Start, Settings, Control Panel, click the Switch to Classic View link, if necessary, and then open the Folder Options icon.

Either way, the view options can be found, appropriately enough, on the View tab, as shown in Figure 2.10.

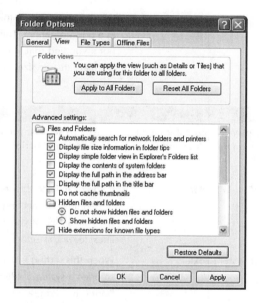

**FIGURE 2.10**    The View tab has quite a few options for customizing Windows Explorer.

The Folder Views group contains two command buttons that you use to define a common view for all your folders:

| | |
|---|---|
| Apply to All Folders | Use Windows Explorer's View menu to customize a folder the way you want. Then display the Folder Options dialog box and click Apply to All Folders. (Note that this button is available only if you display the dialog box from Windows Explorer.) This tells Windows Explorer to display every folder using the same view options as the current folder. |
| Reset All Folders | If you prefer to set up a unique view for each folder, click Reset All Folders to revert everything back to the default Windows XP view. |

Here's a complete look at the various settings in the Files and Folders branch:

| | |
|---|---|
| Automatically Search for Network and Printers | When this setting is activated, Windows XP Folders examines your network and displays all the shared folders and printers in the My Network Places window. If your network has lots of shares, you might prefer to deactivate this feature. |
| Display File Size Information in Folder Tips | When this setting is activated and you hover your mouse pointer over a folder icon, Windows Explorer calculates the size of the files and subfolders within the folder, and displays the size in a pop-up banner. This is useful information, but if you find that your system takes too long to calculate the file size, consider deactivating this setting. |

**NOTE**

If you activate the Display File Size Information in Folder Tips setting, you must also activate the Show Pop-Up Description for Folder and Desktop Items setting, described later.

| | |
|---|---|
| Display Simple Folder View in Explorer's Folders List | If you deactivate this setting, Explorer displays dotted lines connecting folders and subfolders in the Folders bar. If you prefer not to see these lines, leave this setting activated. |
| Display the Contents of System Folders | When this setting is deactivated and you attempt to open a system folder such as the root of the boot drive, Program Files, Windows, and Windows\System, Windows XP displays a These Files Are Hidden message instead. You need to click Show the Contents of This Folder to see what's in the folder. To avoid this extra step, activate this setting. To hide the contents again, display the Task Pane and then click the Hide the Contents of This Folder link. |
| Display the Full Path in the Address Bar | Activate this setting to place the full pathname of the current folder in the Windows Explorer Address bar. The full pathname includes the drive, the names of the parent folders, and the name of the current folder. This is a good idea because it enables you to quickly see where you are in the folder hierarchy, particularly if you're |

| | deep within a set of subfolders. It also means that you're able to edit the path and then move to the new folder by pressing Enter (or clicking Go). |
|---|---|
| Display the Full Path in the Title Bar | This is the same as the previous setting, except that the path appears in the title bar, which is less useful. |
| Hidden Files and Folders | Windows XP hides certain types of files by default (such as BOOT.INI). This makes sense for novice users because they could accidentally delete or rename an important file. However, it's a pain for more advanced users who might require access to these files. You can use these options to tell Windows Explorer which files to display: |

**NOTE**

Files are hidden from view by having their Hidden attribute activated. You can work with this attribute directly by right-clicking a visible file, clicking Properties, and then toggling the Hidden setting on and off.

| | • Do Not Show Hidden Files and Folders— Activate this option to avoid displaying objects that have the hidden attribute set. |
|---|---|
| | • Show Hidden Files and Folders—Activate this option to display the hidden files. |
| Hide File Extensions for Known File Types | When you read Chapter 3, "Mastering File Types," you'll see that file extensions are one of the most crucial Windows XP concepts. That's because file extensions define the file type and automatically associate files with certain applications. Microsoft figures that, crucial or not, the file extension concept is just too hard for new users to grasp. Therefore, right out of the box, Windows Explorer doesn't display file extensions. To overcome this limitation, deactivate this setting. |

**CAUTION**

If you elect not to display file extensions, note that you won't be able to edit the extension when you rename a file. For example, if you have a text file named Index.txt, it will be displayed only as Index with the file extensions hidden. If you edit the filename to Index.htm, Windows XP actually renames the file to Index.htm.txt! To rename extensions, you must display them.

| | |
|---|---|
| Hide Protected Operating System Files | When this setting is activated, Windows XP hides files that have the System attribute activated. This is not usually a problem because you rarely have to do anything with the Windows system files. Deactivate this setting if you need to see one of these files (such as BOOT.INI). When Windows XP asks whether you're sure, click Yes. |
| Launch Folder Windows in a Separate Process | Activating this setting tells Windows XP to create a new thread in memory for each folder you open. This makes Windows Explorer more stable because a problem with one thread won't crash the others. However, this also means that Windows Explorer requires far greater amounts of system resources and memory. Activate this option only if your system has plenty of resources and memory. |
| Remember Each Folder's View Settings | Activate this setting to have Windows Explorer keep track of the view options you set for each folder. The next time you display a folder, Windows Explorer will remember the view options and use them to display the folder. |
| Restore Previous Folder Windows at Logon | If you activate this setting, Windows XP makes note of which folders you have open when you log off. The next time you log on, XP displays those folders again. This is a very useful option if you normally have one or two particular folder windows open all day long because it saves you having to reopen those folders each time you start Windows XP. |
| Show Control Panel in My Computer | Activate this setting to access Control Panel's icon in Windows Explorer. |
| Show Encrypted or Compressed NTFS Files in Color | When this setting is activated, Windows Explorer shows the names of encrypted files in a green font and the names of compressed files in a blue font. This is a useful way to distinguish these from regular files, but you can deactivate it if you prefer to view all your files in a single color. Note that this only applies to files on NTFS partitions because only NTFS supports file encryption and compression. |

| Show Pop-Up Description for Folder and Desktop Items | Some icons display a pop-up banner when you point the mouse at them. For example, the default desktop icons display a pop-up banner that describes each icon. Use this setting to turn these pop-ups on and off. |
| Use Simple File Sharing | When this setting is activated, you can share a folder on your network simply by activating a check box. For better security, I recommend turning off this setting and using permissions, as described in Chapter 22's "Deactivating Simple File Sharing" section. |

## Moving My Documents

The default location of the My Documents folder is `%USERPROFILE%\My Documents`. This is not a great location because it means, usually, that your documents and Windows XP are on the same hard disk partition. If you have to wipe that partition in order to reinstall Windows XP or some other operating system, you'll need to back up your documents first. Similarly, you might have another partition on your system that has lots of free disk space, so you might prefer to store your documents there. For these and other reasons, moving the location of My Documents is a good idea. Here's how:

1. In Windows Explorer or the Windows XP Start menu, right-click My Documents and then click Properties. The property sheet for My Documents appears.

2. In the Target tab, use the Target text box to enter the drive and folder where you want your documents stored. (Or click Move to select the folder using a dialog box.)

3. Click OK. If Explorer asks whether you want to create the new folder and then to move your documents to the new location, click Yes in both cases.

## Customizing the Standard Buttons Toolbar

The Windows Explorer toolbar (known officially as the **Standard Buttons toolbar**) displays just a few buttons, by default. There are some navigation buttons (Back, Forward, and Up), two Explorer bar buttons (Search and Folders), and the Views button. If, like me, you used the old Cut, Copy, and Paste buttons quite often, you probably won't be all that enthusiastic about this new arrangement. Another thing that's less than overwhelming about the new toolbar is its peculiar design. For example, why does the Back button have a text label, but the Forward button doesn't?

All these peculiarities add up to bad toolbar news, but the good news is that they can be remedied because the toolbar is customizable. Here's how it works:

1. Right-click the toolbar and then click Customize in the shortcut menu. The Customize Toolbar dialog box appears, as shown in Figure 2.11.

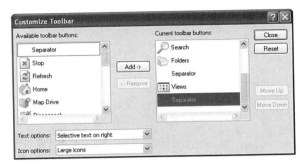

**FIGURE 2.11**    Use this dialog box to create a more sensible toolbar.

2. To add an extra button to the toolbar, select it in the Available Toolbar Buttons list and then click Add. Use the Separator item to add a vertical bar to the toolbar. This is normally used to separate groups of related buttons.

3. To remove a button from the toolbar, select it in the Current Toolbar Buttons list and then click Remove.

4. To change the order of the buttons, highlight any button in the Current Toolbar Buttons list and click Move Up or Move Down.

5. To control the button text, use the Text Options list:

   • Show Text Labels—This option adds text to every button. This makes the buttons much easier to figure out, so I recommend going with this option.

   • Selective Text on Right—This is the default option, and it displays text on only some buttons.

   • No Text Labels—This option displays every button using just its icon. If you already know what each icon represents, selecting this option will give you a bit more room, so you can add extra buttons, if desired.

6. The size of the icons is controlled by the items in the Icon Options list. Select either Small Icons (this is the default) or Large Icons.

7. Click Close to put your new settings into effect.

## Using Windows Explorer's Command-Line Options

The Windows Explorer executable file is `Explorer.exe`, and it resides in the `%SystemRoot%` folder. `Explorer.exe` supports various command-line parameters, which you can take advantage of to control how Windows Explorer starts. Here's the syntax for `Explorer.exe`:

```
Explorer [/N]¦[/E],[/ROOT,[folder]] [/SELECT,subfolder]
```

| | |
|---|---|
| /N | Starts Explorer without the Folders list. |
| /E | Starts Explorer with the Folders list. |
| /ROOT,*folder* | Specifies the *folder* that will be the root of the new Explorer view. In other words, *folder* will appear at the top of the Folders list. If you omit this switch, the desktop is displayed as the root. |
| /SELECT,*subfolder* | Specifies the *subfolder* of the root folder to display in the Folders list. If you don't also include the /ROOT switch, the *subfolder* is only highlighted in the Contents pane. |

**NOTE**

If you run the EXPLORER command without any switches, Windows XP launches My Computer.

For example, if you want to open Explorer with C:\WINDOWS as the root and you want the C:\WINDOWS\SYSTEM32 folder displayed in the Contents pane, use the following command:

```
explorer /e, /root,c:\windows /select,c:\windows\system32
```

Here's another example that displays Explorer with the current user's profile folder selected:

```
explorer /e, /root, /select,%USERPROFILE%
```

# From Here

Here are some places in the book that contain information related to the material in this chapter:

- For an in-depth look at file types, see Chapter 3, "Mastering File Types."

- If you work with digital media files, see Chapter 4, "Working with Digital Media."

- For file maintenance, see the sections in Chapter 12 titled "Deleting Unnecessary Files," "Defragmenting Your Hard Disk," and "Backing Up Your Files."

- To learn how to access network folders and files, see the section in Chapter 22 titled "Accessing Network Resources."

- To share your folders and files on a network, see the section in Chapter 22 titled "Sharing Resources with the Network."

CHAPTER **3**

# Mastering File Types

Amazingly, a long list of useful and powerful Windows XP features are either ignored or given short shrift in the official Microsoft documentation. Whether it's the Windows XP startup options, group policies, or the Registry (to name just three that I discuss in this book), Microsoft prefers that curious users figure these things out for themselves (with, of course, the help of their favorite computer book authors).

The subject of this chapter is a prime example. The idea of the **file type** can be described, without hyperbole, as the very foundation of the Windows XP file system. Not only does Microsoft offer scant documentation and tools for working with file types, but they also seem to have gone out of their way to hide the whole file type concept. As usual, the reason is to block out this aspect of Windows XP's innards from the sensitive eyes of the novice user. Ironically, however, this just creates a whole new set of problems for beginners and more hassles for experienced users.

This chapter brings file types out into the open. You'll learn the basics of file types and then see a number of powerful techniques for using file types to take charge of the Windows XP file system.

## Understanding File Types

To get the most out of this chapter, you need to understand some background about what a file type is and how Windows XP determines and works with file types. The next couple of sections tell you everything you need to know to get you through the rest of the chapter.

## File Types and File Extensions

One of the fictions that Microsoft has tried to foist on the computer-using public is that we live in a "document-centric" world. That is, that people care only about the documents they create and not about the applications they use to create those documents. This is pure hokum. The reality is that applications are still too difficult to use and the capability to share documents between applications is still too problematic. In other words, you can't create documents unless you learn the ins and outs of an application, and you can't share documents with others unless you use compatible applications.

Unfortunately, we're stuck with Microsoft's worship of the document and all the problems that this worship creates. A good example is the hiding of file extensions. As you learned in Chapter 2, "Exploring Expert File and Folder Techniques," Windows XP turns off file extensions by default. Here are just a few of the problems this allegedly document-centric decision creates:

| | |
|---|---|
| Document confusion | If you have a folder with multiple documents that use the same primary name, it's often difficult to tell which file is which. For example, Figure 3.1 shows a folder with 15 different files named `Project`. Windows XP unrealistically expects users to tell files apart just by examining their icons. |

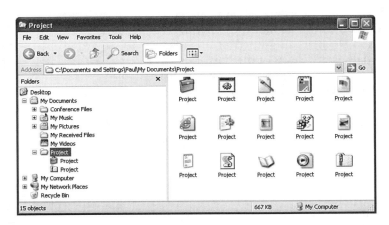

**FIGURE 3.1**   With file extensions turned off, it's often difficult to tell one file from another.

| | |
|---|---|
| The inability to rename extensions | If you have a file named `index.txt` and you want to rename it to `index.html`, you can't do it with file extensions turned off. If you try, you just end up with a file named `index.html.txt`. |
| The inability to save a document under an extension of your choice | Similarly, with file extensions turned off, Windows XP forces you to save a file using the default extension associated with an application. For example, if you're working in Notepad, every file you save must have a `.txt` extension. |

**TIP**

There are two ways to get around the inability to save a document under an extension of your choice, both of which use controls in the Save As dialog box: Surround the filename you want to use with quotation marks; or, in the Save as Type list, select the All Files (\*.\*) option, if it exists.

You can overcome all these problems by turning on file extensions. Why does the lack of file extensions cause such a fuss? Because file extensions *solely and completely* determine the file type of a document. In other words, if Windows XP sees that a file has a .txt extension, it knows the file uses the Text Document file type. Similarly, a file with the extension .bmp uses the Bitmap Image file type.

**NOTE**

As a reminder, you turn on file extensions by selecting Windows Explorer's Tools, Folder Options command, displaying the View tab, and deactivating the Hide File Extensions for Known File Types check box.

The file type, in turn, determines the application that's associated with the extension. If a file has a .txt extension, Windows XP associates that extension with Notepad, so the file will always open in Notepad. Nothing else inherent in the file determines the file type so, at least from the point of view of the user, the entire Windows XP file system rests on the shoulders of the humble file extension.

This method of determining file types is, no doubt, a poor design decision. (For example, there is some danger that a novice user could render a file useless by imprudently renaming its extension.) However, it also leads to some powerful methods for manipulating and controlling the Windows XP file system, as you'll see in this chapter.

## File Types and the Registry

As you might expect, everything Windows XP knows about file types is defined in the Registry. (See Chapter 8, "Getting to Know the Windows XP Registry," for details on understanding and using the Registry.) You use the Registry to work with file types throughout this chapter, so let's see how things work. Open the Registry Editor and examine the HKEY_CLASSES_ROOT key. Notice that it's divided into two sections:

- The first part of HKEY_CLASSES_ROOT consists of dozens of file extension subkeys (such as .bmp and .txt). There are more than 300 such subkeys in a basic Windows XP installation, and there could easily be two or three times that number on a system with many applications installed.

- The second part of HKEY_CLASSES_ROOT lists the various file types that are associated with the registered extensions. When an extension is associated with a particular file type, the extension is said to be **registered** with Windows XP.

HKEY_CLASSES_ROOT also stores information on ActiveX controls in its CLSID subkey. Many of these controls also have corresponding subkeys in the second half of HKEY_CLASSES_ROOT.

To see what this all means, take a look at Figure 3.2. Here, I've highlighted the .txt key, which has txtfile as its Default value.

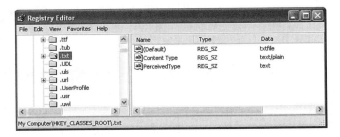

**FIGURE 3.2** The first part of the HKEY_CLASSES_ROOT key contains subkeys for all the registered file extensions.

That Default value is a pointer to the extension's associated file type subkey in the second half of HKEY_CLASSES_ROOT. Figure 3.3 shows the txtfile subkey associated with the .txt extension. Here are some notes about this file type subkey:

- The Default value is a description of the file type (Text Document, in this case).

- The DefaultIcon subkey defines the icon that's displayed with any file that uses this type.

- The shell subkey determines the actions that can be performed with this file type. These actions vary depending on the file type, but Open and Print are common. The Open action determines the application that's associated with the file type. For example, the Open action for a Text Document file type is the following:

```
%SystemRoot%\system32\NOTEPAD.EXE %1
```

**NOTE**

The %1 at the end of the command is a placeholder that refers to the document being opened (if any). If you double-click a file named memo.txt, for example, the %1 placeholder is replaced by memo.txt, which tells Windows to run Notepad and open that file.

**FIGURE 3.3**    The second part of HKEY_CLASSES_ROOT contains the file type data associated with each extension.

## The File Types Tab: A Front-End for HKEY_CLASSES_ROOT

For much of the work you do in this chapter, you won't have to deal with the Registry's HKEY_CLASSES_ROOT key directly. Instead, Windows XP offers a dialog box tab that acts as a front-end for this key. Follow these steps to display this tab:

1. In Windows Explorer, select Tools, Folder Options to display the Folder Options dialog box.

> **NOTE**
>
> You can also get to the Folder Options dialog box by launching the Control Panel's Folder Options icon.

2. Select the File Types tab.

Figure 3.4 shows the File Types tab. The Registered File Types list shows all the file types known to Windows XP, as well as their extensions. When you select a file type, the Opens With line in the Details area shows you the icon and name of the program associated with the file type.

> **TIP**
>
> You can sort the file types to make it easier to find the one you want. In the Registered File Types list, click the Extensions header to sort by extension or click the File Types header to sort by file type.

# Working with Existing File Types

In this section, you'll learn how to work with Windows XP's existing file types. I'll show you how to change the file type description, modify the file type's actions, associate an extension with another file type, and disassociate a file type and an extension.

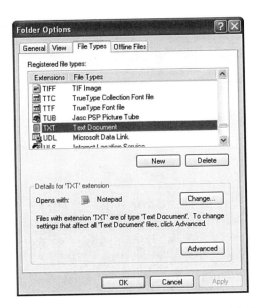

**FIGURE 3.4**    The File Types tab offers a front-end for working with Windows XP's registered file types.

## Editing a File Type

To make changes to an existing file type, follow these steps:

1. Open the Folder Options dialog box and display the File Types tab, as described earlier.

2. Use the Registered File Types list to select the file type you want to work with.

3. Click Advanced. The Edit File Type dialog box appears. Figure 3.5 shows the Edit File Type dialog box for the Text Document type.

4. The text box at the top holds the description of the file type, which you can edit. This description appears in the Registered File Types list and in the New menu (right-click a folder and then click New).

5. You can also work with the following controls:

| | |
|---|---|
| Change Icon | Click this button to display the Change Icon dialog box. Use this dialog box to select a new icon for the file type. |
| Actions | This list shows the actions defined for the file type. I discuss file type actions in more detail in the next section. |

**FIGURE 3.5** Use the Edit File Type dialog box to make changes to an existing file type.

Confirm Open After Download    When this check box is activated and you attempt to download a file from the World Wide Web, Internet Explorer displays the File Download dialog box that asks whether you want to save or open the downloaded file (see Figure 3.6). Otherwise, Internet Explorer just opens the file using its associated application. Here are two points to bear in mind:

- Despite the name of this check box, Internet Explorer displays the File Download dialog box *before* you download the file.

- For many file types, the File Download dialog box includes a check box named Always Ask Before Opening This Type of File. Deactivating this check box is the same thing as deactivating the Confirm Open After Download check box.

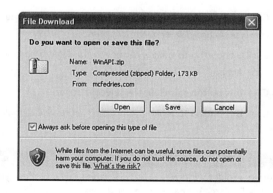

**FIGURE 3.6** If the Confirm Open After Download check box is activated, Internet Explorer displays this dialog box.

| | |
|---|---|
| Always Show Extension | If you activate this check box, Windows XP shows this file type's extension even if you hide extensions globally. |

What if you want Windows XP to *never* show a file type's extension, even if extensions are turned on globally? To set this up, find the appropriate file type subkey in HKEY_CLASSES_ROOT, and add a new string value named NeverShowExt, and leave its value as the empty string. You might have to restart Windows to put this into effect.

| | |
|---|---|
| Browse in Same Window | When this check box is activated, the file type opens within Internet Explorer instead of its associated application. This applies only to Microsoft Office file types that are capable of being displayed within Internet Explorer. |

6. Click OK to return to the File Types tab.

7. Click Close.

## Working with File Type Actions

In the Edit File Type dialog box, the Actions list displays the defined actions for the file type. You usually see two types of actions:

- An action shown in boldface represents the default action for the file type. This is the action that's performed when you double-click one of these files (or highlight a file and press Enter). This action also appears in bold on the file type's shortcut menu (the menu that appears when you right-click a file of that type).

- All other actions are listed on the shortcut menu for the file type.

The buttons beside the Actions list enable you to work with the file type's actions:

| | |
|---|---|
| New | Click this button to create a new action for the file type. See "Creating a New File Type Action," later in this chapter. |
| Edit | Click this button to make changes to the selected action. See "Editing a File Type Action," later in this chapter. |
| Remove | Click this button to delete the selected action. |
| Set Default | Click this button to make the selected action the default for this file type. |

When you want to open a folder window in the two-paned Explorer view, you have to right-click the folder and then click Explore. To make the latter the default action for a folder, edit the Folder file type, select explore in the Actions list, and then click Set Default.

### Associating an Extension with a Different Application

There are many reasons you might want to override Windows XP's default associations and use a different program to open an extension. For example, you might prefer to open text files in WordPad instead of Notepad. Similarly, you might want to open HTML files in Notepad or some other text editor rather than Internet Explorer.

In these cases, you need to associate the extension with the application you want to use instead of the Windows default association. Windows XP gives you two ways to go about this:

| | |
|---|---|
| The Open With dialog box | With this method, right-click any file that uses the extension and then click Open With. (If you've used the Open With dialog box on this extension before, click the Choose Program command from the menu that appears.) In the Open With dialog box, select the program you want to use, activate the Always Use This Program to Open These Files check box, and click OK. |
| The File Types tab | With this method, you use the File Types tab to edit the Open action of the file type. See the next section to learn how to edit a file type action. |

### Editing a File Type Action

Follow these steps to make changes to a file type action:

1. In the File Types tab, select the file type you want to work with.

2. Click the Advanced button. The Edit File Type dialog box appears.

3. In the Actions list, select the action you want to change, and then click Edit. The Editing Action for Type: *Type* dialog box appears (where *Type* is the file type you're working with).

4. (Optional) Use the Action text box to change the name of the action.

5. In the Application Used to Perform Action text box, type the full pathname of the application you want to use for the action. Here are some notes to bear in mind:

   - If the pathname of the executable file contains a space, be sure to enclose the path in quotation marks, like so:

     ```
     "C:\Program Files\My Program\program.exe"
     ```

   - If you'll be using documents that have spaces in their filenames, add the %1 parameter after the pathname:

     ```
     "C:\Program Files\My Program\program.exe" "%1"
     ```

The %1 part tells the application to load the specified file (such as a filename you click), and the quotation marks ensure that no problems occur with multiple-word filenames.

- If you're changing the Print action, be sure to include the /P switch after the application's pathname, like this:

```
"C:\Program Files\My Program\program.exe" /P
```

### Creating a New File Type Action

Instead of replacing an action's underlying application with a different application, you might prefer to create new actions. In our HTML file example, you could keep the default Open action as it is and create a new action—called, for example, Open for Editing—that uses Notepad (or whatever) to open an HTML file. When you highlight an HTML file and pull down the File menu, or right-click an HTML file, the menus that appear will show both commands: Open (for Internet Explorer) and Open for Editing (for Notepad).

To create a new action for an existing file type, follow these steps:

1. In the File Types tab, select the file type you want to work with.

2. Click the Advanced button. The Edit File Type dialog box appears.

3. Click New to display the New Action dialog box.

4. Use the Action text box to enter a name for the action.

---

**TIP**

In the Action text box, if you precede a letter with an ampersand (&), Windows XP designates that letter as the menu accelerator key. For example, entering **Open for &Editing** defines E as the accelerator key. You can then press this letter's key to select the command on either the File menu or the shortcut menu.

---

5. Use the Application Used to Perform Action text box to enter the full pathname of the application you want to use for the new action. (Follow the guidelines that I outlined in the previous section.)

6. Click OK.

7. If you want the new action to be the default, select it and click Set Default.

8. Click OK to return to the File Types tab.

9. Click Close.

## Example: Opening the Command Prompt in the Current Folder

When you're working in Windows Explorer, you might find occasionally that you need to do some work at the command prompt. For example, the current folder might contain multiple files that need to be renamed—a task that's most easily done within a command-line session. Selecting Start, All Programs, Accessories, Command Prompt starts the session in the %USERPROFILE% folder, so you have to use one or more CD commands to get to the folder you want to work in.

An easier way would be to create a new action for the Folder file type that launches the command prompt and automatically displays the current Windows Explorer folder. To do this, follow these steps:

1. Select Folder in the File Types tab.

2. Click Advanced to display the Edit File Type dialog box.

3. Click New to display the New Action dialog box.

4. Type **Open &With Command Prompt** in the Action text box (note that the letter W is the accelerator key).

   ```
   cmd.exe /k cd "%L"
   ```

---
**NOTE**

The `cmd.exe` file is the command prompt executable file. The `/k` switch tells Windows XP to keep the command prompt window open after the CD (change directory) command completes. The `%L` placeholder represents the full pathname of the current folder.

---

---
**TIP**

You can't edit or delete this new action in the Edit File Type dialog box. If you need to make changes to this action, use the following Registry key:

   ```
   HKEY_CLASSES_ROOT\Folder\shell
   ```

---

5. Figure 3.7 shows a completed dialog box. Click OK when you're done. Windows XP adds your new action to the Folder type's Actions list.

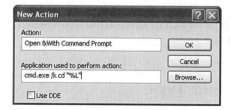

**FIGURE 3.7**     Use the New Action dialog box to define a new action for the file type.

In Figure 3.8, I right-clicked a folder. Notice how the new action appears in the shortcut menu. The command prompt window below is what appears if you click the Open With Command Prompt command.

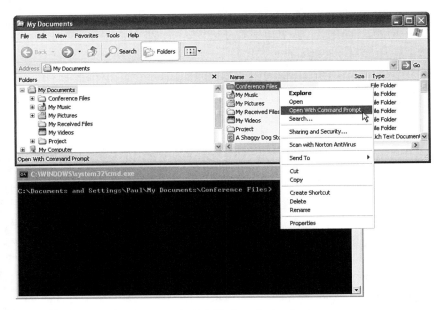

**FIGURE 3.8**    The new action appears in the file type's shortcut menu.

## Disassociating an Application and an Extension

One of the most annoying things a newly installed program can do is change your existing file type associations. Some programs are courteous enough to ask you whether they can change some associations. However, many other programs make the changes without permission. In these cases, you often want to undo the damage by disassociating the new application from the affected extensions. You have two ways to proceed:

- If you want to revert the association back to its original application, use the procedure I outlined earlier in the "Associating an Extension with a Different Application" section.

- If you prefer to have no associated application at all, first display the File Types tab. Then select the file type or extension and click Advanced. In the Actions list, select Open and then click Remove.

## Creating a New File Type

Windows XP comes with a long list of registered file types, but it can't account for every extension you'll face in your computing career. For rare extensions, it's best just to use the Open With dialog box. However, if you have an unregistered extension that you encounter frequently, you should register that extension by creating a new file type for it. The next two sections provide a couple of methods for doing this.

Text files, in particular, seem to come with all kinds of nonstandard (that is, unregistered) extensions. Rather than constantly setting up file types for these extensions or using the Open With dialog box, I created a shortcut for Notepad in my %USERPROFILE\SendTo folder. That way, I can open any text file by right-clicking it and then selecting Send To, Notepad.

## Using Open With to Create a Basic File Type

Our old friend the Open With dialog box provides a quick-and-dirty method for creating a simple file type for an unregistered extension:

1. In Windows Explorer, select the file you want to work with.

2. Select File, Open. (For unregistered file types, Windows XP doesn't display the Open With command.) Windows XP displays a dialog box telling you that it cannot open the file, as shown in Figure 3.9.

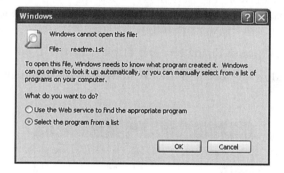

**FIGURE 3.9** Windows XP displays this dialog box when you attempt to open an unregistered file type.

3. Activate the Select the Program from a List option and then click OK. The Open With dialog box appears.

4. In the Programs list, select the application you want to use to open the file or click Browse to choose the program from a dialog box.

5. Use the Type a Description That You Want to Use for This Kind of File text box to enter a description for the new file type.

6. Make sure that the Always Use the Selected Program to Open This Kind of File check box is activated.

7. Click OK.

This method creates a new file type with the following properties:

- In the File Types tab, the new file type appears in the Registered File Types list under the name you entered into the Type a Description type box.

- The number of actions Windows XP creates for the file type depends on the application you selected. If you can use the application to both display and edit the file, Windows XP creates `Open` and `Edit` actions; if you can use the application only to display the file, Windows XP creates just the `Open` action.

- The icon associated with the file is the same as the one used by the associated application.

- In the Registry, the new `HKEY_CLASSES_ROOT` file type name is *ext*`_auto_file`, where *ext* is the file's extension.

## Using the File Types Tab to Create a More Advanced File Type

If you want more control over your new file type, use the File Types tab instead of the Open With dialog box. This method enables you to select a different icon, set up multiple actions, and more. Here are the steps to follow:

1. Open the Folder Options dialog box and display the File Types tab.

2. Click New. Windows XP displays the Create New Extension dialog box shown in Figure 3.10.

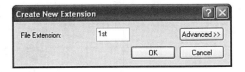

**FIGURE 3.10**    Use the Create New Extension dialog box to define your new file type.

3. Type the File Extension for the new file type.

4. Click OK to return to the File Types tab.

5. Select the new extension in the Registered File Types list.

6. Click Advanced to display the Edit File Type dialog box.

7. Change the file type description and icon, if desired. Follow the steps I outlined in the "Creating a New File Type Action" section to create an Open action for the new file type, as well as any other actions you require (such as Edit or Print).

8. Click OK.

9. Click Close.

## Associating Two or More Extensions with a Single File Type

The problem with creating a new file type is that you often have to reinvent the wheel. For example, let's say you want to set up a new file type that uses the .1st extension. These are usually text files (such as readme.1st) that provide pre-installation instructions, so you probably want to associate them with Notepad. However, this means repeating some or all of the existing Text Document file types. To avoid this, it's possible to tell Windows XP to associate a second extension with an existing file type. Here are the steps to follow:

1. Open the Folder Options dialog box and display the File Types tab.

2. Click New. Windows XP displays the Create New Extension dialog box.

3. Type the File Extension for the new file type.

4. Click Advanced. The dialog box expands as shown in Figure 3.11.

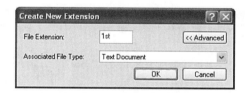

**FIGURE 3.11** The expanded version of the Create New Extension dialog box.

5. Use the Associated File Type list to select the file type for the new extension (such as Text Document).

6. Click OK to return to the File Types tab.

## Customizing the New Menu

One of Windows XP's handiest features is the New menu, which enables you to create a new file without working within an application. In Windows Explorer, select File, New, or right-click inside the Contents pane and select New. In the submenu that appears, you'll see items that create new documents of various file types, including a folder, shortcut, bitmap image, WordPad document, text document, compressed folder, and possibly many others, depending on your system configuration and the applications you have installed.

What mechanism determines whether a file type appears on the New menu? The Registry, of course. To see how this works, start the Registry Editor and open the HKEY_CLASSES_ROOT key. As you've seen, most of the extension subkeys have only a Default setting that's either blank (if the extension isn't associated with a registered file type) or a string file that points to the extension's associated file type.

However, lots of these extension keys also have subkeys and a few of them have a subkey named `ShellNew`, in particular. For example, open the `.bmp` key and you see that it has a subkey named `ShellNew`. This subkey is what determines whether a file type appears on the New menu. Specifically, if the extension is registered with Windows XP and it has a `ShellNew` subkey, the New menu sprouts a command for the associated file type.

The `ShellNew` subkey always contains a setting that determines how Windows XP creates the new file. Four settings are possible:

| | |
|---|---|
| `NullFile` | This setting, the value of which is always set to a null string (""), tells Windows XP to create an empty file of the associated type. Of the file types that appear on the default New menu, three use the `NullFile` setting: Text Document (.txt), Bitmap Image (.bmp), and WordPad Document (.doc). |
| `FileName` | This setting tells Windows XP to create the new file by making a copy of another file. Windows XP has special hidden folders to hold these template files. These folders are user-specific, so you'll find them in `%USERPROFILE%\Templates`. On the default New menu, only the Wave Sound (.wav) file type uses the `FileName` setting, and its value is `sndrec.wav`. To see this value, you need to open the following key: |

> `HKEY_CLASSES_ROOT\.wav\ShellNew`

| | |
|---|---|
| `Command` | This setting tells Windows XP to create the new file by executing a specific command. This command usually invokes an executable file with a few parameters. Two of the New menu's commands use this setting: |

- Shortcut—The `.lnk\ShellNew` key contains the following value for the Command setting:

> `rundll32.exe appwiz.cpl,NewLinkHere %1`

- Briefcase—In the `.bfc\ShellNew` key, you'll see the following value for the Command setting:

> `%SystemRoot%\system32\rundll32.exe %SystemRoot%\`
> `system32\syncui.dll,Briefcase_Create %2!d! %1`

| | |
|---|---|
| `Data` | This setting contains a binary value, and when Windows XP creates the new file, it copies this binary value into the file. The New menu's Compressed (Zipped) Folder command uses this setting, which you can find here: |

> `.zip\CompressedFolder\ShellNew`

> **NOTE**
>
> Some of the extension keys have multiple `ShellNew` subkeys. For example, in a default installation of Windows XP, the `.doc` key has four `ShellNew` subkeys:
>
> `.doc\ShellNew`
> `.doc\Word.Document.6\ShellNew`
> `.doc\WordDocument\ShellNew`
> `.doc\WordPad.Document.1\ShellNew`
>
> Which of these subkeys does Windows XP use when constructing the New menu? It uses the subkey that corresponds to the registered file type. In a default installation of Windows XP, the registered file type for `.doc` files is `WordPad.Document.1`, so for the WordPad Document item on the New menu, Windows XP uses the following subkey:
>
> `.doc\WordPad.Document.1\ShellNew`

3

## Adding File Types to the New Menu

To make the New menu even more convenient, you can add new file types for documents you work with regularly. For any file type that's registered with Windows XP, you follow a simple three-step process:

1. Add a `ShellNew` subkey to the appropriate extension key in `HKEY_CLASSES_ROOT`.

2. Add one of the four settings discussed in the preceding section (`NullFile`, `FileName`, `Command`, or `Data`).

3. Type a value for the setting.

In most cases, the easiest way to go is to use `NullFile` to create an empty file. However, the `FileName` setting can be quite powerful because you can set up a template file containing text and other data.

## Deleting File Types from the New Menu

Many Windows XP applications (such as Microsoft Office) like to add their file types to the New menu. If you find that your New menu is getting overcrowded, you can delete some commands to keep things manageable. To do this, you need to find the appropriate extension in the Registry and delete its `ShellNew` subkey.

> **CAUTION**
>
> Instead of permanently deleting a `ShellNew` subkey, you can tread a more cautious path by simply renaming the key (to, for example, `ShellNewOld`). This will still prevent Windows XP from adding the item to the New menu, but it also means that you can restore the item just by restoring the original key name. Note, however, that some third-party Registry cleanup programs flag such renamed keys for deletion or restoration. The better programs—such as Registry Mechanic (www.pctools.com)—enable you to specify keys that the program should ignore.

# Customizing Windows XP's Open With List

You've used the Open With dialog box a couple of times so far in this chapter. This is a truly useful dialog box, but you can make it even more useful by customizing it. The rest of this chapter takes you through various Open With customizations.

## Opening a Document with an Unassociated Application

From what you've learned in this chapter, you can see the process that Windows XP goes through when you double-click a document:

1. Look up the document's extension in HKEY_CLASSES_ROOT.

2. Examine the Default value to get the name of the file type subkey.

3. Look up the file type subkey in HKEY_CLASSES_ROOT.

4. Get the Default value in the shell\open\command subkey to get the command line for the associated application.

5. Run the application and open the document.

What do you do if you want to bypass this process and have Windows XP open a document in an *unassociated* application? (That is, an application other than the one with which the document is associated.) For example, what if you want to open a text file in WordPad?

One possibility would be to launch the unassociated application and open the document from there. To do so, you'd run the File, Open command (or whatever) and, in the Open dialog box, select All Files (*.*) in the Files of Type list.

That will work, but it defeats the convenience of being able to launch a file directly from Windows Explorer. Here's how to work around this:

1. In Windows Explorer, select the document you want to work with.

2. Select File, Open With. (Alternatively, right-click the document, and then click Open With in the shortcut menu.)

3. The next step depends on the file you're working with:

   - For most files, Windows XP goes directly to the Open With dialog box. In this case, skip to step 4.

   - For a system file, Windows asks whether you're sure that you want to open the file. In this case, click Open With.

   - For some file types, Windows XP displays a submenu of suggested programs. In this case, if you see the alternative program you want, select it. Otherwise, select Choose Program.

4. In the Programs list, select the unassociated application in which you want to open the document. (If the application you want to use isn't listed, click Browse and then select the program's executable file from the dialog box that appears.)

5. To prevent Windows XP from changing the file type to the unassociated application, make sure that the Always Use the Selected Program to Open This Kind of File check box is deactivated.

6. Click OK to open the document in the selected application.

One of the small but useful interface improvements in Windows XP is that the system remembers the unassociated applications that you choose in the Open With dialog box. When you next select the Open With command for the file type, Windows XP displays a menu that includes both the associated program and the unassociated program you chose earlier.

## How the Open With Feature Works

Before you learn about the more advanced Open With customizations, you need to know how Windows XP compiles the list of applications that appear on the Open With list:

- Windows XP checks `HKEY_CLASSES_ROOT\.ext` (where *.ext* is the extension that defines the file type). If it finds an `OpenWith` subkey, the applications listed under that subkey are added to the Open With menu, and they also appear in the Open With dialog box in the Programs list's Recommended Programs branch.

- Windows XP checks `HKEY_CLASSES_ROOT\.ext` to see whether the file type has a `PerceivedType` setting. If so, it means the file type also has an associated **perceived type**. This is a broader type that groups related file types into a single category. For example, the Image perceived type includes files of type BMP, GIF, and JPEG, whereas the Text perceived type includes the files of type TXT, HTM, and XML. Windows XP then checks the following:

  `HKEY_CLASSES_ROOT\SystemFileAssociations\PerceivedType\OpenWithList`

  Here, *PerceivedType* is value of the file type's `PerceivedType` setting. The application keys listed under the `OpenWithList` key are added to the file type's Open With menu and dialog box.

- Windows XP checks `HKEY_CLASSES_ROOT\Applications`, which contains subkeys named after application executable files. If an application subkey has a `\shell\open\command` subkey, and if that subkey's `Default` value is set to the path name of the application's executable file, the application is added to the Open With dialog box.

- Windows XP checks the following key:

  `HKEY_CURRENT_USER\Software\Microsoft\Windows\CurrentVersion\Explorer\`
  `FileExts\.ext\OpenWithList`

Here, *ext* is the file type's extension. This key contains settings for each application that the current user has used to open the file type via Open With. These settings are named a, b, c, and so on, and there's an MRUList setting that lists these letters in the order in which the applications have been used. These applications are added to the file type's Open With menu.

## Removing an Application from a File Type's Open With Menu

When you use the Open With dialog box to choose an alternative application to open a particular file type, that application appears on the file type's Open With menu (that is, the menu that appears when you select the File, Open With command). To remove the application from this menu, open the following Registry key (where *ext* is the file type's extension):

```
HKEY_CURRENT_USER\Software\Microsoft\Windows\CurrentVersion\Explorer\
FileExts\.ext\OpenWithList
```

Delete the setting for the application you want removed from the menu. Also, edit the MRUList setting to remove the letter of the application you just deleted. For example, if the application setting you deleted was named b, delete the letter b from the MRUList setting.

## Removing a Program from the Open With List

Rather than customizing only a single file type's Open With menu, you might need to customize the Open With dialog box for all file types. To prevent a program from appearing in the Open With list, open the Registry Editor and navigate to the following key:

```
HKEY_CLASSES_ROOT/Applications
```

Here you'll find a number of subkeys, each of which represents an application installed on your system. The names of these subkeys are the names of each application's executable file (such as notepad.exe for Notepad). To prevent Windows XP from displaying an application in the Open With list, highlight the application's subkey, and create a new string value named NoOpenWith. (You don't have to supply a value for this setting.) To restore the application to the Open With list, delete the NoOpenWith setting.

> **NOTE**
>
> The NoOpenWith setting only works for applications that are not the default for opening a particular file type. For example, if you add NoOpenWith to the notepad.exe subkey, Notepad will still appear in the Open With list for text documents, but it won't appear for other file types, such as HTML files.

### Adding a Program to the Open With List

You can also add an application to the Open With dialog box for all file types. Again, you head for the following Registry key:

```
HKEY_CLASSES_ROOT/Applications
```

Display the subkey named after the application's executable file. (If the subkey doesn't exist, create it.) Now add the `\shell\open\command` subkey and set the `Default` value to the pathname of the application's executable file.

### Disabling the Open With Check Box

The Open With dialog box enables you to change the application associated with a file type's Open action by activating the Always Use the Selected Program to Open This Kind of File check box. If you share your computer with other people, you might not want them changing this association, either accidentally or purposefully. In that case, you can disable the check box by adjusting the following Registry key:

```
HKEY_CLASSES_ROOT\Unknown\shell\openas\command
```

The `Default` value of this key is the following

```
%SystemRoot%\system32\rundll32.exe %SystemRoot%\system32\shell32.dll,
OpenAs_RunDLL %1
```

To disable the check box in the Open With dialog box, append %2 to the end of the `Default` value:

```
%SystemRoot%\system32\rundll32.exe %SystemRoot%\system32\shell32.dll,
OpenAs_RunDLL %1 %2
```

# From Here

Here are some other places in the book where you'll find related information:

- For a primer on Windows XP file techniques, see Chapter 2, "Exploring Expert File and Folder Techniques."

- To learn about digital media file types, see the sections in Chapter 4 named "A Review of Digital Audio File Formats" and "A Review of Digital Video File Formats."

- For the details on understanding and working with the Registry, see Chapter 8, "Getting to Know the Windows XP Registry."

# Working with Digital Media

The English language is a veritable factory of new words and phrases. Inventive wordsmiths in all fields are constantly forging new additions to the lexicon by blending words, attaching morphemic tidbits to existing words, and creating neologisms out of thin air. Some of these new words strike a chord in popular culture and go through what I call the "cachet-to-cliché" syndrome. In other words, the word is suddenly on the lips of cocktail party participants and water-cooler conversationalists everywhere, and on the fingertips of countless columnists and editorialists. As soon as the word takes root, however, the backlash begins. Rants of the if-I-hear-the-word-*x*-one-more-time-I'll-scream variety start to appear, Lake Superior State University includes the word in its annual list of phrases that should be stricken from the language, and so on.

The word *multimedia* went through this riches-to-rags scenario a few of years ago. Buoyed by the promise of media-rich interactive applications and games, techies and nontechies alike quickly made multimedia their favorite buzzword. It didn't take long, however, for the bloom to come off the multimedia rose.

Part of the problem was that when multimedia first became a big deal in the early '90s, the average computer just wasn't powerful enough to handle the extra demands made on the system. Not only that, but Windows' support for multimedia was sporadic and half-hearted. That's all changed now, however. The typical PC sold today has more than enough horsepower to handle basic multimedia, and Windows XP has a number of slick new features that let developers and end-users alike incorporate multimedia seamlessly into their work. Now it doesn't much matter that the word *multimedia* has more or less been replaced by the phrase *digital media* because what really matters is that people can get down to the more practical matter of creating exciting media-enhanced documents.

The basic digital media features of Windows XP are easy enough to master, but there are plenty of hidden and obscure features that you should know about, and I'll take you through them in this chapter.

# Understanding Digital Audio

When I put together multimedia presentations, videos, and animations, the graphics are what make the audience "ooh" and "aah" during the playback. However, I've often found that what most people comment on *after* the show is, surprisingly, the soundtrack: the music and sound effects that accompany the visuals. It seems that adding bells and whistles (literally) to multimedia makes a big impact on people.

I'm not certain why this happens, but I'm sure that part of the reason has to do with our ears. The ear is a fine and sensitive instrument, attuned to nuance on the one hand, but shamelessly craving novelty on the other. How else do you explain, in a society supposedly in love with the visual image, the relentless popularity of radio after all these years?

I'm guessing that another reason why audio is such an important part of multimedia is that most people are used to their computers being, if not voiceless, at least monotonic. Most mainstream applications are content to utter simple beeps and boops to alert you to an error or otherwise get your attention. Multimedia, however, with its music and unusual sound bites, can provide quite a jolt to people who aren't used to such things (particularly during presentations, where judicious use of sounds can really make an impact).

In other words, there's no reason to think of sound as the poor cousin of flashy videos and graphics. So, let's begin our look at Windows XP media with a primer of digital audio concepts, formats, properties, and hardware. This will help you understand exactly what you're dealing with when you work with digital audio files later.

## Analog-to-Digital Sound Conversion

Sound cards work by converting analog sound waves into digital signals that can be sent to your computer's speakers. To help you evaluate sound cards and choose the appropriate properties for your digital recordings, you should know a bit about how the analog-to-digital conversion takes place.

### The Nature of Sound

When an object such as a violin string or a speaker diaphragm vibrates or moves back and forth, it alternately compresses and decompresses the air molecules around it. This alternating compression and decompression sets up a vibration in the air molecules that propagates outward from the source as a wave. This is called a **sound wave**. When the sound wave reaches your ear, it sets up a corresponding vibration in your eardrum, and you hear the sound created by the object.

Each sound wave has two basic properties:

| | |
|---|---|
| Frequency | This determines the pitch of the sound. It's a measure of the rate at which the sound wave's vibrations are produced. The higher the frequency, the higher the pitch. Frequency is measured in cycles per second, or **hertz** (Hz), where one cycle is a vibration back and forth. |
| Intensity | This is a measure of the loudness of the sound (that is, the strength of the vibration). It's determined by the amplitude of the sound wave. The greater the amplitude, the greater the motion of the sound wave's molecules, and the greater the impact on your eardrum. Amplitude is measured in **decibels** (dB). |

Figure 4.1 shows part of a waveform for a typical sound. The amplitude is found by taking the midpoint of the wave (which is set to 0) and measuring the distance to a positive or negative peak. Because the period from one peak to the next is defined as a cycle, the **frequency** is given by the number of peaks that occur per second.

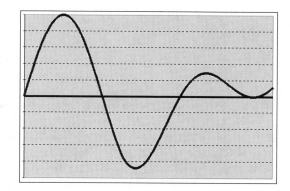

**FIGURE 4.1**    An analog waveform for a sound.

### How an Analog Sound Wave Gets Digitized

Sound waves are inherently analog, so if you want to work with them on a computer, you must convert them to a digital audio format. A sound card has a small chip called an **analog-to-digital converter** (ADC), whose sole purpose is to convert analog sound waves into the digital ones and zeros that computers know and love. (Sound cards also have a **digital-to-analog converter** [DAC] chip that performs the reverse process: converting digitized audio back into an analog wave so that you can hear it.) This is done through a technique called **Pulse Code Modulation** (PCM): taking "snapshots" of the analog wave at discrete intervals and noting the wave's amplitude. These amplitude values form the basis of the digital representation of the wave. Because each snapshot is really a sample of the current state of the wave, this process is called **sampling**.

### Digital Audio Quality I: The Sampling Frequency

One of the major determinants of digital audio quality is the rate at which the sound card samples the analog data. The more samples taken per second—that is, the higher the **sampling frequency**—the more accurately the digitized data will represent the original sound waveform.

To see how this works, consider the chart shown in Figure 4.2. This is a graph of digitized data sampled from the analog waveform shown in Figure 4.1. Each column represents an amplitude value sampled from the analog wave at a given moment. In this case, the sampling frequency is very low, so the shape of the digitized waveform only approximates the analog wave and much data is lost.

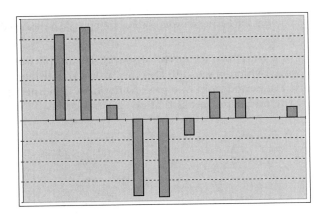

**FIGURE 4.2**   A digitized waveform generated by a low sampling frequency.

To improve the quality and fidelity of the digitized waveform, you need to use a higher sampling frequency. For example, the chart shown in Figure 4.3 shows the resulting digital waveform with a sampling frequency four times greater than the one shown in Figure 4.2. As you can see, the waveform is a much more accurate representation of the original analog wave.

So, what sampling frequency is best? Well, as you'll see later, disk space considerations come into play because higher sampling rates create correspondingly bigger files. However, the general rule of thumb is that, for the most faithful reproduction of analog sound, your sampling frequency should be roughly twice the highest sound frequency you want to reproduce (plus another 10% for good measure).

Human hearing ranges from a low of 20Hz to a high of about 20KHz (20,000Hz). So, for accurate reproduction of anything within the human audible range, you'd sample at a frequency of about 44KHz (two times 20KHz plus 10%). As you'll see a bit later, CD-quality digital audio—the highest quality supported by today's sound hardware—samples at 44.1KHz.

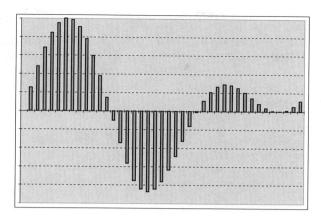

**FIGURE 4.3** To improve the sound quality of the digitized waveform, you need to increase the sampling frequency.

### Digital Audio Quality II: 8-Bit Versus 16-Bit

Another major determinant of digital audio quality is the number of bits used to digitize each sample. This is sometimes called the **sample depth**. To see why sample depth makes a difference, consider a simplified example. Suppose that you're sampling a wave with amplitudes between 0dB and 100dB. If you had only a two-bit sample depth, you'd have only four discrete levels with which to assign amplitudes. If you used, say, 25dB, 50dB, 75dB, and 100dB, all the sampled values would have to be adjusted (by rounding up, for example) to one of these values. Figure 4.4 shows the result. The smooth line shows the original amplitudes, and the columns show the assigned sample values, given a two-bit sample depth. As you can see, much data is lost by having to adjust to the discrete levels.

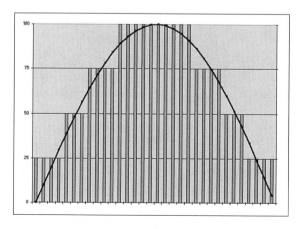

**FIGURE 4.4** The lower the sample depth, the more information that gets lost during sampling.

Fortunately, there is no such thing as 2-bit sampling. Instead, sound cards support two levels of sample depth: 8-bit and 16-bit. The 8-bit sample depth might sound like a lot more, but it means that the digitized amplitude values must be shoehorned into just 256 possible levels, which is a far cry from the infinite number of levels in the original analog waveform. With 16-bit sampling, 65,536 discrete levels are available, which makes a big difference in sound quality.

> **NOTE**
>
> Another way to look at sample depth is to consider a ruler. The accuracy with which you can measure something with a ruler depends on the number of divisions. A ruler with only quarter-inch divisions won't provide as exact a measurement as a ruler with sixteenth-inch divisions. In audio, an 8-bit sample depth is like a ruler with 256 divisions per sample, and a 16-bit sample depth is like a ruler with 65,536 divisions per sample.

### Digital Audio Quality III: Mono Versus Stereo

The final consideration for digital audio quality is the number of channels you want to store. In other words, do you want your audio to be mono (one channel) or stereo (two channels)? The latter provides a richer sound, but only for sound cards that support two channels, and only for systems with two speakers attached to the card.

### Quality Levels and Disk Space Considerations

As you might imagine, the various levels of digital sound quality also affect the size of the resulting audio file. A stereo capture with a 44.1KHz sample rate and a 16-bit sample depth will use approximately 22 times more hard disk area than a mono capture with an 8KHz sampling rate and an 8-bit sample depth. Obviously, you need to think carefully about which options to use when capturing or recording audio. The quality level depends on the amount of disk space you have, your audience, and your need for fidelity. Music files, for example, almost certainly require a higher-quality file than does the spoken word.

To assign some concrete numbers to all this, Table 4.1 lists the number of kilobytes per second used for various combinations of sample frequency, sample depth, and channels. Later, I'll tell you about some audio codecs that can reduce the disk space requirements for audio files.

**TABLE 4.1**   Disk Space Requirements for Various Digital Audio Quality Combinations

| Sample Frequency | Sample Depth | Channels | Disk Space |
|---|---|---|---|
| 8KHz | 8-bit | Mono | 8KBps |
| 8KHz | 8-bit | Stereo | 16KBps |
| 8KHz | 16-bit | Mono | 16KBps |
| 8KHz | 16-bit | Stereo | 32KBps |
| 11.025KHz | 8-bit | Mono | 11KBps |
| 11.025KHz | 8-bit | Stereo | 22KBps |
| 11.025KHz | 16-bit | Mono | 22KBps |

**TABLE 4.1**   Continued

| Sample Frequency | Sample Depth | Channels | Disk Space |
|---|---|---|---|
| 11.025KHz | 16-bit | Stereo | 44KBps |
| 22.05KHz | 8-bit | Mono | 22KBps |
| 22.05KHz | 8-bit | Stereo | 44KBps |
| 22.05KHz | 16-bit | Mono | 22KBps |
| 22.05KHz | 16-bit | Stereo | 88KBps |
| 44.1KHz | 8-bit | Mono | 44KBps |
| 44.1KHz | 8-bit | Stereo | 88KBps |
| 44.1KHz | 16-bit | Mono | 88KBps |
| 44.1KHz | 16-bit | Stereo | 176KBps |

**NOTE**

Three of the combinations in Table 4.1 are standards in the digital audio realm:

| Telephone | 11.025KHz sample frequency, 8-bit sample depth, mono |
| Radio | 22.05KHz sample frequency, 8-bit sample depth, mono |
| CD | 44.1KHz sample frequency, 16-bit sample depth, stereo |

## A Review of Digital Audio File Formats

Audio files come in many different formats, but only a few are of interest to most Windows XP users:

MP3 (`.mp3`)

MP3 (Motion Picture Experts Groups Audio Level 3) is one of the most popular audio file formats. It compresses digital audio by removing extraneous sounds not normally detected by the human ear. This results in high-quality audio files that are one-tenth the size of uncompressed audio, making MP3s ideal for downloading and storing on digital audio players (which are frequently called **MP3 players**, even when they support other audio formats).

WMA (`.wma`)

WMA (Windows Media Audio) is the standard Windows Media Player format. It produces audio files with the same quality as MP3, but compressed to about half the size. WMA is often used for digital audio player storage because it can fit twice the number of songs as MP3.

WAV (`.wav`)

WAV (waveform audio) was once the standard Windows digital audio format. WAV files are created via the PCM technique. All Windows-based sound applications can play WAV files, and each WAV file will sound the same no matter which sound application you use to play it.

| MIDI (`.mid` or `.rmi`) | MIDI (Musical Instrument Digital Interface) is a nonwaveform file that stores musical instructions instead of waveform amplitudes. Sound cards that support MIDI have various synthesized instruments built into their chips. A MIDI file's instructions specify which instrument to play, which note to play, how long the note should be held, and so on. |
| AIFF (`.aif`, `.aifc`, and `.aiff`) | AIFF (Audio Interchange File Format) is a format that began life on the Apple Macintosh. It supports 16-bit 44.1KHz stereo sound files. |
| AU (`.au`) | AU (Sun Audio Format) is the standard UNIX audio format, so it's still one of the standard audio formats on the Internet. A similar UNIX format is SND (Sound; `.snd`), developed by NeXT. |

## Displaying Your Installed Audio Codecs

As their quality increases, sound files take up a progressively bigger chunk of your hard disk. To help reduce the load, a **codec** (coder/decoder) is used to compress digitized audio and then decompress it for playing. Windows XP comes with a number of 32-bit codecs. Follow these steps to see the list of audio codecs installed on your system:

1. Click start, Control Panel, Sound and Audio Devices. The Sound and Audio Devices Properties dialog box appears.

2. Click the Hardware tab.

3. In the Devices list, select Audio Codecs.

4. Click Properties. The Audio Codecs Properties dialog box appears.

5. Click the Properties tab. Windows XP displays a list of your system's installed codecs, as shown in Figure 4.5.

> **NOTE**
>
> Not all sound cards support every available codec. Therefore, the number of codecs that Windows XP adds to your system depends on the sound card you have installed.

## Troubleshooting: Disabling an Audio Codec

If you're having trouble with digital audio, one common cause is conflicting audio codes. For example, you might have two different versions of an **ADPCM** (Adaptive Delta Pulse Code Modulation)—one from Microsoft and one from a third party. You might be able to solve your problem by disabling the third-party codec. Here are the steps to follow to disable an audio codec:

1. Follow steps 1–5 in the previous section to display the Audio Codecs Properties dialog box.

2. Select the codec you want to disable.

**3.** Click Properties to open the codec's property sheet.

**4.** Activate the Do Not Use This Audio Codec option, as shown in Figure 4.6.

**5.** Click OK.

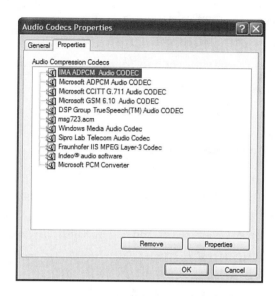

**FIGURE 4.5**    Open the Audio Codecs property sheet to see the list of audio codecs installed on your system.

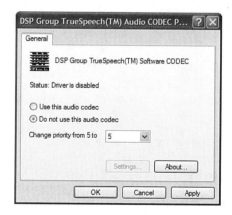

**FIGURE 4.6**    If you suspect conflicting codecs are causing audio problems, disable one of the codecs.

## Troubleshooting: Reinstalling an Audio Codec

Another solution for many audio difficulties is to reinstall a codec that might be damaged. Here are the steps to follow to reinstall a default Windows XP audio codec:

1. Follow steps 1–5 outlined earlier in the "Displaying Your Installed Audio Codecs" section to display the Audio Codecs Properties dialog box.

2. Select the codec you want to reinstall.

3. Click Remove. Windows XP asks you to confirm the deletion.

4. Click Yes. Windows XP tells you that it needs to restart the system.

5. Click Don't Restart Now and then click OK in the next two dialog boxes to return to Control Panel.

6. Double-click the Add Hardware icon.

7. Click Next.

8. Activate the Yes, I Have Already Connected the Hardware option and then click Next.

9. In the Installed Hardware list, select Add a New Hardware Device and click Next.

10. Activate the Install the Hardware That I Manually Select from a List option and click Next.

11. In the Common Hardware Types list, select the Sound, Video and Game Controllers item and click Next.

12. Click Have Disk to display the Install from Disk dialog box.

13. Click Browse and use the Locate File dialog box to open the C:\Windows\System32 folder, select the MMDRIVER.INF file, and click Open.

14. Click OK.

15. If Windows XP warns you that the software has not passed Windows Logo testing, click Continue Anyway. Windows XP displays a list of codecs and drivers, as shown in Figure 4.7.

16. Select the codec you want to install and click Next.

17. Click Next.

18. If Windows XP warns you that the software has not passed Windows Logo testing, click Continue Anyway. Windows XP installs the codec.

19. Click Finish.

20. When Windows XP asks whether you want to restart your system, click Yes.

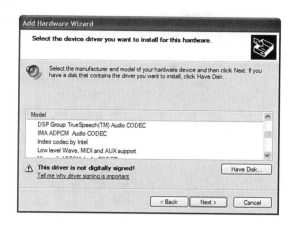

**FIGURE 4.7**    Select the codec you want to reinstall.

# Understanding Digital Video

Although other computer platforms (notably the Macintosh) could work with digital video earlier, for the Windows crowd the big moment came in 1992 with the release of Video for Windows (VfW) 1.0. As long as you installed a video capture card in your machine, you could hook up a camcorder or VCR to your computer. VfW came with a utility called VidCap that would take the incoming video, digitize it, and save the result to a file on your hard disk. You could then use VfW's VidEdit program to manipulate the digitized video frame-by-frame, just as your word processor manipulates text word-by-word.

Digital video has come a long way since then. The original VfW was limited to a puny 160×120-pixel window (hence the epithet "dancing postage stamps" that was often applied to VfW files in those days), and VfW playback limped along at 15 frames per second (fps), which, compared to the full-motion rate of 30fps used by videotape, made some digital videos look jerky. By contrast, today's digital video files run in 720×480-pixel windows (known as **full-screen video**) and play smoothly at 30fps. This section introduces you to the modern-day digital video.

## Understanding Video Compression Schemes

If there were no limit to hard disk capacity, all digital video clips would be captured as raw footage and, provided you had a fast enough processor and a reasonable graphics adapter, there would be no concerns about video quality and tiny window sizes. Hard disks, however, are decidedly not infinite, so video files have to be literally cut down to size. Four factors determine the overall size of a video file:

| | |
|---|---|
| The color depth of the images | Everything else being equal, 8-bit images take up only a third as much space as 24-bit images. |
| The size of the video playback window | A clip designed for a 320×240 window will be less than one-fourth the size of a clip that is designed to run full-screen (720×480). |
| The frame rate | Full-motion videos (30fps) pack twice as much informa tion into a given amount of time than do videos playing at 15fps. |
| The quality of the sound | A video file incorporates synchronized audio as well as video. And, as with video, the higher the quality of the audio, the bigger the audio stream. |

Quality-conscious video producers typically try to maximize as many of these variables as they can, so they capture their footage with as much data as possible. They then use some kind of compression technology to put the squeeze on the massive video files before distributing them. When you play a video clip, Windows XP checks the compression used in the file and then calls the appropriate driver to handle the decompression.

Video compression is one of the most crucial components of digital video because it can have a huge impact on the quality of the resulting file. In general, compression involves trade-offs between file size and image quality. That's because most compression schemes are **lossy**, which means that some redundant information is discarded during the compression process. The higher the compression ratio, the more data that gets lost and the more the image degrades. On the other hand, lower compression ratios improve quality, but at the cost of larger files that might require a fast CPU to decompress.

However, the compression ratio isn't the only characteristic that a video producer must be concerned with. The compression scheme itself is an important consideration as well. If a digital video file is compressed with a codec that Windows XP doesn't recognize, you won't be able to play that video. Happily, Windows XP ships with drivers for many of the most popular codecs in use today (including MPEG-4, Cinepak, Indeo, MPEG-4, RLE, and Microsoft Video 1), so this is less of a concern for producers. Follow these steps to see the list of video codecs installed on your system:

1. Click start, Control Panel, Sound and Audio Devices. The Sound and Audio Devices Properties dialog box appears.

2. Click the Hardware tab.

3. In the Devices list, select Video Codecs.

4. Click Properties. The Video Codecs Properties dialog box appears.

5. Click the Properties tab. Windows XP displays a list of your system's installed codecs, as shown in Figure 4.8.

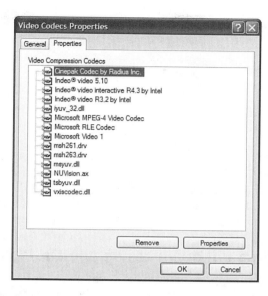

**FIGURE 4.8**   Open the Video Codecs property sheet to see the list of video codecs installed on your system.

## A Review of Digital Video File Formats

Video clips come in many formats, but only a few are of any interest to Windows XP users. Here's a summary of the video formats you're likely to come across in your video travels:

| | |
|---|---|
| MPEG (`.mpeg`, `.mpg`, or `.mp2`) | MPEG (Motion Picture Experts Group) has three main standards: MPEG-1 produces near-VHS quality video; MPEG-2 produces DVD-quality video; MPEG-4 is an enhanced version of MPEG-2 that produces even smaller files. |
| WMV (`.wmv`) | WMV (Windows Media Video) is the default digital video format for Windows Media Player. It's similar to MPEG-4, but produces even smaller files. |
| ASF (`.asf`) | ASF (Active Streaming Format) is another Microsoft digital video technology. ASF allows multiple objects (such as audio objects, video objects, bitmaps, URLs, HTML pages, and programs) to be combined and stored in a single synchronized multimedia stream. |
| VfW (`.avi`) | VfW (Video for Windows) is the standard VfW format that was supported by Windows over the years. The large AVI (Audio Video Interleave) files produced by VfW have caused many producers to move to other formats. |

QuickTime for Windows (.mov)    QuickTime is the digital video format developed by Apple. It's the standard format for Macintosh users, but it has been available for Windows users for a number of years. The big advantage of QuickTime's MOV files is that they can be used on both Mac and Windows machines without alteration. Therefore, because so many video production houses are Mac shops, there are lots of MOV files out there.

### Reinstalling a Video Codec

If you have trouble with a specific codec, removing the codec and then reinstalling it will often solve the problem. Follow the steps for reinstalling an audio codec that I outlined earlier in the "Troubleshooting: Reinstalling an Audio Codec" section.

## Tips for Working with Windows Media Player

You've seen that Windows supports all kinds of digital media formats. In previous versions of Windows, the bad news was that to play those formats you had to master a passel of player programs. In Windows XP, the good news is that you now need to wrestle with only a single program: Windows Media Player. This clever chunk of software is a true one-stop multimedia shop that's capable of playing sound files, music files, audio CDs, animations, movie files, and even DVDs. It can even copy audio CD tracks to your computer, burn music files to a CD, tune in to Internet radio stations, and more.

If you don't see the Windows Media Player icon in the main Start menu, you can open the program by clicking Start, All Programs, Windows Media Player.

### Playing Media Files

Windows XP gives you many indirect ways to play media files via Windows Media Player. Here's a summary:

- Open Windows Explorer, find the media file you want to play, and then double-click the file.

> **NOTE**
>
> To control the media file types that are associated with Windows Media Player, select Tools, Options and display the File Types tab. Activate the check boxes for the file types that you want to open automatically in Windows Media Player. If you don't want Windows Media Player to handle a particular file type, deactivate its check box.

- Insert an audio CD in your CD or DVD drive. If you have a DVD decoder installed on your system, you can also insert a DVD disc in your DVD drive.

- If you have a memory card reader, insert a memory card (such as a CompactFlash card or a MultiMedia Card). If Windows XP asks what you want to do with this disk, select Play the Music Files. If you don't want to be bothered with this dialog box each time, activate the Always Do the Selected Action check box. Click OK.

- Download media from the Internet.

- You can also open files directly from Media Player by pulling down the File menu and selecting either Open (to launch a media file from your computer or from a network location), or Open URL (to launch a media file from the Internet).

---

**TIP**

Many of today's keyboards are media-enhanced, which means they come with extra keys that perform digital media functions such as playing, pausing, and stopping media, adjusting the volume, and changing the track. Also, here are a few Windows Media Player shortcut keys that you might find useful while playing media files:

| | |
|---|---|
| Ctrl+P | Play or pause the current media |
| Ctrl+S | Stop the current media |
| Ctrl+B | Go to the previous track |
| Ctrl+Shift+B | Rewind to beginning of the media |
| Ctrl+F | Go to the next track |
| Ctrl+Shift+F | Fast forward to the end of the media |
| Ctrl+H | Toggle shuffle playback |
| Ctrl+T | Toggle repeat playback |
| Ctrl+1 | Switch to Full mode |
| Ctrl+2 | Switch to Skin mode |
| F8 | Mute sound |
| F9 | Decrease volume |
| F10 | Increase volume |

---

## Setting Windows Media Player's Playback Options

Windows Media Player comes with several options that you can work with to control various aspects of the playback. To see these options, select Tools, Options. The Player tab, shown in Figure 4.9, contains the following settings:

| | |
|---|---|
| Check for Updates | Use these options to determine how often Windows Media Player checks for newer versions of the program. |

---

**TIP**

To prevent Windows Media Player from displaying a message that an update is available, create a string setting named AskMeAgain in the following Registry key and set its value to No:

```
HKLM\SOFTWARE\Microsoft\MediaPlayer\PlayerUpgrade
```

You can also prevent Windows Media Player from automatically updating itself if it detects that a newer version is available. Create the following key, add a DWORD value called DisableAutoUpdate and set its value to 1:

HKLM\SOFTWARE\Policies\Microsoft\WindowsMediaPlayer

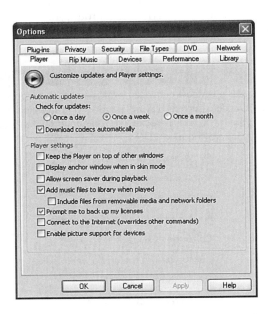

**FIGURE 4.9**   Use the Player tab to configure Windows Media Player's playback options.

| | |
|---|---|
| Download Codecs Automatically | When this check box is activated, Media Player automatically attempts to download and install a codec for any file type that it doesn't recognize. If you prefer to be prompted before the download occurs, deactivate this check box. You can disable this check box using the Group Policy editor (see Chapter 7, "Using Control Panel, Group Policies, and Tweak UI"). Select User Configuration, Administrative Templates, Windows Components, Windows Media Player, Playback and enable the Prevent Codec Download policy. |
| Keep the Player on Top of Other Windows | When this check box is activated, Windows Media Player stays on top of other windows. This is useful if you want to able to access Windows Media Player's playback controls while working in another program. |

Unless you have a large screen running at a high resolution, an always-on-top Windows Media Player window is probably going to get in the way. A better solution is to display the Windows Media Player playback controls in the Windows XP taskbar. To do that, right-click an empty section of the taskbar and then select Toolbars, Windows Media Player. Minimize the Windows Media Player window and the Windows Media Player toolbar appears in the taskbar.

Display Anchor Window When in Skin Mode

When this check box is activated, Media Player displays a small window in the lower-right corner of the screen when you switch to Skin mode (select View, Skin Mode, or press Ctrl+2), as shown in Figure 4.10. With the anchor window displayed, you can click its button to quickly switch to Full mode or change the skin. You can disable this check box using the Group Policy Editor. Select User Configuration, Administrative Templates, Windows Components, Windows Media Player, User Interface and enable the Do Not Show Anchor policy.

Anchor window

**FIGURE 4.10**    Display the Windows Media Player anchor window to quickly restore Full mode or change the skin.

You can use the Group Policy editor to configure Windows Media Player to play only in Skin mode and to specify the skin. Select User Configuration, Administrative Templates, Windows Components, Windows Media Player, User Interface and enable the Set and Lock Skin policy. Also, use the Skin text box to specify the name of a skin file. Note that skin files use the `.wmz` extension and the default skins can be found in the `%ProgramFiles%\ Windows Media Player\Skins` folder.

| | |
|---|---|
| Allow Screen Saver During Playback | When this check box is activated, the Windows XP screensaver is allowed to kick in after the system has been idle for the specified number of minutes. If you're watching streaming video content or a DVD movie, leave this check box deactivated to prevent the screensaver from activating. |
| Add Music Files to Library When Played | When this check box is activated, Windows Media Player adds files that you play to the Library. For example, if you play a downloaded MP3 file, Windows Media Player adds it to the Library in the All Music category. Note that, by default, Windows Media Player doesn't add media from removable media and network shares to the Library. |
| Include Files from Removable Media and Network Folders | When this check box is activated, Media Player adds music files to the Library that you play from removable media, such as a CompactFlash card, as well as from shared network folders. Note that you won't be able to play these items unless the removable media is inserted or the network share is available. |
| Prompt Me to Back Up My Licenses | When this check box is activated, Windows Media Player displays a dialog box to remind you to make a backup copy of a media file license about two weeks after you acquire each license. |
| Connect to the Internet | When this check box is activated, Windows Media Player always connects to the Internet when you select a feature that requires Internet access, such as the Guide (windowsmedia.com) or MSN Music (music.msn.com). This connection occurs even if you have activated the File menu's Work Offline command. |
| Enable Picture Support for Devices | When this check box is activated, Windows Media Player creates an All Pictures category in the Library. If you have an MP3 player or other device that supports JPEG images, you can then synchronize the device and the contents of the All Pictures category. |

## Copying Music from an Audio CD

Windows Media Player comes with the welcome capability to copy (**rip** in the vernacular) tracks from an audio CD to your computer's hard disk. Although this process is straight-forward, as you'll see, there are several options that you need to take into account **before** you start copying. These options include the location of the folder in which the ripped tracks will be stored, the structure of the track filenames, the file format to use, and the quality (bit rate) at which you want to copy the tracks. You control all of these settings in the Rip Music tab of the Options dialog box (select Tools, Options to get there), shown in Figure 4.11.

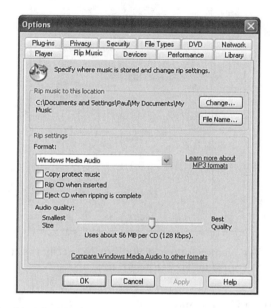

**FIGURE 4.11**   Use the Rip Music tab to specify the options you want to use when copying tracks from an audio CD.

### Selecting a Location and Filename Structure

The Rip Music to This Location group displays the name of the folder that will be used to store the copied tracks. By default, this location is `%UserProfile%\My Documents\My Music`. To specify a different folder (for example, a folder on a partition with lots of free space), click Change and use the Browse for Folder dialog box to choose the new folder.

The default filenames that Windows Media Player generates for each copied track use the following structure:

`Track_Number Song_Title.ext`

Here, `Track_Number` is the song's track number on the CD, `Song_Title` is the name of the song, and `ext` is the extension used by the recording format (such as WMA or MP3). Windows Media Player can also include additional data in the file name such as the artist name, the album name, the music genre, and the recording bit rate. To control which of these details is incorporated into the name, click the File Name button in the Rip Music tab to display the File Name Options dialog box, shown in Figure 4.12. Activate the check boxes beside the details you want in the filenames, and use the Move Up and Move

Down buttons to determine the order of the details. Finally, use the Separator list to choose which character to use to separate each detail.

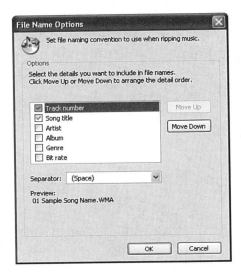

**FIGURE 4.12**   Use the File Name Options dialog box to specify the details you want in the filename assigned to each copied audio CD track.

### Choosing the Recording File Format

Prior to version 10, Windows Media Player supported only a single file format: WMA (Windows Media Audio). This is an excellent music format that provides good quality recordings at high compression rates. If you plan on listening to the tracks only on your computer or on a custom CD, the WMA format is all you need. However, if you have an MP3 player or other device that doesn't recognize WMA files (although most do), you need to use the MP3 recording format. Fortunately, Windows Media Player 10 now provides MP3 encoding support right out of the box. (If you're still using Media Player 9, you need to purchase and install an MP3 encoder.)

If you have multiple encoders installed, use the Format list in the Rip Music tab to choose the encoder you want to use. Note that if you select Windows Media Audio, the Copy Protect Music check box becomes enabled. Here's how this check box affects your copying:

- If Copy Protect Music is activated, Media Player applies a license to each track that prevents you from copying the track to another computer or to any portable device that is SDMI-compliant (SDMI is the Secure Digital Music Initiative; see www.sdmi.org for more information). Note, however, that you are allowed to copy the track to a writeable CD.

- If Copy Protect Music is deactivated, there are no restrictions on where or how you can copy the track. As long as you're copying tracks for personal use, deactivating this check box is the most convenient route to take.

### Specifying the Quality of the Recording

The tracks on an audio CD use the CD Audio Track file format (.cda extension), which represents the raw (uncompressed) audio data. You can't work with these files directly because the CDA format isn't supported by Windows XP and because these files tend to be huge (usually double-digit megabytes, depending on the track). Instead, the tracks need to be converted into a Windows XP–supported format (such as WMA). This conversion always involves compressing the tracks to a more manageable size. However, because the compression process operates by removing extraneous data from the file (that is, it's a *lossy* compression), there's a tradeoff between file size and music quality. That is, the higher the compression, the smaller the resulting file, but the poorer the sound quality. Conversely, the lower the compression, the larger the file, but the better the sound quality. Generally, how you handle this tradeoff depends on how much hard disk space you have to store the files and how sensitive your ear is to the sound quality.

As you saw earlier in this chapter, the recording quality is usually measured in bits per second (this is called the **bit rate**), with higher values producing better quality and larger files. To specify the recording quality, use the Audio Quality slider in the Rip Music tab. Move the slider to the right for higher quality recordings, and to the left for lower quality.

### Copying Tracks from an Audio CD

After you've made your recording choices, you're ready to start ripping tracks. Here are the steps to follow:

1. Insert the audio CD.

2. Click Rip in the Windows Media Player taskbar. Windows Media Player displays a list of the available tracks. To get the track names, connect to the Internet and then click View Album Info.

3. Activate the check boxes beside the tracks you want to copy.

4. Click Rip Music.

## Copying Tracks to a Recordable CD or Device

Windows Media Player can also perform the opposite task: copying media files from your computer to a recordable CD or portable device. Again, there are some settings you should consider before trying out this procedure.

### Setting Recording Options

In Windows Media Player's Options dialog box (select Tools, Options), display the Devices tab, select the device you want to use, and then click Properties. In the property sheet that appears, display the Recording tab. For a recordable CD drive, you have four options (see Figure 4.13):

If you don't see the Recording tab in Windows Media Player, select Start, My Computer, right-click the recordable CD drive icon, click Properties, and then click the Recording tab.

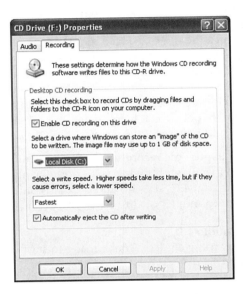

**FIGURE 4.13**    In the property sheet for a CD-R or CD-RW drive, use the Recording tab to enable and configure CD recording.

Enable CD Recording on This Drive

Activate this option to allow Windows Media Player to use the recordable CD drive for recording. You can prevent others from recording to this drive by deactivating this check box.

If you find that the Enable CD Recording on This Drive check box doesn't remain activated, the culprit might be a third-party CD burning program installed on your system. These programs typically disable Windows XP's CD burning features, and one way they do that is to deactivate the Enable CD Recording on This Drive check box. The only workaround is to uninstall the third-party program.

Select a Drive Where Windows Can Store an "Image" of the CD

Before doing the actual recording, Windows Media Player converts your entire playlist into temporary WAV files that get deleted after the recording is complete. Because these are uncompressed files, a full CD's worth could take up as much as 1GB of

|                                        |                                                                                                                                                                                                                                                                                                       |
| -------------------------------------- | ----------------------------------------------------------------------------------------------------------------------------------------------------------------------------------------------------------------------------------------------------------------------------------------------------- |
|                                        | space. Use this list to choose a drive that has at least that much space available.                                                                                                                                                                                                                    |
| Select a Write Speed                   | Use this list to choose how fast you want Windows Media Player to record to the CD. If you have trouble recording, select a slower speed.                                                                                                                                                               |
| Automatically Eject the CD After Writing | When this check box is activated, Windows Media Player ejects the completed CD when the recording is complete. If you prefer to check the contents of the CD after the recording to ensure that the process completed successfully, or if you want to play the new CD, deactivate this check box. |

## Creating a Playlist

Most people find recording is easiest if it's done from a **playlist**, a customized collection of music files. Here's how to create a new playlist:

1. Click Library in the Windows Media Player taskbar.

2. Click Now Playing List, New List, Playlist. Windows Media Player adds the new playlist.

3. For each song you want to include in the new playlist, drag it from the library to the playlist pane.

4. Click New Playlist, Save Playlist As, type a name for the playlist, and then click Save.

> **TIP**
>
> If the music files you want to work with are on your hard disk, you can add them to the playlist using Windows Explorer. To do this, right-click a file or file selection, click Add to Playlist, choose the playlist you want to use, and then click OK.

After your playlist has been created, you can edit the list by highlighting it in the Library's My Playlists branch and then right-clicking the tracks.

## Recording to a CD or Device

Here are the steps to follow to burn music files to a recordable CD or portable device:

1. Insert the recordable CD or attach the portable device.

2. Click Burn in the Windows Media Player taskbar.

3. On the left side of the Burn window, use the drop-down list to choose the playlist or Library item you want to burn.

4. Activate the check boxes beside the tracks that you want to record. Make sure that the total number of minutes that you select isn't greater than the total number of minutes available on the recording device.

5. On the right side of the Burn window, use the drop-down list to select the drive or device that you want to use as the recording destination.

6. Click Start Burn.

# Dealing with Digital Media Files

Previous versions of Windows treated all documents more or less the same. Yes, we've seen innovations such as the Thumbnails view for images and the Web view for folders that showed a preview of some file types in the margin, but the Windows XP designers and programmers went beyond these simple tweaks. They realized that different document types require different user actions. An image, for example, might need to be copied to a CD, set as the desktop background, emailed, or published to the web. They also realized that many of today's users—especially home users—do a lot of work with digital media files: images captured from a digital camera or scanner; music files copied from an audio CD or downloaded from the Internet; and video files created via Windows Movie Maker or a third-party video editing program. The result is that Windows XP has many new features specifically designed to help users manage digital media files. I discuss these new features in this section and show you ways to improve upon them and customize them to suit the way you work.

## Getting the Most Out of Digital Media Files and Windows Explorer

Windows Explorer has three built-in digital media folders:

| | |
|---|---|
| My Pictures | Use this folder for images. The location of this folder is `%UserProfile%\My Documents\My Pictures`. |
| My Music | Use this folder for music and audio files. The location of this folder is `%UserProfile%\My Documents\My Music`. |
| My Videos | Use this folder for video clips and animations. The location of this folder is `%UserProfile%\My Documents\My Video`. |

---

**TIP**

You're free to rename and move all three digital media folders. Windows XP tracks the new names and locations using the My Pictures, My Music, and My Videos settings in the following Registry key:

```
HKCU\Software\Microsoft\Windows\CurrentVersion\Explorer\Shell Folders
```

---

When these folders are open in Windows Explorer, the tasks pane on the left is customized to display tasks related to the folder. For example, when the My Pictures folder is open, the Picture Tasks section contains the following commands:

| | |
|---|---|
| Get Pictures from Scanner or Camera | Click this command to scan an image or download pictures from a digital camera. Note that this command appears only if you have a scanner or camera attached to your computer. |
| View as Slide Show | Click this command to see full-screen versions of each image in the folder. The images change every five seconds. |
| Order Prints Online | Click this link to run the Online Print Ordering Wizard that enables you to send digital images to an online printing service, which will then mail the prints to you. |
| Print Pictures or Print the Selected Pictures or Print This Picture | Click this link to display the Photo Printing Wizard, which enables you to choose the layout (full page, 5×7, and so on) that you want to use to print the selected image or images. |
| Set as Desktop Background | Click this link to display the selected file as the desktop's background image. |
| Copy All Items to CD or Copy to CD | Click this link to copy either all the folder's files or the selected files to a recordable CD. |

The My Music and My Videos folders have their own customized tasks, although not as many as the My Pictures folder.

## Tips for Working with Digital Media Files

Here are a few tips and techniques that you can use to get the most out of working with digital media files in Windows Explorer:

- Take advantage of the new Filmstrip view—In the My Pictures folder, activate the View, Filmstrip command to view the images sequentially, something like a filmstrip.

- Customize the Details view—Windows Explorer's Details view (activate the View, Details command) normally shows only four columns: Name, Size, Type, and Date Modified. However, Windows XP has a number of other columns you can display, such as the dimensions of an image or the bit rate at which a music file was ripped. Select View, Choose Details to open the Choose Details dialog box (see Figure 4.14), or right-click a column heading and click the detail you want to see.

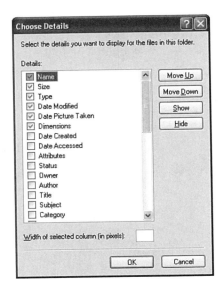

**FIGURE 4.14**    Use the Choose Details dialog box to specify the columns you want to see in Details view.

- Hide filenames in the Thumbnails and Filmstrip views—If you hold down Shift and double-click a folder, Windows Explorer opens the folder without displaying the filenames in the Thumbnails and Filmstrip views. To redisplay the filenames, click a different folder, and then hold down Shift and double-click the original folder.

- Change the default thumbnail size—By default, the images displayed in the Thumbnails view are 96 pixels square. You can change this by adding a DWORD value named ThumbnailSize to one of the following Registry keys and setting it to a decimal value between 32 and 256:

  ```
  HKLM\SOFTWARE\Microsoft\Windows\CurrentVersion\Explorer\
  HKCU\Software\Microsoft\Windows\CurrentVersion\Explorer\
  ```

- Change the default thumbnail quality—When you open a folder in either Thumbnails or Filmstrip view, Windows Explorer creates a file named Thumbs.db and uses it to store the thumbnail versions of each image. The size of this file depends on the quality level that Explorer uses to create the thumbnails: the higher the quality, the larger the file. You can control the quality level by adding a DWORD value named ThumbnailQuality to one of the following Registry keys and setting it to a decimal value between 50 (lowest quality) and 100 (highest quality):

  ```
  HKLM\SOFTWARE\Microsoft\Windows\CurrentVersion\Explorer\
  HKCU\Software\Microsoft\Windows\CurrentVersion\Explorer\
  ```

You can change both the thumbnail size and the thumbnail quality via Tweak UI (see Chapter 7). In the Tweak UI window, open the Explorer, Thumbnails branch.

## Creating a Screensaver Using Digital Images

Rather than displaying an abstract pattern as a screensaver, Windows XP allows you to use a collection of image files. To set this up, follow these steps:

1. Open Control Panel's Display icon, or right-click the desktop and then click Properties.

2. Display the Screen Saver tab.

3. In the Screen Saver list, select My Pictures Slideshow.

4. Click the Settings button to work with the following options:

| | |
|---|---|
| How Often Should Pictures Change? | Use this slider to set the amount of time that each picture is displayed (up to three minutes). |
| How Big Should Pictures Be? | Use this slider to set the maximum size of each picture relative to the screen size. For example, if you choose 50%, then the pictures are displayed up to half the size of the screen. Pictures smaller than that are displayed full-size, whereas pictures larger than that are shrunk to fit. |
| Use Pictures in This Folder | Click Browse to choose the folder from which the screen saver gets its images. The default is the current user's My Pictures folder. |
| Stretch Small Pictures | When this check box is activated, Windows XP expands small pictures so that they take up the percentage of the screen specified by the How Big Should Pictures Be? slider. |
| Show File Names | When this check box is activated, the screensaver shows the path and filename of each image in the upper-left corner. |
| Use Transition Effect Between Pictures | When this check box is activated, the screensaver uses a random transition effect (such as a fade out and fade in) from one picture to the next. |
| Allow Scrolling Through Pictures with the Keyboard | When this check box is activated, you can immediately display the next picture by pressing the Right Arrow key, and you can display the previous picture by pressing the Left Arrow key. |

# Customizing Media Folders

The features available in the My Pictures, My Music, and My Videos folders are actually based on templates that can also be applied to other folders on your system. For example, if you have images located in a folder other than My Pictures, you can set up that folder to use a template that gives it the same features as My Pictures. You can also customize a folder to show a specific image in Thumbnails view and to use an icon other than the generic folder icon.

To get started, open Windows Explorer, right-click the folder you want to work with, and then click Properties. When Windows XP opens the folder's property sheet, display the Customize tab, shown in Figure 4.15.

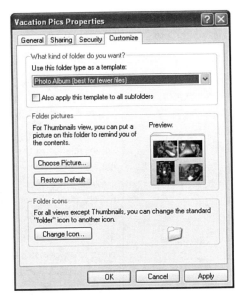

**FIGURE 4.15**   Use the Customize tab to select a template for a folder that contains media files.

## Selecting a Folder Template

In the Use This Folder Type as a Template list, choose one of the following templates:

| | |
|---|---|
| Documents | Choose this template to give the folder the same features as a standard folder. |
| Pictures | Choose this template to give the folder the same features as the My Pictures folder. |
| Photo Album | Choose this template to give the folder the same features as the My Pictures folder, and also display the folder in Filmstrip view by default. |

| Music | Choose this template to give the folder the same features as the My Music folder. |
| Music Artist | Choose this template for a folder that holds music by a single artist. This gives the folder the same features as the My Music folder, and also opens the folder in Thumbnails view, which displays an album art icon for each folder that holds an album by the artist. |
| Music Album | Choose this template for a folder that holds music from a single artist. This gives the folder the same features as the My Music folder, and also opens the folder in Tiles view, which displays an icon for each track from the album. |
| Video | Choose this template to give the folder the same features as the My Videos folder. |

If you want this template to be used for all the folder's subfolders, activate the Also Apply This Template to All Subfolders check box.

## Customizing the Folder Icon

In Thumbnails view, Windows Explorer displays a folder's icon with a picture. For example, if the folder uses the Music Album template, the folder's Thumbnails icon displays a picture of the album cover (assuming that you have an Internet connection and Windows Media Player was able to download the album cover). Similarly, for a folder that uses the Pictures or Photo Album template, its folder icon will display the first four images that reside in the folder.

To change this, click the Choose Picture button and use the Browse dialog box to select the image file you want to appear on the folder's icon.

> **TIP**
>
> Another way to specify the image used in a folder's icon in Thumbnails view is to make a copy of the image inside the folder, and then rename that copy to Folder.jpg. Note that if you use the Choose Picture command to specify a different image, Windows XP ignores the Folder.jpg file. To use the Folder.jpg image again, click the Restore Default button.

This customization applies to folders shown in Thumbnails view. To change the folder icon in other views, click the Change Icon button and use the Change Icon dialog box to choose a new icon.

# From Here

Here are some places in the book that contain information related to the material presented in this chapter:

- For more folder-related customizations, see the section in Chapter 2 titled "Customizing Windows Explorer."

- To learn more about hardware and device drivers, see Chapter 14, "Getting the Most Out of Device Manager."

CHAPTER **5**

# Installing and Running Applications

It's a rare (and no doubt unproductive) user who does nothing but run Windows on his or her computer. After all, when Windows starts, it doesn't do much of anything. No, to get full value for your computing dollar, you have to run an application or two. As an operating system, it's Windows' job to help make it easier for you to run your programs. Whether it's loading them into memory, managing their resources, or printing their documents, Windows has plenty to do behind the scenes. Windows XP also comes with a few tools and techniques that you can use to make your applications run faster and more reliably. In this chapter, you'll learn how to install applications safely, how to launch applications, and how to solve program incompatibility issues.

## Practicing Safe Setups

Outside of hardware woes and user errors (what IT personnel call a **PEBCAK—Problem Exists Between Chair And Keyboard**), most computer problems are caused by improperly installing a program or installing a program that doesn't mesh correctly with your system. It could be that the installation makes unfortunate changes to your configuration files, or that the program replaces a crucial system file with an older version, or that the program just wasn't meant to operate on (or wasn't tested with) a machine with your configuration. Whatever the reason, you can minimize these kinds of problems by understanding the installation process as it relates to user accounts and by following a few precautions before installing a new software package.

## User Accounts and Installing Programs

If you're coming to Windows XP from Windows 9x or Me, you'll find that something as apparently straightforward as installing a program isn't straightforward at all. The biggest hurdle you face is the Windows XP security model, which doesn't let just anyone install a program. If you're logged in with Administrator-level privileges, you'll have no problem launching any installation program. If you're logged in as a member of the Users group (a Limited account), however, Windows XP will cause problems for any installation program that attempts the following:

- Installing files anywhere other than within the %UserProfile% folder (the folder that contains the files of the currently logged-on user)

- Adding or editing Registry keys and settings anywhere other than within the HKEY_CURRENT_USER key

This makes sense because members of the Users group do not have the appropriate privileges to perform either of these actions.

If you're having trouble installing a program for a Limited user, you can usually work around the problem by upgrading the application to one that is Windows XP–compatible, which means the program is supposed to let Limited users install programs safely for their own use. In other words, after a Limited user installs the program, that user can run that program, but no other user can.

The opposite problem occurs when you're logged in as a member of the Administrators group but you don't want an installation program to abuse those privileges. Here's how to fix that:

1. Right-click the installation program's executable file and then click Run As. Windows XP displays the Run As dialog box, shown in Figure 5.1.

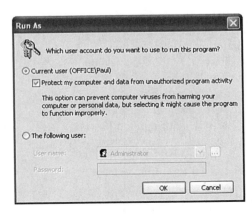

**FIGURE 5.1**    Use the Run As dialog box to ensure that an installation program does not abuse your Administrator-level privileges.

2. In the Run As dialog box, make sure that the Current User option is activated, and also make sure that the Protect My Computer and Data from Unauthorized Program Activity check box is activated.

3. Click OK.

When you launch the installation program, Windows XP will run it as though you were a Limited user.

> **TIP**
>
> You can also use the Run As dialog box to install a program using a different user account. See "Running a Program as a Different User," later in this chapter.

## Running Through a Pre-Installation Checklist

For those who enjoy working with computers, few things are as tempting as a new software package. The tendency is to just tear into the box, liberate the source disks, and let the installation program rip without further ado. This approach often loses its luster when, after a willy-nilly installation, your system starts to behave erratically. That's usually because the application's setup program has made adjustments to one or more important configuration files and given your system a case of indigestion in the process. That's the hard way to learn the hazards of a haphazard installation.

To avoid such a fate, you should always look before you leap. That is, you should follow a few simple safety measures before double-clicking that `setup.exe` file. The next few sections take you through a list of things to check before you install any program.

### Check for Windows XP Compatibility

Check to see whether the program is compatible with Windows XP. The easiest and safest setups occur with programs certified to work with Windows XP. See "Understanding Application Compatibility," later in this chapter, to learn how to tell whether a program is Windows XP–compatible.

### Set a Restore Point

The quickest way to recover from a bad installation is to restore your system to the way it was before you ran the setup program. The only way to do that is to set a system restore point just before you run the program. In Chapter 12, "Maintaining Your Windows XP System," see the section titled "Setting System Restore Points."

### Read `Readme.txt` and Other Documentation

Although it's the easiest thing in the world to skip, you really should peruse whatever setup-related documentation the program provides. This includes the appropriate installation material in the manual, `Readme` text files found on the disk, and whatever else looks promising. By spending a few minutes looking over these resources, you can glean the following information:

- Any advance preparation you need to perform on your system

- What to expect during the installation

- Information you need to have on hand to complete the setup (such as a product's serial number)

- Changes the install program will make to your system or to your data files (if you're upgrading)

- Changes to the program and/or the documentation that were put into effect after the manual was printed

### Virus-Check Downloaded Files

If you downloaded the application you're installing from the Internet, or if a friend or colleague sent you the installation file as an email attachment, you should scan the file using a good (and up-to-date) virus checker.

Although most viruses come to us via the Internet these days, not all of them do. Therefore, there are other situations in which it pays to be paranoid. You should check for viruses before installing if

- You ordered the program directly from an unknown developer.

- The package was already open when you purchased it from a dealer (buying opened software packages is never a good idea).

- A friend or colleague gave you the program on a floppy disk or recordable CD.

### Understand the Effect on Your Data Files

Few software developers want to alienate their installed user base, so they usually emphasize upward compatibility in their upgrades. That is, the new version of the software will almost always be able to read and work with documents created with an older version. However, in the interest of progress, you often find that the data file format used by the latest incarnation of a program is different from its predecessors, and this new format is rarely *downward*-compatible. That is, an older version of the software will usually gag on a data file that was created by the new version. So, you're faced with two choices:

- Continue to work with your existing documents in the old format, thus possibly foregoing any benefits that come with the new format

- Update your files and thus risk making them incompatible with the old version of the program, should you decide to uninstall the upgrade

One possible solution to this dilemma is to make backup copies of all your data files before installing the upgrade. That way, you can always restore the good copies of your documents if the upgrade causes problems or destroys some of your data. If you've already used the upgrade to make changes to some documents, but you want to uninstall the upgrade, most programs have a Save As command that enables you to save the documents in their old format.

## Use the Add or Remove Programs Feature

Double-clicking Control Panel's Add or Remove Programs icon displays the window shown at the top of Figure 5.2. You can use this window to launch a program installation wizard, but most experienced Windows users don't need a wizard to install a program. Instead, Add or Remove Programs is useful for two things:

| | |
|---|---|
| Modifying a program's installation | Clicking the Change or Remove Programs icon displays a list of your computer's installed programs, as shown in Figure 5.2. When you select a program, the window shows you the size of the installation; how frequently the program has been used (rarely, occasionally, or frequently); and when the program was last used. You also get a Change button that you can click to modify the program's installation. (Some programs display a combined Change/Remove button instead.) Depending on the program, modifying its installation might mean adding or removing program features, reinstalling files, or repairing damaged files. |
| Removing a program | Click the Remove (or Change/Remove) button to uninstall the program. Note that each uninstallable item in the Add or Remove Programs list has a corresponding subkey of the following Registry key, as shown in Figure 5.2. |

```
HKLM\SOFTWARE\Microsoft\Windows\
CurrentVersion\Uninstall
```

**TIP**

After you've uninstalled a program, you might find that it still appears in the list of programs in the Add or Remove Programs dialog box. To fix this, open the Registry Editor, display the Uninstall key, and look for the subkey that represents the program. (If you're not sure, click a subkey and examine the `DisplayName` setting, the value of which is the name that appears in the Add or Remove Programs list.) Delete that subkey and the uninstalled program will disappear from the list.

## Save Directory Listings for Important Folders

Another safe setup technique I recommend is to compare the contents of some folders before and after the installation. Windows programs like to add all kinds of files to the `%SystemRoot%` and `%SystemRoot%\System32` folders. To troubleshoot problems, it helps to know which files were installed.

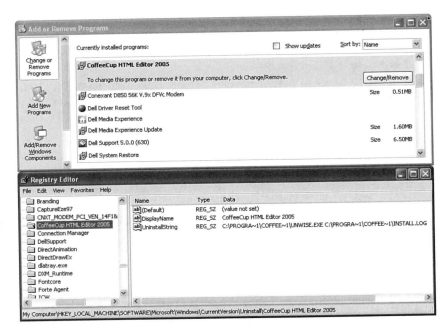

**FIGURE 5.2**    Items that can be uninstalled via Add or Remove Programs have corresponding Registry entries.

To figure this out, write directory listings for both folders to text files. The following two DOS statements use the `DIR` command to produce alphabetical listings of the `%SystemRoot%` and `%SystemRoot%\System32` folders and redirect (using the > operator) these listings to text files:

> **NOTE**
>
> To get to the command prompt, either select Start, All Programs, Accessories, Command Prompt, or select Start, Run, type **cmd**, and click OK. See Appendix B, "Using the Windows XP Command Prompt."

```
dir %SystemRoot% /a-d /on /-p > c:\windir.txt

dir %SystemRoot%\system32 /a-d /on /-p > c:\sysdir.txt
```

When the installation is complete, run the following commands to save the new listings to a second set of text files:

```
dir %SystemRoot% /a-d /on /-p > c:\windir2.txt

dir %SystemRoot%\system32 /a-d /on /-p > c:\sysdir2.txt
```

The resulting text files are long, so comparing the before and after listings is time-consuming. To make this chore easier, use the DOS FC (File Compare) command. Here's the simplified syntax to use with text files:

`FC /L filename1 filename2`

| | |
|---|---|
| `/L` | Compares files as ASCII text |
| `filename1` | The first file you want to compare |
| `filename2` | The second file you want to compare |

> **NOTE**
>
> The FC command can also compare binary files, display line numbers, perform case-insensitive comparisons, and much more. For the full syntax, enter the command `fc /?` at the command prompt.

For example, here's the command to run to compare the files sysdir.txt and sysdir2.txt that you created earlier:

`fc /l c:\sysdir.txt c:\sysdir2.txt > fc-sys.txt`

This statement redirects the FC command's output to a file named fc-sys.txt. Here's an example of the kind of data you'll see in this file when you open it in Notepad:

```
Comparing files C:\sysdir.txt and C:\sysdir2.txt
***** C:\sysdir.txt
08/04/2004  07:00 AM            258,048 WMVDS32.AX
08/04/2004  07:00 AM            264,192 WOW32.DLL
***** C:\SYSDIR2.TXT
08/04/2004  07:00 AM            258,048 WMVDS32.AX
11/22/2004  08:56 PM            913,560 wodFtpDLX.ocx
08/04/2004  07:00 AM            264,192 WOW32.DLL
*****
```

In this case, you can see that a file named wodFtpDLX.ocx has been added between WMVDS32.AX and WOW32.DLL.

> **TIP**
>
> The FC command is useful for more than just directory listings. You could also export Registry keys before and after and then use FC to compare the resulting registration (.reg) files. See Chapter 8, "Getting to Know the Windows XP Registry."

> **TIP**
>
> Most high-end word processors have a feature that enables you to compare two documents (or any file type supported by the program). In Word 2003, for example, open the post-installation file, select Tools, Compare and Merge Documents, and then use the Compare and Merge Documents dialog box to open the pre-installation file. Word examines the documents and then inserts the changes using revision marks.

### Take Control of the Installation

Some setup programs give new meaning to the term *brain-dead*. You slip in the source disk, run `Setup.exe` (or whatever), and the program proceeds to impose itself on your hard disk without so much as a how-do-you-do. Thankfully, most installation programs are a bit more thoughtful than that. They usually give you some advance warning about what's to come, and they prompt you for information as they go along. You can use this newfound thoughtfulness to assume a certain level of control over the installation. Here are a couple of things to watch for:

- Choose your folder wisely—Most installation programs offer to install their files in a default folder. Rather than just accepting this without question, think about where you want the program to reside. Personally, I prefer to use the Program Files folder to house all my applications. If you have multiple hard disks or partitions, you might prefer to use the one with the largest amount of free space. If the setup program lets you select data directories, you might want to use a separate folder that makes it easy to back up the data.

> **TIP**
>
> Most installation programs offer to copy the program's files to a subfolder of `%SystemDrive%\Program Files` (where `%SystemDrive%` is the partition on which Windows XP is installed). You can change this default installation folder by editing the Registry. First, display the following key:
>
>     HKLM\SOFTWARE\Microsoft\Windows\CurrentVersion\
>
> The `ProgramFilesDir` setting holds the default install path. Change this setting to the path you prefer (for example, one that's on a drive with the most free disk space).

- Use the Custom install option—The best programs offer you a choice of installation options. Whenever possible, choose the Custom option, if one is available. This will give you maximum control over the components that are installed, including where and how they're installed.

## Installing the Application

After you've run through this checklist, you're ready to install the program. Here's a summary of the various methods you can use to install a program in Windows XP:

| | |
|---|---|
| Add New Programs Wizard | This wizard is available via Control Panel's Add or Remove Programs icon. It's the standard Windows XP method for installing all types of applications, but it requires too many steps for it to be practical. In the unlikely event that you're not sure which executable to run to install a program, insert the CD or floppy disk, click the Add New Programs icon, and then click the CD or Floppy button. The wizard's dialog boxes lead you through finding the installation program and launching it. The wizard departs at this point and you follow the installation program's instructions. |

**NOTE**

The wizard finds the installation program only if it exists in the CD's root folder. If the wizard fails to find the program, it might be because the program resides in a subfolder (look for a subfolder named Setup or Install).

| | |
|---|---|
| AutoPlay install | If the program comes on a CD or DVD that supports AutoPlay, it's likely that the installation program will launch automatically after you insert the disc into the drive. To prevent the install program from launching automatically, hold down the Shift key while you insert the disc. |
| Run `setup.exe` | For most applications, the installed program is named `setup.exe` (sometimes it's `install.exe`). Use Windows Explorer to find the install program and then double-click it. Alternatively, select Start, Run, enter the path to the `setup.exe` file (such as `e:\setup`), and click OK. |
| Decompress downloaded files | If you downloaded an application from the Internet, the file you receive will be either an `.exe` file or a `.zip` file. Either way, you should always store the file in an empty folder just in case it needs to extract files. You then do one of the following: |

- If it's an `.exe` file, double-click it; in most cases, the install program will launch. In other cases, the program will extract its files and you then launch `setup.exe` (or whatever).

- If it's a `.zip` file, double-click it and Windows XP will open a new compressed folder that shows the contents of the `.zip` file. If you see an installation program, double-click it. It's more likely, however, that you won't see an install program. Instead, the application is ready to go and all you have to do is extract the files to a folder and run the application from there.

Install from an .inf file

Some applications install via an information (.inf) file. To install these programs, right-click the file and then click Install in the shortcut menu that appears.

# Applications and the Registry

As you'll see in Chapter 8, the Registry is perhaps Windows XP's most important component because it stores thousands of settings that Windows needs. The Registry is important for your applications, as well, because most Windows applications use the Registry to store configuration data and other settings.

When you install an application, it typically makes a half-dozen different Registry modifications:

- Program settings
- User settings
- File types
- Application-specific paths
- Shared DLLs
- Uninstall settings

## Program Settings

Program settings are related to the application as a whole: where it was installed, the serial number, and so on. The program settings are placed in a new subkey of `HKEY_LOCAL_MACHINE\Software`:

`HKLM\Software\Company\Product\Version`

Here, `Company` is the name of the program vendor, `Product` is the name of the software, and `Version` is the version number of the program. Here's an example for Office 2003:

`HKLM\Software\Microsoft\Office\11.0`

## User Settings

User settings are user-specific entries, such as the user's name, preferences and options the user has selected, and so on. The user settings are stored in a subkey of `HKEY_CURRENT_USER\Software`:

`HKCU\Software\Company\Product`

## File Types

File types refer to the file extensions used by the program's documents. These extensions are associated with the program's executable file so that double-clicking a document loads the program and displays the document. The extensions and file types are stored as subkeys within HKEY_CLASSES_ROOT. Refer to Chapter 3, "Mastering File Types," for details.

If the application comes with OLE support, it will have a unique **class ID**, which will be stored as a subkey within HKEY_CLASSES_ROOT\CLSID.

## Application-Specific Paths

In computing, a **path** is a listing of the folders that the operating system must traverse to get to a particular file. Windows XP uses a variation on this theme called **application-specific paths**. The idea is that if you enter only the primary name of a program's executable file in the Run dialog box (select Start, Run), Windows XP will find and run the program. For example, WordPad's executable file is Wordpad.exe, so you type **wordpad** in the Run dialog box, click OK, and WordPad opens.

> **NOTE**
> A file's **primary name** is the part of the filename to the left of the dot (.). For example, the primary name of the file Excel.exe is excel.

Windows finds the program because the application's executable file is associated with the particular path to the folder in which the file resides. These application-specific paths are set up in the following key:

HKLM\Software\Microsoft\Windows\CurrentVersion\App Paths

Each application that supports this feature adds a subkey that uses the name of the application's executable file (for example, Wordpad.exe). Within that subkey, the value of the Default setting is the full pathname (drive, folder, and filename) of the executable file. Note, too, that many applications also create a Path setting that specifies a default folder for the application.

> **TIP**
> It's possible to set up your own application-specific paths. See "Creating Application-Specific Paths," later in this chapter.

## Shared DLLs

It's common for multiple applications to share common files such as a dynamic link library (.dll) or an ActiveX control (.ocx). Windows XP uses settings in the following key to keep track of how many applications are sharing a particular DLL:

HKLM\Software\Microsoft\Windows\CurrentVersion\SharedDlls

As you can see in Figure 5.3, the name of each setting is the full pathname of a DLL (or whatever), and the value is the number of applications that share the file.

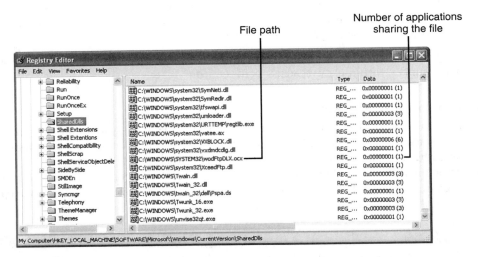

**FIGURE 5.3**    The SharedDlls key keeps a running total of the number of applications that share a particular DLL file.

During the installation of most applications, the setup program checks to see whether any DLLs that it requires are already on the system. If so, it finds the appropriate settings within the SharedDlls key and increases their values by 1.

When you uninstall most applications, the uninstall program decrements the appropriate setting in the SharedDlls key for each DLL used by the application. When the usage counter for a DLL is 0, you see a dialog box asking whether you want to remove the DLL file, as shown in Figure 5.4. If you're certain that the DLL was used only by the application you're removing, click Yes. If you're not sure, click No. (How can you be sure? The only way is if you compared the %SystemRoot% and %SystemRoot%\System folders before and after the install, as I described earlier.)

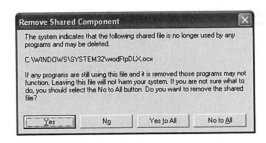

**FIGURE 5.4**    You see this dialog box if a DLL's usage is down to 0 in the SharedDlls Registry key.

> **CAUTION**
>
> It's possible that a DLL with a usage counter of 0 could still be used by another program, particularly a program that doesn't know about the SharedDlls Registry key. A better approach would be to make a note of the DLL's filename, click No, and then move the DLL to another folder. If none of your programs misses the file after a while, it's safe to delete it.

## Uninstall Settings

As I mentioned earlier, most applications also use the Registry to hold data related to uninstalling the application. To store this data, the setup program creates a subkey for the application within the following key:

`HKLM\Software\Microsoft\Windows\CurrentVersion\Uninstall`

# Launching Applications

Launching programs is one of the most fundamental operating system tasks, so it isn't surprising that Windows XP offers an impressive number of ways to go about this:

| | |
|---|---|
| Use the Start menu | Click the Start button to open the Start menu. If you've used the program a lot, it should appear in the list of most frequently used (MFU) applications, so click its icon. Otherwise, click All Programs and open the menus until you see the program icon; then click the icon. |
| Double-click the executable file | Use Windows Explorer to find the application's executable file, and then double-click that file. |
| Double-click a shortcut | If a shortcut points to a program's executable file, double-clicking the shortcut will launch the program. |
| Double-click a document | If you can use the application to create documents, double-clicking one of those documents should launch the program and load the document automatically. (If the document was one of the last 15 that you used, select Start, My Recent Documents, and then click the document in the submenu that appears.) |
| Use the Open With command | If double-clicking a document opens the file in the wrong application, right-click the file and then click Open With. For the details on the Open With command, refer to the section in Chapter 3 titled "Customizing Windows XP's Open With List." |
| Insert a CD or DVD disc | Most CDs and DVDs support Windows XP's AutoPlay feature that automatically starts a default program when the disc is inserted. The program that launches is determined by the |

**5**

contents of the `Autorun.inf` file in the disc's root folder. Open
the file in Notepad and look for the open value in the
`[AutoRun]` section.

---

**TIP**

If you prefer to control what happens after you insert a CD or DVD, you can disable the
AutoRun feature for your CD and DVD drives. Open the Registry Editor and find the following
key:

    HKLM\System\CurrentControlSet\Services\CDRom\

Change the value of the `Autorun` setting to 0.

---

Use the Run dialog box

Select Start, Run (press Windows Logo+R) to display the Run
dialog box. Use the Open text box to specify the application
(click OK when you're done):

- If the application resides within the `%SystemRoot%` or
  `%SystemRoot%\System32` folder, within a folder listed
  as part of the PATH environment variable, or if it has an
  application-specific path in the Registry (as described
  earlier in this chapter), just type the primary name of the
  executable file.

- For all other applications, enter the full pathname (drive,
  folder, and file name) for the executable file.

- You can also enter the full pathname of a document. If
  you want to open the document using a program other
  than the one associated with the document's file type,
  precede the document pathname with the application's
  pathname (separate the two paths with a space).

Use the Scheduled Tasks folder

You can use the Scheduled Tasks folder to run programs
automatically at a given date and time, or on a regular
schedule. Select Start, All Programs, Accessories, System Tools,
Scheduled Tasks, or use Windows Explorer to display the
`%SystemRoot%\Tasks` folder.

In addition to these methods, you can also set up the program to run automatically at
startup, use the Run As command, and create your own application-specific paths. I
discuss these methods in detail in the next three sections. To learn how to launch
programs from the command prompt or a batch file, see the section in Appendix B titled
"Starting Applications from the Command Prompt."

## Launching Applications and Scripts at Startup

If you have one or more programs that you use each day, or that you use as soon as Windows XP starts, you can save yourself the hassle of launching these programs manually by getting Windows XP to do it for you automatically at startup. Similarly, you can also get Windows XP to automatically launch scripts or batch files at startup. You could set up a program or script for automatic startup launch using the Startup folder, the Registry, and the Group Policy snap-in.

### Using the Startup Folder

The Startup folder is a regular file folder, but it has a special place in Windows XP: You can get a program or script to run automatically at startup by adding a shortcut for that item to the Startup folder. (Adding shortcuts to the Startup folder is part of the Start menu customizations that I discuss in more detail in Chapter 10, "Customizing the Windows XP Interface.") Note that the Startup folder appears twice in the Windows XP interface:

- Via the Start menu (click Start, All Programs, Startup).

- Via Windows Explorer as a subfolder in `%SystemDrive%:\Documents and Settings`. Actually, there are three different subfolders you can work with:

| | |
|---|---|
| `\user\Start Menu\Programs\Startup` | Here, *user* is the name of a user defined on the system. A shortcut placed in this folder will run automatically when this user logs on to the system. |
| `\All Users\Start Menu\ Programs\Startup` | A shortcut placed in this folder will run automatically when any user logs on to the system. |
| `\Default User\Start Menu\ Programs\Startup` | A shortcut placed in this folder will be automatically copied to a user's Startup folder when you create a new user account. The Default User subfolder is hidden by default. To display it, select Tools, Folder Options in Windows Explorer, display the View tab, and then activate the Show Hidden Files and Folders option. |

Note that only users with Administrator-level rights can access all three of these subfolders. Users with lesser privileges can work only with their own Startup folder. They can see the All Users version of the Startup folder, but Windows XP prevents them from adding files to it.

> **TIP**
>
> You can prevent the Startup items from running by holding down the Shift key while Windows XP loads (hold down Shift after logging on).

## Using the Registry

The Startup folder method has two drawbacks: Users can easily delete shortcuts from their own Startup folders, and users can bypass Startup items by holding down the Shift key while Windows XP loads. To avoid both problems, you can use the Registry Editor to define your startup items. Assuming that you're logged in as the user you want to work with, the Registry offers two keys:

| | |
|---|---|
| `HKCU\Software\Microsoft\Windows\`<br>`CurrentVersion\Run` | The values in this key run automatically each time the user logs on. |
| `HKCU\Software\Microsoft\Windows\`<br>`CurrentVersion\RunOnce` | The values in this key run only the next time the user logs on, and are then deleted from the key. (This key might not be present in your Registry. In that case, you need to add this key yourself.) |

If you want an item to run at startup no matter who logs on, use the following keys:

| | |
|---|---|
| `HKLM\Software\Microsoft\Windows\`<br>`CurrentVersion\Run` | The values in this key run automatically each time any user logs on. |
| `HKLM\Software\Microsoft\Windows\`<br>`CurrentVersion\RunOnce` | The values in this key run only the next time any user logs on, and are then deleted from the key. Don't confuse this key with the RunOnceEx key. RunOnceEx is an extended version of RunOnce that's used by developers to create more robust startup items that include features such as error handling and improved performance. |

To create a startup item, add a string value to the appropriate key, give it whatever name you like, and then set its value to the full pathname of the executable file or script file that you want to launch at startup.

---

**CAUTION**

Placing the same startup item in both the HKCU and the HKLM hives will result in that item being started twice: once during the initial boot and again at logon.

---

**TIP**

If the program is in the %SystemRoot% folder, you can get away with entering only the name of the executable file. Also, if the program you want to run at startup is capable of running in the background, you can load it in this mode by appending /**background** after the pathname.

---

## Using Group Policies

If you prefer not to edit the Registry directly, or if you want to place a GUI between you and the Registry, XP Professional's Group Policy snap-in can help. (See Chapter 7, "Using

Control Panel, Group Policies, and Tweak UI," for details on using this snap-in.) Note, however, that Group Policy doesn't work directly with the Run keys in the HKLM and HKCU hives. Instead, these are considered to be **legacy keys**, meaning that they're mostly used by older programs. The new keys (new as of Windows 2000, that is) are the following:

```
HKLM\Software\Microsoft\Windows\CurrentVersion\policies\Explorer\Run

HKCU\Software\Microsoft\Windows\CurrentVersion\ Policies\Explorer\Run
```

These keys do not appear in Windows XP by default. You see them only after you specify startup programs in the Group Policy editor, as discussed in the next section. Alternatively, you can add these keys yourself using the Registry Editor.

> **NOTE**
>
> The startup items run in the following order:
>
> ```
> HKLM\Software\Microsoft\Windows\CurrentVersion\RunOnce
>
> HKLM\Software\Microsoft\Windows\CurrentVersion\policies\Explorer\Run
>
> HKLM\Software\Microsoft\Windows\CurrentVersion\Run
>
> HKCU\Software\Microsoft\Windows\CurrentVersion\Run
>
> HKCU\Software\Microsoft\Windows\CurrentVersion\Policies\Explorer\Run
>
> HKCU\Software\Microsoft\Windows\CurrentVersion\RunOnce
> ```
>
> Startup folder (all users)
>
> Startup folder (current user)

**Adding Programs to the Run Keys**    As mentioned, you can either add values to these keys via the Registry Editor, or you can use the Group Policy snap-in. To open the Group Policy window in Windows XP Professional, select Start, Run, type **gpedit.msc**, and then click OK. In the Group Policy window, you have two choices:

- To work with startup programs for all users, select Computer Configuration, Administrative Templates, System, Logon. The items here will affect the Registry keys in the HKLM (all users) Registry hive.

- To work with startup programs for the current user, select User Configuration, Administrative Templates, System, Logon. The items here will affect the Registry keys in the HKCU (current user) hive.

Either way you'll see at least the following three items:

Run These Programs at User Logon    Use this item to add or remove startup programs using the \Policies\Explorer\Run keys in the Registry. To add a program, double-click the item, select the Enabled option, and then click Show. In the Show Contents dialog box, click Add, enter the full pathname

|  | of the program or script you want to run at startup, and then click OK. |
| Do Not Process the Run Once List | Use this item to toggle whether Windows XP processes the RunOnce Registry keys (which I discussed in the previous section). Double-click this item and then activate the Enabled option to put this policy into effect; that is, programs listed in the RunOnce key are not launched at startup. |
| Do Not Process the Legacy Run List | Use this item to toggle whether Windows XP processes the legacy Run keys. Double-click this item and then activate the Enabled option to put this policy into effect; that is, programs listed in the legacy Run key are not launched at startup. |

**Specifying Startup and Logon Scripts**    You also can use the Group Policy snap-in to specify script files to run at startup. You can specify script files at two places:

- Computer Configuration, Windows Settings, Scripts (Startup/Shutdown)—Use the Startup item to specify one or more script files to run each time the computer starts (and before the user logs on). Note that if you specify two or more scripts, Windows XP runs them synchronously. That is, Windows XP runs the first script, waits for it to finish, runs the second script, waits for it to finish, and so on.

- User Configuration, Windows Settings, Scripts (Logon/Logoff)—Use the Logon item to specify one or more script files to run each time any user logs on. Logon scripts are run asynchronously.

Finally, note that Windows XP has policies dictating how these scripts run. For example, you can see the startup script policies by selecting Computer Configuration, Administrative Templates, System, Scripts. There are three items that affect startup scripts:

| Run Logon Scripts Synchronously | If you enable this item, Windows XP runs the logon scripts one at a time. |
| Run Startup Scripts Asynchronously | If you enable this item, Windows XP runs the startup scripts at the same time. |
| Run Startup Scripts Visible | If you enable this item, Windows XP makes the startup script commands visible to the user in a command window. |

For logon scripts, a similar set of policies appears in the User Configuration, Administrative Templates, System, Scripts section.

> **CAUTION**
>
> Logon scripts are supposed to execute before the Windows XP interface is displayed to the user. However, Windows XP's new Fast Logon Optimization can interfere with that by displaying the interface before all the scripts are done. The Fast Logon Optimization feature runs both the computer logon scripts and the user logon scripts asynchronously, which greatly speeds up the logon time since no script has to wait for another to finish.
>
> To prevent this, select Computer Configuration, Administrative Templates, System, Logon and enable the Always Wait for the Network at Computer Startup and Logon setting.

### Using the Scheduled Tasks Folder

Yet another way to set up a program or script to run at startup is to use the Scheduled Tasks folder (select Start, All Programs, Accessories, System Tools, Scheduled Tasks, or use Windows Explorer to display the %SystemRoot%\Tasks folder). When you create a new task, two of the startup options you'll see are

When My Computer Starts

Choose this option to run the program when your computer boots, no matter which user logs in. Note that only someone logged in under the Administrator account can use this option. The tasks will run otherwise, but they won't display.

When I Log On

Choose this option to run the program only when you log on to Windows XP. This is the option to use for accounts other than Administrator.

> **CAUTION**
>
> Note that a bug in Windows XP prevents it from running a scheduled task if your user account doesn't have a password. You need to assign a password to your account and then add the password to the scheduled task. Note that this bug is still not fixed in Service Pack 2.

## Running a Program as a Different User

As I explained earlier in this chapter, some applications—especially installation programs—might fail because the current user account has insufficient privileges to support some program operations. Similarly, a user account might have privileges that are too high to safely run a program. For either case, you can run a program as a different user with any of the following techniques:

- Use the Run As menu command—Right-click the executable file and then click Run As in the shortcut menu. In the Run As dialog box, activate The Following User and then choose a user from the User Name list. Enter the user's Password and click OK.

- Prompt for a user—Create a shortcut to the executable file, right-click the shortcut, and then click Properties. In the Shortcut tab, click Advanced and then activate the

Run with Different Credentials check box. Click OK. When you launch the shortcut, Windows XP will display the Run As dialog box so that you can choose a user.

- Use RUNAS command-line tool—You use RUNAS at the command prompt to specify the username, and Windows XP then prompts you to enter the user's password. Here's the basic syntax (type **RUNAS /?** for the complete list of switches):

```
RUNAS /user:domain\user program
```

| | |
|---|---|
| /user:domain\user | The *user* name under which you want the program to run. Replace *domain* with either the computer name (for a standalone or workgroup machine) or the domain name. |
| *program* | The full path and filename of the application. You need only use the file's primary name if the application resides within the current folder, the %SystemRoot% folder, the %SystemRoot%\System32 folder, or a folder in the PATH variable. |

## Creating Application-Specific Paths

Earlier I told you about application-specific paths, which enable you to launch almost any 32-bit application simply by typing the name of its executable file, either in the Run dialog box or at the command prompt. You don't need to spell out the complete pathname. This pathless execution is handy, but it doesn't work in the following two situations:

- 16-bit applications—These older programs don't store the paths to their executables in the Registry.

- Documents—You can't load a document just by typing its filename in the Run dialog box or at the command prompt unless the document is in the current folder.

To solve both these problems, and to handle the rare case when a 32-bit application doesn't create its own application-specific path, you can edit the Registry to add a path to an executable file (an application-specific path) or to a document (a document-specific path).

In the Registry Editor, open the following key:

```
HKLM\Software\Microsoft\Windows\CurrentVersion\App Paths
```

The App Paths key has subkeys for each installed 32-bit application. Each of these subkeys has one or both of the following settings:

Default—This setting spells out the path to the application's executable file. All the App Paths subkeys have this setting.

Path—This setting specifies one or more folders that contain files needed by the application. An application first looks for its files in the same folder as its executable file. If it can't find what it needs there, it checks the folder or folders listed in the Path setting. Not all App Paths subkeys use this setting.

To create an application-specific path, select the App Paths key, create a new subkey, and assign it the name of the application's executable file. For example, if the program's executable filename is OLDAPP.EXE, name the new subkey OLDAPP.EXE. For this new subkey, change the Default setting to the full pathname of the executable file.

> **TIP**
>
> You don't have to give the new App Paths subkey the name of the executable file. You can use any name you like as long as it ends with .exe and doesn't conflict with the name of an existing subkey.
>
> Why does it have to end with .exe? Unless you specify otherwise, Windows XP assumes that anything you enter in the Run dialog box or at the command prompt ends with .exe. So, by ending the subkey with .exe, you need to type only the subkey's primary name. For example, if you name your new subkey OLDAPP.EXE, you can run the program by typing **oldapp** in the Run dialog box or at the command prompt.

You create document-specific paths the same way. (However, the document's file type must be registered with Windows XP.) In that case, though, the Default setting takes on the full pathname of the document. Again, if you want to load the document just by typing its primary name, make sure that the new App Paths subkey uses the .exe extension.

## Restricting Program Launches for Users

Windows XP has several group policies that enable any member of the Administrators group to restrict the usage of Windows programs for each logged-on user. For example, you can prevent users from running the System Configuration Utility, a program that—in the wrong hands—can do much damage to a system. You can also prevent users from accessing the command prompt (where they could start unauthorized programs) or the Registry Editor.

In the Group Policy editor, select User Configuration, Administrative Templates, System. There are five policies:

| | |
|---|---|
| Prevent Access to the Command Prompt | Enable this policy to prevent the current user from getting to the command prompt. |
| Prevent Access to Registry Editing Tools | Enable this policy to prevent the current user from running the Registry Editor. |
| Run Only Allowed Windows Applications | Enable this policy to specify a list of executable file names that the current user is allowed to run. Note that this policy doesn't prevent users from starting |

other programs at the command prompt, so you should also disable command prompt access.

Don't Run Specified Windows Applications — Enable this policy to specify a list of executable file names that the current user is not allowed to run. Again, users can still run these programs via the command prompt.

Turn Off AutoPlay — Enable this setting to disable the AutoPlay feature for inserted CD or DVD discs.

# Understanding Application Compatibility

Most new software programs are certified as Windows XP–compatible, meaning that they can be installed and run without mishap on any Windows XP system. But what about older programs that were coded before Windows XP was released? They can be a bit more problematic. Because Windows XP is based on the code for Windows 2000—which was in turn based on Windows NT—programs that are compatible with those operating systems will probably (although not definitely) be compatible with Windows XP. But the real problems lie with programs written for Windows 9x and Me. Windows XP—even Windows XP Home—uses a completely different code base than the old consumer versions of Windows, so it's inevitable that some of those legacy programs will either be unstable while running under Windows XP, or they won't run at all.

Why do such incompatibilities arise? One common reason is that the programmers of a legacy application hard-wired certain data into the program's code. For example, installation programs often poll the operating system for its version number. If an application is designed for, say, Windows 95, the programmers might have set things up so that the application installs if and only if the operating system returns the Windows 95 version number. The program might run perfectly well under any later version of Windows, but this simplistic brain-dead version check prevents it from even installing on anything but Windows 95.

Another reason incompatibilities arise is that calls to API (**application programming interface**) functions return unexpected results. For example, the programmers of an old application may have assumed that the **FAT** (**file allocation table**) file system would always be the standard, so when checking for free disk space before installing the program, they'd expect to receive a number that is 2GB or less (the maximum size of a FAT partition). But FAT32 and **NTFS** (**NT file system**) partitions can be considerably larger than 2GB, so a call to the API function that returns the amount for free space on a partition could return a number that blows out a memory buffer and crashes the installation program.

These types of problems might make it seem as though getting older programs to run under Windows XP would be a nightmare. Fortunately, that's not true because the Windows XP programmers did something very smart: Because many of these application incompatibilities are predictable, they gave Windows XP the capability to make allowances for them and so enable many older programs to run under Windows XP without modification. In Windows XP, **application compatibility** refers to a set of concepts and technologies that enable the operating system to adjust its settings or behavior to compensate for the shortcomings of legacy programs. This section shows you how to work with Windows XP's application compatibility tools.

## Determining Whether a Program Is Compatible with Windows XP

One way to determine whether an application is compatible with Windows XP is to go ahead and install it. If the program is not compatible with Windows XP, you might see a dialog box similar to the one shown in Figure 5.5.

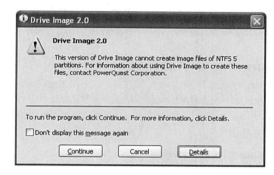

**FIGURE 5.5**    You might see a dialog box such as this if you try to install a program that isn't compatible with Windows XP.

At this point you could click Continue (in some dialog boxes, the button is named Run Program), but this is a risky strategy because you can't be sure how the program will interact with Windows XP. This approach is riskiest of all when dealing with disk utilities, backup software, antivirus programs, and other software that requires low-level control of the system. It's extremely unlikely that Windows XP would ever allow such programs to run, but you should *always* upgrade such products to Windows XP–compatible versions. A much safer route is to click Cancel to abort the installation and then visit the vendor's website or the Windows Update site to see whether a Windows XP–friendly update is available. (You can often get the company's web address by clicking the Details button.)

---

**NOTE**

Where does the information in these dialog boxes come from? In the `%SystemRoot%\AppPatch` folder, Windows XP has a file named `Apphelp.sdb` that contains messages such as the one shown in Figure 5.5 for all known applications that don't have compatibility fixes (discussed later in this section). The `.sdb` files aren't text files, so opening them with Notepad or WordPad will not allow you to read any of these stored messages.

---

A better approach is to find out in advance whether the program is compatible with Windows XP. The most obvious way to do this is to look for the Designed for Windows XP logo on the box. For older programs, check the manufacturer's website to see whether the company tells you that the program can be run under Windows XP or if an upgrade is available. Alternatively, Microsoft has a web page that enables you to search on the name of a program or manufacturer to find out compatibility information: http://www.microsoft.com/windows/catalog/.

What if you're upgrading to Windows XP and you want to know whether your installed software is compatible? The easiest way to find out is to use the Upgrade Advisor tool, which is available on the Windows XP Professional CD. (The Windows XP Home CD doesn't have the Upgrade Advisor.) Insert the Windows XP Professional CD and, when the Welcome to Microsoft Windows XP screen appears, click Check System Compatibility. Run through the Advisor's dialog boxes until you get to the report on system compatibility. This report will list software that doesn't support Windows XP and possibly software that needs to be reinstalled after the Windows XP setup has finished.

## Understanding Compatibility Mode

To help you run programs under Windows XP, especially those programs that worked properly in a previous version of Windows, Windows XP offers a new way to run applications using **compatibility layers**. This means that Windows XP runs the program by doing one or both of the following:

- Running the program in a **compatibility mode**—This involves emulating the behavior of previous version of Windows. Windows XP can emulate the behavior of Windows 95, Windows 98, Windows Me, Windows NT 4.0 with Service Pack 5, or Windows 2000.

- Temporarily changing the system's visual display so that it's compatible with the program—There are three possibilities here: setting the color depth to 256 colors; changing the screen resolution to 640×480; and disabling Windows XP's visual themes.

---

**NOTE**

Windows XP and Microsoft often use the terms *compatibility layer* and *compatibility mode* interchangeably, depending on which compatibility tool you're using. In some cases, the emulations of previous Windows versions are called **operating system modes**.

---

These are the broad compatibility layers supported by Windows XP. As you'll see a bit later, Windows XP also offers fine-tuned control over these and other compatibility settings. For now, however, you have two ways to set up a compatibility layer:

- Right-click the program's executable file or a shortcut to the file, click Properties, and then display the Compatibility tab in the property sheet that appears. To set the compatibility mode, activate the Run this Program in Compatibility Mode For check box (see Figure 5.6), and then use the list to choose the Windows version the program requires. You can also use the check boxes in the Display Settings group to adjust the video mode that Windows XP will switch to when you use the program.

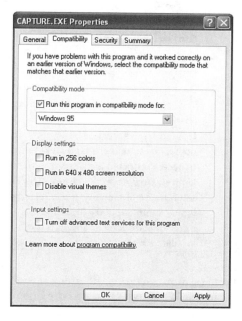

**FIGURE 5.6**    In the property sheet for an executable file, use the Compatibility tab to set the compatibility layer for the program.

- Run the Program Compatibility Wizard by selecting Start, All Programs, Accessories, Program Compatibility Wizard. Use the wizard's windows to select the program's executable file, choose a compatibility mode, set the visual options, and then test the program.

## Scripting Compatibility Layers

What do you do if you have a batch file that needs to run one or more programs within a temporary compatibility layer? You can handle this by using the following command within the batch file before you start the program:

```
SET __COMPAT_LAYER=[!]layer1 [layer2 ...]
```

Here, *layer1* and *layer2* are codes that represent the compatibility layers. Table 5.1 lists the 11 codes you can use.

**TABLE 5.1**    Codes to Use When Scripting Compatibility Layers

| Code | Compatibility Layer |
|------|---------------------|
| Win95 | Windows 95. |
| Win98 | Windows 98 / Windows Me. |
| Win2000 | Windows 2000. |
| NTSP5 | Windows NT 4.0 SP 5. |

**TABLE 5.1**   Continued

| Code | Compatibility Layer |
| --- | --- |
| 256Color | 256 color. |
| 640x480 | 640×480 screen resolution. |
| DisableThemes | Disable visual themes. |
| International | This layer handles incompatibilities caused by double-byte character sets. |
| LUA | **Limited User Access**—This layer redirects some Registry and file operations to nonrestricted areas for users that don't have permission to access restricted areas (such as the HKLM key). |
| LUACleanup | **Limited User Access Cleanup**—This layer removes the Registry settings and files that were redirected using the LUA layer. |
| ProfilesSetup | Profile Setup Support—This layer is used for older programs that install only for the current user; the layer ensures that the program is installed for all users. |

If you've already applied one or more layers to the program using the techniques from the previous section, you can tell Windows XP not to use one of those layers by preceding its keyword with the ! symbol. Also, to turn off the compatibility layers, run the command without any parameters, like so:

```
SET __COMPAT_LAYER=
```

For example, the following commands set the compatibility layers to Windows 95 and 256 colors, run a program, and then remove the layers:

```
SET __COMPAT_LAYER=Win95 256Color
```

```
D:\Legacy\oldapp.exe
```

```
SET __COMPAT_LAYER=
```

> **NOTE**
>
> The compatibility layers created by SET __COMPAT_LAYER also apply to any processes that are spawned by the affected application. For example, if you set the Windows 95 layer for Setup.exe, the same layer will also apply to any other executable called by Setup.exe. You can find more information about the SET __COMPAT_LAYER command and its parameters at http://support.microsoft.com/default.aspx?scid=kb;en-us;286705.

## Using Application Compatibility Toolkit

When you execute a program using a compatibility layer, Windows XP creates an environment within which the program can function properly. For example, a program running under the Win95 layer actually believes that Windows 95 is the operating system.

Windows XP accomplishes that not only by returning the Windows 95 version number when the program calls the `GetVersion` or `GetVersionEx` API functions, but also by "fixing" other incompatibilities between Windows 95 and Windows XP. For example, Windows 95 programs expect components such as Calculator and Solitaire to be in the `%SystemRoot%` folder, but in Windows XP these are in the `%SystemRoot%\System32\` folder. The `Win95` layer intercepts such file calls and reroutes them to the appropriate location.

The `Win95` layer comprises more than 50 such fixes, which are part of a large database of incompatibilities maintained by Microsoft. As of this writing, far more than 200 incompatibilities have been identified, and others might be found in the future. To get access to all these fixes and so get fine-tuned control over the compatibility issues relating to any legacy program, you need to use Application Compatibility Toolkit (ACT).

To install ACT, you have two choices:

- In the Windows XP Professional CD, open the `\SUPPORT\TOOLS\` folder and launch the `Act20.exe` file.

- Download and run the latest version of ACT (version 4.0 as of this writing) from the following Microsoft web page: www.microsoft.com/technet/prodtechnol/windows/appcompatibility/.

The ACT package comprises a number of programs and tools. Some of these are for programmers only, so the next two sections look at the main end-user tool: Compatibility Administrator.

## Using Compatibility Administrator

To create a usable compatibility fix for an application—one that you can use on your own computer or distribute to other computers—you use Compatibility Administrator. Compatibility Administrator stores fixes in databases:

| | |
|---|---|
| System database | This database contains three items: a list of applications for which Microsoft has applied fixes for known problems, a list of the available compatibility fixes, and the defined compatibility modes (that is, the compatibility layers discussed earlier). |
| Installed databases | These are databases that have been installed on this computer. |
| Custom databases | These are databases that contain fixes that you applied to one or more applications. |

There are two ways to start this program:

- If you're using the original version of ACT, select Start, All Programs, Application Compatibility Toolkit, Compatibility Administration Tool.

- If you're using the latest version of ACT, select Start, All Programs, Microsoft Application Compatibility Toolkit, Tools, Compatibility Administrator.

Here's how to create a custom fix database (note that I'm using version 4.0 of Compatibility Administrator for these instructions):

1. A new database is created for you automatically under the Custom Databases branch. Either select this database or create a new one by clicking Custom Database and then selecting File, New.

2. Right-click the new database, click Rename, and then enter a name for the database.

3. To create a new application fix, click the Fix button in the toolbar to launch the Create New Application Fix Wizard.

4. Enter the program's name, vendor, and location, and then click Next. The Compatibility Modes dialog box appears.

5. Choose an operating system mode and use the check boxes in the Select Additional Compatibility Modes list to choose additional layers to apply to the program, as shown in Figure 5.7. Click Next. The Compatibility Fixes dialog box appears.

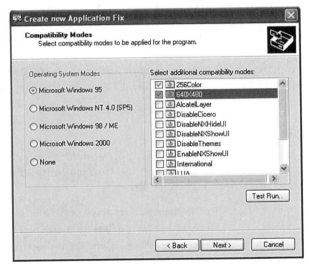

**FIGURE 5.7** Use the Compatibility Modes dialog box to specify an operating system mode and additional compatibility layers.

6. Use the check boxes to apply specific compatibility fixes and then click Next.

7. Compatibility Administrator also needs to know how to identify the program. Click Auto-Generate to have the wizard set up the matching attributes for you, and then click Finish.

Compatibility Administrator adds your program to the database. To try out the program, click it and click Run. Then select View, View Log to see the log that Compatibility Administrator created. Use the log to determine which fixes were required by the program. Then edit the fix to deactivate any fixes that aren't required by the program. To change the fixes, right-click the program's executable filename in the right pane and then click Edit Application Fix.

After you've added all the fixes for all your incompatible programs to the database, save the database file. To enable Windows XP to use the resulting `.sdb` file, you need to install the file by highlighting it and selecting File, Install. To distribute the fix to another computer, copy the `.sdb` file to the machine, launch Compatibility Administrator, and then click Open to open the `.sdb` file. You can then install the database.

# From Here

Here are a few other places where you'll find information related to the material presented in this chapter:

- For more startup options, see Chapter 1, "Customizing and Troubleshooting the Windows XP Startup."

- You can use the Open With list to open a document with a different program. For details, see the section in Chapter 3 titled "Customizing Windows XP's Open With List."

- For more information about group policies, see the section in Chapter 7 titled "Implementing Group Policies with Windows XP."

- For a complete look at the inner workings of the Registry, see Chapter 8.

- To learn how to run programs using a script, see the section in Chapter 9 titled "Programming the WshShell Object."

- To maximize program performance, see the section in Chapter 11 titled "Optimizing Applications."

- To learn how to run programs from the command prompt, see the section in Appendix B titled "Starting Applications from the Command Prompt."

# CHAPTER 6

# Getting the Most Out of User Accounts

Do you share your computer with other people either at work or at home? Then you're no doubt all too aware of one undeniable fact of human psychology: People are individuals with minds of their own! One person prefers Windows in a black-and-purple color scheme; another person just loves that annoying Peace wallpaper; yet another person prefers to have a zillion shortcuts on the Windows desktop; and, of course, everybody uses a different mix of applications. How can you possibly satisfy all those diverse tastes and prevent people from coming to blows?

It's a lot easier than you might think. Windows XP lets you set up a different **user account** for each person who uses the computer. A user account is a username (and an optional password) that uniquely identifies a person who uses the system. The user account enables Windows XP to control the user's **privileges**; that is, the user's access to system resources (**permissions**) and the user's ability to run system tasks (**rights**). Standalone and workgroup machines use *local* user accounts that are maintained on the computer, whereas domain machines use *global* user accounts that are maintained on the domain controller. This chapter looks at local user accounts.

## Understanding Security Groups

Security for Windows XP user accounts is handled mostly (and most easily) by assigning each user to a particular security group. For example, the default Administrator account and all the user accounts you created during the

Windows XP setup process are part of the Administrators group. Each security group is defined with a specific set of permissions and rights, and any user added to a group is automatically granted that group's permissions and rights. There are two main security groups:

| | |
|---|---|
| Administrators | Members of this group have complete control over the computer, meaning they can access all folders and files, install and uninstall programs (including legacy programs) and devices, create, modify, and remove user accounts, install Windows updates, service packs, and fixes, use safe mode, repair Windows, take ownership of objects, and more. |
| Users | Members of this group (also known as **Limited Users** or **Restricted Users**) can access files only in their own folders and in the computer's shared folders, change their account's password, picture, add .NET Passport support, and run programs and install programs that don't require administrative-level rights. |

---

**NOTE**

A .NET Passport is an account—such as a Hotmail or MSN account—that enables you to access the websites and services that comprise the Passport Network, Microsoft's universal login service. For example, a single Hotmail email address and password is all you need to access not only your Hotmail account, but also MSN, Encarta, Windows or MSN Messenger Service, and much more.

---

In addition to those groups, Windows XP also defines up to eight others that you'll use less often:

| | |
|---|---|
| Backup Operators | Members of this group can access the Backup program and use it to back up and restore folders and files, no matter what permissions are set on those objects. |
| Debugger Users | Members of this group can debug processes on the computer, either locally or remotely. |
| Guests | Members of this group have the same privileges as those of the Users group. The exception is the default Guest account, which is not allowed to change its account password. |
| HelpServicesGroup | Members of this group (generally, Microsoft and OEM personnel) can connect to your computer to resolve technical issues using the Remote Assistance feature. |
| Network Configuration Operators | Members of this group have a subset of the Administrator-level rights that enables them to install and configure networking features. |

| | |
|---|---|
| Power Users | Members of this group (also known as **Standard Users**) have a subset of the Administrator group privileges. Power Users can't back up or restore files, replace system files, take ownership of files, or install or remove device drivers. Also, Power Users can't install applications that explicitly require the user to be a member of the Administrators group. |
| Remote Desktop Users | Members of this group can log on to the computer from a remote location using the Remote Desktop feature. |
| Replicator | Members of this group can replicate files across a domain. |

Each user is also assigned a **user profile** that contains all the user's folders and files, as well as the user's Windows settings. The folders and files are stored in `\%SystemDrive%\Documents and Settings\`*user*, where *user* is the username; for the current user, this folder is designated by the `%UserProfile%` variable. This location contains a number of subfolders that hold the user's home folder (My Documents), Internet Explorer cookies (Cookies), desktop icons and subfolders (Desktop), Internet Explorer favorites (Favorites), Start menu items (Start Menu), and more. If a logged-on user has been assigned any group policies, the user's settings are stored in the `HKU\`*sid*`\` Registry key, where *sid* is a SID—a 48-digit **security identifier** (SID) typically in the form S-1-5-*nn*, where *nn* is a variable-length string of numbers interspersed with hyphens. To determine which user is associated with a particular SID, see the following Registry setting:

`HKU\sid\Software\Microsoft\Windows\CurrentVersion\Explorer\`*Logon User Name*

The rest of this chapter shows you the various methods Windows XP offers to create, modify, and remove local user accounts.

## Working with the User Accounts Window

Windows XP has a number of methods for working with user accounts. The most direct route is to launch the Control Panel's User Accounts icon. If you're using a standalone or workgroup computer, you'll see the User Accounts window, which I discuss in this section. (Domain-based computers display the User Accounts dialog box, which I discuss in the next section.)

If you're a member of the Administrators or Power Users group, you create a new user account by following these steps:

1. Click Create a New Account. The Name the New Account window appears.

2. Type the name for the account. The name can be up to 20 characters and must be unique on the system. Click Next. The Pick an Account Type window appears.

3. Activate either Computer Administrator (to add the user to the Administrators group) or Limited (to add the user to the Users group), and then click Create Account.

To modify an existing account, click the account in the User Accounts window to see a list of tasks for changing the account, as shown in Figure 6.1. (If you're a member of the Users or Guests group, launching Control Panel's User Accounts icon takes you directly to the task list.) Depending on your account's privileges, you can then change the account name, create or change the account password, change the picture associated with the account, change the account type, apply a .NET password to the account, or delete the account.

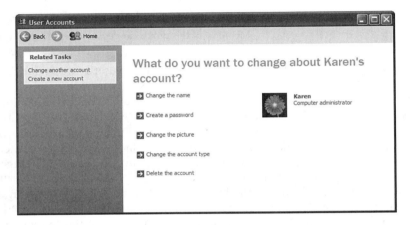

**FIGURE 6.1**    Click a user in the User Accounts window to see this list of tasks for changing the user's account.

# Working with the User Accounts Dialog Box

Control Panel's User Accounts window has one major limitation: It offers only the Administrator and Limited (Users) account types. If you want to assign a user to one of the other groups, you have to use the User Accounts dialog box. You get there by following these steps:

1. Select Start, Run to display the Run dialog box.

2. In the Open text box, type **control userpasswords2**.

3. Click OK. Windows XP displays the User Accounts dialog box, shown in Figure 6.2.

To enable the list of users, make sure that the Users Must Enter a User Name and Password to Use This Computer check box is activated.

## Adding a New User

To add a new user via the User Accounts dialog box, follow these steps:

1. Click Add to launch the Add New User Wizard.

2. Type the new user's username (no more than 20 characters, and it must be unique). You can also type the user's full name and description, but these are optional. Click Next.

3. Type the user's password and type it again in the Confirm Password text box. Click Next.

4. Activate the option that specifies the user's security group: Standard User (Power Users group), Restricted User (Users group), or Other. Activate the latter to assign the user to any of the ten default Windows XP groups.

5. Click Finish.

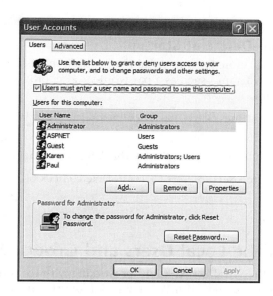

**FIGURE 6.2** The User Accounts dialog box enables you to assign users to any Windows XP security group.

## Performing Other User Tasks

Here's a list of the other tasks you can perform in the User Accounts dialog box:

- Delete a user—Select the user and click Remove. When XP asks you to confirm, click Yes.

- Change the user's name or group—Select the user and click Properties to display the user's property sheet. Use the General tab to change the username; use the Group Membership tab to assign the user to a different group.

- Change the user's password—Select the user and click Reset Password. (Note that this option is not enabled for the Administrator account.) Type the password in the New Password and Confirm New Password text boxes and click OK.

## Requiring Ctrl+Alt+Delete at Startup

Pressing Ctrl+Alt+Delete before logging on adds an extra level of security because it thwarts any malicious program—such as a password-stealing program—that might have been activated at startup.

To require that users must press Ctrl+Alt+Delete before they can log on, follow these steps:

1. In the User Accounts dialog box, display the Advanced tab.

2. Activate the Require Users to Press Ctrl+Alt+Delete check box.

3. Click OK.

# Working with the Local Users and Groups Snap-In

The most powerful of the Windows XP tools for working with users is the Local Users and Groups MMC snap-in that comes with Windows XP Professional. To load this snap-in, Windows XP Professional offers three methods:

- In the User Accounts dialog box (refer to the previous section), display the Advanced tab and then click the Advanced button.

- Select Start, Run, type **lusrmgr.msc**, and click OK.

- Select Start, right-click My Computer, and then click Manage. In the Computer Management window, select System Tools, Local Users and Groups.

Whichever method you use, select the Users branch to see a list of the users on your system, as shown in Figure 6.3.

From here, you can perform the following tasks:

- Add a new user—Make sure that no user is selected and then select Action, New User. In the New User dialog box, type the user name, password, and confirm the password. (I discuss the password-related check boxes in this dialog box later in this chapter; see "User Account Password Options.") Click Create.

- Change a user's name—Right-click the user and then click Rename.

- Change a user's password—Right-click the user and then click Set Password.

- Add a user to a group—Right-click the user and then click Properties to open the user's property sheet. In the Member Of tab, click Add and use the Enter the Object Names to Select box to enter the group name. If you're not sure of the name, click Advanced to open the Select Groups dialog box, click Find Now to list all the groups, select the group, and then click OK. Click OK to close the property sheet.

> **NOTE**
>
> Another way to add a user to a group is to select the Groups branch in the Local Users and Groups snap-in. Right-click the group you want to work with, and then click Add to Group. Now click Add, type the username in the Enter the Object Names to Select box, and then click OK.

- Remove a user from a group—Right-click the user and then click Properties to open the user's property sheet. In the Member Of tab, select the group from which you want the user removed, and then click Remove. Click OK to close the property sheet.

- Change a user's profile—Right-click the user and then click Properties to open the user's property sheet. Use the Profile tab to change the profile path, logon script, and home folder (activate the Local Path option to specify a local folder; or activate Connect to specify a shared network folder).

- Disable an account—Right-click the user and then click Properties to open the user's property sheet. In the General tab, activate the Account Is Disabled check box.

- Delete a user—Right-click the user and then click Delete.

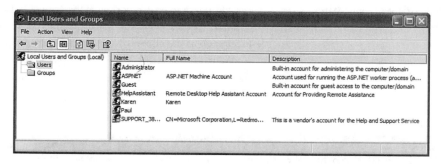

**FIGURE 6.3**   The Users branch lists all the system's users and enables you to add, modify, and delete users.

# Setting Account Policies

Windows XP Professional offers several sets of policies that affect user accounts. There are three kinds of account policies: security options, user rights, and account lockout policies. The next three sections take you through these policies.

## Setting Account Security Policies

To see these policies, you have two choices:

- Open the Group Policy editor (select Start, Run, type **gpedit.msc**, and click OK) and select Computer Configuration, Windows Settings, Security Settings, Local Policies, Security Options, as shown in Figure 6.4.

- Launch the Local Security Settings snap-in (select Start, Run, type **secpol.msc**, and click OK) and select Security Settings, Local Policies, Security Options.

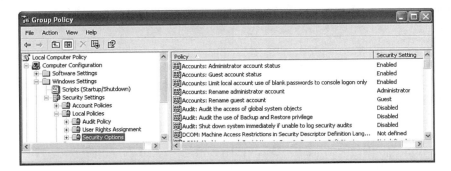

**FIGURE 6.4**    In the Security Options branch, use the five Accounts policies to configure security for your accounts.

The Accounts grouping has five policies:

| | |
|---|---|
| Administrator Account Status | Use this policy to enable or disable the Administrator account. This is useful if you think someone else might be logging on as the Administrator. (A less drastic solution would be to change the Administrator password or rename the Administrator account.) Note that only a different member of the Administrators group can enable a disabled Administrator account. |

> **NOTE**
>
> The Administrator account is always used during a Safe Mode boot, even if you disable the account.

| | |
|---|---|
| Guest Account Status | Use this option to enable or disable the Guest account. |
| Limit Local Account Use of Blank Passwords to Console Logon Only | When this option is enabled, Windows XP allows users with blank passwords to log on to the system directly only by using the Welcome screen or the Log On to Windows dialog box. Such users can't log on via either the RunAs command or remotely over a network. This policy modifies the following Registry setting: |

```
HKLM\SYSTEM\CurrentControlSet\Control\Lsa\limitblankpassworduse
```

Rename Administrator Account          Use this option to change the name of the Administrator account.

Rename Guest Account                  Use this option to change the name of the Guest account.

## Setting User Rights Policies

Windows XP has a long list of policies associated with user rights. To view these policies, you have two choices:

- In the Group Policy editor, select Computer Configuration, Windows Settings, Security Settings, Local Policies, User Rights Assignment, as shown in Figure 6.5.

- In the Local Security Policy snap-in, select Security Settings, Local Policies, User Rights Assignment.

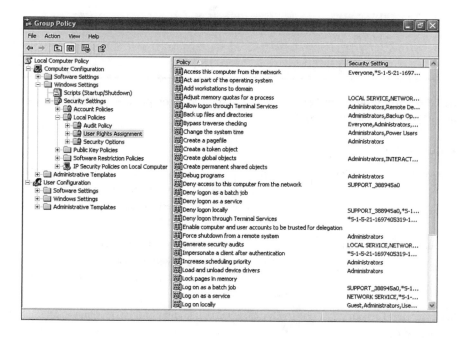

**FIGURE 6.5**    In the User Rights Assignment branch, use the policies to configure the rights assigned to users or groups.

Each policy is a specific task or action, such as Back Up Files and Directories, Deny Logon Locally, and Shut Down the System. For each task or action, the Security Setting column shows the users and groups who can perform the task or to whom the action applies. To change the setting, double-click the policy. Click Add User or Group to add an object to the policy; or delete an object from the policy by selecting it and clicking Remove.

## Setting Account Lockout Policies

Last of all, Windows XP has a few policies that determine when an account gets locked out, which means the user is unable to log on. A lockout occurs when the user fails to log on after a specified number of attempts. This is a good security feature because it prevents an unauthorized user from trying a number of different passwords. Use either of the following methods to view these policies:

- In the Group Policy editor, select Computer Configuration, Windows Settings, Security Settings, Account Policies, Account Lockout, as shown in Figure 6.6.

- In the Local Security Policy snap-in, select Security Settings, Account Policies, Account Lockout Policy.

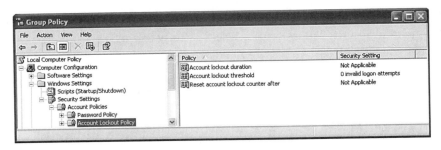

**FIGURE 6.6**    In the Account Lockout Policy branch, use the policies to configure when an account gets locked out of the system.

There are three policies:

| | |
|---|---|
| Account Lockout Duration | This policy sets the amount of time, in minutes, that the user is locked out. Note that, to change this policy, you must set the Account Lockout Threshold (described next) to a nonzero number. |
| Account Lockout Threshold | This policy sets the maximum number of logons the user can attempt before being locked out. Note that after you change this to a nonzero value, Windows XP offers to set the other two policies to 30 minutes. |
| Reset Account Lockout Counter After | This policy sets the amount of time, in minutes, after which the counter that tracks the number of invalid logons is reset to 0. |

# Working with Users and Groups from the Command Line

You can script your user and group chores by taking advantage of the NET USER and NET LOCALGROUP commands. These commands enable you to add users, change passwords, modify accounts, add users to groups, and remove users from groups.

## The NET USER Command

For local users, the NET USER command has the following syntax:

NET USER [*username* [*password* ¦ * ¦ /RANDOM] [/ADD] [/DELETE] [*options*]]

| | |
|---|---|
| *username* | The name of the user you want to add or work with. If you run NET USER with only the name of an existing user, the command displays the user's account data. |
| *password* | The password you want to assign to the user. If you use *, Windows XP prompts you for the password; if you use the /RANDOM switch, Windows XP assigns a random password (containing eight characters, consisting of a random mix of letters, numbers, and symbols), and then displays the pass word on the console. |
| /ADD | Creates a new user account. |
| /DELETE | Deletes the specified user account. |
| *options* | These are optional switches you can append to the command: |
| /ACTIVE:{YES ¦ NO} | Specifies whether the account is active or disabled. |
| /EXPIRES:{*date* ¦ NEVER} | The date (expressed in the system's Short Date format) on which the account expires. |
| /HOMEDIR:*path* | The home folder for the user (make sure that the folder exists). |
| /PASSWORDCHG:{YES ¦ NO} | Specifies whether the user is allowed to change his password. |
| /PASSWORDREQ:{YES ¦ NO} | Specifies whether the user is required to have a password. |
| /PROFILEPATH:*path* | The folder that contains the user's profile. |
| /SCRIPTPATH:*path* | The folder that contains the user's logon script. |
| /TIMES:{*times* ¦ ALL} | Specifies the times that the user is allowed to log on to the system. Use single days or day ranges (for example, Sa or M-F). For times, use 24-hour notation or 12-hour notation with am or pm. Separate the day and time with a comma, separate day/time combinations with semicolons. Here are some examples: |

> M-F,9am-5pm
>
> M,W,F,08:00-13:00
>
> Sa,12pm-6pm;Su,1pm-5pm

**CAUTION**

If you use the /RANDOM switch to create a random password, be sure to make a note of the new password so that you can communicate it to the new user.

Note, too, that if you execute NET USER without any parameters, it displays a list of the local user accounts.

> **TIP**
>
> If you want to force a user to logoff when his logon hours expire, open the Group Policy editor and select Computer Configuration, Windows Settings, Security Settings, Local Policies, Security Options. In the Network Security category, enable the Force Logoff When Logon Hours Expire policy.

## The NET LOCALGROUP Command

NET LOCALGROUP has the following syntax for adding user to or removing users from a group:

```
NET LOCALGROUP [group name1 [name2 ...] {/ADD ¦ /DELETE}
```

| | |
|---|---|
| *group* | This is the name of the security group with which you want to work. |
| *name1* [*name2* ...] | One or more usernames that you want to add or delete, separated by spaces. |
| /ADD | Adds the user or users to the group. |
| /DELETE | Removes the user or users from the group. |

# Creating and Enforcing Bulletproof Passwords

Windows XP sometimes gives the impression that passwords aren't all that important. After all, each user account you specify during setup is supplied with both administrative-level privileges *and* a blank password. That's a dangerous setup, but it's one that's easily remedied by supplying a password to *all* local users. This section gives you some pointers for creating strong passwords and runs through Windows XP's password-related options and policies.

## Creating a Strong Password

Ideally, when you're creating a password for a user, you want to pick one that provides maximum protection without sacrificing convenience. Keeping in mind that the whole point of a password is to select one that nobody can guess, here are some guidelines you can follow when choosing a password:

- Don't be too obvious—Because forgetting a password is inconvenient, many people use meaningful words or numbers so that their password will be easier to remember. Unfortunately, this means that they often use extremely obvious things such as their name, the name of a family member or colleague, their birth date or Social Security number, or even their system username. Being this obvious is just asking for trouble.

- Don't use single words—Many crackers break into accounts by using "dictionary programs" that just try every word in the dictionary. So, yes, *xiphoid* is an obscure word that no person would ever guess, but a good dictionary program will figure it out in seconds flat. Using two or more words in your password (or **pass phrase**, as multiword passwords are called) is still easy to remember, and would take much longer to crack by a brute force program.

- Use a misspelled word—Misspelling a word is an easy way to fool a dictionary program. (Make sure, of course, that the resulting arrangement of letters doesn't spell some other word.)

- Use passwords that are at least eight characters long—Shorter passwords are susceptible to programs that just try every letter combination. You can combine the 26 letters of the alphabet into about 12 million different five-letter word combinations, which is no big deal for a fast program. If you bump things up to eight-letter passwords, however, the total number of combinations rises to 200 *billion*, which would take even the fastest computer quite a while. If you use 12-letter passwords, as many experts recommend, the number of combinations goes beyond mind-boggling: 90 *quadrillion*, or 90,000 trillion!

- Mix uppercase and lowercase letters—Windows XP passwords are case-sensitive, which means that if your password is, say, *YUMMY ZIMA*, trying *yummy zima* won't work. So, you can really throw snoops for a loop by mixing the case. Something like *yuMmY zIMa* would be almost impossible to figure out.

- Add numbers to your password—You can throw more permutations and combinations into the mix by adding a few numbers to your password.

- Include a few punctuation marks and symbols—For extra variety, toss in one or more punctuation marks or special symbols, such as % or #.

- Try using acronyms—One of the best ways to get a password that appears random but is easy to remember is to create an acronym out of a favorite quotation, saying, or book title. For example, if you've just read *The Seven Habits of Highly Effective People*, you could use the password T7HoHEP.

- Don't write down your password—After going to all this trouble to create an indestructible password, don't blow it by writing it on a sticky note and then attaching it to your keyboard or monitor! Even writing it on a piece of paper and then throwing the paper away is dangerous. Determined crackers have been known to go through a company's trash looking for passwords (this is known in the trade as **dumpster diving**). Also, don't use the password itself as your Windows XP password hint.

- Don't tell your password to anyone—If you've thought of a particularly clever password, don't suddenly become unclever and tell someone. Your password should be stored in your head alongside all those "wasted youth" things you don't want anyone to know about.

- Change your password regularly—If you change your password often (say, once a month or so), even if some skulker does get access to your account, at least he'll have it for only a relatively short period.

## User Account Password Options

Each user account has a number of options related to passwords. To view these options, open the Local Users and Groups snap-in (as described earlier in this chapter), right-click the user you want to work with, and then click Properties. There are three password-related check boxes in the property sheet that appears:

| | |
|---|---|
| User Must Change Password at Next Logon | If you activate this check box, the next time the user logs on, she will see a dialog box with the message that she is required to change her password. When the user clicks OK, the Change Password dialog box appears and the user enters her new password. |
| User Cannot Change Password | Activate this check box to prevent the user from changing the password. |
| Password Never Expires | If you deactivate this check box, the user's password will expire. The expiration date is determined by the Maximum Password Age policy, discussed in the next section. |

## Taking Advantage of Windows XP's Password Policies

Windows XP maintains a small set of useful password-related policies that govern settings such as when passwords expire and the minimum length of a password. There are two methods you can use to view these policies:

- In the Group Policy editor, select Computer Configuration, Windows Settings, Security Settings, Account Policies, Password Policy, as shown in Figure 6.7.

- In the Local Security Policy snap-in, select Security Settings, Account Policies, Password Policy.

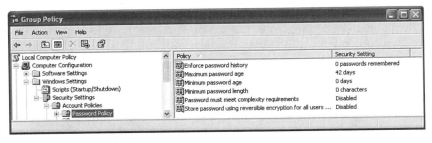

**FIGURE 6.7**    In the Password Policy branch, use the policies to enforce strong passwords and other protections.

There are six policies:

| | |
|---|---|
| Enforce Password History | This policy determines the number of old passwords that Windows XP stores for each user. This is to prevent a user from reusing an old password. For example, if you set this value to 10, the user can't reuse a password until he or she has used at least 10 other passwords. Enter a number between 0 and 24. |
| Maximum Password Age | This policy sets the number of days after which passwords expire. This only applies to user accounts where the Password Never Expires property has been disabled (see the previous section). Enter a number between 1 and 999. |
| Minimum Password Age | This policy sets the numbers of days that a password must be in effect before the user can change it. Enter a number between 1 and 998 (but less than the Maximum Password Age value). |
| Minimum Password Length | This policy sets the minimum number of characters for the password. Enter a number between 0 and 14 (where 0 means no password is required). |
| Password Must Meet Complexity Requirements | If you enable this policy, Windows XP examines each new password and accepts it only if it meets the following criteria: It doesn't contain all or part of the username; it's at least six characters long; and it contains characters from three of the following four categories: uppercase letters, lowercase letters, digits (0–9), and nonalphanumeric characters (such as $ and #). |
| Store Password Using Reversible Encryption for All Users in Domain | Enabling this policy tells Windows XP to store user passwords using reversible encryption. Some applications the require this, but they're rare and you should never need to enable this policy. |

## Recovering from a Forgotten Password

Few things in life are as frustrating as a forgotten password. To avoid this headache, Windows XP offers a couple of precautions that you can take now just in case you forget your password.

The first precaution is called a **password hint**, which is a word, phrase, or other mnemonic device that can help you remember your password. To see the hint, click the question mark (?) button that appears beside the password box in the Welcome screen. To set up a password hint, follow these steps:

1. Launch the Control Panel's User Accounts icon.

2. If you have administrative-level privileges, click the user you want to work with.

3. From here, you have two choices:

   - If the user doesn't have a password, click Create a Password, type the password (twice), and enter the password hint in the Type a Word or Phrase to Use as a Password Hint text box.

   - If the user already has a password, click Change My Password, enter the existing password in all three text boxes, and then enter the password hint in the Type a Word or Phrase to Use as a Password Hint text box.

The second precaution you can take is the Password Reset Disk. This is a floppy disk that enables you to reset the password on your account without knowing the old password. To create a Password Reset Disk, follow these steps:

1. Log on as the user for whom you want to create the disk.

2. Launch the Control Panel's User Accounts icon.

3. Click your account name, if necessary.

4. In the Related Tasks list, click Prevent a Forgotten Password. This launches the Forgotten Password Wizard.

5. Run through the wizard's dialog boxes. (Note that you'll need a blank, formatted disk.)

The password reset disk contains a single file named Userkey.psw, which is an encrypted backup version of your password. If you need to use this disk, follow these steps:

1. Start Windows XP normally.

2. When you get to the logon screen, leave your password blank and press Enter. Windows XP will then ask if you want to use your password reset disk.

3. You have two ways to proceed:

   - If you're using the Welcome screen, click the Use Your Password Reset Disk link.

   - If you're using the Classic logon, click Reset.

4. In the initial Password Reset Wizard dialog box, click Next.

5. Insert the password reset disk and click Next.

6. Type a new password (twice), type a password hint, and click Next.

7. Click Finish.

# Sharing Your Computer Securely

If you're the only person who uses your computer, you don't have to worry all that much about the security of your user profile—that is, your files and Windows XP settings. However, if you share your computer with other people, either at home or at the office, you need to set up some kind of security to ensure that each user has his "own" Windows and can't mess with anyone else's (either purposely or accidentally). Here's a list of security precautions to set up when sharing your computer (these techniques have been discussed earlier in this chapter, except where noted):

- Create an account for each user—Everyone who uses the computer, even if they use it only occasionally, should have her own user account. (If a user needs to access the computer rarely, or only once, activate the Guest account and let him use that. You should disable the Guest account after the user has finished his session.)

- Remove unused accounts—If you have accounts set up for users who no longer require access to the computer, you should delete those accounts.

- Limit the number of administrators—Members of the Administrators group can do *anything* in Windows XP, including granting themselves privileges that they might not have by default. These all-powerful accounts should be kept to a minimum. Ideally, your system should have just one: the Administrator account.

- Rename the Administrator account—Renaming the Administrator account ensures that no other user can be certain of the name of the computer's top-level user.

- Don't display the last logged-on user—If you're using the Classic logon, tell Windows XP not to display the name of the user who last logged on to the system. In the Group Policy editor, select Computer Configuration, Windows Settings, Security Settings, Local Policies, Security Options, and then enable the Interactive Logon: Do Not Display Last User Name policy.

- Put all other accounts in the Users (Limited) group—Most users can perform almost all of their everyday chores with the permissions and rights assigned to the Users group, so that's the group you should use for all other accounts.

- Use strong passwords on all accounts—Supply each account with a strong password so that no user can access another's account by logging on with a blank or simple password.

- Set up each account with a screensaver and be sure the screensaver resumes to the Welcome screen—To do this, launch Control Panel's Display icon, navigate to the Screen Saver tab, choose a screensaver, and then activate the On Resume, Display Welcome Screen check box.

- Use disk quotas—To prevent users from taking up an inordinate amount of hard disk space (think MP3 downloads), set up disk quotas for each user. To enable quotas, right-click a hard disk in Windows Explorer, and then click Properties to display the disk's property sheet. Display the Quota tab and activate the Enable Quota Management check box.

6

# From Here

Here are a few other places to turn to for information related to user accounts and other aspects of this chapter:

- For some logon tips and techniques, see the section in Chapter 1 titled "Useful Windows XP Logon Strategies."

- For the details on group policies, see the section in Chapter 7 titled "Implementing Group Policies with Windows XP."

- To learn how to work with the Registry, see Chapter 8, "Getting to Know the Windows XP Registry."

- For information on sharing Outlook Express within a single user account, see the section in Chapter 19 titled "Working with Identities."

- You need to set up user accounts for the people with whom you want to share resources in a peer-to-peer network. For the details, see the section in Chapter 22 titled "Sharing Resources with the Network."

# PART II

# Unleashing Essential Windows XP Power Tools

## IN THIS PART

# CHAPTER 7

# Using Control Panel, Group Policies, and Tweak UI

$M$y goal in this book is to help you unleash the true power of Windows XP, and my premise is that this goal can't be met by toeing the line and doing only what the manual or Help system tells you. Rather, I believe you can reach this goal only by taking various off-the-beaten track routes that go beyond Windows orthodoxy.

This chapter is a perfect example. The three tools that I discuss—Control Panel, system policies, and Tweak UI—aren't difficult to use, but they put an amazing amount of power and flexibility into your hands. I discuss them in this early chapter because you'll be using these important tools throughout the rest of the book. However, you can scour the Windows XP manual and Help system all day long and you'll find only a few scant references to Control Panel, and nothing at all on system policies or Tweak UI. To be sure, Microsoft is just being cautious because these *are* powerful tools, and the average user can wreak all kinds of havoc if these features are used incorrectly. However, your purchase of this book is proof that you are not an average user; so, by following the instructions in this chapter, I'm sure you'll have no trouble at all using these tools.

## Operating Control Panel

Control Panel is a folder that contains a large number of icons—there are 30 or so (depending on your version of XP) in the default Windows XP setup, but depending on your system configuration, 40 or more icons could be available. Each of these icons deals with a specific area of the Windows XP configuration: hardware, applications, fonts, printers, multimedia, and much more.

Opening an icon displays a dialog box containing various properties related to that area of Windows. For example, launching the Add or Remove Programs icon enables you to install or uninstall third-party applications and Windows XP components.

To display the Control Panel folder, use any of the following techniques:

- Select Start, Control Panel.
- In Windows Explorer's Folders list, select the `Desktop\My Computer\Control Panel` folder.
- In My Computer, click the Control Panel link.

---

**TIP**

You can also display Control Panel in My Computer's contents list by selecting the Tools, Folder Options command, displaying the View tab, and activating the Show Control Panel in My Computer check box. To learn how to convert the Start menu's Control Panel link to a menu of Control Panel icons, see "Putting Control Panel on the Start Menu," later in this chapter.

---

By default, Windows XP displays Control Panel in Category View, which divides the underlying icons into various categories. In most cases, you click a category and then click the icon you want to work with. This setup might help novice users, but it just delays the rest of us unnecessarily. Therefore, your first Control Panel task should be to click the Switch to Classic View link, which displays all the Control Panel icons, as shown in Figure 7.1. (The collection of icons that appear in the Control Panel window varies depending on the hardware and software installed on your machine.) Note that Windows XP remembers the last view you used, so the Classic View will now appear each time you launch Control Panel.

## Reviewing the Control Panel Icons

To help you familiarize yourself with what's available in Control Panel, this section offers summary descriptions of the Control Panel icons found in a standard Windows XP installation. Note that your system might have extra icons, depending on your system's configuration and the programs you have installed.

| | |
|---|---|
| Accessibility Options | Enables you to customize input—the keyboard and mouse—and output—sound and display—for users with special mobility, hearing, or vision requirements. |
| Add Hardware | Launches the Add Hardware Wizard, which searches for new Plug and Play devices on your system, and can run a more in-depth hardware detection to look for non-Plug and Play devices. You can also use this wizard to install device drivers by hand by choosing the one you want from a list or from a disc that came with your device. |

**FIGURE 7.1**    Switch Control Panel to the Classic View to see all the icons in one window.

Add or Remove Programs

Enables you to install and uninstall applications, add and remove Windows XP components, and, if you have Windows XP Service Pack 1 or later installed, change the default programs for the web browser, email client, instant messaging program, and more.

Administrative Tools

Displays a window with more icons, each of which enables you to administer a particular aspect of Windows XP:

- Component Services—Enables you to configure and administer COM (Component Object Model) components and COM+ applications.

- Computer Management—Enables you to manage a local or remote computer. You can examine hidden and visible shared folders, set group policies, access Device Manager, manage hard disks, and much more.

- Data Sources (ODBC)—Enables you to create and work with data source names, which are connection strings that you use to connect to local or remote databases.

- Event Viewer—Enables you to examine Windows XP's list of events, which are unusual or noteworthy occurrences on your system, such as a service that doesn't start, the installation of a device, or an application error.

- Local Security Policy—Displays the Local Security Settings snap-in, which enables you to set up security policies on your system. See "Setting Account Security Policies" in Chapter 6, "Getting the Most Out of User Accounts," and "Implementing Group Policies with Windows XP" later in this chapter.

- Performance—Enables you to monitor the performance of your system using System Monitor (in Chapter 11, "Tuning Windows XP's Performance," see "Monitoring Performance with System Monitor"), performance logs, and alerts.

- Services—Displays a list of the system services available with Windows XP. System services are background routines that enable the system to perform tasks such as network logon, disk management, Plug and Play, Internet Connection Sharing, and much more. You can pause, stop, and start services, as well as configure how services load at startup.

| | |
|---|---|
| Automatic Updates | Enables you to configure XP's Automatic Updates feature, including setting up a schedule for the download and installation of updates. |
| Bluetooth Devices | Enables you to add, configure, and manage devices that use the Bluetooth wireless networking standard. This icon appears only if you've installed a Bluetooth device on your system. |
| Date and Time | Enables you to set the current date and time, select your time zone, and set up an Internet time server to synchronize your system time. |
| Display | Offers a large number of customization options for the desktop, screen saver, video card, monitor, and other display components. |
| Folder Options | Enables you to customize the display of Windows XP's folders, set up whether Windows XP uses single- or double-clicking, work with file types, and configure offline files. |
| Fonts | Displays the Fonts folder, from which you can view, install, and remove fonts. |
| Game Controllers | Enables you to calibrate joysticks and other game devices. |
| Internet Options | Displays a large collection of settings for modifying Internet properties (how you connect, the Internet Explorer interface, and so on). |
| Keyboard | Enables you to customize your keyboard, work with keyboard languages, and change the keyboard driver. |
| Mouse | Enables you to set various mouse options and to install a different mouse device driver. |
| Network Connections | Enables you to create, modify, and launch connections to a network or the Internet. |

| | |
|---|---|
| Network Setup Wizard | Launches the Network Setup Wizard, which takes you step by step through the process of setting up and configuring your computer for network use. |
| Phone and Modem Options | Enables you to configure telephone dialing rules and to install and configure modems. |
| Portable Media Devices (Service Pack 2) | Displays a list of your system's installed portable media devices, including Flash drives, memory cards, memory card readers, and so on. |
| Power Options | Enables you to configure power management properties for powering down system components (such as the monitor and hard drive), defining low-power alarms for notebook batteries, enabling hibernation, and configuring an uninterruptible power supply. |
| Printers and Faxes | Enables you to install and configure printers and the Windows XP Fax service. |
| Regional and Language Options | Enables you to configure international settings for country-dependent items such as numbers, currencies, times, and dates. |
| Scanners and Cameras | Enables you to install and configure document scanners and digital cameras. |
| Scheduled Tasks | Displays the Scheduled Tasks folder, which you use to set up a program to run on a schedule. |
| Security Center (Service Pack 2) | Displays the Security Center window, which shows the current status of Windows Firewall, Automatic Updates, and Virus Protection. You can also manage security settings for the Internet, Windows Firewall, and Automatic Updates. |
| Sounds and Audio Devices | Enables you to control the system volume, map sounds to specific Windows XP events (such as closing a program or minimizing a window), specify settings for audio, voice, and other multimedia devices. |
| Speech | Enables you to configure Windows XP's text-to-speech feature. |
| System | Gives you access to a large number of system properties, including the computer name and workgroup, Device Manager and hardware profiles, and settings related to performance, startup, System Restore, Automatic Updates, Remote Assistance, and the Remote Desktop. |
| Tablet and Pen Settings (Tablet PC Edition) | Displays settings for configuring handwriting, the digital pen, and other aspects of Windows XP Tablet PC Edition. |
| Taskbar and Start Menu | Enables you to customize the taskbar and Start menu. |
| User Accounts | Enables you to set up and configure user accounts. |

| Windows Firewall (Service Pack 2) | Enables you to activate and configur Windows Firewall. |
| Wireless Network Setup Wizard (Service Pack 2) | Launches the Wireless Network Setup Wizard, which takes you step by step through the process of configuring a secure wireless network. |

## Understanding Control Panel Files

Many of the Control Panel icons are represented by **Control Panel extension** files, which use the .cpl extension. These files reside in the %SystemRoot%\System32 folder. When you open Control Panel, Windows XP scans the System32 folder looking for CPL files, and then displays an icon for each one.

The CPL files offer an alternative method for launching individual Control Panel dialog boxes. The idea is that you run control.exe and specify the name of a CPL file as a parameter. This bypasses the Control Panel folder and opens the icon directly. Here's the syntax:

```
control CPLfile [,option1 [, option2]]
```

| CPLfile | The name of the file that corresponds to the Control Panel icon you want to open (see Table 7.1 later in this chapter). |
| option1 | This option is obsolete and is included only for backward compatibility with batch files and scripts that use Control.exe for opening Control Panel icons. |
| option2 | The tab number of a multitabbed dialog box. Many Control Panel icons open a dialog that has two or more tabs. If you know the specific tab you want to work with, you can use the option2 parameter to specify an integer that corresponds to the tab's relative position from the left side of the dialog box. The first (leftmost) tab is 0, the next tab is 1, and so on. |

---

**NOTE**

If the dialog box has multiple rows of tabs, count the tabs from left to right and from bottom to top. For example, if the dialog box has two rows of four tabs each, the tabs in the bottom row are numbered 0 to 3 from left to right, and the tabs in the top row are numbered 4 to 7 from left to right.

Also, note that even though you no longer use the option1 parameter, you must still display its comma in the command line.

---

For example, to open Control Panel's System icon with the Hardware tab displayed, run the following command:

```
control sysdm.cpl,,2
```

Table 7.1 lists the various Control Panel icons and the appropriate command line to use. (Note, however, that some Control Panel icons—such as Taskbar and Start Menu—can't be accessed by running `Control.exe`.)

**TABLE 7.1**    Command Lines for Launching Individual Control Panel Icons

| Control Panel Icon | Command |
|---|---|
| Accessibility Options | control access.cpl |
| Add Hardware | control hdwwiz.cpl |
| Add or Remove Programs | control appwiz.cpl |
| Administrative Tools | control admintools |
| Automatic Updates | control wuaucpl.cpl |
| Date and Time | control timedate.cpl |
| Display | control desk.cpl |
| Folder Options | control folders |
| Fonts | control fonts |
| Game Controllers | control joy.cpl |
| Internet Options | control inetcpl.cpl |
| Keyboard | control keyboard |
| Mouse | control mouse |
| Network Connections | control ncpa.cpl |
| Phone and Modem Options | control telephon.cpl |
| Power Options | control powercfg.cpl |
| Printers and Faxes | control printers |
| Regional and Language Options | control intl.cpl |
| Scanners and Cameras | control scannercamera |
| Scheduled Tasks | control schedtasks |
| Security Center | control wscui.cpl |
| Sounds and Audio Devices | control mmsys.cpl |
| System | control sysdm.cpl |
| Tablet and Pen Settings | control tabletpc.cpl |
| User Accounts | control nusrmgr.cpl |
| Windows Firewall | control firewall.cpl |

**NOTE**

If you find your Control Panel folder is bursting at the seams, you can trim it down to size by removing those icons you never use. There are a number of ways you can do this in Windows XP, but the easiest is probably via group policies. I discuss group policies in detail later in this chapter, and I include an example technique that shows you how to use policies to configure access to Control Panel. See "Example: Controlling Access to Control Panel," later in this chapter.

## Easier Access to Control Panel

Control Panel is certainly a useful and important piece of the Windows XP package. It's even more useful if you can get to it easily. I'll close this section by looking at a few methods for gaining quick access to individual icons and the entire folder.

### Alternative Methods for Opening Control Panel Icons

Access to many Control Panel icons is scattered throughout the Windows XP interface, meaning that there's more than one way to launch an icon. Many of these alternative methods are faster and more direct than using the Control Panel folder. Here's a summary:

| | |
|---|---|
| Date and Time | Double-click the clock in the taskbar's system tray. |
| Display | Right-click the desktop and then click Properties. |
| Folder Options | In Windows Explorer, select Tools, Folder Options. |
| Fonts | In Windows Explorer, open the `%SystemRoot%\Fonts` folder. |
| Internet Options | In Internet Explorer, select Tools, Internet Options. Alternatively, click Start, right-click Internet, and then click Internet Properties. |
| Network Connections | In Windows Explorer, open My Network Places and click View Network Connections in the Network Tasks list. |
| Power Options | On a notebook computer, right-click the Power Meter icon in the taskbar's notification area and then click Open Power Meter. |
| Printers and Faxes | Select Start, Printers and Faxes. |
| Scheduled Tasks | Select Start, All Programs, Accessories, System Tools, Scheduled Tasks. Alternatively, in Windows Explorer open the `%SystemRoot%\Tasks` folder. |
| System | Right-click My Computer icon and then click Properties. |
| Taskbar and Start Menu | Right-click an empty section of the taskbar or Start button and then click Properties. |

### Putting Control Panel on the Taskbar

For one-click access to the icons, create a new Control Panel toolbar on the taskbar by following these steps:

1. Right-click an empty section of the taskbar and then click Toolbars, New Toolbar. The New Toolbar dialog box appears.

2. Select My Computer, Control Panel.

3. Click OK.

From here, you can customize the Control Panel toolbar to fit all the icons on your screen (for example, by turning off the icon titles). See Chapter 10, "Customizing the Windows XP Interface," to learn how to tweak taskbar toolbars.

### Putting Control Panel on the Start Menu

You can turn the Start menu's Control Panel command into a menu that displays the Control Panel icons by following these steps:

1. Launch Control Panel's Taskbar and Start menu icon.

2. Display the Start Menu tab, ensure that the Start Menu option is activated, and then click Customize. The Customize Start Menu dialog box appears.

3. Display the Advanced tab.

4. In the Start Menu Items list, find the Control Panel item and activate the Display as a Menu option.

5. You can also add the Network Connections icon directly to the Start menu. Find the Network Connections item and activate either the Display as Connect to Menu option or the Link to Network Connections Folder option.

6. To add the Administrative Tools icon directly to the Start menu, find the System Administrative Tools item and activate the Display on the All Programs Menu and the Start Menu option.

7. Click OK.

# Implementing Group Policies with Windows XP

Group policies—which are available only with Windows XP Professional—are settings that control how Windows XP works. You can use them to customize the Windows XP interface, restrict access to certain areas, specify security settings, and much more.

Group policies are mostly used by system administrators who want to make sure that novice users don't have access to dangerous tools (such as the Registry Editor), or who want to ensure a consistent computing experience across multiple machines. Group policies are also ideally suited to situations in which multiple users share a single computer. However, group policies are also useful on single-user standalone machines, as you'll see throughout this book.

## Working with Group Policies

You implement group policies using the Group Policy editor, a Microsoft Management Console snap-in. To start the Group Policy editor, select Start, Run and then use either of the following methods:

- To implement group policies for the local computer, type **gpedit.msc** and click OK.

- To implement group policies for a remote computer, type **gpedit.msc /gpcomputer:"*name*"**, where ***name*** is the name of the remote machine, and click OK.

---

**NOTE**

You must be logged on to Windows XP Professional with administrative-level privileges to use the Group Policy editor.

---

The Group Policy window that appears is divided into two sections:

| | |
|---|---|
| Left pane | This pane contains a treelike hierarchy of policy categories, which is divided into two main categories: Computer Configuration and User Configuration. The Computer Configuration policies apply to all users and are implemented before the logon. The User Configuration policies apply only to the current user and, therefore, are not applied until that user logs on. |
| Right pane | This pane contains the policies for whichever category is selected in the left pane. |

The idea, then, is to open the tree's branches to find the category you want. When you click the category, its policies appear in the right pane. For example, Figure 7.2 shows the Group Policy window with the Computer Configuration, Administrative Templates, System, Logon category highlighted.

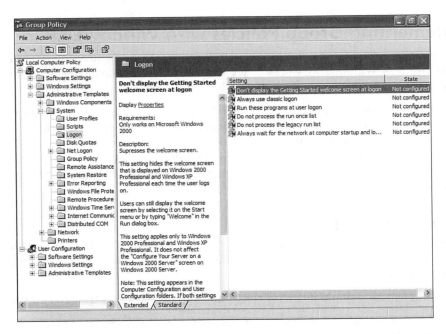

**FIGURE 7.2**   When you select a category in the left pane, the category's policies appear in the right pane.

> **TIP**
>
> Windows XP Professional comes with another tool called the Local Security Policy editor, which displays only the policies found in the Group Policy editor's Computer Configuration, Windows Settings, Security Settings branch. To launch the Local Security Policy editor, select Start, Run, enter **secpol.msc**, and click OK.

In the right pane, the Setting column tells you the name of the policy, and the State column tells you the current state of the policy. Click a policy to see its description on the left side of the pane. To configure a policy, double-click it. The type of window you see depends on the policy:

- For simple policies, you see a window similar to the one shown in Figure 7.3. These kinds of policies take one of three states: Not Configured (the policy is not in effect), Enabled (the policy is in effect and its setting is enabled), and Disabled (the policy is in effect but its setting is disabled).

**FIGURE 7.3**    Simple policies are Not Configured, Enabled, or Disabled.

- Other kinds of policies also require extra information when the policy is enabled. For example, Figure 7.4 shows the window for the Run These Programs at User Logon policy. When Enabled is activated, the Show button appears; you use it to specify one or more programs that run when the computer starts.

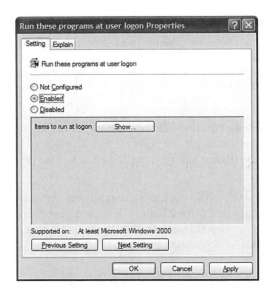

**FIGURE 7.4**    More complex policies also require extra information such as, in this case, a list of programs to run at logon.

## Example: Controlling Access to Control Panel

You can use group policies to hide and display Control Panel icons and to configure other Control Panel access settings. To see how this works, follow these steps:

1.  In the Group Policy editor, select User Configuration, Administrative Templates, Control Panel.

2.  Configure one or more of the following policies:

| | |
|---|---|
| Prohibit Access to the Control Panel | If you enable this policy, users can't access Control Panel using the Start menu, Windows Explorer, or the `control.exe` executable. |
| Hide Specified Control Panel Applets | If you enable this policy, you can hide specific Control Panel icons. To do this, click Show, click Add, enter the name of the icon you want to hide (such as Game Controllers) or the name of the CPL file (such as `Joy.cpl`), and then click OK. |
| Show Only Specified Control Panel Applets | If you enable this policy, you hide all Control Panel icons except the ones that you specify. To do this, click Show, click Add, enter the name of the icon you want to show (such as Game Controllers) or the name of the CPL file (such as `Joy.cpl`), and then click OK. |

Force Classic Control Panel Style

If you enable this policy, Control Panel is always displayed in the Classic View and the user can't change to the Category View. If you disable this policy, Control Panel is always displayed in the Category View and the user can't change to the Classic View.

3. When you've finished with a policy, click OK or Apply to put the policy into effect.

> **TIP**
>
> Another way to hide and display Control Panel icons is to use Tweak UI, which I describe in the next section. Tweak UI's Control Panel tab offers check boxes for each CPL file. Activate a check box to display the icon; deactivate a check box to hide the icon.

Note, too, that group policies also enable you to customize the behavior of some Control Panel icons. When you open the Control Panel branch, you'll see four sub-branches that correspond to four Control Panel icons: Add or Remove Programs, Display, Printers and Faxes, and Regional and Language Options. In each case, you use the policies in a particular sub-branch to hide dialog box tabs (or **pages** as the Group Policy editor calls them), specify default settings, and more.

## Tweaking Your System with Tweak UI

Some of the Windows XP developers weren't satisfied with having worked on just the Windows XP code. In their off-hours (I presume), they cobbled together a number of small programs designed to make your Windows life a bit easier and a bit more fun. The result was the Microsoft PowerToys for Windows XP. (Don't be fooled by the "Microsoft" part of the name. These programs are *not* supported by Microsoft, so if you have any problems with them, you're on your own.) There are links to download the eleven PowerToys here: www.microsoft.com/windowsxp/downloads/ powertoys/xppowertoys.mspx.

In all cases, double-click the downloaded file to install the PowerToy. In particular, be sure to download and install the Tweak UI PowerToy, which I discuss in this section. Tweak UI acts as a front-end for a large number of user interface customization options. Most of these options are controls for adding and working with Registry settings. As with the Registry Editor and the System Policy editor, I'll be using various Tweak UI settings throughout the rest of this book.

To launch Tweak UI, select Start, All Programs, PowerToys for Windows XP, Tweak UI. Windows XP displays the Tweak UI window. Use the tree on the left to select the customization category you want to work with, and then use the settings that appear on the right to tweak the system.

For example, if you select the Control Panel branch, Tweak UI displays a number of check boxes that correspond to Control Panel options, as shown in Figure 7.5. Deactivate the check box for any icon you do not want to display in Control Panel.

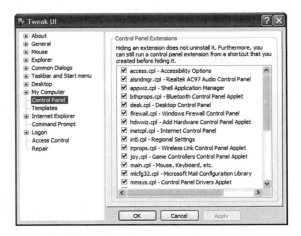

**FIGURE 7.5**   Tweak UI offers a simple interface for customizing a wealth of Windows XP options, including Control Panel's icons.

# From Here

You'll find Control Panel and Tweak UI techniques sprinkled throughout the book. Here are some other sections in the book that contain material related to group policies:

- In Chapter 1, see "Setting Logon Policies."

- In Chapter 5, see "Launching Applications and Scripts at Startup."

- In Chapter 6, see "Setting Account Policies" and "Taking Advantage of Windows XP's Password Policies."

- In Chapter 10, see "Modifying the Start Menu and Taskbar with Group Policies."

- In Chapter 14, see "Working with Device Security Policies."

- In Chapter 22, see "Connecting to Remote Group Policies."

- In Chapter 24, see "Some Group Policy Problems."

# CHAPTER 8

# Getting to Know the Windows XP Registry

As you learn throughout this book, a big part of unleashing Windows XP involves customizing the interface and the accessories either to suit your personal style or to extract every last ounce of performance from your system. For the most part, these customization options are handled via the following mechanisms:

- Control Panel
- Group policies
- Property sheets for individual objects
- Program menu commands and dialog boxes
- Command-line switches

But there is another, even more powerful mechanism you can use to customize Windows XP: the Registry. No, it doesn't have a pretty interface like most of the other customization options, and many aspects of the Registry give new meaning to the word arcane, but it gives you unparalleled access to facets of Windows XP that would be otherwise out of reach. This chapter introduces you to the Registry and its structure, and it shows you how to make changes to the Registry by wielding the Registry Editor.

## A Synopsis of the Registry

When you change the desktop wallpaper using Control Panel's Display icon, the next time you start your computer, how does Windows XP know which wallpaper you selected? If you change your video display driver, how does Windows XP know to use that driver at startup and not the original driver loaded during Setup? In other words, how does Windows XP remember the various settings and options either that you've selected yourself or that are appropriate for your system?

The secret to Windows XP's prodigious memory is the Registry. The Registry is a central repository Windows XP uses to store anything and everything that applies to the configuration of your system. This includes all the following:

- Information about all the hardware installed on your computer

- The resources used by those devices

- A list of the device drivers that Windows XP loads at startup

- Settings used internally by Windows XP

- File type data that associates a particular type of file with a specific application

- Wallpaper, color schemes, and other interface customization settings

- Other customization settings for things such as the Start menu and the taskbar

- Settings for accessories such as Windows Explorer and Internet Explorer

- Internet and network connections and passwords

- Settings and customization options for many applications

It's all stored in one central location, and, thanks to a handy tool called the Registry Editor, it's yours to play with (carefully!) as you see fit.

## A Brief History of Configuration Files

It wasn't always this way. In the early days of DOS and Windows (version 1!), system data was stored in two humble files: CONFIG.SYS and AUTOEXEC.BAT, those famous (or infamous) Bobbsey twins of configuration files.

When Windows 2.0 was born (to little or no acclaim), so too were born another couple of configuration files: WIN.INI and SYSTEM.INI. These so-called **initialization files** were also simple text files. It was WIN.INI's job to store configuration data about Windows and about Windows applications; for SYSTEM.INI, life consisted of storing data about hardware and system settings. Not to be outdone, applications started creating their own INI files to store user settings and program options. Before long, the Windows directory was festooned with dozens of these INI garlands.

The air became positively thick with INI files when Windows 3.0 rocked the PC world. Not only did Windows use WIN.INI and SYSTEM.INI to store configuration tidbits, but it also created new INIs for Program Manager (PROGMAN.INI), File Manager (WINFILE.INI), Control Panel (CONTROL.INI), and more.

It wasn't until Windows 3.1 hit the shelves that the Registry saw the light of day, albeit in a decidedly different guise from its Windows XP descendant. The Windows 3.1 Registry was a database used to store registration information related to OLE (object linking and embedding) applications.

Finally, Windows for Workgroups muddied the configuration file waters even further by adding a few new network-related configuration files, including `PROTOCOL.INI`.

### The Registry Puts an End to INI Chaos

This INI inundation led to all kinds of woes for users and system administrators alike. Because they were just text files in the main Windows directory, INIs were accidents waiting for a place to happen. Like sitting ducks, they were ripe for being picked off by an accidental press of the Delete key from a novice's fumbling fingers. There were so many of the darn things that few people could keep straight which INI file contained which settings. There was no mechanism to help you find the setting you needed in a large INI file. And the linear, headings-and-settings structure made it difficult to maintain complex configurations.

To solve all these problems, the Windows 95 designers decided to give the old Windows 3.1 Registry a promotion, so to speak. Specifically, they set it up as the central database for all system and application settings. The Registry essentially maintains this structure in Windows XP.

Here are some of the advantages you get with this revised Registry:

- The Registry files (discussed in the next section) have their Hidden, System, and Read-Only attributes set, so it's much tougher to delete them accidentally. Even if a user somehow managed to blow away these files, Windows XP maintains backup copies for easy recovery.

- Not only does the Registry serve as a warehouse for hardware and operating system settings, but applications are free to use the Registry to store their own configuration morsels, instead of using separate INI files.

- If you need to examine or modify a Registry entry, the Registry Editor utility gives you a hierarchical, treelike view of the entire Registry database (more on this topic later).

- The Registry comes with tools that enable you to search for specific settings and to query the Registry data remotely.

That's not to say that the Registry is a perfect solution. Many of its settings are totally obscure, it uses a structure that only a true geek could love, and finding the setting you need is often an exercise in guesswork. Still, most of these problems can be overcome with a bit of practice and familiarity, which is what this chapter is all about.

## Understanding the Registry Files

As you'll see a bit later, the Registry's files are binary files, so you can't edit them directly. Instead, you use a program called the Registry Editor, which enables you to view, modify, add, and delete any Registry setting. It also has a search feature to help you find settings, and export and import features that enable you to save settings to and from a text file.

To launch the Registry Editor, select Start, Run, type **regedit**, and click OK. Figure 8.1 shows the Registry Editor window that appears. (Your Registry Editor window might look different if someone else has used the program previously. Close all the open branches in the left pane to get the view shown in Figure 8.1.)

**FIGURE 8.1**    Running the REGEDIT command launches the Registry Editor, a front-end that enables you to work with the Registry's data.

The Registry Editor is reminiscent of Windows Explorer, and it works in basically the same way. The left side of the Registry Editor window is similar to Explorer's Folders pane, except that rather than folders, you see keys. For lack of a better phrase, I'll call the left pane the **Keys pane**.

## Navigating the Keys Pane

The Keys pane, like Explorer's Folders pane, is organized in a treelike hierarchy. The five keys that are visible when you first open the Registry Editor are special keys called **handles** (which is why their names all begin with HKEY). These keys are referred to collectively as the Registry's **root keys**. I'll tell you what to expect from each of these keys later (see the section called "Getting to Know the Registry's Root Keys," later in this chapter).

These keys all contain subkeys, which you can display by clicking the plus sign (+) to the left of each key, or by highlighting a key and pressing the plus-sign key on your keyboard's numeric keypad. When you open a key, the plus sign changes to a minus sign (-). To close a key, click the minus sign or highlight the key and press the minus-sign key on the numeric keypad. Again, this is just like navigating folders in Explorer.

You often have to drill down several levels to get to the key you want. For example, Figure 8.2 shows the Registry Editor after I've opened the HKEY_CURRENT_USER key, and then the Control Panel subkey, and then clicked the Mouse subkey. Notice how the status bar tells you the exact path to the current key, and that this path is structured just like a folder path.

---

**NOTE**

To see all the keys properly, you likely will have to increase the size of the Keys pane. To do this, use your mouse to click and drag the split bar to the right. Alternatively, select View, Split, use the Right Arrow key to adjust the split bar position, and then press Enter.

---

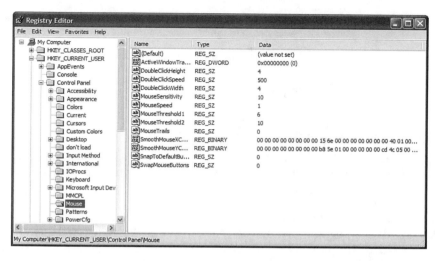

**FIGURE 8.2**    Open the Registry's keys and subkeys to find the settings you want to work with.

## Understanding Registry Settings

If the left side of the Registry Editor window is analogous to Explorer's Folders pane, the right side is analogous to Explorer's Contents pane. In this case, the right side of the Registry Editor window displays the settings contained in each key (so I'll call it the **Settings pane**). The Settings pane is divided into three columns:

| | |
|---|---|
| Name | This column tells you the name of each setting in the currently selected key (analogous to a filename in Explorer). |
| Type | This column tells you the data type of the setting. There are five possible data types: |

- REG_SZ—This is a string value.

- REG_MULTI_SZ—This is a series of strings.

- REG_EXPAND_SZ—This is a string value that contains an environment variable name that gets "expanded" into the value of that variable. For example, the %SystemRoot% environment variable holds the folder in which Windows XP was installed. So, if you see a Registry setting with the value %SystemRoot%\System32\, and Windows XP is installed in C:\Windows, the setting's expanded value is C:\Windows\System32\.

- REG_DWORD—This is a double word value: a 32-bit hexadecimal value arranged as eight digits. For example, 11 hex is 17 decimal, so this number would be represented in DWORD form as 0x00000011 (17). (Why "double word"? A 32-bit value represents four bytes of data, and because a word in programming circles is defined as two bytes, a four-byte value is a **double word**.)

- REG_BINARY—This value is a series of hexadecimal digits.

Data         This column displays the value of each setting.

## Getting to Know the Registry's Root Keys

The root keys are your Registry starting points, so you need to become familiar with what kinds of data each key holds. The next few sections summarize the contents of each key.

### HKEY_CLASSES_ROOT

HKEY_CLASSES_ROOT—usually abbreviated as HKCR—contains data related to file extensions and their associated programs, the objects that exist in the Windows XP system, as well as applications and their Automation information. There are also keys related to shortcuts and other interface features.

The top part of this key contains subkeys for various file extensions. You see .bmp for BMP (Paint) files, .doc for DOC (WordPad) files, and so on. In each of these subkeys, the Default setting tells you the name of the registered file type associated with the extension. (I discussed file types in more detail in Chapter 3, "Mastering File Types.") For example, the .txt extension is associated with the txtfile file type.

These registered file types appear as subkeys later in the HKEY_CLASSES_ROOT branch, and the Registry keeps track of various settings for each registered file type. In particular, the shell subkey tells you the actions associated with this file type. For example, in the shell\open\command subkey, the Default setting shows the path for the executable file that opens. Figure 8.3 shows this subkey for the txtfile file type.

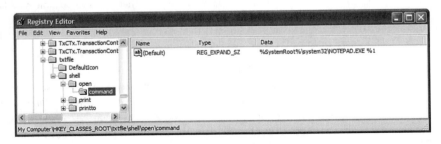

**FIGURE 8.3**   The registered file type subkeys specify various settings associated with each file type, including its defined actions.

HKEY_CLASSES_ROOT is actually a copy (or an **alias**, as these copied keys are called) of the following HKEY_LOCAL_MACHINE key:

HKEY_LOCAL_MACHINE\Software\Classes

The Registry creates an alias for HKEY_CLASSES_ROOT to make these keys easier for applications to access and to improve compatibility with legacy programs.

HKEY_CURRENT_USER

HKEY_CURRENT_USER—usually abbreviated as HKCU—contains data that applies to the user that's currently logged on. It contains user-specific settings for Control Panel options, network connections, applications, and more. Note that if a user has group policies set on his account, his settings are stored in the HKEY_USERS\sid subkey (where sid is the user's security ID). When that user logs on, these settings are copied to HKEY_CURRENT_USER. For all other users, HKEY_CURRENT_USER is built from the user's profile file, Ntuser.dat.

> **TIP**
>
> How do you find out each user's SID? First, open the following Registry key:
>
> HKLM\SOFTWARE\Microsoft\Windows NT\CurrentVersion\ProfileList\
>
> Here you'll find a list of SIDs. The ones that begin S-1-5-21 are the user SIDs. Highlight one of these SIDs and then examine the ProfileImagePath setting, which will be of the form %SystemDrive%\Documents and Settings\user, where user is the username associated with the SID.

Here's a summary of the most important HKEY_CURRENT_USER subkeys:

| | |
|---|---|
| AppEvents | Contains sound files that play when particular system events occur (such as maximizing of a window) |
| Control Panel | Contains settings related to certain Control Panel icons |
| Identities | Contains settings related to Outlook Express, including mail and news options and message rules |
| Keyboard Layout | Contains the keyboard layout as selected via Control Panel's Keyboard icon |
| Network | Contains settings related to mapped network drives |
| Software | Contains user-specific settings related to installed applications and Windows |

HKEY_LOCAL_MACHINE

HKEY_LOCAL_MACHINE (HKLM) contains non–user-specific configuration data for your system's hardware and applications. There are three subkeys that you'll use most often:

| | |
|---|---|
| Hardware | Contains subkeys related to serial ports and modems, as well as the floating-point processor. |
| Software | Contains computer-specific settings related to installed applications. The Classes subkey is aliased by HKEY_CLASSES_ROOT. The Microsoft subkey contains settings related to Windows (as well as any other Microsoft products you have installed on your computer). |
| System | Contains subkeys and settings related to Windows startup. |

∞

HKEY_USERS

HKEY_USERS (HKU) contains settings that are similar to those in HKEY_CURRENT_USER. HKEY_USERS is used to store the settings for users with group policies defined, as well as the default settings (in the .DEFAULT subkey) which get mapped to a new user's profile.

HKEY_CURRENT_CONFIG

HKEY_CURRENT_CONFIG (HKCC) contains settings for the current hardware profile. If your machine uses only one hardware profile, HKEY_CURRENT_CONFIG is an alias for HKEY_LOCAL_MACHINE\SYSTEM\ControlSet001. If your machine uses multiple hardware profiles, HKEY_CURRENT_CONFIG is an alias for HKEY_LOCAL_MACHINE\SYSTEM\ControlSet*nnn*, where *nnn* is the numeric identifier of the current hardware profile. This identifier is given by the Current setting in the following key:

HKLM\SSYSTEM\CurrentControlSet\Control\IDConfigDB

## Understanding Hives and Registry Files

The Registry database actually consists of a number of files that contain a subset of the Registry called a **hive**. A hive consists of one or more Registry keys, subkeys, and settings. Each hive is supported by several files that use the extensions listed in Table 8.1.

**TABLE 8.1**    Extensions Used by Hive Supporting Files

| Extension | File Contains |
| --- | --- |
| None | A complete copy of the hive data |
| .alt | A backup copy of the hive data |
| .log | A log of the changes made to the hive data |
| .sav | A copy of the hive data as of the end of the text mode portion of the Windows XP setup |

Table 8.2 shows the supporting files for each hive (note that all of these files might not appear on your system).

**TABLE 8.2**    Supporting Files Used by Each Hive

| Hive | Files |
| --- | --- |
| HKLM\SAM | %SystemRoot%\System32\config\SAM |
| | %SystemRoot%\System32\config\SAM.LOG |
| | %SystemRoot%\System32\config\SAM.SAV |
| HKLM\Security | %SystemRoot%\System32\config\SECURITY |
| | %SystemRoot%\System32\config\SECURITY.LOG |
| | %SystemRoot%\System32\config\SECURITY.SAV |
| HKLM\Software | %SystemRoot%\System32\config\SOFTWARE |
| | %SystemRoot%\System32\config\SOFTWARE.LOG |
| | %SystemRoot%\System32\config\SOFTWARE.SAV |
| HKLM\System | %SystemRoot%\System32\config\SYSTEM |
| | %SystemRoot%\System32\config\SYSTEM.ALT |

**TABLE 8.2**     Continued

| Hive | Files |
|------|-------|
|  | %SystemRoot%\System32\config\SYSTEM.LOG |
|  | %SystemRoot%\System32\config\SYSTEM.SAV |
| HKU\.DEFAULT | %SystemRoot%\System32\config\DEFAULT |
|  | %SystemRoot%\System32\config\DEFAULT.LOG |
|  | %SystemRoot%\System32\config\DEFAULT.SAV |

Also, each user has her own hive, which is mapped to HKEY_CURRENT_USER during logon. The supporting files for each user hive are stored in \Documents and Settings\\*user*, where *user* is the username. In each case, the Ntuser.dat file contains the hive data, and the Ntuser.log file tracks the hive changes. (If a user has group policies set on her account, the user data is stored in an HKEY_USERS subkey.)

> **NOTE**
> You can also work with a Registry on a remote computer over a network. See the "Connecting to a Remote Registry" section in Chapter 22, "Setting Up and Accessing a Small Network."

# Keeping the Registry Safe

The sheer wealth of data stored in one place makes the Registry convenient, but it also makes it very precious. If your Registry went missing somehow, or if it got corrupted, Windows XP simply would not work. With that scary thought in mind, let's take a moment to run through several protective measures. The techniques in this section should ensure that Windows XP never goes down for the count because you made a mistake while editing the Registry.

> **TIP**
> If you share your computer with other people, you might not want to give them access to the Registry Editor. You can prevent any user from using this tool by running the Group Policy editor (refer to Chapter 7, "Using Control Panel, Group Policies, and Tweak UI"). Open User Configuration, Administrative Templates, System, and then enable the Prevent Access to Registry Editing Tools policy. Note that *you* won't be able to use the Registry Editor, either. However, you can overcome that by temporarily disabling this policy prior to running the Registry Editor.

## Backing Up the Registry

Windows XP maintains what is known as the **system state**: the crucial system files that Windows XP requires to operate properly. Included in the system state are the files used during system startup, the Windows XP–protected system files, and, naturally, the Registry files. The Backup utility has a feature that enables you to easily back up the current system state, so it's probably the most straightforward way to create a backup copy of the Registry should anything go wrong.

> **NOTE**
>
> You must be logged on as a member of the Administrators group or the Backup Operators groups to back up the system state.

Here are the steps to follow to back up the system state:

1. Select Start, All Programs, Accessories, System Tools, Backup. (Note that if you're using Windows XP Home, you might need to install Backup from the Windows XP CD. I explain how this is done in Chapter 12, "Maintaining Your Windows XP System.")

2. If the Backup or Restore Wizard appears, click the Advanced Mode link.

3. Display the Backup tab.

4. In the folder tree, open the Desktop branch and then the My Computer branch, if they're not open already.

5. Activate the System State check box.

6. Choose your other backup options, click Start Backup, and then follow the usual backup procedure.

> **CAUTION**
>
> Depending on the configuration of your computer, the system state can be quite large—hundreds of megabytes. Therefore, make sure that the destination you choose for the backup has enough free space to handle such a large file.

## Saving the Current Registry State with System Restore

Another easy way to save the current Registry configuration is to use Windows XP's System Restore utility. This program takes a snapshot of your system's current state, including the Registry. If anything should go wrong with your system, the program then enables you to restore a previous configuration. It's a good idea to set a system restore point before doing any work on the Registry. I show you how to work with System Restore in Chapter 12.

> **TIP**
>
> Another way to protect the Registry is to ensure that its keys have the appropriate permissions. By default, Windows XP gives members of the Administrators group full control over the Registry, and it gives individual users control over the HKCU key when that user is logged on. (Refer to Chapter 6, "Getting the Most Out of User Accounts," for more information on users, groups, and permissions.) To adjust the permissions, right-click the key in the Registry Editor, and then click Permissions. Make sure that only administrators have the Full Control check box activated.

## Protecting Keys by Exporting Them to Disk

If you're just making a small change to the Registry, backing up all of its files might seem like overkill. Another approach is to back up only the part of the Registry that you're working on. For example, if you're about to make changes within the HKEY_CURRENT_USER key, you could back up just that key, or even a subkey within HKCU. You do that by exporting the key's data to a registration file, which is a text file that uses the .reg extension. That way, if the change causes a problem, you can import the .reg file back into the Registry to restore things to the way they were.

### Exporting a Key to a .reg File

Here are the steps to follow to export a key to a registration file:

1.  Open the Registry Editor and select the key you want to export.

2.  Select File, Export to display the Export Registry File dialog box.

3.  Select a location for the file.

4.  Use the File Name text box to type a name for the file.

5.  If you want to export only the currently highlighted key, make sure that the Selected Branch option is activated. If you'd prefer to export the entire Registry, activate the All option.

6.  If you'll be importing this file into a system running Windows 9x, Windows Me, or Windows NT, use the Save As Type list to choose the Win9x/NT 4 Registration Files (*.reg) item.

7.  Click Save.

---

### Finding Registry Changes

One common Registry scenario is to make a change to Windows XP using a tool such as the Group Policy editor or Tweak UI, and then try and find which Registry setting (if any) was affected by the change. However, because of the sheer size of the Registry, this is usually a needle-in-a-haystack exercise that ends in frustration. One way around this is to export some or all the Registry before making the change and then export the same key or keys after making the change. You can then use the FC (file compare) utility at the command prompt to find out where the two files differ. Here's the FC syntax to use for this:

```
FC /U pre_edit.reg post-edit.reg > reg_changes.txt
```

Here, change pre_edit.reg to the name of the registration file you exported before editing the Registry; change post_edit.reg to the name of the registration file you exported after editing the Registry; and change reg_changes.txt to the name of a text file to which the FC output is redirected. Note that the /U switch is required since registration files use the Unicode character set.

---

8

### Importing a .reg File

If you need to restore the key that you backed up to a registration file, follow these steps:

1. Open the Registry Editor.

2. Select File, Import to display the Import Registry File dialog box.

3. Find and select the file you want to import.

4. Click Open.

5. When Windows XP tells you the information has been entered into the Registry, click OK.

> **NOTE**
>
> You also can import a .reg file by locating it in Windows Explorer and then double-clicking the file.

> **CAUTION**
>
> Many applications ship with their own .reg files for updating the Registry. Unless you're sure that you want to import these files, avoid double-clicking them. They might end up overwriting existing settings and causing problems with your system.

# Working with Registry Entries

Now that you've had a look around, you're ready to start working with the Registry's keys and settings. In this section, I'll give you the general procedures for basic tasks, such as modifying, adding, renaming, deleting, and searching for entries, and more. These techniques will serve you well throughout the rest of the book when I take you through some specific Registry modifications.

## Changing the Value of a Registry Entry

Changing the value of a Registry entry is a matter of finding the appropriate key, displaying the setting you want to change, and editing the setting's value. Unfortunately, finding the key you need isn't always a simple matter. Knowing the root keys and their main subkeys, as described earlier, will certainly help, and the Registry Editor also has a Find feature that's invaluable (I'll show you how to use it later).

To illustrate how this process works, let's work through an example: changing your registered owner name and company name. During the Windows XP installation process, Setup might have asked you to enter your name and, optionally, your company name. (If you upgraded to Windows XP, this data was brought over from your previous version of Windows.) These registered names appear in several places as you work with Windows XP:

- If you open Control Panel's System icon, your registered names appear in the General tab of the System Properties dialog box.

- If you select Help, About in most Windows XP programs, your registered names appear in the About dialog box.

- If you install a 32-bit application, the installation program uses your registered names for its own records (although you usually get a chance to make changes).

With these names appearing in so many places, it's good to know that you can change either or both names (for example, if you give the computer to another person). The secret lies in the following key:

`HKLM\SOFTWARE\Microsoft\WindowsNT\CurrentVersion`

To get to this key, you open the branches in the Registry Editor's tree pane: `HKEY_LOCAL_MACHINE`, and then `SOFTWARE`, and then `Microsoft`, and then `WindowsNT`. Finally, click the `CurrentVersion` subkey to select it. Here you see a number of settings, but two are of interest to us (see Figure 8.4):

| | |
|---|---|
| `RegisteredOrganization` | This setting contains your registered company name. |
| `RegisteredOwner` | This setting contains your registered name. |

**TIP**

If you have keys that you visit often, you can save them as favorites to avoid trudging through endless branches in the keys pane. To do this, navigate to the key and then select Favorites, Add to Favorites. In the Add to Favorites dialog box, edit the Favorite Name text box, if desired, and then click OK. To navigate to a favorite key, pull down the Favorites menu and select the key name from the list that appears at the bottom of the menu.

Now you open the setting for editing by using any of the following techniques:

- Select the setting name and either select Edit, Modify or press Enter.

- Double-click the setting name.

- Right-click the setting name and click Modify from the context menu.

The dialog box that appears depends on the value type you're dealing with, as discussed in the next few sections. Note that edited settings are written to the Registry right away, but the changes might not go into effect immediately. In many cases, you need to exit the Registry Editor and then either log off or restart Windows XP.

8

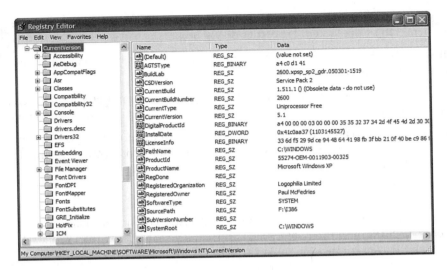

**FIGURE 8.4**    Navigate to `HKLM\SOFTWARE\Microsoft\WindowsNT\CurrentVersion` to see your registered names.

### Editing a String Value

If the setting is a `REG_SZ` value (as it is in our example), a `REG_MULTI_SZ` value, or a `REG_EXPAND_SZ` value, you see the Edit String dialog box, shown in Figure 8.5. Use the Value Data text box to enter a new string or modify the existing string, and then click OK. (For a `REG_MULTI_SZ` multistring value, Value Data is a multiline text box. Type each string value on its own line. That is, after each string, press Enter to start a new line.)

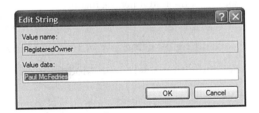

**FIGURE 8.5**    You see the Edit String dialog box if you're modifying a string value.

### Editing a DWORD Value

If the setting is a `REG_DWORD` value, you see the Edit DWORD Value dialog box shown in Figure 8.6. In the Base group, select either Hexadecimal or Decimal, and then use the Value Data text box to enter the new value of the setting. (If you chose the Hexadecimal option, enter a hexadecimal value; if you chose Decimal, enter a decimal value.)

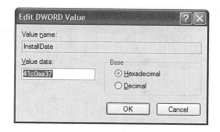

**FIGURE 8.6** You see the Edit DWORD Value dialog box if you're modifying a string value.

### Editing a Binary Value

If the setting is a REG_BINARY value, you see an Edit Binary Value dialog box like the one shown in Figure 8.7.

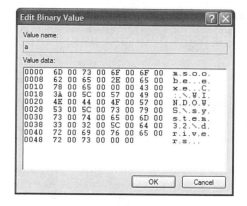

**FIGURE 8.7** You see the Edit Binary Value dialog box if you're modifying a binary value.

For binary values, the Value Data box is divided into three vertical sections:

| | |
|---|---|
| Starting byte number | The four-digit values on the left of the Value Data box tell you the sequence number of the first byte in each row of hexadecimal numbers. This sequence always begins at 0, so the sequence number of the first byte in the first row is 0000. There are eight bytes in each row, so the sequence number of the first byte in the second row is 0008, and so on. You can't edit these values. |
| Hexadecimal numbers (bytes) | The eight columns of two-digit numbers in the middle section display the setting's value, expressed in hexadecimal numbers, where each two-digit number represents a single byte of information. You can edit these values. |

ANSI equivalents

The third section on the right side of the Value Data box shows the ANSI equivalents of the hexadecimal numbers in the middle section. For example, the first byte of the first row is the hexadecimal value 6D, which represents the lowercase letter m. You can also edit the values in this column.

### Editing a `.reg` File

If you exported a key to a registration file, you can edit that file and then import it back into the Registry. To make changes to a registration file, find the file in Windows Explorer, right-click the file, and then click Edit. Windows XP opens the file in Notepad.

> **TIP**
>
> If you need to make global changes to the Registry, export the entire Registry and then load the resulting registration file into WordPad or some other word processor or text editor. Use the application's Replace feature (carefully!) to make changes throughout the file. If you use a word processor for this, be sure to save the file as a text file when you're done. You can then import the changed file back into the Registry.

### Creating a `.reg` File

You can create registration files from scratch and then import them into the Registry. This is a handy technique if you have some customizations that you want to apply to multiple systems. To demonstrate the basic structure of a registration file and its entries, Figure 8.8 shows two windows. The top window is the Registry Editor with a key named `Test` highlighted. The settings pane contains six sample settings: the `(Default)` value and one each of the five types of settings (binary, `DWORD`, expandable string, multistring, and string). The bottom window shows the `Test` key in Notepad as an exported registration file (`test.reg`).

> **TIP**
>
> If you want to add a comment to a `.reg` file, start a new line and begin the line with a semicolon (;).

Windows XP registration files always start with the following header:

```
Windows Registry Editor Version 5.00
```

> **TIP**
>
> If you're building a registration file for a Windows 9x, Me, or NT 4 system, change the header to the following:
>
> ```
> REGEDIT4
> ```

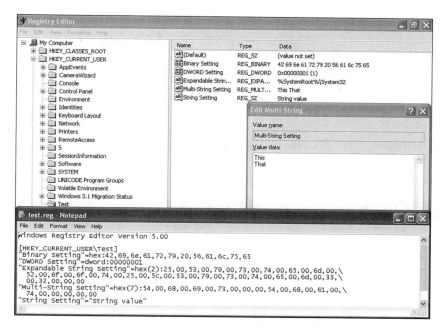

**FIGURE 8.8**    The settings in the Test key shown in the Registry Editor correspond to the data shown in the `test.reg` file shown in Notepad.

Next is an empty line followed by the full path of the Registry key that will hold the settings you're adding, surrounded by square brackets:

`[HKEY_CURRENT_USER\Test]`

Below the key are the setting names and values, which use the following general form:

`"SettingName"=identifier:SettingValue`

| | |
|---|---|
| *SettingName* | The name of the setting. Note that you use the @ symbol to represent the key's Default value. |
| *identifier* | A code that identifies the type of data. REG_SZ values don't use an identifier, but the other four types do: |
| dword | Use this identifier for a DWORD value. |
| hex | Use this identifier for a binary value. |
| hex(2) | Use this identifier for an expandable string value. |
| hex(7) | Use this identifier for a multistring value. |
| *SettingValue* | This is the value of the setting, which you enter as follows: |
| String | Surround the value with quotation marks. |
| DWORD | Enter an eight-digit DWORD value. |

| | |
|---|---|
| Binary | Enter the binary value as a series of two-digit hexadecimal numbers, separating each number with a comma. |
| Expandable string | Convert each character to its hexadecimal equivalent and then enter the value as a series of two-digit hexadecimal numbers, separating each number with a comma, and separating each character with 00. |
| Multistring | Convert each character to its hexadecimal equivalent and then enter the value as a series of two-digit hexadecimal numbers, separating each number with a comma, and separating each character with 00, and separating each string with space (00 hex). |

**TIP**

To delete a setting using a .REG file, set its value to a hyphen (-), as in this example:

```
Windows Registry Editor Version 5.00

[HKEY_CURRENT_USER\Test]
"BinarySetting"=-
```

To delete a key, add a hyphen to the start of the key name, as in this example:

```
Windows Registry Editor Version 5.00

[-HKEY_CURRENT_USER\Test]
```

## Renaming a Key or Setting

You won't often need to rename existing keys or settings. Just in case, though, here are the steps to follow:

1. In the Registry Editor, find the key or setting you want to work with, and then highlight it.

2. Select Edit, Rename, or press F2.

3. Edit the name and then press Enter.

**CAUTION**

Rename only those keys or settings that you created yourself. If you rename any other key or setting, Windows XP might not work properly.

## Creating a New Key or Setting

Many Registry-based customizations don't involve editing an existing setting or key. Instead, you have to create a new setting or key. Here's how you do it:

1. In the Registry Editor, select the key in which you want to create the new subkey or setting.

2. Select Edit, New. (Alternatively, right-click an empty section of the Settings pane and then click New.) A submenu appears.

3. If you're creating a new key, select the Key command. Otherwise, select the command that corresponds to the type of setting you want: String Value, Binary Value, DWORD Value, Multi-String Value, or Expandable String Value.

4. Type a name for the new key or setting.

5. Press Enter.

### Deleting a Key or Setting

Here are the steps to follow to delete a key or setting:

1. In the Registry Editor, select the key or setting that you want to delete.

2. Select Edit, Delete, or press Delete. The Registry Editor asks whether you're sure.

3. Click Yes.

---

**CAUTION**

Again, to avoid problems, you should delete only those keys or settings that you created your-self. If you're not sure about deleting a setting, try renaming it instead. If a problem arises, you can also return the setting back to its original name.

---

# Finding Registry Entries

The Registry contains only five root keys, but these root keys contain hundreds of subkeys. The fact that some root keys are aliases for subkeys in a different branch only adds to the confusion. If you know exactly where you're going, the Registry Editor's tree-like hierarchy is a reasonable way to get there. If you're not sure where a particular subkey or setting resides, however, you could spend all day poking around in the Registry's labyrinthine nooks and crannies.

To help you get where you want to go, the Registry Editor has a Find feature that enables you to search for keys, settings, or values. Here's how it works:

1. In the Keys pane, select My Computer at the top of the pane (unless you're certain of which root key contains the value you want to find; in this case, you can high-light the appropriate root key instead).

2. Select Edit, Find or press Ctrl+F. The Registry Editor displays the Find dialog box, shown in Figure 8.9.

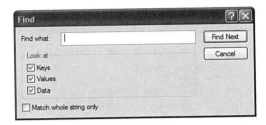

**FIGURE 8.9**    Use the Find dialog box to search for Registry keys, settings, or values.

3. Use the Find What text box to enter your search string. You can enter partial words or phrases to increase your chances of finding a match.

4. In the Look At group, activate the check boxes for the elements you want to search. For most searches, you want to leave all three check boxes activated.

5. If you want to find only those entries that exactly match your search text, activate the Match Whole String Only check box.

6. Click the Find Next button. The Registry Editor highlights the first match.

7. If this isn't the item you want, select Edit, Find Next (or press F3) until you find the setting or key you want.

When the Registry Editor finds a match, it displays the appropriate key or setting. Note that if the matched value is a setting name or data value, Find doesn't highlight the current key. This is a bit confusing, but just remember that the current key always appears at the bottom of the Keys pane.

## From Here

Here's a list of a some chapters and sections of the book that contain information related to what you learned about the Registry in this chapter:

- For the details on file types and how they relate to the HKEY_CLASSES_ROOT key, see Chapter 3, "Mastering File Types."

- Windows XP has three main programs that serve as front-ends for the Registry, and I discuss them in Chapter 7, "Using Control Panel, Group Policies, and Tweak UI."

- To learn how to read, add, and modify Registry entries programmatically, see the section "Working with Registry Entries" in Chapter 9.

- Many of the Registry values are generated by Windows XP's customization features. I discuss many of these features in Chapter 10, "Customizing the Windows XP Interface."

- For a broad look at Windows XP memory features, as well as how to use the System Monitor, see Chapter 11, "Tuning Windows XP's Performance."

- To learn how to use System Restore and Backup, see Chapter 12, "Maintaining Your Windows XP System."

- To better understand the Registry's hardware-related keys, head for Chapter 14, "Getting the Most Out of Device Manager."

- For information on connecting to a remote Registry on your network, see the section in Chapter 22 titled "Connecting to a Remote Registry."

8

# Programming the Windows Script Host

In Appendix C, "Automating Windows XP with Batch Files," you learn how to tame the command prompt by creating **batch files**—small, executable text files that run one or more commands. You'll see that with a little ingenuity and a dash of guile, it's possible to make batch files perform some interesting and useful tasks. Indeed, for many years, batch files were the only way to automate certain kinds of tasks. Unfortunately, the batch file world is relentlessly command-line–oriented. So, with the exception of being able to launch Windows programs, batch files remain ignorant of the larger Windows universe.

If you're looking to automate a wider variety of tasks in Windows, you need to supplement your batch file knowledge with scripts that can deal with the Registry, shortcuts, files, and network drives, and that can even interact with Windows programs via Automation. The secret to these powerful scripts is the **Windows Script Host** (**WSH**). This chapter introduces you to the Windows Script Host, shows you how to execute scripts, and runs through the various elements in the Windows Script Host object model.

## WSH: Your Host for Today's Script

As you might know, Internet Explorer is really just an empty container application that's designed to host different data formats, including ActiveX controls, various file formats (such as Microsoft Word documents and Microsoft Excel worksheets), and several ActiveX scripting engines. A **scripting engine** is a dynamic link library (DLL) that provides programmatic support for a particular scripting language. Internet Explorer supports two such scripting engines: VBScript (VBScript.dll) and JavaScript (JSscript.dll). This enables web programmers to write small programs—**scripts**—that interact with the user, control the browser, set cookies, open and close windows, and more. Although these scripting engines don't offer full-blown programmability (you can't compile scripts, for example), they do offer modern programming structures such as loops, conditionals, variables, objects, and more. In other words, they're a huge leap beyond what a mere batch file can do.

The Windows Script Host is also a container application, albeit a scaled-down application in that its only purpose in life is to host scripting engines. Right out of the box, the Windows Script Host supports both the VBScript and JavaScript engines. However, Microsoft designed the Windows Script Host to be a universal host that can support any ActiveX-based scripting engine. Therefore, there are also third-party vendors offering scripting engines for languages such as Perl, Tcl, and Rexx.

The key difference between Internet Explorer's script hosting and the Windows Script Host is the environment in which the scripts run. Internet Explorer scripts are web page–based, so they control and interact with either the web page or the web browser. The Windows Script Host runs scripts within the Windows XP shell or from the command prompt, so you use these scripts to control various aspects of Windows. Here's a sampling of the things you can do:

- Execute Windows programs

- Create and modify shortcuts

- Use Automation to connect and interact with Automation-enabled applications such as Microsoft Word, Outlook, and Internet Explorer

- Read, add, and delete Registry keys and items

- Access the VBScript and JavaScript object models, which give you access to the file system, runtime error messages, and more

- Use pop-up dialog boxes to display information to the user, and even determine which button the user clicked to dismiss the dialog box

- Read environment variables

- Deal with network resources, including mapping and unmapping network drives, accessing user data (such as the username and user domain), and connecting and disconnecting network printers

Clearly, we've gone *way* beyond batch files!

What about speed? After all, you wouldn't want to load something that's the size of Internet Explorer each time you need to run a simple script. That's not a problem because, as I've said, the Windows Script Host does nothing but host scripting engines, so it has much less memory overhead than Internet Explorer. That means that your scripts run quickly. For power users looking for a Windows-based batch language, the Windows Script Host is a welcome tool.

This chapter does not teach you how to program in either VBScript or JavaScript and, in fact, assumes that you're already proficient in one or both of these languages. If you're looking for a programming tutorial, my *Absolute Beginner's Guide to VBA* (Que, 2004) is a good place to start (VBScript is a subset of VBA—Visual Basic for Applications). For JavaScript, try my *Special Edition Using JavaScript* (Que, 2001).

# Scripts and Script Execution

Scripts are simple text files that you create using Notepad or some other text editor. You can use a word processor such as WordPad to create scripts, but you must make sure that you save these files using the program's Text Only document type. For VBScript, a good alternative to Notepad is the editor that comes with either Visual Basic or any program that supports VBA (such as the Office suite). Just remember that VBScript is a subset of VBA (which is, in turn, a subset of Visual Basic), so not all objects and features are supported.

In a web page, you use the <SCRIPT> tag to specify the scripting language you're using, as in this example:

```
<SCRIPT LANGUAGE="VBScript">
```

With the Windows Script Host, the scripting language is specified using the script file's extension:

- For VBScript, save your text files using the .vbs extension (which is registered as the following file type: VBScript Script File).

- For JavaScript, use the .js extension (which is registered as the following file type: JScript Script File).

As described in the next three sections, you have three ways to run your scripts: by launching the script files directly, by using WSscript.exe, or by using CScript.exe.

## Running Script Files Directly

The easiest way to run a script from within Windows is to launch the .vbs or .js file directly. That is, you either double-click the file in Windows Explorer, or type the file's path and name in the Run dialog box. Note, however, that this technique does not work at the command prompt. For that, you need to use the CScript program, which is described a bit later.

## Using WScript for Windows-Based Scripts

The .vbs and .js file types have an open method that's associated with WScript (WScript.exe), which is the Windows-based front-end for the Windows Script Host. In

6

other words, launching a script file named MyScript.vbs is equivalent to entering the following command in the Run dialog box:

**wscript myscript.vbs**

The WScript host also defines several parameters that you can use to control how the script executes. Here's the full syntax:

```
WSCRIPT filename arguments //B //D //E:engine //H:host //I //Job:xxxx
➡//S //T:ss //X
```

| | |
|---|---|
| *filename* | Specifies the name, including the path, if necessary, of the script file. |
| *arguments* | Specifies optional arguments required by the script. An **argument** is a data value that the script uses as part of its procedures or calculations. |
| //B | Runs the script in batch mode, which means script errors and Echo method output lines are suppressed. (I discuss the Echo method later in this chapter.) |
| //D | Enables Active Debugging. If an error occurs, the script is loaded into the Microsoft Script Debugger (if it's installed) and the offending statement is highlighted. |
| //E:*engine* | Executes the script using the specified scripting *engine*, which is the scripting language to be used to run the script. |
| //H:*host* | Specifies the default scripting host. For *host*, use either CScript or WScript. |
| //I | Runs the script in interactive mode, which displays script errors and Echo method output lines. |
| //Job:*xxxx* | In a script file that contains multiple jobs, executes only the job with ID equal to *xxxx*. |
| //S | Saves the specified WSCRIPT arguments as the default for the current user; the following Registry key is used to save these settings: HKCU\Software\Microsoft\Windows Script Host\Settings |
| //TT:*ss* | Specifies the maximum time in seconds (*ss*) that the script can run before it is shut down automatically. |
| //X | Executes the entire script in the Microsoft Script Debugger (if it's installed). |

### Creating Script Jobs

A script **job** is a section of code that performs a specific task or set of tasks. Most script files contain a single job. However, it's possible to create a script file with multiple jobs. To do this, first surround the code for each job with the <script> and </script> tags, and then surround those with the <job> and </job> tags. In the <job> tag, include the id attribute and set it to a unique value that identifies the job. Finally, surround all the jobs with the <package> and </package> tags. Here's an example:

```
<package>
<job id="A">
<script language="VBScript">
    WScript.Echo "This is Job A."
</script>
</job>

<job id="B">
<script language="VBScript">
     WScript.Echo "This is Job B."
</script>
</job>
</package>
```

Save the file using the .wsf (Windows Script File) extension.

For example, the following command runs MyScript.vba in batch mode with a 60-second maximum execution time:

```
wscript myscript.vbs //B //TT:60
```

## Using CScript for Command-Line Scripts

The Windows Script Host has a second host front-end application called CScript (CScript.exe), which enables you to run scripts from the command line. At its simplest, you launch CScript and use the name of the script file (and its path, if required) as a parameter, as in this example:

```
cscript myscript.vbs
```

The Windows Script Host displays the following banner and then executes the script:

```
Microsoft (R) Windows Script Host Version 5.6 for Windows
Copyright (C) Microsoft Corporation 1996-2001. All rights reserved.
```

As with WScript, the CScript host has an extensive set of parameters you can specify:

```
CSCRIPT filename arguments //B //D //E:engine //H:host //I //Job:xxxx
➥//S //T:ss //X //U //LOGO //NOLOGO
```

This syntax is almost identical to that of WScript, but adds the following three parameters:

| | |
|---|---|
| //LOGO | Displays the Windows Script Host banner at startup |
| //NOLOGO | Hides the Windows Script Host banner at startup |
| //U | Uses Unicode for redirected input/output from the console |

## Script Properties and .wsh Files

In the last two sections, you saw that the WScript and CScript hosts have a number of parameters you can specify when you execute a script. It's also possible to set some of these options by using the properties that are associated with each script file. To see these properties, right-click a script file and then click Properties. In the properties sheet that appears, display the Script tab, shown in Figure 9.1. You have two options:

| | |
|---|---|
| Stop Script After Specified Number of Seconds | If you activate this check box, Windows shuts down the script after it has run for the number of seconds specified in the associated spin box. This is useful for scripts that might hang during execution. For example, a script that attempts to enumerate all the mapped network drives at startup might hang if the network is unavailable. |
| Display Logo When Script Executed in Command Console | As you saw in the previous section, the CScript host displays some banner text when you run a script at the command prompt. If you deactivate this check box, the Windows Script Host suppresses this banner (unless you use the //LOGO parameter). |

When you make changes to these properties, the Windows Script Host saves your settings in a new file that has the same name as the script file, except with the .wsh (Windows Script Host Settings) extension. For example, if the script file is MyScript.vbs, the settings are stored in MyScript.wsh. These .wsh files are text files organized into sections, much like .ini files. Here's an example:

```
[ScriptFile]
Path=C:\Documents and Settings\Paul\My Documents\myscript.vbs
[Options]
Timeout=0
DisplayLogo=1
```

To use these settings when running the script, use either WScript or CScript and specify the name of the .wsh file:

```
wscript myscript.wsh
```

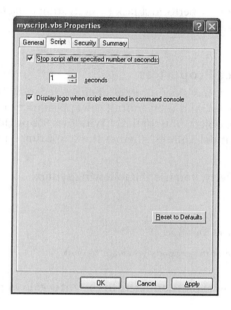

**FIGURE 9.1**    In a script file's properties sheet, use the Script tab to set some default options for the script.

> **NOTE**
>
> Rather than setting properties for individual scripts, you might prefer to set global properties that apply to the WScript host itself. These settings are then applied to every script that's run using the WScript host. To do this, run WScript.exe without any parameters. This displays the properties sheet for WScript, which contains only the Script tab shown earlier in Figure 9.1. The settings you choose here are then stored in the following Registry key:
>
> ```
> HKLM\Software\Microsoft\Windows Script Host\Settings
> ```

## Programming Objects

Although this chapter isn't a programming primer per se, I'd like to take some time now to run through a few quick notes about programming objects. This will serve you well throughout the rest of the chapter as I take you on a tour of the Windows Script Host object model.

The dictionary definition of an object is "anything perceptible by one or more of the senses, especially something that can be seen and felt." In scripting, an **object** is an application element that exposes an interface to the programmer, who can then perform the programming equivalent of seeing and feeling:

- You can make changes to the object's *properties* (this is the seeing part).

- You can make the object perform a task by activating a *method* associated with the object (this is the feeling part).

## Working with Object Properties

Every programmable object has a defining set of characteristics. These characteristics are called the object's **properties**, and they control the appearance and position of the object. For example, the WScript object (the top-level Windows Script Host object) has an Interactive property that determines whether the script runs in interactive mode or batch mode.

When you refer to a property, you use the following syntax:

*Object.Property*

> *Object*      The name of the object
>
> *Property*    The name of the property you want to work with

For example, the following expression refers to the Interactive property of the WScript object:

WScript.Interactive

### Setting the Value of a Property

To set a property to a certain value, you use the following syntax:

*Object.Property = value*

Here, *value* is an expression that specifies the value to which you want to set the property. As such, it can be any of the scripting language's recognized data types, which usually include the following:

- A numeric value

- A string value, enclosed in double quotation marks (such as "My Script Application")

- A logical value (in VBScript: True or False; in JavaScript: true or false)

For example, the following VBScript statement tells the Windows Script Host to run the script using interactive mode:

WScript.Interactive = True

### Returning the Value of a Property

Sometimes you need to know the current setting of a property before changing the property or performing some other action. You can find out the current value of a property by using the following syntax:

```
variable = Object.Property
```

Here, *variable* is a variable name or another property. For example, the following statement stores the current script mode in a variable named currentMode:

```
currentMode = WScript.Interactive
```

## Working with Object Methods

An object's properties describe what the object is, whereas its **methods** describe what the object *does*. For example, the WScript object has a Quit method that enables you to stop the execution of a script.

How you refer to a method depends on whether the method requires any arguments. If it doesn't, the syntax is similar to that of properties:

```
Object.Method
```

| | |
|---|---|
| *Object* | The name of the object |
| *Method* | The name of the method you want to run |

For example, the following statement shuts down a script:

```
WScript.Quit
```

If the method requires arguments, you use the following syntax:

```
Object.Method(Argument1, Argument2, ...)
```

> **NOTE**
> In VBScript, the parentheses around the argument list are necessary only if you'll be storing the result of the method in a variable or object property. In JavaScript, the parentheses are always required.

For example, the WshShell object has a RegWrite method that you use to write a key or value to the Registry. (I discuss this object and method in detail later in this chapter; see "Working with Registry Entries.") Here's the syntax:

```
WshShell.RegWrite strName, anyValue[, strType]
```

| | |
|---|---|
| *strName* | The name of the Registry key or value |
| *anyValue* | The value to write, if *strName* is a Registry value |
| *strType* | The data type of the value |

---

**Argument Naming Conventions**

When presenting method arguments in this chapter, I'll follow Microsoft's naming conventions, including the use of the following prefixes for the argument names:

| Prefix | Data Type |
|---|---|
| any | Any type |
| b | Boolean |
| int | Integer |
| nat | Natural numbers |
| obj | Object |
| str | String |

For many object methods, not all the arguments are required. In the RegWrite method, for example, the *strName* and *anyValue* arguments are required, but the *strType* argument is not. Throughout this chapter, I differentiate between required and optional arguments by surrounding the optional arguments with square brackets—for example, [*strType*].

---

For example, the following statement creates a new value named Test and sets it equal to Foo:

```
WshShell.RegWrite "HKCU\Software\Microsoft\Windows Script Host\Test",
➥"Foo", "REG_SZ"
```

## Assigning an Object to a Variable

If you're using JavaScript, you assign an object to a variable using a standard variable assignment:

```
var variableName = ObjectName
```

| | |
|---|---|
| *variableName* | The name of the variable |
| *ObjectName* | The object you want to assign to the variable |

In VBScript, you assign an object to a variable by using the Set statement. Set has the following syntax:

```
Set variableName = ObjectName
```

| | |
|---|---|
| *variableName* | The name of the variable |
| *ObjectName* | The object you want to assign to the variable |

You'll see later on that you must often use Automation to access external objects. For example, if you want to work with files and folders in your script, you must access the scripting engine object named `FileSystemObject`. To get this access, you use the `CreateObject` method and store the resulting object in a variable, like so:

```
Set fs = CreateObject("Scripting.FileSystemObject")
```

## Working with Object Collections

A **collection** is a set of similar objects. For example, `WScript.Arguments` is the set of all the arguments specified on the script's command line. Collections are objects, too, so they have their own properties and methods, and you can use the properties and methods to manipulate one or more objects in the collection.

The members of a collection are called the **elements** of the collection. You can refer to individual elements by using an **index**. For example, the following statement refers to the first command-line argument (collection indexes always begin at 0):

```
WScript.Arguments(0)
```

If you don't specify an element, the Windows Script Host assumes that you want to work with the entire collection.

### VBScript: Using `For Each...Next` **Loops for Collections**

As you might know, VBScript provides the `For...Next` loop that enables you to cycle through a chunk of code a specified number of times. For example, the following code loops 10 times:

```
For counter = 1 To 10
    Code entered here is repeated 10 times
Next counter
```

A useful variation on this theme is the `For Each...Next` loop, which operates on a collection of objects. You don't need a loop counter because VBScript loops through the individual elements in the collection and performs on each element whatever operations are inside the loop. Here's the structure of the basic `For Each...Next` loop:

```
For Each element In collection
    [statements]
Next
```

| | |
|---|---|
| `element` | A variable used to hold the name of each element in the collection |
| `collection` | The name of the collection |
| `statements` | The statements to be executed for each element in the collection |

The following code loops through all the arguments specified on the script's command line and displays each argument:

```
For Each arg In WScript.Arguments
    WScript.Echo arg
Next
```

### JavaScript: Using Enumerators and for Loops for Collections

To iterate through a collection in JavaScript, you must do two things: create a new Enumerator object, and use a for loop to cycle through the enumerated collection.

To create a new Enumerator object, use the new keyword to set up an object variable (where *collection* is the name of the collection you want to work with):

```
var enum = new Enumerator(collection)
```

You then set up a special for loop:

```
for (; !enumerator.atEnd(); enumerator.moveNext())
{
    [statements];
}
```

>  *enumerator*  The Enumerator object you created
>
>  *statements*  The statements to be executed for each element in the collection

The Enumerator object's moveNext method runs through the elements in the collection, whereas the atEnd method shuts down the loop after the last item has been processed. The following code loops through all the arguments specified on the script's command line and displays each argument:

```
var args = new Enumerator(WScript.Arguments);
for (; !args.atEnd(); args.moveNext())
{
    WScript.Echo(args.item());
}
```

# Programming the WScript Object

The WScript object represents the Windows Script Host applications (WScript.exe and CScript.exe). You use this object to get and set certain properties of the scripting host, as well as to access two other objects: WshArguments (the WScript object's Arguments property) and WshScriptEngine (accessed via the WScript object's GetScriptEngine method). WScript also contains the powerful CreateObject and GetObject methods, which enable you to work with Automation-enabled applications.

## Displaying Text to the User

The WScript object method that you'll use most often is the Echo method, which displays text to the user. Here's the syntax:

```
WScript.Echo [Argument1, Argument2,...]
```

Here, *Argument1*, *Argument2*, and so on, are any number of text or numeric values that represent the information you want to display to the user. In the Windows-based host (WScript.exe), the information is displayed in a dialog box; in the command-line host (CScript.exe), the information is displayed at the command prompt (much like the command-line ECHO utility).

## Shutting Down a Script

You use the WScript object's Quit method to shut down the script. You can also use Quit to have your script return an error code by using the following syntax:

```
WScript.Quit [intErrorCode]
```

    *intErrorCode*        An integer value that represents the error code you want to return

You could then call the script from a batch file and use the ERRORLEVEL environment variable to deal with the return code in some way. (See Appendix C for more information on ERRORLEVEL.)

## Scripting and Automation

Applications such as Internet Explorer and Word come with (or **expose**, in the jargon) a set of objects that define various aspects of the program. For example, Internet Explorer has an Application object that represents the program as a whole. Similarly, Word has a Document object that represents a Word document. By using the properties and methods that come with these objects, it's possible to programmatically query and manipulate the applications. With Internet Explorer, for example, you can use the Application object's Navigate method to send the browser to a specified web page. With Word, you can read a Document object's Saved property to see whether the document has unsaved changes.

This is powerful stuff, but how do you get at the objects that are exposed by these applications? You do that by using a technology called **Automation**. Applications that support Automation implement object libraries that expose the application's native objects to Automation-aware programming languages. Such applications are called **Automation servers**, and the applications that manipulate the server's objects are called **Automation controllers**. The Windows Script Host is an Automation controller that enables you to write script code to control any server's objects.

This means that you can use an application's exposed objects more or less as you use the Windows Script Host objects. With just a minimum of preparation, your script code can refer to and work with the Internet Explorer Application object or the Microsoft Word Document object, or any of the hundreds of other objects exposed by the applications on your system. (Note, however, that not all applications expose objects. Outlook Express and most of the built-in Windows XP programs—such as WordPad and Paint—do not expose objects.)

### Creating an Automation Object with the `CreateObject` Method

The WScript object's `CreateObject` method creates an Automation object (specifically, what programmers call an **instance** of the object). Here's the syntax:

```
WScript.CreateObject(strProgID)
```

> *strProgID*          A string that specifies the Automation server application and the type of object to create. This string is called a **programmatic identifier**, which is a label that uniquely specifies an application and one of its objects. The programmatic identifier always takes the following form:
>
> > `AppName.ObjectType`
>
> Here, *AppName* is the Automation name of the application, and *ObjectType* is the object class type (as defined in the registry's HKEY_CLASSES_ROOT key). For example, here's the programmatic ID for Word:
>
> > `Word.Application`

Note that you normally use `CreateObject` within a `Set` statement, and that the function serves to create a new instance of the specified Automation object. For example, you could use the following statement to create a new instance of Word's `Application` object:

```
Set objWord = CreateObject("Word.Application")
```

Note that there's nothing else you need to do to use the Automation object. With your variable declared and an instance of the object created, you can use that object's properties and methods directly. Listing 9.1 shows a VBScript example (you must have Word installed for this to work).

**LISTING 9.1**    A VBScript Example That Creates and Manipulates a Word Application Object

```
' Create the Word Application object
'
Set objWord = WScript.CreateObject("Word.Application")
'
' Create a new document
'
objWord.Documents.Add
'
' Add some text
'
objWord.ActiveDocument.Paragraphs(1).Range.InsertBefore "Automation test."
'
' Save the document
'
objWord.ActiveDocument.Save
'
```

**LISTING 9.1**   Continued

```
' We're done, so quit Word
'
objWord.Quit
```

This script creates and saves a new Word document by working with Word's `Application` object via Automation. The script begins by using the `CreateObject` method to create a new Word `Application` object, and the object is stored in the `objWord` variable. From here, you can wield the `objWord` variable just as though it were the Word `Application` object.

For example, the `objWord.Documents.Add` statement uses the `Documents` collection's `Add` method to create a new Word document, and the `InsertBefore` method adds some text to the document. Then the `Save` method displays the Save As dialog box so that you can save the new file. With the Word-related chores complete, the `Application` object's `Quit` method is run to shut down Word. For comparison, Listing 9.2 shows a JavaScript procedure that performs the same tasks.

**LISTING 9.2**   A JavaScript Example That Creates and Manipulates a Word Application Object

```
// Create the Word Application object
//
var objWord = WScript.CreateObject("Word.Application");
//
// Create a new document
//
objWord.Documents.Add();
//
// Add some text
//
objWord.ActiveDocument.Paragraphs(1).Range.InsertBefore("Automation test.");
//
// Save the document
//
objWord.ActiveDocument.Save();
//
// We're done, so quit Word
//
objWord.Quit();
```

9

**Making the Automation Server Visable**

The `CreateObject` method loads the object, but doesn't display the Automation server unless user interaction is required. For example, you see Word's Save As dialog box when you run the Save method on a new document (as in Listings 9.1 and 9.2). Not seeing the Automation server is the desired behavior in most Automation situations. However, if you *do* want to see what the Automation server is up to, set the Application object's `Visible` property to `True`, as in this example:

```
objWord.Visible = True
```

## Working with an Existing Object Using the GetObject Method

If you know that the object you want to work with already exists or is already open, the `CreateObject` method isn't the best choice. In the example in the previous section, if Word is already running, the code will start a second copy of Word, which is a waste of resources.

For these situations, it's better to work directly with the existing object. To do this, use the `GetObject` method:

```
WScript.GetObject(strPathname, [strProgID])
```

| | |
|---|---|
| *strPathname* | The pathname (drive, folder, and filename) of the file you want to work with (or the file that contains the object you want to work with). If you omit this argument, you have to specify the *strProgID* argument. |
| *strProgID* | The **programmatic ID** that specifies the Automation server application and the type of object to work with (that is, the *AppName.ObjectType* class syntax). |

Listing 9.3 shows a VBScript procedure that puts the `GetObject` method to work.

**LISTING 9.3**    A VBScript Example That Uses the `GetObject` Method to Work with an Existing Instance of a Word `Document` Object

```
' Get the Word Document object
'
Set objDoc = WScript.GetObject("C:\GetObject.doc", "Word.Document")
'
' Get the word count
'
WScript.Echo objDoc.Name & " has " & objDoc.Words.Count & " words."
'
' We're done, so quit Word
'
objDoc.Application.Quit
```

The `GetObject` method assigns the Word `Document` object named `GetObject.doc` to the `objDoc` variable. Again, after you've set up this reference, you can use the object's properties and methods directly. For example, the `Echo` method uses `objDoc.Name` to return the filename and `objDoc.Words.Count` to determine the number of words in the document.

Note that even though you're working with a `Document` object, you still have access to Word's `Application` object. That's because most objects have an `Application` property that refers to the `Application` object. In the script in Listing 9.3, for example, the following statement uses the `Application` property to quit Word:

```
objDoc.Application.Quit
```

### Exposing VBScript and JavaScript Objects

One of the most powerful uses for scripted Automation is accessing the object models exposed by the VBScript and JavaScript engines. These models expose a number of objects, including the local file system. This enables you to create scripts that work with files, folders, and disk drives, read and write text files, and more. You use the following syntax to refer to these objects:

```
Scripting.ObjectType
```

`Scripting` is the Automation name of the scripting engine, and *ObjectType* is the class type of the object.

> **NOTE**
>
> This section just gives you a brief explanation of the objects associated with the VBScript and JavaScript engines. For the complete list of object properties and methods, please see the following site: msdn.microsoft.com/scripting.

### Programming the `FileSystemObject`

`FileSystemObject` is the top-level file system object. For all your file system scripts, you begin by creating a new instance of `FileSystemObject`:

In VBScript:

```
Set fs = WScript.CreateObject("Scripting.FileSystemObject")
```

In JavaScript:

```
var fs = WScript.CreateObject("Scripting.FileSystemObject");
```

Here's a summary of the file system objects you can access via Automation and the top-level `FileSystemObject`:

| | |
|---|---|
| `Drive` | This object enables you to access the properties of a specified disk drive or UNC network path. To reference a `Drive` object, use either the `Drives` collection (discussed next) or the `FileSystemObject` object's `GetDrive` method. For example, the following VBScript statement references drive C: |

```
Set objFS = WScript.CreateObject("Scripting.
➥FileSystemObject")
Set objDrive = objFS.GetDrive("C:")
```

Drives

This object is the collection of all available drives. To reference this collection, use the FileSystemObject object's Drives property:

```
Set objFS = WScript.CreateObject("Scripting.
➥FileSystemObject")
Set objDrives = objFS.Drives
```

Folder

This object enables you to access the properties of a specified folder. To reference a Folder object, use either the Folders collection (discussed next) or the FileSystemObject object's GetFolder method:

```
Set objFS = WScript.CreateObject("Scripting.
➥FileSystemObject")
Set objFolder = objFS.GetFolder("C:\My Documents")
```

Folders

This object is the collection of subfolders within a specified folder. To reference this collection, use the Folder object's Subfolders property:

```
Set objFS = WScript.CreateObject("Scripting.
➥FileSystemObject")
Set objFolder = objFS.GetFolder("C:\Windows")
Set objSubfolders = objFolder.Subfolders
```

File

This object enables you to access the properties of a specified file. To reference a File object, use either the Files collection (discussed next) or the FileSystemObject object's GetFile method:

```
Set objFS = WScript.CreateObject("Scripting.
➥FileSystemObject")
Set objFile = objFS.GetFile("c:\autoexec.bat")
```

Files

This object is the collection of files within a specified folder. To reference this collection, use the Folder object's Files property:

```
Set objFS = WScript.CreateObject("Scripting.
➥FileSystemObject")
Set objFolder = objFS.GetFolder("C:\Windows")
Set objFiles = objFolder.Files
```

TextStream

This object enables you to use sequential access to work with a text file. To open a text file, use the FileSystemObject object's OpenTextFile method:

```
Set objFS = WScript.CreateObject("Scripting.
➥FileSystemObject")
Set objTS= objFS.OpenTextFile("C:\Boot.ini")
```

Alternatively, you can create a new text file by using the FileSystemObject object's CreateTextFile method:

```
Set objFS = WScript.CreateObject("Scripting.FileSystemObject")
Set objTS= objFS.CreateTextFile("C:\Boot.ini")
```

Either way, you end up with a TextStream object, which has various methods for reading data from the file and writing data to the file. For example, the following script reads and displays the text from C:\Autoexec.bat:

```
Set objFS = WScript.CreateObject("Scripting.FileSystemObject")
Set objTS = objFS.OpenTextFile("C:\Boot.ini")
strContents = objTS.ReadAll
WScript.Echo strContents
objTS.Close
```

# Programming the WshShell Object

WshShell is a generic name for a powerful object that enables you to query and interact with various aspects of the Windows shell. You can display information to the user, run applications, create shortcuts, work with the Registry, and control Windows' environment variables. The next few sections discuss each of the useful tasks.

## Referencing the WshShell Object

WshShell refers to the Shell object that is exposed via the Automation interface of WScript. Therefore, you must use CreateObject to return this object:

```
Set objWshShell = WScript.CreateObject("WScript.Shell")
```

From here, you can use the objWshShell variable to access the object's properties and methods.

## Displaying Information to the User

You saw earlier that the WScript object's Echo method is useful for displaying simple text messages to the user. You can gain more control over the displayed message by using the WshShell object's Popup method. This method is similar to the MsgBox function used in Visual Basic and VBA in that it enables you to control both the dialog box title and the buttons that are displayed, as well as to determine which of those buttons the user pressed. Here's the syntax:

WshShell.Popup(*strText*, [*nSecondsToWait*], [*strTitle*], [*intType*])

| | |
|---|---|
| *WshShell* | The WshShell object. |
| *strText* | The message you want to display in the dialog box. You can enter a string up to 1,024 characters long. |
| *nSecondsToWait* | The maximum number of seconds the dialog box will be displayed. |
| *strTitle* | The text that appears in the dialog box title bar. If you omit this value, Windows Script Host appears in the title bar. |

| | |
|---|---|
| *intType* | A number or constant that specifies, among other things, the command buttons that appear in the dialog box (see the next section). The default value is 0. |

For example, the following statements display the dialog box shown in Figure 9.2:

```
Set objWshShell = WScript.CreateObject("WScript.Shell")
objWshShell.Popup "Couldn't find Memo.doc!", , "Warning"
```

**FIGURE 9.2**    A simple message dialog box produced by the Popup method.

---

**TIP**

For long messages, VBScript wraps the text inside the dialog box. If you prefer to create your own line breaks, use VBScript's Chr function and the carriage-return character (ASCII 13) between each line:

```
WshShell.Popup "First line" & Chr(13) & "Second line"
```

For JavaScript, use \n instead:

```
WshShell.Popup("First line" + "\n" + "Second line");
```

---

### Setting the Style of the Message

The default Popup dialog box displays only an OK button. You can include other buttons and icons in the dialog box by using different values for the *intType* parameter. Table 9.1 lists the available options.

**TABLE 9.1**    The Popup Method's *intType* Parameter Options

| VBScript Constant | Value | Description |
|---|---|---|
| **Buttons** | | |
| vbOKOnly | 0 | Displays only an OK button. This is the default. |
| vbOKCancel | 1 | Displays the OK and Cancel buttons. |
| vbAbortRetryIgnore | 2 | Displays the Abort, Retry, and Ignore buttons. |
| vbYesNoCancel | 3 | Displays the Yes, No, and Cancel buttons. |
| vbYesNo | 4 | Displays the Yes and No buttons. |
| vbRetryCancel | 5 | Displays the Retry and Cancel buttons. |

**TABLE 9.1** Continued

| VBScript Constant | Value | Description |
| --- | --- | --- |
| **Icons** | | |
| vbCritical | 16 | Displays the Critical Message icon. |
| vbQuestion | 32 | Displays the Warning Query icon. |
| vbExclamation | 48 | Displays the Warning Message icon. |
| vbInformation | 64 | Displays the Information Message icon. |
| **Default Button** | | |
| vbDefaultButton1 | 0 | The first button is the default (that is, the button selected when the user presses Enter). |
| vbDefaultButton2 | 256 | The second button is the default. |
| vbDefaultButton3 | 512 | The third button is the default. |

You derive the *intType* argument in one of two ways:

- By adding the values for each option
- By using the VBScript constants separated by plus signs (+)

The script in Listing 9.4 shows an example and Figure 9.3 shows the resulting dialog box.

**LISTING 9.4**   A VBScript Example That Uses the Popup Method to Display the Dialog Box Shown in Figure 9.3

```
' First, set up the message
'
strText = "Are you sure you want to copy" & Chr(13)
strText = strText & "the selected files to drive A?"
strTitle = "Copy Files"
intType = vbYesNoCancel + vbQuestion + vbDefaultButton2
'
' Now display it
'
Set objWshShell = WScript.CreateObject("WScript.Shell")
intResult = objWshShell.Popup(strText, ,strTitle, intType)
```

Here, three variables—strText, strTitle, and intType—store the values for the Popup method's *strText*, *strTitle*, and *intType* arguments, respectively. In particular, the following statement derives the *intType* argument:

```
intType = vbYesNoCancel + vbQuestion + vbDefaultButton2
```

You also could derive the *intType* argument by adding up the values that these constants represent (3, 32, and 256, respectively), but the script becomes less readable that way.

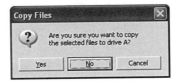

**FIGURE 9.3**    The dialog box that's displayed when you run the script.

### Getting Return Values from the Message Dialog Box

A dialog box that displays only an OK button is straightforward. The user either clicks OK or presses Enter to remove the dialog from the screen. The multibutton styles are a little different, however; the user has a choice of buttons to select, and your script should have a way to find out which button the user chose. You do this by storing the Popup method's return value in a variable. Table 9.2 lists the seven possible return values.

**TABLE 9.2**    The Popup Method's Return Values

| VBScript Constant | Value | Button Selected |
|---|---|---|
| vbOK | 1 | OK |
| vbCancel | 2 | Cancel |
| vbAbort | 3 | Abort |
| vbRetry | 4 | Retry |
| vbIgnore | 5 | Ignore |
| vbYes | 6 | Yes |
| vbNo | 7 | No |

To process the return value, you can use an If...Then...Else or Select Case structure to test for the appropriate values. For example, the script shown earlier used a variable called intResult to store the return value of the Popup method. Listing 9.5 shows a revised version of the script that uses a VBScript Select Case statement to test for the three possible return values.

**LISTING 9.5**    A Script That Uses a Select Case Statement to Process the Popup Method's Return Value

```
' First, set up the message
'
strText = "Are you sure you want to copy" & Chr(13)
strText = strText & "the selected files to drive A?"
strTitle = "Copy Files"
intType = vbYesNoCancel + vbQuestion + vbDefaultButton2
'
' Now display it
'
Set objWshShell = WScript.CreateObject("WScript.Shell")
intResult = objWshShell.Popup(strText, ,strTitle, intType)
'
```

**LISTING 9.5**  Continued

```
' Process the result
'
Select Case intResult
    Case vbYes
        WScript.Echo "You clicked ""Yes""!"
    Case vbNo
        WScript.Echo "You clicked ""No""!"
    Case vbCancel
        WScript.Echo "You clicked ""Cancel""!"
End Select
```

## Running Applications

When you need your script to launch another application, use the Run method:

WshShell.Run strCommand, [intWindowStyle], [bWaitOnReturn]

| | |
|---|---|
| *WshShell* | The WshShell object. |
| *strCommand* | The name of the file that starts the application. Unless the file is in the Windows folder, you should include the drive and folder to make sure that the script can find the file. |
| *intWindowStyle* | A constant or number that specifies how the application window will appear: |

| intWindowStyle | Window Appearance |
|---|---|
| 0 | Hidden |
| 1 | Normal size with focus |
| 2 | Minimized with focus (this is the default) |
| 3 | Maximized with focus |
| 4 | Normal without focus |
| 6 | Minimized without focus |

| | |
|---|---|
| *bWaitOnReturn* | A logical value that determines whether the application is run asynchronously. If this value is True, the script halts execution until the user exits the launched application; if this value is False, the script continues running after it has launched the application. |

Here's an example:

```
Set objWshShell = WScript.CreateObject("WScript.Shell")
objWshShell.Run "Control.exe Inetcpl.cpl", 1, True
```

This Run method launches Control Panel's Internet Properties dialog box.

---

**NOTE**

To learn more about launching individual Control Panel icons using `Control.exe`, refer to "Operating Control Panel" in Chapter 7, "Using Control Panel, Group Policies, and Tweak UI."

---

## Working with Shortcuts

The Windows Script Host enables your scripts to create and modify shortcut files. If you're writing scripts for other users, you might want to take advantage of this capability to display shortcuts for new network shares, Internet sites, instruction files, and so on.

### Creating a Shortcut

To create a shortcut, use the `CreateShortcut` method:

*WshShell*`.CreateShortcut(`*strPathname*`)`

| | |
|---|---|
| *WshShell* | The `WshShell` object. |
| *strPathname* | The full path and filename of the shortcut file you want to create. Use the `.lnk` extension for a file system (program, document, folder, and so on) shortcut; use the `.url` extension for an Internet shortcut. |

The following example creates and saves a shortcut on a user's desktop:

```
Set WshShell = objWScript.CreateObject("WScript.Shell")
Set objShortcut = objWshShell.CreateShortcut("C:\Documents and Settings\
➥Paul\Desktop\test.lnk")
objShortcut.Save
```

### Programming the `WshShortcut` Object

The `CreateShortcut` method returns a `WshShortcut` object. You can use this object to manipulate various properties and methods associated with shortcut files.

This object contains the following properties:

| | |
|---|---|
| `Arguments` | Returns or sets a string that specifies the arguments used when launching the shortcut. For example, suppose that the shortcut's target is the following: |
| | `C:\Windows\Notepad.exe C:\Boot.ini` |
| | In other words, this shortcut launches Notepad and loads the Boot.ini file. In this case, the `Arguments` property would return the following string: |
| | `C:\Boot.ini` |
| `Description` | Returns or sets a string description of the shortcut. |

FullName                    Returns the full path and filename of the shortcut's target. This will be
                            the same as the *strPathname* value used in the CreateShortcut
                            method.

Hotkey                      Returns or sets the hotkey associated with the shortcut. To set this value,
                            use the following syntax:

                                *WshShortcut*.Hotkey = *strHotKey*

                            *WshShortcut*—The WshShortcut object.

                            *strHotKey*—A string value of the form *Modifier+Keyname*, where
                            *Modifier* is any combination of Alt, Ctrl, and Shift, and *Keyname* is one
                            of A through Z or 0 through 9.

                            For example, the following statement sets the hotkey to Ctrl+Alt+7:

                            objShortcut.Hotkey = "Ctrl+Alt+7"

IconLocation                Returns or sets the icon used to display the shortcut. To set this value,
                            use the following syntax:

                                *WshShortcut*.IconLocation = *strIconLocation*

                            *WshShortcut*—The WshShortcut object.

                            *strIconLocation*—A string value of the form *Path,Index*, where *Path* is
                            the full pathname of the icon file, and *Index* is the position of the icon
                            within the file (where the first icon is 0).

                            Here's an example:

                                objShortcut.IconLocation =
                                "C:\Windows\System32\Shell32.dll,21"

TargetPath                  Returns or sets the path of the shortcut's target.

WindowStyle                 Returns or sets the window style used by the shortcut's target. Use the
                            same values that I outlined earlier for the Run method's *intWindowStyle*
                            argument.

WorkingDirectory            Returns or sets the path of the shortcut's working directory.

**NOTE**

If you're working with Internet shortcuts, bear in mind that they support only two properties:
FullName and TargetPath (the URL target).

The `WshShortcut` object also supports two methods:

| | |
|---|---|
| Save | Saves the shortcut file to disk. |
| Resolve | Uses the shortcut's `TargetPath` property to look up the target file. Here's the syntax: |

> `WshShortcut.Resolve = intFlag`

*WshShortcut*—The `WshShortcut` object.

*intFlag*—Determines what happens if the target file is not found:

| intFlag | **What Happens** |
|---|---|
| 1 | Nothing |
| 2 | Windows continues to search subfolders for the target file |
| 4 | Updates the `TargetPath` property if the target file is found in a new location |

Listing 9.6 shows a complete example of a script that creates a shortcut.

**LISTING 9.6**    A Script That Creates a Shortcut File

```
Set objWshShell = WScript.CreateObject("WScript.Shell")
Set objShortcut = objWshShell.CreateShortcut("C:\Documents and Settings\Paul
➥\Desktop\Edit BOOT.INI.lnk")
With objShortcut
    .TargetPath = "C:\Windows\Notepad.exe"
    .Arguments = "C:\Boot.ini"
    .WorkingDirectory = "C:\"
    .Description = "Opens BOOT.INI in Notepad"
    .Hotkey = "Ctrl+Alt+7"
    .IconLocation = "C:\Windows\System32\Shell32.dll,21"
    .WindowStyle = 3
    .Save
End With
```

## Working with Registry Entries

You've seen throughout this book that the Registry is one of Windows' most crucial data structures. However, the Registry isn't a tool wielded only by Windows. Most 32-bit applications make use of the Registry as a place to store setup options, customization values selected by the user, and much more. Interestingly, your scripts can get in on the act as well. Not only can your scripts read the current value of any Registry setting, but they can also use the Registry as a storage area. This enables you to keep track of user settings, recently used files, and any other configuration data that you'd like to save between sessions. This section shows you how to use the WshShell object to manipulate the Registry from within your scripts.

### Reading Settings from the Registry

To read any value from the Registry, use the WshShell object's RegRead method:

`WshShell.RegRead(strName)`

| | |
|---|---|
| *WshShell* | The WshShell object. |
| *strName* | The name of the Registry value or key that you want to read. If *strName* ends with a backslash (\), RegRead returns the default value for the key; otherwise, RegRead returns the data stored in the value. Note, too, that *strName* must begin with one of the following root key names: |

| Short Name | Long Name |
|---|---|
| HKCR | HKEY_CLASSES_ROOT |
| HKCU | HKEY_CURRENT_USER |
| HKLM | HKEY_LOCAL_MACHINE |
| N/A | HKEY_USERS |
| N/A | HKEY_CURRENT_CONFIG |

The script in Listing 9.7 displays the name of the registered owner of this copy of Windows XP.

**LISTING 9.7**    A Script That Reads the RegisteredOwner Setting from the Registry

```
Set objWshShell = WScript.CreateObject("WScript.Shell")
strSetting = "HKLM\SOFTWARE\Microsoft\Windows NT\CurrentVersion\
➥RegisteredOwner"
strRegisteredUser = objWshShell.RegRead(strSetting)
WScript.Echo strRegisteredUser
```

### Storing Settings in the Registry

To store a setting in the Registry, use the WshShell object's RegWrite method:

`WshShell.RegWrite strName, anyValue [, strType]`

| | |
|---|---|
| *WshShell* | The WshShell object. |
| *strName* | The name of the Registry value or key that you want to set. If *strName* ends with a backslash (\), RegWrite sets the default value for the key; otherwise, RegWrite sets the data for the value. *strName* must begin with one of the root key names detailed in the RegRead method. |
| *anyValue* | The value to be stored. |

| | |
|---|---|
| *strType* | The data type of the value, which must be one of the following: REG_SZ (the default), REG_EXPAND_SZ, REG_DWORD, or REG_BINARY. |

The following statements create a new key named ScriptSettings in the HKEY_CURRENT_USER root:

```
Set objWshShell = WScript.CreateObject("WScript.Shell")
objWshShell.RegWrite "HKCU\ScriptSettings\", ""
```

The following statements create a new value named NumberOfReboots in the HKEY_CURRENT_USER\ScriptSettings key, and set this value to 1:

```
Set objWshShell = WScript.CreateObject("WScript.Shell")
objWshShell.RegWrite "HKCU\ScriptSettings\NumberOfReboots", 1, "REG_DWORD"
```

### Deleting Settings from the Registry

If you no longer need to track a particular key or value setting, use the RegDelete method to remove the setting from the Registry:

```
WshShell.RegDelete(strName)
```

| | |
|---|---|
| *WshShell* | The WshShell object. |
| *strName* | The name of the Registry value or key that you want to delete. If *strName* ends with a backslash (\), RegDelete deletes the key; otherwise, RegDelete deletes the value. *strName* must begin with one of the root key names detailed in the RegRead method. |

To delete the NumberOfReboots value used in the previous example, you would use the following statements:

```
Set objWshShell = WScript.CreateObject("WScript.Shell")
objWshShell.RegDelete "HKCU\ScriptSettings\NumberOfReboots"
```

## Working with Environment Variables

Windows XP keeps track of a number of **environment variables** that hold data such as the location of the Windows folder, the location of the temporary files folder, the command PATH, the primary drive, and much more. Why would you need such data? One example would be for accessing files or folders within the main Windows folder. Rather than guessing that this folder is C:\Windows, it would be much easier to just query the %SystemRoot% environment variable. Similarly, if you have a script that accesses files in a user's My Documents folder, hard-coding the username in the file path is inconvenient because it means creating custom scripts for every possible user. Instead, it would be much easier to create just a single script that references the %UserProfile% environment variable. This section shows you how to read environment variable data within your scripts.

The defined environment variables are stored in the Environment collection, which is a property of the WshShell object. Windows XP environment variables are stored in the "Process" environment, so you reference this collection as follows:

```
WshShell.Environment("Process")
```

Listing 9.8 shows a script that runs through this collection, adds each variable to a string, and then displays the string.

**LISTING 9.8**    A Script That Displays the System's Environment Variables

```
Set objWshShell = WScript.CreateObject("WScript.Shell")
'
' Run through the environment variables
'
strVariables = ""
For Each objEnvVar In objWshShell.Environment("Process")
    strVariables = strVariables & objEnvVar & Chr(13)
Next
WScript.Echo strVariables
```

Figure 9.4 shows the dialog box that appears (your mileage may vary).

**FIGURE 9.4**    A complete inventory of a system's environment variables.

If you want to use the value of a particular environment variable, use the following syntax:

```
WshShell.Environment("Process")("strName")
```

> WshShell    The WshShell object
>
> strName    The name of the environment variable

Listing 9.9 shows a revised version of the script from Listing 9.6 to create a shortcut. In this version, the Environment collection is used to return the value of the %UserProfile% variable, which is used to contrast the path to the current user's Desktop folder.

**LISTING 9.9**    A Script That Creates a Shortcut File Using an Environment Variable

```
Set objWshShell = WScript.CreateObject("WScript.Shell")
strUserProfile = objWshShell.Environment("Process")("UserProfile")
Set objShortcut = objWshShell.CreateShortcut(strUserProfile & _
                "\Desktop\Edit BOOT.INI.lnk")
With objShortcut
    .TargetPath = "C:\Windows\Notepad.exe"
    .Arguments = "C:\Boot.ini"
    .WorkingDirectory = "C:\"
    .Description = "Opens BOOT.INI in Notepad"
    .Hotkey = "Ctrl+Alt+7"
    .IconLocation = "C:\Windows\System32\Shell32.dll,21"
    .WindowStyle = 3
    .Save
End With
```

# Programming the WshNetwork Object

WshNetwork is a generic name for an object that enables you to work with various aspects of the Windows network environment. You can determine the computer name and username, you can enumerate the mapped network drives, you can map new network drives, and more. The next couple of sections show you how to work with this object.

## Referencing the WshNetwork Object

WshNetwork refers to the Network object that is exposed via the Automation interface of WScript. This means you use CreateObject to return this object, as shown here:

```
Set objWshNetwork = WScript.CreateObject("WScript.Network")
```

From here, you use the WshNetwork variable to access the object's properties and methods.

## WshNetwork Object Properties

The WshNetwork object supports three properties:

| ComputerName | Returns the network name of the computer |
| UserDomain | Returns the network domain name of the current user |
| UserName | Returns the username of the current user |

## Mapping Network Printers

The WshNetwork object supports several methods for working with remote printers. For example, to map a network printer to a local printer resource, use the WshNetwork object's AddWindowsPrinterConnection method:

*WshNetwork*.AddPrinterConnection *strPrinterPath*

| *WshNetwork* | The WshNetwork object |
| *strPrinterPath* | The UNC path to the network printer |

Here's an example:

```
Set objWshNetwork = WScript.CreateObject("WScript.Network")
objWshNetwork.AddWindowsPrinterConnection "\\ZEUS\printer"
```

To remove a remote printer mapping, use the WshNetwork object's RemovePrinterConnection method:

*WshNetwork*.RemovePrinterConnection *strPrinterPath* [, *bForce*] [, *bUpdateProfile*]

| *WshNetwork* | The WshNetwork object |
| *strPrinterPath* | The UNC path to the network printer |
| *bForce* | If True, the resource is removed even if it is currently being used |
| *bUpdateProfile* | If True, the printer mapping is removed from the user's profile |

Here's an example:

```
Set objWshNetwork = WScript.CreateObject("WScript.Network")
objWshNetwork.RemovePrinterConnection "\\ZEUS\inkjet"
```

## Mapping Network Drives

The WshNetwork object supports several methods for mapping network drives. To map a shared network folder to a local drive letter, use the WshNetwork object's MapNetworkDrive method:

*WshNetwork*.MapNetworkDrive *strLocalName*, *strRemoteName*,
➥[*bUpdateProfile*], [*strUser*], [*strPassword*]

| | |
|---|---|
| *WshNetwork* | The WshNetwork object. |
| *strLocalName* | The local drive letter to which the remote share will be mapped (for example, F:). |
| *strRemoteName* | The UNC path for the remote share. |
| *bUpdateProfile* | If True, the drive mapping is stored in the user's profile. |
| *strUser* | Use this value to enter a username that might be required to map the remote share (if you're logged on as a user who doesn't have the proper permissions, for example). |
| *strPassword* | Use this value to enter a password that might be required to map the remote drive. |

Here's an example:

```
Set objWshNetwork = WScript.CreateObject("WScript.Network")
objWshNetwork.MapNetworkDrive "Z:", "\\ZEUS\SharedDocs"
```

To remove a mapped network drive, use the WshNetwork object's RemoveNetworkDrive:

WshNetwork.RemoveNetworkDrive *strName*, [*bForce*], [*bUpdateProfile*]

| | |
|---|---|
| *WshNetwork* | The WshNetwork object. |
| *strName* | The name of the mapped network drive you want removed. If you use a network path, all mappings to that path are removed; if you use a local drive letter, only that mapping is removed. |
| *bForce* | If True, the resource is removed even if it is currently being used. |
| *bUpdateProfile* | If True, the network drive mapping is removed from the user's profile. |

Here's an example:

```
Set objWshNetwork = WScript.CreateObject("WScript.Network")
objWshNetwork.RemoveNetworkDrive "Z:"
```

# Example: Scripting Internet Explorer

To give you a taste of the power and flexibility of scripting—particularly Automation programming—I'll close this chapter by showing you how to program a specific Automation server: Internet Explorer. You'll see that your scripts can control just about everything associated with Internet Explorer:

- The position and dimensions of the window
- Whether the menu bar, toolbar, and status bar are displayed

- The current URL

- Sending the browser backward and forward between navigated URLs

## Displaying a Web Page

To get started, I'll show you how to use the `InternetExplorer` object to display a specified URL. You use the `Navigate` method to do this, and this method uses the following syntax:

```
InternetExplorer.Navigate URL [, Flags,] [ TargetFramename] [, PostData]
➡[ ,Headers]
```

| | |
|---|---|
| *InternetExplorer* | A reference to the `InternetExplorer` object with which you're working. |
| *URL* | The address of the web page you want to display. |
| *Flags* | One of (or the sum of two or more of) the following integers that control various aspects of the navigation: |

|  |  |
|---|---|
| 1 | Opens the *URL* in a new window |
| 2 | Prevents the *URL* from being added to the history list |
| 4 | Prevents the browser from reading the page from the disk cache |
| 8 | Prevents the *URL* from being added to the disk cache |

| | |
|---|---|
| *TargetFrameName* | The name of the frame in which to display the *URL*. |
| *PostData* | Specifies additional POST information that HTTP requires to resolve the hyperlink. The most common uses for this argument are to send a web server the contents of a form, the coordinates of an imagemap, or a search parameter for an ASP file. If you leave this argument blank, this method issues a GET call. |
| *Headers* | Specifies header data for the HTTP header. |

Here's an example:

```
Set objIE = CreateObject("InternetExplorer.Application")
objIE.Navigate "http://www.microsoft.com/"
```

## Navigating Pages

Displaying a specified web page isn't the only thing the `InternetExplorer` object can do. It also has quite a few methods that give you the ability to navigate backward and forward through visited web pages, refresh the current page, stop the current download, and more. Here's a summary of these methods:

| | |
|---|---|
| GoBack | Navigates backward to a previously visited page |
| GoForward | Navigates forward to a previously visited page |
| GoHome | Navigates to Internet Explorer's default Home page |
| GoSearch | Navigates to Internet Explorer's default Search page |
| Refresh | Refreshes the current page |
| Refresh2 | Refreshes the current page using the following syntax: |

Refresh2(*Level*)

| | | |
|---|---|---|
| *Level* | | A constant that determines how the page is refreshed: |
| | 0 | Refreshes the page with a cached copy |
| | 1 | Refreshes the page with a cached copy only if the page has expired |
| | 3 | Performs a full refresh (doesn't use a cached copy) |

| | |
|---|---|
| Stop | Cancels the current download or shuts down dynamic page objects, such as background sounds and animations. |

## Using the InternetExplorer Object's Properties

Here's a summary of many of the properties associated with the InternetExplorer object:

| | |
|---|---|
| Busy | Returns True if the InternetExplorer object is in the process of downloading text or graphics. This property returns False when the complete document has been downloaded. |
| FullScreen | A Boolean value that toggles Internet Explorer between the normal window and a full-screen window in which the title bar, menu bar, toolbar, and status bar are hidden. |
| Height | Returns or sets the window height. |
| Left | Returns or sets the position of the left edge of the window. |
| LocationName | Returns the title of the current document. |
| LocationURL | Returns the URL of the current document. |
| MenuBar | A Boolean value that toggles the menu bar on and off. |
| StatusBar | A Boolean value that toggles the status bar on and off. |
| StatusText | Returns or sets the status bar text. |
| ToolBar | A Boolean value that toggles the toolbar on and off. |
| Top | Returns or sets the position of the top edge of the window. |
| Type | Returns the type of document currently loaded in the browser. |

| `Visible` | A Boolean value that toggles the object between hidden and visible. |
| `Width` | Returns or sets the window width. |

## Running Through a Sample Script

To put some of the properties and methods into practice, Listing 9.10 shows a sample script.

**LISTING 9.10**  A Script That Puts the `InternetExplorer` Object Through Its Paces

```
Option Explicit
Dim objIE, objWshShell, strMessage, intResult

' Set up the Automation objects
Set objIE = WScript.CreateObject("InternetExplorer.Application")
Set objWshShell = WScript.CreateObject("WScript.Shell")

' Navigate to a page and customize the browser window
objIE.Navigate "http://www.wordspy.com/"
objIE.Toolbar = False
objIE.StatusBar = False
objIE.MenuBar = False

' Twiddle thumbs while the page loads
Do While objIE.Busy
Loop

' Get the page info
strMessage = "Current URL:  " & objIE.LocationURL & vbCrLf & _
    "Current Title: " & objIE.LocationName & vbCrLf & _
    "Document Type: " & objIE.Type & vbCrLf & vbCrLf & _
    "Would you like to view this document?"

' Display the info
intResult = objWshShell.Popup(strMessage, , "Scripting IE", vbYesNo + vbQuestion)

' Check the result
If intResult = vbYes Then

    ' If Yes, make browser visible
    objIE.Visible = True
Else

    ' If no, bail out
    objIE.Quit
```

**LISTING 9.10**    Continued

```
End If
Set objIE = Nothing
Set objWshShell = Nothing
```

The script begins by creating instances of the InternetExplorer and WScript Shell objects. The Navigate method displays a page, and then the toolbar, status bar, and menu bar are turned off. A Do...Loop checks the Busy property and loops while it's True. In other words, this loop won't exit until the page is fully loaded. Then a string variable is used to store the URL, title, and type of the page, and this string is then displayed in a Popup box, which also asks whether the user wants to see the page. If the user clicks Yes, the browser is made visible; if the user clicks No, the Quit method shuts down the browser.

# From Here

Here are some sections of the book that contain information related to the scripting techniques you learned in this chapter:

- To learn how to run scripts when you start your Windows XP system, see the section "Specifying Startup and Logon Scripts" in Chapter 5, "Installing and Running Applications."

- To learn more about the Registry, see Chapter 8, "Getting to Know the Windows XP Registry."

- I show you a script that displays the available free space on all your drives in the "Checking Free Disk Space" section of Chapter 12, "Maintaining Your Windows XP System."

- For some examples of security-related scripts, see Chapter 21, "Implementing Windows XP's Internet Security and Privacy Features."

- You can also "program" Windows XP using batch files. See Appendix C for more information.

# PART III

# Unleashing Windows XP Customization and Optimization

## IN THIS PART

# Customizing the Windows XP Interface

Microsoft spent countless hours and untold millions of dollars testing and retesting the Windows XP user interface (UI) in its usability labs. It's important, however, to remember that Windows XP is an operating system designed for the masses. With an installed base running in the hundreds of millions, it's only natural that the Windows UI would incorporate lots of "lowest-common-denominator" thinking. So, in the end, you have an interface that most people find easy to use most of the time; an interface that's skewed toward accommodating neophytes and the newly digital; an interface designed for a typical computer user, whoever the heck that is.

In other words, unless you consider yourself a typical user (and your purchase of this book proves otherwise), Windows XP in its right-out-of-the-box getup won't be right for you. Fortunately, you'll find no shortage of options and programs that will help you remake Windows XP in your own image, and that's just what this chapter shows you how to do. After all, you weren't produced by a cookie cutter, so why should your operating system look like it was?

Having said that, I should also point out that it's my philosophy that the litmus test of any interface customization is a simple question: Does it improve productivity? I've seen far too many tweaks that fiddle uselessly with some obscure setting, resulting in little or no improvement to the user's day-to-day Windows experience. This may be fine for people with lots of time to kill, but most of us don't have that luxury, so efficiency and productivity must be the goals of the customization process. (Note that this does not preclude aesthetic improvements to the Windows XP interface. A better-looking Windows provides a happier computing experience, and a happier worker is a more productive worker.)

To that end, I devote most of this chapter to the most common of computing tasks: launching programs and documents. This chapter is packed with useful tips and techniques for rearranging Windows XP to help you get your programs and documents up and running as quickly and as easily as possible.

# Customizing the Start Menu for Easier Program and Document Launching

The whole purpose of the Start menu is, as its name implies, to start things, particularly programs and documents. Yes, you can also launch these objects via shortcut icons on the desktop, but that's not a great alternative because the desktop is covered most of the time by windows. So, if you want to get something going in Windows XP, the vast majority of the time you're going to have to do it via the Start menu. The good news is that Windows XP's Start menu is wonderfully flexible and is geared, in fact, to launching objects with as few mouse clicks or keystrokes as possible. To get to that state, however, you have to work with a few relatively obscure options and settings, which you'll learn about in the next few sections.

## Getting More Favorite Programs on the Start Menu

The Start menu is divided vertically into two sections, as shown in Figure 10.1:

| | |
|---|---|
| Favorite programs | This is the left side of the Start menu, which appears by default with a white background. This side includes the fixed Internet and E-mail icons at the top, and below them are shortcut icons for the six programs that you've used most frequently. |
| Built-in features | This is the right side of the Start menu, which appears by default with a light blue background. It contains icons for various built-in Windows XP features. |

The list of favorite programs is one of the best features in Windows XP because it ensures that the programs you use most often are always just a couple of mouse clicks away. If there's a downside to this feature, it's that it displays a maximum of six icons, so many frequently used programs get left off the list. However, if you have enough room, you can tell Windows XP to display up to 30 icons in this area. Here's how:

1. Open the Control Panel's Taskbar and Start Menu icon. The Taskbar and Start Menu Properties dialog box appears.

2. Select the Start Menu tab.

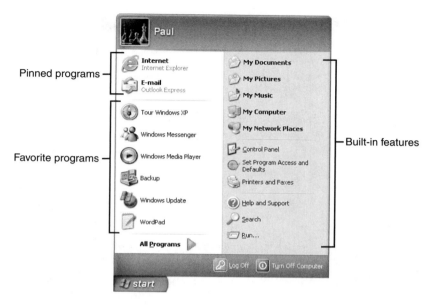

Pinned programs

Favorite programs

Built-in features

**FIGURE 10.1**    The Start menu lists favorite programs on the left and built-in icons for XP features on the right.

**TIP**

A quick way to go directly to the Start Menu tab is to right-click either the Start button or an empty section of the Start menu and then click Properties.

3. Make sure that the Start Menu option is activated and then click the Customize button to its right. The Customize Start Menu dialog box appears, as shown in Figure 10.2.

4. Use the Number of Programs on Start Menu spin box to specify the number of favorite programs you want to display.

5. If you want to start over with a fresh list of frequent programs, click the Clear List button.

**TIP**

If you need to get rid of only one or two icons from the Start menu's frequent programs list, display the Start menu, right-click an icon you want to delete, and then click Remove from This List.

10

**FIGURE 10.2**    Use the Customize Start Menu dialog box to set the maximum number of shortcut icons that appear in the Start menu's list of favorite programs.

6.  If you don't think you have enough screen space to display all the icons, activate the Small Icons option. This significantly reduces the amount of space each icon takes up on the Start menu.

7.  Click OK.

---

**TIP**

To prevent a program from appearing on the Start menu's frequent programs list, open the Registry Editor and display the following key:

    HKCR\Applications\program.exe

Here, *program.exe* is the name of the program's executable file. (If the key doesn't exist, create it.) Create a string value called NoStartPage and set its value to the null string (" "). You can also do this via Tweak UI. Open the Taskbar, XP Start Menu branch and deactivate the check boxes for the programs that you don't want to appear on the Start menu.

---

## Customizing the Internet and E-mail Icons

Above the Start menu's favorite programs list is the **pinned programs** list (pointed out in Figure 10.1), which contains two icons that appear permanently on the Start menu:

Internet     By default, this icon launches the Internet Explorer web browser.

E-mail      By default, this icon launches the Outlook Express email client.

---

**NOTE**

If your computer's manufacturer or reseller preinstalled Windows XP, you might notice that the manufacturer or reseller altered the default Internet and email programs to support other software packaged with your computer. However, you should be able to further modify the defaults to reflect your own preferences.

---

If you have multiple web browsers or email clients installed on your computer, you can customize these icons to launch a different program. Here are the steps to follow:

1. Display the Customize Start Menu dialog box, as described in the previous section.

2. If you want the Internet icon to appear on the Start menu, leave the Internet check box activated; otherwise, deactivate it and continue with step 4.

3. If the Internet check box is activated, use the list to its right to choose the web browser you want associated with the icon.

4. If you want the E-mail icon to appear on the Start menu, leave the E-mail check box activated; otherwise, deactivate it and continue with step 6.

5. If the E-mail check box is activated, use the list to its right to choose the email client you want associated with the icon.

6. Click OK.

Note, too, that it's also possible to change the text and the icon used for the Internet item on the Start menu. You do this by first displaying the following key in the Registry Editor:

```
HKLM\SOFTWARE\Clients\StartMenuInternet\client\
```

Here, *client* is the name of the executable file of the program associated with the icon (such as `Iexplorer.exe` for Internet Explorer). The (Default) setting controls the icon text, and the (Default) setting of the `DefaultIcon` subkey controls the icon.

Customizing the text and icon for the email item is similar. You'll find the necessary settings here:

```
HKLM\Software\Clients\Mail\client\
```

Here, *client* is the name of the program associated with the icon (such as Outlook Express). The (Default) setting controls the icon text, and the (Default) setting of the `DefaultIcon` subkey controls the icon. Note that you might have to create this subkey.

## Setting Program Access and Defaults

You can modify Windows XP (with Service Pack 1 or later installed) to use other programs as the default for activities such as web browsing, email, instant messaging, and media playing. This enables you to have your favorite programs available in more convenient locations and to have those programs launch automatically in certain situations.

Your version of Windows XP is most likely set up to use Internet Explorer, Outlook Express, Windows Messenger, and Windows Media Player as the default programs for web browsing, email, instant messaging, and media playing, respectively. This means that Internet Explorer and Outlook Express are associated with the Start menu's Internet and E-mail items. Also, it means these programs launch automatically in response to certain events. For example, an audio CD you insert plays in Windows Media Player.

You can set up as defaults any other programs you have installed for web browsing, email, instant messaging, and media playing. You can also disable access to programs so that other users cannot launch them on your computer. Here are the steps to follow (you must be logged on with Administrator-level privileges):

1. Select Start, Set Program Access and Defaults. Windows XP displays the Add or Remove Programs window with the Set Program Access and Defaults item selected.

2. Click the configuration you want to start with:

| | |
|---|---|
| Computer Manufacturer | This configuration appears if your computer vendor defined its own program defaults. |
| Microsoft Windows | This configuration is the Windows default as defined by Microsoft. |
| Non-Microsoft | This configuration is generated by Windows XP if you have one or more non-Microsoft programs available in any of the categories (such as a web browser or email program). |
| Custom | Use the item to configure your own default programs. |

3. If you activated the Custom configuration, you see options similar to those shown in Figure 10.3. You can do two things with this configuration:

   • Activate the option buttons of the programs you prefer to use as the system defaults.

   • Deactivate the Enable Access to This Program check box for any program that you don't want other users to have access to.

4. Click OK to put the new defaults into effect.

## Pinning a Favorite Program Permanently to the Start Menu

The Start menu's list of favorite programs is such a time-saving feature that it can be frustrating if a program drops off the list. Another aggravation is that the icons often change position because Windows XP displays the programs in order of popularity. When you display the Start menu, this constant shifting of icons can result in a slight hesitation while you look for the icon you want. (This is particularly true if you've expanded the maximum number of icons.) Contrast both of these problems with the blissfully static nature of the pinned programs list's Internet and E-mail icons, which are always where you need them, when you need them.

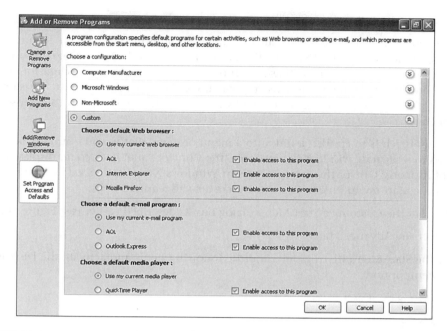

**FIGURE 10.3**    In Service Pack 1 or later, use the Set Program Access and Defaults feature to set up a custom program configuration for your system.

You can get the same effect with other shortcuts by adding—or **pinning**—them to the pinned programs list. To do this, first open the Start menu and find the shortcut you want to work with. Then you have two choices:

- Right-click the shortcut and then click Pin to Start Menu.

- Drag the shortcut and drop it in the pinned programs list.

You can also use this technique to pin shortcuts residing on the desktop to the pinned programs lists. If you decide later on that you no longer want a shortcut pinned to the Start menu, right-click the shortcut and then click Unpin from Start Menu.

---

**TIP**

When you display the Start menu, you can select an item quickly by pressing the first letter of the item's name. If you add several shortcuts to the pinned programs list, however, you might end up with more than one item that begins with the same letter. To avoid conflicts, rename each of these items so that they begin with a number. For example, renaming "Backup" to "1 Backup" means you can select this item by pressing 1 when the Start menu is displayed. (To rename a Start menu item, right-click the item and then click Rename.)

---

10

## Streamlining the Start Menu by Converting Links to Menus

The right side of the Start menu contains a number of built-in Windows XP features, which are set up as links. That is, you click an item and a window or a program runs in response. That's fine for items such as Search or Run, but it's not very efficient for an item such as Control Panel where you're usually looking to launch a specific icon. It seems wasteful to have to open the Control Panel window, launch the icon, and then close Control Panel.

A better approach is to convert a link into a menu of items that would normally be displayed in a separate window. For example, the Control Panel item could display a menu of its icons. One of the nicer features in Windows XP is that it's easy to convert many of the Start menu links into menus. Here are the required steps:

1. Display the Customize Start Menu dialog box as described earlier (see Figure 10.2).

2. Select the Advanced tab.

3. In the Start Menu Items group, find the following items and activate the Display as a Menu option:

   Control Panel

   My Computer

   My Documents

   My Music

   My Pictures

4. In the Start Menu Items group, activate the Favorites check box to add a menu of your Internet Explorer favorites to the Start menu.

5. In the Start Menu Items group, find the Network Connections item and activate the Display as Connect to Menu option. This gives you a menu of network connections, and you can launch any connection by selecting it from the menu.

6. In the Start Menu Items group, find the System Administrative Tools item and activate the Display on the All Programs Menu and the Start Menu option. This gives you an Administrative Tools menu that offers shortcuts to features such as Computer Management snap-in, the Performance monitor, and the Local Security Policy editor.

7. Make sure that the List My Most Recently Opened Documents check box is activated. This adds the My Recent Documents menu to the Start menu, which displays the last 15 documents that you worked with.

8. Click OK to return to the Taskbar and Start Menu Properties dialog box.

9. Click OK.

## Adding, Moving, and Removing Other Start Menu Icons

In addition to the main Start menu, the icons on the All Programs menu and submenus can be customized to suit the way you work. Using the techniques I discuss in this section you can perform the following Start menu productivity boosts:

- Move important features closer to the beginning of the All Programs menu hierarchy

- Remove features you don't use

- Add new commands for features not currently available on the All Programs menu (such as the Registry Editor)

Windows XP offers three methods for adding and removing Start menu shortcuts, and I explain each of them in the next three sections.

### Dragging and Dropping onto the Start Button

The quickest way to add a shortcut is to drag an executable file from Windows Explorer and then do either of the following:

| | |
|---|---|
| Drop it on the Start button | This pins the shortcut to the Start menu. |
| Hover over the Start button | After a second or two, the main Start menu appears. Now hover the file over All Programs until the menu appears, and then drop the file where you want the shortcut to appear. |

### Working with the Start Menu Folder

The All Programs shortcuts are stored in two places within %SystemDrive%\Documents and Settings\:

- The *user*\Start Menu\Programs subfolder, where *user* is the name of the current user. Shortcuts in this subfolder appear only when the user is logged on to Windows XP.

- The All Users\Start Menu\Programs subfolder. Shortcuts in this folder appear to all users.

> **TIP**
>
> A quick way to get to the current user's Start Menu folder is to right-click the Start button and then click Explore.

By working with this folder, you get the most control over not only where your Start menu shortcuts appear, but also the names of those shortcuts. Here's a summary of the techniques you can use:

- Within the Programs folder and its subfolders, you can drag existing shortcuts from one folder to another.

- To create a new shortcut, drag the executable file and drop it inside the folder you want to use. Remember that if you want to create a shortcut for a document or other nonexecutable file, right-drag the file and then select Create Shortcut(s) Here when you drop the file.

- You can create your own folders within the Programs folder hierarchy and they'll appear as submenus within the All Programs menu.

- You can rename a shortcut the same way you rename any file.

- You can delete a shortcut the same way you delete any file.

### Working with All Programs Menu Shortcuts Directly

Many of the chores listed in the previous section are more easily performed by working directly within the All Programs menu itself. That is, you open the All Programs menu, find the shortcut you want to work with, and then use any of these techniques:

- Drag the shortcut to another section of its current menu

- Drag the shortcut to another menu or to the Recycle Bin

- Right-click the shortcut and then select a command (such as Delete) from the context menu

# Customizing the Taskbar for Easier Program and Document Launching

In Windows XP, the taskbar acts somewhat like a mini-application. The purpose of this "application" is to display a button for each running program and to enable you to switch from one program to another. And like most applications these days, the taskbar also has its own toolbars that, in this case, enable you to launch programs and documents.

## Displaying the Built-In Taskbar Toolbars

In Service Pack 2, the Windows XP taskbar comes with five default toolbars:

Address
This toolbar contains a text box into which you can type a local address (such as a folder or file path), a network address (a UNC path), or an Internet address. When you press Enter or click the Go button, Windows XP loads the address into Windows Explorer (if you entered a local or network folder address), an application (if you entered a file path), or Internet Explorer (if you entered an Internet address). In other words, this toolbar works just like the Address Bar used by Windows Explorer and Internet Explorer.

| | |
|---|---|
| Links | This toolbar contains several buttons that link to predefined Internet sites. This is the same as the Links toolbar that appears in Internet Explorer. |
| Windows Media Player | This toolbar contains controls for playing media. When you activate this toolbar, it appears when you minimize the Windows Media Player window. |
| Quick Launch | This is a collection of one-click icons that launch Internet Explorer or Media Player, or clear the desktop. Other applications—such as Microsoft Office—also add icons to this toolbar. |
| Desktop | This toolbar contains all the desktop icons, as well as an icon for Internet Explorer and submenus for My Documents, My Computer, and My Network Places. |

To toggle these toolbars on and off, you must first right-click an empty spot on the taskbar. In the shortcut menu that appears, click Toolbars and then click the toolbar you want to work with.

## Setting Some Taskbar Toolbar Options

After you've displayed a toolbar, there are a number of options you can set to customize the look of the toolbar and to make the toolbars easier to work with. Right-click an empty section of the toolbar and then click one of the following commands:

| | |
|---|---|
| View | This command displays a submenu with two options: Large Icons and Small Icons. These commands determine the size of the toolbar's icons. For example, if a toolbar has more icons than can be shown given its current size, switch to the Small Icons view. |
| Show Text | This command toggles the icon titles on and off. If you turn on the titles, it makes it easier to decipher what each icon does, but you'll see fewer icons in a given space. |
| Show Title | This command toggles the toolbar title (displayed to the left of the icons) on and off. |

### Creating New Taskbar Toolbars

In addition to the predefined taskbar toolbars, you can also create new toolbars that display the contents of any folder on your system. For example, if you have a folder of programs or documents that you launch regularly, you can get one-click access to those items by displaying that folder as a toolbar. Here are the steps to follow:

1. Right-click an empty spot on the toolbar, and then click Toolbars, New Toolbar. Windows XP displays the New Toolbar dialog box.

10

2. Use the folder list provided to highlight the folder you want to display as a toolbar. (Or click Make New Folder to create a new subfolder within the currently highlighted folder.)

3. Click OK. Windows XP creates the new toolbar.

## Putting Taskbar Toolbars to Good Use

Now that you know how to display, create, and customize taskbar toolbars, you can take advantage of them to get one-click access to large numbers of programs and documents. The basic idea is to create a toolbar, populate its folder with shortcuts to programs and documents, and then display the toolbar on the left side of the screen for easy access. Here's how it's done:

> **NOTE**
>
> Before you begin these steps, make sure that the taskbar isn't locked. Right-click an empty section of the taskbar and then click Lock the Taskbar to deactivate it. Also, make sure that the desktop is visible by minimizing all open windows (right-click the taskbar and then click Show the Desktop).

1. Create a new folder.

2. Create shortcuts in this new folder for your favorite documents and programs.

3. Create a new taskbar toolbar that displays the contents of the new folder.

4. Drag the left edge of the new toolbar and drop it on the desktop. Windows XP displays the toolbar as a window.

5. Drag the toolbar window to the left edge of the screen and drop it when the toolbar expands to fill the left edge.

6. Right-click an empty section of the toolbar and activate the Show Title, Show Text, and Always on Top commands. The Always on Top command ensures that the toolbar is always visible, even if other windows are maximized.

As you can see in Figure 10.4, the new toolbar is displayed on the left. Here are some notes about this arrangement:

- You can size the toolbar by dragging (in this case) the right edge to the left or right.

- If you prefer, you can display the toolbar on the right or top edge of the window. To move it, first drag it from the edge and drop it on the desktop. Then drag the toolbar window and drop it on the edge you want to use.

- If you have enough room, you can display multiple toolbars on one edge of the window. For example, you could add the Quick Launch and Links toolbars for easy access to their shortcuts. To do this, display the other toolbar, drag it off the taskbar, drop it on the desktop, and then drag the toolbar window to the edge of the window and drop it on the toolbar that's already in place. You might need to drag the top edge of the toolbar up or down to see its icons.

**FIGURE 10.4**   The new toolbar appears on the left edge of the screen and is visible even when other windows are maximized.

### Improving Productivity by Setting Taskbar Options

The taskbar comes with a few options that can help you be more productive either by saving a few mouse clicks or by giving you more screen room to display your applications. Follow these steps to set these taskbar options:

1. Right-click the taskbar and then click Properties. (Alternatively, open Control Panel's Taskbar and Start Menu icon.) The Taskbar and Start Menu Properties dialog box appears with the Taskbar tab displayed, as shown in Figure 10.5.

2. Activate or deactivate the following options, as required to boost your productivity:

| | |
|---|---|
| Lock the Taskbar | When this check box is activated, you can't resize the taskbar and you can't resize or move any taskbar toolbars. This is useful if you share your computer with other users and you don't want to waste time resetting the taskbar if it's changed by someone else. |

10

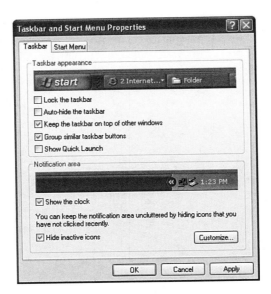

**FIGURE 10.5**    Use the Taskbar tab to set up the taskbar for improved productivity.

| | |
|---|---|
| Auto-Hide the Taskbar | When this check box is activated, Windows XP reduces the taskbar to a thin, blue line at the bottom of the screen when you're not using it. This is useful if you want a bit more screen room for your applications. To redisplay the taskbar, move the mouse to the bottom of the screen. Note, however, that you should consider leaving this option deactivated if you use the taskbar frequently; otherwise, auto-hiding it will slow you down because it takes Windows XP a second or two to restore the taskbar when you hover the mouse over it. |
| Keep the Taskbar on Top of Other Windows | If you deactivate this option, Windows XP hides the taskbar behind any window that's either maximized or moved over the taskbar. To get to the taskbar, you need to either minimize or move the window or you need to press the Windows logo key. This isn't a very efficient way to work, so I recommend leaving this option activated. |
| Group Similar Taskbar Buttons | See the next section, "Controlling Taskbar Grouping," for more information on this setting. |
| Show Quick Launch | Activate this check box to display the Quick Launch toolbar, discussed earlier (refer to "Displaying the Built-In Taskbar Toolbars"). Quick Launch is a handy way to access Internet Explorer, the desktop, and Windows Media Player (as well as any other shortcuts you add to the Quick Launch folder), so I recommend activating this option. |
| Show the Clock | Leave this check box activated to keep the clock displayed in the notification area. |

Hide Inactive Icons    When this check box is activated, Windows XP hides notification area icons that you haven't used for a while. This gives the taskbar a bit more room to display program buttons, so leave this option activated if you don't use the notification area icons all that often. If you don't use the icons frequently, deactivate this option to avoid having to click the arrow to display the hidden icons.

**NOTE**

If your notification area is crowded with icons, it's inefficient to display all the icons if you use only a few of them. Instead of showing them all, leave the Hide Inactive Icons check box activated and click Customize. For the icons you use often, click the item's Behavior column and then click Always Show in the list that appears. This tells Windows XP to always display the icon in the notification area.

3. Click OK.

## Controlling Taskbar Grouping

One of the new things built into the Windows XP taskbar is the grouping feature. When the taskbar fills up with buttons, Windows XP consolidates icons from the same program into a single button, as shown in Figure 10.6. To access one of these grouped windows, you click the button and then click the window you want.

**TIP**

You can close all of a group's windows at once by right-clicking the group button and then clicking Close Group.

**FIGURE 10.6**    When the taskbar gets filled with buttons, Windows XP groups similar windows into a single button, as shown here with Windows Explorer and Internet Explorer.

The grouping feature makes it easier to read the name of each taskbar button, but the price is a slight efficiency drop because it takes two clicks to activate a window instead of one. If you don't like this tradeoff, you can disable the grouping feature by right-clicking the taskbar, clicking Properties, and then deactivating the Group Similar Taskbar Buttons check box.

**TIP**

Another way to prevent grouping is to give the taskbar more room to display buttons. The easiest way to do that is to resize the taskbar by dragging its top edge up until the taskbar

10

expands. If this doesn't work, the taskbar is probably locked. Unlock it by right-clicking the taskbar and then clicking Lock the Taskbar.

Alternatively, you can tweak the grouping feature to suit the way you work. To do this, open the Registry Editor and head for the following key:

`HKCU\Software\Microsoft\Windows\CurrentVersion\Explorer\Advanced\`

Add a `DWORD` value called `TaskbarGroupSize` and set it to one of the following values:

| | |
|---|---|
| 0 | When the grouping kicks in (that is, when the taskbar gets full), Windows XP will group the buttons from only the applications that you have used the least. |
| 1 | When the grouping kicks in, Windows XP will group the buttons from only the application that has the most windows open. If a second application surpasses the number of open windows in the first application, the second application's windows will be grouped as well. |
| x | Windows XP will group any application that has at least x windows open, where x is a number between 2 and 99. Note that the grouping occurs even if the taskbar is not full. |

Note that you must log off or restart Windows XP to put the new setting into effect. Note, too, that you can also change this setting via Tweak UI. Display the Taskbar, Grouping item.

## Modifying the Start Menu and Taskbar with Group Policies

You've seen throughout this book that the group policies offer unprecedented control over the Windows XP interface without having to modify the Registry directly. This is particularly true of the Start menu and taskbar, which boast more than 40 policies that do everything from removing Start menu links such as Run and Help to hiding the taskbar's notification area. To see these policies, launch the Group Policy editor and select User Configuration, Administrative Templates, Start Menu and Taskbar.

Most of the policies are straightforward: By enabling them, you remove a feature from the Start menu or taskbar. For example, enabling the Remove Run Menu from Start Menu policy hides the Start menu's Run command for the current user. This is a handy feature if you're trying to restrict a user to using only those programs and documents that appear on the Start menu. Here are a few policies that I think are the most useful:

| | |
|---|---|
| Remove Drag-and-Drop Context Menus on the Start Menu | Enable this policy to prevent the current user from rearranging the Start menu using drag-and-drop techniques. |
| Prevent Changes to Taskbar and Start Menu Settings | Enable this policy to prevent the current user from accessing the Taskbar and Start Menu Properties dialog box. |

| | |
|---|---|
| Remove Access to the Context Menus for the Taskbar | Enable this policy to prevent the current user from seeing the taskbar's shortcut (also called **context**) menus by right-clicking the taskbar. |
| Do Not Keep History of Recently Opened Documents | Enable this policy to prevent Windows XP from tracking the current user's recently opened documents. |
| Clear History of Recently Opened Documents on Exit | Enable this policy to remove all documents from the current user's recent documents list whenever Windows XP exits. |
| Remove Balloon Tips on Start Menu Items | Enable this policy to prevent the current user from seeing the balloon tips that Windows XP displays when it prompts you about new hardware being detected, downloading automatic updates, and so on. |
| Remove User Name from Start Menu | Enable this policy to prevent the current user's name from appearing at the top of the Start menu. This is a good idea if you need more room on the Start menu for the pinned or frequent program lists. |
| Hide the Notification Area | Enable this policy to prevent the current user from seeing the taskbar's notification area. |
| Do Not Display Custom Toolbars in the Taskbar | Enable this policy to prevent the current user from adding custom toolbars to the taskbar. |

## Using Screen Space Efficiently

How images appear on your monitor and how efficiently you use the monitor's viewable area is a function of two measurements: the **color quality** and the screen resolution. The color quality is a measure of the number of colors available to display images on the screen. Color quality is usually expressed in either bits or total colors. For example, a 4-bit display can handle up to 16 colors (because 2 to the power of 4 equals 16). The most common values are 16-bit (65,536 colors), 24-bit (16,777,216 colors), and 32-bit (16,777,216 colors).

The **screen resolution** is a measure of the density of the pixels used to display the screen image. The pixels are arranged in a row-and-column format, so the resolution is expressed as rows by columns, where **rows** is the number of pixel rows and **columns** is the number of pixel columns. For example, an 800 by 600 resolution means screen images are displayed using 800 rows of pixels and 600 columns of pixels.

How does all this affect productivity?

- In general, the greater the number of colors, the sharper your screen image will appear. Sharper images, especially text, are easier to read and put less strain on the eyes.

10

---

**Sharpening Text with ClearType**

If you read a lot of onscreen text, particularly if you use a notebook or an LCD screen, activate Windows XP's ClearType feature, which drastically reduces the jagged edges of screen fonts and makes text super-sharp and far easier to read than regular screen text. To activate this feature, launch Control Panel's Display icon, select the Appearance tab, and click Effects. In the Effects dialog box, make sure that the Use the Following Method to Smooth Edges of Screen Fonts check box is activated and then select ClearType from the list below it. Click OK and then click OK in the Display Properties dialog box to put the new setting into effect. Note, too, that you can customize some ClearType settings using the ClearType Tuner PowerToy, available from Microsoft's PowerToys for Windows XP site (www.microsoft.com/windowsxp/downloads/powertoys/xppowertoys.mspx).

---

- At higher resolutions, individual screen items—such as icons and dialog boxes—appear smaller because these items tend to have a fixed height and width, expressed in pixels. For example, a dialog box that's 400 pixels wide will appear half as wide as the screen at 800 by 600. However, it will appear to be only one quarter of the screen width at 1,600 by 1,024 (a common resolution for very larger monitors). This means that at higher resolutions your maximized windows will appear larger, so you'll get a larger work area.

The key thing to bear in mind about all this is that there's occasionally a tradeoff between color quality and resolution. That is, depending on how much video memory is installed on your graphics adapter, you might have to trade higher resolution for lower color quality, or vice versa.

To change the screen resolution and color quality, follow these steps:

1. Open the Control Panel's Display icon to get the Display Properties dialog box onscreen.

2. Display the Settings tab, as shown in Figure 10.7.

3. To set the resolution, drag the Screen Resolution slider left or right.

4. To set the color quality, choose an item from the Color Quality list.

5. Click OK. Windows XP performs the adjustment and then displays a dialog box asking if you want to keep the new setting.

6. Click Yes.

---

**NOTE**

If your graphics adapter or monitor can't handle the new resolution or color quality, you'll end up with a garbled display. In this case, just wait for 15 seconds and Windows XP will restore the resolution to its original setting.

---

**FIGURE 10.7**    Use the Settings tab to set the screen resolution and color quality.

# From Here

Here's a list of sections in this book where you'll find information related to the topics in this chapter:

- To learn how to personalize Windows Explorer, see "Customizing Windows Explorer" in Chapter 2.

- For the details on customizing the New menu and the Open With list, see the sections in Chapter 3 titled "Customizing the New Menu" and "Customizing Windows XP's Open With List."

- To learn how to customize digital media folders, see "Customizing Media Folders" in Chapter 4.

- For the details on group policies and Tweak UI, see Chapter 7, "Using Control Panel, Group Policies, and Tweak UI."

- To learn more about the Registry, see Chapter 8, "Getting to Know the Windows XP Registry."

- To learn how to personalize Internet Explorer, see "Customizing Internet Explorer" in Chapter 18.

# Tuning Windows XP's Performance

We often wonder why our workaday computer chores seem to take just as long as they ever did, despite the fact that our hardware is, generally speaking, bigger, better, and faster than ever. The answer to this apparent riddle is related to Parkinson's Law of Data, which states that data expands to fill the space available for storage. On a more general level, Parkinson's Law could be restated as follows: The increase in software system requirements is directly proportional to the increase in hardware system capabilities. A slick new chip is released that promises a 30% speed boost; software designers, seeing the new chip gain wide acceptance, add extra features to their already bloated code to take advantage of the higher performance level; then another new chip is released, followed by another software upgrade—and the cycle continues *ad nauseum* as these twin engines of computer progress lurch codependently into the future.

So, how do you break out of the performance deadlock created by the immovable object of software code bloat meeting the irresistible force of hardware advancement? By optimizing your system to minimize the effects of overgrown applications and to maximize the native capabilities of your hardware. Learning how to optimize memory, applications, and hard disks is the key to unleashing your system's performance potential, and that's exactly what I'll show you how to do in this chapter.

## Monitoring Performance

Performance optimization is a bit of a black art in that every user has different needs, every configuration has different operating parameters, and every system can react in a unique and unpredictable way to performance tweaks. What this means is that if you want to optimize your system, you have to get to know how it works, what it needs, and how it reacts to changes. You can do this by just using the system and paying attention to how things look and feel, but a more rigorous approach is often called for. To that end, the next few sections take you on a brief tour of Windows XP's performance monitoring capabilities.

## Monitoring Performance with Task Manager

The Task Manager utility is excellent for getting a quick overview of the current state of the system. To get it on-screen, press Ctrl+Alt+Delete. If the Windows Security dialog box appears, click the Task Manager button.

> **TIP**
>
> To bypass the Windows Security dialog box, right-click an empty section of the taskbar and then click Task Manager.

The Processes tab, shown in Figure 11.1, displays a list of the programs, services, and system components that are currently running on your system. The processes are displayed in the order in which they were started, but you can change the order by clicking the column headings. (To return to the original, chronological order. you must shut down and restart Task Manager.)

**FIGURE 11.1**    The Processes tab lists your system's running programs and services.

In addition to the name of each process and the user who started the process, you also see two performance measures:

| CPU | The values in this column tell you the percentage of CPU resources that each process is using. If your system seems sluggish, look for a process that is consuming all or nearly all of the CPU's resources. Most programs will monopolize the CPU occasionally for short periods, but a program that is stuck at 100 (percent) for a long time most likely has some kind of problem. In that case, try shutting down the program. If that doesn't work, click the program's process and then click End Process. Click Yes when Windows XP asks whether you're sure that you want to do this. |
| Mem Usage | This value tells you approximately how much memory the process is using. This value is less useful because a process might genuinely require a lot of memory to operate. However, if this value is steadily increasing for a process that you're not using, it could indicate a problem and you should shut down the process. |

**TIP**

The four default columns in the Processes tab aren't the only data available to you. Select the View, Select Columns command to see a list of more than two dozen items that you can add to the Processes tab.

The Performance Tab, shown in Figure 11.2, offers a more substantial collection of performance data, particularly for that all-important component, your system's memory.

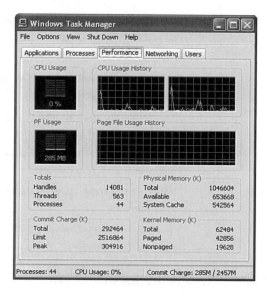

**FIGURE 11.2**    The Performance tab lists various numbers related to your system's memory components.

The graphs show you both the current value and the values over time for the **CPU usage** (the total percentage of CPU resources that your running processes are using) and the Page File Usage.

What is a page file? Your computer can address memory beyond what is physically installed on the system. This nonphysical memory is called **virtual memory**, and it's implemented by using a piece of your hard disk that's set up to emulate physical memory. This hard disk storage is actually a single file called a **page file** (or sometimes a **paging file** or a **swap file**). When physical memory is full, Windows XP makes room for new data by taking some data that's currently in memory and swapping it out to the page file. The PF Usage graph shows the current size of the page file, and the Page File Usage History graphs shows the relative size of the page file over time.

Below the graphs are various numbers. The items in the Totals group appeal only to programmers, so we'll skip them. Here's what the other values mean:

> **NOTE**
>
> The memory values are listed in kilobytes. To convert to megabytes, divide by 1,024.

| | |
|---|---|
| Physical Memory Total | The total amount of physical RAM in your system. |
| Physical Memory Available | The amount of physical RAM that Windows XP has available for your programs. Note that Windows XP does not include the system cache (see the next item) in this total. |
| Physical Memory System Cache | The amount of physical RAM that Windows XP has set aside to store recently used programs and documents. |
| Commit Charge Total | The combined total of physical RAM and virtual memory the system is using. |
| Commit Charge Limit | The combined total of physical RAM and virtual memory available to the system. |
| Commit Charge Peak | The maximum combined total of physical RAM and virtual memory the system has used so far in this session. |
| Kernel Memory Total | The total amount of RAM used by the Windows XP system components and device drivers. |
| Kernel Memory Paged | The amount of kernel memory that is mapped to pages in virtual memory. |
| Kernel Memory Nonpaged | The amount of kernel memory that cannot be mapped to pages in virtual memory. |

Here are some notes related to these values that will help you monitor memory-related performance issues:

- If the Physical Memory Available value approaches zero, it means your system is starved for memory. You might have too many programs running or a large program is using lots of memory.

- If the Physical Memory System Cache value is much less than half the Physical Memory Total value, it means your system isn't operating as efficiently as it could because Windows XP can't store enough recently used data in memory. Because Windows XP gives up some of the system cache when it needs RAM, close down programs you don't need.

- If the Commit Charge Total value remains higher than the Physical Memory Total value, it means Windows XP is doing a lot of work swapping data to and from the page file, which greatly slows performance.

- If the Commit Charge Peak value is higher than the Physical Memory Total value, it means at some point in the current session Windows XP had to use the page file. If the Commit Charge Total value is currently less than Physical Memory Total value, the peak value might have been a temporary event, but you should monitor the peak over time, just to make sure.

In all of these situations, the quickest solution is to reduce the system's memory footprint either by closing documents or by closing applications. For the latter, use the Processes tab to determine which applications are using the most memory and then shut down the ones you can live without for now. The better, but more expensive, solution is to add more physical RAM to your system. This decreases the likelihood that Windows XP will need to use the paging file, and it also enables Windows XP to increase the size of the system cache, which greatly improves performance.

---

**TIP**

If you're not sure which process corresponds to which program, display the Applications tab, right-click a program, and then click Go to Process. Task Manager displays the Processes tab and selects the process that corresponds to the program.

---

## Monitoring Performance with System Monitor

For more advanced performance monitoring, Windows XP offers the System Monitor tool, which you can get to by selecting Start, Run, typing **perfmon.msc**, and clicking OK. The System Monitor appears, as shown in Figure 11.3.

System Monitor's job is to provide you with real-time reports on how various system settings and components are performing. Each item is called a **counter** and the displayed counters are listed at the bottom of the window. Each counter is assigned a different colored line, and that color corresponds to the colored lines shown in the graph. Note, too, that you can get specific numbers for a counter—the most recent value, the average, the minimum, and the maximum—by clicking a counter and reading the boxes just below the graphs.

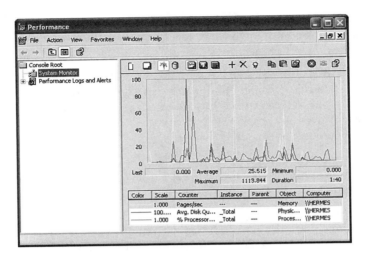

**FIGURE 11.3**    Use System Monitor to keep an eye on various system settings and components.

The idea is that you should configure System Monitor to show the processes you're interested in (page file size, free memory, and so on) and then keep System Monitor running while you perform your normal chores. By examining the System Monitor readouts from time to time, you gain an appreciation of what is typical on your system. Then, if you run into performance problems, you can check System Monitor to see whether you've run into any bottlenecks or anomalies.

By default, System Monitor shows only the Kernel Processor Usage setting, which tells you the percentage of time the processor is busy. To add another setting to the System Monitor window, follow these steps:

1. Right-click a counter and then click Add Counters. The Add Counters dialog box appears.

2. Use the Performance Object list to select a counter category (such as Memory, Paging File, or Processor).

3. Activate the Select Counters from List option.

4. Select the counter you want and then click Add. If you need more information about the item, click the Explain button.

5. Repeat step 4 to add any other counters you want to monitor.

6. Click OK.

Now that you know how to monitor performance, it's time to get practical with a few specific optimizations. The rest of this chapter shows you how to optimize items such as the Windows XP startup, applications, the hard disk, virtual memory, and more.

# Optimizing Startup

One of the longest-running debates in computer circles involves the question of whether or not to turn off the computer when you're not using it. The "off" camp believes that shutting down the computer reduces hard disk wear and tear (because the disk's platter's spin full-time, even when the computer is idle), prevents damage from power surges or power failures that occur while the machine is off, and saves energy. The "on" camp believes that cold starts are hard on many computer components, that energy can be saved by taking advantage of power-saving features, and that leaving the computer running is more productive because it avoids the lengthy startup process.

In the end, I believe it's the overall boot time that usually determines which of these camps you belong to. If the startup time is just unbearably long, you'll certainly be more inclined to leave your computer running all the time. Fortunately, Windows XP has made great strides on improving startup times, which are now routinely measured in seconds instead of minutes. However, if you're convinced that turning off the computer is a sensible move but you hate waiting even for Windows XP's faster startup process, the next few sections provide you with a few tips for improving startup performance even more.

## Reducing or Eliminating BIOS Checks

Many computers run through one or more diagnostic checks at system startup. For example, it's common for machines to check the integrity of the system memory chips. That seems like a good idea, but it can take an interminable amount of time to complete on a system with a great deal of memory. Access your system's BIOS settings and turn off these checks to reduce the overall time of the computer's Power-On Self Test.

> **NOTE**
>
> How you access your computer's BIOS settings (also called the **CMOS setup**) depends on the manufacturer. You usually have to press a function key (usually F1, F2, or F10), a key such as Delete or Esc, or a key combination. During the POST, you should see some text on the screen that tells you what key or key combination to press.

## Reducing the OS Choices Menu Timeout

If you have two or more operating systems on your computer, you see Windows XP's OS Choices menu at startup. If you're paying attention to the startup, you can press the Enter key as soon as this menu appears and your system will boot the default operating system. If your mind is focused elsewhere, however, the startup will be delayed 30 seconds until the default choice is selected automatically. If this happens to you frequently, you can reduce that 30-second timeout to speed up the startup. There are four ways to do this:

- Edit the BOOT.INI file. In the [boot loader] section, change the timeout value.

- Select Start, Run, type **msconfig -4**, and click OK. In the System Configuration Utility's BOOT.INI tab, modify the value in the Timeout text box.

- Run Control Panel's System icon to get to the System Properties dialog box. Display the Advanced tab, click Settings in the Startup and Recovery group, and then adjust the value of the Time to Display List of Operating Systems spin box.

- At the command prompt, enter the following command (replace *ss* with the number of seconds you want to use for the timeout):

```
BOOTCFG /Timeout ss
```

> **TIP**
>
> If your system has multiple hardware profiles, the Hardware Profile menu also appears for 30 seconds before choosing the default profile. You can reduce this timeout by launching Control Panel's System icon, selecting the Hardware tab, and then clicking Hardware Profiles. In the Hardware Profiles dialog box, activate the Select the First Profile Listed If I Don't Select a Profile In option and use the spin box below it to set the reduced timeout.

## Turning Off the Startup Splash Screen

In BOOT.INI, use the /NOGUIBOOT switch as described in Chapter 1, "Customizing and Troubleshooting the Windows XP Startup" (refer to the section "Using the BOOT.INI Switches"). This prevents the Windows XP splash screen from appearing, which will shave a small amount of time from the startup.

> **CAUTION**
>
> Using /NOGUIBOOT means that you won't see any startup blue-screen errors. In other words, if a problem occurs, all you'll know for sure is that your system has hung, but you won't know why. For this reason, the small performance improvement represented by using /NOGUIBOOT is likely not enough to offset the lack of startup error messages.

## Upgrading Your Device Drivers

Device drivers that are designed to work with Windows XP will generally load faster than older drivers. Therefore, you should check each of your device drivers to see whether a Windows XP–compatible version exists and, where available, upgrade to that driver as described in Chapter 14, "Getting the Most Out of Device Manager" (see the section "Updating a Device Driver").

## Using an Automatic Logon

One of the best ways to reduce startup time frustration is to ignore the startup altogether by doing something else (such as getting a cup of coffee) while the boot chores occur. This strategy is foiled if the startup is interrupted by the logon process. If you're the only person who uses your computer, you can overcome this problem by setting up Windows

XP to log you on automatically. I discussed this in Chapter 1; refer to the section "Setting Up an Automatic Logon."

> **Not Requiring Ctrl+Alt+Delete**
>
> If you must log on, and if you're using the classic logon method (that is, you're not using Windows XP's Welcome screen), Windows XP usually asks you to press Ctrl+Alt+Delete before it displays the Log On to Windows dialog box. You can save a startup step by eliminating this usually unnecessary procedure. I showed you how to do this in Chapter 6, "Getting the Most Out of User Accounts" (refer to the section "Requiring Ctrl+Alt+Delete at Startup").

## Reducing or Eliminating Startup Programs

By far the biggest startup bottleneck is the array of programs scheduled to launch automatically when Windows XP loads. Loading many small programs or just a couple of large programs can slow the startup to an excruciating crawl. Use the techniques I discussed in Chapter 5, "Installing and Running Applications," (refer to the section "Launching Applications and Scripts at Startup") to reduce the number of startup programs to only these you absolutely need to run first.

## Using Hibernation Mode

**Hibernation mode**, which is supported by most new PCs, saves the current contents of memory (running programs, open documents, and so on) to a file on your hard disk and then shuts down the computer. When you turn the machine back on, Windows XP bypasses the usual startup routines and restores the memory contents from the hibernation file. The result is that your system is back on its feet in just a few seconds.

Before you can use hibernation, you need to make sure that it's enabled on your system by first opening Control Panel's Power Options icon. In the Power Options Properties dialog box, display the Hibernate tab and activate the Enable Hibernation check box.

To put the computer into hibernation, you have two ways to proceed:

- If you use the Welcome screen, select Start, Turn Off Computer, hold down the Shift key, and then click Hibernate.

- If you use the Classic logon screen, select Start, Shut Down and then select Hibernate from the list.

> **CAUTION**
>
> The contents of your system's memory are stored in a file called `Hiberfil.sys` in the root folder of the `%SystemDrive%` (usually C:). This is hardwired into the system and can't be changed. Therefore, before enabling hibernation, make sure that you have plenty of free space on the `%SystemDrive%`. Note that `Hiberfil.sys` will be as large as the amount of RAM on your system. If you have 512MB RAM, the hibernation file will also be approximately 512MB.

### Configuring the Prefetcher

**Prefetching** is a Windows XP performance feature that analyzes disk usage and then reads into memory the data that you or your system accesses most frequently. The prefetcher can be used to speed up booting, application launching, or both. You configure the prefetcher using the following Registry setting:

```
HKLM\SYSTEM\CurrentControlSet\Control\SessionManager\Memory Management\
PrefetchParameters\EnablePrefetcher
```

Set this value to 1 for application-only prefetching, 2 for boot-only prefetching, or 3 for both application and boot prefetching. I recommend setting this value to 2 for boot-only prefetching. This will improve boot performance and, on most systems, have little or no effect on application performance because commonly used application launch files are probably in the RAM cache anyway.

# Optimizing Applications

Running applications is the reason we use Windows XP, so it's a rare user who doesn't want his applications to run as fast as possible. The next few sections offer some pointers for improving the performance of applications under Windows XP.

### Adding More Memory

All applications run in RAM, of course, so the more RAM you have, the less likely it is that Windows XP will have to store excess program or document data in the page file on the hard disk, which is a real performance killer. In Task Manager or System Monitor, watch the Available Memory value. If it starts to get too low, you should consider adding RAM to your system.

### Installing to the Fastest Hard Drive

If your system has multiple hard drives, install your applications on the fastest drive. This will enable Windows XP to access the application's data and documents faster.

### Optimizing Application Launching

As discussed in the previous section, Windows XP's prefetcher component can optimize disk files for booting, application launching, or both. It probably won't make much difference, but experiment with setting the Registry's EnablePrefetcher value to 1 to optimize application launching.

### Getting the Latest Device Drivers

If your application works with a device, check with the manufacturer or Windows Update to see whether a newer version of the device driver is available. In general, the newer the driver, the faster its performance. I show you how to update device drivers in Chapter 14; see the section titled "Updating a Device Driver."

## Optimizing Windows XP for Programs

You can set up Windows XP so that it is optimized to run programs. This involves two things:

- **Processor scheduling**, which determines how much time the processor allocates to the computer's activities. In particular, processor scheduling differentiates between the **foreground program**—the program in which you are currently working—and **background programs**—programs that perform tasks, such as printing or backing up, while you work in another program.

- The **system cache**, a portion of memory that holds recently used data for faster access. In terms of memory usage, the bigger the system cache, the less memory is available for your programs, which can reduce performance.

Optimizing programs means configuring Windows XP so that it gives more CPU time and memory to your programs. This is the default in Windows XP, but it's worth your time to make sure that this default configuration is still the case on your system. Here are the steps to follow:

1. Launch Control Panel's System icon to display the System Properties dialog box.

2. Display the Advanced Tab.

3. In the Performance group, click Settings to display the Performance Options dialog box.

4. Display the Advanced tab, shown in Figure 11.4.

5. In the Processor Scheduling group, activate the Programs option.

6. In the Memory Usage group, activate the Programs option.

7. Click OK.

8. When Windows XP tells you the changes require a restart, click OK to return to the System Properties dialog box.

9. Click OK. Windows XP asks whether you want to restart your system.

10. Click Yes.

## Setting the Program Priority in Task Manager

You can improve the performance of a program by adjusting the priority given to the program by your computer's processor. The processor enables programs to run by doling out thin slivers of its computing time to each program. These time slivers are called **cycles** because they are given to programs cyclically. For example, if you have three programs running—A, B, and C—the processor gives a cycle to A, one to B, another to C, and then back to A again. This cycling happens quickly, appearing seamless when you work with each program.

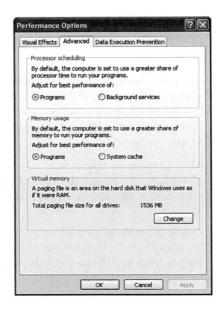

**FIGURE 11.4**    In the Performance Options dialog box, use the Advanced tab to optimize Windows XP for programs.

The **base priority** is a ranking that determines the relative frequency with which a program gets processor cycles. A program given a higher frequency gets more cycles, which improves the program's performance. For example, suppose that you raise the priority of program A. The processor might give a cycle to A, one to B, another to A, one to C, another to A, and so on.

Follow these steps to change a program's priority:

1. Launch the program you want to work with.

2. Open Task Manager, as described earlier in this chapter (refer to "Monitoring Performance with Task Manager").

3. Display the Processes tab.

4. Right-click your application's process to display its shortcut menu.

5. Click Set Priority, and then click (from highest priority to lowest) Realtime, High, or AboveNormal.

---

**TIP**

After you've changed the priority of one or more programs, you might forget the values that you have assigned to each one. To help, you can view the priority for all the items in the Processes tab. Click View and then click Select Columns to display the Select Columns dialog box. Activate the Base Priority check box and click OK. This adds a Base Priority column to the Processes list.

---

# Optimizing the Hard Disk

Windows XP uses the hard disk to fetch application data and documents as well as to temporarily store data in the page file. Therefore, optimizing your hard disk can greatly improve Windows XP's overall performance, as described in the next few sections.

## Examining Hard Drive Performance Specifications

If you're looking to add another drive to your system, your starting point should be the drive itself: specifically, its theoretical performance specifications. Compare the drive's average seek time with other drives (the lower the value the better). Also, pay attention to the rate at which the drive spins the disk's platters. A 7,200 RPM (or higher) drive will have noticeably faster performance than, say, a 5,400 RPM drive.

## Performing Hard Drive Maintenance

For an existing drive, optimization is the same as maintenance, so you should implement the maintenance plan I discuss in Chapter 12, "Maintaining Your Windows XP System." For a hard disk, this means doing the following:

- Keep an eye on the disk's free space to make sure that it doesn't get too low.
- Periodically clean out any unnecessary files on the disk.
- Uninstall any programs or devices you no longer use.
- Check all partitions for errors frequently.
- Defragment partitions on a regular schedule.

## Disabling Compression and Encryption

If you use NTFS on a partition, Windows XP enables you to compress files to save space, as well as to encrypt files for security. (See "Converting FAT16 and FAT32 Partitions to NTFS," later in this chapter.) From a performance point of view, however, you shouldn't use compression and encryption on a partition if you don't have to. Both technologies slow down disk accesses because of the overhead involved in the compression/decompression and encryption/decryption processes.

## Turning Off the Indexing Service

The Indexing Service is a Windows XP background process that indexes the contents of a drive on-the-fly as you add or delete data. This greatly speeds up content-based file searches because Windows XP knows the contents of each file. However, you should consider turning off the Indexing Service for a drive if you don't do much file searching. To do this, follow these steps:

1. Select Start, My Computer.
2. Right-click the drive you want to work with and then click Properties. Windows XP displays the drive's property sheet.

3. On the General tab, deactivate the Allow Indexing Service to Index This Disk for Fast File Searching check box.

4. Click OK.

## Enabling Write Caching

You should also make sure that your hard disk has **write caching** enabled. Write caching means that Windows XP doesn't flush changed data to the disk until the system is idle, which improves performance. The downside is that a power outage or system crash means the data never gets written, so the changes are lost. The chances of this happening are minimal, so I recommend leaving write caching enabled, which is the Windows XP default. To make sure, follow these steps:

1. Launch Control Panel's System icon to display the System Properties dialog box.

2. Display the Hardware tab.

3. Click Device Manager to launch the Device Manager window.

4. Open the Disk Drives branch and double-click your hard disk to display its property sheet.

5. In the Policies tab, make sure that the Enable Write Caching on the Disk check box is activated.

6. Click OK.

## Converting FAT16 and FAT32 Partitions to NTFS

The NTFS file system is your best choice if you want optimal hard disk performance because, in most cases, NTFS outperforms both FAT16 and FAT32. (This is particularly true with large partitions and with partitions that that have lots of files.) Note, however, that for best NTFS performance you should format a partition as NTFS and then add files to it. If this isn't possible, Windows XP offers the CONVERT utility for converting a FAT16 or FAT32 drive to NTFS:

```
CONVERT volume /FS:NTFS [/V] [/CvtArea:filename] [/NoSecurity] [/X]
```

| | |
|---|---|
| *volume* | Specifies the drive letter (followed by a colon) or volume name you want to convert. |
| /FS:NTFS | Specifies that the file system is to be converted to NTFS. |
| /V | Uses verbose mode, which gives detailed information during the conversion. |
| /CvtArea:*filename* | Specifies a contiguous placeholder file in the root directory that will be used to store the NTFS system files. |

| | |
|---|---|
| `/NoSecurity` | Specifies that the default NTFS permissions are not to be applied to this volume. All the converted files and folders will be accessible by everyone. |
| `/X` | Forces the volume to dismount first if it currently has open files. |

For example, running the following command at the command prompt converts drive C to NTFS:

```
convert c: /FS:NTFS
```

Note, however, that if Windows XP is installed on the partition you're trying to convert, you'll see the following message:

```
Convert cannot gain exclusive access to the C: drive, so it cannot
convert it now. Would you like to schedule it to be converted the
next time the system restarts? <Y/N>
```

In this case, press Y to schedule the conversion.

Note that if you make the move to NTFS, either via formatting a partition during Setup or by using the CONVERT utility, you can implement a couple of other tweaks to maximize NTFS performance. I cover these tweaks in the next two sections.

## Turning Off 8.3 Filename Creation

To support legacy applications that don't understand long filenames, for each file NTFS keeps track of a shorter name that conforms to the old 8.3 standard used by the original DOS file systems. The overhead involved in tracking two names for one file isn't much for a small number of files, but it can become onerous if a folder has a huge number of files (300,000 or more).

To disable the tracking of an 8.3 name for each file, enter the following statement at the command prompt:

**FSUTIL BEHAVIOR SET DISABLE8DOT3 1**

Note, too, that you can do the same thing by changing the value of the following Registry setting to 1 (note that the default value is 0):

```
HKLM\SYSTEM\CurrentControlSet\Control\FileSystem\NtfsDisable8dot3NameCreation
```

## Disabling Last Access Timestamp

For each folder and file, NTFS stores an attribute called Last Access Time that tells you when the folder or file was last accessed by the user. If you have folders that have a large number of files and if you use programs that access the files frequently, writing the Last

Access Time data can slow down NTFS. To disable writing of the Last Access Time attribute, enter the following statement at the command prompt:

```
FSUTIL BEHAVIOR SET DISABLELASTACCESS 1
```

You can achieve the same effect by changing the value of the following Registry setting to 1 (note that the default value is 0):

```
HKLM\SYSTEM\CurrentControlSet\Control\FileSystem\NtfsDisableLastAccessUpdate
```

# Optimizing Virtual Memory

No matter how much main memory your system boasts, Windows XP still creates and uses a page file for virtual memory. To maximize page file performance, you should make sure that Windows XP is working with the page file optimally. The next few sections present some techniques that help you do just that.

### Storing the Page File Optimally

The location of the page file can have a major impact on its performance. There are three things you should consider:

- Store the page file on the hard disk that has the fastest access time—You'll see later in this section that you can tell Windows XP which hard disk to use for the page file. If you have multiple hard disks (not just multiple partitions of a single disk), you should store the page file on the disk that has the fastest access time.

- Store the page file on an uncompressed partition—Windows XP is happy to store the page file on a compressed NTFS partition. However, as with all file operations on a compressed partition, the performance of page file operations suffers because of the compression and decompression required. Therefore, you should store the page file on an uncompressed partition.

- Store the page file on the hard disk that has the most free space—Windows XP expands and contracts the page file dynamically depending on the system's needs. To give Windows XP the most flexibility, make sure that the page file resides on a hard disk that has a lot of free space.

See "Changing the Paging File's Location and Size," later in this chapter, for the details on moving the page file.

### Splitting the Page File

If you have two or more physical drives (not just two or more partitions on a single physical drive), splitting the page file over each drive can improve performance because it means Windows XP can extract data from each drive's page file simultaneously. For example, if your current initial page file size is 384MB, you'd set up a page file on a drive with a 192MB initial size, and another page file on a second drive with a 192MB initial size.

Again, see "Changing the Paging File's Location and Size" to learn how to split the page file.

## Customizing the Page File Size

By default, Windows XP sets the initial size of the page file to 1.5 times the amount of RAM in your system, and it sets the maximum size of the page file to 3 times the amount of RAM. For example, on a system with 256MB RAM, the page file's initial size will be 384MB and its maximum size will be 768MB. The default values work well on most systems, but you might want to customize these sizes to suit your own configuration. Here are some notes about custom page file sizes:

- The less RAM you have, the more likely it is that Windows XP will use the page file, so the Windows XP default page file sizes make sense. If your computer has less than 512MB RAM, you should leave the page file sizes as is.

- The more RAM you have, the less likely it is that Windows XP will use the page file. Therefore, the default initial page file size is too large and the disk space reserved by Windows XP is wasted. On systems with 512MB RAM or more, you should set the initial page file size to half the RAM size, while leaving the maximum size at three times RAM, just in case.

- If disk space is at a premium and you can't move the page file to a drive with more free space, set the initial page file size to 2MB (the minimum size supported by Windows XP). This should eventually result in the smallest possible page file, but you'll see a bit of a performance drop because Windows XP will often have to dynamically increase the size of the page file as you work with your programs.

- You might think that setting the initial size and the maximum size to the same (relatively large; say, two or three times RAM) value would improve performance because it would mean that Windows XP would never resize the page file. In practice, however, it has been shown that this trick does *not* improve performance, and in some cases can actually decrease performance.

- If you have a large amount of RAM (at least 1GB), you might think that Windows XP would never need virtual memory, so that it would be okay to turn off the page file. This won't work, however, because Windows XP needs the page file anyway, and some programs might crash if no virtual memory is present.

See "Changing the Paging File's Location and Size" to learn how to customize the page file size.

## Watching the Page File Size

Monitor the page file performance to get a feel for how it works under normal conditions, where *normal* means while running your usual collection of applications and your usual number of open windows and documents.

Start up all the programs you normally use (and perhaps a few extra, for good measure) and then watch System Monitor's Process\Page File Bytes and Process\Page File Bytes Peak counters.

## Changing the Paging File's Location and Size

The page file is named `Pagefile.sys` and it's stored in the root folder of the `%SystemDrive%`. Here's how to change the hard disk that Windows XP uses to store the page file as well as the page file sizes:

1. If necessary, defragment the hard disk that you'll be using for the page file. See Chapter 12's "Defragmenting Your Hard Disk" section.

2. Launch Control Panel's System icon to display the System Properties dialog box.

3. In the Advanced tab's Performance group, click Settings to display the Performance Options dialog box.

4. In the Advanced tab's Virtual Memory group, click Change. Windows XP displays the Virtual Memory dialog box, shown in Figure 11.5.

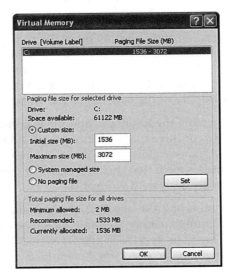

**FIGURE 11.5**    Use the Virtual Memory dialog box to select a different hard disk to store the page file.

5. Use the Drive list to select the hard drive you want to use.

6. Select a page file size option:

Custom Size    Activate this option to set your own page file sizes using the Initial Size (MB) and Maximum Size (MB) text boxes. Ensure that Windows XP is able to dynamically resize the page file as needed by entering a maximum size that's larger than the initial size.

| | |
|---|---|
| System Managed Size | Activate this option to let Windows XP manage the page file sizes for you. |
| No Paging File | Activate this option to disable the page file on the selected drive. |

## 11

> **TIP**
>
> If you want to move the page file to another drive, first select the original drive and then activate the No Paging File option to remove the page file from that drive. Select the other drive and choose either Custom Size or System Managed Size to add a new page file to that drive.

> **TIP**
>
> If you want to split the page file over a second drive, leave the original drive as is, select the second drive, and choose either Custom Size or System Managed Size to create a second page file on that drive.

7. Click Set.

Exit all the dialog boxes. If you changed the drive or if you decreased either the initial size or the maximum size, you need to restart your computer to put the changes into effect.

## Defragmenting the Page File

As Windows XP dynamically sizes the page file, it's possible that it can become fragmented, resulting in a small performance hit. Windows XP manipulates the page file in relatively large blocks, so fragmentation rarely occurs. However, if you're looking to eke out every last drop of performance on your machine, you should probably ensure that the page file is defragmented.

> **TIP**
>
> To determine whether the page file is defragmented, run Disk Defragmenter and analyze the partition that contains the page file. View the analysis report and, in the Volume Information list, find the Pagefile Fragmentation item. The Total Fragments value tells you the number of fragments used by the page file.

Unfortunately, Windows XP Disk Defragmenter tool does *not* defragment the page file. To accomplish this, you have to temporarily move or disable the page file. Here are the steps to follow:

1. Display the Virtual Memory dialog box as described in the previous section.

2. You have two ways to proceed:

- If you have a second hard drive on your system, first set up a page file on the other hard drive using the same initial and maximum values of the original page file. Then select the original drive and reduce the initial and maximum sizes to 0 for the page file.

- If you have only one hard drive, activate No Paging File to disable the page file.

3. Restart your computer.

4. Defragment the hard drive that contained the original page file.

5. Display the Virtual Memory dialog box and restore the original page file settings.

6. Restart your computer.

# More Optimization Tricks

The rest of this chapter takes you through three tricks for eking out a bit more performance from your system: adjusting power option, disabling fast user switching, and turning off visual effects.

## Adjusting Power Options

Windows XP's power management options can shut down your system's monitor or hard disk to save energy. Unfortunately, it takes a few seconds for the system to power up these devices again, which can be frustrating when you want to get back to work. There are two things you can do to eliminate or reduce this frustration:

- Don't let Windows XP turn off the monitor and hard disk—Run Control Panel's Power Options icon to display the Power Options Properties dialog box. In the Power Schemes tab, use the Power Schemes list to select the Always On item (this is optional) and select Never in the Turn Off Monitor and Turn Off Hard Disks lists. For good measure, you should also make sure that Never is selected in the System Standby and System Hibernates lists.

- Don't use a screensaver—Again, it can take a few seconds for Windows XP to recover from a screensaver. To ensure that you're not using one, launch Control Panel's Display icon, select the Screen Saver tab, and choose (None) in the Screen Saver list. If you're worried about monitor wear and tear, use the Blank or Windows XP screensavers, which are relatively lightweight and exit quickly. Also, be sure to deactivate the On Resume, Display Welcome Screen check box to avoid having to log on all over again each time you exit the screen saver.

## Turning Off Fast User Switching

Windows XP's Fast User Switching feature enables multiple users to keep programs and documents running concurrently, which makes it easy to quickly switch from one user to another. Of course, having multiple sets of running programs and open documents adds to the memory and resource requirements of your system, which slows down performance for all users. In other words, the time saved by switching users quickly is most likely lost several times over by overall slower performance.

Therefore, you should disable Fast User Switching by following these steps:

1. Launch Control Panel's User Accounts icon.

2. Click the Change the Way Users Log On or Off link.

3. Deactivate the Use Fast User Switching check box.

4. Click Apply Options.

## Reducing the Use of Visual Effects

Windows XP uses a large number of visual effects to enhance the user's overall Windows experience. For example, Windows XP animates the movement of windows when you minimize or maximize them; it fades or scrolls in menus and tooltips; and it adds small visual touches such as shadows under menus and the mouse pointer. Most of these effects serve merely cosmetic purposes and are drains (albeit small ones) on system performance. If you don't need some or all of these effects, there are various methods you can use to turn them off:

- Launch Control Panel's Display Icon, select the Appearance tab, and click Effects. In the Effects dialog box (see Figure 11.6), deactivate the following check boxes:

  Use the Following Transition Effect for Menus and Tooltips

  Use the Following Method to Smooth Edges of Screen Fonts

  Show Shadows Under Menus

  Show Windows Contents While Dragging

  Hide Underlined Letters for Keyboard Navigation Until I Press the Alt Key

- While you have the Display Properties dialog box open, select the Settings tab and choose Medium (16 bit) in the Color Quality list. Using fewer colors gives your graphics card less to do, which should speed up video performance. Also, click Advanced, display the Troubleshooting tab, and make sure that the Hardware Acceleration slider is set to Full.

- Launch Control Panel's System icon, display the Advanced tab, and click Settings in the Performance group. In the Visual Effects tab of the Performance Options dialog box (see Figure 11.7), either activate the Adjust for Best Performance option (which deactivates all the check boxes) or activate Custom and then deactivate the check boxes for the effects you want to disable.

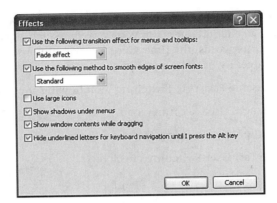

**FIGURE 11.6**    Turn off most of the check boxes in the Effects dialog box to improve performance.

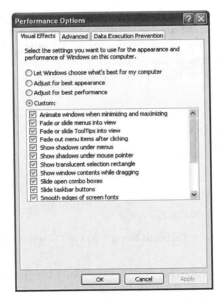

**FIGURE 11.7**    Turn off the check boxes in the Visual Effects tab to improve performance.

- Launch Tweak UI and select the Mouse branch. Move the Menu Speed slider all the way to the left (Fast). This eliminates the delay when you hover the mouse over a menu item that displays a submenu. This is equivalent to setting the following Registry value to 0:

```
HKCU\Control Panel\Desktop\MenuShowDelay
```

# From Here

Here's a list of sections in this book where you'll find information related to Windows XP performance tuning:

- To learn how to logon automatically, refer to the section in Chapter 1 titled "Setting Up an Automatic Logon."

- To learn more about the Indexing Service, refer to the section in Chapter 2 titled "Searching Faster with the Indexing Service."

- To control the number of applications that load at startup, refer to the section in Chapter 5 titled "Launching Applications and Scripts at Startup."

- To learn about the Ctrl+Alt+Delete logon requirement, refer to the section in Chapter 6 titled "Requiring Ctrl+Alt+Delete at Startup."

- To learn about hard drive maintenance, see Chapter 12, "Maintaining Your Windows XP System."

- To learn how to update to a newer device driver, see the section in Chapter 14 titled "Updating a Device Driver."

CHAPTER **12**

# Maintaining Your Windows XP System

Computer problems, like the proverbial death and taxes, seem to be one of those constants in life. Whether it's a hard disk giving up the ghost, a power failure that trashes your files, or a virus that invades your system, the issue isn't *whether* something will go wrong, but rather *when* it will happen. Instead of waiting to deal with these difficulties after they've occurred (what I call **pound-of-cure mode**), you need to become proactive and perform maintenance on your system in advance (**ounce-of-prevention mode**). This will not only reduce the chances that something will go wrong, but it will also set up your system to more easily recover from any problems that do occur. This chapter shows you various Windows XP utilities and techniques that can help you do just that. At the end of the chapter, I give you a step-by-step plan for maintaining your system and checking for the first signs of problems.

## Checking Your Hard Disk for Errors

Our hard disks store our programs and, most importantly, our precious data, so they have a special place in the computing firmament. They ought to be pampered and coddled to ensure a long and trouble-free existence, but that's rarely the case, unfortunately. Just consider everything that a modern hard disk has to put up with:

- General wear and tear—If your computer is running right now, its hard disk is spinning away at between 5,400 and 10,000 revolutions per minute. That's right: Even though you're not doing anything, the hard disk is hard at work. Because of this constant activity, most hard disks simply wear out after a few years.

- The old bump-and-grind—Your hard disk includes **read/write heads** that are used to read data from and write data to the disk. These heads float on a cushion of air just above the spinning hard disk platters. A bump or jolt of sufficient intensity can send them crashing onto the surface of the disk, which could easily result in trashed data. If the heads happen to hit a particularly sensitive area, the entire hard disk could crash. Notebook computers are particularly prone to this problem.

- Power surges—The current that is supplied to your PC is, under normal conditions, relatively constant. It's possible, however, for your computer to be assailed by massive power surges (for example, during a lightning storm). These surges can wreak havoc on a carefully arranged hard disk.

So, what can you do about it? Windows XP comes with a program called Check Disk that can check your hard disk for problems and repair them automatically. It might not be able to recover a totally trashed hard disk, but it can at least let you know when a hard disk might be heading for trouble.

Check Disk performs a battery of tests on a hard disk, including looking for invalid file-names, invalid file dates and times, bad sectors, and invalid compression structures. In the hard disk's file system, Check Disk also looks for the following errors:

- Lost clusters

- Invalid clusters

- Cross-linked clusters

- File system cycles

The next few sections explain these errors in more detail.

## Understanding Clusters

Large hard disks are inherently inefficient. When you format a disk, the disk's magnetic medium is divided into small storage areas called **sectors**, which usually hold up to 512 bytes of data. A large hard disk can contain tens of millions of sectors, so it would be too inefficient for Windows XP to deal with individual sectors. Instead, Windows XP groups sectors into **clusters**, the size of which depends on the file system and the size of the partition, as shown in Table 12.1.

**TABLE 12.1**  Default Cluster Sizes for Various File Systems and Partition Sizes

| Partition Size | FAT16 Cluster Size | FAT32 Cluster Size | NTFS Cluster Size |
|----------------|--------------------|--------------------|--------------------|
| 7MB–16MB       | 2KB                | N/A                | 512 bytes          |
| 17MB–32MB      | 512 bytes          | N/A                | 512 bytes          |
| 33MB–64MB      | 1KB                | 512 bytes          | 512 bytes          |
| 65MB–128MB     | 2KB                | 1KB                | 512 bytes          |

**TABLE 12.1**   Continued

| Partition Size | FAT16 Cluster Size | FAT32 Cluster Size | NTFS Cluster Size |
|---|---|---|---|
| 129MB–256MB | 4KB | 2KB | 512 bytes |
| 257MB–512MB | 8KB | 4KB | 512 bytes |
| 513MB–1,024MB | 16KB | 4KB | 1KB |
| 1,025MB–2GB | 32KB | 4KB | 2KB |
| 2GB–4GB | 64KB | 4KB | 4KB |
| 4GB–8GB | N/A | 4KB | 4KB |
| 8GB–16GB | N/A | 8KB | 4KB |
| 16GB–32GB | N/A | 16KB | 4KB |
| 32GB–2TB | N/A | N/A | 4KB |

Still, each hard disk has many thousands of clusters, so it's the job of the file system to keep track of everything. In particular, for each file on the disk, the file system maintains an entry in a **file directory**, a sort of table of contents for your files. (On an NTFS partition, this is called the **Master File Table**, or **MFT**.)

## Understanding Lost Clusters

A **lost cluster** (also sometimes called an **orphaned cluster**) is a cluster that, according to the file system, is associated with a file, but that has no link to any entry in the file directory. Lost clusters are typically caused by program crashes, power surges, or power outages.

If Check Disk comes across lost clusters, it offers to convert them to files in either the file's original folder (if Check Disk can determine the proper folder) or in a new folder named Folder.000 in the root of the %SystemDrive%. (If that folder already exists, Check Disk creates a new folder named Folder.001 instead.) In that folder, Check Disk converts the lost clusters to files with names like File0000.chk and File0001.chk.

You can take a look at these files (using a text editor) to see whether they contain any useful data and then try to salvage the data. Most often, however, these files are unusable and most people just delete them.

## Understanding Invalid Clusters

An **invalid cluster** is one that falls under one of the following three categories:

- A file system entry with an illegal value. In the FAT16 file system, for example, an entry that refers to cluster 1 is illegal because a disk's cluster numbers start at 2.

- A file system entry that refers to a cluster number larger than the total number of clusters on the disk.

- A file system entry that is marked as unused, but is part of a cluster chain.

In this case, Check Disk asks whether you want to convert these lost file fragments to files. If you say yes, Check Disk truncates the file by replacing the invalid cluster with an

EOF (**end of file**) marker and then converts the lost file fragments to files. These are probably the truncated portion of the file, so you can examine them and try to piece everything back together. More likely, however, you just have to trash these files.

## Understanding Cross-Linked Clusters

A **cross-linked cluster** is a cluster that has somehow been assigned to two different files (or twice in the same file). Check Disk offers to delete the affected files, copy the cross-linked cluster to each affected file, or ignore the cross-linked files altogether. In most cases, the safest bet is to copy the cross-linked cluster to each affected file. This way, at least one of the affected files should be usable.

## Understanding Cycles

In an NTFS partition, a **cycle** is a corruption in the file system whereby a subfolder's parent folder is listed as the subfolder itself. For example, a folder name C:\Data should have C:\ as its parent; if C:\Data is a cycle, C:\Data—the same folder—is listed as the parent instead. This creates a kind of loop in the file system that can cause the cycled folder to "disappear."

## Running the Check Disk GUI

Check Disk has two versions: a GUI version and a command-line version. See the next section to learn how to use the command-line version. Here are the steps to follow to run the GUI version of Check Disk:

1. In Windows Explorer, right-click the drive you want to check and then click Properties. The drive's property sheet appears.

2. Display the Tools tab.

3. Click the Check Now button. The Check Disk window appears, as shown in Figure 12.1.

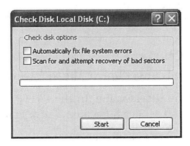

**FIGURE 12.1**    Use Check Disk to scan a hard disk partition for errors.

4. Activate one or both of the following options, if desired:

| | |
|---|---|
| Automatically Fix File System Errors | If you activate this check box, Check Disk will automatically repair any file system errors that it finds. If you leave this option deactivated, Check Disk just reports on any errors it finds. |
| Scan for and Attempt Recovery of Bad Sectors | If you activate this check box, Check Disk performs a sector-by-sector surface check of the hard disk surface. If Check Disk finds a bad sector, it automatically attempts to recover any information stored in the sector and it marks the sector as defective so that no information can be stored there in the future. |

**5.** Click Start.

**6.** If you activated the Automatically Fix File System Errors check box and are checking a partition that has open system files, Check Disk will tell you that it can't continue because it requires exclusive access to the disk. It will then ask whether you want to schedule the scan to occur the next time you boot the computer. Click Yes to schedule the disk check.

**7.** When the scan is complete, Check Disk displays a message letting you know and a report on the errors it found, if any.

## The AUTOCHK Utility

If you click Yes when Check Disk asks whether you want to schedule the scan for the next boot, the program adds the AUTOCHK utility to the following Registry setting:

```
HKLM\SYSTEM\CurrentControlSet\Control\Session Manager\BootExecute
```

This setting specifies the programs that Windows XP should run at boot time when the Session Manager is loading. AUTOCHK is the automatic version of Check Disk that runs at system startup. If you want the option of skipping the disk check, you need to specify a timeout value for AUTOCHK. You change the timeout value by using the AutoChkTimeOut setting in the same Registry key:

```
HKLM\SYSTEM\CurrentControlSet\Control\Session Manager\BootExecute
```

Set this to the number of seconds you want to use for the timeout. Another way to do this is to use the CHKNTFS /T:[time] command, where time is the number of seconds to use for the timeout. (If you exclude time, CHKNTFS returns the current timeout setting.) For example, the following command sets the timeout to 60 seconds:

```
CHKNTFS /T:60
```

When AUTOCHK is scheduled with a timeout value greater than 0, you see the following the next time you restart the computer:

```
A disk check has been scheduled.
To skip disk checking, press any key within 10 second(s).
```

You can bypass the check by pressing a key before the timeout expires.

## Running Check Disk from the Command Line

Here's the syntax for Check Disk's command-line version:

```
CHKDSK [volume [filename]] [/F] [/V] [/R] [/X] [/I] [/C] [/L:[size]]
```

| | |
|---|---|
| *volume* | The drive letter (followed by a colon) or volume name. |
| *filename* | On FAT16 and FAT32 disks, the name of the file to check. Include the path if the file isn't in the current folder. |
| /F | Tells Check Disk to automatically fix errors. This is the same as running the Check Disk GUI with the Automatically Fix File System Errors option activated. |
| /V | Runs Check Disk in verbose mode. On FAT16 and FAT32 drives, Check Disk displays the path and name of every file on the disk; on NTFS drives, displays cleanup messages, if any. |
| /R | Tells Check Disk to scan the disk surface for bad sectors and recover data from the bad sectors, if possible. This is the same as running the Check Disk GUI with the Scan for and Attempt Recovery of Bad Sectors option activated. |
| /X | On NTFS nonsystem disks that have open files, forces the volume to dismount, invalidates the open file handles, and then runs the scan (the /F switch is implied). |
| /I | On NTFS disks, tells Check Disk to check only the file system's index entries. |
| /C | On NTFS disks, tells Check Disk to skip the checking of cycles within the folder structure. This is a rare error, so using /C to skip the cycle check can speed up the disk check. |
| /L:[*size*] | On NTFS disks, tells Check Disk to set the size of its log file to the specified number of kilobytes. The default size is 65,536, which is plenty big enough for most systems, so you should never need to change the size. Note that if you include this switch without the *size* parameter, Check Disk tells you the current size of the log file. |

# Checking Free Disk Space

Hard disks with capacities measured in the tens of gigabytes are commonplace even in low-end systems nowadays, so disk space is much less of a problem than it used to be. Still, you need to keep track of how much free space you have on your disk drives, particularly the %SystemDrive%, which usually stores the virtual memory page file.

One way to check disk free space is to view My Computer using the Details view, which includes columns for Total Size and Free Space, as shown in Figure 12.2. Alternatively, right-click the drive in Windows Explorer and then click Properties. The disk's total capacity, as well as its current used and free space, appear in the General tab of the disk's property sheet.

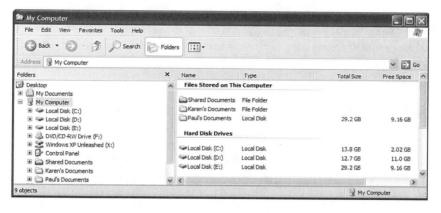

**FIGURE 12.2**    Display My Computer in Details view to see the total size and free space on your system's disks.

Listing 12.1 presents a VBScript procedure that displays the status and free space for each drive on your system.

**LISTING 12.1**    A VBScript Example That Displays the Status and Free Space for Your System's Drives

```
Option Explicit
Dim objFSO, colDiskDrives, objDiskDrive, strMessage

' Create the File System Object
Set objFSO = CreateObject("Scripting.FileSystemObject")

' Get the collection of disk drives
Set colDiskDrives = objFSO.Drives

' Run through the collection
strMessage = "Disk Drive Status Report" & vbCrLf & vbCrLf
For Each objDiskDrive in colDiskDrives
```

**LISTING 12.1**    Continued

```
' Add the drive letter to the message
strMessage = strMessage & "Drive: " & objDiskDrive.DriveLetter & vbCrLf

' Check the drive status
If objDiskDrive.IsReady = True Then

    ' If it's ready, add the status and the free space to the message
    strMessage = strMessage & "Status: Ready" & vbCrLf
    strMessage = strMessage & "Free space: " & objDiskDrive.FreeSpace
    strMessage = strMessage & vbCrLf & vbCrLf
Else

    ' Otherwise, just add the status to the message
    strMessage = strMessage & "Status: Not Ready" & vbCrLf & vbCrLf
End If
Next

' Display the message
Wscript.Echo strMessage
```

This script creates a `FileSystemObject` and then uses its `Drives` property to return the system's collection of disk drives. Then a `For Each...Next` loop runs through the collection, gathering the drive letter, the status, and, if the disk is ready, the free space. It then displays the drive data as shown in Figure 12.3.

**FIGURE 12.3**    The script displays the status and free space for each drive on your system.

# Deleting Unnecessary Files

If you find that a hard disk partition is getting low on free space, you should delete any unneeded files and programs. Windows XP comes with a Disk Cleanup utility that enables you to remove certain types of files quickly and easily. Before discussing this utility, let's look at a few methods you can use to perform a spring cleaning on your hard disk by hand:

- Uninstall programs you don't use—If you have an Internet connection, you know it's easier than ever to download new software for a trial run. Unfortunately, that also means it's easier than ever to have unused programs cluttering your hard disk. Use the Control Panel's Add or Remove Programs icon to uninstall these and other rejected applications.

- Delete downloaded program archives—Speaking of program downloads, your hard disk is also probably littered with Zip files or other downloaded archives. For those programs you use, you should consider moving the archive files to a removable medium for storage. For programs you don't use, you should delete the archive files.

- Remove Windows XP components that you don't use—If you don't use some Windows XP components, use the Control Panel's Add or Remove Programs icon to remove those components from your system.

- Delete application backup files—Applications often create backup copies of existing files and name the backups using either the .bak or .old extension. Use Windows Explorer's Search utility to locate these files and delete them.

After you've performed these tasks, you should run the Disk Cleanup utility, which can automatically remove some of the preceding file categories, as well as several other types of files. Here's how it works:

1. Select Start, All Programs, Accessories, System Tools, Disk Cleanup. The Select Drive dialog box appears.

2. Select the disk drive you want to work with and then click OK. Disk Cleanup scans the drive to see which files can be deleted, and then displays a window similar to the one shown in Figure 12.4.

> **TIP**
>
> Windows XP offers two methods for bypassing the Select Drive dialog box. One is to right-click the disk drive in Windows Explorer and then click the Disk Cleanup button in the General tab of the drive's property sheet. The other is to select Start, Run, and type `cleanmgr /d`*`drive`*, where *drive* is the letter of the drive you want to work with (for example, `cleanmgr /dc`).

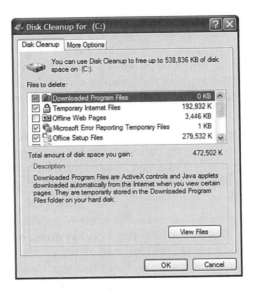

**FIGURE 12.4**    Disk Cleanup can automatically and safely remove certain types of files from a disk drive.

3. In the Files to Delete list, activate the check box beside each category of file you want to remove. If you're not sure what an item represents, select it and read the text in the Description box. Note, too, that for most of these items you can click View Files to see what you'll be deleting.

4. Click OK. Disk Cleanup asks whether you're sure that you want to delete the files.

5. Click Yes. Disk Cleanup deletes the selected files.

---

**Saving Disk Cleanup Settings**

It's possible to save your Disk Cleanup settings and run them again at any time. This is handy if you want to, for example, delete all your downloaded program files and temporary Internet files at shutdown. Launch the command prompt and then enter the following command:

```
cleanmgr /sageset:1
```

Note that the number 1 in the command is arbitrary: You can enter any number between 0 and 65535. This launches Disk Cleanup with an expanded set of file types to delete. Make your choices and click OK. What this does is save your settings to the Registry; it doesn't delete the files. To delete the files, open the command prompt and enter the following command:

```
cleanmgr /sagerun:1
```

You can also create a shortcut for this command, add it to a batch file, or schedule it with the Task Scheduler.

# Defragmenting Your Hard Disk

Windows XP comes with a utility called Disk Defragmenter that's an essential tool for tuning your hard disk. Disk Defragmenter's job is to rid your hard disk of **file fragmentation**.

*File fragmentation* is one of those terms that sounds scarier than it actually is. It simply means that a file is stored on your hard disk in scattered, noncontiguous bits. This is a performance drag because it means that when Windows XP tries to open such a file, it must make several stops to collect the various pieces. If a lot of files are fragmented, it can slow even the fastest hard disk to a crawl.

Why doesn't Windows XP just store files contiguously? Recall that Windows XP stores files on disk in clusters, and that these clusters have a fixed size, depending on the disk's capacity. Recall too that Windows XP uses a file directory to keep track of each file's whereabouts. When you delete a file, Windows XP doesn't actually clean out the clusters associated with the file. Instead, it just marks the deleted file's clusters as unused.

To see how fragmentation occurs, let's look at an example. Suppose that three files are stored on a disk—FIRST.TXT, SECOND.TXT, and THIRD.TXT—and that they use up four, three, and five clusters, respectively. Figure 12.5 shows how they might look on the disk.

**FIGURE 12.5**   Three files before fragmentation.

If you now delete SECOND.TXT, clusters 5, 6, and 7 become available. But suppose that the next file you save—call it FOURTH.TXT—takes up five clusters. What happens? Well, Windows XP looks for the first available clusters. It finds that 5, 6, and 7 are free, so it uses them for the first three clusters of FOURTH.TXT. Windows continues and finds that clusters 13 and 14 are free, so it uses them for the final two clusters of FOURTH.TXT. Figure 12.6 shows how things look now.

As you can see, FOURTH.TXT is stored noncontiguously—in other words, it's fragmented. Although a file fragmented in two pieces isn't that bad, it's possible for large files to become split into dozens of blocks.

## Running the Disk Defragmenter Tool

Before using Disk Defragmenter, you should perform a couple of housekeeping chores:

- Delete any files from your hard disk that you don't need, as described in the previous section. Defragmenting junk files only slows down the whole process.

- Check for file system errors by running Check Disk as described earlier in this chapter (refer to "Checking Your Hard Disk for Errors").

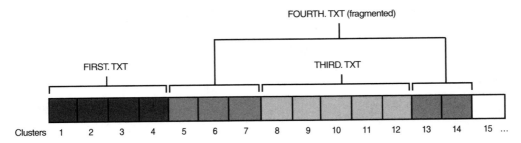

**FIGURE 12.6**    A fragmented file.

Follow these steps to use Disk Defragmenter:

1. Select Start, All Programs, Accessories, System Tools, Disk Defragmenter. Alternatively, in Windows Explorer, right-click the drive you want to defragment, click Properties, and then display the Tools tab in the dialog box that appears. Click the Defragment Now button. Either way, the Disk Defragmenter window appears.

2. Select the drive you want to defragment.

3. Click Analyze. Disk Defragmenter analyzes the fragmentation of the selected drive and then displays its recommendation (for example, You should defragment this volume, as shown in Figure 12.7).

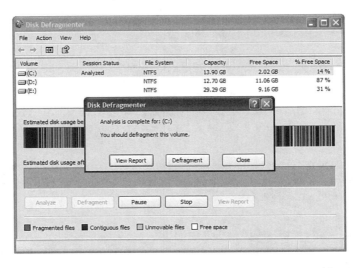

**FIGURE 12.7**    Use Disk Defragmenter to eliminate file fragmentation and improve hard disk performance.

4. If you want more information, click View Report. If you don't want to defragment the drive, click Close. If you want to defragment the drive, click Defragment.

> **TIP**
>
> In some cases, you can defragment a drive even further by running Disk Defragmenter on the drive twice in a row. (That is, run the defragment, and when it's done, immediately run a second defragment on the same drive.)

## Defragmenting from the Command Line

If you want to schedule a defragment or perform this chore from a batch file, you have to use the DEFRAG command-line utility. Here's the syntax:

```
DEFRAG volume [-a] [-f] [-v]
```

| | |
|---|---|
| volume | Specifies the drive letter (followed by a colon) of the disk you want to defragment. |
| -a | Tells DEFRAG only to analyze the disk. |
| -f | Forces DEFRAG to defragment the disk, even if it doesn't need defragmenting or if the disk has less than 15% free space. (DEFRAG normally requires at least that much free space because it needs an area in which to sort the files.) |
| -v | Runs DEFRAG in verbose mode, which displays both the analysis report and the defragmentation report. |

# Setting System Restore Points

One of the biggest causes of Windows instability in the past was the tendency for some newly installed programs to simply not get along with Windows. It could be an executable file that didn't mesh with the Windows system or a Registry change that caused havoc on other programs or on Windows. Similarly, hardware installs often caused problems by adding faulty device drivers to the system or by corrupting the Registry.

To help guard against software or hardware installations that bring down the system, Windows XP offers the System Restore feature. It's job is straightforward, yet clever: to take periodic snapshots—called **restore points** or **checkpoints**—of your system, each of which includes the currently installed program files, Registry settings, and other crucial system data. The idea is that if a program or device installation causes problems on your system, you use System Restore to revert your system to the most recent restore point before the installation.

System Restore automatically creates restore points under the following conditions:

- Every 24 hours—This is called a **system checkpoint** and it's set once a day as long as your computer is running. If your computer isn't running, the system checkpoint is created the next time you start your computer, assuming that it has been at least 24 hours since that previous system checkpoint was set.

> **NOTE**
>
> The system checkpoint interval is governed by the `RPGlobalInterval` setting in the following Registry key:
>
>     HKLM\SOFTWARE\Microsoft\Windows NT\CurrentVersion\SystemRestore
>
> The value is in seconds, and the default is 86400 (24 hours). If you often change your system configuration, you might prefer a shorter interval of, say, 28800 (8 hours). Note, too, that you can also adjust the `RPSessionInterval` value, which controls the intervals, in seconds, that system checkpoints are created during each Windows XP session (the default is 0, meaning that the feature is turned off). Finally, the `RPLifeInterval` value determines the number of days that Windows XP maintains restore points. The default is 7776000 (90 days).

- Before installing certain applications—Some newer applications—notably Office 2000 and later—are aware of System Restore and will ask it to create a restore point prior to installation.

- Before installing a Windows Update patch—System Restore creates a restore point before you install a patch either by hand via the Windows Update site or via the Automatic Updates feature.

- Before installing an unsigned device driver—Windows XP warns you about installing unsigned drivers. If you choose to go ahead, the system creates a restore point before installing the driver.

- Before restoring backed-up files—When you use the Windows XP Backup program to restore one or more backed-up files, System Restore creates a restore point just in case the restore causes problems with system files.

- Before reverting to a previous configuration using System Restore—Sometimes reverting to an earlier configuration doesn't fix the current problem or it creates its own set of problems. In these cases, System Restore creates a restore point before reverting so that you can undo the restoration.

It's also possible to create a restore point manually using the System Restore user interface. Here are the steps to follow:

1. Select Start, All Programs, Accessories, System Tools, System Restore. The System Restore window appears.

2. Activate the Create a Restore Point option and click Next.

3. Use the Restore Point Description text box to enter a description for the new checkpoint and then click Create. System Restore creates the restore point and displays the Restore Point Created window.

4. Click Close.

**TIP**

To change how much disk space System Restore uses to store checkpoints, open the Control Panel's System icon and display the System Restore tab. Highlight the drive you want to work with and then click Settings. Use the Disk Space Usage slider to set the amount of disk space you want. Note, too, that you can toggle System Restore on and off by using the Turn Off System Restore on this Drive check box.

# Backing Up Your Files

In theory, theory and practice are the same thing; in practice, they're not. That old saw applies perfectly to data backups. In theory, backing up data is an important part of everyday computing life. After all, we know that our data is valuable to the point of being irreplaceable, and you saw earlier that there's no shortage of ways that a hard disk can crash: power surges, rogue applications, virus programs, or just simple wear and tear. In practice, however, backing up our data always seems to be one of those chores we'll get to "tomorrow." After all, that old hard disk seems to be humming along just fine, thank you—and anyway, who has time to work through the few dozen floppy disks you need for even a small backup?

When it comes to backups, theory and practice don't usually converge until that day you start your system and you get an ugly `Invalid system configuration` or `Hard disk failure` message. Believe me: Losing a hard disk that's crammed with unsaved (and now lost) data brings the importance of backing up into focus real quick. To avoid this sorry fate, you have to find a way to take some of the pain out of the practice of backing up. Fortunately, you can do two things to make backups more painless:

- Use the Backup accessory that comes with Windows XP Professional. This program has a few nice features that make it easy to select files for backup and to run backups regularly.

**NOTE**

If you're using Windows XP Home, Backup is not installed by default; instead, you need to install Backup from the Windows XP CD. In the VALUEADD\MSFT\NTBACKUP folder, launch the Ntbackup.exe file.

- Practice what I call "real-world" backups. In short, these are backups that protect only your most crucial files. I explain this in more detail in the next section.

## Some Thoughts on Real-World Backups

It's a rare computer user these days who doesn't know that backing up is important. So, why do so many of us put off backing up? I think the main reason is that it's often a difficult or inconvenient process. However, there are a few things you can do to make backing up easier. Here are some ideas that I use to make my backup chores more palatable:

- Forget floppies, if possible—Backing up to floppy disks ranks just above root canal on the Top Ten Most Unpleasant Chores list. The reason, of course, is that a standard 3 1/2-inch floppy disk holds a mere 1.39MB (*not* 1.44MB) of data. If your hard disk contains hundreds of megabytes, you'll have to back up to hundreds of floppy disks, which hurts just to think about it.

- Try a tape drive—Tape drives are the de facto backup standard, and come in many different capacities. You can back up hundreds of megabytes or even multiple gigabytes for an extremely low cost.

- Try other backup media—The big downfall for tape drives is their relatively slow access times. Fortunately, there are much faster media available. These include CD-R and CD-RW drives; removable media such as USB flash drives and memory cards; a second hard disk (*not* a second partition on the same hard disk!); and a network folder.

- Consider online backups—If your ISP provides you with disk space for a website, use it to back up your most important files. Note, too, that there are also companies that will sell you online disk space for backups.

- Back up data, not programs—Although a full system backup can come in handy, it isn't strictly necessary. The only irreplaceable files on your system are those you created yourself, so they're the ones you should spend the most time protecting.

- Keep data together—You save an immense amount of backup time if you store all your data files in one place. It could be the My Documents folder, a separate partition, or a separate hard disk. In each case, you can select all the data files for backup simply by activating a single folder or drive check box.

- Back up downloaded archives—If space is at a premium, you can leave program files out of your backup job because they can always be reinstalled from their source disks. The exceptions to this are downloaded programs. To avoid having to find and download these files again, make backup copies of the archives.

> **NOTE**
>
> The *real* backup dilemma in these modern times isn't protecting our documents and downloads, but preserving the innumerable patches, updates, and security fixes associated not only with Windows XP, but also applications such as Microsoft Office. The only way to truly recover these aspects of your system is to create a ghost image of your system using a third-party program such as Norton Ghost (www.symantec.com).

- Don't always run the full backup—You can speed up your backup times by taking advantage of Backup's different backup types:

| | |
|---|---|
| Normal | Backs up all the files in the backup job. Each file is marked (that is, its archive bit is turned off) to indicate that the file has been backed up. |

Incremental    Backs up only those files that have changed since the last Normal or Incremental backup. This is the fastest type because it includes only the minimum number of files. Again, the files are marked to indicate they've been backed up.

Differential    Backs up only those files that have changed since the last nondifferential backup. Files are *not* marked to indicate they've been backed up. So, if you run this type of backup again, the same files get backed up (plus any others that have changed in the meantime).

Copy    Makes copies of the selected files. This type of backup does not mark the files as having been backed up.

Daily    Backs up only those files that were modified on the day you ran the backup. Files are marked as having been backed up.

Your overall backup strategy might look something like this:

1. Perform a normal backup of all your documents once a month or so.

2. Do a differential backup of modified files once a week.

3. Do an incremental or daily backup of modified files every day.

## Defining a Backup Job

In backup lingo, a **backup job** is a file that defines your backup. It includes three things:

- A list of the files you want to include in your backup

- The backup options you selected, including the type of backup you want to use

- The destination drive and folder for the backed-up files

Here are the steps to follow to define and run a backup job:

1. Select Start, All Programs, Accessories, System Tools, Backup. The Backup or Restore Wizard appears.

2. Click the Advanced Mode link to display the Backup Utility window.

3. Select the Backup tab, shown in Figure 12.8.

4. Select Tools, Options to display the Options dialog box, and then set the following options, as desired (click OK when you're done):

   - To specify the backup type, display the Backup Type tab and then use the Default Backup Type list to select the backup type you want to use.

   - To verify that the backed-up data contains no errors, display the General tab and activate the Verify Data After the Backup Operation check box. Note, however, that this roughly doubles the length of the backup operation.

- To exclude files based on the file type, display the Exclude Files tab and click Add New (the one under the Files Excluded for All Users list) to display the Add Excluded Files dialog box. In the Registered File Type list, select the file type you want to exclude and click OK.

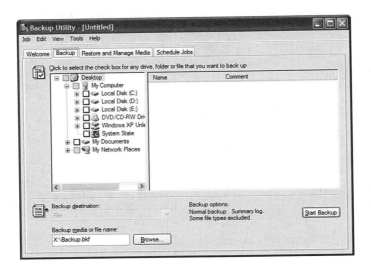

**FIGURE 12.8**    Use the Backup tab to define a backup job.

5. Use the folder and file lists to activate the check boxes for the drives, folders, and files you want to include in the backup job.

> **NOTE**
>
> To back up the Registry, your system's boot files, and its COM+ Class Registration Database, activate the System State check box.

6. Use the Backup Destination list to choose a backup device.

7. If you chose File in step 6, use the Backup Media or File Name text box to enter the drive, path, and filename for the backup file.

8. Select Job, Save Selections. If you're creating a new backup job, enter a name in the Save As dialog box and then click Save.

9. Click Start Backup to perform the backup.

# Running the Automated System Recovery Preparation Wizard

The worst-case scenario for PC problems is a system crash that renders your hard disk or system files unusable. Your only recourse in such a case is to start from scratch with either a reformatted hard disk or a new hard disk. This usually means that you have to reinstall Windows XP and then reinstall and reconfigure all your applications. In other words, you're looking at the better part of a day or, more likely, a few days, to recover your system.

However, Windows XP comes with a utility called Automated System Recovery that, with a little advance planning on your part, can help you recover from a crash in just a few steps. What kind of advance planning is required? Just two things:

- You must run the Automated System Recovery Preparation Wizard. This wizard backs up your system files and creates a disk that enables you to restore your system.

- You must run a full backup of all your data and application files.

---

**NOTE**

If you're not replacing your hard disk and if you have your application files and data files on a separate partition, you don't have to back up that partition because you won't be formatting it.

---

Because your system, application, and data files change regularly, to ensure a smooth recovery, you must do both of these things regularly. Here are the steps to following to run the Automated System Recovery Preparation Wizard:

1. Select Start, All Programs, Accessories, System Tools, Backup. The Backup or Restore Wizard appears.

2. Click the Advanced Mode link to display the Backup Utility window.

3. In the Welcome tab, click the Automated System Recovery Wizard button. Alternatively, select Tools, ASR Wizard. The Automated System Recovery Preparation Wizard appears.

4. Click Next. The wizard prompts you for a backup destination for your system files.

5. Choose the Backup Media Type and then enter the backup media name or filename. Click Next.

---

**CAUTION**

Don't back up the system files to the `%SystemDrive%` partition because it is the partition you'll be formatting as part of your recovery effort.

---

6. Click Finish. The wizard backs up your system files. When it's done, it prompts you to insert a floppy disk in drive A.

7. Insert a blank, formatted disk and click OK. The wizard copies the files `Asr.sif`, `Asrpnp.sif`, and `Setup.log` to the disk and lets you know when it has finished.

8. Click OK.

To learn how to recover your system using Automated System Recovery, see Chapter 13, "Troubleshooting and Recovering from Problems."

# Checking for Updates and Security Patches

Microsoft is constantly working to improve Windows XP with bug fixes, security patches, new program versions, and device driver updates. All of these new and improved components are made available online, so you should check for updates and patches often.

## Checking the Windows Update Website

The main online site for Windows XP updates is the Windows Update website, which you load into Internet Explorer by selecting Start, All Programs, Windows Update. You should visit this site regularly to look for crucial new components that can make Windows XP more reliable and more secure.

Windows XP also comes with a vastly improved automatic updating feature, which can download and install updates automatically. If you prefer to know what's happening with your computer, it's possible to control the automatic updating by following these steps:

1. Launch Control Panel's System icon to get to the System Properties dialog box.

2. Display the Automatic Updates tab, shown in Figure 12.9.

3. Activate one of the following options to determine how Windows XP performs the updating:

Automatic          This option tells Windows XP to download and install updates automatically. Windows XP checks for new updates on the date (such as Every Day or Every Sunday) and time you specify. For example, you might prefer to choose a time when you won't be using your computer.

**CAUTION**

Some updates require your computer to be rebooted to put them into effect. In such cases, if you activate the Automatic option, Windows XP will automatically reboot your system. This could lead to problems if you have open documents with unsaved changes or if you need a particular program to be running at all times. You can work around these problems by saving your work constantly, by setting up an automatic logon (refer to "Setting Up an Automatic Logon" in Chapter 1, "Customizing and Troubleshooting the Windows XP Startup"), and by putting any program you need to fun in your Startup folder (refer to "Using the Startup Folder" in Chapter 5, "Installing and Running Applications").

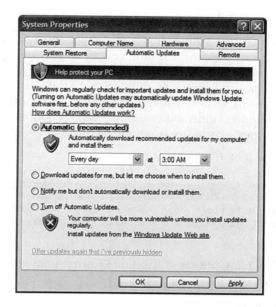

**FIGURE 12.9**   Use the Automatic Updates tab to configure Windows XP's automatic updating.

| | |
|---|---|
| Download Updates for Me, but Let Me Choose When to Install Them | If you activate this option, Windows XP checks for new updates and then automatically downloads any updates that are available. Windows XP then displays an icon in the notification area to let you know that the updates are ready to install. Click the icon to see the list of updates. If you see an update that you don't want to install, deactivate its check box. Click Install to install the updates. |
| Notify Me but Don't Automatically Download or Install Them | If you activate this option, Windows XP checks for new updates and then, if any are available, displays an icon in the notification area to let you know that the updates are ready to download. Click the icon to see the list of updates. If you see an update that you don't want to download, deactivate its check box. Click Start Download to initiate the download. When the download is complete, Windows XP displays an icon in the notification area to let you know that the updates are ready to install. Click the icon and then click Install to install the updates. |
| Turn Off Automatic Updates | Activate this option to prevent Windows XP from checking for new updates. |

4. Click OK to put the new settings into effect.

## Checking for Security Vulnerabilities

Microsoft regularly finds security vulnerabilities in components such as Internet Explorer and Windows Media Player. Fixes for these problems are usually made available via Windows Update. However, to ensure that your computer is safe, you should download and regularly run the Microsoft Baseline Security Analyzer (MSBA). This tool not only scans your system for missing security patches, but it also looks for things such as weak passwords and other Windows vulnerabilities. Download the tool here: www.microsoft.com/technet/security/tools/mbsahome.mspx.

After you've installed the tool, follow these steps to use it:

> **NOTE**
>
> The instructions in this section cover MBSA version 1.21. At the time of writing, Microsoft was beta-testing version 2.0, which might be released by the time you read this.

1. Select Start, All Programs, Microsoft Baseline Security Analyzer 1.21. The program's Welcome screen appears.

2. Click Scan a Computer.

3. Your computer should be listed in the Computer Name list. If not, enter it manually. Alternatively, use the IP Address text boxes to enter your computer's IP address.

4. Use the Options check boxes to specify the security components you want to check. For most scans, you should leave all the options activated.

5. Click Start Scan. The program checks your system and displays a report on your system's security (and usually offers remedies for any vulnerability it finds). Figure 12.10 shows a sample report.

# Verifying Digitally Signed Files

In Chapter 14, "Getting the Most Out of Device Manager," you learn that digitally unsigned drivers are often the cause of system instabilities. To ensure that you don't accumulate unsigned drivers on your system (particularly if you share your computer with other users), you should regularly run the Signature Verification Tool. This program scans your entire system (or, optionally, a specific folder) for unsigned drivers. Follow these steps to run this tool:

1. Select Start, Run, enter **sigverif**, and click OK. The File Signature Verification window appears.

2. Click Advanced to display the Advanced File Signature Verification Settings dialog box.

3. Activate the Look for Other Files That Are Not Digitally Signed option.

4. In the Look in This Folder text box, enter **SystemRoot\System32\drivers**, where *SystemRoot* is the folder in which Windows XP is installed (such as C:\Windows).

5. Click OK.

6. Click Start to begin the verification process.

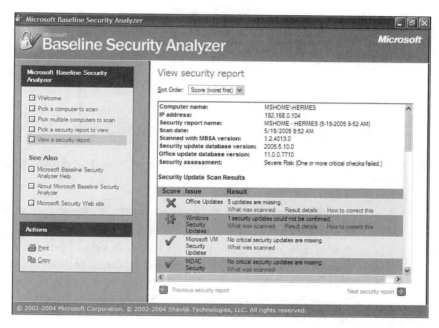

**FIGURE 12.10**    A sample report generated by Microsoft Baseline Security Analyzer.

When the verification is complete, the program displays a list of the unsigned driver files, as shown in Figure 12.11. The results for all the scanned files are written to the log file Sigverif.txt, which is copied to the %SystemRoot% folder when you close the window that shows the list of unsigned drivers. In the Status column of Sigverif.txt, look for files listed as Not Signed. If you find any, consider upgrading these drivers to signed versions. In Chapter 14, see the section titled "Updating a Device Driver."

# Reviewing Event Viewer Logs

Windows XP constantly monitors your system for unusual or noteworthy occurrences. It might be a service that doesn't start, the installation of a device, or an application error. These occurrences are called **events** and Windows XP tracks them in three different event logs:

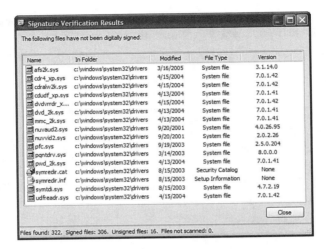

**FIGURE 12.11**    When the Signature Verification Tool completes its work, it displays a list of the unsigned drivers on your system.

| | |
|---|---|
| Application | This log stores events related to applications, including Windows XP programs and third-party applications. |
| Security | This log stores events related to system security, including logons, user accounts, and user privileges. Note that this log doesn't record anything until you turn on Windows XP's security auditing features. You do so by opening Windows XP Professional's Local Security Settings snap-in (select Start, Run, type **secpol.msc**, and click OK) and selecting Local Policies, Audit Policy. You can then enable auditing for any of the several polices listed. |
| System | This log stores events generated by Windows XP and components such as system services and device drivers. |

---

**NOTE**

The System log catalogs device driver errors, but remember that Windows XP has other tools that make it easier to see device problems. As you'll see in Chapter 14 (see "Troubleshooting with Device Manager"), Device Manager displays an icon on devices that have problems, and you can view a device's property sheet to see a description of the problem. Also, the System Information utility (`Msinfo32.exe`) reports hardware woes in the System Information, Hardware Resources, Conflicts/Sharing branch and the System Information, Components, Problem Devices branch.

---

You should scroll through the Application and System event logs regularly to look for existing problems or for warnings that could portend future problems. The Security log isn't as important for day-to-day maintenance. You need to use it only if you suspect a security issue with your machine; for example, if you want to keep track of who logs on to the computer. To examine these logs, you use the Event Viewer snap-in, available via either of the following techniques:

- Select Start, Run, type **eventvwr.msc**, and then click OK.

- Open Control Panel's Administrative Options icon and launch the Event Viewer icon.

Figure 12.12 shows a typical Event Viewer window. Use the tree in the left pane to select the log you want to view: Application, Security, or System.

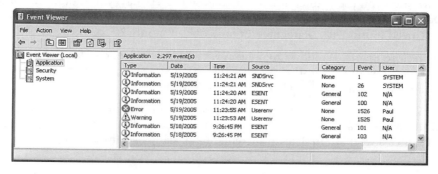

**FIGURE 12.12**    Use the Event Viewer to monitor events generated by applications and Windows XP.

When you select a log, the right pane displays the available events, including the event's date, time, and source, its type (Information, Warning, or Error), and other data. To see a description of an event, double-click it or select it and press Enter.

---

**TIP**

Rather than monitoring the event logs by hand, Windows XP comes with a couple of tools that can help automate the process. The Eventquery.vbs script enables you to query the log files for specific event types, IDs, sources, and more. Search Help and Support for *eventquery* to get the script's command-line syntax. Also, you can set up an **event trigger** that will perform some action when a particular event occurs. You do this using the Eventtriggers.exe utility. Search Help and Support for *eventtriggers* to get the full syntax for this tool.

---

## Setting Up a 10-Step Maintenance Schedule

Maintenance is effective only if it's done regularly, but there's a fine line to be navigated. If maintenance is performed too often, it can become a burden and interfere with more interesting tasks; if it's performed too seldom, it becomes ineffective. So, how often should you perform the 10 maintenance chores listed in this chapter? Here's a 10-step maintenance plan:

1. Check your hard disk for errors. Run a basic scan about once a week. Run a more thorough disk surface scan once a month. The surface scan takes a long time, so run it when you won't be using your computer for a while.

2. Check free disk space. Do this once about once a month. If you have a drive where the free space is getting low, check it approximately once a week.

3. Delete unnecessary files. If free disk space isn't a problem, run this chore once every two or three months.

4. Defragment your hard disk. How often you defragment your hard disk depends on how often you use your computer. If you use it every day, you should run Disk Defragmenter about once a week. If your computer doesn't get heavy use, you probably need to run Disk Defragmenter only once a month or so.

5. Set restore points. Windows XP already sets regular system checkpoints, so you need only create your own restore points when you're installing a program or device or making some other major change to your system.

6. Back up your files. Perform a full backup of all your documents, as well as a backup of the system state, about once a month. Carry out a differential backup of modified files once a week. Complete an incremental or daily backup of modified files every day.

7. Check Windows Update. If you've turned off automatic updating, you should check in with the Windows Update website about once a week.

8. Check for security vulnerabilities. Run the Microsoft Baseline Security Analyzer once a month. You should also pay a monthly visit to Microsoft's Security site to keep up to date on the latest security news, get security and virus alerts, and more: www.microsoft.com/security/.

9. Verify digitally signed files. If other people use your computer regularly, you should run the Signature Verification Tool every couple of months.

10. Review Event Viewer logs. If your system appears to be working fine, you need only check the Application and System log files weekly or every couple of weeks. If the system has a problem, check the logs daily to look for Warning or Error events.

Remember, as well, that Windows XP offers a number of options for running most of these maintenance steps automatically:

- If you want to run a task every day, set it up to launch automatically at startup, as described in Chapter 5, "Installing and Running Applications."

- Use the Task Scheduler (Start, All Programs, Accessories, System Tools, Scheduled Tasks) to set up a program on a regular schedule. Note that some programs, particularly Disk Defragmenter, can't be scheduled in their GUI form. You need to use the command-line version instead.

- The Backup program enables you to schedule backup jobs. In the Backup Utility window, display the Schedule Jobs tab and click Add Job.

- Use the Automatic Updates feature instead of checking for Windows updates by hand.

## From Here

Here's a list of sections in the book where you'll find related information on Windows XP maintenance:

- To learn how to log on automatically, see the section in Chapter 1 titled "Setting Up an Automatic Logon."

- For the details on launching programs automatically at system startup, see the section in Chapter 5 titled "Launching Applications and Scripts at Startup."

- For more about scripting Windows XP, see Chapter 9, "Programming the Windows Script Host."

- If, despite your diligent maintenance, you run into problems, see Chapter 13, "Troubleshooting and Recovering from Problems." Also, see the section titled "Troubleshooting Device Problems" in Chapter 14.

# Troubleshooting and Recovering from Problems

A long time ago, somebody proved mathematically that it was impossible to make any reasonably complex software program problem-free. As the number of variables increase, as the interactions of subroutines and objects become more complex, and as the underlying logic of a program grows beyond the ability of a single person to grasp all at once, errors inevitably creep into the code. Given Windows XP's status as possibly the most complex software ever created, the bad news is that there are certainly problems lurking in the weeds. (Actually, considering the immense complexity of Windows XP—its lines of code are numbered in the tens of millions—it's borderline miraculous that there have been, to date, relatively few problems reported.) However, the good news is that the overwhelming majority of these problems will be extremely obscure and will appear only under the rarest circumstances.

This doesn't mean that you're guaranteed a glitch-free computing experience—far from it. The majority of computer woes are caused by third-party programs and devices, either because they have inherent problems themselves or because they don't get along well with Windows XP. Using software, devices, and device drivers designed for Windows XP can help tremendously, as can the maintenance program I outlined in Chapter 12, "Maintaining Your Windows XP System." But computer problems, like the proverbial death and taxes, are certainties in life, so you need to know how to troubleshoot and resolve the problems that will inevitably come your way. In this chapter I help you do just that by showing you my favorite techniques for determining problem sources, and by taking you through all of Windows XP's recovery tools.

---

**The Origins of the Word "Bug"**

Software glitches are traditionally called bugs, although many developers shun the term because it comes with too much negative baggage these days. Microsoft, for example, prefers the euphemistic term **issues**. There's a popular and appealing tale of how this sense of the word bug came about. As the story goes, in 1947 an early computer pioneer named Grace Hopper was working on a system called the Mark II. While investigating a problem, she found a moth among the machine's vacuum tubes, so from then on glitches were called bugs. A great story, to be sure, but this tale was *not* the source of the computer glitch sense of bug. In fact, engineers had already been referring to mechanical defects as bugs for at least 60 years before Ms. Hopper's discovery. As proof, the *Oxford English Dictionary* offers the following quotation from an 1889 edition of the *Pall Mall Gazette*:

Mr. Edison, I was informed, had been up the two previous nights discovering 'a bug' in his phonograph—an expression for solving a difficulty, and implying that some imaginary insect has secreted itself inside and is causing all the trouble.

---

# Troubleshooting Strategies: Determining the Source of a Problem

One of the ongoing mysteries that all Windows XP users experience at one time or another is what might be called the now-you-see-it-now-you-don't problem. This is a glitch that plagues you for a while and then mysteriously vanishes without any intervention on your part. (This also tends to occur when you ask a nearby user or someone from the IT department to look at the problem. Like the automotive problem that goes away when you take the car to a mechanic, computer problems will often resolve themselves as soon as a knowledgeable user sits down at the keyboard.) When this happens, most people just shake their heads and resume working, grateful to no longer have to deal with the problem.

Unfortunately, most computer ills aren't resolved so easily. For these more intractable problems, your first order of business is to track down the source of the glitch. This is, at best, a black art, but it can be done if you take a systematic approach. Over the years, I've found that the best approach is to ask a series of questions designed to gather the required information and/or to narrow down what might be the culprit. The next few sections take you through these questions.

## Did You Get an Error Message?

Unfortunately, most computer error messages are obscure and do little to help you resolve a problem directly. However, error codes and error text can help you down the road, either by giving you something to search for in an online database (see "Troubleshooting Using Online Resources," later in this chapter) or by providing information to a tech support person. Therefore, you should always write down the full text of any error message that appears.

If the error message is lengthy and you can still use other programs on your computer, don't bother writing down the full message. Instead, while the message is displayed, press Print Screen to place an image of the current screen on the clipboard. Then open Paint or some other graphics program, paste the screen into a new image, and save the image. If you think you'll be sending the image via email to a tech support employee or someone else who can help with the problem, consider saving the image as a monochrome or 16-color bitmap or, if possible, a JPEG file, to keep the image size small.

If the error message appears before Windows XP starts, but you don't have time to write it down, press the Pause Break key to pause the startup. After you record the error, press Ctrl+Pause Break to resume the startup.

If Windows XP itself handles the error, it displays a Windows Error Reporting dialog box similar to the one shown in Figure 13.1. It also lets you know that Windows XP has generated an error report and asks whether you want to send it to Microsoft.

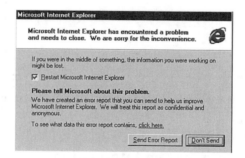

**FIGURE 13.1**    If Windows XP handles a program error, it displays a Windows Error Reporting dialog box similar to this one.

This error report was built by the Dr. Watson debugging tool, which springs into action when an error is detected and then creates an error log in the following folder:

`%AllUsersProfile%\Application Data\Microsoft\Dr Watson`

To see the contents of the error log, either click the Click Here link in the dialog box, or display the folder just mentioned and open the `drwatsn32.log` text file.

You can customize the contents of the Dr Watson error log as well as the operation of the program. Select Start, Run, type **drwtsn32** in the Run dialog box, and then click OK. The dialog box that appears enables you to change the log location, turn log contents on and off, control program options, and view application error logs.

## Does an Error or Warning Appear in the Event Viewer Logs?

Open the Event Viewer and examine the Application and System logs. (Refer to the section in Chapter 12 titled "Reviewing Event Viewer Logs" for more information about the Event Viewer.) In particular, look in the Type column for Error or Warning events. If you see any, double-click each one to read the event description. Figure 13.2 shows an example.

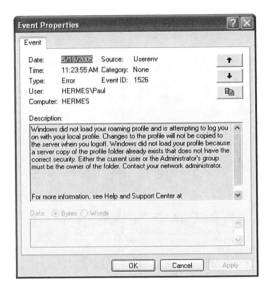

**FIGURE 13.2**    In the Event Viewer, look for Error or Warning events in the Application and System logs.

## Does an Error Appear in System Information?

Select Start, All Programs, Accessories, System Tools, System Information to launch the System Information utility. (Alternatively, select Start, Run, type **msinfo32**, and click OK.) In the Hardware Resources\Conflicts\Sharing category, look for device conflicts. Also, see whether any devices are listed in the Components\Problem Devices category, as shown in Figure 13.3.

## Did the Error Begin with a Past Hardware or Software Change?

A good troubleshooting clue is when the onset of an error coincided with a previous hardware or software change. To investigate this possibility, launch the System Information utility (as described in the previous section) and select View, System History. This displays a history of the changes made to your system in each of the main categories: Hardware Resources, Components, and Software Environment. If you know when the problem began, you can look through the history items to see whether a change occurred at the same time and so might be the cause of the problem.

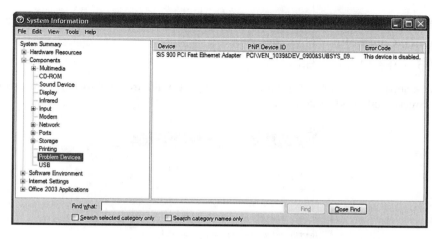

**FIGURE 13.3**    You can use the System Information utility to look for device conflicts and problems.

## Did You Recently Edit the Registry?

Improper Registry modifications can cause all kinds of mischief. If the problem occurred after editing the Registry, try restoring the changed key or setting. Ideally, if you exported a backup of the offending key, you should import the backup. I showed you how to back up the Registry in Chapter 8, "Getting to Know the Windows XP Registry." Refer to the section titled "Keeping the Registry Safe."

## Did You Recently Change Any Windows Settings?

If the problem started after you changed your Windows configuration, try reversing the change. Even something as seemingly innocent as activating the screensaver can cause problems, so don't rule anything out. If you've made a number of recent changes and you're not sure about everything you did, or if it would take too long to reverse all the changes individually, use System Restore to revert your system to the most recent checkpoint before you made the changes. See "Recovering Using System Restore," later in this chapter.

## Did Windows XP "Spontaneously" Reboot?

When certain errors occur, Windows XP will reboot itself. This apparently random behavior is actually built into the system in the event of a system failure (also called a **stop error** or a **blue screen of death**—BSOD). By default, Windows XP writes an error event to the system log, dumps the contents of memory into a file, and then reboots the system. So, if your system reboots, check the Event Viewer to see what happened.

You can control how Windows XP handles system failures by following these steps:

1. Launch Control Panel's System icon.

2. Display the Advanced tab.

3. Click Settings in the Startup and Recovery group. Figure 13.4 shows the Startup and Recovery dialog box that appears.

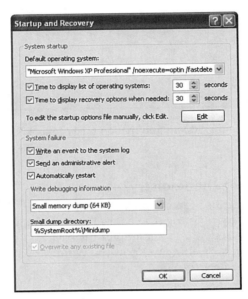

**FIGURE 13.4**    Use the Startup and Recovery dialog box to configure how Windows XP handles system failures.

4. Configure how Windows XP handles system failures using the following controls in the System Failure group:

| | |
|---|---|
| Write an Event to the System Log | Leave this check box activated to have the system failure recorded in the system log. This enables you to view the event in the Event Viewer. |
| Send an Administrative Alert | If you're on a network, when this option is activated, Windows XP sends an alert message to the administrator of the network when the system failure occurs. |
| Automatically Restart | This is the option that, when activated, causes your system to reboot when a stop error occurs. Deactivate this check box to avoid the reboot. |
| Write Debugging Information | This list determines what information Windows XP saves to disk (in the folder specified in the text box below the list) when a system |

failure occurs. This information—it's called a **memory dump**—contains data that can help a tech support employee determine the cause of the problem. You have four choices:

- None—No debugging information is written.

- Small Memory Dump (64 KB)—This option writes the minimum amount of useful information that could be used to identify what caused the stop error. This 64KB file includes the stop error number and its description, the list of running device drivers, and the processor state.

- Kernel Memory Dump—This option writes the contents of the kernel memory to the disk. (The **kernel** is the Windows XP component that manages low-level functions for processor-related activities such as scheduling and dispatching threads, handling interrupts and exceptions, and synchronizing multiple processors.) This dump includes memory allocated to the kernel, the hardware abstraction layer, and the drivers and programs used by the kernel. Unallocated memory and memory allocated to user programs are not included in the dump. This information is the most useful for troubleshooting, so I recommend using this option.

- Complete Memory Dump—This option writes the entire contents of RAM to the disk.

**CAUTION**

Windows XP first writes the debugging information to the paging file—`Pagefile.sys` in the root folder of the `%SystemDrive%`. When you restart the computer, Windows XP then transfers the information to the dump file. Therefore, you need to have a large enough paging file to handle the memory dump. This is particularly true for the Complete Memory Dump option, which requires the paging file to be as large as the physical RAM, plus one megabyte. The file size of the Kernel Memory Dump is typically about a third of physical RAM, although it may be as large as 800MB. I showed you how to check and adjust the size of the paging file in the section titled "Changing the Paging File's Location and Size" in Chapter 11, "Tuning Windows XP's Performance."

| Overwrite Any Existing File | When this option is activated, Windows XP overwrites any existing dump file with the new dump information. If you deactivate this check box, Windows XP creates a new dump file with each system failure. Note that this option is enabled only for the Kernel Memory Dump and the Complete Memory Dump (which by default write to the same file: `%SystemRoot%\Memory.dmp`). |

## Did You Recently Change Any Application Settings?

If so, try reversing the change to see whether doing so solves the problem. If that doesn't help, check to see whether an upgrade or patch is available. Also, some applications come with a Repair option that can fix corrupted files. Otherwise, try reinstalling the program.

> **NOTE**
>
> If a program freezes, you won't be able to shut it down using conventional methods. If you try, you might see a dialog box warning you that the program is not responding. If so, click End Now to force the program to close. Alternatively, right-click the taskbar and then click Task Manager. When you display the Applications tab, you should see your stuck application listed, and the Status column will likely say Not responding. Click the program and then click End Task.

## Did You Recently Install a New Program?

If you suspect a new program is causing system instability, restart Windows XP and try operating the system for a while without using the new program. (If the program has any components that load at startup, be sure to deactivate them, as I described in Chapter 1, "Customizing and Troubleshooting the Windows XP Startup"; refer to the section titled "Custom Startups with BOOT.INI.") If the problem doesn't reoccur, the new program is likely the culprit. Try using the program without any other programs running.

You should also examine the program's readme file (if it has one) to look for known problems and possible workarounds. It's also a good idea to check for a Windows XP–compatible version of the program. Again, you can also try the program's Repair option or you can reinstall the program.

Similarly, if you recently upgraded an existing program, try uninstalling the upgrade.

> **TIP**
>
> One common cause of program errors is having one or more program files corrupted because of bad hard disk sectors. Before you reinstall a program, run a surface check on your hard disk to identify and block off bad sectors. I showed you how to do a hard disk surface scan in Chapter 12; refer to the section titled "Checking Your Hard Disk for Errors."

> **TIP**
>
> When a program crashes, Windows XP displays a dialog box to let you know and it asks whether you want to send an error report to Microsoft. If you never choose to send the report, this dialog box can be annoying. To turn it off, launch Control Panel's System icon, display the Advanced tab, and then click Error Reporting. Activate the Disable Error Reporting option. Alternatively, leave the Enable Error Reporting option activated and deactivate the Programs check box.

## Did You Recently Install a New Device?

If you recently installed a new device or if you recently updated an existing device driver, the new device or driver might be causing the problem. Check Device Manager to see whether there's a problem with the device. Follow my troubleshooting suggestions in Chapter 14, "Getting the Most Out of Device Manager"; see the section titled "Troubleshooting Device Problems."

## Did You Recently Install an Incompatible Device Driver?

As you'll see in Chapter 14, Windows XP allows you to install drivers that aren't Windows XP–certified, but it also warns you that this is a bad idea. Incompatible drivers are one of the most common sources of system instability, so whenever possible you should uninstall the driver and install one that is designed for Windows XP. If you can't uninstall the driver, Windows XP automatically set a system restore point before it installed the driver, so you should use that to restore the system to its previous state. (See "Recovering Using System Restore," later in this chapter.)

## Did You Recently Apply an Update from Windows Update?

Before you install an update from the Windows Update site, Windows XP creates a system restore point (usually called *Software Distribution Service 2.0*). If your system becomes unstable after installing the update, use System Restore to revert to the pre-update configuration.

> **TIP**
>
> If you have Windows XP set up to perform automatic updating, you can keep tabs on the changes made to your system by examining the `WindowsUpdate.log` file, which you'll find in the `%SystemRoot%` folder. You can also review your Windows Update changes by going to the Windows Update site (select Start, All Programs, Windows Update) and clicking the View Installation History link.

## Did You Recently Install a Windows XP Hotfix or Service Pack?

It's ironic that hotfixes and Service Packs that are designed to increase system stability will occasionally do the opposite and cause more problems than they fix:

- If you've applied a hotfix, you can often remove it using Control Panel's Add or Remove Programs icon. Look for a Windows XP Hotfix entry in the Change or Remove Programs list. If you have multiple hotfixes listed, make sure that you remove the correct one. To be sure, check with either the Microsoft Security site or the Microsoft Knowledge Base, both of which I discuss in the next section. Note, however, that many hotfixes cannot be uninstalled. You can try using System Restore to revert to a recent restore point, but there's no guarantee this will work.

- If you installed a Service Pack and you elected to save the old system files, you can uninstall the Service Pack using Control Panel's Add or Remove Programs icon. Look for a Windows XP Service Pack entry in the Change or Remove Programs list.

# General Troubleshooting Tips

Figuring out the cause of a problem is often the hardest part of troubleshooting, but by itself it doesn't do you much good. When you know the source, you need to parlay that information into a fix for the problem. I discussed a few solutions in the previous section, but here are a few other general fixes you need to keep in mind:

- Close all programs—You can often fix flaky behavior by shutting down all your open programs and starting again. This is a particularly useful fix for problems caused by low memory or low system resources.

- Log off Windows XP—Logging off clears the RAM and so gives you a slightly cleaner slate than merely closing all your programs.

- Reboot the computer—If there are problems with some system files and devices, logging off won't help because these objects remain loaded. By rebooting the system, you reload the entire system which is often enough to solve many computer problems.

- Turn off the computer and restart—You can often solve a hardware problem by first shutting your machine off. Wait for 30 seconds to give all devices time to spin down, and then restart.

- Check connections, power switches, and so on—Some of the most common (and some of the most embarrassing) causes of hardware problems are the simple physical things: making sure that a device is turned on; checking that cable connections are secure; and ensuring that insertable devices are properly inserted.

- Use the Help and Support Center—Microsoft greatly improved the quality of the Help system in Windows XP. The Help and Support Center (select Start, Help and Support) is awash in articles and advice on using Windows XP. However, the real strength of Help and Support is, in my opinion, the Support side. In the Help and Support Center home page, click the Fixing a Problem link to see more links for general troubleshooting and for fixing specific problems related to software, multimedia, email, networking, and more. Note, too, that the Help and Support Center offers a number of **Troubleshooters**—guides that take you step-by-step through troubleshooting procedures.

# Troubleshooting Using Online Resources

The Internet is home to an astonishingly wide range of information, but its forte has always been computer knowledge. Whatever problem you have, there's a good chance that someone out there has run into the same thing, knows how to fix it, and has posted the solution on a website or newsgroup, or would be willing to share it with you if asked. True, finding what you need is sometimes difficult, and you often can't be sure how accurate some of the solutions are. However, if you stick to the more reputable sites and if you get second opinions on solutions offered by complete strangers, you'll find the online world an excellent troubleshooting resource. Here's my list of favorite online resources:

| | |
|---|---|
| Microsoft Product Support Services | This is Microsoft's main online technical support site. Through this site you can access frequently asked questions about Windows XP, see a list of known problems, download files, and send questions to Microsoft support personnel: support.microsoft.com/. |
| Microsoft Knowledge Base | The Microsoft Product Support Services site has links that enable you to search the Microsoft Knowledge Base, which is a database of articles related to all Microsoft products including, of course, Windows XP. These articles provide you with information about Windows XP and instructions on using Windows XP features. But the most useful aspect of the Knowledge Base is for trouble-shooting problems. Many of the articles were written by Microsoft support personnel after helping customers overcome problems. By searching for error codes or keywords, you can often get specific solutions to your problems. |
| Microsoft TechNet | This Microsoft site is designed for IT professionals and power users. It contains a huge number of articles on all Microsoft products. These articles give you technical content, program instructions, tips, scripts, downloads, and troubleshooting ideas: www.microsoft.com/technet/. |
| Windows Update | Check this site for the latest device drivers, security patches, Service Packs, and other updates: windowsupdate.microsoft.com/. |
| Microsoft Security | Check this site for the latest information on Microsoft's security and privacy initiatives, particularly security patches: www.microsoft.com/security/. |
| Vendor websites | All but the tiniest hardware and software vendors maintain websites with customer support sections that you can peruse for upgrades, patches, workarounds, frequently asked questions, and sometimes chat or bulletin board features. |
| Newsgroups | There are computer-related newsgroups for hundreds of topics and products. Microsoft maintains its own newsgroups via the msnews.microsoft.com server, and Usenet has a huge list of groups in the alt and comp hierarchies. Before asking a question in a newsgroup, be sure to search Google Groups to see whether your question has been answered in the past: groups.google.com/. |

13

# Recovering from a Problem

Ideally, solving a problem will require a specific tweak to the system: a Registry setting change, a driver upgrade, a program uninstall. But sometimes you need to take more of a "big picture" approach to revert your system to some previous state in the hope that you'll leap past the problem and get your system working again. Windows XP offers five ways to try such an approach—last known good configuration, System Restore, Recovery Console, reinstalling Windows XP, and Automated System Recovery—which should be used in that order. The next five sections discuss these tools.

## Booting Using the Last Known Good Configuration

Each time Windows XP starts successfully in Normal mode, the system makes a note of which **control set**—the system's drivers and hardware configuration—was used. Specifically, it enters a value in the following Registry key:

```
HKLM\SYSTEM\Select\LastKnownGood
```

For example, if this value is 1, it means that control set 1 was used to start Windows XP successfully:

```
HKLM\SYSTEM\ControlSet001
```

If you make driver or hardware changes and then find that the system won't start, you can tell Windows XP to load using the control set that worked the last time. (That is, the control set that doesn't include your most recent hardware changes.) This is called the **last known good configuration**, and the theory is that by using the previous working configuration, your system should start because it's bypassing the changes that caused the problem. Here's how to start Windows XP using the last known good configuration:

1.  Restart your computer.

2.  When the OS Choices menu appears, press F8 to display the Advanced Options menu. (If your system doesn't display the OS Choices menu, press F8 immediately after your system finishes the Power-On Self Test, which is usually indicated by a single beep.)

3.  Select the Last Known Good Configuration option.

## Recovering Using System Restore

The Last Known Good Configuration option is most useful when your computer won't start and you suspect that a hardware change is causing the problem. You might think that you can also use the last known good configuration if Windows XP starts but is unstable, and you suspect a hardware change is causing the glitch. Unfortunately, that won't work because when you start Windows XP successfully in normal mode, the hardware change is added to the last known good configuration. To revert the system to a previous configuration when you can start Windows XP successfully, you need to use the System Restore feature.

I showed you how to use System Restore to set restore points in Chapter 12 (refer to the section titled "Setting System Restore Points"). Remember, too, that Windows XP creates automatic restore points each day and when you perform certain actions (such as installing an uncertified device driver). To revert your system to a restore point, follow these steps:

1. Select Start, All Programs, Accessories, System Tools, System Restore.

2. Make sure that the Restore My Computer to an Earlier Time option is activated and click Next. The Select a Restore Point window appears, as shown in Figure 13.5.

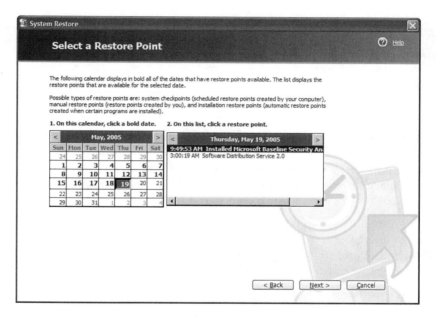

**FIGURE 13.5**   Use the Select a Restore Point window to choose the restore point you want to revert to.

3. Use the calendar to click the date on which the restore point was made. System Restore displays that day's restore points in a box to the right of the calendar.

4. Click the restore point you want to restore. Here are some common restore points you might come across:

| | |
|---|---|
| Restore Operation | A restore point set prior to a previous use of System Restore to revert the system to an earlier state |
| System Checkpoint | A restore point that Windows XP creates automatically each day |
| Software Distribution Service 2.0 | A restore point set prior to installing a Windows XP update |
| Unsigned Driver Install | A restore point set prior to installing an unsigned device driver |

5. Click Next. System Restore asks you to close all open programs and warns you not to do anything with your computer until the restore is done.

6. Click Next. System Restore begins reverting to the restore point. When it's done, it restarts your computer and displays the Restoration Complete window.

7. Click OK.

> **TIP**
>
> System Restore is available in safe mode. So, if Windows XP won't start properly, and if using the last known good configuration doesn't work, perform a safe mode startup and run System Restore from there.

## Recovering Using the Recovery Console

If Windows XP won't start normally, your first troubleshooting step is almost always to start the system in safe mode. When you make it to Windows XP, you can investigate the problem and make the necessary changes (such as disabling or rolling back a device driver). But what if your system won't even start in Safe mode?

Your next step should be booting with the last known good configuration. And if that doesn't work either? Don't worry, there's still hope in the form of the Recovery Console, a command-line tool that enables you to launch recovery tools, stop and start services, access files, and replace corrupted system files. Here's how to use it:

1. Insert the Windows XP Professional CD-ROM.

2. Restart your computer. If your system prompts you to boot from the CD, press the required key or key combination.

> **TIP**
>
> If your system won't boot from the Windows XP CD, you need to adjust the system's BIOS settings to allow this. Restart the computer and look for a startup message that prompts you to press a key or key combination to modify the BIOS settings (which might be called *Setup* or something similar). Find the boot options and either enable a CD-based boot or make sure that the option to boot from the CD comes before the option to boot from the hard disk.

3. When the Welcome to Setup screen appears, press R to choose the To Repair a Windows XP Installation Using Recovery Console option. The Recovery Console displays a list of the Windows installations on your computer.

4. Type the number that corresponds to your main Windows XP installation and press Enter. Recovery Console prompts you to enter the Administrator password.

5. Type the password and press Enter. The Recovery Console command-line prompt appears.

The Recovery Console is similar to the Windows XP command prompt, but it offers only limited access to the files and folders: the %SystemRoot% folder; the root folder of any partition; and the contents of any floppy disk, CD-ROM, or other removable disk.

Here are some troubleshooting notes to bear in mind when working at the Recovery Console:

- You have a large but limited set of commands at your disposal. To see a list of those commands, type **help** and press Enter.

- If Windows XP won't start because the BOOT.INI file is corrupted or improperly configured, you can repair it by running the BOOTCFG /REBUILD command.

- To repair bad sectors on the hard disk, run the CHKDSK command. Note, however, that CHKDSK has only two switches when you run it from the Recovery Console: /P and /R. In most cases, you'll use /R (which implies /P) to repair any bad sectors. I should point out that the /P switch is available only in the Recovery Console; you can't use /P in the command-line version of CHKDSK.

- If Windows XP won't start because a system file is corrupted, use the COPY command to copy the file from the Windows XP CD's I386 folder to the appropriate folder in the %SystemDrive%. This works for both regular and compressed files. If the file exists with a compressed cabinet (.cab) file, use the EXPAND command instead.

- If another operating system has taken over the partition boot sector, or if you suspect the partition boot sector is corrupt, you can fix the problem by running the FIXBOOT command.

- If you suspect that your computer won't start because the Master Boot Record is corrupted, you can repair it by running the FIXMBR command.

- You can display a list of all the available device drivers and services by running the LISTSVC command. If a driver or service is preventing Windows XP from starting, you can work around this by disabling the driver or service. You do this by running the DISABLE *servicename* command, where *servicename* is the name of the driver or service. Run ENABLE *servicename* to enable the driver or service.

- When you're finished working with the Recovery Console, type **exit** and press Enter.

**Recovery Console Group Policies**

If you run the SET command in the Recovery Console, you'll see a list of four environment variables that control your ability to access and copy data while in the Recovery Console:

| | |
|---|---|
| AllowWildCards | This variable determines whether you can use the ? and * wild card characters in Recovery Console commands. |
| AllowAllPaths | This variable determines whether you can use the CD command to change to any folder on the hard disk. |

| | |
|---|---|
| `AllowRemovableMedia` | This variable determines whether you can copy files from the hard disk to a removable disk. |
| `NoCopyPrompt` | This variable determines whether the Recovery Console warns you when the `COPY` command will overwrite an existing file. |
| | Each variable is set to `FALSE`, by default. Unfortunately, if you attempt to use `SET` to change the value of any variable, Recovery Console tells you that the `SET` command is disabled. To enable this command, you need to adjust a group policy setting. (Of course, if you can't start Windows XP, this won't do you much good now. However, I'm letting you know about it just in case you need it for future troubleshooting missions.) In the Group Policy editor, open the Computer Configuration, Windows Settings, Security Settings, Local Policies, Security Options branch. Enable the Recovery Console: Allow Floppy Copy and Access to All Drives and All Folders policy. |
| | Note, too, that you can also enable the Recovery Console: Allow Automatic Administrative Logon policy. Doing this prevents you from being prompted for a password when you start the Recovery Console. This is quite dangerous, of course, so enable this policy only if you're sure that no one else has access to your computer. |

## Reinstalling Windows XP

If you can't get Windows XP back on its feet using the Recovery Console, you might be able to fix things by reinstalling Windows XP over the existing installation. This won't affect your data or any personal settings you've adjusted, but it might cure what's ailing Windows XP either by restoring the system to its default settings or by installing fresh copies of corrupted system files. Here are the steps to follow to reinstall Windows XP:

1. Insert the Windows XP Professional CD-ROM.

2. Restart your computer. If your system prompts you to boot from the CD, press the required key or key combination.

3. When the Welcome to Setup screen appears, press Enter to choose the To Set Up Windows XP Now option.

4. When the Licensing Agreement appears, press F8 to accept it. Setup then displays a list of Windows XP installations on your computer.

5. If you have more one Windows XP installation, select the one you want to fix.

6. Press R to choose the To Repair the Selected Windows XP Installation option.

### Recovering Using Automated System Recovery

If nothing can get Windows XP up and running again, you have no choice but to start with a clean slate. This means either formatting the %SystemDrive% partition or, if hard disk errors are the culprit, replacing your hard disk. This will be less catastrophic if you followed my advice and used the Automated System Recovery Preparation Wizard to make backups of your system files (refer to the section in Chapter 12 titled "Running the Automated System Recovery Preparation Wizard"). If so, here are the steps to follow to recover your system:

1. Insert the Windows XP Professional CD-ROM.

2. Restart your computer. If your system prompts you to boot from the CD, press the required key or key combination. Watch the bottom of the screen for the following prompt:

   ```
   Press F2 to run Automated System Recovery (ASR)...
   ```

3. Press F2. Setup asks you to insert the ASR disk.

4. Insert the disk and then press any key. Setup continues the Windows XP installation. Note that, along the way, Setup automatically formats the %SystemDrive% partition.

From here, the Setup program proceeds normally, except that it uses the information on the ASR disk to restore your system files and settings from the backup you made using the ASR Preparation Wizard. If you also backed up your application and data files, use the Backup utility to restore them now.

## From Here

Here's a list of other places in the book where you'll find information related to troubleshooting:

- In Chapter 1, refer to the section titled "Troubleshooting Windows XP Startup."

- In Chapter 5, refer to the section titled "Practicing Safe Setups."

- In Chapter 8, refer to the section titled "Keeping the Registry Safe."

- Refer to Chapter 12, "Maintaining Your Windows XP System."

- In Chapter 14, see the section titled "Troubleshooting Device Problems."

- See Chapter 24, "Troubleshooting Network Problems."

# Getting the Most Out of Device Manager

*Man is a shrewd inventor, and is ever taking the hint of a new machine from his own structure, adapting some secret of his own anatomy in iron, wood, and leather, to some required function in the work of the world.*

*—Ralph Waldo Emerson*

Emerson's concept of a machine was decidedly low-tech ("iron, wood, and leather"), but his basic idea is still apt in these high-tech times. Man has taken yet another "secret of his own anatomy"—the brain—and used it as the "hint of a new machine"—the computer. And although even the most advanced computer is still a mere toy compared to the breathtaking complexity of the human brain, some spectacular advancements have been made in the art of hardware in recent years.

One of the hats an operating system must wear is that of an intermediary between you (or your software) and your hardware. Any operating system worth its salt has to translate incomprehensible "device-speak" into something you can make sense out of, and it must ensure that devices are ready, willing, and able to carry out your commands. Given the sophistication and diversity of today's hardware market, however, that's no easy task.

The good news is that Windows XP brings to the PC world support for a broad range of hardware, from everyday devices such as keyboards, mice, printers, monitors, and video, sound, and network cards, to more exotic hardware fare such as IEEE 1394 (FireWire) controllers, Flash storage readers, and infrared devices. However, although this hardware support is broad, it's not all that deep, meaning that Windows XP doesn't have built-in support for many older devices. So, even though lots of hardware vendors have taken at least some steps towards upgrading their devices and drivers, managing hardware is still one of Windows XP's trickier areas. This chapter should help as I take you through lots of practical techniques for installing, updating, and troubleshooting devices in Windows XP.

# Understanding Windows XP's Device Support

Let's begin our examination of hardware issues by looking at a few of the innovations the Windows operating system brings to device management. But first, let's recap how people dealt with devices before Windows came along.

## Device Support: The Bad Old Days

Installing and configuring hardware has always been the bête noire of PC owners. Sure, getting cards and drives into their particular slots or bays wasn't a big deal, as long as you were at least minimally dexterous (and could stomach the idea of dealing with your computer's innards). It was the "before" and "after" phases that gave most people ulcers and prematurely gray hair. The before phase usually consisted of adjusting jumpers and setting **DIP** (dual inline package) switches; the after phase involved configuring a few more device parameters by using some kind of setup program.

What was the purpose of all this adjusting, setting, and configuring? To coax the device into working with our hardware and to avoid conflicts with other devices. For most devices, this required configuring three resources: the Interrupt Request Line (IRQ), the Input/Output (I/O) port address, and the Direct Memory Access (DMA) channel.

### The IRQ

The **IRQ** is a hardware line over which a device (such as a keyboard or a sound card) can send signals (called **interrupts**) to get the attention of the processor when the device is ready to accept or send data. The basic problem is that although you need a separate IRQ for each device that needs one, only 16 IRQs are available to go around. That might sound like plenty, but many of these IRQs are used by system devices. Table 14.1 lists a very basic IRQ distribution in a simple PC.

**TABLE 14.1**    IRQ Distribution in a Simple Computer

| IRQ | Device |
| --- | --- |
| 0 | System timer |
| 1 | Keyboard |
| 2 | Programmable interrupt controller |
| 3 | PCI slot or serial port 2 (COM2) |
| 4 | Serial port 1 (COM1) |
| 5 | PCI slot or parallel port 2 (LPT2) |
| 6 | Floppy disk controller |

**TABLE 14.1**    Continued

| IRQ | Device |
|-----|--------|
| 7 | Parallel port 1 (LPT1) |
| 8 | Real-time clock |
| 9 | Microsoft ACPI-compliant system |
| 10 | PCI slot |
| 11 | PCI slot |
| 12 | Mouse |
| 13 | Numeric data processor |
| 14 | Primary IDE channel |
| 15 | Secondary IDE channel |

In the old days, you often had only two or three unallocated IRQs for all your other devices: sound card, network card, SCSI controller, video adapter, and whatever other devices you've stuffed inside your machine. An **IRQ conflict**—either two devices trying to use the same IRQ or software that thinks a device is using one IRQ when in fact it's using another—was the cause of many hardware problems.

### The I/O Port Address

An **I/O port** is a small block of memory (typically 8 bytes, 16 bytes, or 32 bytes) that acts as a communications channel between a device and the processor or a device driver. After a device has used its IRQ to catch the attention of the processor, the actual exchange of data or commands takes place through the device's I/O port address. Each I/O port address is expressed as a range of hexadecimal numbers. For example, the first I/O port on most systems is used by the Direct Memory Access controller, and its address is the 16-byte range 00000000– 0000000F.

There are 65,535 I/O ports available—more than enough to satisfy all your device needs. As with IRQs, however, no two devices can share an I/O port, so conflicts can lead to problems. Note also that many devices use multiple I/O port addresses. In this case, the I/O port is expressed as a range of hexadecimal numbers.

### The DMA Channel

A **DMA channel** is a connection, maintained by a DMA controller chip, that enables a device to transfer data directly to and from memory without going through the processor (as it does with an I/O port). The processor tells the DMA controller chip what device to work with and what data is needed. The DMA controller chip then uses the channel to perform the complete data transfer without involving the processor. Modern computers support eight DMA channels, as shown in Table 14.2.

**TABLE 14.2**    DMA Channel Distribution in a Typical Computer

| DMA Channel | Device |
|-------------|--------|
| 0 | Available |
| 1 | Available |
| 2 | Floppy disk controller |

14

**TABLE 14.2** Continued

| DMA Channel | Device |
| --- | --- |
| 3 | Available |
| 4 | DMA controller |
| 5 | Available |
| 6 | Available |
| 7 | Available |

As with the other resources, problems can arise when two devices attempt to use the same DMA channel. This is a rarer problem, however, because few devices use DMA and most of the DMA channels are available.

### More Device Woes

It's bad enough just trying to make sense of all these acronyms and abbreviations, but installing hardware devices is a lonely business because you're on your own. The situation has improved somewhat because some device setup programs have improved in recent years, and the resources for many recent devices are software selectable. However, we're still left with lots of troubling questions:

- How do you know which resources a device is currently using?

- If a device isn't working properly, which resource—IRQ, I/O port, or DMA channel—is causing the problem?

- Is the problem a conflict with an existing device, or is it that the software trying to access the device is referencing the wrong resource?

- How do you handle computers that use multiple configurations, such as a notebook computer that has a docking station?

- How do you handle all the different PC Card (PCMCIA) configurations and standards?

- What if you change your hardware? Do you have to constantly adjust the resources for your devices?

What the PC world needed badly was a way to manage devices easily. In other words, some kind of new approach to device management was needed that would provide two things:

- A central repository for hardware information that showed you not only the peripherals attached to your system, but also which resources they were using and whether any devices were in conflict with each other.

- "Smart" devices and software that could examine the resources currently being used and configure the devices accordingly.

## Device Support in Windows XP

Windows XP is the boldest and most ambitious attempt yet by the PC community to solve the thorny problem of device management. From day one, Microsoft designed this operating system to offer greatly improved support for all kinds of peripherals, including rewritable DVD drives, wireless devices, Universal Serial Bus (USB) 2.0, and FireWire (IEEE 1394). To that end, Windows XP comes loaded with device management features, including the following:

- Plug and Play support—This is the big news for people who are sick of wrestling with IRQs and other hardware mysteries. The theory behind Plug and Play (PnP) is simple: PnP-compliant hardware can report its current configuration and adjust itself automatically to a new configuration to avoid conflicts with other devices. Windows XP supports PnP, which means it can work with the reports given by these devices and automatically load or unload the appropriate device drivers. (For a more detailed treatment of Plug and Play, see the section titled "Installing Plug and Play Devices" later in this chapter.)

- Device Manager and the Registry—To satisfy the need for a central repository of device information, Windows XP serves up two related features: Device Manager and the Registry. Device Manager provides a graphical outline of all the devices on your system. It can show you the current configuration of each device (including the IRQ, I/O ports, and DMA channel used by each device). And it even enables you to adjust a device's configuration (assuming that the device doesn't require you to make physical adjustments to, say, a DIP switch or jumper). The Device Manager actually gets its data from, and stores modified data in, the Registry. (I'll show you how to use Device Manager later in this chapter; see the later section "Managing Your Hardware with Device Manager." For the Registry, refer to Chapter 8, "Getting to Know the Windows XP Registry.")

- Add Hardware Wizard—When you install Windows XP, the Setup program runs a hardware detection routine to automatically detect the devices in your system and the resources used by each device. The hardware detection feature is also available after you've installed Windows XP, in the form of the Add Hardware Wizard. You can use this wizard to have Windows XP check your system for new hardware, or you can use it to specify new devices by hand.

- IRQ sharing—Windows XP supports a relatively new PCI hardware feature called **IRQ sharing**. This means that, for devices on the PCI bus, Windows XP is capable of managing the interrupt requests in such a way that two or more devices can share the same IRQ without conflicting with each other.

- **Advanced Programmable Interrupt Controller** (**APIC**) support—APIC is a powerful interrupt controller that is faster and more robust than the old **Programmable Interrupt Controller** (PIC), and the APIC usually supplies 24 IRQs instead of the 16 supplied in PIC systems.

# Tips and Techniques for Installing Devices

When working with Windows 2000 and Windows NT, there was one cardinal rule for choosing a device to attach to your Windows XP system: Check the hardware compatibility list! This was a list of devices that were known to work with Windows. Like its operating system ancestors, Windows XP also maintains a list of compatible hardware, only now it's called the Windows Catalog. You can get to this website by entering the following address in your web browser: www.microsoft.com/windows/catalog/.

If you see your device (and, in some cases, the correct device version) in the hardware list, you can install it secure in the knowledge that it will work properly with Windows XP. If you don't see the device, all is not lost because you still have two other options:

- Check the box for some indication that the device works with Windows XP or contains drivers for Windows XP. Seeing the Designed for Windows XP logo on the box is the best way to be sure that the device works with Windows XP.

- Check the manufacturer's website to see whether an updated Windows XP driver or device setup program is available.

## Installing Plug and Play Devices

The Holy Grail of device configuration is a setup in which you need only to insert or plug in a peripheral and turn it on (if necessary), and your system configures the device automatically. In other words, the system not only recognizes that a new device is attached to the machine, but it also gleans the device's default resource configuration and, if required, resolves any conflicts that might have arisen with existing devices. And, of course, it should be able to perform all this magic without your ever having to flip a DIP switch, fiddle with a jumper, or fuss with various IRQ, I/O port, and DMA combinations.

Plug and Play is an attempt by members of the PC community to reach this Zen-like hardware state. Did they succeed? Yes, Plug and Play works like a charm, but only if your Windows XP system meets the following criteria:

- It has a Plug and Play BIOS—One of the first things that happens inside your computer when you turn it on (or do a hardware reboot) is the ROM BIOS (basic input/output system) code performs a Power-On Self Test to check the system hardware. If you have a system with a Plug and Play BIOS, the initial code also enumerates and tests all the Plug and Play–compliant devices on the system. For each device, the BIOS not only activates the device, but also gathers the device's resource configuration (IRQ, I/O ports, and so forth). When all the Plug and Play devices have been isolated, the BIOS then checks for resource conflicts and, if there are any, takes steps to resolve them.

- It uses Plug and Play devices—Plug and Play devices are the extroverts of the hardware world. They're only too happy to chat with any old Plug and Play BIOS or operating system that happens along. What do they chat about? The device essentially identifies itself to the BIOS (or the operating system if the BIOS isn't Plug and

Play–compliant) by sending its **configuration ID**, which tells the BIOS what the device is and which resources it uses. The BIOS then configures the system's resources accordingly.

Plug and Play is built in to every device that connects via a USB or IEEE 1394 port, and it comes with all PC Card devices and almost all interface cards that connect to the PCI bus. Other devices that connect via the serial, parallel, or PS/2 ports aren't necessarily Plug and Play–compliant, but almost all of these devices manufactured in the past few years are. Interface cards that connect to the legacy ISA bus are not Plug and Play–compliant.

Before you install a Plug and Play device, check to see whether the hardware came with a setup program on a floppy disk, a CD, or as part of the downloaded package. If it did, run that program and, if you're given any setup options, be sure to install at least the device driver. Having the driver loaded on the system will help Windows XP install the device automatically.

**CAUTION**

Only members of the Administrators group can install device drivers, so be sure to log in as a member of that group before installing the device. Alternatively, you can log in as another user and then enter your Administrator username and password when prompted during the installation.

How Windows reacts when you install a Plug and Play device that is designed for Windows XP depends on how you installed the device:

- If you **hot-swapped** a device such as a PC Card or a printer, Windows XP recognizes the device immediately and installs the driver for it.

- If you turned your computer off to install the device, Windows XP recognizes it the next time you start the machine, and installs the appropriate driver.

Either way, an icon appears in the system tray and a balloon tip titled Found New Hardware pops up to tell you that your new hardware is installed and ready for use.

If Windows XP did not find a device driver for the new hardware, it automatically runs the Found New Hardware Wizard. The wizard first asks whether it can connect to Windows Update to search for the latest drivers.

If you bypass Windows Update—if you allow the connection but Windows XP doesn't find an appropriate driver—the wizard gives you two choices to proceed:

| | |
|---|---|
| Install the Software Automatically | Activate this option if you have a floppy disk or CD that contains a Windows XP–compatible device driver for the hardware. Insert the disk or CD and click Next. Windows XP examines the system's disk drives, locates the driver, and then installs its. If the wizard finds more than one driver, it asks you to choose the one you want from a list. |

14

| Install from a List or Specific Location | Activate this option if you've downloaded a driver from the Internet or if you have a disk or CD that has a driver that isn't compatible with Windows XP. Click Next. |

If you choose the latter option and click Next, you see the dialog box shown in Figure 14.1.

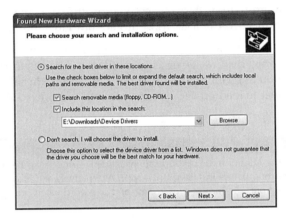

**FIGURE 14.1**    This dialog box appears if you elected to install the device driver from a list or a specific location.

Again, you have two ways to proceed:

| Search for the Best Driver in These Locations. | Activate this option if you've downloaded the device driver from the Internet. If the driver is on a floppy disk or CD, leave the Search Removable Media check box activated; otherwise, deactivate it. If the driver is on your hard disk or a network drive, activate the Include This Location in the Search check box and then enter the full path of the folder that contains the driver. Click Next. |

---

**CAUTION**

If the downloaded driver is contained within a compressed file (such as a Zip file), be sure to decompress the file before moving on to the next wizard step.

---

| Don't Search. I Will Choose the Driver to Install. | Activate this option if you have a floppy disk or CD containing a device driver that isn't compatible with Windows XP. Note that you should also choose this option if you want to use one of Windows XP's built-in drivers that you think might be a close enough match |

for the device. Click Next, choose the appropriate hard
ware type, and click Next again. In the next wizard
dialog box, you have two choices:

- If you have a floppy disk or CD, insert it, click
  Have Disk, type *d*:\, where *d* is the letter of the
  drive that holds the disk or CD, and click OK.

- If you want to pick an existing Windows XP driver,
  activate the Show Compatible Hardware check
  box, select the driver that closely matches your
  device, and then click Next.

## Installing Legacy Devices

When it comes to installing legacy devices (that is, devices that don't support Plug and
Play), your best bet by far is to run the setup program that the manufacturer supplies
either on a floppy disk, a CD, or as part of the driver download. If you're asked, choose
the Windows XP driver, if one is available. If no Windows XP driver is available, the
Windows 2000 driver will work in most cases. If the device only has drivers for Windows
NT, Windows 9x, or Windows Me, these almost certainly will not work with Windows XP,
so there's no point in installing them. Go to the manufacturer's website and look for a
Windows XP (or, at worst, a Windows 2000) driver to download.

If you don't have a setup program for the device, Windows XP might still be able to
support the hardware using one of its legacy device drivers. To do this, you need to run
one of Windows XP's hardware wizards. Some of these wizards are device-specific, so you
should use those where appropriate:

- Joystick or other game device—Launch Control Panel's Game Controllers icon and
  then click Add.

- Modem—Launch Control Panel's Phone and Modem Options icon, display the
  Modems tab, and click Add.

- Printer—Select Start, Printers and Faxes, and then click the Add a Printer link.

- Scanner or digital camera—Launch Control Panel's Scanners and Cameras icon, and
  then click the Add an Imaging Device link.

For all other devices, connect the device and then run the Add Hardware Wizard:

1. Launch Control Panel's Add Hardware icon.

2. In the wizard's initial dialog box, click Next. The wizard searches for new Plug and
   Play hardware.

3. When the wizard asks whether the hardware is connected, activate the Yes, I Have Already Connected the Hardware option and click Next. The wizard displays a list of installed hardware.

4. At the bottom of the list, select Add a New Hardware Device and click Next.

5. You now have two choices:

| | |
|---|---|
| Search for and Install the Hardware Automatically | Activate this option if you have a device that the wizard is capable of locating using hardware detection. This route often works with modems, printers, video cards, and network cards. Click Next to start the detection process. If the detection failed, the wizard will let you know. In this case, click Next and proceed with step 6. |
| Install the Hardware That I Manually Select from a List | Activate this option to pick out the device by hand. Click Next. |

6. Select the hardware category that applies to your device. If you don't see an appropriate category, select Show All Devices. Click Next.

7. Depending on the hardware category you selected, a new wizard might appear. (For example, if you chose the Modems category, the Install New Modem Wizard appears.) In this case, follow the wizard's dialog boxes. Otherwise, a dialog box appears with a list of manufacturers and models. You have two choices:

   • Specify your device by first selecting the device's manufacturer in the Manufacturers list and then selecting the name of the device in the Models list.

   • If you have a manufacturer's floppy disk, CD, or downloaded file, click Have Disk, enter the appropriate path and filename in the Install from Disk dialog box, and click OK.

8. Click Next. Windows XP installs the device.

9. Click Finish to complete the wizard.

## Controlling Driver Signing Options

Device drivers that meet the Designed for Windows XP specifications have been tested for compatibility with Microsoft and then given a digital signature. This signature tells you that the driver works properly with Windows XP and that it hasn't been changed since it was tested. (For example, the driver hasn't been infected by a virus or Trojan horse program.) When you're installing a device, if Windows XP comes across a driver that has not been digitally signed, it displays a dialog box similar to the one shown in Figure 14.2.

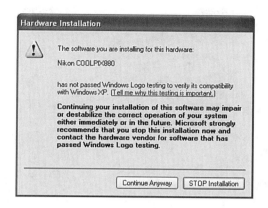

**FIGURE 14.2**   Windows XP displays a dialog box similar to this one when it comes across a device driver that does not have a digital signature.

If you click STOP Installation, Windows XP aborts the driver installation and you won't be able to use the device. This is the most prudent choice in this situation because an unsigned driver can cause all kinds of havoc, including lock-ups, **BSODs** (Blue Screens of Death), and other system instabilities. You should check the manufacturer's website for a Windows XP–compatible driver, or upgrade to a newer model that's supported by Windows XP.

Having said all that, although not installing an unsigned driver is the *prudent* choice, it's not the most *convenient* choice because in most cases you probably want to use the device now rather than later. The truth is that most of the time these unsigned drivers cause no problems and work as advertised, so it's probably safe to continue with the installation. In any case, Windows XP always sets a restore point prior to the installation of an unsigned driver, so you can always restore your system to its previous state should anything go wrong.

> **NOTE**
>
> Test your system thoroughly after installing the driver: Use the device, open and use your most common applications, and run some disk utilities. If anything seems awry, use the restore point to roll back the system to its previous configuration.

By default, Windows XP gives you the option of either continuing or aborting the installation of the unsigned driver. You can change this behavior to automatically accept or reject all unsigned drivers by following these steps:

1. Launch Control Panel's System icon.

2. Display the Hardware tab.

3. Click Driver Signing. Windows XP displays the Driver Signing Options dialog box, shown in Figure 14.3.

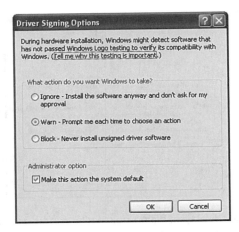

**FIGURE 14.3**    Use the Driver Signing Options dialog box to specify how Windows XP should handle unsigned device drivers.

4.  Choose an option in the What Action Do You Want Windows to Take? group:

Ignore       Choose this option if you want Windows XP to install all unsigned drivers.

Warn        Choose this option if you want Windows XP to warn you about an unsigned driver by displaying the dialog box in Figure 14.2.

Block        Choose this option if you want Windows XP not to install any unsigned drivers.

5.  If you want this action to apply to all the users of the computer, leave the Make This Action the System Default check box activated.

6.  Click OK.

> **TIP**
>
> There are some device drivers that Windows XP knows will cause system instabilities. Windows XP will simply refuse to load these problematic drivers, no matter which action you choose in the Driver Signing Options dialog box. In this case, you'll see a dialog box similar to the one in Figure 14.2, except this one tells you that the driver will not be installed and your only choice is to cancel the installation.

## Managing Your Hardware with Device Manager

Windows XP stores all its hardware data in the Registry, but it provides Device Manager to give you a graphical view of the devices on your system. To display Device Manager, first use any of the following techniques:

- Launch Control Panel's System icon

- Right-click My Computer and click Properties in the shortcut menu

In the System Properties dialog box that appears, display the Hardware tab and then click Device Manager.

**TIP**

A quick way to go directly to the Device Manager snap-in is to select Start, Run, type `devmgmt.msc`, and click OK. Note, too, that you can display the System Properties dialog box quickly by pressing [Windows logo key]+Pause/Break.

Device Manager's default display is a treelike outline that lists various hardware types. To see the specific devices, click the plus sign (+) to the left of a device type. For example, opening the DVD/CD-ROM Drives branch displays all the DVD and CD-ROM drives attached to your computer, as shown in Figure 14.4.

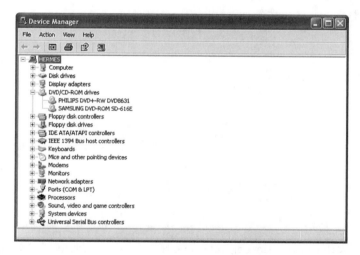

**FIGURE 14.4**    Device Manager organizes your computer's hardware in a tree-like hierarchy organized by hardware type.

## Controlling the Device Display

Device Manager's default view is by hardware type, but it also offers several other views, all of which are available on the snap-in's View menu:

Devices by Connection          This view displays devices according to what they are connected to within your computer. For example, to see which devices are connected to the PCI bus, on most systems you'd open the ACPI branch, and then the Microsoft ACPI-Compliant System branch, and finally the PCI Bus branch.

Resources by Type

This view displays devices according to the **hardware resources** they require. Your computer's resources are the communications channels by which devices communicate back and forth with software. There are four types: Interrupt Request (IRQ), Input/Output (IO), Direct memory access (DMA), and Memory (a portion of the computer's memory that's allocated to the device and is used to store device data). For example, Figure 14.5 shows Device Manager with devices displays by IRQ.

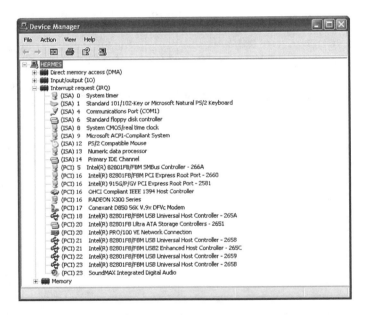

**FIGURE 14.5**  With Device Manager, you can display your system's devices according to the IRQ they use.

Resources by Connection

This view displays the computer's allocated resources according to how they're connected within the computer.

Show Hidden Devices

When you activate this command, Device Manager displays those non–Plug and Play devices that you normally don't need to adjust or troubleshoot. It also displays **nonpresent devices**, which are those that have been installed but aren't currently attached to the computer.

## Viewing Device Properties

Each device listed in Device Manager has its own property sheet. You can use these properties not only to learn more about the device (such as the resources it's currently using), but also to make adjustments to the device's resources, change the device driver, alter the device's settings (if it has any), and make other changes.

To display the property sheet for a device, double-click the device or click the device and then select Action, Properties. The number of tabs you see depends on the hardware, but most devices have at least the following:

| | |
|---|---|
| General | This tab gives you general information such as the name of the device, its hardware type, and the manufacturer's name. The Device Status group tells you whether the device is working properly, and gives you status information if it's not (see "Troubleshooting with Device Manager," later in this chapter). You use the Device Usage list to enable or disable a device (see "Managing Hardware Profiles," later in this chapter). |
| Driver | This tab gives you information about the device driver and offers several buttons to managing the driver. See "Working with Device Drivers," next. |
| Resources | This tab tells you the hardware resources used by the device. |

## Working with Device Drivers

For most users, device drivers exist in the nether regions of the PC world, shrouded in obscurity and the mysteries of assembly language programming. As the middlemen brokering the dialogue between Windows XP and our hardware, however, these complex chunks of code perform a crucial task. After all, it's just not possible to unleash the full potential of your system unless the hardware and the operating system coexist harmoniously and optimally. To that end, you need to ensure that Windows XP is using appropriate drivers for all your hardware. You do that by updating to the latest drivers and by rolling back drivers that aren't working properly.

### Updating a Device Driver

Follow these steps to update a device driver:

1. If you have a floppy disk or CD with the updated driver, insert the disk or CD. If you downloaded the driver from the Internet, decompress the driver file, if necessary.

2. In Device Manager, click the device you want to work with.

3. Select Action, Update Driver. (You can also open the device's property sheet, display the Driver tab, and click Update Driver.) The Hardware Update Wizard appears.

4. This wizard works the same way as the Found New Hardware Wizard discussed earlier in this chapter so follow the instructions given in the "Installing Plug and Play Devices" section.

### Rolling Back a Device Driver

If an updated device driver is giving you problems, you have two ways to fix things:

- If updating the driver was the last action you performed on the system, restore the system to the most recent restore point.

- If you've updated other things on the system in the meantime, a restore point might restore more than you need. In that case, you need to roll back just the device driver that's causing problems.

Follow these steps to roll back a device driver:

1. In Device Manager, open the device's property sheet.

2. Display the Driver tab.

3. Click Roll Back Driver.

## Uninstalling a Device

When you remove a Plug and Play device, the BIOS informs Windows XP that the device is no longer present. Windows XP, in turn, updates its device list in the Registry, and the peripheral no longer appears in the Device Manager display.

If you're removing a legacy device, however, you need to tell Device Manager that the device no longer exists. To do that, follow these steps:

1. Click the device in the Device Manager tree.

2. Select Action, Uninstall. (Alternatively, open the device's property sheet, display the Driver tab, and click Uninstall.)

3. If you've defined multiple hardware profiles (as described later, in the "Managing Hardware Profiles" section), Windows XP will ask whether you want to remove the device from all the profiles or just from a specific profile. Select the appropriate option.

4. When Windows XP warns you that you're about to remove the device, click OK.

# Managing Hardware Profiles

In most cases, your hardware configuration will remain relatively static. You might add the odd new device or remove a device, but these are permanent changes. Windows XP merely updates its current hardware configuration to compensate.

In some situations, however, you might need to switch between hardware configurations regularly. A good example is a notebook computer with a docking station. When the computer is undocked, it uses its built-in keyboard, mouse, and display; when the computer is docked, however, it uses a separate keyboard, mouse, and display. To make it easier to switch between these different configurations, Windows XP enables you to set up a hardware profile for each setup. It then becomes a simple matter of your selecting the profile you want to use at startup; Windows XP handles the hard part of loading the appropriate drivers.

> **NOTE**
>
> Generally speaking, you don't need to bother with hardware profiles if your computer has a Plug and Play BIOS and you're using Plug and Play devices. Plug and Play detects any new hardware configuration automatically and adjusts accordingly. For example, Plug and Play supports hot docking of a notebook computer: While the machine is running, you can insert it into, or remove it from, the docking station, and Plug and Play handles the switch without breaking a sweat. Hardware profiles are useful when you have configurations that require major hardware changes and you don't want to wait for the Plug and Play process to redetect each changed device.

Before creating a new hardware profile, install the drivers you need for all the hardware you'll be using. If the hardware isn't currently attached, that's okay; just be sure to specify the appropriate devices by hand in the Add Hardware Wizard. The important thing is to make sure that all the drivers you need are installed.

After that's done, display the System Properties dialog box as described earlier and select the Hardware tab. Click the Hardware Profiles button to display the Hardware Profiles dialog box. On most systems, you see a single profile named Profile 1. This profile includes all the installed device drivers. The idea is that you create a new profile by making a copy of this configuration, and then you tell Windows XP which devices to include in each profile.

To make a copy of the profile, click the Copy button, type a name for the new profile in the Copy Profile dialog box, and click OK. (If you want to rename a profile, highlight the profile, click Rename, enter the new name in the Rename Profile dialog box, and click OK.)

Now that you have multiple profiles in place, you need to tell Windows XP which devices go with which profile. Follow these steps:

1. If you want to work with the new profile, restart your computer and select the profile from the menu that appears at startup.

2. Open Device Manager and find the device you want to work with.

3. Display the device's property sheet.

4. In the General tab's Device Usage list, choose one of the following options (you'll see one or more of the following three choices, depending on the device):

| | |
|---|---|
| Use this Device (Enable) | Select this option to include the device in the profile. |
| Do Not Use This Device in the Current Hardware Profile (Disable) | If you select this option, Windows XP disables the device only in the current hardware profile. |

| Do Not Use This Device in Any Hardware Profiles (Disable) | If you select this option, Windows XP disables the device in every hardware profile. |

5. Click OK.

# Working with Device Security Policies

The Group Policy editor offers several device-related policies. To see them, open the Group Policy editor and select Local Computer Policy, Computer Configuration, Windows Settings, Security Settings, Local Policies, Security Options. Here are the policies in the Devices category:

| Allow Undock Without Having to Log On | When this policy is enabled, users can undock a notebook computer without having to log on to Windows XP (that is, they can undock the computer by pressing the docking station's eject button). If you want to restrict who can do this, disable this policy. |

> **TIP**
>
> To control who can undock the computer, display Local Computer Policy, Computer Configuration, Windows Settings, Security Settings, Local Policies, User Rights Assignment. Use the Remove Computer from Docking Station policy to assign the users or groups who have this right.

| Allowed to Format and Eject Removable Media | Use this policy to determine the groups that are allowed to format floppy disks and eject CDs and other removable media. |
| Prevent Users from Installing Printer Drivers | Enable this policy to prevent users from installing a network printer. Note that this doesn't affect the installation of a local printer. |
| Restrict CD-ROM Access to Locally Logged-On User Only | Enable this policy to prevent network users from operating the computer's CD-ROM or DVD drive at the same time as a local user. If no local user is accessing the drive, the network user can access it. |
| Restrict Floppy Access to Locally Logged-On User Only | Enable this policy to prevent network users from operating the computer's floppy drive at the same time as a local user. If no local user is accessing the drive, the network user can access it. |
| Unsigned Driver Installation Behavior | This policy determines the action Windows XP takes if it comes across an unsigned device driver. There are three choices: Silently Succeed; Warn but Allow Installation; and Do Not Allow Installation. |

# Troubleshooting Device Problems

Windows XP has excellent support for most newer devices, and most major hardware vendors have taken steps to update their devices and drivers to run properly with Windows XP. If you use only recent, Plug and Play–compliant devices that qualify for the Designed for Windows XP logo, you should have a trouble-free computing experience (at least from a hardware perspective). Of course, putting *trouble-free* and *computing* next to each other is just asking for trouble. Hardware is not foolproof; far from it. Things still can, and will, go wrong, and, when they do, you'll need to perform some kind of troubleshooting. (Assuming, of course, that the device doesn't have a physical fault that requires a trip to the repair shop.) Fortunately, Windows XP also has some handy tools to help you both identify and rectify hardware ills.

## Troubleshooting with Device Manager

Device Manager not only provides you with a comprehensive summary of your system's hardware data, but it also doubles as a decent troubleshooting tool. To see what I mean, check out the Device Manager tab shown in Figure 14.6. See how the icon for the SiS 900 PCI Fast Ethernet Adapter device has an X superimposed on it? This tells you that there's a problem with the device.

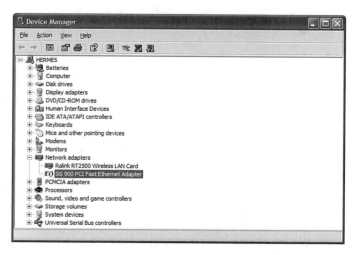

**FIGURE 14.6**   The Device Manager uses icons to warn you if there's a problem with a device.

If you examine the device's properties, as shown in Figure 14.7, the Device Status area tells you a bit more about what's wrong. As you can see in Figure 14.7, the problem here is that the device won't start. Either try Device Manager's suggested remedy or click the Troubleshooting button to launch Windows XP's hardware troubleshooter.

> **NOTE**
>
> Device Manager has several dozen error codes. See the following Microsoft Knowledge Base article for a complete list of the codes as well as solutions to try in each case: support.microsoft.com/default.aspx?scid=kb;en-us;Q310123.

**FIGURE 14.7**   The Device Status area tells you if the device isn't working properly.

Device Manager uses three different icons to give you an indication of the device's current status:

- A black exclamation mark (!) on a yellow field tells you that there's a problem with the device.

- A red X tells you that the device is disabled or missing.

- A blue i on a white field tells you that the device's Use Automatic Settings check box (on the Resources tab) is deactivated and that at least one of the device's resources was selected manually. Note that the device might be working just fine, so this icon doesn't indicate a problem. If the device isn't working properly, however, the manual setting might be the cause. (For example, the device might have a DIP switch or jumper set to a different resource.)

If a device is flagged on your system, but you don't notice any problems, you can usually get away with just ignoring the flag. I've seen lots of systems that run perfectly well with flagged devices, so this falls under the "If it ain't broke[el]" school of troubleshooting. The danger here is that tweaking your system to try to get rid of the flag can cause other—usually more serious—problems.

## Troubleshooting Device Driver Problems

Outside of problems to the hardware itself, device drivers are the cause of most device woes. Here are a few tips and pointers for correcting device driver problems:

- Reinstall the driver—A driver might be malfunctioning because one or more of its files have become corrupted. You can usually solve this by reinstalling the driver. Just in case a disk fault caused the corruption, you should check the partition where the driver is installed for errors before reinstalling. (In Chapter 12, "Maintaining Your Windows XP System," refer to the section titled "Checking Your Hard Disk for Errors" for instructions on checking a disk for errors.)

- Upgrade to a signed driver—Unsigned drivers are accidents waiting for a place to happen in Windows XP, so you should upgrade to a signed driver, if possible. How can you tell if an installed driver is unsigned? Open the device's property sheet, display the Driver tab, and click Driver Details. Signed driver files have a certificate icon with a green checkmark; unsigned files have no icon. Refer to "Updating a Device Driver," earlier in this chapter.

- Disable an unsigned driver—If an unsigned driver is causing system instability and you can't upgrade the driver, try disabling it. In the General tab of the device's property sheet, select Do Not Use This Device (Disable) in the Device Usage list.

- Use the Signature Verification Tool—This program checks your entire system (or, optionally, a specific folder) for unsigned drivers. In Chapter 12, refer to the section titled "Verifying Digitally Signed Files" to learn how to use this program.

- Try the manufacturer's driver supplied with the device—If the device came with its own driver, try either updating the driver to the manufacturer's or running the device's setup program.

- Download the latest driver from the manufacturer—Device manufacturers often update drivers to fix bugs, add new features, and tweak performance. Go to the manufacturer's website to see whether an updated driver is available. (See "Tips for Downloading Device Drivers," next.)

- Try Windows Update—The Windows Update website often has updated drivers for downloading. Select Start, All Programs, Windows Update and let the site scan your system. Then click the Driver Updates link to see which drivers are available for your system.

- Roll back a driver—If the device stops working properly after you update the driver, try rolling it back to the old driver. (Refer to "Rolling Back a Device Driver," earlier in this chapter.)

## Tips for Downloading Device Drivers

Finding device drivers on the World Wide Web is an art in itself. I can't tell you how much of my life I've wasted rooting around manufacturer websites trying to locate a device driver. Most hardware vendor sites seem to be optimized for sales rather than service, so although you can purchase, say, a new printer with just a mouse click or two, downloading a new driver for that printer can take a frustratingly long time. To help you avoid such frustration, here are some tips from my hard-won experience:

- If the manufacturer offers different sites for different locations (such as different countries), always use the company's "home" site. Most mirror sites aren't true mirrors, and (Murphy's Law still being in effect) it's usually the driver you're looking for that a mirror site is missing.

- The temptation when you first enter a site is to use the search feature to find what you want. This works only sporadically for drivers, and the site search engines almost always return marketing or sales material first.

- Instead of the search engine, look for an area of the site dedicated to driver downloads. The good sites will have links to areas called Downloads or Drivers, but it's far more common to first have to go through a Support or Customer Service area.

- Don't try to take any shortcuts to where you *think* the driver might be hiding. Trudge through each step the site provides. For example, it's common to have to select an overall driver category, and then a device category, and then a line category, and then the specific model you have. This is tedious, but it almost always gets you where you want to go.

- If the site is particularly ornery, the preceding method might not lead you to your device. In that case, try the search engine. Note that device drivers seem to be particularly poorly indexed, so you might have to try lots of search text variations. One thing that usually works is searching for the exact filename. How can you possibly know that? A method that often works for me is to use Google (www.google.com) or Google Groups (groups.google.com) or some other web search engine to search for your driver. Chances are someone else has looked for your file and will have the filename (or, if you're really lucky, a direct link to the driver on the manufacturer's site).

- When you get to the device's download page, be careful which file you choose. Make sure that it's a Windows XP driver, and make sure that you're not downloading a utility program or some other nondriver file.

- When you finally get to download the file, be sure to save it to your computer rather than opening it. If you reformat your system or move the device to another computer, you'll be glad you have a local copy of the driver so that you don't have to wrestle with the whole download rigmarole all over again.

## Troubleshooting Resource Conflicts

On modern computer systems that support the Advanced Configuration and Power Interface (ACPI), use PCI cards, and external Plug and Play–compliant devices, resource conflicts have become almost nonexistent. That's because the ACPI is capable of managing the system's resources to avoid conflicts. For example, if a system doesn't have enough IRQ lines, ACPI will assign two or more devices to the same IRQ line and manage the devices so that they can share the line without conflicting with each other. To see which devices are sharing an IRQ line, activate Device Manager's View, Resources by Connection command, and then double-click the Interrupt Request (IRQ) item.

ACPI's success at allocating and managing resources is such that Windows XP doesn't allow you to change a device's resources, even if you'd want to do such a thing. If you open a device's property sheet and display the Resources tab, you'll see that none of the settings can be changed.

If you use legacy devices in your system, however, conflicts could arise because Windows XP is unable to properly manage the device's resources. If that happens, Device Manager will let you know there's a problem. To solve it, first display the Resources tab on the device's property sheet. The Resource Settings list shows you the resource type on the left and the resource setting on the right. If you suspect that the device has a resource conflict, check the Conflicting Device List box to see whether any devices are listed. If the list displays only No conflicts, the device's resources aren't conflicting with another device.

If there is a conflict, you need to change the appropriate resource. Some devices have multiple configurations, so one easy way to change resources is to select a different configuration. To try this, deactivate the Use Automatic Settings check box and then use the Setting Based On drop-down list to select a different configuration. Otherwise, you need to play around with the resource settings by hand. Here are the steps to follow to change a resource setting:

1. In the Resource Type list, select the resource you want to change.

2. Deactivate the Use Automatic Settings check box, if it's activated.

3. For the setting you want to change, either double-click it or select it and then click the Change Setting button. (If Windows XP tells you that you can't modify the resources in this configuration, select a different configuration from the Setting Based On list.) A dialog box appears that enables you to edit the resource setting.

4. Use the Value spin box to select a different resource. Watch the Conflict Information group to make sure that your new setting doesn't step on the toes of an existing setting.

5. Click OK to return to the Resources tab.

6. Click OK. If Windows XP asks whether you want to restart your computer, click Yes.

> **TIP**
>
> An easy way to see which devices are either sharing resources or are conflicting is via the System Information utility. Select Start, Run, type **msinfo32**, and click OK. (Alternatively, select Start, All Programs, Accessories, System Tools, System Information.) Open the Hardware Resources branch and then click Conflicts/Sharing.

14

# From Here

Here's a list of places elsewhere in the book where you'll find information related to devices:

- For hard disk techniques, refer to "Optimizing the Hard Disk" in Chapter 11 and "Checking Your Hard Disk for Errors" in Chapter 12.

- To learn how to use the Signature Verification tool to look for unsigned device drivers, refer to the section in Chapter 12 titled "Verifying Digitally Signed Files."

- For other troubleshooting techniques, refer to Chapter 13, "Troubleshooting and Recovering from Problems."

- To learn how modems work, see the section in Chapter 15 titled "Getting Started with Modem Communications."

- For information on networking hardware, see the section in Chapter 22 titled "Hardware: NICs and Other Network Knickknacks."

# PART IV

# Unleashing Windows XP Modem Communications

## IN THIS PART

# 15

# Getting Started with Modem Communications

Thanks to falling prices and expanding services, broadband Internet connections (mostly via DSL and cable) are growing at a healthy clip and are now used by a majority of Internet users. However, many online users still connect via the humble modem. If you're one of those users, or you support such users, this chapter gives you some background in modem communications and shows you how to get your modem's mojo working. Chapter 16, "Putting Your Modem to Work," shows you how to work a few modem-dependent Windows XP programs: Phone Dialer, HyperTerminal, and the Windows XP Fax service.

## A Modem Communications Primer

Computers are essentially solitary beasts that prefer to keep their own company. However, that's not to say that PCs don't have a social side as well; you just have to work a bit to dig it out. There are three ways to go about this:

- Add network interface cards to the computers, and then sling some cable around (or use wireless devices) to set up a **local area network** (LAN). You'll learn how this is done in Chapter 22, "Setting Up and Accessing a Small Network."

- Use a special cable (or infrared) to connect the serial ports of two computers, and then use a direct cable connection to exchange files between them. I don't discuss this in the book, but it's easy enough to establish the connection. Select Start, All Programs, Accessories, Communications, New Connection

Wizard. In the first New Connection Wizard dialog box, click Next, activate Set Up an Advanced Connection, and click Next. Then activate Connect Directly to Another Computer, click Next, and follow the rest of the dialog boxes.

- Attach a modem to your computer and use it to connect to remote systems.

The third method is the focus of this chapter. As an appetizer, this section presents a bit of background info that serves to get you comfortable with the underlying principles of modem communications. This knowledge will make it much easier for you to set up and work with your modem, and it will be invaluable when you need to troubleshoot the inevitable communications problems.

## Modems: The Inside Story

Modems are, by now, a ubiquitous feature of the PC terrain, but they remain more mysterious than the other peripherals. Perhaps it's the alphabet soup of modem standards, or the inherent complexities of modem-to-modem communications, or just all those strange sounds modems make when they converse with one another. To help you penetrate the mysteries of the modem, this section examines the inner workings of these electronic marvels.

### The Modulation/Demodulation Thing

In Chapter 4, "Working with Digital Media," I explained a bit about how sound waves are created. When you speak into a telephone, a diaphragm inside the mouthpiece vibrates. This vibration is converted into an electromagnetic wave that mirrors the amplitude and frequency of the original analog wave created by your voice. This wave travels along the telephone lines, and at the destination, electromagnets in the receiver vibrate another diaphragm that reproduces your voice.

Note that this process is entirely analog, from the original sound wave of your voice, to the electromagnetic wave that traverses the phone system, to the reconstituted sound wave created by the receiver. Computers, of course, are resolutely digital, so this analog state of affairs just won't do. For a computer to send data along a telephone line, the individual bits that make up the data must be converted into some kind of analog wave.

This digital-to-analog process is called **modulation**. In essence, the 1s and 0s that compose digital data are converted into signals (or symbols) that can be represented as tones that fall within the frequency range of the human voice (between 300Hz and 3,000Hz). These tones can then be sent along regular telephone lines, where they're converted back into their original digital format. This reconversion process is called **demodulation**. The device that modulates the data, sends the resulting tones, and demodulates the tones on the receiving end is a **modulator/demodulator**, or as it's more familiarly known, a **modem**. Now you know why modems make such a racket while they're communicating with each other: It's all those tones exchanged back and forth.

> **NOTE**
>
> Although most telephone systems are analog, digital phone lines are cropping up with increasing frequency. These lines work by sampling the voice, much like the way a sound card samples analog audio. The samples are then sent across the lines as bits without the need of modulation or demodulation, and so without the need of a modem.

## The Difference Between Baud and Bits Per Second

The speed at which modems transmit data is called the **data transfer rate**, and it's measured in **bits per second** (bps). The current standards for the data transfer rate are 14,400bps on the low end and 56,000bps on the high end. Another measure of transmission speed does, however, exist—the **baud rate**—and the two terms are often confused.

The baud rate defines the number of symbols (which might be variations in, say, voltage or frequency, depending on the modulation standard being used) per second that can be exchanged between two modems. Each of these symbols, however, can incorporate multiple bits of data. For example, a 2,400-baud modem might be able to cram six bits of data into a symbol, thus resulting in a data transfer rate of 14,400bps.

In the old days, modems incorporated only a single bit per baud, so the bps and baud rates were synonymous. Now, however, all modems support multibit baud rates, so the only true measure of a modem's transmission speed is bps.

## Understanding Modem Standards

For modems to communicate with each other successfully, they must speak the same language—*language* in this sense meaning, among other things, the type of modulation used, the data transfer rate, how errors are handled, and whether any data compression is used.

At one time, there were almost as many modem languages as there were modem manufacturers, resulting in what I call the Tower of Babel problem in communications. In other words, you could never be sure that the modem you were trying to connect with would have the faintest idea what your modem was saying. To solve this problem, the major players in the data communications game put together a series of modem standards to help ensure compatibility between devices from different manufacturers. These standards cover three aspects of modem communications: modulation, error correction, and data compression.

> **NOTE**
>
> You might still see some modems described as *Hayes compatible*. This is a holdover from the days when Hayes modems were the market leader, so other modems had to fall in line with the Hayes standard to gain consumer acceptance. In this case, however, the standard had nothing to do with modem communications. Instead, it defined a command set used by applications to control the modem. For example, the command ATDT (attention dial tone) tells the modem to get a dial tone. By now, however, every modem supports this command set (which is usually just called the AT **command set** because most of the commands begin with AT), so being Hayes compatible is no longer a big deal.

15

**Modulation Standards**    When a modem modulates digital data into a carrier wave, the receiving modem must understand how this modulation was performed in order to reverse the procedure during demodulation. This is, for obvious reasons, the most crucial aspect of modem compatibility, so having modulation standards is critical. These standards are set by a United Nations umbrella group called the International Telecommunication Union-Telecommunications Standardization Section (ITU-TSS; it was formerly another mouthful: the Consultative Committee on International Telephone and Telegraph, or CCITT). The ITU-TSS consists of representatives from modem manufacturers, telephone companies, and government agencies.

As modem technology improved, new standards had to be hammered out, so numerous modulation standards have been implemented over the years. Here's a review of the most common ones.

> **NOTE**
>
> When speaking the name of any modulation standard, the *V.* part is pronounced as *vee dot.* So, for example, the standard V.90 is pronounced *vee dot ninety.*

| | |
|---|---|
| V.22 | This is a 1,200bps standard that was used mostly outside of the United States and Canada. (The corresponding standard used in the United States and Canada was called Bell 212A, which was a standard implemented by Bell Labs.) |
| V.22bis | This is a 2,400bps standard, and the first of the international standards. (The *bis* part is French for *again* or *encore.*) |
| V.29 | This is the standard for half-duplex (that is, one-way) communication at 9,600bps. It's used for Group III fax transmissions and so is the standard facsimile implementation in fax/modems. |
| V.32 | This is the standard for full-duplex (that is, two-way) communications at 9,600bps. This standard incorporates a technique called **trellis coding** that enables on-the-fly error checking and reduces the effect of line noise. |
| V.32bis | This standard defines full-duplex transmission at 14,400bps. It's basically the same as V.32, except that the number of bits per signal change was upped from four in V.32 to six in V.32bis (both standards operate at 2,400 baud). |
| V.32fast or V.FC | These standards upped the V.32 and V.32bis transmissions to 28,800bps, but they've been replaced by V.34. |
| V.34 | This is the standard for full-duplex transmission at 33,600bps. |
| V.90 | This is the standard for full-duplex transmission at 56,000bps for **downloads** (data coming into your computer) and 33,600bps for **uploads** (data going out of your computer). |
| V.92 | This is the standard for full-duplex transmission at 56,000bps for downloads and 48,000bps for uploads. V.92 also boasts a Quick Connect feature that |

cuts modem connect time in half, as well as a **Modem On Hook (MOH)** feature that enables you to initiate and receive voice phone calls while a modem connection is active. V.92 represents the current state of the art for analog modem communications. Despite their latest-and-greatest status, V.92 modems are relatively inexpensive, so you should shoot for V.92 if you're in the market for a modem.

Most experts used to believe that V.34 represented the ceiling for analog transmission speed. However, modem companies continued to push the transmission rate envelope. U.S. Robotics and 3Com, for example, introduced x2 technology, which allowed for 56Kbps rates over standard phone lines. A competing technology called **K56**—also known as **K56Flex**—was also available, and eventually the combined standard V.90 was established. How was this speed increase achieved? V.34 treats the entire network as though it were analog, so it's limited to 33,600bps. However, V.90 takes advantage of the fact that most of the network involved in modem communications is digital. In particular, the connection between a service provider and the switched telephone network is, in most cases, entirely digital. This means that no download modulation is necessary. In other words, the data that is downloaded to your modem doesn't have to go through the costly digital-to-analog conversion, so it can make the most use out of the wider bandwidth on digital telephone networks. So, with V.90, downloaded data can achieve theoretical rates of up to 56,000bps, while uploaded data still transfers at 33,600bps. V.92 gets rid of most of the upload modulation as well, so uploaded data can transfer at up to 48,000bps.

Does it work? Well, in practice, you're not likely to see true 56Kbps transmission rates due to line noise and other factors. However, rates in the 35Kbps to 50Kbps range are achievable, thus making V.92 a viable alternative.

**Error Correction Standards**    One of the problems with analog telephone lines is that they suffer from line noise and other factors that can wreak havoc on the carefully crafted symbols sent by modems. To ensure that data arrives intact, the ITU-TSS has set up **error correction standards**. These standards enable the receiving modem to check the integrity of incoming symbols and, if it finds a problem, ask the originating modem to resend the data.

The current standard for error correction is V.42, which incorporates two protocols: **Link Access Procedure for Modems (LAPM)** and **Microcom Networking Protocol** (MNP) 4. Both protocols correct errors by asking that corrupted data be retransmitted. The default protocol is LAPM because it's a bit faster than MNP 4.

**Compression Standards**    If you apply compression to a folder, NTFS compresses the files by replacing redundant character strings with tokens. Many modern modems can perform the same process on your outgoing data. In other words, the modem first uses a compression technique to reduce the size of the data and then converts the compressed data into symbols. This means that less data is sent, thus reducing upload times.

15

> **NOTE**
>
> To apply compression to a folder, right-click the folder and then click Properties. In the General tab of the folder's property sheet, click Advanced and then activate the Compress Contents to Save Disk Space check box. Note that with Windows XP you can only compress folders on NTFS partitions (although there are third-party utilities that enable you to compress folders on any file system).

Of course, the receiving modem must be able to decompress the data, so the ITU-TSS has implemented compression standards. The current standard is V.44, which can compress data up to 6:1. The old standard was V.42bis, which can compress data up to 4:1. (Most modems also support another compression scheme called **MNP 5**. However, this scheme provides a maximum compression ratio of only 2:1.)

> **CAUTION**
>
> Data compression sounds great, but it really works only on text transfers. Because binary files contain few redundant character strings, they can't be compressed all that much, so you won't see a significant increase in throughput. In fact, if you're dealing with files that have already been compressed (such as ZIP files), data compression might lead to slower download times because compressing an already-compressed file generally increases the size of the file.

## A Review of Modem Types

Modems come in various shapes and sizes, and most brand-name models provide similar features. If you're looking to purchase a modem, your main criterion should be that the modem supports the ITU-TSS standards, especially one of the modulation standards (such as V.90). Also, many modems come with built-in fax capabilities (these are required if you want to use the Windows XP Fax service, as described in Chapter 16; see the section titled "Sending and Receiving Faxes"), so look for V.29 compatibility as well.

After standards compliance, your next criterion will be the type of modem (or fax/modem) you need. Here's a summary of the three main types:

External    These modems are standalone boxes you connect to a serial port with a special cable. (You can also get USB modems that plug into a USB port.) Although external modems require a separate power source and tend to be more expensive than an equivalent internal modem, they have several advantages. For one, they can be transported between machines fairly easily. For another, most external modems have a series of LED indicators on their front panel that tell you the current state of the modem. These lights can be invaluable during troubleshooting. Here's a summary of the LEDs that appear on most external modems and what each light represents:

| LED | Description |
| --- | --- |
| AA | Auto Answer—When lit, indicates that the modem will answer incoming calls automatically. |

| LED | Description |
|---|---|
| CD | Carrier Detect—Lights up when the modem receives a valid data signal from a remote modem. This indicates that data transmission is possible, and the light remains on during the entire connection. |
| CS | Clear to Send—Lights up when the modem has determined that it's okay for an application to start sending data. (See the discussion of flow control in the later section "Modem-to-Modem Communications.") |
| MR | Modem Ready—Lights up when the modem's power is turned on. |
| OH | Off Hook—Lights up when the modem takes control of the phone line (which is the modem equivalent of taking the telephone receiver off the hook). |
| RD | Receive Data—Lights up when the modem receives data. |
| RS | Request to Send—Lights up when your computer has asked the modem whether it's okay to start sending data. |
| SD | Send Data—Lights up when the modem sends data. |
| TR | Terminal Ready—Lights up when the modem receives a **DTR (data terminal ready**) signal from the computer. This means that the current communications program is ready to start sending data. |
| Internal | These modems are cards you insert into a slot on your computer's expansion bus. This type of modem is convenient because no external power source is required, it's one less device taking up valuable desk space, and no external serial port is used up. Most modem jockeys, however, dislike internal modems because of the lack of LED indicators for troubleshooting. (As you'll see later, though, Windows XP does provide an icon during modem connections that shows you the state of the RD and SD signals.) |
| PC Card | These are modems that use the credit-card–size, PC Card (PCMCIA) format and plug directly into a PC Card slot. If possible, look for PC Card modems that accept an RJ-11 jack directly because these kinds are more reliable than the "dongles" used by some PC Card modems. |

15

## Serial Ports: Communicating One Bit at a Time

The link between your computer and your modem is the **serial port** (also known as a **COM port** or **RS-232 port**). For an external modem, this link usually comes in the form of a serial cable that runs from the port to an interface in the back of the modem. The exception is the pocket modem, which usually plugs into the serial port directly. For internal and PC Card modems, the serial port is built right into the modem's circuitry.

They're called *serial* ports because they transmit and receive data one bit at a time, in a series. (This is opposed to working with data in *parallel*, in which multiple bits are transmitted simultaneously.) As such, serial ports can be used by many kinds of devices that require two-way communication, such as mice, infrared adapters, bar code scanners, and, of course, modems.

### Serial Port Pin Configurations

Like most computer interfaces, serial ports send and receive data and signals via wires that correspond to single bits. For a serial port, these wires are metal pins that come in two configurations: 9-pin and 25-pin, as illustrated in Figure 15.1. From the context of modem communications, there is no essential difference between the 9-pin and 25-pin connectors, other than their layout. Table 15.1 shows the pin assignments for the 9-pin connector, and Table 15.2 shows the partial pin assignments for the 25-pin connector (the other pins can be safely ignored).

9-pin serial port

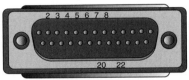

25-pin serial port

**FIGURE 15.1**   The 9-pin and 25-pin serial port connectors.

**TABLE 15.1**   Pin Assignments for a 9-Pin Serial Port Connector

| Pin Number | Signal |
| --- | --- |
| 1 | Carrier Detect (CD) |
| 2 | Receive Data (RD) |
| 3 | Transmit Data (TD) |
| 4 | Data Terminal Ready (DTR) |
| 5 | Signal Ground |
| 6 | Data Set Ready (DSR) |
| 7 | Request To Send (RTS) |
| 8 | Clear To Send (CTS) |
| 9 | Ring Indicator |

**TABLE 15.2**   Partial Pin Assignments for a 25-Pin Serial Port Connector

| Pin Number | Signal |
| --- | --- |
| 2 | Transmit Data (TD) |
| 3 | Receive Data (RD) |
| 4 | Request To Send (RTS) |
| 5 | Clear To Send (CTS) |
| 6 | Data Set Ready (DSR) |
| 7 | Signal Ground |
| 8 | Carrier Detect (CD) |
| 20 | Data Terminal Ready (DTR) |
| 22 | Ring Indicator |

The key pins in both layouts are Transmit Data (TD) and Receive Data (RD). The computer uses the TD pin to send the individual bits of outgoing serial data to the modem. For incoming data, the modem uses the RD pin to get the bits into the computer. See "Modem-to-Modem Communications" later in this chapter to learn the functions of some of the other wires.

### The UART: The Heart of the Serial Port

You might be wondering how the computer's processor and the serial port can possibly get along with each other. After all, the CPU deals with data in parallel: the eight bits (one byte) that are required to represent a single character of information. I've just told you, however, that serial ports are one-bit wonders. How do you reconcile these seemingly incompatible ways of looking at data?

The answer is a special chip that resides inside every serial port (or sometimes on the computer's motherboard): the **Universal Asynchronous Receiver/Transmitter (UART)**. (For an internal or PC Card modem, the UART chip sits on the card itself.) It's the UART's job, among other things, to take the computer's native parallel data and convert it into a series of bits that can be spit out of the serial port's TD line. On the other end, individual bits streaming into the destination serial port's RD line are reassembled by the UART into the parallel format that the processor prefers.

It's clear, then, that the role of the UART in data communications is crucial. In fact, the UART is often the source of transmission bottlenecks that can hold up the entire process. To see why, consider what happens when serial data arrives via the modem. The UART assembles the incoming bits until it has a full byte, and it stores this byte in a special memory buffer. It then notifies the CPU—by generating an interrupt request—that data is waiting. Under ideal conditions, the CPU grabs the data from the buffer immediately, the UART processes the next byte, and the cycle repeats. However, what if the CPU is busy with some other task when it receives the interrupt request? The UART continues processing the incoming bits, and if the processor can't get to the buffered data in time, the UART simply overwrites the existing buffer with the new data. This means, at best, that the lost byte must be retransmitted, and the overall performance of the download suffers as a result. (At worst, you might lose the character altogether!)

This isn't usually a problem at relatively slow data transfer rates (for example, up to 9,600bps), but it can cause all kinds of problems with modern modems running at up to 56,600bps. To prevent these overruns, you need a UART that can keep up with the deluge. Here's a summary of the various UART types and their suitability for fast data transfer rates:

| | |
|---|---|
| 8250 | This was the chip used in the original IBM PC XT. Its design calls for a one-byte data buffer, so it isn't suitable for high-speed transfers. |
| 16450 | This was the chip used in the IBM PC AT and compatible machines. Although it sported some improvements over 8250 (essentially the capability of working with computers that have higher internal clock speeds), it still used the one-byte data buffer, so it too is limited to 9,600bps. |

15

| | |
|---|---|
| 16550 | This chip represented a huge improvement over its predecessors. The major innovation was a 16-byte **FIFO (first in, first out)** buffer that enabled the UART to handle high-speed data transfers, and reduced retransmissions and dropped characters. Also, the 16550 had a variable interrupt trigger that the user could configure to send an interrupt to the CPU when the buffer reached a certain number of bytes. (You'll see later that Windows XP lets you configure this trigger.) The 16550, however, had a defective FIFO buffer that often caused data loss. |
| 16550A | This is a replacement chip that fixes the bugs in the 16550 but is otherwise identical. The 16550A (or the updated 16550AF, 16550AN, or 16550AFN) is the chip of choice for modems that support data transfer rates of 14,400bps and up. Almost all modern systems have this type of UART. |

# Modem-to-Modem Communications

Modem communications is one of those ideas that, after you learn a bit of background, you wonder how on earth your system actually pulls it off. I mean, you're talking about tens of thousands of bits per second busily bustling between two computers, all the while negotiating compression routines, FIFO buffers, parallel-to-serial UART conversions, modulations, and who knows what else. To combine all of these complex technologies and achieve a remarkably high level of accuracy is an amazing achievement. To help you appreciate some of the hoops your computer, serial port, and modem have to jump through to accomplish this wizardry, this section takes a closer look at just how two modems communicate with each other.

## Flow Control: The Communications Traffic Cop

Modem downloads come in fast and furious, so what's your computer supposed to do if it isn't ready to receive any data? Conversely, what if you're sending data and the remote system indicates that it can't receive any more data just now? How does your modem tell the CPU to stop processing data temporarily?

These kinds of situations fall under the rubric of **flow control**, which defines how the computer and the modem communicate with each other to coordinate data exchanges and prevent overruns when one device isn't ready to receive information from the other. There are two types of flow control: software and hardware.

### Software Flow Control (XON/XOFF)

With **software flow control**, the computer and modem send signals to each other that indicate whether they're ready to receive data. For example, suppose that you're downloading a file and the computer needs to pause the download briefly while it attends to some other chores. To do this, it sends to the remote system's modem a special "hold your horses" signal called **XOFF**. (In data communications circles, *X* stands for transfer, so *XOFF* means *transfer off.*) XOFF is an ASCII control code character (ASCII 19 or Ctrl+S) that gets shipped out to the remote system just like any other character. When the computer decides it's okay to resume the download, it notifies the remote system by sending a signal called **XON** (which is another control code character: ASCII 17 or Ctrl+Q). Because of these two signals, software flow control is also known as **XON/XOFF flow control**.

> **NOTE**
>
> If you find that a data transfer has halted, it might be because your system has inadvertently sent an XOFF flow control signal. Try pressing Ctrl+Q to send an XON signal. If the remote system supports software flow control, this might be enough to get the transfer going again.

### Hardware Flow Control (RTS/CTS)

Because of the high overhead associated with software flow control, it becomes inefficient at data transfer rates higher than 2,400bps. For higher speeds, **hardware flow control** is a much better option. That's because instead of firing an entire character out to the remote device, hardware flow control just uses individual serial port lines to send signals. Hardware flow control uses two of these lines: RTS and CTS (which is why this method is also called **RTS/CTS flow control**).

For example, suppose that your modem wants to stop the computer from sending any more data (because, for example, it has lost its Carrier Detect signal and so doesn't have a connection with the remote system). To do that, all it does is turn off its CTS (Clear To Send) signal. The computer reads that the serial port's CTS wire is off, so it stops processing data for the modem.

Similarly, the processor's willingness to accept more data from the modem is controlled by the RTS (Request To Send) wire. If the processor turns off RTS, the modem reads that the serial port's RTS wire is off, so it pauses the data transfer.

## Data Bits: The Crux of the Matter

The role of the serial port's UART chip is to convert the eight parallel bits that PCs use to represent data into a series of eight consecutive bits suitable for squeezing through the serial port's TD (Transmit Data) wire.

The problem, though, is that not all computer systems use eight bits to represent their characters. All PCs do, because they need the eight bits to represent all 256 characters in the ASCII character set (because each bit can use one of two states—on or off, 1 or 0—and 2 to the power of 8 is 256). Most mainframe systems, however, use only seven bits to represent characters because they recognize only the first 128 ASCII characters (2 to the power of 7 is 128). The number of bits used to represent a character is called the **data bits** setting or the **character length**.

So, one of the most important parameters when a remote system is involved is the number of data bits it uses. Problems can arise, for example, if you send eight-bit bytes to a system that knows how to deal with only seven of them. In PC systems, fortunately, the first 128 ASCII characters have a 0 as their eighth bit, so it can be safely discarded during communication with seven-bit systems.

## Start and Stop Bits: Bookends for Your Data

The data coursing through your computer is transferred from place to place at extremely high speeds by using exquisitely timed procedures to coordinate the transfers. This type of communications is called **synchronous** because it depends on timing signals.

The vagaries of modem communications, however, prevent such precise timing, so modems use **asynchronous** communications. In asynchronous communications, as long as the remote system is willing and able to receive data, the data is just sent out whenever it's ready to go.

But with no timing involved, knowing where one character ends and the next begins becomes a problem. You might think that you could just use the number of data bits. For example, if your system and the remote system both use eight-bit bytes, you could simply define every eighth bit as the starting point for each character. Unfortunately, that approach would work only in a perfect world that boasted noiseless telephone lines and error-free data transfers. In the real world, in the journey between here and there, legitimate bits can become missing, and extraneous "bits" (that is, line noises) can get tossed into the mix.

To help the receiving end delimit incoming characters, the sending system's UART tacks on extra bits on both sides of the data. At the front of the data, the UART adds a start bit that defines the beginning of each character. This is followed by the data bits, and then the UART appends a **stop bit** to mark the end of the character.

The start bit is always the same, but different systems require different length stop bits. Most systems use a single stop bit, but a few rare cases insist on two stop bits. (You also read about systems that require 1 1/2 stop bits. *Half* a bit? It doesn't make sense until you remember that these "bits" I'm talking are really electromagnetic pulses traveling along an analog carrier wave. Each pulse consumes a predefined amount of time—say, 1/14,400th of a second—so 1 1/2 bits is really just 1 1/2 pulses.)

At the receiving end, the UART busies itself by stripping off the start and stop bits before recombining the data bits into a full byte.

## Parity: A Crude Error Check

The start and stop bits can tell the receiving modem it has received corrupted data. For example, if the modem is expecting eight data bits but gets seven or nine, it knows that something has gone haywire, and it can ask that the bit be retransmitted.

What if, however, a voltage spike or some line noise doesn't add or subtract bits from a character, but instead *changes* one of the existing bits? The receiving modem still gets the appropriate number of data bits, so it won't know that anything has gone awry. To cover this kind of trouble, many systems that use seven-bit characters also use **parity checking**. In this technique, an extra bit—called the **parity bit**—is added to the data bits (but before the stop bit). The parity bit is set to either 1 or 0, depending on the type of parity checking used:

| Even parity | In this method, you first sum all the 1s in the data bits and see whether you end up with an odd or even number. Your goal is to send out an even number of 1s, so you use (or, technically, the UART uses) the extra parity bit to ensure this. For example, suppose that the data bits are 0000111. The sum of the 1s here is 3, which is odd, so the parity bit must be set to 1 to give you an even number of 1s. So, the UART sends out 10000111. Similarly, suppose that your data bits are 1000001. The sum of the 1s is 2, which is even, so the parity bit can be set to 0, like so: 01000001. |
| --- | --- |
| Odd parity | This is the opposite of even parity. Again, you first sum all the 1s in the data bits and see whether you end up with an odd or even number. In this case, however, your goal is to send out an odd number of 1s, and you manipulate the parity bit accordingly. |

Most systems use even parity. (Two other kinds of parity—*mark* and *space*—exist, but these are virtually obsolete.)

How does this help the receiving system check the data? Well, if it's using even parity, the receiving system's UART checks the incoming bits and adds up all the 1s. If it finds an odd number of 1s, it knows that a bit was changed en route, so it can ask for a retransmit. Of course, if a voltage spike changes several bits, the number of 1s might remain even, so the receiving UART wouldn't detect an error. Therefore, parity is only a crude error-checking mechanism.

> **NOTE**
>
> When setting up a connection to a remote system, you need to make sure that the three settings I've just talked about—data bits, stop bits, and parity—match the parameters expected by the remote computer. If you're not sure which settings to use, note that two combinations are the most common: seven data bits, even parity, one stop bit (usually written as 7-E-1); and eight data bits, no parity, one stop bit (8-N-1). The former combination is often used to connect to large online services that use mainframes (such as CompuServe); the latter works for most bulletin board systems and PC-to-PC connections.

## Terminal Emulation: Fitting in with the Online World

When you use your modem to connect to a remote computer, you are, essentially, operating that computer from your keyboard and seeing the results onscreen. In other words, your computer has become a **terminal** attached to the remote machine.

It's likely, however, that the remote computer is completely different from the one you're using. It could be a mainframe or a minicomputer, for example. In that case, it isn't likely that the codes produced by your keystrokes will correspond exactly with the codes used by the remote computer. Similarly, some of the return codes won't make sense to your machine. So, for your computer to act like a true terminal, some kind of translation is needed between the two systems. This translation is called **terminal emulation** because it forces your system to emulate the kind of terminal that the remote computer normally deals with.

Most communications programs give you a choice of terminal emulation methods, such as ANSI for other DOS/Windows computers, TTY for teletype terminals, or specific terminal types, such as the DEC VT100 and VT52.

## File Transfers: A Matter of Protocol

You'll probably spend most of your modem time on the Internet. However, you can also use your modem to connect to other services, where you can chat with others, access data, and also transfer files back and forth. When you receive a file from a remote computer, it's called **downloading**; when you send a file to a remote computer, it's called **uploading**.

For your downloads and uploads to succeed, your system and the remote system must agree on which file **transfer protocol** to use. The protocol governs various aspects of the file transfer ritual, including starting and stopping, the size of the data packets being sent (in general, the larger the packet, the faster the transfer), how errors are handled, and so on. Many different file transfer protocols are available, but as you'll see later, Windows XP supports the following seven:

| | |
|---|---|
| Xmodem | Designed in 1977, this was the first protocol for PCs. Because it uses only a simple error-checking routine and sends data in small, 128-byte packets, Xmodem should be used only as a last resort. |
| 1K Xmodem | This is an updated version of Xmodem that uses 1024-byte data packets and an improved 16-bit **cyclic redundancy check** (CRC) error-checking protocol. This makes 1K Xmodem more reliable than plain Xmodem and, as long as the telephone lines are relatively noise-free, much faster as well. |
| Kermit | This is a flexible protocol that can handle the seven-bit bytes used by mainframes and minicomputers. It's very slow, however, and you should avoid it if the remote machine supports any other protocol. |
| Ymodem | This protocol provides all the benefits of 1K Xmodem (including 1024-byte packets and CRC error control) but also implements multiple-file transfers and the exchange of file data, including the name and size of each file. |
| Ymodem-G | This protocol is the same as Ymodem, except that it performs no error checking. Instead, it relies on the built-in error checking of modern modems (such as V.42 and MNP 4). |

| Zmodem | This is the fastest of the file transfer protocols and the most reliable. Zmodem doesn't use a fixed packet size. Instead, it adjusts the size of each packet based on the line conditions. For error checking, Zmodem uses a 32-bit CRC for enhanced reliability. Zmodem is, by far, the choice among online aficionados. |
| Zmodem with Crash Recovery | This version of the Zmodem protocol offers crash protection. This means that if the file transfer bails out before completing, you can restart and the Zmodem protocol resumes the transfer where it left off. |

## Configuring Serial Ports

As you've seen so far, serial ports play a vital role in modem communications. To make sure that your serial ports are ready to do their duty, you might want to set a few properties. Here's how it's done:

1. Double-click Control Panel's System icon to display the System Properties dialog box.

2. In the Hardware tab, click Device Manager.

3. Open the Ports (COM and LPT) branch.

4. Double-click the COM port you want to work with. The COM port's property sheet appears.

5. Display the Port Settings tab, shown in Figure 15.2. These drop-down lists set up default communications settings for the port. You don't need to adjust these values for your modem's port, however, because the settings you specify for the modem will override the ones you see here. You need to change these values only if you'll be attaching some other kind of device to the port.

6. Click Advanced to display the Advanced Settings dialog box.

7. Make sure that the Use FIFO Buffers check box is activated, and make sure the UART's Receive Buffer and Transmit Buffer sliders are all the way to the right (High). (See "Modifying Advanced Port Settings," later in this chapter, for more information on these buffers.)

8. Click OK to return to the COM port's property sheet.

9. Click OK and, if necessary, restart your computer.

**FIGURE 15.2**    The Port Settings tab controls various communications parameters.

# Installing and Configuring a Modem

Before you can use Phone Dialer, HyperTerminal, the Windows XP Fax service, or any other communications software, you need to tell Windows XP what kind of modem you have. After that's done, you need to configure the modem to suit the types of online sessions you plan to run. To that end, the next few sections take you through the rigmarole of installing and configuring your modem.

## Installing a Modem

If you have an internal or PC Card modem, chances are Windows XP will recognize the modem automatically and install the necessary drivers. If not, here are the steps to follow to install your modem:

1. Double-click Control Panel's Phone and Modem Options icon. The Phone and Modem Options dialog box appears.

2. Display the Modems tab.

3. Click Add. The Add Hardware Wizard appears.

4. Click Next.

5. Windows XP queries your system's serial ports to see whether a modem is attached. When it's finished, Windows XP displays the message Your modem has been set up successfully. Click Finish.

If Windows XP cannot find your modem or if your modem isn't attached to your computer yet, follow these steps to specify the modem by hand:

1. Double-click Control Panel's Phone and Modem Options icon. The Phone and Modem Options dialog box appears.

2. Display the Modems tab.

3. Click Add. The Add Hardware Wizard appears.

4. Activate the Don't Detect My Modem; I Will Select It from a List check box.

5. Click Next. Windows XP displays a list of standard modem types.

6. In the Models list, select the standard modem type that corresponds to your modem. (Alternatively, click Have Disk to install the drivers from a disc provided by the modem manufacturer.)

7. Click Next. The wizard asks you to select a serial port.

8. Select the appropriate port and click Next. Windows XP installs your modem.

9. Click Finish.

## Working with Different Dialing Locations

If you have a notebook computer, you can set up multiple dialing locations. For example, you could have one location for dialing from the office that uses extra digits to access an outside line and uses your corporate calling card. You could then have a second location for home that doesn't require anything extra to access an outside line and disables your call waiting service.

> **CAUTION**
>
> If you travel with your notebook and use a modem to connect to the office or the Internet, watch out for the digital phone systems that are used by many hotels. Analog modems aren't compatible with digital systems, so you end up frying your modem if you attempt to connect over a digital line. Unfortunately, digital phone jacks look identical to regular analog jacks, so you need to ask the hotel staff what kind of phone jacks the hotel uses. Note, however, that almost all hotel phones now come with a data jack, and it's perfectly safe to plug your modem into that jack. Just avoid plugging the modem into any wall jacks.

### Creating a New Dialing Location

The location information you entered while installing Windows XP (if Setup detected your modem) or while installing your first modem is stored in a location called My Location. To set up another location, follow these steps:

1. Double-click Control Panel's Phone and Modem Options icon. The Phone and Modem Options dialog box appears.

2. Display the Dialing Rules tab.

3. Click New to display the New Location dialog box.

4. Type a name in the Location Name text box.

5. Configure the location as described in the next section.

### Modifying Dialing Location Properties

Windows XP keeps track of various dialing properties that you can apply before connecting with your modem. These properties determine how Windows XP dials the modem. For example, the Country setting determines the country code used for long-distance calls (this is 1 in the United States and Canada), and the Area Code setting lets Windows XP determine whether the outgoing call is long distance.

You can change these and other dialing parameters by following these steps:

1. Double-click Control Panel's Phone and Modem Options icon. The Phone and Modem Options dialog box appears.

2. Display the Dialing Rules tab.

3. In the Locations list, select the location you want to work with.

4. Click Edit to display the Edit Location dialog box, shown in Figure 15.3.

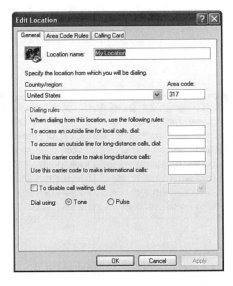

**FIGURE 15.3**    Use this dialog box to adjust the settings that Windows XP uses to dial your modem.

5. Configure the location using the following controls:

| | |
|---|---|
| Country/Region | Use this list to set the country code from which you'll be dialing. |
| Area Code | Use this text box to set the area code from which you'll be dialing. |
| To Access an Outside Line for Local Calls, Dial | Use this text box to enter the code that must be dialed to get an outside line for local calls (such as 9). |
| To Access an Outside Line for Long-Distance Calls, Dial | Use this text box to enter the code that must be dialed to get an outside line for long distance calls (such as 8). |
| Use this Carrier Code to Make Long-Distance Calls | Use this text box to enter the code required by your long-distance carrier for long-distance calls. |
| Use this Carrier Code to Make International Calls | Use this text box to enter the code required by your long-distance carrier for international calls. |
| To Disable Call Waiting, Dial | To deactivate call waiting before making the call, activate this check box and then either type the appropriate code in the text box or select one of the existing codes from the list. |

**CAUTION**

The extra beeps that call waiting uses to indicate an incoming call can wreak havoc on modem communications, so you should always disable call waiting before initiating a data call. The sequences *70, 70#, and 1170 usually disable call waiting, but you should check with your local phone company to make sure.

| | |
|---|---|
| Dial Using | Activate either Tone or Pulse, as appropriate for your telephone line. |

## Specifying an Area Code Rule

Area codes are getting increasingly confusing. There are two situations that are causing the weirdness:

- Calling the same area code—In this situation, you don't usually have to bother with the area code. However, some phone systems insist that you include the area code even if the other number is in the same area code. In some cases, these are long-distance calls, so you even have to dial a 1 (or some other country or region code) to start the call.

- Calling a different area code—This situation normally requires that you dial a 1 (or whatever), followed by the area code, followed by the number. However, in some larger cities, the phone company has actually run out of numbers in the main area code, so they've created a whole new area code for the city. These aren't usually long-distance calls, however, so even though you have to include the area code, you don't usually have to dial a 1 to get started.

Note that in both cases, the area code might apply to only certain phone number prefixes. (The prefix is the first three digits of the seven-digit number.) If you have to make any calls in these situations, you need to define a new area code rule to handle it. Here's how it's done:

1. Double-click Control Panel's Phone and Modem Options icon. The Phone and Modem Options dialog box appears.

2. Display the Dialing Rules tab.

3. In the Locations list, select the location you want to work with.

4. Click Edit to display the Edit Location dialog box.

5. Display the Area Code Rules tab.

6. Click New to display the New Area Code Rule dialog box, shown in Figure 15.4.

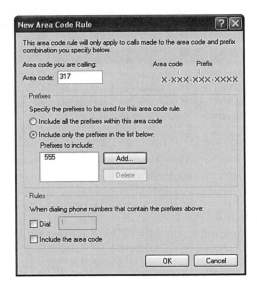

**FIGURE 15.4**    Use the New Area Code Rule dialog box to add an area code rule to a dialing location.

7. Use the Area Code text box to type the area code you'll be calling.

8. If the rule will apply only to certain phone number prefixes, activate the Include Only the Prefixes in the List Below option. Then click Add, type the prefix (or prefixes, separated by spaces or commas), and click OK.

9. If you need to dial a country code (such as 1) before the area code, activate the Dial check box and use the text box to type the number.

10. To force Windows XP to dial this area code, activate the Include the Area Code check box.

11. Click OK.

### Specifying a Calling Card

When you're on the road, you'll often find yourself having to make calls that cost money. For example, if you're in a hotel that charges for calls, you might want the charge to go through your calling card.

For this type of situation, Windows XP enables you to specify a calling card to use when making the call. Here's the simplest route to take:

1. Double-click Control Panel's Phone and Modem Options icon. The Phone and Modem Options dialog box appears.

2. Display the Dialing Rules tab.

3. In the Locations list, select the location you want to work with.

4. Click Edit to display the Edit Location dialog box.

5. Display the Calling Card tab.

6. In the Card Types list, select the type of calling card you have.

7. Type your account number.

8. Type your personal ID number (PIN).

9. Click OK.

If your calling card isn't in the list, click New to get to the New Calling Card dialog box. Alternatively, if your card is listed, you might need to adjust its settings. In that case, select the card and then click Edit to get the Edit Calling Card dialog box (which is identical to the New Calling Card dialog box). This dialog box has four tabs, so let's see what each one holds.

The General tab is as good a place as any to start. Here you need to enter three things: the calling card name (this will appear in the Card Types list), your account number, and your PIN.

You use the Long Distance tab to specify the steps that must be followed to make a long distance call. The first thing to do is specify your card's access number for long-distance calls. After that's done, you define the steps by clicking the buttons below the Calling Card Dialing Steps box. There are six buttons for your clicking finger to tickle:

| | |
|---|---|
| Access Number | Click this button to add the long-distance access number to the steps. |
| PIN | Click this button to add your PIN to the steps. |

| | |
|---|---|
| Wait for Prompt | Click this button to display a dialog box with various things that the system must wait for before continuing the dialing. You can have the system wait for a dial tone, a completed voice message, or a specified number of seconds. |
| Account Number | Click this button to add your account number to the steps. |
| Destination Number | Click this button to add the number you're calling to the steps. You also get a dialog box in which you can tell Windows XP to also dial the country code and area code. |
| Specify Digits | Click this button to add one or more digits (as well as * and #) to the steps. |

The idea is that you click these buttons in the order that they must appear in the card's calling sequence. If you make a mistake, use the Move Up and Move Down buttons to shuffle things around. If your card requires different sequences for international and local calls, follow the same steps using the International and Local Calls tabs. When you're done, click OK to return to the New Location dialog box. Then click OK to return to the Phone and Modem Options dialog box.

## Modifying the Modem's General Properties

Your modem has all kinds of properties you can play with to alter how the device works and to troubleshoot problematic connections. To see these properties, select the modem in the Modems tab and then click the Properties button. In the property sheet that appears, display the Modem tab, shown in Figure 15.5, which offers the following controls:

| | |
|---|---|
| Speaker Volume | This slider determines how loud your modem sounds (although not all modems support this feature). Because modems can make quite a racket, you might consider setting the volume low or even off while using it in public or in a quiet office. If adjusting this slider to its lowest setting still doesn't turn off your modem's sounds, check out the "Modifying the Modem's Advanced Properties" section later in this chapter. The Advanced tab has an Extra Settings text box in which you can enter the ATM0 command, which mutes the modem. |
| Maximum Speed | This setting determines the maximum throughput (in bps) that the modem can handle. This speed depends on the modulation protocol, data compression used, and a few other factors. Later, I'll show you a test you can run to determine the maximum speed for your modem (see "Testing the Modem" later in this chapter). Your modem won't necessarily use this speed. Instead, it will determine the optimum speed based on the remote system and the line conditions. |

> **NOTE**
>
> If you're having trouble connecting and the serial port doesn't use a 16550 UART, be sure to set the Maximum Speed value to no more than 9600.

Wait for Dial Tone Before Dialing

When this check box is activated, the modem won't dial unless it can detect a dial tone, which is usually what you want. However, there are three circumstances in which you might want to deactivate this option:

- Your phone system gives you an immediate dial tone. In this case, deactivating this check box might slightly decrease the connection time because the modem no longer waits for the dial tone.

- The modem can't recognize the dial tone (this often happens in foreign countries).

- You have to dial manually or with the assistance of an operator.

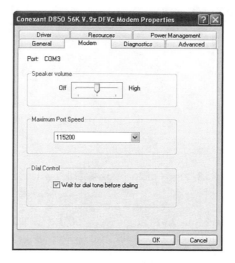

**FIGURE 15.5**  Use the Modem tab to control the modem's port, speaker volume, and maximum speed.

## Modifying the Modem's Advanced Properties

The Advanced tab of the modem's property sheet has a text box named Extra Initialization Commands. Any text you enter into this box is used by Windows XP to initialize the modem. Use this text box to add AT commands or other initialization settings, as described in your modem manual. Note that these commands are sent to the modem *after* Windows XP has sent the modem's default initialization string.

For example, you can get most modems to dial faster by changing the value of the S11 register, which sets the number of milliseconds between numbers dialed. The default on most modems is about 70, so try lowering this number gradually until the dialing no longer works. On my modem, I put ATS11=40 in the Extra Initialization Commands text box.

---

**NOTE**

You can also enter AT commands by hand using a program such as HyperTerminal. I show you how to do this in Chapter 16. See the section titled "Entering AT Commands in HyperTerminal."

---

### Modifying Advanced Port Settings

In the Advanced tab, clicking the Advanced Port Settings button displays the Advanced Settings dialog box, shown in Figure 15.6. You use this dialog box to control the FIFO buffers used by the serial port's UART chip. (This applies only to serial ports that have a 16550-compatible UART. The type of UART you have is one of the things displayed in the modem diagnostics test I told you about earlier.)

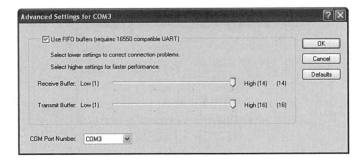

**FIGURE 15.6**   The Advanced Settings dialog box enables you to customize the FIFO buffers for a 16550 UART.

Recall from our earlier discussion that the purpose of the UART is to convert the CPU's outgoing bytes into bits for modem transmission, as well as to convert the modem's incoming bits into bytes for the CPU. The FIFO buffers are storage areas that the UART uses to hold incoming (the **receive buffers**) and outgoing (the **transmit buffers**) bytes. When a certain number of these buffers are full, the UART generates an interrupt to let the CPU know what's going on.

The two sliders determine when these interrupts are sent:

- Moving the sliders to the right means that more buffers must be full before an interrupt is sent. This means fewer interrupts are generated, so performance increases.

- Moving the sliders to the left means that fewer buffers must be full before an interrupt is sent. This gives the CPU more opportunity to deal with the buffers, so you're less likely to have transmission problems.

### Modifying Default Preferences

In the Advanced tab, clicking the Change Default Preferences button displays the modem's Default Preferences dialog box, The Call Preference group has two options:

| | |
|---|---|
| Disconnect a Call If Idle for More Than $x$ Mins | If you activate this check box, Windows XP monitors the connection for activity. If there is no activity within the specified number of minutes, Windows XP disconnects the call. (Note that this check box will be disabled if your modem doesn't support this property.) |

---

**CAUTION**

Forgetting that your modem is connected to a remote system is easy to do. If you pay money for your connection time—either a per-minute connect fee or a long distance charge—be sure to activate the Disconnect a Call If Idle for More Than $x$ Mins check box. For the idle time, enter a value between 1 and 42 minutes.

---

| | |
|---|---|
| Cancel the Call If Not Connected Within $x$ Secs | If you activate this check box, Windows XP gives the modem the specified number of seconds to connect to the remote system. If the connection doesn't happen within that time, Windows XP cancels the call. If you're connecting to a system that takes a while to connect (such as an international call), adjust the number of seconds accordingly (you can enter any integer value between 1 and 254). |

The Data Connection Preferences group has options that enable you to configure the various modem protocols, including error correction, compression, flow control, and modulation. Besides setting the default port speed, you can also use the following lists:

| | |
|---|---|
| Data Protocol | Use this list to select or disable the modem's built-in error-checking protocol (such as V.42 or MNP 4). Select Standard EC to enable the modem to negotiate the error correction method with the remote mode; select Forced EC to require that the modem use V.42 (if the remote modem doesn't support V.42, the connection is canceled); select None to disable error checking. (Disable error checking only if you are having trouble connecting to the remote modem.) |
| Compression | Use this list to enable or disable the modem's built-in data compression protocol (such as V.44 or V.42bis). As explained earlier, you can use compression for text and binary files, but you should disable it for compressed file transfers. |
| Flow Control | Use this list to select or disable flow control. Select Hardware (RTS/CTS), Xon/Xoff (software), or None. |

15

In the Advanced tab, use the Data Bits, Parity, and Stop Bits lists to set the default values for these connection parameters. For some modems, you can also use the Modulation list to specify whether the modem uses its default modulation protocol (the Standard option) or some other proprietary protocol.

## Testing the Modem

After you've configured your modem, you should test it to make sure that things are working correctly. To do this, follow these steps:

1. Double-click Control Panel's Phone and Modem Options icon. The Phone and Modem Options dialog box appears.

2. Display the Modems tab.

3. Select the modem you want to test.

4. Click Properties to display the modem's property sheet.

5. Display the Diagnostics tab.

6. Click Query Modem. Windows XP attempts to communicate with the modem and then displays the results in the Command and Response lists, as shown in Figure 15.7.

7. Click OK.

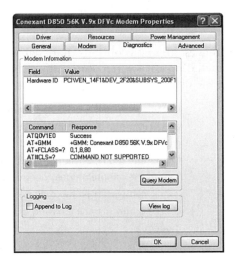

**FIGURE 15.7**    Use the Diagnostics tab to test your modem.

# From Here

This chapter represents only the beginning of your look at Windows XP communications. Here's what's in store in chapters to come:

- To learn how to use the Phone Dialer program, see the section in Chapter 16 titled "Getting Your Modem to Dial Voice Calls for You."

- To learn how to use HyperTerminal, see the section in Chapter 16 titled "Using HyperTerminal for Modem-to-Modem Connections."

- To learn how to use the Windows XP Fax service, see the section in Chapter 16 titled "Sending and Receiving Faxes."

- To learn how to use NetMeeting, see the section in Chapter 16 titled "Remote Collaboration with Microsoft NetMeeting."

- If you'll be using your modem to connect to the Internet, see the chapters in Part V, "Unleashing Windows XP for the Internet."

- If you're on the road, you can use your modem to connect to your network. See Chapter 23, "Making Remote Network Connections ."

15

# Putting Your Modem to Work

W ith your modem now installed and configured in Windows XP, you're ready to put it to good use. To that end, this chapter gets the practical side of your modem education off the ground by showing how to use several of Windows XP communications accessories. I begin by showing you how to use Phone Dialer to get your modem to dial voice calls for you. From there, I turn to more serious modem matters by showing how to use HyperTerminal to connect to bulletin board systems and online services, and the Windows XP Fax service to send and receive faxes.

## Getting Your Modem to Dial Voice Calls for You

If you don't have a speed-dial phone on your desk, Windows XP can provide you with the next best thing: Phone Dialer. This is a simple telephony application that accepts a phone number and then uses your modem to dial the number for you automatically.

To take advantage of Phone Dialer, you need to make the following arrangements with your phone cables:

- Run one phone cable from your phone to the Phone jack on your modem

- Run a second phone cable from your modem's Line jack to the phone jack on your wall

When that's done, you can get into Phone Dialer by selecting Start, Run, typing **dialer** in the Run dialog box, and then clicking OK. You see the Phone Dialer window, shown in Figure 16.1.

> **TIP**
>
> If you plan on using Phone Dialer regularly, consider setting up a shortcut for it on your Start menu (for instance, in the Communications folder). The `Dialer.exe` file is located in the `%SystemDrive%\Program Files\Windows NT` folder.

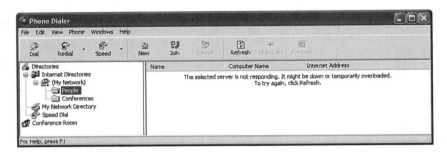

**FIGURE 16.1**    Phone Dialer is only too happy to use your modem to dial voice calls for you.

## Placing a Voice Call

Phone Dialer has a number of sophisticated features, but getting it to dial a phone number through your modem is as simple as following these steps:

1. Click Dial or select Phone, Dial. Phone Dialer displays the Dial dialog box, shown in Figure 16.2.

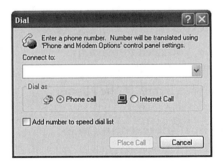

**FIGURE 16.2**    Use the Dial dialog box to specify the phone number you want to call.

2. In the Connect To text box, type the phone number you want to dial.

3. Activate the Phone Call option.

4. If you will be calling this number regularly, you can have Phone Dialer add the number to its Speed Dial directory by activating the Add Number to Speed Dial List check box.

5. Click Place Call. After a couple of seconds, you'll hear the number being dialed through your modem's speaker.

6. Pick up the telephone receiver and proceed with your call.

7. When the call is done, click Disconnect.

---

**TIP**

The Phone Dialer uses the dialing properties you established earlier for your modem. If you want to change the properties (to use a calling card, for example), you can access the Phone and Modem Options dialog box from within Phone Dialer. Select Edit, Options to display the Options dialog box. In the Lines tab, click Phone and Modem Options.

---

**NOTE**

If you want to see a list of phone calls you've made, including the phone number and duration of the call, select Phone Dialer's View, Call Log command.

---

If you want to dial the same number again later, you have two choices:

- Click Redial (or select Phone, Redial) and then click the number from the list that appears

- Click Dial (or select Phone, Dial) and then select the number from the Connect To list

Note that Phone Dialer keeps track of only the last ten numbers you dialed, including both voice and Internet calls.

## Configuring Windows Firewall to Allow Incoming Internet Calls

By default, Windows Firewall blocks data coming through port 1720. Unfortunately, this is the port that Phone Dialer uses to establish phone calls over the Internet or your network. So, if you want to use Phone Dialer to place Internet calls (as I describe in the next section), you must unblock port 1720 by following these steps:

1. On the computer that will be receiving the Internet call, open Control Panel's Windows Firewall icon.

2. Display the Exceptions tab.

3. Click the Add Port button to display the Add a Port dialog box. Figure 16.3 shows a completed version of this dialog box.

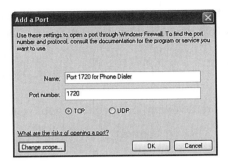

**FIGURE 16.3**    Use the Add a Port dialog box to add port 1720 to Windows Firewall's list of exceptions.

4. Use the Name text box to type a name for the unblocked port (such as "Port 1720 for Phone Dialer").

5. In the Port Number text box, type **1720**.

6. Make sure that the TCP option is activated.

7. If you want to restrict who can access port 1720 on this computer, click Change Scope to display the Change Scope dialog box. You have three options (click OK when you're done):

Any Computer                    Activate this option to allow any computer—including any computer connected to the Internet—to access port 1720.

My Network (Subnet) Only    Activate this option to allow only computers on your network subnet (as defined by your subnet mask) to access port 1720.

> **NOTE**
>
> For more information on IP addresses and subnets, see Chapter 17, "Implementing TCP/IP for Internet Connections."

Custom List                      Activate this option to specify a custom list of network subnets or individual IP addresses, separated by commas.

8. Click OK to return to the Windows Firewall dialog box. The port appears in the Programs and Services list.

9. Click OK.

## Placing an Internet or Network Call

In addition to voice calls, you can also use Phone Dialer to place calls over the Internet or over your network. In this case, the telephone handset is replaced by the computer's microphone and speakers. If each person also has a web cam attached to the computer, you can use Phone Dialer to place a video call over the Internet or your network.

Here are the steps to follow to place a call over the Internet or your network:

1. Click Dial (or select Phone, Dial) to display the Dial dialog box.

2. In the Connect To text box, type the IP address or computer name for the person you want to dial.

3. Activate the Internet Call option.

4. If you will be calling this address or computer name regularly, you can have Phone Dialer add the number to its Speed Dial directory by activating the Add Number to Speed Dial List check box.

5. Click Place Call. Phone Dialer contacts the remote computer, which sees an active call window like the one shown in Figure 16.4.

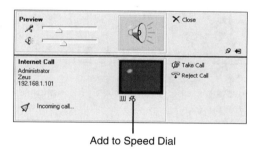

Add to Speed Dial

**FIGURE 16.4**   When you place a call over the Internet or your network, the remote user sees this active call window and must click Take Call to complete the connection.

6. If you see a Windows Security Alert dialog box asking whether to block TAPI 3.0 Dialer (that is, Phone Dialer), click Unblock.

7. The remote computer must click Take Call.

8. When the call is done, click Disconnect.

## Setting Phone Dialer's Options

Phone Dialer has a few options you can use to configure your phone dialing. For example, if you have multiple modems or multiple lines on your phone, you can tell Phone Dialer which ones to use. To work with these options, select Edit, Options to display the Options dialog box. You use the controls in the Lines tab, shown in Figure 16.5, to configure the lines that Phone Dialer uses for calls and conferences:

Preferred Line for Calling         Activate either Phone or Internet to set the default call types that Phone Dialer uses when you initiate a call.

Line Used For                  Use the Phone Calls, Internet Calls, and Internet Conferences lists to
                               choose the line you want to use for each type of call. If you have
                               multiple modems attached to your computer, choose the modem
                               you want to use in the Phone Calls list. You should leave both
                               Internet Calls and Internet Conferences set to <Auto-Select> to allow
                               Phone Dialer to choose the appropriate line.

**FIGURE 16.5**   Use the Lines tab in the Options dialog to configure the lines that Phone
Dialer uses for calls and conferences.

You use the controls in the Audio/Video tab, shown in Figure 16.6, to configure Phone
Dialer's sound and video options:

Sound Settings                 Click this button to open the Sounds and Audio Devices property
                               sheet. This is the same as double-clicking Control Panel's Sounds and
                               Audio Devices icon.

Use the Telephone Handset      Activate this check box to use a USB telephone handset for all
Connected to This PC for       your calls.
All Calls

Enable Acoustic Echo           Activate this check box to prevent hearing your own voice through
Cancellation                   your computer's speakers on Internet calls.

Devices Used for Calling       Use the Line list to select the type of call you want to configure
                               (Phone Calls, Internet Calls, or Internet Conferences). Then use the
                               Audio Record, Audio Playback, and Video Recording lists to select the
                               device you want to use for each action. You can choose <Use
                               Preferred Device> (as defined in the Sounds and Audio Devices
                               property sheet), <None>, or an installed device.

**FIGURE 16.6**   Use the Audio/Video tab to configure Phone Dialer's sound and video options.

## Quick Connections with Speed Dial

Phone Dialer is certainly handy, but it becomes downright useful when you take advantage of the Speed Dial feature. If you have numbers that you call frequently, add the numbers to the Speed Dial list to make them accessible with just a couple of mouse clicks.

Follow these steps to add a number to the Speed Dial list:

1. Pull down the Speed list and click Edit Speed Dial List (or select Edit, Speed Dial List). The Edit Speed Dial List dialog box appears.

2. Click Add to display the Speed Dial dialog box.

3. Use the Display Name text box to type a name for the Speed Dial entry.

4. Use the Number or Address text box to type the phone number, IP address, or computer name that you want associated with this Speed Dial entry.

5. In the Dial As group, activate Phone Call, Internet Call, or Internet Conference, as appropriate.

6. Click OK. Phone Dialer adds the new Speed Dial item to the Entries list.

7. Repeat steps 2–6 to add other Speed Dial list entries.

8. To make changes to an entry, select it in the Entries list and click Edit.

9. To change the order of the Speed Dial list items, select an item in the Entries list and then click either Move Up or Move Down.

10. When you're done, click OK.

16

> **TIP**
>
> You can also add a Speed Dial list entry on the fly. When you initiate a call, the active call window has an Add to Speed Dial icon (refer to Figure 16.4). Click this icon to display the Speed Dial dialog box.

To place a speed dial call, you have three choices:

- In the Speed Dial branch of the Phone Dialer window, click the Speed Dial entry and then click Speed. Alternatively, double-click the Speed Dial entry.

- Pull down the Speed button and click the Speed Dial entry.

- Select Phone, Speed Dial, and then select the Speed Dial entry in the submenu that appears.

# Using HyperTerminal for Modem-to-Modem Connections

These days, the most common reason for including a modem in your computer is to connect to the Internet. However, many people still use their modems to connect to remote devices (such as electronic test analyzers), telecommunications equipment, as well as to other modems and thus propel themselves into the world of (non-Internet) online services and bulletin board systems (**BBSs**). To do this, you need a communications program (or **terminal** program) that can operate your modem and handle the behind-the-scenes dirty work of dialing, connecting, downloading, and uploading.

In Windows XP, the terminal program of choice is called *HyperTerminal*, and it should serve the needs of all but the most discriminating modem jockeys. HyperTerminal integrates seamlessly with Windows XP's communications subsystem, and it offers several terminal emulation options, as well as support for most popular file transfer protocols, such as 1K Xmodem and Zmodem. The next few sections show you how to use HyperTerminal to set up, dial, and work with online connections.

To get HyperTerminal started, select Start, All Programs, Accessories, Communications, HyperTerminal. If you see a dialog box recommending that you make HyperTerminal your default Telnet program, activate the Don't Ask Me This Question Again check box and then click Yes (or No, if you prefer to use Windows XP's Microsoft Telnet Client or a different Telnet program).

## Creating a New HyperTerminal Connection

When you start HyperTerminal, the Connection Description dialog box appears. If you don't want to create a connection, click Cancel; otherwise, follow the steps I outline in the next few sections. Note that you set up the connection in three stages: defining the basic connection options, defining the connection's settings, and specifying the connection's modem properties.

### Defining the Basic Connection Options

Here are the steps to follow to get the basic connection options in place:

1. If the Connection Description dialog box, shown in Figure 16.7, isn't already onscreen, select File, New Connection.

**FIGURE 16.7**    When you start a new HyperTerminal connection, the Connection Description dialog box appears.

2. Use the Name text box to enter a descriptive name for the connection. Note that this entry will also serve as the primary name of the new HyperTerminal file (with the .HT extension), so you should follow Windows XP's rules for long filenames.

3. Use the Icon list to select an icon for the connection and then click OK. The Connect To dialog box, shown in Figure 16.8, appears.

**FIGURE 16.8**    Use the Connect To dialog box to supply HyperTerminal with the dialing details for your connection.

4. Fill in the country/region code, area code, and phone number for the remote system.

5. In the Connect Using drop-down list, you have four choices:

- Choose the modem you want to use for the connection.

- If you want to use HyperTerminal to connect to a PC via a serial cable that runs between the two machines' serial ports, choose the appropriate serial port.

- If your computer is part of a Virtual Private Network (**VPN**), select Microsoft VPN Adapter.

- If the remote computer understands TCP/IP and you have the TCP/IP protocol installed on your machine (this is the default on all Windows XP systems; see Chapter 17), select TCP/IP (Winsock).

6. Click OK. HyperTerminal displays the Connect dialog box.

At this point, the connection is set up to use the default settings you defined for your modem. If you want to use those settings, you can either click Dial to connect to the remote system or click Cancel to get to the main HyperTerminal window. I suggest clicking Cancel because then you can save the connection (by selecting File, Save). See "Connecting to a Remote System" later in this chapter to learn how to connect from the HyperTerminal window.

### Defining the Connection's Modem Properties

If you don't want to use the default modem settings, HyperTerminal enables you to define alternative settings for the connection. If you want to change the dialing properties for the connection, click the Dialing Properties button in the Connect dialog box. (If you canceled the Connect dialog box earlier, you can display it again by selecting Call, Connect.)

To change other settings (such as the connect speed and the terminal emulation), first display the property sheet for the connection by using either of the following methods:

- In the HyperTerminal window, select File, Properties.

- In the Connect dialog box, click Modify.

Figure 16.9 shows the property sheet that appears. The Connect To tab enables you to change the basic options (icon, country code, area code, and so on).

For modem-related settings, click the Configure button to display the modem's properties sheet. This dialog box offers the same settings you saw in Chapter 15, "Getting Started with Modem Communications," with the following additions:

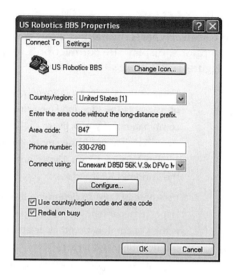

**FIGURE 16.9**   The property sheet for a connection.

| | |
|---|---|
| Operator Assisted (Manual) Dial | This check box is on the General tab of the modem property sheet. When you activate this option, each time you connect to the remote system, HyperTerminal displays a dialog box to prompt you to dial the phone number manually. This option is useful in hotels or in other situations when you might need to speak to an operator before you can dial. When you hear the remote modem, click the Connect button in the dialog box and then hang up the receiver. |
| Bring Up Terminal Window Before Dialing | This check box is on the Advanced tab of the modem property sheet. When you activate this check box, each time you connect to the remote system, HyperTerminal displays the Pre-Dial Terminal Screen before it dials the modem. You can use this screen to enter modem commands (see your modem manual for a list of applicable commands). You enter your commands and then click the window's Continue button. |
| Bring Up Terminal Window After Dialing | This check box is on the Advanced tab of the modem property sheet. When you activate this check box, HyperTerminal displays the Post-Dial Terminal Screen after it has connected to the remote system. Again, you can use this screen to enter modem commands. |

### Defining the Connection's Settings

To finish defining the connection, HyperTerminal has a few other options up its electronic sleeve. To view these options, display the connection's properties sheet, and select the Settings tab, shown in Figure 16.10. Here's the rundown:

| | |
|---|---|
| Function, Arrow, and Ctrl Keys Act As | These options determine how HyperTerminal reacts when you press any of the function keys, arrow keys, or Ctrl key combinations. If you activate the Terminal Keys option, HyperTerminal sends the keystrokes to the remote modem; if you activate Windows Keys, HyperTerminal applies the keystrokes to the Windows XP interface. |
| Backspace Key Sends | Use these options to determine the key or key combination that HyperTerminal sends when you press Backspace. Note that Ctrl+H is the key combination that deletes the previously typed character on most UNIX systems. |
| Emulation | Use this drop-down list to choose the terminal emulation you want to use with the remote system. The Auto Detect option tells HyperTerminal to attempt to determine the remote terminal type automatically. If you choose one of the specific terminal emulations, you can also click the Terminal Setup button to configure various aspects of the emulation. The available options depend on the emulation. |
| Telnet Terminal ID | If you'll be using HyperTerminal as your Telnet client, use this text box to enter the terminal type you want to use. |
| Backscroll Buffer Lines | This setting determines the number of lines displayed by the remote system that HyperTerminal stores in its buffer. You can scroll up or down through this buffer by using the scrollbars or the Page Up and Page Down keys. |
| Play Sound When Connecting or Disconnecting | This check box determines whether HyperTerminal beeps the speaker whenever it connects and disconnects. |
| Input Translation | Click this button to select the character encoding system used by the host system: Shift-JIS (Japanese Industrial Standard) or Standard JIS. |
| ASCII Setup | Clicking this button displays the ASCII Setup dialog box. These controls set various options for ASCII text you send to the remote system, as well as ASCII text that you receive. |

---

> **TIP**
>
> If you want to see the characters that you type in the HyperTerminal window, click ASCII Setup and then activate the Echo Typed Characters Locally check box.

**FIGURE 16.10**    Use the Settings tab to define terminal emulation and a few other options for the connection.

## Connecting to a Remote System

After you have your connection set up to your liking, you're ready to dial in. HyperTerminal gives you a couple of methods of establishing a connection with the remote system:

- When you save your first connection, HyperTerminal adds a new HyperTerminal subfolder to the Start menu's Communications folder. Select Start, All Programs, Accessories, Communications, HyperTerminal (the folder, not the program icon). In the submenu that appears, select the icon of the connection you want to launch.

- In the HyperTerminal program, select File, Open and use the dialog box that appears to open the connection.

In either case, you then click the Dial button in the Connect dialog box that appears. HyperTerminal dials the modem and connects with the remote system. Text from the remote computer appears in the HyperTerminal window, as shown in Figure 16.11. The status bar tells you the length of time you've been connected, and also indicates various connection settings.

## Performing File Transfers

If the remote system has a file you want to download, HyperTerminal makes it easy. After you've told the online service the name of the file you want to receive or send and the protocol to use, the service says something like `Ready to send/receive file. Please initiate file transfer.` At this point, you tell HyperTerminal that a file transfer is about to take place by using one of the following techniques:

16

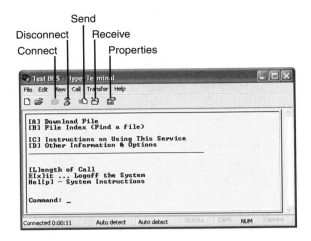

**FIGURE 16.11**    HyperTerminal connected to a remote system.

- For a download, either select Transfer, Receive File or click the Receive button in the toolbar (refer to Figure 16.11).

- For an upload, either select Transfer, Send File or click the Send button in the toolbar (refer to Figure 16.11).

- For a text file upload, select Transfer, Send Text File.

Note that in some cases, HyperTerminal selects the appropriate command for you automatically.

If you're downloading, the Receive File dialog box, shown in Figure 16.12, appears. In the Place Received File in the Following Folder text box, type the name of the folder in which you want to store the file. If you're not sure of the folder's name, click the Browse button, choose a folder in the Select a Folder dialog box that appears, and click OK to return to the Receive File dialog box. To select a protocol, drop down the Use Receiving Protocol list and choose the same protocol you selected in the remote system. Click the Receive button when you're ready to proceed with the transfer.

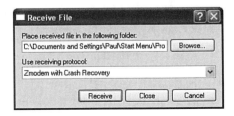

**FIGURE 16.12**    Use the Receive File dialog box to select a folder in which to store the file and a protocol.

If you're uploading, either the Send File dialog box or the Send Text File dialog box appears. Select the file to send, use the Protocol drop-down list to choose the same protocol you selected in the remote system, and click Send to make it so.

Whether you're sending or receiving, HyperTerminal displays the progress of the transfer in a dialog box. If for any reason you need to abort the transfer before it's complete, you can click the Cancel button. You can also click Skip File to bypass the current file in a multifile transfer.

When the transfer is complete, HyperTerminal returns control to the service, and you can continue with other service options or log off.

## Disconnecting from the Remote System

When you've finished working with the remote system, disconnecting is as easy as selecting Call, Disconnect or clicking the toolbar's Disconnect button (refer to Figure 16.11).

## Connecting to Another Computer

In addition to the usual online services and BBS computers, you can also use HyperTerminal to connect to another PC and then chat with the remote user or send files back and forth. All that's required is that both computers be running HyperTerminal or some other terminal program and that one of the modems be set up to answer incoming calls.

To set up HyperTerminal for a PC-to-PC connection, follow these steps:

1. Create a new HyperTerminal connection, following these instructions:

   - If your computer is doing the dialing, enter the phone number of the remote PC.

   - If your computer is doing the answering, the phone number doesn't matter, but because HyperTerminal requires one anyway, you can just enter a bogus number.

   - Make sure that both computers are set up with the same connection settings (speed, data bits, emulation, and so on).

   - When HyperTerminal prompts you to dial, click Cancel.

2. Select File, Properties to display the property sheet for the connection, and select the Settings tab.

3. Click the ASCII Setup button to display the ASCII Setup dialog box.

4. Activate the following check boxes:

   Send Line Ends with Line Feeds

   Echo Typed Characters Locally

   Append Line Feeds to Incoming Line Ends

   Wrap Lines That Exceed Terminal Width

16

5. Click OK to return to the property sheet.

6. Click OK.

To make the connection, one computer dials and the other waits for the incoming call. When you see the ring indicator on the modem or hear the phone ring, type your modem's answer command and press Enter. You need to check your modem manual for the correct command, but on most modems you use either ATA or just A. (You can avoid this step if your modem supports automatic answering. If it does, check your manual to see how to set it up.)

After the connection has been established, you can send messages back and forth by typing onscreen and pressing Enter after each line. File transfers work just as I described earlier.

### Entering AT Commands in HyperTerminal

If you're familiar with the AT command set, you might need to send a command or two to your modem. If so, here are the steps to follow to send commands via HyperTerminal:

1. Start HyperTerminal.

2. Enter a name for the connection (for example, **AT Commands**), select an icon, and click OK.

3. In the Phone Number dialog box, use the Connect using drop-down list to choose Com*x*, where *x* is the port number to which your modem is attached, and then click OK.

4. When the port property sheet appears, click OK. The HyperTerminal window appears.

5. Select File, Properties, activate the Settings tab, and click ASCII Setup.

6. In the ASCII Setup dialog box, activate the Send Line Ends with Line Feeds check box and make sure that the Echo Typed Characters Locally Check Box is deactivated. Click OK.

7. Click OK to return to HyperTerminal.

You can now enter AT commands in the terminal window. Don't forget to save your connection so that you can reuse it at any time.

# Sending and Receiving Faxes

Remember when, a couple of decades or so ago, the fax machine (or the *facsimile machine*, as it was called back then) was the hottest thing around, the new kid on the telecommunications block? How amazing it seemed that we could send a letter or memo or even a picture through the phone lines and have it emerge seconds later across town or even across the country. Sure, the fax that came slithering out the other end was a little fuzzier than the original, and certainly a lot slimier, but it sure beat using the post office.

Nowadays, though, faxing is just another humdrum part of the workaday world, and any business worth its salt has a fax machine on standby. Increasingly, however, dedicated fax machines are giving way to **fax modems**—modems that have the capability of sending and receiving faxes in addition to their regular communications duties. Not only does this make faxing affordable for small businesses and individuals, but it also adds a new level of convenience to the whole fax experience:

- You can send faxes from your computer without having to print the document.

- Because faxes sent via computer aren't scanned (as they are with a fax machine), the document that the recipient gets is sharper and easier to read.

- You can use your printer to get a hard copy of a fax on regular paper, thus avoiding fax paper (which, besides being inherently slimy, has an annoying tendency to curl).

- You can send binary files along with your faxes, provided that both the sending and the receiving fax modems support this feature.

## Installing the Fax Service

If you want to get into the fax fast lane, look no further than the Fax service. If you don't have this service on your system, follow these steps to install it:

1. Open Control Panel's Add or Remove Programs icon.

2. In the Add or Remove Programs window, click Add/Remove Windows Components. The Windows Components Wizard appears.

3. Activate the Fax Services check box and then click Next. Windows XP Setup installs the Fax service.

4. Click Finish.

The rest of this chapter shows you how to configure the Fax service and how to use it to send and receive faxes.

## Starting the Fax Console

You begin your faxing duties at the Fax Console, which you open by selecting Start, All Programs, Accessories, Communications, Fax, Fax Console. (Alternatively, select Start Printers and Faxes. In the Printers and Faxes window, double-click the Fax icon.) The first time you do this, the Fax Configuration Wizard appears. The next section takes you through this wizard's steps.

## Configuring the Fax Service

Follow these steps to configure the Fax service:

1. In the initial Fax Configuration Wizard dialog box, click Next. The wizard displays the Sender Information dialog box.

2. Use this dialog box to enter your name, fax number, address, and so on. Remember that this information will be added automatically to your fax cover pages, so enter only data that you want your fax recipients to see. When you're done, click Next. You now see the Select Device for Sending or Receiving Faxes dialog box.

> **NOTE**
>
> Instead of the Select Device for Sending or Receiving Faxes dialog box, you might see the final wizard dialog box instead. When you click Finish, a Windows Security Alert dialog box appears letting you know that Windows XP is blocking the Fax Console program. If this happens, click Unblock. In the Fax Console window, select Tools, Configure Fax to restart the Fax Configuration Wizard.

3. This dialog box has the following controls (click Next when you've made your choices):

| | |
|---|---|
| Please Select the Fax Device | This is a list of the fax/modems installed on your computer. If you have more than one, use the list to choose the one you want to perform the faxing chores. |
| Enable Send | Activate this check box if you want to be able to send faxes from your computer. |
| Enable Receive | Activate this check box if you want to be able to receive faxes on your computer. When this check box is activated, the following two controls come into play: |

| | | |
|---|---|---|
| | Manual Answer | Activate this option to answer incoming calls manually (as described in the "Answering Calls Manually" section, later in this chapter). |
| | Automatically Answer After *x* Rings | Activate this option to have the Fax service answer incoming calls auto-matically (as described in the "Answering Calls Automatically" section, later in this chapter). |

4. The wizard now prompts you for your **Transmitting Subscriber Identification**, or **TSID**. Type the text (such as your name or your company name) and click Next.

> **NOTE**
>
> Windows XP assigns a name to your fax machine. This is known in the trade as the **TSID—Transmitting Subscriber Identification** (or sometimes **Transmitting Station Identifier**). When the other person receives your fax, your TSID is displayed at the top of each page. If the other person is receiving on a computer, the TSID appears in the TSID line (or some similar field, depending on the program the recipient is using). Unfortunately, the default TSID in Windows XP is *Fax*, which redefines the word *uninspiring*. To fix this, edit the TSID as described in step 4. For example, it's common to change it to a name—such as your company name, your department name, or your own name—followed by your fax number.

5. If you elected to receive faxes, the wizard asks you for your **Called Subscriber Identification**, or **CSID**. This identifies your computer to the fax sender. This isn't as important as the TSID, so enter whatever you like and click Next.

6. If you'll be receiving faxes, the wizard now wonders what you want to do with incoming faxes (click Next when you're done):

Print It On

Activate this check box to have Windows XP automatically print any received fax. Use the list that becomes activated to choose the printer you want to use.

Store a Copy in a Folder

Activate this check box to store a second copy of each fax in the folder that you specify. The original copy of the fax is saved in the Fax Console, which you learn about in the next section.

7. Click Finish.

## Examining the Fax Console

When the wizard exits, you end up with the Fax Console window onscreen, as shown in Figure 16.13. The Fax Console is where you'll do your fax work in Windows XP.

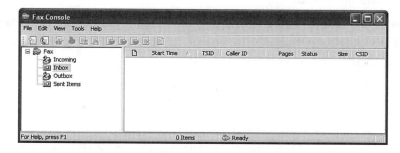

**FIGURE 16.13**    The Fax Console is your home base for Windows XP faxing.

The Fax Console includes four folders that store fax-related things:

Incoming

This folder displays information about the fax that is currently being received. For example: During fax reception, the Status column displays In progress and the Extended Status column displays Answered and then Receiving.

Inbox

This folder stores the incoming faxes that were received successfully. Note that the TSID column shows the name or phone number of the sender.

| Outbox | This folder stores data about the fax that is currently being sent. For example: During the send, the Status column displays `In progress` and the Extended Status column displays `Transmitting`. |
|--------|------|
| Sent Items | This folder stores a copy of the faxes that you have sent successfully. |

## Sending a Fax

To fax something to a friend or colleague (or, heck, even a total stranger), Windows XP gives you two ways to proceed:

- You can fax a simple note by sending just a cover page.
- You can fax a more complex document by sending it to the Windows XP fax "printer."

### Specifying Send Options

Before getting to the specifics of sending a fax, let's take a quick look at the various options that the Fax service provides for sending. To see these options, follow these steps:

1. Select Tools, Fax Printer Configuration to display the Fax Properties dialog box.

2. Display the Devices tab.

3. If you have multiple fax/modems installed on your computer, select the fax/modem you want to use to send faxes.

4. Click Properties. The modem's property sheet appears.

5. The Send tab, shown in Figure 16.14, has the following options:

| Enable Device to Send | Activate this check box to enable the Fax service's Send feature. |
|--------|------|
| TSID | Use this text box to type the transmitting subscriber identification that appears at the top of all your outgoing faxes. |
| Include Banner | When you activate this option, the Fax service includes text banner across the top edge of each page of the outgoing fax. This text includes your TSID, page number, and the recipient's fax number. |
| Number of Retries | This value determines the number of times the Fax service attempts to send a fax if it encounters a busy signal or some other error. |
| Retry After | This value determines the number of minutes the Fax service waits between retries. |
| Discount Rate Start | You'll see later on that you can tell the Fax service to send a fax "when discount rates apply," which means when your phone rates |

are discounted (such as after midnight). Use the Discount Rate Start spin box to specify the start time for your discounted phone rates.

Discount Rate Stop                    Use this spin box to specify the end time for your discounted phone rates.

6. Click OK in each open dialog box.

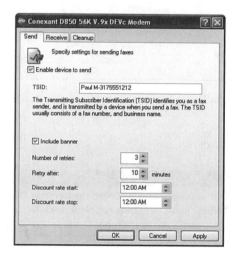

**FIGURE 16.14**   Use the Send tab of the modem's property sheet to configure the Fax service's sending options.

### Sending a Cover Page Fax

Let's start with the simple cover page route. This is handled by the Send Fax Wizard, which you can launch by using any of the following methods:

- In the Fax Console, select File, Send a Fax.

- From the Printers and Faxes window, click the task pane's Send a fax link. Alternatively, select File, Send Fax.

- Select Start, All Programs, Accessories, Communications, Fax, Send a Fax.

Here's what happens when the Send Fax Wizard arrives on the scene:

1. The initial dialog box isn't much use, so just click Next to continue. The Send Fax Wizard displays the Recipient Information dialog box, shown in Figure 16.15.

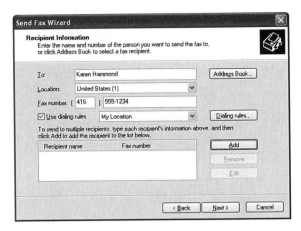

**FIGURE 16.15**   The Send Fax Wizard takes you through the steps necessary to send a simple cover page fax.

2. Fill in the following fields:

> **TIP**
>
> If the recipient is in your Address Book and you have the Fax field filled in (in either the Business or the Home tab), click Address Book, select the recipient, click To, and then click OK. The Send Fax Wizard adds the person's name and fax number to the recipient list.

| | |
|---|---|
| To | Type the name of the fax recipient. |
| Location | If you're calling long distance and you need to start the dialing with a number other than 1, activate the Use Dialing Rules check box and then use the Location list to select the country code for the fax recipient's phone number. |
| Fax Number | Use these two text boxes to enter the area code (if necessary) and phone number for the fax recipient. Note that you can't enter the area code unless you activate the Use Dialing Rules check box. |

3. Click Add. This isn't necessary if you're sending the fax to a single recipient or if you inserted the recipient via the Address Book.

4. If you want to send the fax to several people, repeat steps 2 and 3 as necessary.

5. When you're ready to move on, click Next. The Preparing the Cover Page dialog box appears.

6. Fill in the following fields (click Next when you're done):

| Cover Page Template | Select the cover page you want to use. See the "Working with Fax Cover Pages" section later in this chapter to find out about these predefined cover pages. |
| --- | --- |
| Subject Line | Type the subject of the fax. |
| Note | Type your cover page message. |

7. The wizard now asks you for the time you want the fax sent:

| Now | Sends the fax right away |
| --- | --- |
| When Discount Rates Apply | Sends the fax as soon as possible after your discount rates begin (as you specified in the previous section) |
| Specific Time in the Next 24 Hours | Sends the fax at the specified time |

8. Set the fax priority to High, Normal, or Low, and then click Next.

9. In the final wizard dialog box, click Preview Fax to check out the fax in the Windows Picture and Fax Viewer.

10. When you're ready to ship the fax, click Finish. The Fax Monitor window replaces the wizard so that you can see what's happening with the fax.

## Faxing from an Application

The other (and probably more common) method of sending a fax is to send a document directly from an application. You don't need applications with special features to do this, either. That's because when you install the Fax service, it adds a new printer driver to Windows XP. This printer driver, however, doesn't send a document to the printer. Instead, it renders the document as a fax and sends it to your modem.

To try this, follow these steps:

1. Create the document that you want to ship.

2. Select the program's File, Print command to get to the Print dialog box.

3. Select Fax as the printer and then click Print. The Send Fax Wizard appears.

4. Follow the steps outlined in the previous steps to set the fax options. With this method you don't have to bother with a cover page. If you'd still like to include one, activate the Select a Cover Page Template with the Following Information check box when you get to the Preparing the Cover Page dialog box.

**TIP**

You can use Windows XP's Photo Printing Wizard to fax a scanned image or photo. After you scan the picture, right-click the resulting file and then click Print to start the Photo Printing Wizard. (If you have the task pane displayed, you can also select the file and then click the Print this Picture link.) Click Next in the first two dialog boxes. In the Printing Options dialog box, select Fax in the What Printer Do You Want to Use? list. Click Next in the rest of the wizard's dialog boxes. When the wizard "prints" the image, the Send Fax Wizard appears.

## Working with Fax Cover Pages

I've mentioned fax cover pages a couple of times so far in this chapter, so it's time to take a closer look. In the fax world, a cover page performs the same function as an email message header: It specifies who is supposed to receive the fax and who sent it. Unlike an email message header, which is meant to be read and interpreted by a mail server or gateway, a fax cover sheet is meant for human consumption. In a company or department in which several people share a fax machine, the cover page clarifies who is supposed to get the fax. And when that person does read the message, she can use the rest of the information to see who sent the fax.

The Fax service comes with four prefabricated cover pages:

| | |
|---|---|
| Confidential | This cover page includes the word *confidential* on it, so it's useful for faxes that you want only the recipient to see. |
| FYI | This cover page includes the phrase *for your information* on it, so use it for faxes that don't require a response. |
| Generic | This cover page has no extra text on it, so use it for basic faxes. |
| Urgent | This cover page includes the word *urgent* on it, so it's good for faxes that you want read and responded to as soon as possible. |

You can use these pages as circumstances dictate, you can modify them to suit your style, or you can create new pages from scratch.

### Starting the Fax Cover Page Editor

To edit and create fax cover pages, the Fax service comes with the Fax Cover Page Editor application. To start this program, use either of the following techniques:

- Select Start, All Programs, Accessories, Communications, Fax, Cover Page Editor.

- In the Fax Console, select Tools, Personal Cover Pages. In the Personal Cover Pages dialog box, click New.

At this point you might see the Cover Page Editor Tips dialog box. If you don't want to deal with this dialog box each time you start the Cover Page Editor, deactivate the Show Tips at Startup check box and then click OK. Figure 16.16 shows the Fax Cover Page Editor window that appears.

> **NOTE**
>
> To open one of the four sample cover pages, select File, Open and then look in the following folder:
>
> `%SystemDrive%\Documents and Settings\All Users\Application Data\Microsoft\`
>
> `Windows NT\MSFax\Common Coverpages`

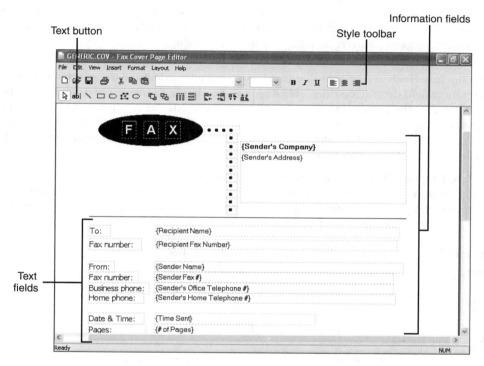

**FIGURE 16.16**    The Fax service provides the Fax Cover Page Editor so that you can edit and create cover pages to use with your faxes.

### Editing a Cover Page

Keeping in mind that cover pages are always sent as bitmaps, the idea behind the Cover Page Editor is to create a template for the bitmap. So, as you might expect, the Cover Page Editor is really a graphics application that specializes in working with fax bitmaps. The templates you work with consist of three types of fields: information, text, and graphics.

**Inserting Information Fields**    Information fields are placeholders for data. For example, the {Sender's Company} field (information fields always appear surrounded by braces) tells the Fax service to insert the name of the sender's company each time you use this cover page when you send a fax. With the Cover Page Editor, you can insert fields for recipient, sender, and message data:

- For the recipient, you can insert fields for the person's name, fax number, company, address, and much more. This information is gleaned from the properties sheet for the recipient's address. Select Insert, Recipient to see a complete list of the available fields.

- For the sender, you can insert fields for the name, fax number, company, address, telephone numbers, and more. Select Insert, Sender to see the available fields.

- For the message, the available fields include the note text, the Subject line, the time the fax was sent, the number of pages, and the number of attachments. Selecting Insert, Message displays a menu that lists these fields.

**Inserting Text Fields**    Text fields are text boxes that either describe the contents of each information field or provide titles, subtitles, and headings. To insert a text field, click the Text button on the Drawing toolbar, drag the mouse inside the cover page to create a box for the field, and enter your text. To change the text in an existing field, double-click it. (Note, too, that you can format text fields by using the buttons on the Style toolbar or by selecting Format, Font or Format, Align Text.)

**Inserting Graphics Fields**    Graphics fields are bitmap objects that you can use for logos or separators or just to add some style to the cover page. The Cover Page Editor's Drawing toolbar enables you to create many kinds of drawing objects, including lines, rectangles, circles, and polygons. Table 16.1 lists the buttons available on this toolbar.

**TABLE 16.1**    The Cover Page Editor's Drawing Toolbar Buttons

| Button | Name | Description |
|---|---|---|
|  | Line | Creates a straight line. |
|  | Rectangle | Creates a rectangle. (Hold down Shift while dragging to create a square.) |
|  | Rounded Rectangle | Creates a rectangle with rounded corners. |
|  | Polygon | Creates a polygon. |
|  | Ellipse | Creates an ellipse. (Hold down Shift while dragging to create a circle.) |
|  | Bring To Front | Moves the selected object in front of any objects that overlap it. You can also select Layout, Bring to Front or press Ctrl+F. |

**TABLE 16.1**    Continued

| Button | Name | Description |
|--------|------|-------------|
| | Send To Back | Moves the selected object behind any objects that overlap it. You can also select Layout, Send to Back or press Ctrl+B. |
| | Space Across | Spaces the selected objects evenly across the page. You can also select Layout, Space Evenly, Across. |
| | Space Down | Spaces the selected objects evenly down the page. You can also select Layout, Space Evenly, Down. |
| | Align Left | Aligns the selected objects along their left edges. You can also select Layout, Align Objects, Left. |
| | Align Right | Aligns the selected objects along their right edges. You can also select Layout, Align Objects, Right. |
| | Align Top | Aligns the selected objects along their top edges. You can also select Layout, Align Objects, Top. |
| | Align Bottom | Aligns the selected objects along their bottom edges. You can also select Layout, Align Objects, Bottom. |

## Receiving Faxes

This section explains how the Fax service handles incoming faxes and shows you how to view those faxes when they're sitting in your Inbox.

### Specifying Receive Options

Before getting to the specifics of receiving a fax, let's take a quick look at the various options that the Fax service provides for receiving. To see these options, follow these steps:

1. In the Fax Console, select Tools, Fax Printer Configuration to display the Fax Properties dialog box.

2. Display the Devices tab.

3. If you have multiple fax/modems installed on your computer, select the fax/modem you want to use to send faxes.

4. Click Properties. The modem's property sheet appears.

5. The Receive tab, shown in Figure 16.17, has the following options:

| | |
|---|---|
| Enable Device to Receive | Activate this check box if you want to be able to receive faxes on your computer. |
| CSID | Use this text box to type your Called Subscriber Identification. |
| Manual | Activate this option to answer incoming calls manually (as described later in the "Answering Calls Manually" section, later in this chapter). |
| Automatically After *x* Rings | Activate this option to have the Fax service answer incoming calls automatically (as described later in the "Answering Calls Automatically" section, later in this chapter). |
| Print It On | Activate this check box to have Windows XP automatically print any received fax. Use the list that becomes activated to choose the printer you want to use. |
| Store a Copy in Folder | Activate this check box to store a second copy of each fax in the folder that you specify. The original copy of the fax is saved in the Fax Console. |

**FIGURE 16.17**    Use the Receive tab to configure the Fax service for receiving incoming faxes.

### Answering Incoming Calls

How the Fax service handles incoming calls from remote fax systems depends on how you set up your fax/modem: manually or automatically. I describe both options in the next two sections.

**Answering Calls Automatically**    Enabling the Answer After *x* Rings option is the easiest way to handle incoming calls. In this mode, the Fax service constantly polls the modem's serial port for calls. When it detects a call coming in, it waits for whatever number of rings you specified (which can be as few as one ring or as many as 99) and then leaps into action. Without any prodding from you, it answers the phone and immediately starts conversing with the remote fax machine. The Fax Monitor window appears onscreen so that you can see the progress of the transfer, as shown in Figure 16.18.

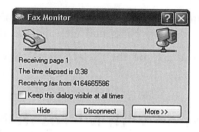

**FIGURE 16.18**    The Fax Monitor appears when the Fax service answers the incoming call.

> **TIP**
>
> If you find the Fax service's sounds (such as the ringing associated with an incoming call) annoying, you can disable them. In the Fax Console, select Tools, Fax Printer Configuration and then display the Tracking tab. Click Configure Sound Settings and then deactivate the check boxes for each sound you want to silence.

**Answering Calls Manually**    If you work with the Fax service in manual mode, when a call comes in you hear a ringing tone and the taskbar's notification area pops up a message that says The line is ringing. Click that message to receive the fax. If you happen to have the Fax Monitor open already, click the Answer Now button.

This mode is ideal if you receive both voice calls and fax calls on the same phone line. Here's the basic procedure you need to follow for incoming calls:

1. When the phone rings, pick up the receiver.

2. If you hear a series of tones, you know that a fax is on its way. In this case, click the notification message or the Answer Now button, as described earlier.

3. The Fax service initializes the modem to handle the call. Wait until the Fax service reports Receiving fax in the Fax Monitor window and then hang up the receiver. If you hang up before you see this message, you disconnect the call.

**Working with Received Faxes**

Depending on the size of the fax transmission, the Fax service takes from a few seconds to a few minutes to process the data. Eventually, though, your fax appears in the Inbox. From there, you can perform the following chores:

- Read the fax—Double-click the fax in the Fax Console's Inbox folder (or select the fax and then select File, View). This launches the Windows Picture and Fax Viewer, which displays your fax and enables you to annotate it.

- Print the fax—Select the fax and then select File, Print.

- Save the fax as an image—Select the fax and then select File, Save As. Use the Save As dialog box to choose a name and location for the file and then click Save. Note that the fax is saved as a TIF image.

- Email the fax as an attachment—Select the fax and then select File, Mail To. Use the New Message window to set up the e-mail message and then click Send.

- Delete the fax—Select the fax and then select File, Delete (or just press the Delete key).

# Remote Collaboration with Microsoft NetMeeting

As remote connection technologies improve, commuters find themselves morphing into telecommuters, and employees often end up with more freedom than ever to work where they want, when they want. In this new age of distance computing, the traditional definition of an office needs to be modified to include modern incarnations that are more virtual than physical.

In addition, the manner in which employees interact with each other also needs to be rethought. If members of, say, the editorial department are scattered all over the city, state, or even country, regular meetings just aren't possible. Sure, there is always email or company web pages (or even that almost-forgotten device, the telephone) to keep distance workers informed, but these methods lack the interaction of a true meeting.

If you have users or colleagues who must collaborate regularly but who are too far-flung to meet face-to-face, Microsoft NetMeeting might be the solution. NetMeeting is a communication and collaboration tool that allows users to establish conferences over an Internet, a network, or a modem connection. Within these conferences, remote users can interact in various ways:

- They can have voice conversations using sound card/microphone combinations.

- They can exchange files.

- They can chat by sending text messages in real time.

- They can use an electronic Whiteboard to collaborate on drawings.

- They can share applications and even work together on the same document.

The rest of this chapter shows you how to set up NetMeeting and then takes you through all of its collaboration features. (Although NetMeeting isn't strictly a modem tool, I've included it here because it fits into the communications theme of this chapter.)

## Configuring NetMeeting

Assuming you have an Internet or network connection set up, let's run through the steps necessary to configure NetMeeting. Begin by selecting Start, Run, typing **conf** in the Run dialog box, and then clicking OK. The first time you do this, Windows XP launches the NetMeeting Wizard. Follow these steps to use this wizard to configure NetMeeting.

> **TIP**
>
> If you plan on using NetMeeting regularly, consider setting up a shortcut for it on your Start menu (for instance, in the Communications folder). The `Conf.exe` file is located in the `%SystemDrive%\Program Files\NetMeeting` folder.

1. The initial dialog box just gives you an overview of NetMeeting's capabilities, so click Next to proceed.

2. The next dialog box asks for some personal data. At a minimum, you have to specify your first and last names and your email address to coax NetMeeting into continuing. (Don't worry: you can tell NetMeeting not to publish this information if you'd prefer to be incognito.) When you're done, click Next.

3. You can find other NetMeeting users (and they can find you), by logging in to a directory server (also known as an **Internet Locator Server**). You have two options (click Next when you've made your choices):

   | | |
   |---|---|
   | Log On to a Directory Server When NetMeeting Starts | If you activate this check box, NetMeeting will automatically log you in to one of these servers at startup. Use the Server Name list to select the directory server. |
   | Do Not List My Name in the Directory | Activate this check box if you don't want the personal data you entered in the previous dialog box to be published on the server. |

4. Now the wizard wonders what connection speed you'll be using for your NetMeeting collaborations. (Not surprisingly, the faster the connection, the better NetMeeting performs. However, for best results, you shouldn't select a connection speed that's faster than the one you'll be using.) Activate the appropriate connection speed and then click Next.

5. In the next dialog box, you can choose whether the wizard adds shortcuts for NetMeeting on your desktop and the Quick Launch bar. Click Next.

6. NetMeeting now launches the Audio Tuning Wizard, which checks your sound card to see whether it supports full-duplex (two-way) or half-duplex (one-way) sound. First, make sure that no other programs that use your sound card are running. This includes Windows Media Player, programs that use the sound card to broadcast messages ("You have mail!"), multimedia software, and so on. When that's done, click Next.

7. The Audio Tuning Wizard first checks to see whether you have multiple audio devices in your computer. If you do, you'll see a dialog box that enables you to select your Recording and Playback devices. Make your choices and then click Next.

16

8. In the Audio Tuning Wizard's next dialog box, click Test to play a sound, and then adjust the Volume slider to taste. Click Next when you're done.

9. You use the next dialog box to adjust the input (microphone) volume. Make sure that you have your sound card microphone plugged in and at the ready. Then speak into the microphone using your normal voice (the wizard displays some suggested text to read). As you speak, the wizard adjusts the Record Volume slider automatically. Keep speaking until the slider stabilizes. When the recording is complete, click Next.

10. Click Finish in the final wizard dialog box to continue loading NetMeeting.

11. If the Windows Security Alert dialog box appears, click Unblock to stop Windows Firewall from blocking NetMeeting.

The NetMeeting window appears, as shown in Figure 16.19.

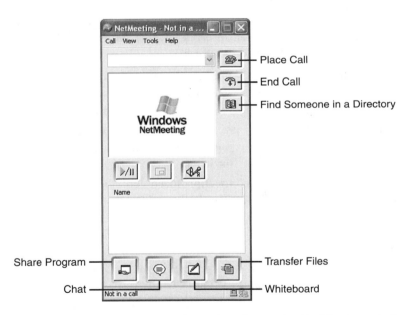

**FIGURE 16.19**    When you finish your configuration chores, the NetMeeting window appears.

---

**NOTE**

Windows Firewall must be configured to allow Internet-based NetMeeting connections. Here are the ports NetMeeting uses for its connections:

| Port | Purpose | Protocol |
|------|---------|----------|
| 389 | Internet locator service | TCP |
| 522 | User location service | TCP |

| Port | Purpose | Protocol |
|------|---------|----------|
| 1503 | T.120 | TCP |
| 1720 | H.323 call setup | TCP |
| 1731 | Audio call control | TCP |

In other words, Windows Firewall must be configured to allow TCP connections on ports 389, 522, 1503, 1720, and 1731.

## Placing NetMeeting Calls

After NetMeeting has been configured and you have the Internet or network connection established, you can get right down to business. In this section, I'll show you how to make calls in NetMeeting, place speed dial calls, and more.

### Placing Simple Calls

If you know who you want to call, NetMeeting is simple to use. Here are the steps to follow:

1. Select the Call, New Call command, or press Ctrl+N. (You can also click the Place Call button.) You'll see the Place a Call dialog box, shown in Figure 16.20.

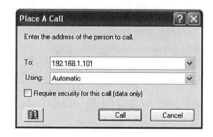

**FIGURE 16.20**  Use this dialog box to tell NetMeeting who you want to call.

2. In the To text box, specify the person you want to call by entering one of the following:

   - If you want to contact someone with a voice call, type the recipient's phone number.

> **NOTE**
>
> Voice calls in NetMeeting must go through a gateway server on your network. To specify the gateway, select Tools, Options to open the Options dialog box. In the General tab, click Advanced Calling to display the Advanced Calling Options dialog box. Activate the Use a Gateway to Call Telephones and Videoconferencing Systems check box, and then use the Gateway text box to enter the computer name or IP address of the gateway system. Note that some networks use a **gatekeeper**, a computer that enables you to connect to other people and

other computers. In this case, activate the Use a Gatekeeper to Place Calls check box instead, and then enter the computer's name or IP address in the Gatekeeper text box.

- If the person is logged on to a directory server, type the server name, a slash (/), and then the person's email address, as in this example:

  ```
  logon.netmeeting.microsoft.com/username@domain.com
  ```

- If you're on a network, type the name that the person's computer uses on the network, or the computer's IP address.

- If the person is connected to the Internet, type the IP address of their computer.

3. In the Using list, select either Network or Directory. (Alternatively, you can select Automatic and let NetMeeting figure it out.)

4. Click Call.

When NetMeeting finds the user and places the call, the other person hears a ring and sees the dialog shown in Figure 16.21. The remote user clicks Accept to answer the call, or clicks Ignore to reject the call. (NetMeeting automatically rejects an incoming call if it isn't answered after five rings.)

**FIGURE 16.21**   This dialog box appears when there is an incoming NetMeeting call.

If the call goes through, your name and the remote user's name are added to the Name list, and NetMeeting displays In a call in the status bar, as shown in Figure 16.22.

Here are some notes to bear in mind when you're connected:

- To talk to the other person, just speak into your microphone. If the sound cards used by you and the remote user can handle full-duplex audio, both of you can speak at the same time. If the cards support only half-duplex audio, only one of you can speak at a time.

- If the remote user complains that your voice isn't loud enough, you can increase your microphone volume or the remote user can increase his speaker volume.

- To find out the email address and other particulars about the remote user (depending on what that person entered into her NetMeeting configuration), right-click the user and select Properties from the context menu.

- Users who have voice capability are shown with an icon in the audio column. Similarly, users with video capability have an icon in the video column.

- In a conference, only two people can communicate by voice or video at one time. If a third person joins the conference, that person can communicate only via Chat, Whiteboard, or some other NetMeeting feature.

**FIGURE 16.22**    NetMeeting with a call in progress.

16

### Ending a Call

When it's time to end a NetMeeting call, use any of the following techniques to hang up:

- Select Call, Hang Up

- Click the End Call button

- Select Call, Exit or close the NetMeeting window

NetMeeting disconnects the call. If you began the conference and it includes three or more people, NetMeeting displays the warning that hanging up will disconnect everyone you invited. To disconnect everyone in the conference, click Yes.

### Using the SpeedDial Feature

If you call certain people frequently, you can use NetMeeting's SpeedDial feature to connect to these users with only a couple of mouse clicks or keystrokes. Follow these steps to create a SpeedDial entry:

1. Select Call, Create SpeedDial to display the Create SpeedDial dialog box.

2. In the Address text box, type the person's computer name, IP address, or directory entry. (You can't create telephone number SpeedDial entries.)

3. In the Call Using list, select either Directory or Network.

4. Make sure that the Add to SpeedDial option is activated.

5. Click OK.

After you've added someone to the SpeedDial, you can call that person by selecting Call, Directory to open the Find Someone window. In the Select a Directory list, select Speed Dial to display your SpeedDial list, and the double-click the entry you want to call.

---

**TIP**

The list of SpeedDial entries has two columns: Name and Address. Unfortunately, NetMeeting puts the entry's address value in both columns, which is the opposite of helpful. To fix this, open the SpeedDial folder:

```
%SystemDrive%\Program Files\NetMeeting\SpeedDial
```

Here you'll see a shortcut for each SpeedDial entry. Rename each shortcut to the name of the person it represents. Now return to the Find Someone window and reselect SpeedDial in the Select a Directory list. This time the shortcut names you created appear in the Name list.

---

**TIP**

If you want to give other people a SpeedDial shortcut that connects to you, create a new SpeedDial entry that uses your computer name, IP address, or directory entry. Activate the Save on the Desktop option and click OK. Display the desktop, right-click the shortcut icon, and then select Send To, Mail Recipient. Send the message to the person you want to call you.

---

### Hanging a "Do Not Disturb" Sign

If you have NetMeeting running but you don't want to accept any new calls for a while, you can hang an electronic Do Not Disturb sign by activating the Call, Do Not Disturb command (click OK in the dialog box that appears). While this command is active, others attempting to call you will receive a message telling them The other party did not accept your call.

## Exchanging Files in NetMeeting

Assuming that you've established a connection with one or more remote users, NetMeeting makes it easy to send files back and forth. To transfer a file, follow these steps:

1. Display the File Transfer window by using any of the following techniques:

   • Select Tools, File Transfer

   • Press Ctrl+F

   • Click the Transfer Files toolbar button

2. Select File, Add Files to display the Select a File to Send dialog box.

3. Select the file you want to ship and then click Add.

4. Repeat steps 2 and 3 to add other files, if necessary.

5. Use the drop-down list to select the file recipient: either Everyone or a specific user.

6. To send files, you have two choices:

   • To send a single file, select the file and then select File, Send a File.

   • To send all the files, select File, Send All.

NetMeeting begins sending the file and displays the progress of the operation in the status bar.

On the remote end, the user sees a dialog box similar to the one shown in Figure 16.23. There are three ways to proceed:

   • To have NetMeeting store the file on your hard drive without further ado, click Accept. Alternatively, you can wait until the download is complete and then click Close.

   • To cancel the file transfer (or to remove the file after the transfer is finished), click Delete.

   • To work with the file after the transfer has finished, click Open.

**FIGURE 16.23**   This dialog box appears when a remote user attempts to send you a file.

**NOTE**

NetMeeting stores the files that are transferred to your computer in the following folder:

```
%SystemDrive%\Program Files\NetMeeting\Received Files
```

To change this folder, open the File Transfer window and select File, Change Folder. Use the Browse for Folder dialog box to select the new folder, and then click OK.

## Using the Chat Feature

If you don't have a microphone, NetMeeting's audio features won't do you much good. That doesn't mean you can't communicate with remote callers, however. For simple text communications in real time, NetMeeting's Chat feature is perfect.

To run Chat, use any of the following methods:

- Select Tools, Chat
- Press Ctrl+T
- Click the Chat toolbar button

The Chat window that appears is shown in Figure 16.24.

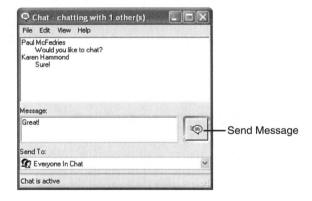

To use Chat, follow these steps:

1. Type your message in the Message text box
2. Use the Send To list to select the recipient of the message
3. Press Enter or click the Send Message button to the right of the Message text box

Messages appear in the upper text box, along with the name of each person who sent them.

Chat also has a couple of customization features. Select View, Options to display the Options dialog box. Here's a summary of the available settings:

| | |
|---|---|
| Information Display | Use these check boxes to specify how much information Chat displays about each message. In addition to the person's name, you can also choose to display the date and time that each message is sent. |
| Entire Message Is on One Line | If you activate this option, each Chat message is displayed on a single line across the window. |
| Wrap (Message Appears Next to Information Display) | If you activate this option, the messages are wrapped within the Chat window, and they appear beside the person's name (or whatever is checked in the Information display group). |
| Wrap (Message Appears Below Information Display) | If you activate this option (this is the Chat default), the messages again are wrapped within the Chat window, but they appear below the displayed information. |
| Fonts | Use these buttons to set the font for received messages, received private messages, sent messages, and sent private messages. |

## Using the Whiteboard

Whiteboards have become a standard feature in boardrooms and conference rooms. Presenters, facilitators, and meeting leaders use them to record action points, highlight important information, and draw charts and diagrams.

If you're running a remote conference via NetMeeting, you can use its Whiteboard feature for the same purposes. The Whiteboard is basically a revamped version of the Paint window that enables you to enter text, highlight information, and draw lines and shapes. Everything you add to the Whiteboard is reflected on the other users' screens, so they see exactly what you're typing and drawing. You can create multiple Whiteboard pages, and even save pages for later use.

To work with the Whiteboard, each user must display it by using any of the following techniques:

- Select Tools, Whiteboard
- Press Ctrl+W
- Click the Whiteboard toolbar button

For basic operations, you use Whiteboard just as you use Paint. That is, you select a tool to work with, select a line width (if applicable for the tool), select a color, and then draw your shape or type your text. However, Whiteboard has quite a few other techniques that aren't found in the Paint program. Here's a summary:

Figure 16.25 shows the Whiteboard window that appears.

16

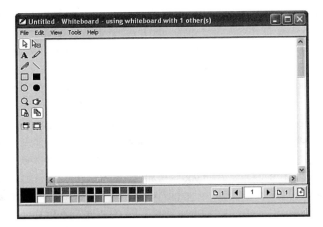

**FIGURE 16.25** Use the Whiteboard to draw text and pictures that can be seen by the other users in the conference.

- Locking the Whiteboard contents—To prevent the other users from changing the Whiteboard screen while you work, either select View, Lock Contents or click the Lock Contents tool.

- Using the remote pointer—Whiteboard has a remote pointer that, when activated, appears on each user's Whiteboard. To activate it, either select View, Remote Pointer or click the Remote Pointer On tool. When the pointer appears, use the mouse to drag it around the screen.

- Displaying the contents of another window in the Whiteboard—Whiteboard has a Select Window feature that enables you to display the contents of another open window inside the Whiteboard. To activate this feature, either select Tools, Select Window or click the Select Window tool. Click OK in the Whiteboard Select Window dialog box that appears, and then click the window you want to display.

- Displaying part of the screen in the Whiteboard—Rather than an entire window, you might prefer to display only part of the screen in the Whiteboard. To do this, either select Tools, Select Area or click the Select Area tool. Click OK in the Whiteboard Select Area dialog box that appears, and then use the mouse to select the screen area you want to display.

- Clearing the Whiteboard—If you want to start over, you can clear the contents of the Whiteboard either by selecting Edit, Clear Page or by pressing Ctrl+Delete. Click Yes when NetMeeting asks you to confirm the deletion.

- Adding another page to the Whiteboard—The Whiteboard is capable of displaying multiple pages. To add a new page, either select Edit, Insert Page After or click the Insert New Page button.

- Navigating Whiteboard pages—When you have multiple pages in the Whiteboard, you can navigate among them by pressing Ctrl+Page Up (to move to the next page) or Ctrl+Page Down (to move to the previous page). Note that as you move from page to page, the remote users' Whiteboards also change pages. You can also use the following navigation buttons:

  Previous Page

  Next Page

- Deleting a Whiteboard page—To remove the current page from the Whiteboard, select Edit, Delete page.

- Preventing remote users from seeing your changes—If you want to make some changes to a page without the other users seeing them, deactivate the View, Synchronize command, move to the page and make your changes, and then activate View, Synchronize again. The remote users will remain on the original page while you make your edits.

- Saving the Whiteboard—If you think you'll need to use your Whiteboard again, select File, Save and then choose a location and name for the new file. (Whiteboard files use the .nmw extension.) To reuse the Whiteboard, select File, Open and choose the Whiteboard file from the Open dialog box.

## Sharing Programs

Chat and the Whiteboard are handy features, but their functionality is limited to text and simple drawings or screenshots. For truly collaborative computing, you need the ability to run a program on one computer and display what's happening on the remote machines. An even better scenario is one in which all the users can work with an application at the same time.

The good news is that NetMeeting can handle both situations, albeit with a few quirks and security concerns. The next two sections take you through NetMeeting's program sharing features.

> **CAUTION**
>
> Program sharing works best when all users have their screens set to the same resolution. If a user running at high resolution (for example, 1,024×768) shares a maximized application with a user running at low resolution (for example , 800×600), the user with the lower resolution sees only part of the shared program's window. However, that user can still see more of the window by scrolling vertically and horizontally within the window that contains the shared program.

16

### Demonstrating a Program

NetMeeting's default method for application sharing is to select one of your running programs to share, and the program's window appears on the other users' screens. However, only you can access the program's features and edit the program's documents. This is perfect if you just want to demonstrate a feature or display a document.

To share an application in this way, follow these steps:

1. Use any of the following techniques to start the Sharing feature:

   - Select Tools, Sharing

   - Press Ctrl+S

   - Click the Share Program button on the toolbar

2. As you can see in Figure 16.26, the Sharing window appears with a list of your running applications. Click the application you want to share.

3. Click Share. A copy of the application's window is sent to each user.

4. If you want to share multiple programs, repeat steps 2 and 3 for each program you want to work with.

5. If you're sharing over a network or a fast connection, activate the Share in True Color check box to enable each user to see the window in full color.

6. Activate the window you want to share.

> **TIP**
>
> If you have data in an application window that you want to hide from others, use another open window to cover that portion of the shared window. The remote users will see a pattern over the obscured section of the window.

Any actions you perform within this window (including mouse movements) are mirrored on the remote screens.

### Allowing Remote Users to Assume Control

Instead of merely demonstrating a program to the other users, you might prefer a more interactive approach that allows each user to work with the shared application. This is called **giving a remote user control**. After you've shared an application, you switch to this mode by following these steps:

1. Return to the Sharing window.

2. Click Allow Control.

3. Set the control options:

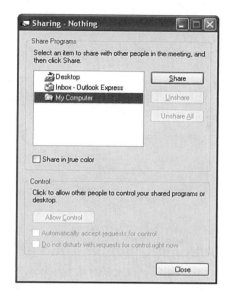

**FIGURE 16.26**   Use the Sharing dialog box to choose the running program you want to share with the remote users.

| | |
|---|---|
| Automatically Accept Requests for Control | Activate this check box to enable remote users to assume control without your permission. |
| Do Not Disturb with Requests for Control Right Now | Activate this check box to temporarily prevent remote users from assuming control. This is useful if you want to leave control turned on, but you require the control yourself for a short time. |

4. Activate the window you're sharing.

---

**CAUTION**

When you allow other people to assume control over a program, they can use it just as though they were sitting at your keyboard. Depending on the program, this might include the ability to open, save, and delete files, or even to launch programs. Therefore, exercise some caution when allowing others to control certain programs.

---

On the remote user's screen, the **Control** window (that is, the window within which the shared program appears) displays controllable in the title bar. To request control of the window, the remote user has two choices:

- Select Control, Request Control
- Double-click the shared window

On your screen, the Request Control dialog box appears (unless you activated the Automatically Accept Requests for Control check box). Click Accept to allow the user to assume control of the window, or click Reject to prevent the user from taking control.

### Stopping Program Sharing

To end the program sharing, either exit the shared program or return to the Sharing window and perform one of the following:

- If you only want to stop others from assuming control of the program, click Prevent Control.

- To stop sharing the program, select it in the list of programs and then click Unshare. If you're sharing multiple programs, you can stop sharing all of them at once by clicking Unshare All.

## Setting NetMeeting Options

To finish our look at NetMeeting, this section shows you how to customize the program using its extensive list of properties. To work with these options, select Tools, Options to display the Options dialog box.

The options in the General tab control a mixed bag of NetMeeting settings. Here's a review:

| | |
|---|---|
| My Directory Information | The controls in this group display the personal NetMeeting data that you specified when configuring the program. Feel free to edit this information as needed. |
| Directory | Use this list to specify the default directory server you want NetMeeting to use. |
| Do Not List My Name in the Directory | Activate this check box if you prefer that your data not appear in the directory server. |
| Log On to the Directory Server When NetMeeting Starts | If you activate this check box, NetMeeting will log you on to the directory server each time you start the program. |
| Run NetMeeting in the Background When Windows Starts | Activate this check box to launch NetMeeting automatically when you start Windows XP. |
| Show the NetMeeting Icon on the Taskbar | This check box toggles the NetMeeting icon on and off in the taskbar's notification area. |
| Bandwidth Settings | Click this button to select your connection speed. |
| Advanced Calling | Click this button to enable and configure a gatekeeper or gateway server on your network. |

The options in the Security tab enable you to configure secure calling:

| | |
|---|---|
| Incoming Calls | Activate this check box to force NetMeeting to accept only secure incoming calls. |
| Outgoing Calls | Activate this check box to force NetMeeting to place all your calls as secure calls. |
| Use Privacy (Encryption) Only | Activate this option to use the standard NetMeeting Certificate to encrypt your secure calls. |
| Use this Certificate for Privacy and Authentication | Activate this option to use a digital ID to both encrypt your calls and to authenticate yourself as the caller. Use the list below this option to select the digital ID you want to use. |

> **NOTE**
>
> For the details of encryption, authentication, and digital IDs, see Chapter 21, "Implementing Windows XP's Internet Security and Privacy Features."

The Audio tab controls various settings related to the audio portion of the NetMeeting show. Here's a summary:

> **NOTE**
>
> Not all sound cards support all the options in the Audio tab. If a check box is disabled, your sound card doesn't support that feature.

| | |
|---|---|
| Enable Full-Duplex Audio So I Can Speak While Receiving Audio | This check box toggles full-duplex (two-way) audio on and off. |
| Enable Auto-Gain Control | NetMeeting's Auto-Gain feature adjusts the microphone volume based on the volume of your voice. That is, if you speak quietly, NetMeeting increases the microphone volume to compensate; if you speak loudly, the value is decreased accordingly. If a noisy work environment causes the microphone level to fluctuate unpredictably, deactivate this check box to shut off automatic gain. |
| Automatically Adjust Microphone Volume While in a Call | This is similar to the Auto-Gain feature. If your sound card doesn't support auto-gain, activate this check box instead. |
| Enable DirectSound for Improved Audio Performance | Activate this check box to use DirectSound, which reduces the delay between the time that audio is sent and when it is heard. |
| Tuning Wizard | Click this button to run the Audio Tuning Wizard. This is a good idea if you change your sound card or the speed of |

|  | your connection. (You can also launch the Audio Tuning Wizard by selecting Tools, Audio Tuning Wizard. Note that this command is unavailable while you're in an audio conference.) |
|---|---|
| Advanced | Click this button if you'd like to configure your own audio codecs. In the Advanced Compression Settings dialog box, activate the Manually Configure Compression Settings check box. Then use the Preferred Codec for Audio Compression list to choose the default codec. |
| Silence Detection | The sensitivity of your microphone to the detection of silence is a measure of how it handles background noises. A high sensitivity setting means the microphone will pick up back ground noises. By default, NetMeeting adjusts this sensitivity automatically (that is, the Adjust Silence Detection Automatically option button is activated). If you prefer to make the adjustments yourself, activate the Let Me Adjust Silence Detection Myself option, and then use the slider to choose a setting (move the slider to the right for higher sensitivity; move it to the left for lower sensitivity). |

If you have video capability on your system, use the controls in the Video tab to set up your video conferencing:

| Automatically Send Video at the Start of Each Call | Activate this check box to configure NetMeeting to start sending the video immediately after connecting to the remote user. |
|---|---|
| Automatically Receive Video at the Start of Each Call | When this check box is activated, NetMeeting displays the incoming video stream when the call connects. If you'd prefer not to see incoming video, deactivate this check box. |
| Send Image Size | These options determine the default size of the video image you send. |
| Video Quality | As usual with video applications, in NetMeeting there is a trade-off between video speed and video quality. You can use this slider to set the level of quality you prefer. Move the slider to the left for a better frame rate; move the slider to the right for higher quality within each frame. |
| The Video Capture Device I Wish to Use Is | This list shows you the video device NetMeeting is using. If you have more than one device on your system, use this list to select the one you want to use. Click the Source button to display the Video Source dialog box, which enables you to |

| | adjust various settings related to the device. Click Format to set video capture properties, if your capture card supports this option. |
|---|---|
| Show Mirror Image in Preview Video Window | Activate this check box to show your video preview as though you were looking in a mirror. (Note that only you see this mirror image; the remote user sees the normal image.) |

## From Here

Here's a list of other parts of the book that contain information related to what you learned in this chapter:

- For information on installing and configuring a modem in Windows XP, refer to Chapter 15, "Getting Started with Modem Communications."

- For more information about IP addresses and subnets, see Chapter 17, "Implementing TCP/IP for Internet Connections."

- For the details on encryption, authentication, and digital IDs, see Chapter 21, "Implementing Windows XP's Internet Security and Privacy Features."

- If you're on the road, you can use your modem to connect to your network. See Chapter 23, "Making Remote Network Connections."

16

# PART V

# Unleashing Windows XP for the Internet

## IN THIS PART

# Implementing TCP/IP for Internet Connections

One of the problems facing network administrators these days is the need to support multiple protocols. If the network includes older Windows NT servers and Windows machines, NetBEUI is often the protocol of choice. Throw in some NetWare nodes, and you also need IPX/SPX. If any UNIX boxes are on the network or if the network has an Internet gateway, TCP/IP must also be supported. Diverse networks might also need to support AppleTalk, Banyan VINES, and who knows what else.

Increasingly, administrators are throwing up their hands and saying, "Enough already!" Instead of putting up with the headache of supporting umpteen protocols, they're simplifying both their networks and their lives by implementing a single protocol on *all* their network machines. That protocol is TCP/IP, thanks to its near-universal support by networking vendors, its large packet size and speed, its robustness, and its unmatched scalability.

But TCP/IP isn't just for network honchos. The explosion of interest in the Internet has thrust TCP/IP into the spotlight. That's because TCP/IP is the *lingua franca* of Internet communication, and you can't get online without it. So, even if you're using a standalone machine with no network in sight, you'll need to know how to implement TCP/IP in Windows XP to take advantage of all the Net has to offer.

This chapter will help you do just that. Whether you work with one machine or one thousand, you'll find everything you need to know to install and configure TCP/IP in the Windows XP environment.

# Understanding TCP/IP

If there's a downside to TCP/IP, it's that compared to other protocols, TCP/IP is much more complex to implement and manage. However, we're still not talking about brain surgery here. With just a smattering of background info, the mysteries of TCP/IP will become clear and your configuration chores will become downright comprehensible. That's my goal in this section: to give you enough knowledge about TCP/IP plumbing to stand you in good stead when you get down to the brass tacks of actually setting up, using, and, if necessary, troubleshooting TCP/IP.

## What Is TCP/IP?

Although people often speak of TCP/IP as being a protocol, it is in fact a suite of protocols (more than 100 in all!) housed under one roof. Here's a summary of the most important of these protocols:

| | |
|---|---|
| Internet Protocol (IP) | This is a connectionless protocol that defines the Internet's basic packet structure and its addressing scheme, and that also handles routing of packets between hosts. |
| Transmission Control Protocol (TCP) | This is a connection-oriented protocol that sets up a connection between two hosts and ensures that data is passed between them reliably. If packets are lost or damaged during transmission, TCP takes care of retransmitting the packets. |
| File Transfer Protocol (FTP) | This protocol defines file transfers among computers on the Internet. |
| Simple Mail Transport Protocol (SMTP) | This protocol describes the format of Internet email messages and how messages get delivered. |
| Post Office Protocol (POP) | This protocol specifies how an email client connects to and downloads messages from a mail server. |
| Internet Message Access Protocol (IMAP) | This protocol defines how to manage received messages on a remote server, including viewing headers, creating folders, and searching message data. |
| Hypertext Transport Protocol (HTTP) | This protocol defines the format of Uniform Resource Locator (URL) addresses and how World Wide Web data is transmitted between a server and a browser. |
| Network News Transport Protocol (NNTP) | This protocol defines how Usenet newsgroups and postings are transmitted. |

Of these, IP and TCP are the most important for our purposes, so the next two sections look at these protocols in greater detail.

> ### The TCP/IP Stack
>
> You'll often see references to the **TCP/IP stack**. Networks are always implemented in a layered model that begins with the *application* and *presentation* layers at the top (these layers determine how programs interact with the operating system and user, respectively) and the *data-link* and *physical* layers at the bottom (these layers govern the network drivers and network adapters, respectively). In between, you have a three-layer stack of protocols:
>
> Session layer—These are protocols that let applications communicate across the network. This is where protocols such as FTP and SMTP reside.
>
> Transport layer—These are connection-oriented protocols which ensure that data is transmitted correctly. This is where TCP resides.
>
> Network layer—These are connectionless protocols that handle the creation and routing of packets. This is where IP resides.

## Understanding IP

As the name *Internet Protocol* implies, the Internet, in a very basic sense, *is* IP. That's because IP has a hand in everything that goes on in the Internet:

- The structure of all the data being transferred around the Internet is defined by IP.

- The structure of the address assigned to every host computer and router on the Internet is defined by IP.

- The process by which data gets from one address to another (this is called **routing**) is defined by IP.

Clearly, to understand the Internet (or, on a smaller scale, an **intranet**: the implementation of Internet technologies for use within a corporate organization), you must understand IP. In turn, this understanding will make your life a lot easier when it comes time to implement TCP/IP in Windows XP.

### The Structure of an IP Datagram

Network data is broken down into small chunks called **packets**. These packets include not only the data (such as part of a file), but also *header information* that specifies items such as the destination address and the address of the sender. On the Internet, data is transmitted in a packet format defined by IP. These IP packets are known as **datagrams**.

The datagram header can be anywhere from 160 to 512 bits in length, and it includes information such as the address of the host that sent the datagram and the address of the host that is supposed to receive the datagram. Although you don't need to know the exact format of a datagram header to implement TCP/IP, Table 17.1 spells it out in case you're interested.

**TABLE 17.1**    The Structure of a Datagram Header

| Field | Bits | Description |
| --- | --- | --- |
| Version | 0 to 3 | Specifies the format of the header. |
| Internet Header Length | 4 to 7 | The length of the header, in words (32 bits). |
| Type of Service | 8 to 15 | Specifies the quality of service desired (for example, this field can be used to set precedence levels for the datagram). |
| Total Length | 16 to 31 | The length of the datagram, including the header and data. Because this is a 16-bit value, datagrams can be as large as 65,536 bytes. |
| Identification | 32 to 47 | An identifying value that lets the destination reassemble a fragmented datagram. (Some systems can't handle packets larger than a particular size, so they'll fragment datagrams as needed. The header is copied to each fragment, and the next two fields are altered as necessary.) |
| Flags | 48 to 50 | One flag specifies whether a datagram can be fragmented. If it can't, and the host can't handle the datagram, it discards the datagram. If the datagram can be fragmented, another flag indicates whether this is the last fragment. |
| Fragment Offset | 51 to 63 | If the datagram is fragmented, this field specifies the position in the datagram of this fragment. |
| Time to Live | 64 to 71 | Specifies the maximum number of hosts through which the datagram can be routed. Each host decrements this value by 1, and if the value reaches 0 before arriving at its destination, the datagram is discarded. This prevents runaway datagrams from traversing the Internet endlessly. |
| Protocol | 72 to 79 | Represents the session layer protocol being used (such as FTP or SMTP). |
| Header Checksum | 80 to 95 | Used to check the integrity of the header (not the data). |
| Source Address | 96 to 127 | The IP address of the host that sent the datagram. |
| Destination Address | 128 to 159 | The IP address of the host that is supposed to receive the datagram. |
| Options | 160 and over | This field can contain anywhere from 0 to 352 bits, and it specifies extra options such as security. |

The rest of the datagram is taken up by the data that is to be transmitted to the destination host.

### The Structure of an IP Address

You saw in the preceding section that the addresses of both the source and the destination hosts form an integral part of every IP datagram. This section looks at the structure of these **IP addresses**. When setting up TCP/IP in Windows XP, you might have to enter the IP address of your computer (and, if you're an administrator, each computer on your network), as well as several other IP addresses. Similarly, you saw in Chapter 16, "Putting Your Modem to Work," that you could use an IP address to place a "call" to another person on your network or on the Internet. In other words, IP addresses come up a lot these days, so you need to know how they work.

An **IP address** is a 32-bit value assigned to a computer by a network administrator or, if you've signed up for an Internet account, by your **Internet service provider** (**ISP**). As you'll see in a minute, these addresses are designed so that every host and router on the Internet or within a TCP/IP network has a unique address. That way, when an application needs to send data to a particular locale, it knows that the destination address it plops into the datagram header will make sure that everything ends up where it's supposed to.

**Dotted-Decimal Notation**    The problem with IP addresses is their "32-bitness." For example, here's the IP address of my web server:

11001101110100000111000100000010

Not very inviting, is it? To make these numbers easier to work with, the TCP/IP powers-that-be came up with the **dotted-decimal notation** (also known in the trade as **dotted-quad notation**). This notation divides the 32 bits of an IP address into four groups of 8 bits each (each of these groups is called a **quad**), converts each group into its decimal equivalent, and then separates these numbers with dots.

Let's look at an example. Here's my web server's IP address grouped into four eight-bit quads:

11001101 11010000 01110001 00000010

Now you convert each quad into its decimal equivalent. When you do, you end up with this:

```
11001101 11010000 01110001 00000010
   205       208      113       2
```

> **TIP**
>
> You can convert a value from binary to decimal using Windows XP's Calculator. Select Start, All Programs, Accessories, Calculator and then, in the Calculator window, select View, Scientific. Activate the Bin option, use the text box to type the 1's and 0's of the binary value you want to convert, and activate the Dec option.

Now you shoehorn dots between each decimal number to get the dotted-decimal form of the address:

205.208.113.2

**IP Address Classes**    So, how is it possible, with millions of hosts on the Internet the world over, to ensure that each computer has a unique IP address? The secret is that each network that wants on the Internet must sign up with a domain registrar (such as VeriSign.com or Register.com). In turn, the registrar assigns that network a block of IP addresses that the administrator can then dole out to each computer (or, in the case of an ISP, to each customer). These blocks come in three classes: A, B, and C.

In a **class A network**, the registrar assigns the first (that is, the leftmost) 8 bits of the address: The first bit is 0, and the remaining seven bits are an assigned number. Two to the power of 7 is 128, so 128 class A networks are possible. The dotted-decimal versions of these IP addresses begin with the numbers 0 (that is, 00000000) through 127 (that is, 01111111). However, 0 isn't used and 127 is used for other purposes, so there are really only 126 possibilities.

> **NOTE**
>
> The numbers assigned by the registrar are called **network IDs,** and the numbers assigned by the network administrator are called **host IDs.** For example, consider the following address from a class A network: 115.123.234.1. The network ID is 115 (or it's sometimes written as 115.0.0.0), and the host ID is 123.234.1.

The number 126 might seem small, but consider that the remaining 24 address bits are available for the network to assign locally. In each quad, you have 254 possible numbers (0 and 255 aren't used), so you have 254×254×254 possible addresses to assign, which comes out to a little more than 16 million. In other words, you need to have a large system to rate a class A network. (If you do have such a system, don't bother petitioning the registrar for a block of IP addresses because all the class A networks were snapped up long ago by behemoths such as IBM.) Figure 17.1 shows the layout of the IP addresses used by class A networks.

> **NOTE**
>
> Bear in mind that you need to register your network with the registrar only if you require Internet access. If you're just creating an internal TCP/IP network, you can create your own block of IP addresses and assign them at will.

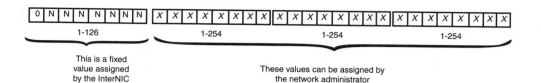

**FIGURE 17.1**    The IP address structure for class A networks.

In a **class B network**, the registrar assigns the first 16 bits of the address: The first two bits are 10, and the remaining 14 bits are an assigned number. This allows for a total of 16,384 (2 to the power of 14) class B networks, all of which have a first quad dotted-decimal value between 128 (that is, 10000000) and 191 (that is, 10111111). Note that, as with class A networks, all the possible class B numbers have been assigned.

Again, the network administrator can dole out the remaining 16 bits to the network hosts. Given 254 possible values in each of the two quads, that produces a total of 64,516 possible IP addresses. Figure 17.2 shows the layout of class B network IP addresses.

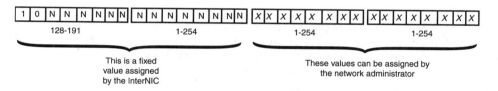

**FIGURE 17.2**    The IP address structure for class B networks.

In a **class C network**, the registrar assigns the first 24 bits of the address: The first 3 bits are 110, and the remaining 21 bits are an assigned number. So, the total number of class C networks available is 2,097,152 (2 to the power of 21), all of which have a first quad dotted-decimal value between 192 (that is, 11000000) and 223 (that is, 11011111).

This leaves only the remaining eight bits in the fourth quad for network administrators to assign addresses to local computers. Again, 0 and 255 aren't used, so a class C network has a total of 254 possible IP addresses. The layout of class C network IP addresses is shown in Figure 17.3.

> **NOTE**
>
> Because the first quad of an IP address is eight bits, the range of possible values should be between 0 and 255, but class A, B, and C networks usurp only 0 through 223. What happened to 224 through 255? Well, the values between 224 and 239 are used for special multicast protocols (these are **class D addresses**), and the values between 240 and 255 are used for experimental purposes (these are **class E addresses**).

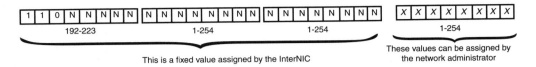

FIGURE 17.3    The IP address structure for class C networks.

### IP Routing

So far you've seen that IP datagrams include the source and destination IP addresses in their headers and that these addresses use the dotted-decimal notation. The next question is, how do the datagrams get from the source to the destination? The answer is that IP also defines how datagrams travel from host to host in a process called **routing**. (Each leap from one host to the next is called a **hop**.)

When IP is ready to send data, it compares the addresses in the datagram header to see whether the source and destination reside on the same network. If they do, IP just hands the packets over to the LAN for delivery, and the data is sent directly to the destination. If the addresses are on different networks, however, the packets must be routed outside of the network.

**Subnet Masks**    At first blush, deciding whether the source and destination hosts are on the same network sounds easy: just compare the network IDs of the two addresses. For example, consider the following two addresses:

Source                          200.100.55.101

Destination                   200.100.66.72

These are class C networks, so the source address has a network ID of 200.100.55, and the destination has a network ID of 200.100.66. Therefore, they're on different networks. Or are they? One of the consequences of having no more class A and class B address blocks is that many large corporations can handle their addressing needs only by obtaining multiple blocks of class C addresses. So, it's entirely possible that the 200.100.55 and 200.100.66 network IDs belong to the same company and could therefore be part of the same network! If so, IP should look at only the first two quads (200.100) to determine whether the addresses are on the same network.

So, how does IP know to compare the first one, two, or three quads? By using a **subnet mask**. A **subnet** is a subsection of a network that uses related IP addresses. On a class C network, for example, you could define the first 127 addresses to be on one subnet and the second 127 addresses to be on another subnet. On a larger scale, from the point of view of the Internet—which you can think of as being *the* network—each class A, B, and C network is a subnet.

The subnet mask is a 32-bit value that is usually expressed in the same dotted-decimal notation used by IP addresses. The purpose of the subnet mask is to let IP separate the network ID (or, as you saw in the preceding example, part of the network ID) from the full IP address and thus determine whether the source and destination are on the same network. Table 17.2 spells out the default subnet masks used for each type of network class.

**TABLE 17.2**   Normal Subnet Masks Used for Each Network Class

| Network | Subnet Mask | Bit Values |
| --- | --- | --- |
| Class A | 255.0.0.0 | 11111111 00000000 00000000 00000000 |
| Class B | 255.255.0.0 | 11111111 11111111 00000000 00000000 |
| Class C | 255.255.255.0 | 11111111 11111111 11111111 00000000 |

When IP applies the subnet mask to an IP address, the part of the mask that is all 0's strips off the corresponding section of the address. Consider the following example:

| | IP Address | Mask | Result |
| --- | --- | --- | --- |
| Source | 205.208.113.2 | 255.255.255.0 | 205.208.113.0 |
| Destination | 205.208.113.50 | 255.255.255.0 | 205.208.113.0 |

The mask produces the same result, so these two addresses are on the same network. Now consider the example I used earlier. In this case, we need to use a nonstandard mask of 255.255.0.0:

| | IP Address | Mask | Result |
| --- | --- | --- | --- |
| Source | 200.100.55.101 | 255.255.0.0 | 200.100.0.0 |
| Destination | 200.100.66.72 | 255.255.0.0 | 200.100.0.0 |

**NOTE**

The operation of the subnet mask is a bit more complex than I've let on. It's actually a two-step process. In the first step, the IP addresses are both compared bit by bit with the subnet mask using a Boolean AND operation—if both bits are 1, a 1 is returned; otherwise, a 0 is returned:

**Source:**

| | |
| --- | --- |
| 205.208.113.2 | 11001101 11010000 01110001 00000010 |
| 255.255.255.0 | 11111111 11111111 11111111 00000000 |
| Result of AND | 11001101 11010000 01110001 00000000 |

17

**Destination:**

| | |
|---|---|
| 205.208.113.50 | 11001101 11010000 01110001 00110010 |
| 255.255.255.0 | 11111111 11111111 11111111 00000000 |
| Result of AND | 11001101 11010000 01110001 00000000 |

Now the two results are compared bit by bit using a **Boolean Exclusive Or** (XOR) operation—if both bits are 0 or both bits are 1, a 0 is returned; otherwise, a 1 is returned:

| | |
|---|---|
| Source Result | 11001101 11010000 01110001 00000000 |
| Destination Result | 11001101 11010000 01110001 00000000 |
| Result of XOR | 00000000 00000000 00000000 00000000 |

If the result of the XOR operation is all 0's, the source and destination are on the same network.

**Routing and the Default Gateway**    As I said, if IP determines that the source and destination exist on the same network, it hands the datagrams over to the LAN for immediate delivery. If the destination is outside the network, however, IP's routing capabilities come into play.

**Routing** is the process by which a datagram travels from the source host to a destination host on another network. The first part of the routing process involves defining a default gateway. This is the IP address of a computer or dedicated router on the same network as the source computer. When IP sees that the destination is on a different network, it sends the datagrams to the default gateway.

When the gateway gets the datagrams, it checks the IP header for the destination address and compares that address to its internal list of other gateways and network addresses on the Internet. In some cases, the gateway will be able to send the datagrams directly to the destination. More likely, though, the gateway will only be able to forward the packet to another system that's en route to the destination. This system repeats the procedure: It checks the destination and forwards the datagrams accordingly. Although many hops might be involved, the datagrams will eventually arrive at their destination.

---

**NOTE**

Actually, if the datagram has to perform too many hops, it might never reach its destination. That's because each datagram is supplied with a **Time to Live** (TTL) value in its header (as described earlier). If the TTL value is 64, for example, and if the datagram has made 64 hops before getting to its destination, it's discarded without a second thought. The TTL is useful for preventing datagrams from running amok and wandering the Internet's highways and byways endlessly.

---

**TIP**

If you're curious about how many hops it takes to get from here to there (wherever *there* might be), TCP/IP provides a way to find out. You use a utility called TRACERT. I'll show you how it works later in this chapter (see "Wielding the TCP/IP Utilities").

### Dynamic IP Addressing

If your network just has a few computers and if the organization of the network is static (the computers attached to the network remain attached at all times), it's easiest to assign an IP address to every computer from the block of addresses supplied by the registrar.

Managing IP addresses, however, can become quite cumbersome if the network has many computers or if the network configuration changes constantly, thanks to users logging on to the network remotely or computers being moved from one subnet to another. One way to solve this problem is to assign IP addresses to network computers dynamically. In other words, when a computer logs on to the network, it is assigned an IP address from a pool of available addresses. When the computer logs off, the address it was using is returned to the pool.

The system that manages this dynamic allocation of addresses is called **Dynamic Host Configuration Protocol** (**DHCP**), and the computers that implement DHCP are called DHCP servers.

### Domain Name Resolution

Of course, when you're accessing an Internet resource such as a website or FTP site, you don't use IP addresses. Instead, you use friendlier names such as www.mcfedries.com and ftp.domain.net. That's because TCP/IP, bless its heart, lets us mere humans use English-language equivalents of IP addresses. So, in the same way that IP addresses can be seen as network IDs and host IDs, these English-language alternatives are broken down into **domain names** and **hostnames**.

When you sign up with a registrar, what you're really doing is registering a domain name that is associated with your network. In my case, I'm registered under the domain name mcfedries.com, which points to my network ID of 205.208.113. The computers—or hosts—on my network have their own hostnames. For example, I have one machine with the hostname hermes, so its full Internet name is hermes.mcfedries.com (this machine's IP address is 205.208.113.4); similarly, my web server's hostname is www, so its full Internet name is www.mcfedries.com (its IP address is 205.208.113.2).

Even though domain names and hostnames look sort of like IP addresses (a bunch of characters separated by dots), there's no formula that translates one into the other. Instead, a process called **name resolution** is used to look up hostnames and domain names to find their underlying IP addresses (and vice versa). Three mechanisms are used to perform this task: the HOSTS file, the Domain Name System, and the Windows Internet Name System.

**The LMHOSTS File**    The simplest method of mapping a hostname to an IP address is to use an LMHOSTS file. This is a simple text file that implements a two-column table with IP addresses in one column and their corresponding hostnames in the other, like so:

```
127.0.0.1 localhost
205.208.113.2 www.mcfedries.com
205.208.113.4 hermes.mcfedries.com
```

17

The address 127.0.0.1 is a special IP address that refers to your computer. If you send a packet to 127.0.0.1, it comes back to your machine. For this reason, 127.0.0.1 is called a **loopback** address. You just add an entry for every host on your network.

For a sample LMHOSTS file—named LMHOSTS.SAM—, see the following folder on your computer:

```
%SystemRoot%\System32\Drivers\Etc
```

You can use this file as a start by copying it to a file in the same folder named LMHOSTS (no extension). Note, however, that after you have the LMHOSTS file set up for your network, you must copy it to *every* machine on the network.

**The Domain Name System**    The LMHOSTS system is fine for resolving hostnames within a network, but with millions of hosts worldwide, it's obviously impractical for resolving the names of computers that reside outside of your subnet.

You might think that because the registrar handles all the registration duties for domains, your TCP/IP applications could just query some kind of central database at the registrar to resolve hostnames. There are two problems with this approach: The number of queries this database would have to handle would be astronomical (and thus extremely slow), and you'd have to contact the registrar every time you added a host to your network.

Instead of one central database of hostnames and IP addresses, the Internet uses a distributed database system called the **Domain Name System** (DNS). The DNS databases use a hierarchical structure to organize domains. The **generic top-level domains (gTLDs)** in this hierarchy consist of fourteen categories, as described in Table 17.3.

**TABLE 17.3**   Generic Top-Level Domains in the DNS

| Domain | What It Represents |
| --- | --- |
| com | Commercial businesses |
| edu | Educational institutions |
| gov | Governments |
| int | International organizations |
| mil | Military organizations |
| net | Networking organizations |
| org | Nonprofit organizations |
| aero | The aviation industry |
| biz | Businesses or firms |
| coop | Cooperatives |
| info | Organizations providing information services |
| museum | Museums and museum professionals |
| name | Individual or personal Internet |
| pro | Registered professionals such as accountants, doctors, lawyers, and engineers |

Top-level domains also exist for various countries. Table 17.4 lists a few of these **country code top-level domains (ccTLDs)**.

**TABLE 17.4**    Some Country Code Top-Level Domains in the DNS

| Domain | The Country It Represents |
| --- | --- |
| at | Austria |
| au | Australia |
| ca | Canada |
| ch | Switzerland |
| cn | China |
| de | Germany |
| dk | Denmark |
| es | Spain |
| fi | Finland |
| fr | France |
| hk | Hong Kong |
| ie | Ireland |
| il | Israel |
| jp | Japan |
| mx | Mexico |
| nl | Netherlands |
| no | Norway |
| nz | New Zealand |
| ru | Russia |
| se | Sweden |
| uk | United Kingdom |
| us | United States |

Below these top-level domains are the domain names, such as whitehouse.gov and microsoft.com. From there, you can have subdomains (subnetworks) and then hostnames at the bottom of the hierarchy. The database maintains a record of the corresponding IP address for each domain and host.

To handle name resolution, the DNS database is distributed around the Internet to various computers called **DNS servers**, or simply **name servers**. When you set up TCP/IP, you specify one of the DNS servers, and your TCP/IP software uses this server to resolve all hostnames into their appropriate IP addresses.

**The Windows Internet Name Service**    Earlier, I told you about how DHCP can be used to assign IP addresses to hosts dynamically. On a Microsoft TCP/IP network, how are these addresses coordinated with hostnames? By using a name resolution feature called the **Windows Internet Name Service (WINS)**. WINS maps **NetBIOS names** (the names you assign to computers in the Identification tab of the Network properties sheet) to the IP addresses assigned via DHCP.

17

## Understanding TCP

IP is a connectionless protocol, so it doesn't care whether datagrams ever reach their eventual destinations. It just routes the datagrams according to the destination address and then forgets about them. This is why IP is also called an *unreliable* protocol.

We know from experience, however, that the Internet is reliable (most of the time!). Where does this reliability come from if not from IP? It comes from the rest of the TCP/IP equation: TCP. You can think of TCP as IP's better half because through TCP, applications can make sure that their data gets where it's supposed to go and that it arrives there intact.

To help you visualize the difference between IP and TCP, imagine IP as analogous to sending a letter through the mail. You put the letter in an envelope, address the envelope, and drop it in a mailbox. You don't know when the letter gets picked up, how it gets to its destination, or even *whether* it gets there.

Suppose, however, that after mailing the letter you were to call up the recipient and say that a letter was on its way. You could give the recipient your phone number and have that person call you when she receives the letter. If the letter doesn't arrive after a preset length of time, the recipient could let you know so that you could resend it.

That phone link between you and the recipient is analogous to what TCP does for data transfers. TCP is a connection-oriented protocol that sets up a two-way communications channel between the source and the destination to monitor the IP routing.

### TCP Sockets

In the TCP scheme of things, this communications channel is called a **socket**, and it has two components on each end:

| | |
|---|---|
| IP address | You've already seen that each IP datagram header includes both the source and the destination IP address. For a TCP socket, these addresses are analogous to the sender and receiver having each other's phone number. |
| Port number | Having a phone number might not be enough to get in touch with someone. If the person works in an office, you might also have to specify his extension. Similarly, knowing the IP address of a host isn't enough information for TCP. It also must know which application sent the datagram. After all, in a multitasking environment such as Windows XP, you could be running a web browser, an email client, and an FTP program all at the same time. To differentiate between programs, TCP uses a 16-bit number called a *port* that uniquely identifies each running process. |

> **NOTE**
>
> On the source host, the port number usually specifies an application. On the destination host, the port can also specify an application, but it's more likely that the port is a fixed number that is used by an Internet service. For example, FTP uses port 21, SMTP uses port 25, and HTTP uses port 80.

### The Structure of a TCP Segment

When a TCP/IP application sends data, it divides the data into a number of **TCP segments**. These segments include part of the data along with a header that defines various parameters used in the TCP communication between the source and the destination. These TCP segments are then encapsulated within the data portion of an IP datagram and sent on their way.

Wait a minute. If TCP segments are sent inside IP datagrams, and I just said that IP is unreliable, how can TCP possibly be reliable? The trick is that, unlike straight IP, TCP expects a response from its TCP counterpart on the receiving end. Think of it this way: Imagine mailing a letter to someone and including a Post-it Note on the letter that specifies your phone number and tells the recipient to call you when he or she receives the letter. If you don't hear back, you know he didn't get the letter. To ensure reliable communications, TCP includes an electronic "Post-it Note" in its header that does two things:

- When the application requests that data be sent to a remote location, TCP constructs an initial segment that attempts to set up the socket interface between the two systems. No data is sent until TCP hears back from the receiving system that the sockets are in place and that it's ready to receive the data.

- When the sockets are ready to go, TCP starts sending the data within its segments and always asks the receiving TCP to acknowledge that these data segments have arrived. If no acknowledgment is received, the sending TCP retransmits the segment.

As with IP, you don't need to know the exact format of a TCP header. In case you're curious, however, I've laid it all out in Table 17.5.

**TABLE 17.5**  The Structure of a TCP Segment Header

| Field | Bits | Description |
|---|---|---|
| Source Port | 0 to 15 | The source port number. |
| Destination Port | 16 to 31 | The destination port number. |
| Sequence Number | 32 to 63 | In the overall sequence of bytes being sent, this field specifies the position in this sequence of the segment's first data byte. |
| Acknowledgment Number | 64 to 95 | If the ACK Control Bit is set (see the Control Bits entry), this field contains the value of the next sequence number the sender of the segment is expecting the receiver to acknowledge. |
| Data Offset | 96 to 99 | The length of the TCP segment header, in 32-bit words. This tells the receiving socket where the data starts. |

17

**TABLE 17.5**   Continued

| Field | Bits | Description |
|---|---|---|
| Reserved | 100 to 105 | This field is reserved for future use. |
| Control Bits | 106 to 111 | These codes specify various aspects of the communication. When set to 1, each bit controls a particular code, as listed here: |
| | | 106   URG: Urgent Pointer field significant. |
| | | 107   ACK: Acknowledgment Number field is to be used. |
| | | 108   PSH: Push function. |
| | | 109   RST: Reset the connection. |
| | | 110   SYN: Synchronize sequence numbers. This bit is set when the connection is opened. |
| | | 111   FIN: No more data from sender, so close the connection. |
| Window | 112 to 127 | The number of data bytes that the sender can currently accept. This **sliding window** lets the sender and receiver vary the number of bytes sent and thus increase efficiency. |
| Checksum | 128 to 143 | This value lets the receiver determine the integrity of the data. |
| Urgent Pointer | 144 to 159 | If the URG Control Bit is set, this field indicates the location in the data where urgent data resides. |
| Options | 160 and over | This variable-length field specifies extra TCP options such as the maximum segment size. |

## TCP Features

To ensure that IP datagrams are transferred in an orderly, efficient, and reliable manner, TCP implements the following six features:

| | |
|---|---|
| Connection opening | On the sending host, a process (such as a web browser) issues a request to send data (such as a URL) to a destination host (such as a web server). TCP creates an initial segment designed to open the connection between the sender and the receiver (the browser and server). In this initial contact, the two systems exchange IP addresses and port numbers (to create the socket interface) and set up the flow control and sequencing (discussed next). |
| Flow control | One of the parameters that the sending and receiving hosts exchange is the number of bytes each is willing to accept at one |

time. That way, one system doesn't end up sending more data than the other system can handle. This value can move up or down as circumstances change on each machine, so the systems exchange this information constantly to ensure efficient data transfers.

| | |
|---|---|
| Sequencing | Every segment is assigned a sequence number (or, technically, the first data byte in every segment is assigned a sequence number). This technique lets the receiving host reassemble any segments that arrive out of order. |
| Acknowledgment | When TCP transmits a segment, it holds the segment in a queue until the receiving TCP issues an acknowledgment that it has received the segment. If the sending TCP doesn't receive this acknowledgment, it retransmits the segment. |
| Error detection | A checksum value in the header lets the receiver test the integrity of an incoming segment. If the segment is corrupted, the receiver fires back an error message to the sender, which then immediately retransmits the segment. |
| Connection closing | When the process on the sending host indicates that the connection should be terminated, the sending TCP sends a segment that tells the receiver that no more data will be sent and that the socket should be closed. |

These features illustrate why Internet communications are generally reliable. They show that TCP acts as a sort of chaperone for the IP datagrams traveling from host to host.

# Installing and Configuring TCP/IP

TCP/IP is a complex set of protocols (I've really only scratched the surface here), but the good news is that it's much easier to implement than it is to understand. With this chapter's background info in hand, after you've installed the protocol, configuring a computer to use TCP/IP becomes a simple matter of plugging in a few values. Here's what you need to know before getting started:

- Whether your network or ISP uses dynamic IP addressing.

- If dynamic addressing isn't used, the IP address that has been assigned to your computer and the appropriate subnet mask for your network.

- The IP address of your network's default gateway.

- The hostname of your computer and the domain name of your network.

- Whether your network uses DNS—If it does, you need to know the IP address of one or more DNS servers.

- Whether your network uses WINS—If it does, you need to know the IP address of your WINS server.

- Which network clients and services use TCP/IP—For each of these clients and services, you need to bind the TCP/IP protocol.

After you have all of this information in hand (which you can get from your network administrator or your ISP), you're ready to install TCP/IP on your computer.

## Installing the TCP/IP Protocol

In default Windows XP installations, the TCP/IP protocol is installed automatically. Therefore, you should have TCP/IP on your system already. To be certain, the following steps show you how to check that the protocol is installed and how to install the protocol if, for some reason, it's not already on your system:

1. In Control Panel, launch the Network Connections icon. (Alternatively, select Start, All Programs, Accessories, Communications, Network Connections.) The Network Connections window appears.

2. Right-click the network connection you want to work with (such as Local Area Connection) and then click Properties.

3. Depending on the connection, display the tab that includes the list named This Connection Uses the Following Items (this list appears either on the General tab or the Networking tab).

4. Examine the list to see whether it includes an item named Internet Protocol (TCP/IP). If so, make sure that this item's check box is activated and then click OK. Otherwise, proceed to step 5 to install the TCP/IP protocol.

5. Click the Install button to display the Select Network Component Type dialog box.

6. Select Protocol and click Add. The Select Network Protocol dialog box appears.

7. In the Manufacturer list, select Microsoft.

8. In the Network Protocol list, select TCP/IP.

9. Click OK. Windows XP adds TCP/IP to the list of network items.

10. Activate the check box beside Internet Protocol (TCP/IP).

11. Click Close.

---

**NOTE**

Windows XP is quite flexible when it comes to having multiple TCP/IP configurations. For example, you might need to use TCP/IP on your LAN with one configuration and through your ISP with a different configuration. In this case, you use the New Connection Wizard to create and configure each connection.

## Configuring the TCP/IP Protocol

With TCP/IP safely ensconced on your system, you now need to configure it to your liking. To do this, first follow these steps to get started:

1. In Control Panel, launch the Network Connections icon. (Alternatively, select Start, All Programs, Accessories, Communications, Network Connections.) The Network Connections window appears.

2. Right-click the network connection you want to work with (such as Local Area Connection) and then click Properties.

3. Depending on the connection, display the tab that includes the list named This Connection Uses the Following Items (this list appears on either the General tab or the Networking tab).

4. Select Internet Protocol (TCP/IP).

5. Click Properties to display the Internet Protocol (TCP/IP) Properties dialog box, which contains several controls for configuring TCP/IP. The next few sections take you though each of these controls.

### Configuring the IP Address

Your IP address is assigned either automatically or permanently, and you use the following two option buttons to specify this:

| | |
|---|---|
| Obtain an IP Address Automatically | Activate this option if your network uses DHCP or if your ISP supplies you with an IP address on the fly whenever you log on. |
| Use the Following IP Address | Activate this option if your computer has been assigned a permanent IP address. Type this address in dotted-decimal notation in the IP Address text box. Also, you'll need to type the appropriate dotted-decimal subnet mask in the Subnet Mask text box, and the IP address of network or ISP gateway in the Default Gateway text box. |

### Configuring the DNS Servers

The address of the DNS servers is also assigned either automatically or permanently, and you use the following two option buttons to specify this:

| | |
|---|---|
| Obtain DNS Server Address Automatically | Activate this option if your network or ISP supplies the DNS server addresses on the fly whenever you log on. |
| Use the Following DNS Server Addresses | Activate this option if your network or ISP uses permanent DNS server addresses. Type the address of the main DNS server in dotted-decimal notation in the |

Preferred DNS Server text box. Also, type the address of a secondary DNS server in dotted-decimal notation in the Alternate DNS Server text box.

Figure 17.4 shows the TCP/IP property sheet with assigned IP and DNS server addresses.

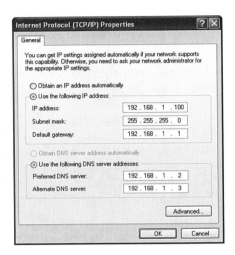

**FIGURE 17.4**    The General tab with an IP address and a subnet mask filled in.

# Wielding the TCP/IP Utilities

Windows XP TCP/IP comes with a few command-line utilities that you can use to review your TCP/IP settings and troubleshoot problems. Here's a list of the available utilities:

| | |
|---|---|
| ARP | This utility displays (or modifies) the IP-to-Ethernet or IP-to-Token Ring address translation tables used by the Address Resolution Protocol (ARP) in TCP/IP. Enter the command `arp -?` for the syntax. |
| NBTSTAT | This utility displays the protocol statistics and the current TCP/IP connections using NBT (NetBIOS over TCP/IP). Enter `nbtstat -?` for the syntax. |
| NETSTAT | This utility displays the protocol statistics and current TCP/IP connections. The command `netstat -?` displays the syntax. |
| PING | This utility can check a network connection to a remote computer. This is one of the most commonly used TCP/IP diagnostic tools, so I describe it more detail in the next section. |
| ROUTE | This utility can be used to manipulate a network routing table (LMHOSTS). Enter `route -?` for the syntax. |
| TRACERT | This utility can check the route taken to a remote host. I explain this valuable diagnostic command in more detail later. |

IPCONFIG

This utility displays the current TCP/IP network configuration. If you run the command ipconfig without any switches, the utility returns your system's current IP address, subnet mask, and default gateway. If you run the command ipconfig /all, the utility returns more detailed information, as shown in Figure 17.5.

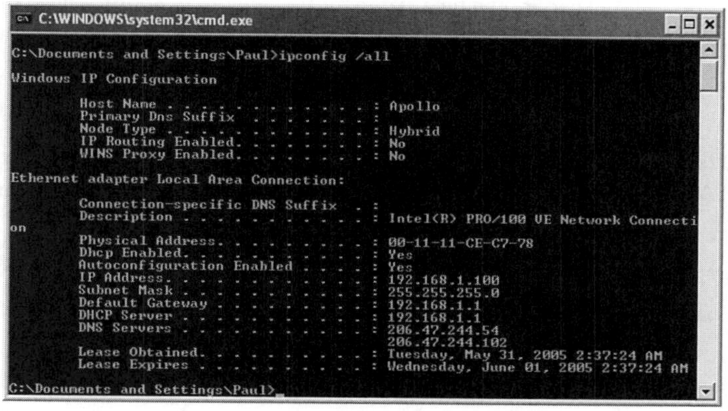

**FIGURE 17.5**    The IPCONFIG utility displays information about the TCP/IP configuration.

## The PING Command

As you might know, a submarine can detect a nearby object by using sonar to send out a sound wave and then seeing whether the wave is reflected. This is called **pinging** an object.

TCP/IP has a PING command that performs a similar function. PING sends out a special type of IP packet—called an **Internet Control Message Protocol (ICMP) echo packet**—to a remote location. This packet requests that the remote location send back a response packet. PING then tells you whether the response was received. In this way, you can check your TCP/IP configuration to see whether your host can connect with a remote host.

Here's the PING syntax:

```
ping [-t] [-a] [-n count] [-l size] [-f] [-i TTL] [-v TOS] [-r count]
   ➥[-s count] [[-j host-list] ¦ [-k host-list]] [-w timeout] target_name
```

| | |
|---|---|
| -t | Pings the specified *target_name* until you interrupt the command. |
| -a | Specifies not to resolve IP addresses to hostnames. |
| -n *count* | Sends the number of echo packets specified by *count*. The default is 4. |
| -l *size* | Sends echo packets containing the amount of data specified by *size*. The default is 32 bytes; the maximum is 8192. |
| -f | Sends a Do Not Fragment flag in the packet's header. The flag ensures that the packet won't be fragmented by gateways along the route. |

| | |
|---|---|
| -i *TTL* | Sets the Time To Live field to the value specified by *TTL* (the default is 32). |
| -v *TOS* | Sets the Type Of Service field to the value specified by *TOS*. |
| -r *count* | Records the route of the outgoing packet and the returning packet in the Record Route field. A minimum of 1 to a maximum of 9 hosts must be specified by *count*. |
| -s *count* | Specifies the time stamp for the number of hops specified by *count*. |
| -j *host-list* | Routes packets by means of the list of hosts specified by *host-list*. Consecutive hosts may be separated by intermediate gateways (loose source routed). The maximum number allowed by IP is 9. |
| -k *host-list* | Routes packets by means of the list of hosts specified by *host-list*. Consecutive hosts may not be separated by intermediate gateways (strict source routed). The maximum number allowed by IP is 9. |
| -w *timeout* | Specifies a time-out interval in milliseconds. The default is 1000 (1 second). |
| *target_name* | Specifies either the IP address or the hostname (a fully qualified domain name) of the remote host you want to ping. |

Here's an example that uses PING on the Google.com domain:

```
C:\>ping google.com

Pinging google.com [216.239.37.99] with 32 bytes of data:

Reply from 216.239.37.99: bytes=32 time=37ms TTL=242
Reply from 216.239.37.99: bytes=32 time=37ms TTL=242
Reply from 216.239.37.99: bytes=32 time=49ms TTL=242
Reply from 216.239.37.99: bytes=32 time=37ms TTL=242

Ping statistics for 216.239.37.99:
    Packets: Sent = 4, Received = 4, Lost = 0 (0% loss),
Approximate round trip times in milli-seconds:
    Minimum = 37ms, Maximum = 49ms, Average = 40ms
```

Here you see that each echo packet received a reply. If you can't connect to the remote host, PING returns a Request timed out message for each packet.

If you can't connect to a remote host, here are some notes on using PING to troubleshoot TCP/IP problems:

- First, check to see whether you can use PING successfully on the loopback address: ping 127.0.0.1. If you can't, make sure that you restarted Windows XP after installing TCP/IP. If PING still doesn't work on the loopback address, you might need to remove TCP/IP and reinstall it.

- If your loopback test works properly, try using PING on your computer's IP address. (If you're using DHCP, run the IPCONFIG utility to get your current IP address.) If you don't get a successful echo, it could be that you entered an invalid IP address or subnet mask.

- The next test you should run is on your default gateway. If you can't successfully ping the gateway, you won't be able to access remote Internet sites. In this case, check the IP address you entered for the gateway. Make sure that TCP/IP is bound to the network adapter you're using.

- If you get this far, now try using PING on the remote host you're trying to contact. If you're unsuccessful, check to make sure that you're using the correct IP address for the host and that the gateway (router) is set up to route IP packets.

- You can also try pinging the remote host by both its IP address and its hostname. If you get a response with the IP address but not the hostname, you likely have a name resolution problem.

## The TRACERT Command

If you can't ping a remote host, it could be that your echo packets are getting held up along the way. To find out, you can use the TRACERT (trace route) command:

```
tracert [-d] [-h maximum_hops] [-j host-list] [-w timeout] target_name
```

| | |
|---|---|
| -d | Specifies not to resolve IP addresses to hostnames. |
| -h maximum_hops | Specifies the maximum number of hops to search for the target_name (the default is 30). |
| -j host-list | Specifies loose source route along the host-list. |
| -w timeout | Waits the number of milliseconds specified by timeout for each reply. |
| target_name | Specifies the hostname of the destination computer. |

TRACERT operates by sending ICMP echo packets with varying TTL values. Recall that TTL places a limit on the number of hops that a packet can take. Each host along the packet's route decrements the TTL value until, when the TTL value is 0, the packet is discarded (assuming that it hasn't reached its destination by then).

In TRACERT, the ICMP packets specify that whichever host decrements the echo packet to 0 should send back a response. So, the first packet has a TTL value of 1, the second has a TTL value of 2, and so on. TRACERT keeps sending packets with incrementally higher TTL values until either a response is received from the remote host or a packet receives no response. Here's an example of a TRACERT command in action:

```
C:\>tracert google.com

Tracing route to google.com [216.239.57.99]
over a maximum of 30 hops:
```

```
1     <1 ms    <1 ms    <1 ms    192.168.1.1
2      8 ms     8 ms     8 ms    64.230.197.178
3      6 ms     6 ms     6 ms    64.230.221.201
4      6 ms     6 ms     6 ms    64.230.234.249
5      8 ms     6 ms     7 ms    64.230.233.93
6     17 ms    17 ms    16 ms    core1-chicago23-pos0-0.in.bellnexxia.net
                                 ➥[206.108.103.130]
7     17 ms    17 ms    17 ms    bx2-chicago23-pos11-0.in.bellnexxia.net
                                 ➥[206.108.103.138]
8     17 ms    17 ms    17 ms    so-4-3-3.cr1.ord2.us.above.net [208.184.233.185]
9     18 ms    17 ms    18 ms    so-0-0-0.cr2.ord2.us.above.net [64.125.29.186]
10    36 ms    36 ms    36 ms    so-5-2-0.cr1.dca2.us.above.net [64.125.30.225]
11    47 ms    46 ms    46 ms    so-4-1-0.mpr2.atl6.us.above.net [64.125.29.41]
12    48 ms    48 ms    48 ms    64.124.229.173.google.com [64.124.229.173]
13    48 ms    48 ms    48 ms    216.239.48.23
14    49 ms    49 ms    49 ms    216.239.46.44
15   100 ms   100 ms   100 ms    216.239.47.129
16    99 ms    99 ms    99 ms    216.239.49.250
17    99 ms    99 ms    99 ms    66.249.95.65
18    99 ms    99 ms    99 ms    66.249.94.27
19   102 ms   101 ms   101 ms    216.239.49.97
20    99 ms   100 ms    99 ms    216.239.57.99
```

Trace complete.

The first column is the hop number (that is, the TTL value set in the packet). Notice that, in my case, it took 20 hops to get to google.com. The next three columns contain round-trip times for an attempt to reach the destination with that TTL value. (Asterisks indicate that the attempt timed out.) The last column contains the hostname (if it was resolved) and the IP address of the responding system.

---

### Changing the Default TTL Value

One of the reasons your packets might not be getting to their destination is that the default TTL value used by Windows XP might be set too low. The default is 32, as compared to 64 in most UNIX systems. To increase this value, start the Registry Editor and highlight the following key:

HKEY_LOCAL_MACHINE\System\CurrentControlSet\Services\Tcpip\Parameters

Select Edit, New, DWORD Value, type **DefaultTTL**, and press Enter. Change the value of this new setting to 80 hexadecimal or 128 decimal.

---

# From Here

Here's a list of chapters where you'll find related information:

- For examples of IP addresses in action, refer to the sections titled "Getting Your Modem to Dial Voice Calls for You" and "Remote Collaboration with Microsoft NetMeeting" in Chapter 16, "Putting Your Modem to Work."

- For practical network knowledge, see the chapters in Part VI, "Unleashing Windows XP Networking."

- To get the scoop on working at the command prompt, see Appendix B, "Using the Windows XP Command Prompt."

17

# Exploring the Web with Internet Explorer

As I write this, Internet Explorer is by far the most dominant web browser with, depending on which source you use, anywhere from 85% to 90% of the market. (This is down about 5% since the Firefox browser was released in late 2004.) And because most computer-savvy people have also been on the Internet for a number of years, it's safe to say that Internet Explorer is probably one of the most familiar applications available today. Or perhaps I should say that the *basics* of Internet Explorer are familiar to most people. However, as with any complex program, there are hidden pockets of the browser that most people don't know about. Significantly, many of these seldom-seen areas are not as obscure as you might think. Lots of these features can be put to good use immediately to make your web surfing easier, more efficient, and more productive. In this chapter, I take you on a tour of a few of my favorite Internet Explorer nooks and crannies and I show you how they can improve your web experience.

## Understanding Web Page Addresses

Let's begin by examining that strange creature, the World Wide Web address, officially known as a **Uniform Resource Locator** (**URL**). A web page's address usually takes the following form:

http://*host.domain/directory/file.name*

| | |
|---|---|
| *host.domain* | The domain name of the host computer where the page resides |
| *directory* | The host computer directory that contains the page |
| *file.name* | The page's filename. Note that most web pages use the extensions `.html` and `.htm`. |

Here are some notes about URLs:

- The *http* part of the URL signifies that the TCP/IP protocol to be used for communication between the web browser and the web server is **HTTP** (**Hypertext Transfer Protocol**), which is used for standard web pages. Other common protocols are **https** (**Secure Hypertext Transfer Protocol**; secure web pages), **ftp** (**File Transfer Protocol**; file downloads), and **file** (for opening local files within the browser).

- Most web domains use the www prefix and the com suffix (for example, www.mcfedries.com). Other popular suffixes are edu (educational sites), gov (government sites), net (networking companies), and org (nonprofit sites). Note, too, that most servers don't require the www prefix (for example, mcfedries.com).

- Directory names and filenames are case-sensitive on most web hosts (those that run UNIX servers, anyway).

> **NOTE**
>
> Most websites use one or more default filenames, the most common of which are `index.html` and `index.htm`. If you omit the filename from the URL, the web server will display the default page.

## Tips and Techniques for Better Web Surfing

Surfing web pages with Internet Explorer is straightforward and easy, but even experienced uses might not be aware of all the ways that they can open and navigate pages. Here's a review of all the techniques you can use to open a web page in Windows XP:

- Type a URL in any Address bar—Internet Explorer and all Windows XP folder windows have an Address bar. To open a page, type the URL in the Address bar and press Enter.

- Type a URL in the Run dialog box—Select Start, Run, type the URL you want in the Run dialog box, and click OK.

> **CAUTION**
>
> When you type a URL in the Run dialog box, you must include the *www* portion of the address. For example, typing **microsoft.com** won't work, but typing **www.microsoft.com** will. If the URL doesn't have a *www* component—for example, support.microsoft.com—then you must add *http://* to the front of the address.

- Select a URL from the Address bar—Internet Explorer's Address bar doubles as a drop-down list that holds the last 15 addresses you entered.

- Use the Open dialog box for remote pages—Select File, Open (or press Ctrl+O) to display the Open dialog box, type the URL, and click OK.

- Use the Open dialog box for local pages—If you want to view a web page that's on your computer, display the Open dialog box, enter the full path (drive, folder, and filename), and click OK. Alternatively, click Browse, find the page, click Open, and then click OK.

- Select a favorite—Pull down the Favorites menu and click the site you want to open.

- Click a Links bar button—The Links bar contains seven buttons that take you to predefined web pages. For example, the Windows button takes you to the Windows home page. (You can add buttons to the Links bar, remove existing buttons, and more. See "Customizing the Links Bar for One-Click Surfing," later in this chapter.)

- Click a web address in an Outlook Express message—When Outlook Express recognizes a web address in an email message (that is, an address that begins with http://, https://, ftp://, www//, and so on), it converts the address into a link. Clicking the link opens the address in Internet Explorer. Note, too, that many other programs are URL-aware, including the Microsoft Office suite of programs.

After you've opened a page, you usually move to another page by clicking a link: either a text link or an imagemap. However, there are more techniques you can use to navigate to other pages:

- Open a link in another window—If you don't want to leave the current page, you can force a link to open in another Internet Explorer window by right-clicking the link and then clicking Open in New Window. (You can open a new window for the current page by selecting File, New, Window, or by pressing Ctrl+N.)

---

**TIP**

You can also hold down the Shift key and click a link to open that link in a new browser window.

---

- Retrace the pages you've visited—Click Internet Explorer's Back button to return to a page you visited previously in this session. (Alternatively, select View, Go To, Back or press Alt+Left arrow.) After you've gone back to a page, click the Forward button to move ahead through the visited pages. (You can also select View, Go To, Forward or press Alt+Right arrow.) Note, too, that the Back and Forward buttons also serve as drop-down lists. Click the downward-pointing arrow to the right of each button to see the list.

- Return to the start page—When you launch Internet Explorer without specifying a URL, you usually end up at MSN, the default start page (http://www.msn.com/; note, however, that many computer manufacturers change the default start page).

You can return to this page at any time by selecting View, Go To, Home Page, or by clicking the Home button in the toolbar (you can also press Alt+Home).

- Use the History bar—If you click the toolbar's History button or select the View, Explorer Bar, History command, Internet Explorer adds a History bar to the left side of the window. This bar lists the sites you've visited over the past 20 days. Just click a URL to go to a site. The items you see in the History bar are based on the contents of the %UserProfile%\Local Settings\History folder. See "Using the Handy History Bar," later in this chapter, for more on the History bar.

## Taking Advantage of the Address Bar

Internet Explorer's Address bar (and the Address bars that appear in all Windows XP folder windows) appears to be nothing more than a simple type-and-click mechanism. However, it's useful for many things, and comes with its own bag of tricks for making it even easier to use. Here's a rundown:

- Internet Explorer maintains a list of the last 15 URLs you typed into the Address bar. To access this list, press F4 and then use the Up and Down Arrow keys to select an item from the list.

### Clearing the Address Bar List

One way to clear the Address bar list is to clear the History files. You do this by selecting Tools, Internet Options and, in the General tab, clicking Clear History. If you prefer to preserve the History files, note that Internet Explorer stores the last 15 typed URLs in the following Registry key:

```
HKCU\Software\Microsoft\Internet Explorer\TypedURLs
```

You can therefore clear the Address bar list by closing all Internet Explorer windows and deleting the settings url1 through url15 in this key. Here's a script that will also do this:

```
Option Explicit
Dim objWshShell, i
Set objWshShell = WScript.CreateObject("WScript.Shell")
For i = 1 to 15
    objWshShell.RegDelete "HKCU\Software\Microsoft\Internet Explorer\
    ➥TypedURLs\url" & i

Next 'i
objWshShell.Popup "Finished deleting typed URLs", , "Delete Typed URLs"
```

Note that if there are fewer than 15 addresses in this history list, you will get a Windows Script Host error stating the following:

```
Unable to remove registry key "HKCU\Software\Microsoft\Internet
\Explorer\TypedURLs\urln,
```

Here, *n* is one greater than the number of history items found in the list. The message can be safely ignored; all the history items have been removed from the list.

- To edit the Address bar text, press Alt+D to select it.

- The Address bar's AutoComplete feature monitors the address as you type. If any previously entered addresses match your typing, those addresses appear in a list. To choose one of those addresses, use the down arrow to select it and then press Enter. The quickest way to use AutoComplete is to begin typing the site's domain name. For example, if you want to bring up http://www.microsoft.com/, start typing the *microsoft* part. If you start with the full address, you have to type http://www. or just www., and then one other character.

- Internet Explorer assumes that any address you enter is for a website. Therefore, you don't need to type the http:// prefix because Internet Explorer will add it for you automatically.

- Internet Explorer also assumes that most web addresses are in the form http://www.*something*.com. Therefore, if you simply type the *something* part and press Ctrl+Enter, Internet Explorer will automatically add the http://www. prefix and the .com suffix. For example, you can get to the Microsoft home page (http://www.microsoft.com) by typing **microsoft** and pressing Ctrl+Enter.

- Some websites use frames to divide a web page into multiple sections. Some of these sites offer links to other websites but, annoyingly, those pages appear within the first site's frame structure. To break out of frames, drag a link into the Address bar.

- To search from the Address bar (AutoSearch), first type your search text. As you type, Internet Explorer adds `Search for "text"` below the Address bar, where `text` is your search text. When you've finished your search text, press Tab to select the `Search for` item and then press Enter. Alternatively, precede your search text with the word `go`, `find`, or `search`, or with a question mark (?), as in these examples:

```
go vbscript
find autosearch
search neologisms
? registry
```

## Creating a Shortcut to a URL

Another way to navigate websites via Internet Explorer is to create shortcuts that point to the appropriate URLs. To do this, use either of the following techniques:

- Copy the URL to the Clipboard, create a new shortcut (open the folder in which you want to store the shortcut and then select File, New, Shortcut), and then paste the URL into the Type the Location of the Item text box.

- You can create a shortcut for the currently displayed page by using the page icon that appears in the Address bar (to the left of the address). Drag this icon and drop it on the desktop (or whatever folder you want to use to store the shortcut).

- You can create a shortcut for any hypertext link by dragging the link text from the page.

18

After your shortcut is in place, you can open the website by launching the shortcut's icon.

## Using the Handy History Bar

You saw earlier (refer to "Tips and Techniques for Better Web Surfing") how you can click the Back and Forward buttons to follow your own footsteps on the World Wide Web. However, Internet Explorer wipes those lists clean when you return to the home page or exit the program. What do you do when you want to revisit a site from a previous session? Happily, Internet Explorer keeps track of the addresses of all the pages you perused for the last 20 days.

The list of these pages is stored in a special screen area called the History bar, and you can view it using either of the following methods:

- Click the History button in the toolbar

- Select the View, Explorer Bar, History command

You'll then see the History bar on the left side of the window. To bring a site into view, follow these steps:

1. Click the day you want to work with. Internet Explorer displays a list of the domains you visited on that day.

2. Click the domain of the website that contains the page you want to see. Internet Explorer opens the domain to reveal all the pages you visited within that site.

3. Click the name of the page you want. Internet Explorer displays a cached version of the page in the right side of the content area, as shown in Figure 18.1.

# Searching the Web

Veteran surfers, having seen a wide range of what the Web has to offer, usually prefer to tackle the Web using a targeted approach that enables them to quickly find information and do research. This means using one or more of the Web's many search engines. It's usually best to deal directly with a search engine site, but Internet Explorer also offers some default searching options. For example, you saw earlier in this chapter (refer to "Taking Advantage of the Address Bar") that you can run searches directly from the Address bar.

History button

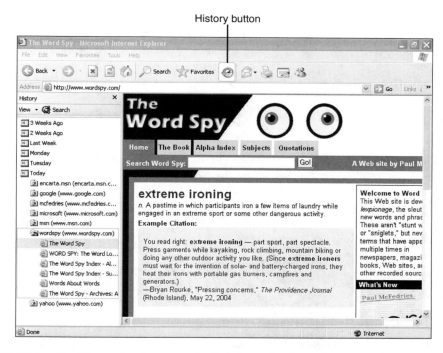

**FIGURE 18.1**    The History bar keeps track of all the web addresses you called on in the last 20 days.

You can also run searches from the built-in Search bar, which you can display either by clicking the Search toolbar button or by selecting View, Explorer Bar, Search. Internet Explorer adds the Search bar to the left side of the window, as shown in Figure 18.2.

> **TIP**
>
> You can also press Ctrl+E to toggle the Search bar on and off.

Enter your search terms in the text box and then press Enter (or click Search). When the search is complete, the right side of the Internet Explorer window shows links to the matching sites. You also have the following web search options:

| | |
|---|---|
| Automatically Send Your Search to Other Search Engines | When you click this link, Internet Explorer submits your search text to another search engine (such as HotBot) and then displays links for a few more search engines (such as MSN and Google). Click one of those links to submit the text to that search engine. You can also click Send Search to More Search Engines to see more engines. |
| Highlight Words on the Results Page | When you click this link, Internet Explorer asks which words you want to highlight in the search results. You have |

18

options for each search term as well as a Highlight Other Text option, which includes a text box in which you enter another word or phrase. Click the option you want and then click Highlight Next to highlight the first instance of the chosen term. Continue clicking Highlight Next to high light subsequent instances.

Change Current Search     Use this text box to edit your search text or enter new search terms.

Start a New Search     Click this link to return to the original Search bar layout and start over again.

**FIGURE 18.2** Use the Search bar to enter quick searches.

## Changing the Default Search Engine

By default, Internet Explorer initially submits the search text to the MSN search engine. (The default search engine is also the one that Internet Explorer uses for the Address bar AutoSearch.) If you prefer to use a different search engine as the default, follow these steps:

1. Display the Search bar. If the Search bar is already displayed and is showing the results of a search, click the Start a New Search link.

2. Click Change Preferences.

3. Click Change Internet Search Behavior.

4. In the Select the Default Search Engine list, click the search engine you prefer.

5. Click OK.

## Setting Up Other Search Engines for Address Bar Searching

Address bar–based searching with the search text preceded by keywords such as go or ? is often the quickest route for simple searches. Unfortunately, you're limited to using only Internet Explorer's default search engine. What if you regularly use several search engines depending on the search text or the results you get? In that case, it's still possible to set up an AutoSearch for any number of other search engines. Here are a few sample steps that create an AutoSearch URL for Google searches:

1. Run the Registry Editor and display the following key:

   ```
   HKCU\Software\Microsoft\Internet Explore\SearchURL
   ```

2. Create a new subkey. The name of this subkey will be the text that you enter into the Address bar before the search text. For example, if you name this subkey google, you'll initiate an Address bar search by typing **google** *text*, where *text* is your search text.

3. Highlight the new subkey and open its (Default) value for editing.

4. Type the URL that initiates a search for the search engine, and specify **%s** as a place-holder for the search text. For Google, the URL looks like this

   ```
   http://www.google.com/search?q=%s
   ```

5. You also need to specify the characters or hexadecimal values that Internet Explorer will substitute for characters that have special meaning within a query string: space, percent (%), ampersand (&), and plus (+). To do this, add the following settings to the new subkey:

   | Name | Type | Data |
   | --- | --- | --- |
   | <blank> | REG_SZ | + |
   | % | REG_SZ | %25 |
   | & | REG_SZ | %26 |
   | + | REG_SZ | %2B |

Figure 18.3 shows a completed example. The text that you type in the Address bar before the search string—that is, the name of the new subkey—is called the **search prefix**. Although I used google as the search prefix in my example, ideally it should be a single character (such as g for Google or a for AltaVista) to minimize typing. Note, too, that you can also use Tweak UI to create search prefixes. Launch Tweak UI and select the Internet Explorer, Search branch. Then click Create to set up the search prefix and the search URL.

18

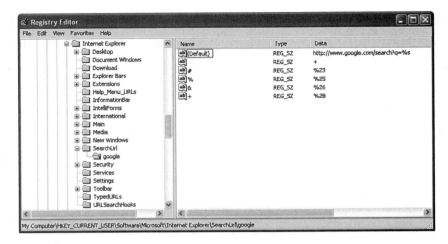

**FIGURE 18.3**    A sample search prefix for the Google search engine.

How do you know the proper URL to use for a search engine? What I do is go to the search engine site and then run a search with a single word. When the results appear, I examine the URL in the Address bar, which almost always takes the following general form:

*ScriptURL?QueryString*

Here, *ScriptURL* is the address of the site's search script, and *QueryString* is the data sent to the script. In most cases, I just copy the URL and substitute %s for my search text when I'm setting up my search prefix. Often I'll experiment with reducing the query string to the minimum necessary for the search to execute properly. For example, a typical Google search might produce a URL such as the following:

http://www.google.com/search?hl=en&lr=&ie=UTF-8&oe=UTF-8&q=mcfedries&

➥btnG=Google+Search

In the query string, each item is separated by an ampersand (&), so what I do is delete one item at a time until either the search breaks or I'm down to the search text (q=mcfedries in the earlier query string). To save you some legwork, here are the minimal search URLs for a number of search sites:

| | |
|---|---|
| All the Web: | http://www.alltheweb.com/search?query=%s&cat=web |
| AltaVista: | http://www.altavista.com/cgi-bin/query?q=%s |
| AOL Search: | http://search.aol.com/aolcom/search?query=%s |
| Ask Jeeves: | http://web.ask.com/web?q=%s |
| Encarta (Dictionary only): | http://encarta.msn.com/encnet/features/ |
| | dictionary/DictionaryResults.aspx?search=%s |
| Encarta (General): | http://encarta.msn.com/encnet/refpages/search.aspx?q=%s |

| | |
|---|---|
| Excite: | http://msxml.excite.com/info.xcite/search/web/%s |
| Lycos: | http://search.lycos.com/default.asp?query=%s |
| MSN: | http://search.msn.com/results.asp?q=%s |
| Yahoo: | http://search.yahoo.com/bin/search?p=%s |

# The Favorites Folder: Sites to Remember

The sad truth is that much of what you'll see on the Web will be utterly forgettable and not worth a second look. However, there are all kinds of gems out there waiting to be uncovered—sites you'll want to visit regularly. Instead of memorizing the appropriate URLs, jotting them down on sticky notes, or plastering your desktop with shortcuts, you can use Internet Explorer's handy Favorites feature to keep track of your choice sites.

The Favorites feature is really just a folder (you'll find it in your `%UserProfile%` folder) that you use to store Internet shortcuts. The advantage of using the Favorites folder as opposed to any other folder is that you can add, view, and link to the Favorites folder shortcuts directly from Internet Explorer.

## Adding a Shortcut to the Favorites Folder

When you find a site that you'd like to declare as a favorite, follow these steps:

1. Select the Favorites, Add to Favorites command. The Add Favorite dialog box appears.

2. Make sure that the Make Available Offline check box is deactivated. (See "Reading Pages Offline," later in this chapter, for the complete story on viewing web pages offline.)

3. The Name text box displays the title of the page. This is the text that appears when you later view the list of your favorites. Feel free to edit this text if you like.

4. Internet Explorer enables you to set up subfolders to hold related favorites. If you don't want to bother with this, skip down to step 8. Otherwise, click the Create In button to expand the dialog box as shown in Figure 18.4.

5. Select the folder in which you want the new folder to appear.

6. Click New Folder to display the Create New Folder dialog box.

7. Type in the name of the new folder and then click OK. Windows XP takes you back to the expanded Add Favorite dialog box.

8. Select the folder in which you want to store the favorite.

9. Click OK.

18

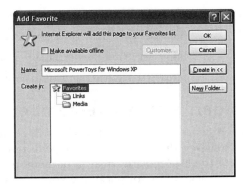

**FIGURE 18.4**   Use this dialog box to add a shortcut to the Favorites folder.

---

**TIP**

Internet Explorer offers two methods for quickly adding a site to the Favorites folder:

- If the current page has a link to the site you want to save, click and drag the link to the Favorites menu.
- If you want to save the current page, instead, click and drag the icon from the Address bar to the Favorites menu.

When the Favorites menu pulls down, drag the item to the position you want (you can even hover over submenus to open them) and then drop the item.

---

## Opening an Internet Shortcut from the Favorites Folder

The purpose of the Favorites folder, of course, is to give you quick access to the sites you visit regularly. To link to one of the shortcuts in your Favorites folder, you have three choices:

- In Internet Explorer, the Favorites menu contains the complete list of your Favorites folder shortcuts. To link to a shortcut, pull down this menu and select the shortcut you want.

- Click the Favorites toolbar button, or select View, Explorer Bar, Favorites, to display the Favorites Bar, as shown in Figure 18.5. Click a link in the Favorites Bar.

---

**TIP**

You can also toggle the Favorites bar on and off by pressing Ctrl+I.

---

- Select Start, Favorites and then click the favorite you want from the submenu that appears.

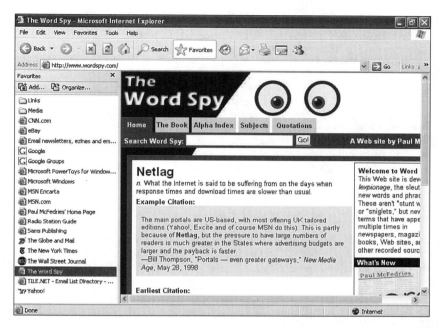

**FIGURE 18.5**    The Favorites bar keeps your favorite links visible at all times.

---

**TIP**

If the Favorites submenu doesn't appear on your Start menu, right-click the Start button, click Properties, and then click the Customize button beside the Start Menu option (which should be activated). In the Advanced tab's Start Menu Items list, activate the Favorites Menu check box, and then click OK.

---

## Maintaining Favorites

When you have a large number of favorites, you need to do some regular maintenance to keep things organized. This involves creating new subfolders, moving favorites between folders, changing URLs, deleting unused favorites, and more. Here's a summary of a few maintenance techniques you'll use most often:

- To change the URL of a favorite, display the Favorites list, find the item you want to work with, and right-click it. In the context menu, click Properties and then use the property sheet to adjust the URL.

- To move a favorite, display the Favorites list, find the item you want to work with, and then drag the item to another spot on the menu (or into a submenu).

- To delete a favorite, display the Favorites list, find the item you want to work with, right-click it, and then click Delete.

18

- To sort the favorites alphabetically, pull down the Favorites menu, right-click anywhere inside the menu, and then click Sort By Name.

- To send a favorite via email, display the Favorites list, right-click the favorites, and then select Send To, Mail Recipient.

---

**Allowing Internet Shortcut Attachments in Outlook**

If you use Microsoft Outlook 2003 as your email client, the program blocks certain outgoing attachment types, including Internet shortcuts. Therefore, after you've selected the Mail Recipient command, the message window displays a message telling you that it has blocked access to the "potentially unsafe attachment." To work around this problem, open the Registry Editor and navigate to the following key:

```
HKCU\Software\Microsoft\Office\11.0\Outlook\Security
```

Create a new string value named `Level1Remove`, open the new value, and type `.url`. This tells Outlook not to block attachments that use the `.url` extension. You can add multiple extensions to the `Level1Remove` value; separate each one with a semicolon.

---

## Viewing the Favorites Folder

If you want to work with the Favorites folder directly, select Favorites, Organize Favorites, or click Organize in the Favorites bar. Figure 18.6 shows the Organize Favorites window that appears. From here, you can rename shortcuts, delete shortcuts, and create new subfolders to organize your shortcuts. Click Close when you're done.

---

**TIP**

You can also open the Organize Favorites dialog box by pressing Ctrl+B. Note, too, that this dialog box is sizable. Use your mouse to drag any edge to get the size you want.

---

**NOTE**

You can also work with the Favorites folder in Explorer or My Computer. Open your `%UserProfile%` folder and select the `Favorites` subfolder.

---

## Sharing Favorites with Other Browsers

Many users like to run Internet Explorer along with another browser such as Firefox or Netscape on their machines. Unfortunately, these browsers store saved sites differently: Internet Explorer uses *favorites*, whereas Firefox and Netscape use *bookmarks*. However, Internet Explorer has a feature that enables you to either export favorites to a bookmark file or import bookmarks as favorites. Here's how it's done:

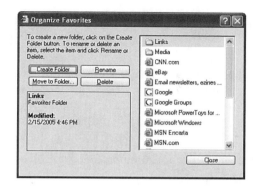

**FIGURE 18.6** Use the Organize Favorites dialog box to perform maintenance chores on the URL shortcut files.

1. In Internet Explorer, select File, Import and Export. The Import/Export Wizard makes an appearance.

2. Click Next.

3. Select one of the following:

| | |
|---|---|
| Import Favorites | Select this option to import Firefox or Netscape bookmarks as favorites. When you click Next, the wizard asks you for the path to the bookmark.htm file. Click Next when you're done. |
| Export Favorites | Select this option to export your favorites as Netscape bookmarks. When you click Next, the wizard first asks you which Favorites folder you want to export. Click Next again and the wizard prompts you to enter the path to the bookmark.htm file. Click Next once you've done that. |

4. This wizard performs the requested operation and then displays a dialog box to let you know when it's complete. Click Finish.

## Reading Pages Offline

After you've spent some time on the Web, you'll likely find you have a long list of favorites, and that they fall into one of the following three categories:

- Sites that remain relatively constant over time—These are sites that contain good information for research or fun features for entertainment. You usually access them only as needed.

- Sites that change frequently—These are sites that have constantly updated information, such as news or "something-of-the-day" features. To keep up with these sites, you might consider storing them in a Favorites subfolder named, say, Daily Links, and browsing each favorite daily to look for new content.

- Sites that change content only occasionally—These are sites that update on an irregular schedule. They're problematic because you never know when the content will change.

The second and third categories are workable if you have just a few sites in each category. However, they quickly chew up a lot of connection time if you end up with a large number of these sites. If you have many frequently changing sites, you spend a great deal of connection time reading the new content; if you have many occasionally changing sites, you waste a lot of connection time looking for changed content.

In other words, there are two connection time problems to solve:

- Reading a large number of frequently changing sites

- Searching for changed content in a large number of occasionally changing sites

Internet Explorer solves both problems with its offline pages feature. The idea is that for each of your pages saved as a favorite, you can tell Internet Explorer to also make the page available offline. This means that a local copy of the page is stored in the `%SystemRoot%\Offline Web Pages` folder. There is also an associated synchronize feature that you can run to tell Internet Explorer to go online and check for (and download) updated versions of the offline pages. These features solve the above problems as follows:

- Having the changed pages on your computer means that you can read them without going online.

- When the synchronization is complete, Internet Explorer indicates which pages have changed, so you know from a glance which ones to read.

---

**NOTE**

You might be wondering whether the synchronization feature has a problem with pages that automatically display the current date. After all, this "data" changes every day, even if the real content of the page does not. The good news is that this isn't a problem because the current date is almost always generated using JavaScript code, a Java applet, or some sort of server-side script. Because the page's underlying code doesn't change, Internet Explorer doesn't flag the page as updated.

---

**TIP**

Another problem that the offline pages feature solves is the increasing use of metered connection charges by hotels. That is, the more time you spend connected to a local ISP, the more money the hotel charges you. If you download the pages you want to read offline before you go on the road, you might not need to connect to the Internet at all at the hotel (except, say, to quickly check your email). Even at the hotel, you can save money by downloading the pages you want and then reading them offline.

---

## Setting Up a Page for Offline Reading

To set up a page for offline reading, you have two ways to get started:

- For a page that's already set up as a favorite—Pull down the Favorites menu, right-click the favorite, and then click Make Available Offline.

- For all other pages—Open the page in Internet Explorer and then select Favorites, Add to Favorites (or click Add in the Favorites bar). In the Add Favorite dialog box, activate the Make Available Offline check box and then click Customize.

Either way, the Offline Favorite Wizard appears. Here's how to wield this wizard:

1. The first dialog box just offers an introduction, so click Next. (You might want to activate the In the Future, Do Not Show This Introduction Screen check box to avoid this useless dialog box down the road.)

2. As shown in Figure 18.7, the next wizard dialog box wonders whether you also want to view pages that are linked to the favorite page (which could be pages on the same site or on different sites):

   No    Activating this option tells Internet Explorer not to bother downloading linked pages.

   Yes   Activating this option tells Internet Explorer to download the linked pages. Use the Download Pages *x* Links Deep from This Page spin box to specify how many levels of links you want downloaded.

---

**CAUTION**

Be careful when you set the depth of the links you want to download. Going one level deep means you also download as many other pages as there are links in the offline page, which is probably not too bad on most pages. However, going two levels deep means you also download all the pages that are linked in these other pages. That could easily mean hundreds of extra page downloads. If you go three levels deep, you could be talking about thousands of pages saved to your computer. Only go two or three levels deep if you're certain that the resulting download will be manageable.

---

3. Click Next. The wizard now asks how you want the page synchronized:

   Only When I Choose Synchronize    Activate this option to perform the synchronization by hand.
   from the Tools Menu               Click Next and skip to step 5.

   I Would Like to Create a          Activate this option to set up a schedule for automatic
   New Schedule                      synchronizations. Click Next and proceed to step 4.

4. If you elected to set up a schedule, the wizard displays a dialog box with the following controls (click Next when you're done):

18

**FIGURE 18.7**    Use the Offline Favorite Wizard to set up a page for offline viewing.

| | |
|---|---|
| Every x Days | Sets the interval, in days, that Internet Explorer uses to run the synchronization. |
| At | Sets the time at which Internet Explorer runs the synchronization. |
| Name | Makes up a name for this new synchronization schedule. |
| If My Computer Is Not Connected | Activating this check box tells Internet Explorer to connect to the Internet automatically to perform the synchronization. |

---

**CAUTION**

Having Internet Explorer automatically connect is great for running unattended synchronizations (in the middle of the night, for example). However, this will work only if you connect to your ISP without having to input login data using the Post-Dial Terminal Screen.

---

5. The wizard now asks whether the page requires a password. If not, activate No; if so, activate Yes and then enter your username and password (twice).

6. Click Finish. Internet Explorer synchronizes the page.

## Synchronizing Offline Pages

With all that done, you can synchronize your offline content at any time by using either of the following techniques:

- Select the Tools, Synchronize command—In the Items to Synchronize dialog box, leave the check boxes activated for the pages you want to download, and then click Synchronize.

- To synchronize an individual page, pull down the Favorites menu, right-click the page, and then click Synchronize.

When that's done, you can go offline (by activating the File, Work Offline command) and view the updated content by selecting the pages from the Favorites menu. You can tell the pages that have changed content by looking for a small, red dot in the upper-left corner of the page's icon on the Favorites menu, as shown in Figure 18.8.

Grayed-out pages aren't available offline

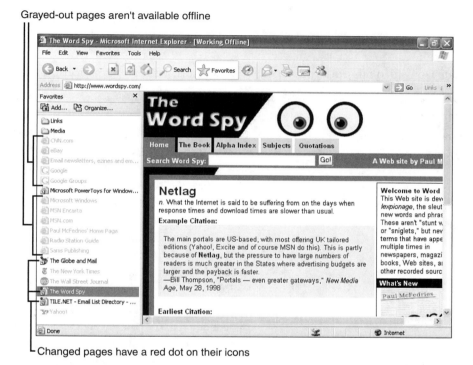

Changed pages have a red dot on their icons

**FIGURE 18.8**   Internet Explorer uses a red dot to indicate offline pages with changed content.

## Changing Offline Page Properties

To change any options for an offline page, follow these steps:

1. Select Tools, Synchronize to display the Items to Synchronize dialog box.

2. Select the item you want to work with and then click Properties. Internet Explorer displays a property sheet for the offline page.

3. In the Web Document tab, use the Make This Page Available Offline check box to toggle offline availability on and off.

4. The Schedule tab offers two options that control how the page is synchronized:

| | |
|---|---|
| Only When I Choose Synchronize from the Tools Menu | Activate this option to run the synchronization by hand. |
| Using the Following Schedule(s) | Activate this option to synchronize the page on a schedule. In the list below it, activate the check boxes beside each schedule you want to use. Use the Add, Remove, and Edit buttons to create, delete, and change schedules. |

5. The Download tab, shown in Figure 18.9, is loaded with useful options:

| | |
|---|---|
| Download Pages *x* Links Deep from This Page | Use this spin box to set the number of levels of linked pages that Internet Explorer downloads. |
| Follow Links Outside of This Page's Web Site | If you leave this check box activated, Internet Explorer will download a linked page even if it's not within the same site as the offline page. If you prefer to stick to the offline page's site, deactivate this check box. |
| Limit Hard-Disk Usage for This Page to *x* Kilobytes | Activate this check box and use the associated spin box to restrict the amount of hard disk space used by the offline page. This is a good idea if you decide to down load pages more than one level deep because that could easily lead to hundreds of pages being down loaded. |
| Advanced | Click this button to display the Advanced Download Options dialog box, which you use to tell Internet Explorer not to download certain page components (such as image, sound, and video files, ActiveX controls, and Java applets), as well as to follow links only to HTML pages (rather than, say, links to documents or files). |
| When This Page Changes, Send E-mail To | Activate this check box if you want Internet Explorer to alert you via email when an offline page has new content. You also need to fill in the E-mail Address and the Mail Server (SMTP) text boxes. |
| If the Site Requires a User Name and Password | If you have to log in to the website, click Login and use the resulting dialog box to specify your username and password (twice). |

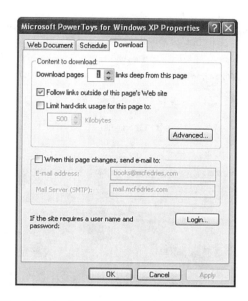

**FIGURE 18.9**   Use the Download tab to control various options related to how the offline page is downloaded to your computer.

6. Click OK to return to the Items to Synchronize dialog box.

7. Click Close.

## Changing Synchronization Settings

In addition to properties for individual offline pages, Internet Explorer also maintains a separate collection of settings that apply to the synchronization feature as a whole. These settings provide you with alternative ways to set up automatic synchronizations (such as when you log on or when your computer has been idle for a while).

To work with these settings, first select Tools, Synchronize to display the Items to Synchronize dialog box, and then click the Setup button. Internet Explorer displays the Synchronization Settings dialog box shown in Figure 18.10.

This dialog box sports three tabs:

| | |
|---|---|
| Logon/Logoff | Use this tab to select offline pages that you want automatically synchronized when you log on to your network (or just when you log on to your computer). |
| On Idle | Use this tab to select offline pages that you want automatically synchronized when your computer has been idle. To set the idle time, click Advanced. |

18

Scheduled                    Use this tab to create and edit synchronization tasks. A **synchronization task** is
                             a collection of offline pages that are automatically synchronized on a regular
                             schedule. Clicking the Add button invokes the Scheduled Synchronization
                             Wizard, which takes you through the process of creating a synchronization
                             task.

When you're done, click OK to return to the Items to Synchronize dialog box and then
click Close.

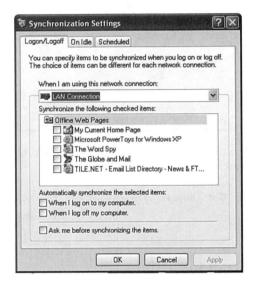

**FIGURE 18.10**    Use the Synchronization Settings dialog box to set up Internet Explorer for
automatic synchronizing of offline pages.

# Customizing Internet Explorer

Internet Explorer is chock full of customization options that enable you to set up the
program for the way you work and surf. The rest of this chapter examines what I think
are the most useful of Internet Explorer's long list of customization features.

---

**TIP**

You can brand your version of Internet Explorer by setting up a custom window title, a custom
browser logo, and custom toolbar buttons. You can do all of this via the Group Policy editor.
Run the program and select User Configuration, Windows Settings, Internet Explorer
Maintenance, Browser User Interface. Use the Browser Title, Custom Logo, and Browser Toolbar
Customizations settings to perform the customizations.

---

## Customizing the Links Bar for One-Click Surfing

The Links bar gives you one-click access to web pages, and so is more convenient than even the Favorites folder (unless you have the Favorites bar displayed). To take full advantage of this convenience, you'll want to redesign the Links bar so that its links and setup are suitable for the way you work. Here's a list of a few techniques and options you can use to work with and customize the Links bar:

> **NOTE**
>
> Before you can perform certain operations on the Links bar (such as moving it), you might have to unlock the Internet Explorer toolbars. Right-click any toolbar and then deactivate the Lock the Toolbars command.

- Moving the Links bar—By default, the Links bar appears to the right of the Address bar with only the title displayed. Unfortunately, this means that you have to click twice to launch a link, which defeats the purpose of the toolbar. To get the one-click access back, move your mouse over the Links label and then drag the bar just below the Address bar, where it will snap into place.

- Changing button positions—The positions of the Links bar buttons are not permanent. To move any button, use your mouse to drag the button left or right along the Links bar.

- Renaming a button—Right-click the button and then click Rename. Use the Rename dialog box to edit the name and then click OK.

- Changing the URL for a button—Right-click a button and then click Properties. Use the URL text box to edit the URL for the button.

- Creating a new link button—To add a new Links bar button for the current page, drag the page icon from the Address bar and drop it on the Links bar. To add a new button for a hypertext link, drag the link and drop it on the Links bar. If you've already saved the page as a favorite, pull down the Favorites menu, drag the icon from the menu and drop it inside the Links bar. If the page title is long, you'll likely want to rename it to something shorter to avoid wasting precious Links bar space.

- Deleting a link—To remove a button from the Links bar, right-click it and then click Delete.

> **TIP**
>
> The Links bar buttons are URL shortcut files located in the %UserProfile\Favorites\Links folder. You can use this folder to work with the shortcuts directly. Perhaps most importantly, you can also use the folder to create subfolders. When you click a subfolder in the Links bar, it drops down a list of the URL shortcuts that are in that subfolder.

18

**TIP**

After you have customized your Links bar to suit your style, you can make it even more convenient by displaying it as part of the taskbar. To do this, right-click an empty section of the taskbar, and then click Toolbars, Links.

## Controlling the Web Page Cache

In the same way that a disk cache stores frequently used data for faster performance, Internet Explorer also keeps a cache of files from web pages you've visited recently. This cache is maintained on a per-user basis and is located in the following folder:

```
%UserProfile%\Local Settings\Temporary Internet Files
```

Internet Explorer uses these saved files to display web pages quickly the next time you ask to see them or while you are offline.

To control the cache, select Tools, Internet Options and display the General tab. Use the following buttons in the Temporary Internet files group:

| | |
|---|---|
| Delete Files | Clicking this button cleans out the Temporary Internet Files folder |
| Settings | Clicking this button displays the Settings dialog box (see Figure 18.11) |

**FIGURE 18.11**   Use this dialog box to control how the Internet Explorer cache works.

You have the following options:

| | |
|---|---|
| Check for Newer Versions of Stored Pages | Activate an option in this group to determine when Internet Explorer checks for updated versions of cache files: |

- Every Visit to the Page—Activating this option tells Internet Explorer to check for a new version of a page every time you navigate to that page. This always ensures that you see the most current data, but it can slow down your browsing, especially if you often redisplay a particular page in the same session.

- Every Time You Start Internet Explorer—Activating this option tells Internet Explorer to check for a new version of a page only once in each browser session. That is, when you visit a page for the first time in a session, Internet Explorer compares the current page content with the cached version; when you subsequently visit the same page in the current session, Internet Explorer does not check for changes. This option also tells Internet Explorer to check a page for changes at least once each day, but no more than once each day. For example, if you visited a page yesterday and the same browser session continues into today, Internet Explorer will check for changes if you revisit the page today; conversely, if you visit a page today and then shut down and restart the browser session on the same day, Internet Explorer will not check for changes if you revisit the page.

- Automatically—Activating this option tells Internet Explorer to determine the best method for updating the cache. Specifically, Internet Explorer monitors how frequently a page's content changes and will modify its updating frequency accordingly.

- Never—Activating this option tells Internet Explorer to never check for updated pages.

**NOTE**

No matter which cache update option you choose, you can view the most up-to-date version of a page at any time by selecting the View, Refresh command. (You can also press F5 or click the Refresh button.)

| | |
|---|---|
| Amount of Disk Space to Use | Use this slider to set the size of the cache, as a percentage of the hard disk's capacity. A larger cache speeds up website browsing but also uses more hard drive space. |
| Move Folder | Clicking this button enables you to change the folder used for the cache. For example, you could move the cache to a partition with more free space (so that you can increase the cache size) or to a faster hard drive (to improve cache performance).Note that you must restart your computer if you move the cache folder. |
| View Files | Clicking this button displays the Temporary Internet Files folder. |

| | |
|---|---|
| View Objects | Clicking this button displays the Downloaded Program Files folder, which holds the Java applets and ActiveX controls that have been downloaded and installed on your system. |

## Setting Internet Explorer Options

You had a brief introduction to the Internet Options dialog box in the previous section. However, this dialog box is loaded with useful options and settings that enable you to control dozens of aspects of Internet Explorer's behavior and look. These include not only cosmetic options such as the fonts and colors used by the program, but also more important concerns, such as your home page and the level of security that Internet Explorer uses.

To display these options, you have several ways to proceed:

- In Internet Explorer, select View, Internet Options
- In Control Panel, double-click the Internet Options icon
- Select Start, right-click the Internet icon, and then click Internet Properties

Whichever method you use, you see the Internet Options (or Internet Properties) dialog box, shown in Figure 18.12. The next few sections discuss the details of most of the controls in this dialog box.

> **NOTE**
>
> I don't discuss the Security and Privacy tabs here. For the details on these important tabs, see Chapter 21, "Implementing Windows XP's Internet Security and Privacy Features."

## Changing the Home Page

In Internet Explorer, the **home page** is what the browser views when you start a new session. The default home page is usually MSN.com, but most computer manufacturers substitute their own pages.

To change the home page, display the General tab and then click one of the following buttons:

| | |
|---|---|
| Use Current | For this button, first navigate to the page you want to use. Then open the Internet Options dialog box and click Use Current to change the home page to the current page. |
| Use Default | Click this button to revert to Internet Explorer's default home page. |
| Use Blank | Click this button if you'd prefer to launch Internet Explorer without loading a home page. |

**FIGURE 18.12**    Use the Internet Options dialog box to customize Internet Explorer to suit the way you work.

**TIP**

Another way to change the home page is to first surf to the page you want to use, and then click and drag the icon from the Address bar and drop it on the Home toolbar button.

## Configuring the Page History

The General tab has a History group that controls various options related to the History folder (refer to the "Using the Handy History Bar" section, earlier in this chapter):

Days to Keep Pages in History    Use this spin box to set the maximum number of days that Internet Explorer will store a URL in its History list. Enter a value between 1 and 99. If you do not want Internet Explorer to keep any pages in the History folder, enter **0**.

Clear History    Click this button to remove all URLs from the History folder.

## Setting More General Options

The General tab also boasts four buttons at the bottom:

Colors    Click this button to display the Colors dialog box. From here, you can deactivate the Use Windows Colors check box to set the default text and background colors used in the Internet Explorer window. (If you leave this check box activated, Internet Explorer uses the colors defined in the Display property sheet.) You can also use the Visited and Unvisited buttons to set the default link

18

| | |
|---|---|
| | colors. Finally, activate the Use Hover Color check box to have Internet Explorer change the color of a link when you position the mouse pointer over the link. (Use the Hover button to set the color.) |
| Fonts | Click this button to display the Fonts dialog box, which enables you to determine how web page fonts appear within Internet Explorer. |

---

**TIP**

To change the size of the fonts Internet Explorer uses, select View, Text Size, and then choose a relative font size from the cascade menu (for example, Larger or Smaller). If you have a mouse with a wheel button, hold down Ctrl while pressing and turning the wheel. This changes the onscreen text size on the fly.

---

| | |
|---|---|
| Languages | Click this button to display the Language Preferences dialog box, which enables you to add one or more languages to Internet Explorer. This makes it possible for Internet Explorer to handle pages in foreign languages. You can also use this dialog box to set up relative priorities for the designated languages. |
| Accessibility | Click this button to display the Accessibility dialog box. From here, you can tell Internet Explorer to ignore the colors, font styles, and font sizes specified on any web page. You can also specify your own style sheet to use when formatting web pages. |

## Using the Content Advisor

The World Wide Web is a vast information source, much of which is helpful or educational or, at worst, innocuous. However, no central authority or government directs the Web, which means that controlling what gets put on it is nearly impossible. As a result, many sites display content that is unsuitable for children, or that is otherwise objectionable to some viewers. Profanity, nudity, sex, and violence are all on the Web—sometimes in extreme form.

If you have children who access the Web, if you want to avoid objectionable content yourself, or if you run an office and do not want employees viewing obscene materials, Internet Explorer can help. The Content Advisor feature enables you to set up ratings that determine the maximum acceptable level of content in four categories: language, nudity, sex, and violence. To view any site that displays content beyond these ratings, the user must enter a supervisor password.

Follow these steps to enable and configure the Content Advisor:

1. In the Internet Options dialog box, display the Content tab.

2. In the Content Advisor group, click Enable to display the Content Advisor dialog box.

3. Use the Select a Category to View the Rating Levels list to click the category you want to work with.

4. Click and drag the rating slider to set the maximum level that unauthorized users can view (see Figure 18.13). If a site is rated higher, users must enter the supervisor password to download the site.

**FIGURE 18.13**   Click and drag the rating slider to set the maximum website rating for the current category that unauthorized users can view.

5. Repeat steps 3 and 4 until you've set the rating for all the categories you want to restrict.

6. Click OK. The Create Supervisor Password dialog box appears.

7. Type the supervisor password in both the Password and Confirm Password text boxes and, optionally, type a hint in the Hint text box.

8. Click OK. Internet Explorer lets you know that the Content Advisor is now enabled.

9. Click OK.

> **TIP**
>
> You can also restrict web content by site. For example, if you know of a site that you never want unauthorized users to view, regardless of the page ratings, you can specify that site's address as never viewable. In the Content Advisor dialog box, click the Approved Sites tab, type the site address in the Allow this Web Site text box, and then click Never.

To make changes to the Content Advisor's ratings or other options, click the Settings button in the Content tab to redisplay the Content Advisor dialog box. There are three important settings in the Content Advisor's General tab that you should know about:

| | |
|---|---|
| Users Can See Sites That Have No Rating | Activate this check box if you want users to be able to view only rated sites. Many sites aren't rated, so activating this option will seriously restrict users' surfing. This, of course, might be exactly what you want. |
| Supervisor Can Type a Password to Allow Users to View Restricted Content | Deactivate this check box to prevent users from entering the supervisor password to see sites rated higher than their permissions allow. (After deactivating this option, if you or another supervisor want to view restricted content, you must temporarily disable Content Advisor. In the Content tab of the Internet Options dialog box, click Disable, type your password, and click OK.) |
| Change Password | Click this button to change your supervisor password. Type your old password, type your new password, confirm your new password, type a password hint, and then click OK. |

---

**Third-Party Filtering Programs**

There are many third-party programs that filter out content deemed objectionable to children. Among the most popular in this category are CYBERsitter (www.cybersitter.com), Net Nanny (www.netnanny.com), and CyberPatrol (www.cyberpatrol.com). Yahoo! has a list of these software packages at the following address:

http://dir.yahoo.com/Business_and_Economy/Shopping_and_Services/

Communication_and_Information_Management/Internet_and_

World_Wide_Web/Software/Blocking_and_Filtering/Titles/

---

## Specifying Internet Explorer Programs

The controls in the Programs tab, shown in Figure 18.14, determine the applications used to read mail, view Usenet newsgroups, and handle other types of Internet files:

| | |
|---|---|
| HTML Editor | This list specifies the default program that runs when you click the Edit with *Program* feature. For example, if you select Notepad, you can load the source code of the current page into Notepad by selecting File, Edit with Notepad or by clicking the Edit with Notepad toolbar button. |
| E-mail | This drop-down list determines the program you use to send Internet email. To launch the email program from within Internet Explorer, select Tools, Mail and News and then select a command such as Read Mail or New Message. You can also start a new message by selecting File, New, Message. |

| | |
|---|---|
| Newsgroups | This drop-down list determines the Usenet newsreader to use while reading newsgroups from within Internet Explorer. To launch the newsreader from within Internet Explorer, select Tools, Mail and News, Read News. You can also start a newsgroup post by selecting File, New, Post. |
| Internet Call | This drop-down list determines the program used to place voice calls over the Internet. To launch the program from within Internet Explorer, select File, New, Internet Call. |
| Calendar | This list sets the program you use as a calendar. |
| Contact List | This list sets the program you use for your contacts database. To create a new contact within Internet Explorer, select File, New, Contact. |

**FIGURE 18.14**    Use the Programs tab to enable Internet Explorer's newsreader features.

## Understanding Internet Explorer's Advanced Options

Internet Explorer has a huge list of customization features found in the Advanced tab of the Internet Options dialog box (see Figure 18.15). Many of these settings are obscure, but there are lots that are extremely useful for surfers of all stripes. This section runs through all of these settings.

> **TIP**
>
> The advanced options can be set for users via the Group Policy editor. Run the program and open the User Configuration, Windows Settings, Internet Explorer Maintenance branch. Right-click Internet Explorer Maintenance and then click Preference Mode. Click the Advanced branch that is added to the Internet Explorer Maintenance section. Double-click the Internet Settings item to work with the advanced options.

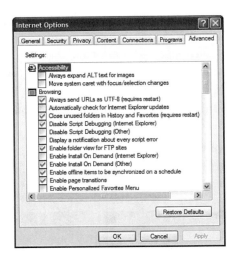

**FIGURE 18.15**    In the Internet Options dialog box, the Advanced tab contains a long list of Internet Explorer customization settings.

The Accessibility group has two options:

Always Expand ALT Text for Images

Most webmasters define a text description for each image they include on a page. If you tell Internet Explorer not to show images (see the later discussion of the Show Pictures check box), all you see are boxes where the images should be, and each box contains the text description (which is known as **alt text**, where *alt* is short for *alternate*). Activating this check box tells Internet Explorer to expand the image box horizontally so that the alt text appears on a single line.

Move System Caret with Focus/ Selection Changes

Activating this check box tells Internet Explorer to move the system caret whenever you change the focus. (The **system caret** is a visual indication of what part of the screen currently has the focus. If a text box has the focus, the system caret is a blinking, vertical bar; if a check box or option button has the focus, the system caret is a dotted outline of the control name.) This is useful if you have a screen reader or screen magnifier that uses the position of the system caret to determine what part of the screen should be read or magnified.

Here are the options in the Browsing group:

Always Send URLs as UTF-8

When activated, this check box tells Internet Explorer to send web page addresses using the UTF-8 standard, which is readable in any language. If you're having trouble accessing a page that uses non-English characters in the URL, the server might not be able to handle UTF-8, so deactivate this check box. You need to restart Internet Explorer if you change this setting.

Automatically Check for Internet Explorer Updates

When activated, this option tells Internet Explorer to check (approximately every 30 days) to see whether a newer version of the program is available. This is a useful and easy method for keeping up with the latest Internet Explorer updates and security patches.

Close Unused Folders in History and Favorites

When this check box is activated, Internet Explorer keeps unused folders closed when you display the History bar and the Favorites bar. That is, if you open a folder and then open a second folder, Internet Explorer automatically closes the first folder. This makes the History and Favorites lists easier to navigate, so it's usually best to leave this option activated. You need to restart Internet Explorer if you change this setting.

Disable Script Debugging (Internet Explorer)

This check box toggles the script debugger (if one is installed) on and off within Internet Explorer only. You should need to activate this option only if you're a page designer and you have scripts in your pages that you need to debug before uploading them to the Web.

Disable Script Debugging (Other)

This is similar to the Disable Script Debugging (Internet Explorer) option, except that it toggles the script debugger (again, if one is installed) on and off within any application other than Internet Explorer that can display web content (such as Outlook Express).

Display a Notification About Every Error

If you activate this check box, Internet Explorer Script displays a dialog box to alert you to JavaScript or VBScript errors on a page. If you leave this option deactivated, Internet Explorer displays an error message in the status bar. To see the full error message, double-click the status bar message. Again,

18

|  | only script programmers will want to enable this option, and only when they're debugging scripts. Many websites are poorly programmed and contain script errors, so enabling this option means that you'll have to deal with lots of annoying dialog boxes as you surf. |
|---|---|
| Enable Folder View for FTP Sites | When this option is activated and you access an FTP (File Transfer Protocol) site, Internet Explorer displays the contents of the site using the familiar Windows folder view. This makes it easy to drag and drop files from the FTP to your hard disk (and possibly perform other file maintenance chores, depending on what permissions you have at the site). |
| Enable Install On Demand (Internet Explorer) | When this check box is activated, Internet Explorer examines each web page for elements that require a specific browser feature. If that feature isn't installed, and that feature comes with setup instructions in a cabinet information file, Internet Explorer asks whether you want to install the feature. If you find that a page doesn't appear to work properly, a missing component could be the problem, so try enabling this option. |

**NOTE**

For a list of the features supported by Install On Demand, see the following web page:
msdn.microsoft.com/workshop/author/behaviors/reference/methods/installable.asp

| Enable Install On Demand (Other) | This is similar to the Enable Install On Demand (Internet Explorer) option, except that activating this check box tells Internet Explorer to prompt you to install features that come with their own installation program. Only the Windows Virtual Machine (Java support, which is not installed by default in Windows XP) can be installed this way. |
|---|---|
| Enable Offline Items to Be Synchronized on a Schedule | This check box toggles the synchronization updates on and off. Deactivating this check box is a good idea if you're going out of town for a few days and don't want offline pages updated while you're away. |
| Enable Page Transitions | This check box toggles Internet Explorer's support for page transitions on and off—websites that use a server that supports FrontPage extensions can define |

|  | various page transitions (such as wipes and fades). However, these transitions often slow down your browsing, so I recommend turning them off. |
| Enable Personalized Favorites Menu | When this check box is activated, Windows XP's personalized menu feature gets applied to Internet Explorer's Favorites menu. This means that Internet Explorer hides favorites that you haven't visited in a while. To see the hidden favorites, click the down ward-pointing arrow at the bottom of the menu. Personalized menus reduce the command clutter that can confuse novice users, but they just slow down experienced users. I recommend leaving this option turned off. |
| Enable Third-Party Browser Extensions | When this check box is activated, Internet Explorer supports third-party extensions to its interface. For example, the Google toolbar is a third-party extension that integrates the Google search engine into Internet Explorer as a toolbar. If you deactivate this check box, these third-party extensions don't appear and can't be displayed. Deactivating this check box is a good way to turn off some (but, unfortunately, not all) of those annoying third-party toolbars that install themselves without permission. You need to restart Internet Explorer if you change this setting. |
| Enable Visual Styles on Buttons and Controls in Web Pages | When this check box is activated, Internet Explorer applies the current Windows XP visual style to all web pages for objects such as form buttons. If you deactivate this check box, Internet Explorer applies its default visual style to all page elements. |
| Force Offscreen Compositing Even Under Terminal Server | If you activate this check box, Internet Explorer performs all **compositing**—the combining of two or more images—in memory before displaying the result onscreen. This avoids the image flashing that can occur when running Internet Explorer under Terminal Services, but it can reduce performance significantly. I recommend leaving this option unchecked. You need to restart Internet Explorer if you change this setting. |
| Notify When Downloads Complete | If you leave this check box activated, Internet Explorer leaves its download progress dialog box onscreen after the download is complete (see Figure 18.16). This enables you to click Run to launch the |

18

downloaded file or to click Open Folder to display the file's destination folder. If you deactivate this check box, Internet Explorer closes this dialog box as soon as the download is over.

---

**TIP**

You can also force Internet Explorer to close the Download Complete dialog box automatically by activating the Close this Dialog Box When Download Completes check box.

---

**FIGURE 18.16**    When Internet Explorer completes a file download, it leaves this dialog box onscreen to help you deal with the file.

Reuse Windows for Launching Shortcuts

When this check box is activated, Windows looks for an already-open Internet Explorer window when you click a web page shortcut (such as a web address in an Outlook Express email message). If such a window is open, the web page is loaded into that window. This is a good idea because it prevents Internet Explorer windows from multiplying unnecessarily. If you deactivate this option, Windows always loads the page into a new Internet Explorer window.

Show Friendly HTTP Error Messages

When this check box is activated, Internet Explorer intercepts the error messages (for, say, pages not found) generated by web servers and replaces them with its own messages that offer more information as well as possible solutions to the problem. If you deactivate this option, Internet Explorer displays the error message generated by the web server. However, I recommend deactivating this option because the web server error messages are often customized to be more helpful than the generic messages reported by Internet Explorer.

Show Friendly URLs

This check box determines how URLs appear in the status bar when you hover the mouse over a link or imagemap. Activate this check box to see only the filename of the linked page; deactivate this check box to see the full URL of the linked page. I prefer to see the full URL so that I know exactly where a link will take me (particularly if the link will take me to a different site).

Show Go Button in Address Bar

When this check box is activated, Internet Explorer adds a Go button to the right of the Address bar. You click this button to open whatever URL is shown in the Address bar. The usefulness of this button is dubious (it's usually easiest just to press Enter after typing an address), but it doesn't hurt anything.

Underline Links

Use these options to specify when Internet Explorer should format web page links with an underline. The Hover option means that the underline appears only when you position the mouse pointer over the link. Many websites use colored text, so it's often difficult to recognize a link without the underlining. Therefore, I recommend that you activate the Always option.

Use Inline AutoComplete

This check box toggles the Address bar's inline AutoComplete feature on and off. When inline AutoComplete is on, Internet Explorer monitors the text that you type in the Address bar. If your text matches a previously typed URL, Internet Explorer automatically completes the address by displaying the matching URL in the Address bar. It also displays a drop-down list of other matching URLs. When inline AutoComplete is off, Internet Explorer displays only the drop-down list of matching URLs.

**18**

**NOTE**

If you want to prevent Internet Explorer from displaying the drop-down list of matching URLs, click the Content tab's AutoComplete button to display the AutoComplete Settings dialog box. Deactivate the Web Addresses check box. Note that Internet Explorer's AutoComplete feature also applies to web forms. That is, AutoComplete can also remember data that you've typed into a form—including usernames and passwords—and then enter that data automatically when you use the form again. You can control this web form portion of AutoComplete by using the other check boxes in the Use AutoComplete For section of the AutoComplete Settings dialog box.

| | |
|---|---|
| Use Passive FTP (for Firewall and DSL Modem Compatibility) | In a normal FTP session, Internet Explorer opens a connection to the FTP server (for commands) and then the FTP server opens a second connection back to the browser (for the data). If you're on a network with a firewall, however, incoming connections from a server aren't allowed. With passive FTP, the browser establishes the second (data) connection itself. So, if you're on a firewalled network (or are using a DSL modem) and you can't establish an FTP connection, activate this check box. |
| Use Smooth Scrolling | This check box toggles a feature called smooth scrolling on and off. When you activate this check box to enable smooth scrolling, pressing Page Down or Page Up causes the page to scroll down or up at a preset speed. If you deactivate this check box, pressing Page Down or Page Up causes the page to instantly jump down or up. |

**TIP**

When reading a web page, you can scroll down one screen by pressing the spacebar. To scroll up one screen, press Shift+Spacebar.

The check boxes in the HTTP 1.1 Settings branch determine whether Internet Explorer uses the HTTP 1.1 protocol:

| | |
|---|---|
| Use HTTP 1.1 | This check box toggles Internet Explorer's use of HTTP 1.1 to communicate with web servers. (HTTP 1.1 is the standard protocol used on the Web today.) You should deactivate this check box only if you're having trouble connecting to a website. This tells Internet Explorer to use HTTP 1.0, which might solve the problem. |
| Use HTTP 1.1 Through Proxy Connections | This check box toggles on and off the use of HTTP 1.1 only when connecting through a proxy server. |

The check boxes in the Microsoft VM branch are related to Internet Explorer's Java Virtual Machine:

| | |
|---|---|
| Java Console Enabled | This check box toggles the Java console on and off. The Java console is a separate window in which the output and error messages from a Java applet are displayed. If you activate this option (which requires that you restart Internet Explorer), you can view the |

| | |
|---|---|
| | Java console by selecting the View, Java Console command. You should need to use the Java Console only if you're debugging a Java application. |
| Java Logging Enabled | This check box toggles Internet Explorer's Java logging on and off. When it's on, Internet Explorer logs Java applet error messages to a file named Javalog.txt in the %SystemRoot%\Java folder. This is useful for troubleshooting Java problems. |
| JIT Compiler for Virtual Machine Enabled | This check box toggles Internet Explorer's internal just-in-time (JIT) Java compiler on and off. This compiler is used to compile and run Java applets using native Windows code. In many cases, this causes the Java applet to run much faster than the regularly compiled code. However, it might break some applets or cause them to run slower than normal. You need to restart Internet Explorer if you change this setting. |

The options in the Multimedia branch toggle various multimedia effects on and off:

| | |
|---|---|
| Enable Automatic Image Resizing | If you activate this check box, Internet Explorer automatically shrinks large images so that they fit inside the browser window. This is useful if you're running Windows XP with a small monitor or a relatively low resolution, and you're finding that many website images don't fit entirely into the browser window. |

**TIP**

If Enable Automatic Image Resizing is activated, you can restore an image to its normal size by first hovering the mouse pointer over the image. After a couple of seconds, Internet Explorer displays Automatic Image Resizing icon in the lower-right corner of the image (see Figure 18.17). Click that icon to expand the image to its normal size.

| | |
|---|---|
| Enable Image Toolbar | When this check box is activated and you hover the mouse pointer over an image, Internet Explorer displays a toolbar in the upper-left corner of the image, as shown in Figure 18.17. You can use this toolbar to save or print the image, send the image via email, or open the My Pictures folder. Internet Explorer also displays the Fit Image to Window button in the lower-right corner of the image. Click this button to resize the image to fit inside the browser window. |

18

Image Toolbar

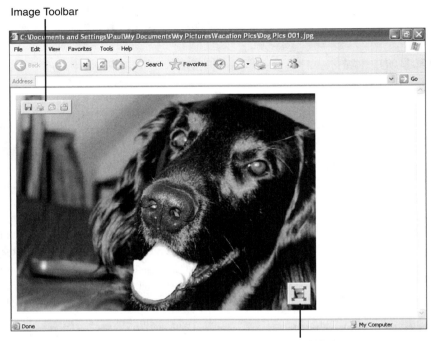

Fit Image to Window

**FIGURE 18.17**    When you hover the mouse pointer over an image, Internet Explorer can display the Image toolbar in the upper-left corner of the image and the Automatic Image Resizing icon in the lower-right corner.

| | |
|---|---|
| Play Animations in Web Pages | This check box toggles animated GIF images on and off. Most animated GIFs are unwelcome annoyances, so you'll probably greatly improve your surfing experience by clearing this check box. If you turn this option off and you want to view an animation, right-click the box and then click Show Picture. |
| Play Sounds in Web Pages | This check box toggles web page sound effects on and off. Because the vast majority of web page sounds are extremely bad MIDI renditions of popular tunes, turning off sounds will save your ears. |
| Play Videos in Web Pages | This check box toggles Internet Explorer's support for inline AVI files on and off. If you turn this setting off, the only way to view a video is to turn the option back on and then refresh the page. |

| | |
|---|---|
| Show Image Download Placeholders | If you activate this check box, Internet Explorer displays a box that is the same size and shape as the image it is downloading. |
| Show Pictures | This check box toggles web page images on and off. If you're using a slow connection, turn off this option and Internet Explorer will show only a box where the image would normally appear. (If the designer has included ALT text, that text will appear inside the box.) If you want to view a picture, right-click the box and then click Show Picture. |
| Smart Image Dithering | This check box toggles image dithering on and off. **Dithering** is a technique that slightly alters an image in order to make jagged edges appear smooth. |

In the Printing group, the Print Background Colors and Images check box determines whether Internet Explorer includes the page's background when you print the page. Many web pages use solid colors or fancy images as backgrounds, so you'll print these pages faster if you leave this setting deactivated.

The options in the Search from the Address Bar group control Internet Explorer's Address bar searching:

| | |
|---|---|
| Display Results, and Go to the Most Likely Site | Activate this option to display the search engine's results in the Search bar and to display the best match in the main browser window. |
| Do Not Search from the Address Bar | Activate this option to disable Address bar searching. |
| Just Display the Results in the Main Window | Activate this option to display in the main browser window a list of the sites that the search engine found. |
| Just Go to the Most Likely Site | Activate this option to display the search engine's best match in the main browser window. |

The Security branch has many options related to Internet Explorer security. I discuss these options in Chapter 21.

# From Here

Here's a list of some other places in the book where you'll find information related to what you learned in this chapter:

- To learn how to control Internet Explorer via scripting, refer to the section titled "Example: Scripting Internet Explorer" in Chapter 9, "Programming the Windows Script Host."

- For information on placing Internet phone calls, refer to the sections titled "Getting Your Modem to Dial Voice Calls for You" and "Remote Collaboration with Microsoft NetMeeting" in Chapter 16, "Putting Your Modem to Work."

- For the details on sending and receiving email using Outlook Express, see Chapter 19, "Communicating with Internet Email."

- For information on the newsgroup capabilities of Outlook Express, see Chapter 20, "Participating in Internet Newsgroups."

- To learn about the security and privacy features in Internet Explorer, see Chapter 21, "Implementing Windows XP's Internet Security and Privacy Features."

# Communicating with Internet Email

If software programs can have inferiority complexes, Outlook Express would be a prime candidate. After all, it has always been considered the poor cousin of Outlook, Microsoft's flagship email client. But I think that's a bad rap because Outlook Express 6, the version that ships with Windows XP, is a mature, full-featured client that does just about everything Outlook does. (The exception is that Outlook Express doesn't support scripting. But that's a mark in its favor these days because it seems that most email virus programmers target Outlook and its capability to run scripts embedded in messages.) More than that, Outlook Express even comes with a few of its own unique features. The problem, though, is that many people don't know just what Outlook Express is capable of.

My goal in this chapter is to give you a taste of what Outlook Express can do. I take you through subjects such as setting up accounts, processing messages, customizing columns, setting read and send options, maintaining Outlook Express, and working with identities, all of which will help you perform your email chores faster and more efficiently.

## Setting Up Mail Accounts

If you haven't yet started Outlook Express—and so haven't yet defined your first mail account—or if you have multiple accounts and need to set up the others, this section shows you how to do it within Outlook Express.

## Specifying Basic Account Settings

Here are the steps to follow to set up an email account with just the basic settings (which should be enough to get most accounts up and running):

1. Start the Internet Connection Wizard using one of the following techniques:

    - Start Outlook Express for the first time.

    - In Outlook Express, select Tools, Accounts to display the Internet Accounts dialog box, and then click Add, Mail.

2. Type your **display name**—this is the name that will appear in the From field when you send a message—and click Next.

3. Type the email address for the account and click Next.

4. Specify your mail server data (click Next when you're done):

| | |
|---|---|
| My Incoming Mail Server Is a x Server | Use this list to select the incoming mail server type: POP3, IMAP, or HTTP (World Wide Web–based email). |
| Incoming Mail (POP3, IMAP, or HTTP) Server | Type the domain name for your incoming mail server. |
| Outgoing Mail (SMTP) Server | Type the domain name for your outgoing mail server. |

5. Type your account name (your username) and your password, and then click Next.

6. If you have another email client installed on your system (such as Microsoft Outlook), you might see the Import Messages and Address Book dialog box. You have two choices (click Next when you're done):

| | |
|---|---|
| Import From | Activate this option if you want to import data from the other client. If Outlook Express shows multiple clients, click the client you want to use. After you've clicked Next, you're asked whether you want to import just the client's messages, its address book, or both. Make your choice and click Next. |
| Do Not Import at This Time | Activate this option to bypass the import. |

7. Click Finish.

When the wizard completes its labors, your new account appears in the Mail tab of the Internet Accounts dialog box, as shown in Figure 19.1.

## Setting the Default Account

If you have more than one account, you should specify one of them as the default account. The default account is the one Outlook Express uses automatically when you send a message. To set the default account, select it in the Mail tab and then click Set as Default.

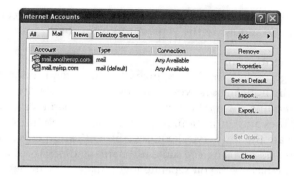

**FIGURE 19.1**    Your Internet email accounts are listed in the Mail tab.

> **NOTE**
>
> It *is* possible to send a message using any of your accounts. However, sending a message using anything other than the default account requires an extra step. See "Sending Messages," later in this chapter.

## Specifying Advanced Account Settings

Although the basic account settings that you specify using the Internet Connection Wizard suffice in most cases, many accounts require a more advanced setup. For example, your Internet Service Provider (**ISP**) might require a different SMTP port or you might prefer to leave your messages on the server.

To work with these more advanced settings, select an account and then click Properties. The property sheet that appears contains a number of tabs, and most of the controls in this dialog box are straightforward. The next four sections take you through some of the other options and show how useful they can be.

> **NOTE**
>
> I discuss the options in the Security tab as well as other email security issues in Chapter 21, "Implementing Windows XP's Internet Security and Privacy Features."

### Using a Different Reply Address

It's occasionally useful to have replies sent to a different address. For example, if you're sending a message requesting feedback from a number of people, you might prefer that the return messages go to a colleague or assistant for collating or processing. Similarly, if you send a work-related message from a personal account, you might want replies sent to your work account.

To specify a different reply address, display the General tab in the account's property sheet, and then type the address in the Reply Address text box.

### Enabling SMTP Authentication
With spam such a big problem these days, many ISPs now require **SMTP authentication** for outgoing mail, which means that you must log on to the SMTP server to confirm that you are the person sending the mail (as opposed to some spammer spoofing your address). If your ISP uses authentication, display the Servers tab in the accounts property sheet, and then activate the My Server Requires Authentication check box. By default, Outlook Express logs you on using the same username and password as your incoming mail server. If your ISP has given you separate logon data, clicking Settings, activate the Log On Using option, type your account name and password, and click OK.

### Specifying a Different SMTP Port
For security reasons, some ISPs insist that all their customers' outgoing mail must be routed through the ISP's Simple Mail Transport Protocol (**SMTP**) server. This usually isn't a problem if you're using an email account maintained by the ISP, but it can lead to problems if you're using an account provided by a third party (such as your website host):

- Your ISP might block messages sent using the third-party account because it thinks you're trying to relay the message through the ISP's server (a technique often used by spammers).

- You might incur extra charges if your ISP allows only a certain amount of SMTP bandwidth per month or a certain number of sent messages, whereas the third-party account offers higher limits or no restrictions at all.

- You might have performance problems, with the ISP's server taking much longer to route messages than the third-party host.

You might think that you can solve the problem by specifying the third-party host's SMTP server in the account settings. However, this doesn't usually work because outgoing email is sent by default through port 25; when you use this port, you must also use the ISP's SMTP server.

To work around this, many third-party hosts offer access to their SMTP server via a port other than the standard port 25. To configure an email account to use a nonstandard SMTP port, display the Advanced tab in the account's property sheet, and then use the Outgoing Mail (SMTP) text box to type the port number specified by the third-party host.

### Checking the Same Account from Two Different Computers
In today's increasingly mobile world, it's common to have to check the same email account from multiple devices. For example, you might want to check your business account not only using your work computer, but also using your home computer or your notebook while traveling, or using a PDA or other portable device while commuting.

Unfortunately, after you've downloaded a message, the message is deleted from the server and you can't access it from any other device. If you need to check mail on multiple devices, the trick is to leave a copy of the message on the server after you download it. That way the message will still be available when you check messages using another device.

To tell Outlook Express to leave a copy of each message on the server, display the Advanced tab in the account's property sheet, and then activate the Leave a Copy of Messages on the Server check box. You can also activate the following options:

| | |
|---|---|
| Remove from Server After *X* Days | If you activate this check box, Outlook Express automatically deletes the message from the server after the number of days specified in the spin box. |
| Remove from Server When Deleted from 'Deleted Items' | If you activate this check box, Outlook Express deletes the message from the server only when you permanently delete the message on your system. |

Here's a good strategy to follow:

- On your main computer, activate the Leave a Copy of Messages on the Server check box *and* the Remove from Server After *X* Days check box. Set the number of days long enough so that you have time to download the messages using your other devices.

- On all your other devices, activate only the Leave a Copy of Messages on the Server check box.

This strategy ensures that you can download messages on all your devices, but it prevents messages from piling up on the server.

> **NOTE**
>
> There are other occasions when you'd prefer to leave messages temporarily on the server. For example, if you're on the road, you might want to download the messages to a notebook or to some other computer that you're using temporarily. By leaving the messages on the server, you can still download them to your main computer when you return to the office or to your home. Similarly, you might want to download your messages into another email client for testing purposes or to take advantage of features in that client that aren't found in Outlook Express.

## Handling Incoming Messages

Incoming email messages are stored in your mailbox on your ISP's server until you use an email client such as Outlook Express to retrieve them. The easiest way to do that is to let Outlook Express check for and download new messages automatically. This feature is controlled by several settings within the Options dialog box. Select Tools, Options and make sure that the General tab is displayed, as shown in Figure 19.2.

19

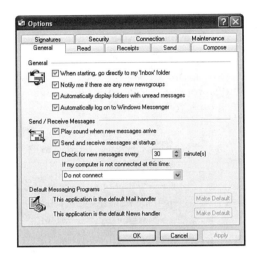

**FIGURE 19.2**   The General tab has a couple of options related to retrieving messages.

Here are the settings related to retrieving messages:

| | |
|---|---|
| Play Sound When New Messages Arrive | When this option is activated, Outlook Express plays a sound whenever one or more messages are down loaded. (If multiple messages arrive, Outlook Express only plays the sound once.) This is useful only if you don't get very many messages and if you leave Outlook Express running in the background while maintaining a connection to the Internet. In any other scenario the sound is either annoying or redundant, so consider deactivating this check box. |

**TIP**

It's possible to change the sound that indicates a new message has arrived. Launch Control Panel's Sound and Audio Devices icon and then display the Sounds tab. In the Program Events list, select New Mail Notification and then click Browse to choose the sound file you want Outlook Express to play when new messages are delivered.

| | |
|---|---|
| Send and Receive Messages at Startup | When this check box is activated, Outlook Express connects with the server to check for waiting messages as soon as you start the program. (It also sends any messages that are waiting in the Outbox folder.) Note that if your computer is not connected to the Internet, Outlook Express will attempt to establish a connection. This is true even if you select Do Not Connect in the If My Computer Is Not Connected at This Time list |

| | |
|---|---|
| | (described later). If you prefer to stay offline at startup, deactivate this check box. |
| Check for New Messages Every *X* Minute(s) | When this option is activated, Outlook Express automatically checks for new messages using the interval specified in the spin box. You can enter a time between 1 and 480 minutes. |
| If My Computer Is Not Connected at This Time | If the Check for New Messages Every *X* Minute(s) check box is activated, use this list to specify what Outlook Express should do if your computer is not connected to the Internet when the time comes to check for new messages: |

- Do Not Connect—Choose this option to prevent Outlook Express from initiating a connection.

- Connect Only When Not Working Offline— Choose this option to tell Outlook Express to connect only when the program is in online mode.

- Connect Only When Working Offline—Choose this option to tell Outlook Express to connect only when the program is in offline mode.

**NOTE**

To put Outlook Express in offline mode, pull down the File menu and activate the Work Offline command. To return to online mode, deactivate this command.

If you elected not to have Outlook Express check for new mail automatically, you can use any of the following techniques to check the server by hand:

- To receive messages on all your accounts—Select Tools, Send and Receive, Receive All, or click the Send/Recv button's arrow to drop down the list, and then click Receive All.

- To receive messages on only a single account—Select Tools, Send and Receive and then select the account you want to work with, or click the Send/Recv button's arrow to drop down the list, and then click the account.

- To send and receive messages on all your accounts—If you also have messages waiting in your Outbox, select Tools, Send and Receive, Send and Receive All, or click the Send/Recv toolbar button.

**19**

**TIP**

A quick way to send and receive messages on all your accounts is to press Ctrl+M or F5.

## Processing Messages

Each new message that arrives is stored in the Inbox folder's message list and appears in a bold font. To view the contents of any message, select it in the message list and Outlook Express then displays the message text in the preview pane. If you find the preview pane too confining, you can open the selected message in its own window by double-clicking it.

When you have a message selected, you can do plenty of things with it (in addition to reading it, of course). You can print it, save it to a file, move it to another folder, reply to it, delete it, and more. Most of these operations are straightforward, so I'll just summarize the basic techniques here:

- Dealing with attachments—If a message has an attachment, you'll see a paper clip icon in the Inbox folder's Attachment column, as well as in the upper-right corner of the preview pane. You have two choices:

  To open the attachment: Click the preview pane's paper clip icon and then click the name of the file.

  To save the attachment: Click the preview pane's paper clip icon and then click Save Attachments. You can also select the File, Save Attachments command.

- Moving a message to a different folder—Later in this chapter, I'll show you how to create new folders you can use for storing related messages. To move a message to another folder, use your mouse to drag the message from the Inbox folder and then drop it on the destination folder.

- Saving a message—Instead of storing the message in a folder, you might prefer to save it to a file. To do this, select File, Save As and then use the Save As dialog box to select a location, enter a filename, and select a file type.

- Saving a message as stationery—If you receive a formatted message and you like the layout, you can save it as stationery for your own use. To do so, select File, Save As Stationery.

- Printing a message—To print a copy of the message, select File, Print.

- Replying to a message—Outlook Express gives you two reply options:

  | | |
  |---|---|
  | Replying to the Message Author | This option sends the reply to only the person who sent the original message. Any names in the Cc line are ignored. To use this option, select Message, Reply to Sender or press Ctrl+R. You can also click the Reply button on the toolbar. |
  | Reply to All of the Message Recipients | This option sends the reply not only to the original author, but also to anyone else mentioned in the Cc line. To use this option, select Message, Reply to All or press Ctrl+Shift+R. You can also click the Reply All button on the toolbar. |

- Forwarding a message—You can forward a message to another address by using either of the following commands:

| | |
|---|---|
| Forward | Select Message, Forward, press Ctrl+F, or click the Forward toolbar button. The full text of the original message is inserted into the body of the new message and a greater than sign (>) is appended to the beginning of each line. |
| Forward as Attachment | Select Message, Forward as Attachment. In this case, Outlook Express packages the original message as an attachment, but it makes no changes to the message. The user who receives the forwarded message can then open this attachment and view the original message exactly as you received it. |

- Deleting a message—To get rid of a message, select it in the folder and then press Delete (or Ctrl+D) or click the toolbar's Delete button. If the message is open, press Ctrl+D or click the Delete button. Note that Outlook Express doesn't really delete the message. Instead, it just moves it to the Deleted Items folder. If you change your mind and decide to keep the message, open the Deleted Items folder and move the message back. To remove a message permanently, open the Deleted Items folder and delete the message from there.

## Customizing the Message Columns

The default columns in Outlook Express tell you the basic information you need for any message. More information is available, however. For example, you might want to know the date and time the message was sent, the size of the message and to whom the message was sent. These items can be displayed as columns in the message list. Here are the steps to follow to customize the Outlook Express columns:

1. Select View, Columns. (You can also right-click any column header and then click Columns.) Outlook Express displays the Columns dialog box, shown in Figure 19.3.

2. To add a column, either activate its check box or select it and click Show.

3. To remove a column, either deactivate its check box or select it and click Hide.

4. To change the order of the columns, select a column and then use the Move Up and Move Down buttons to position the column where you want it. (Columns listed top to bottom are displayed left to right in the message list.)

5. To control the width of a column, select it and then enter a new value in the The Selected Column Should Be $X$ Pixels Wide text box.

6. Click OK.

19

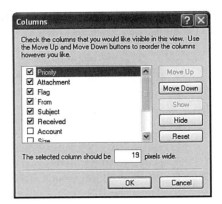

**FIGURE 19.3**    Use the Columns dialog box to customize the columns displayed in the message list.

Here are a few more column customization tricks:

- To change the width of a displayed column, use your mouse to drag the right edge of the column's header to the left or right.

- To change the width of a displayed column to fit its widest entry, double-click the right edge of the column's header.

- To change the position of a column, use your mouse to drag the column's header left or right.

## Setting Read Options

To help you work with your correspondence, Outlook Express has a number of options related to reading messages. To view them, select Tools, Options to open the Options dialog box, and then display the Read tab, shown in Figure 19.4.

> **NOTE**
>
> For a discussion of the options in newsgroups, see Chapter 20, "Participating in Internet Newsgroups."

Here's a review of the controls in this tab:

| | |
|---|---|
| Mark Message Read After Displaying for *X* Second(s) | Deactivate this check box to prevent Outlook Express from removing the boldfacing while you're reading a message. Alternatively, you can use the spin box to adjust how long it takes Outlook Express to remove the bold (the maximum is 60 seconds). |

**FIGURE 19.4**    Use the Read tab to set various properties related to reading messages.

---

**Marking Messages as Read**

You can also control the marking of read messages via the Edit menu using the following commands:

Mark As Read—Turns off boldfacing for the current message or messages. Alternatively, press Ctrl+Q or Ctrl+Enter, or right-click the message and then click Mark as Read.

Mark As Unread—Turns on boldfacing for the current message or messages. You can also press Ctrl+Shift+Enter or right-click the message and then click Mark as Unread.

Mark Conversation as Read—Turns off boldfacing for all the messages in the conversation associated with the current message. (A **conversation** or thread is a group of messages that have the same subject line, ignoring the Re: and Fw: prefixes added to replies and forwards.) Alternatively, press Ctrl+T. Note that for this command to work, you have to group messages by conversation by selecting the View, Current View, Group Messages By Conversation command.

Mark All Read—Turns off boldfacing on all messages in the current folder. You can also press Ctrl+Shift+A.

---

**NOTE**

Note that you can ask Outlook Express to display only unread messages by selecting the View, Current View, Hide Read Messages command. (Select View, Current View, Show All Messages to return to the regular view.)

---

Automatically Expand Grouped Messages

When you group messages by conversation (by selecting the View, Current View, Group Messages By Conversation command), Outlook Express displays only the first message in the group and includes a plus sign

|  | (+) to its left. You need to click the plus sign to see the other messages in the conversation. If you prefer to see all the messages in the conversation automatically, activate this check box. |
| Automatically Download Message When Viewing in the Preview Pane | When you're working with a Web-based email account (such as Hotmail) or a newsgroup, deactivate this check box to prevent Outlook Express from downloading message text when the message header is selected. When you're ready to receive the text, press the spacebar. |
| Read All Messages in Plain Text | Activate this check box to convert all HTML messages to plain text, which helps to thwart web bugs and malicious scripts. I discuss these and other security-related issues in Chapter 21. |
| Show ToolTips in the Message List for Clipped Items | When this check box is activated, Outlook Express displays clipped information (such as a subject line that's cut off at the end because the Subject column is too narrow) in a ToolTip when you hover the mouse pointer over the item. |
| Highlight Watched Messages | Use this list to specify the color that Outlook Express uses to display messages marked as watched. To mark a message as watched, you first need to display the Watch/Ignore column (refer to "Customizing the Message Columns," earlier in this chapter). Then click inside the column beside the message to add an eyeglasses icon to the column and to format the message in the specified color. |
| Fonts | Click this button to display the Fonts dialog box, which displays a list of the character sets installed on your computer. For each character set, you can specify a proportional and fixed-width font, as well as a font size and encoding. You can also specify which character set to use as the default. |
| International Settings | Click this button to display the International Read Settings dialog box. Activate the Use Default Encoding for All Incoming Messages to apply the encoding shown in the Default Encoding box to all your messages. |

# Sending Messages

Composing a basic message in Outlook Express is straightforward, and it isn't all that much different from composing a letter or memo in WordPad. There are a number of ways to get started, however, not all of them well known. Here's a summary:

- In Outlook Express, select Compose, New Message, press Ctrl+N, or click the Create Mail toolbar button.

- In Internet Explorer, select Tools, Mail and News, and then choose one of the following commands:

| | |
|---|---|
| New Message | Select this command to start an empty email message. |
| Send a Link | Select this command to create a new message with a URL shortcut file attached. This file is a shortcut for the current website that the recipient can click to load that site into Internet Explorer. |
| Send Page | Select this command to create a new message with the current web page as the content of the message. |

- In a web page, click a mailto link. This creates a new message addressed to the recipient specified by the link.

- In Windows Explorer, right-click a file and then click Send To, Mail Recipient. This creates a new message with the file attached.

From here, if you have multiple email accounts, use the From list to select the account from which you want to send the message. Use the To field to enter the address of the recipient; use the Cc field to enter the address of a recipient that you want to receive a copy of the message; and use the Bcc field to enter the addresses of any recipients you want to receive blind copies of the message. (The Bcc field is not displayed by default. To see it, select the View, All Headers command.) Note that in each field you can specify multiple recipients by separating each address with a semicolon (;).

Use the Subject field to enter a brief description of the message, and then use the box below the Subject field to enter your message. To send your message, you have two choices:

- Select File, Send Message (or press Alt+S)—This tells Outlook Express to send the message out to the Internet right away.

- Select File, Send Later—This command tells Outlook Express to store the message in the Outbox folder. If you choose this route, Outlook Express displays a dialog box telling you that your message is stored in the Outbox folder. Click OK. When you're ready to send the message, select the Tools, Send and Receive, Send All command in the Outlook Express window.

## Taking Control of Your Messages

Outlook Express offers many more options for composing messages than the simple steps outlined in the previous section. Here's a summary of the other features and techniques you can use to modify your outgoing messages:

- Choosing the message format—Pull down the Format menu and select either Rich Text (HTML) or Plain Text. If you select the HTML sending format, use any of the formatting options found on the Format menu or the Formatting toolbar. Remember, however, that not all systems will transfer the rich text formatting.

- Setting the message priority—Select Tools, Set Priority, and then choose the level—High, Normal, or Low—from the submenu that appears. Alternatively, drop down the Priority toolbar list and then click the level you want.

- Attaching a file—Select Insert, File Attachment, or click the Attach toolbar button, use the Insert Attachment dialog box to select a file, and then click Attach. Outlook Express adds an Attach box below the Subject line and displays the name and size of the file. To remove the attachment, click it in the Attach box and then press Delete.

---

**TIP**

Another way to attach a file to a message is to drag the file from Windows Explorer and drop it in the body of the message.

---

- Inserting a file into the message—Depending on the type of object you want to work with, Outlook Express gives you two methods of inserting objects:

| | |
|---|---|
| Inserting file text | If you have text in a separate file that you want to add to the message, select the Insert, Text from File command. In the Insert Text File dialog box that appears, select the file and then click Open. Outlook Express adds the file's contents to the message. |
| Inserting an image | To insert an image file into the message, select Insert, Picture. In the Picture dialog box that appears, use the Picture Source text box to enter the path and filename (or click Browse). |

- Applying stationery—Email stationery is a predefined message format that includes a background image and text. This is essentially a web page to which you can also add your own text. You choose a stationery by selecting the Format, Apply Stationery command, and then picking out the stationery you want from the submenu that appears. Note that you can also begin a message with a specific stationery by selecting the Message, New Message Using command in Outlook Express and then selecting the stationery. (Alternatively, drop down the Create Mail toolbar list and click the stationery you want.)

**Working with Stationery**

To set a default stationery, select Tools, Options and then display the Compose tab. In the Stationery group, activate the Mail check box and then click the Select button to the right of that check box. Use the Select Stationery dialog box to choose the default stationery and then click OK. Note that the stationery files are HTML files, so if you know how to create your own web pages, you can also create your own stationery. Another way to create stationery is to click Create New in the Compose tab. (This button is also available in the Select Stationery dialog box.) This launches the Stationery Setup Wizard that takes you through the steps required to create a custom stationery.

- Inserting a signature—A **signature** is text that appears at the bottom of a message. Most people use a signature to provide their email and web addresses, their company contact information, and perhaps a snappy quote or epigram that reflects their personality. If you've defined a signature (see the next section), you can insert it into the body of the message at the current cursor position by selecting Insert, Signature. If you've defined multiple signatures, select the one you want from the submenu that appears.

- Requesting a read receipt—To ask the recipient's email client to send you a read receipt, select the Tools, Request Read Receipt command. Note that you can also set up Outlook Express to request a read receipt for all outgoing messages. In the Outlook Express window, select Tools, Options and then display the Receipts tab. Activate the Request a Read Receipt for All Sent Messages check box, and then click OK.

- Digitally signing or encrypting a message—I cover these options in Chapter 21.

## Creating a Signature

As I mentioned in the previous section, a signature is a few lines of text that provide contact information and other data. Outlook Express enables you to define a signature and then have it appended to the bottom of every outgoing message (or you can insert it by hand in individual messages). To do this, you must first follow these steps to define a signature:

1. In the main Outlook Express window, select Tools, Options to open the Options dialog box.

2. Display the Signatures tab.

3. Click New to add a new signature to the Signatures list.

4. The default name for each new signature (such as Signature #1) is not very informative. To define a new name, click the signature, click Rename, type the new name, and then press Enter.

5. You now have two choices:

| Type the signature text by hand | Activate the Text option and then type your signature in the box provided. |
| Get the signature from a text file | Activate the File option and then enter the full path to the file in the box provided. (Or click Browse to choose the file from a dialog box.) |

6. If you want Outlook Express to add the signature to all of your messages, activate the Add Signatures to All Outgoing Messages check box.

7. If you'd rather use the signature only on original messages, leave the Don't Add Signature to Replies and Forwards check box activated.

8. The default signature is the one that's added automatically if you activated the Add Signatures to All Outgoing Messages check box. To set a signature as the default, select it in the Signatures list and then click Set as Default.

9. To associate a signature with one or more accounts, select the signature in the Signatures list and then click Advanced. In the Advanced Signature Settings dialog box, activate the check box beside each account that you want to use the signature. Click OK.

10. Click OK to put the signature options into effect.

## Creating an Email Shortcut for a Recipient

If you don't leave Outlook Express open all day, when you need to send a message it can seem like a lot of work to start the program, compose the new message, send it, and then close Outlook Express. You can save yourself a couple of steps by creating an email shortcut on your desktop or in a folder such as Quick Launch for a particular recipient. When you open the shortcut, a new email message window appears, already addressed to the recipient. You then fill in the rest of the message and send it, all without starting Outlook Express.

Follow these steps to create an email shortcut:

1. Display the desktop or open the folder in which you want to create the shortcut.

2. Right-click the desktop or folder and then select New, Shortcut. The Create Shortcut dialog box appears.

3. In the text box, type the following (where *address* is the email address of the recipient; see the example in Figure 19.5):

    ```
    mailto:address
    ```

**FIGURE 19.5**   Type **mailto:*address*** to create an email shortcut for an email recipient.

**4.** Click Next.

**5.** Type a title for the shortcut (such as the person's name or email address).

**6.** Click Finish.

## Setting Send Options

Outlook Express offers a number of options for sending email. Select Tools, Options, and in the Options dialog box that appears, display the Send tab, shown in Figure 19.6.

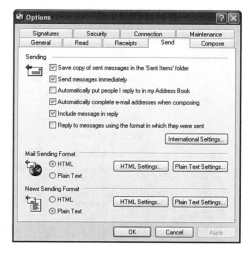

**FIGURE 19.6**   Outlook Express's options for sending email.

Here's a quick rundown of the options in the Sending group:

| | |
|---|---|
| Save Copy of Sent Messages in the 'Sent Items' Folder | When this check box is activated, Outlook Express saves a copy of each message you send in the Sent Items folder. It's a good idea to leave this option checked because it gives you a record of the messages you send. |
| Send Messages Immediately | When this check box is activated, Outlook Express passes your message to the SMTP server as soon as you click the Send button. If you deactivate this option, clicking the Send button when composing a message only stores that message in the Outbox folder. This is useful if you have a number of messages to compose and you use a dial-up connection to the Internet. That is, you could compose all your messages offline and store them in the Outbox folder. You could then connect to the Internet and send all your messages at once. |
| Automatically Put People I Reply to in My Address Book | When this option is activated, each time you reply to a message Outlook Express takes the recipient's name and email address and adds them to your Address Book. This only serves to clutter your Address Book with names you'll never or rarely use, so I recommend deactivating this check box. |
| Automatically Complete E-Mail Addresses When Composing | When this check box is activated, Outlook Express monitors the email addresses you enter when composing a message. If you've entered a similar address before, the program will complete the rest of the address automatically. |
| Include Message in Reply | When this check box is activated, Outlook Express includes the original message text as part of the new message when you reply to or forward a message. This is a good idea because including the original message text serves as a reminder to the original author of what you're responding to. |

**TIP**

Including the original message text in replies is useful, but you should rarely have to include the entire reply. It's good email etiquette to delete unnecessary parts of the original message; keep only the text that applies directly to your response.

Reply to Messages Using the Format in Which They Were Sent

When this check box is activated, Outlook Express automatically selects either the HTML or Plain Text sending format depending on the format used in the original message. If you'd prefer to always use your default sending format, deactivate this check box.

The Mail Sending Format group contains two options buttons that determine whether your messages contain formatting: HTML and Plain Text. If you activate the HTML button, Outlook Express enables you to apply a number of formatting options to your messages. In effect, your message becomes a miniature web page and can be formatted in much the same way that a web page can. Note, however, that this formatting will be visible only to recipients who have an HTML-enabled mail client. Clicking the HTML Settings button beside the HTML option displays the HTML Settings dialog box, shown in Figure 19.7.

**FIGURE 19.7**   Use this dialog box to work with settings associated with the HTML sending format.

Here's a synopsis of the available options:

Encode Text Using

SMTP supports only 7-bit ASCII data, so binary messages or messages that include full 8-bit values (such as foreign characters), must be encoded. This list determines how (or whether) Outlook Express encodes message text:

- None—Tells Outlook Express not to encode the text.
- Quoted Printable—Use this encoding if your messages have full 8-bit values. This encoding converts each of these characters into an equal sign (=) followed by the character's hexadecimal representation. This ensures SMTP compatibility. (Note that most 7-bit ASCII characters are not encoded.)
- Base 64—Use this encoding if your message contains binary data. This encoding uses the Base64 alphabet, which is a set of 64 character/value pairs: A through Z is 0 through 25; a through z is 26 through 51; 0 through 9 is 52 through 61; + is 62 and / is 63. All other characters are ignored.

| | |
|---|---|
| Allow 8-Bit Characters in Headers | When this check box is activated, characters that require eight bits—including ASCII 128 or higher, foreign character sets, and double-byte character sets—will be allowed within the message header without being encoded. If you leave this check box deactivated, these characters are encoded. |
| Send Pictures with Messages | When this check box is activated, any pictures embedded in the message or used as the message background will be sent along with the message text. |
| Indent Message on Reply | When this check box is activated and you reply to a message, Outlook Express displays the original message indented below your reply. |
| Automatically Wrap Text at *X* Characters, When Sending | This spin box determines the point at which Outlook Express wraps text onto a new line. Many Internet systems can't read lines longer than 80 characters, so you shouldn't select a value higher than that. Note that the Quoted Printable and Base 64 encoding schemes require 76-character lines, so this option is available only if you select None in the Encode Text Using list. |

If you activate the Plain Text option instead, Outlook Express sends your message as regular text, without any formatting. Clicking the Plain Text Settings button displays the Plain Text Settings dialog box, shown in Figure 19.8.

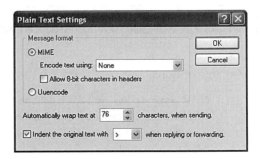

**FIGURE 19.8**    Use this dialog box to work with settings associated with the Plain Text sending format.

This dialog box includes many of the same options as the HTML Settings dialog box shown earlier. Here's what's different:

| | |
|---|---|
| MIME | **MIME** stands **for Multipurpose Internet Mail Extensions** and it's the standard encoding format for text-based messages. Each of the encoding options I discussed above is MIME-based. |
| Uuencode | This is an older encoding format that is primarily used when sending binary files to newsgroups. |

| Indent the Original Text with > When Replying or Forwarding | It's standard on the Internet that original message text in a plain text reply be indicated with a greater than sign (>) at the beginning of each line. (Colons are also sometimes used.) When this check box is activated, Outlook Express prefaces each line of the original message with whatever character you specify in the list. |
| --- | --- |

## Maintaining Outlook Express

For the most part, Outlook Express is a set-it-and-forget-it application. After the program and your accounts have been set up, you can just go about your email business with worrying about Outlook Express itself. However, to ensure trouble-free and worry-free operation, here's a list of a few maintenance chores you should perform from time-to-time:

- Remove clutter from your inbox—Few things in business life are more daunting and frustrating than an inbox bursting at the seams with a huge list of new or unprocessed messages. To prevent this from happening, you should regard the Inbox folder as just a temporary holding area for all your incoming messages. Periodically throughout the day, you should perform the following routine to keep your Inbox clean:

    If a message doesn't require a response, file it or delete it. Note that by *file it,* I mean move it to some other folder. You should have folders set up for all major recipients, projects, customers, or categories that you deal with.

    If a message requires a response and you can answer it without further research or without taking a lot of time, answer it immediately and then either delete or file the message.

    If a message requires a response but you can't send a reply right away, move the message to a folder designated for messages that require further action. You can then handle those messages later in the day when you have some time.

---

**TIP**

Before moving the message to whatever you've designated as your "action items" folder, be sure to mark the message as unread. That way you'll be able to see at a glance whether there are items in that folder and how many there are.

---

- Clean out your Deleted Items folder—This folder is a good safeguard to help you recover accidentally deleted messages. However, after a while it's extremely unlikely that you'll need to recover a message from this folder. Therefore, you should regularly delete messages from the Deleted Items folder. I recommend leaving the last two weeks' worth of deleted messages and deleting everything older.

19

- Keep your spam filters up to date—I'll show you how to filter out spam messages in Chapter 21 (see the section titled "Filtering Out Spam"). Unfortunately, new spam messages appear every day. When you start to see repeats—the same message, the same subject line phrase, the same sender, and so on—update your filters to block the new messages.

- Look for Outlook Express patches and updates—Pay a visit to Windows Update to see whether Microsoft has released any security patches or updates for Outlook Express.

- Back up your messages—Outlook Express keeps your messages in various **message stores**, each of which is a `.dbx` file that holds the messages contained in a folder. For example, the Inbox folder messages are kept in a file named `Inbox.dbx`. You'll find these message stores in the following folder

  ```
  %UserProfile%\Local Settings\Application Data\Identities\CLSID\Microsoft\
  Outlook Express
  ```

  Here, *CLSID* is a 32-digit class ID that Outlook Express generated for your default Outlook Express identity. You should include the contents of this folder in your backups and run those backups regularly.

  ---

  **TIP**

  You can change the location of the message stores. In Outlook Express, select Tools, Options and then display the Maintenance tab. Click the Store Folder button and, in the Store Location dialog box, click Change. Use the Browse for Folder dialog box to choose the new location, and then click OK. Note, too, that the Outlook Express store location is held in the following Registry setting (where *CLSID* is your 32-digit identity number for Outlook Express):

  ```
  HKCU\Identities\CLSID\Software\Microsoft\Outlook Express\5.0\Store Root
  ```

  ---

- Back up your addresses—You should also include your Address Book in your backups. The Address Book's file name is *User*.wab, where *User* is your username, and it's stored in the following folder:

  ```
  %AppData%\Microsoft\Address Book
  ```

  ---

  **NOTE**

  The `%AppData%` environment variable refers to the `Application Data` folder for the current user:

  ```
  %UserProfile%\Application Data
  ```

  ---

- Back up your accounts—If you have multiple accounts, re-creating them on a new system or in the event of a crash can be a lot of work. To lessen the drudgery, make backups of your accounts by saving them to Internet Account Files (`.iaf` extension). In Outlook Express, select Tools, Accounts and then display the Mail tab. Select an account and then click Export. In the Export Internet Account dialog box, choose a location and then click Save. Note that you can also do this with News and Directory Service accounts.

---

**TIP**

An even easier way to back up your accounts is to export the following Registry key:

`HKCU\Software\Microsoft\Internet Account Manager\Accounts`

Here you'll find subkeys for each of your Outlook Express accounts (usually named `00000001`, `00000002`, and so on).

---

- Back up your Outlook Express data—Your defined Outlook Express rules, signatures, and settings are stored in the following Registry key:

  `HKCU\Identities\`*`CLSID`*`\Software\Microsoft\Outlook Express\5.0\Store Root`

  Again, *CLSID* is your 32-digit identity number for Outlook Express. Regularly export this key to save this important Outlook Express data.

- Compact your folders—When you move or delete messages, Outlook Express removes the corresponding data from the corresponding message store (`.dbx` file). This results in gaps within the file. To remove these gaps and reduce the size of the file, you need to compact the folder. To do this, select the folder in Outlook Express and then select File, Folder, Compact. If you've been moving and deleting messages from a number of folders, you can get Outlook Express to compact all your folders in one pass by selecting the File, Folder, Compact All Folders command.

# Filtering Incoming Messages

Just a couple of years ago, my email chores took up only a few minutes of each workday. Now it takes me up to two or three hours to get through the hundreds of messages I receive every day. What's interesting about this is that it's by no means unusual. Most people find that when they really get into Internet email, the messages really start to pile up quickly.

To help ease the crunch, Outlook Express offers **mail rules**. You can set up these rules to handle incoming messages for you automatically. Of course, these rules are limited in what they can do, but what they *can* do isn't bad:

- If you'll be out of the office for a few days or if you'll be on vacation, you can create a rule to mail out an automatic reply that lets the sender know you received the message but won't be able to deal with it for a while.

- If you have multiple email accounts, you can set up a rule to redirect incoming messages into separate folders for each account.

One of the problems with redirecting messages to other folders is that it's less convenient to read those messages. Outlook Express helps by bolding the name of any folder that contains unread messages. (It also tells you how many unread messages are in each folder.) Outlook Express also opens the folder tree to reveal any folders that have unread messages. (To make sure that this option is turned on, select Tools, Options and, in the General tab, check that the `Automatically display folders with unread messages` setting is activated.)

- You can create a rule to redirect incoming messages into separate folders for specific people, projects, or mailing lists.

- If you receive unwanted messages from a particular source (such as a spammer), you can set up a rule to automatically delete those messages. I take you through some specific anti-spam rules in Chapter 21.

## Blocking Senders

For the latter, note that Outlook Express also comes with a Blocked Senders list. If you put an address on this list, Outlook Express watches for messages from that address and deletes them automatically. To use this feature, follow these steps:

1. Select a message that comes from the address you want to block.

2. Select Message, Block Sender. Outlook Express adds the address to the Blocked Senders list and asks whether you want to delete all messages from that address.

3. Click Yes to delete the messages, or click No to leave them.

To view the Blocked Senders list, select Tools, Message Rules, Blocked Senders List. Outlook Express opens the Message Rules dialog box and displays the Blocked Senders tab. From here, you can add another blocked sender, or modify or delete an existing blocked sender.

## Creating a Mail Rule

For more general situations, you need to set up mail rules. Here's how it works:

1. Select the Tools, Message Rules, Mail command. Outlook Express displays the New Mail Rule dialog box.

2. In the Select the Conditions for Your Rule list, activate the check box beside the rule condition you want to use to pick out a message from the herd. Outlook Express adds the condition to the Rule Description text box. Note that you're free to select multiple conditions.

3. The condition shown in the Rule Description text box will probably have some underlined text. You need to replace that underlined text with the specific criterion you want to use (such as a word or an address). To do that, click the underlined

text, type the criterion in the dialog box that appears and click Add. Most conditions support multiple criteria (such as multiple addresses or multiple words in a Subject line), so repeat this step as necessary. When you're done, click OK. Outlook Express updates the Rule Description text box with the text you entered, as shown in Figure 19.9.

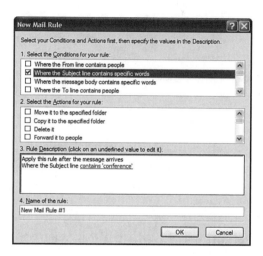

**FIGURE 19.9**   Click underlined text in the Rule Description text box to edit the text to the criterion you want for your rule.

> **TIP**
>
> If you add multiple words or phrases to a rule criterion, you can make that criterion use Boolean operators such as AND, OR, and NOT. To do this, click the Options button in the dialog box that appears in step 3. To make an AND criterion, activate Message Matches All of the X Below (where X depends on the condition—for example, *words* or *people*); to make an OR criterion, activate Message Matches Any One of the X Below; to make a NOT criterion, activate Message Does Not Contain the X Below.

4. In the Select the Actions for your rule list, activate the check box beside the action you want Outlook Express to take with messages that meet your criteria. Again, you might have to click underlined text in the Rule Description text box to complete the action. Also, you can select multiple actions.

5. If you selected multiple conditions, Outlook Express assumes that all the conditions must be true before invoking the rule (Boolean AND). To change this, click and in the Rule Description text box, activate the Messages Match Any One of the Criteria option, and click OK.

6. Use the Name of the Rule text box to type a descriptive name for the rule.

7. Click OK. Outlook Express drops you off at the Mail Rules tab of the Message Rules dialog box.

Whichever method you used, here are a few notes to bear in mind when working with the list of rules:

- **Toggling rules on and off**—Use the check box beside each rule to turn the rule on and off.

- **Setting rule order**—Some rules should be processed before others. For example, if you have a rule that deletes spam, you want Outlook Express to process that rule before sending out a vacation reply. To adjust the order of a rule, select it and then click either Move Up or Move Down.

- **Modifying a rule**—To edit a rule, select it and click Modify.

- **Applying a rule**—If you want to apply a rule to existing inbox messages or to messages in a different folder, click Apply Now. Select the rule you want to apply (or click Select All to apply them all). To choose a different folder, click Browse. When you're ready, click Apply Now.

- **Deleting a rule**—Select the rule and click Remove. When Outlook Express asks whether you're sure, click Yes.

# Finding a Message

Although you'll delete many of the messages that come your way, it's unlikely that you'll delete all of them. So, over time, you'll probably end up with hundreds or more likely thousands, of messages stored throughout various folders. What happens if you want to find a particular message? Even if you curmudgeonly delete everything that comes your way, your Sent Items folder will still eventually contain copies of the hundreds or thousands of missives you've shipped out. What if you want to find one of those messages?

For both incoming and outgoing messages, Outlook Express offers a decent Find Message feature that can look for messages based on addresses, subject lines, body text, dates, and more.

## Simple Searches

If you're not fussy about what part of the message Find uses to look for a particular word, and if you already know which folder holds the message you want, Outlook Express offers a simplified Find feature for quick-and-dirty searches. Here are the steps to follow:

1. Use the Folders list to select the folder in which you want to search.

2. Select Edit, Find, Message in this Folder. (Alternatively, either press Shift+F3 or pull down the Find toolbar list and select Message in this Folder.) Outlook Express displays the Find dialog box shown in Figure 19.10.

**FIGURE 19.10**    Use the Find dialog box to perform simple searches within a folder.

3. Use the Look For text box to type a word or two that you want to use as the search criteria. Find will look in the From, To, and Subject fields for the search text. If you also want Find to look in the body of the messages, activate the Search All the Text in Downloaded Messages check box.

> **NOTE**
>
> When entering your search criteria, bear in mind that if you include multiple words, Find will match only messages that contain *all* the words. Also, Find matches only whole words, so it won't match partial words, and the search is not case sensitive.

4. Click Find Next. Find examines the messages and, if it locates a match, it selects the message.

5. If this isn't the message you're looking for, select Edit, Find, Next. (You can also either press F3 or pull down the Find toolbar list and select Next.)

## Advanced Searches

If you want to search specific message fields, if you want to specify different criteria for each field, or if you want to include specialized criteria such as the message date or whether a message has attachments, you need to use the full-fledged Find Message feature.

To try it out, you have two ways to get started:

- Select the Edit, Find, Message command. (The alternatives are to press Ctrl+Shift+F or to click the Find toolbar button.)

- If you have the Find dialog box displayed, click the Advanced Find button.

Figure 19.11 shows the Find Message dialog box that appears. Use the following controls to set the search criteria:

| | |
|---|---|
| Browse | Select the folder to search. If you want the search to include the subfolders of the selected folder, leave the Include Subfolders check box activated. |
| From | Type one or more words that specify the email address or display the name of the sender you want to find. |

**19**

As with Find, the individual Find Message criteria match only those messages that contain *all* the words you enter, match only whole words, and are not case sensitive. Note, too, that Find Message only looks for messages that match all the criteria you enter.

The Find Message feature in Outlook Express is quite slow, particularly if you have a message store with thousands of messages. If you search for messages frequently, there are third-party tools available that can search your email much faster. A good choice is Google Desktop Search (desktop.google.com).

| | |
|---|---|
| To | Type one or more words that specify the email address or display name of the recipient you want to find. |
| Subject | Type one or more words that specify the Subject line you want to find. |
| Message | Type one or more words that specify the message body you want to find. |
| Received Before | Select the latest received date for the message you want to find. |
| Received After | Select the earliest received date for the message you want to find. |
| Message Has Attachment(s) | Activate this check box to find only messages that have attached files. |
| Message Is Flagged | Activate this check box to find only messages that have been flagged. |

**FIGURE 19.11**    Use the Find Message dialog box to look for specific messages in a folder.

After you've defined your search criteria, click Find Now. If Outlook Express finds any matches, it displays them in a message list at the bottom of the dialog box. From here, you can open a message or use any of the commands in the menus to work with the messages (reply, forward, move to another folder, delete, and so on).

# Finding a Person

In an effort to create a kind of white pages for the Internet, a number of companies have set up **directory servers** that contain databases of names and email addresses. Using a standard Internet protocol called the **Lightweight Directory Access Protocol** (**LDAP**), email clients and other programs can use these directory servers to perform simple searches for names and addresses.

Outlook Express supports LDAP and is set up to provide ready access to several of the most popular directory servers. To see the complete list, select Tools, Accounts and then display the Directory Service tab. If your company runs its own directory server, you can add it to this list by clicking Add, Directory Service and following the Internet Connection Wizard's dialog boxes.

To perform a search on a directory server or to search the Windows Address Book, follow these steps:

1. Select the Edit, Find, People command. (Alternatively, press Ctrl+E or pull down the Find toolbar list and select People.) Outlook Express displays the Find People dialog box.

2. Use the Look In list to select either Address Book (to search the Windows Address Book) or a directory service.

> **NOTE**
>
> To get more information about the selected directory service, click the Web Site button to open the service's home page in Internet Explorer. Note, too, that in most cases you can use the website to add your own name and address to the service.

3. You have two searching options:

    - If you know the name of a person and want to find out his or her email address, use the Name text box to type the person's name. (You can enter the exact name or a partial name.)

    - If you know the email address of a person and want to find out his or her name, use the E-mail text box to type the person's exact email address.

4. Click Find Now. Outlook Express accesses the directory server and runs the query. If the server reports any matches, they're displayed at the bottom of the dialog box.

# Working with Identities

Sharing a computer with colleagues or family members is problematic on many levels. For example, one person's soothing wallpaper might be another person's constant eyesore, and a younger person's high resolution screen might be an older person's text-too-tiny-to-read squintfest.

19

These sorts of cosmetic differences can be overcome with compromises or, in a pinch, by setting up different users (as I described in Chapter 6, "Getting the Most Out of User Accounts"). Even better, each user gets her own set of Outlook Express email accounts and folders, so logging on to your own user account means that you see only your own email accounts, Outlook Express folders, and messages.

If you can't or won't set up separate user accounts (if, for example, you don't want the hassle of logging off and logging on, or if you don't have the permissions to create user accounts), you can still share a single copy of Outlook Express. You do this by using a feature called **identities**, and it works much like the user accounts feature in Windows. That is, you configure Outlook Express so that each person using it has their own identity. Only one person can be logged on to Outlook Express at a time, and that person sees only his own accounts and his own folders. For extra protection, each identity can be protected by a password.

## Creating a New Identity

Outlook Express already has a default identity in place, and it's called **Main Identity** (I show you how to rename identities a bit later). Follow these steps to set up another identity:

1. Select File, Identities, Add New Identity. Outlook Express displays the New Identity dialog box.

2. Type the name of the new identity in the Type Your Name text box.

3. To protect the identity with a password, activate the Require a Password check box. Outlook Express displays the Enter Password dialog box. Type the password in both the New Password and Confirm New Password text boxes, and then click OK to return to the New Identity dialog box.

4. Click OK. Outlook Express asks whether you want to switch to the new identity.

5. Click Yes. Outlook Express closes, restarts, and launches the Internet Connection Wizard to set up the initial account for the new identity.

6. Run through the wizard's dialog boxes as described earlier in this chapter (refer to "Setting Up Mail Accounts").

When the wizard is complete, you're dropped off at the Outlook Express window, which is logged on to the new identity. To reiterate, being logged on to an identity means the following:

- Only that identity's accounts are available.

- Only that identity's messages and folders are visible.

- Only that identity's contacts are listed in the Address Book and Contacts list.

> **TIP**
>
> Although the logged-on identity sees only its contacts, it's possible to share contacts among identities. In the Address Book, add the contacts you want to share to the Shared Contacts folder. For contacts that already exist, drag them from the identity's Address Book and drop them on the Shared Contacts folder.

- That identity can customize Outlook Express and the new settings will affect only that identity's version of the program.

## Switching Identities

To switch from one identity to another, follow these steps:

1. Select File, Switch Identity. The Switch Identities dialog box appears.

2. Use the list of identities to select the one you want to use.

3. Use the Password text box to enter the identity's password, if applicable.

4. Click OK. Outlook Express closes and then restarts with the chosen identity logged on.

> **NOTE**
>
> How do you know which identity is currently logged on? The easiest way to tell is to look at the Outlook Express title bar. For example, if the Inbox folder is currently displayed, the title bar will say Inbox - Outlook Express - *Identity*, where *Identity* is the name of the current identity.

## Managing Identities

If you need to change the name or password for an identity, delete an identity, or perform some other identity maintenance, follow these steps:

1. Select File, Identities, Manage Identities. (Alternatively, click the Manage Identities button in the Switch Identities dialog box.) Outlook Express displays the Manage Identities dialog box, shown in Figure 19.12.

2. Use the Identities list to select the identity you want to work with.

3. In addition to the New button (which enables you to create a new identity from here), there are two other command buttons available:

| | |
|---|---|
| Remove | Click this button to delete the selected identity. Note that you can't delete the Main Identity. |
| Properties | Click this button to change the selected identity's name or password. |

19

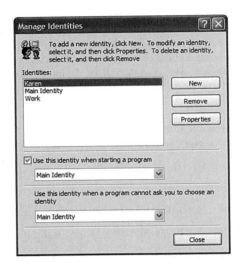

**FIGURE 19.12**   Use the Manage Identities dialog box to make changes to your Outlook Express identities.

4. Other programs might also be identity-aware (an example is the Windows Messenger program that ships with Windows XP). To determine which identity is logged on when you start those programs, make sure that the Use This Identity When Starting a Program check box is activated, and then use the drop-down list to choose which identity you want logged on.

5. If an identity-ignorant program needs to request that Outlook Express create a new email message, the program won't be able to ask you (or Outlook Express) which identity to use. For these situations, pick out the default identity from the Use This Identity When a Program Cannot Ask You to Choose an Identity list.

6. Click Close.

## Logging Off Your Identity

As a convenience, Outlook Express leaves you logged on to your identity when you exit the program in the usual way (that is, by selecting File, Exit or by pressing Alt+F4). This means Outlook Express uses your identity the next time you start the program.

However, if someone else starts the program in the meantime, they'll be logged on to your identity and will have access to all your accounts and messages. That obviously defeats the purpose of identities. To prevent this from happening, always *log off* your identity when you shut down Outlook Express. You do that by selecting File, Exit and Log Off Identity.

> **NOTE**
>
> Another way to log off Outlook Express is to select File, Switch Identities and then click the Log Off Identity button in the Switch Identities dialog box.

The next time you (or anyone else) launches Outlook Express, the first thing that appears is the Identity Login dialog box. Select the identity you want to use, type a password, if necessary, and click OK.

### Identities—Storage Locations and the Registry

I mentioned earlier that Outlook Express maintains a `.dbx` file for each folder. To see these files, first go to the following folder:

`%UserProfile%\Local Settings\Application Data\Identities`

Here you find a subfolder for each Outlook Express identity. Unfortunately, the folder names are obscure 32-character user IDs that bear no resemblance to the identity name. How do you know which folder applies to which identity (say, for backup purposes)? The only way to tell is to head for the following Registry key:

`HKEY_CURRENT_USER\Identities`

There you find subkeys that use the same 32-character user IDs. Select the subkey you want and then look for the `Username` setting, which tells you the identity name. When you know which folder is which, open it and head for the `Microsoft\Outlook Express` subfolder, which is where the `.dbx` files are stored.

## From Here

Here's a list of chapters where you'll find related information:

- For information on user accounts, refer to Chapter 6, "Getting the Most Out of User Accounts."

- To learn other ways to communicate with Windows XP, refer to Chapter 16, "Putting Your Modem to Work."

- You can also use Outlook Express as a newsreader. For the details, see Chapter 20, "Participating in Internet Newsgroups."

- For information on Outlook Express security and privacy issues, see Chapter 21, "Implementing Windows XP's Internet Security and Privacy Features."

19

# Participating in Internet Newsgroups

The vast majority of the attention, buzz, and hype about the Internet is centered on the World Wide Web. That's not surprising because it's the easiest Net service for novices to use, and it's where all the cutting-edge development is taking place. The rest of the Internet services fall into two categories: those that have fallen into disuse (anybody remember Gopher?) and those that just keep on keeping on.

A good example of the latter type of service is Usenet. Usenet is, in essence, a collection of topics available for discussion. These discussion groups (or **newsgroups**, as they're normally called) are open to all and sundry, and they usually won't cost you a dime (aside from the usual connection charges, of course; note, too, that some ISPs charge extra for newsgroup access).

Will you find anything interesting in these discussion groups? Well, let's put it this with way: With more than 100,000 (that's right, one hundred *thousand*) groups to choose from, if you can't find anything that strikes your fancy, you'd better check your pulse. (Not all service providers offer the complete menu of Usenet groups, so the number available to you might be considerably less than 100,000.) On the other hand, most of Usenet has no central control, which means that many newsgroups have degenerated into a collection of rambling, off-topic posts and unsolicited commercial email. (One wag has likened Usenet to a *verbal landfill*.) Not all groups are this bad, but you'll need to be cautious when choosing which discussions you join.

In this chapter, I'll now turn your attention (if I may) to the Usenet service. I'll give you some background about Usenet, and then I'll show you how to wield the newsreader portion of the Outlook Express show.

> **NOTE**
>
> Usenet began its life back in 1979 at Duke University. A couple of resident computer whizzes (James Elliot and Tom Truscott) needed a way to easily share research, knowledge, and smart-aleck opinions among Duke students and faculty. So, in true hacker fashion, they built a program that would do just that. Eventually, other universities joined in, and the thing just mushroomed. Today, tens of millions of people participate in Usenet, sending hundreds of thousands of messages a day.

## Some Usenet Basics

To get your Usenet education off on the right foot, this section looks at a few crucial concepts that will serve as the base from which you can explore the rest of Usenet:

| | |
|---|---|
| **article** | An individual message in a newsgroup discussion. |
| **follow up** | To respond to an article. (Also: **follow-up**; the response itself.) |
| **hierarchy** | Usenet divides its discussion groups into several classifications, or *hierarchies*. There are several so-called **mainstream** hierarchies: |

| | |
|---|---|
| biz | Business |
| comp | Computer hardware and software |
| misc | Miscellaneous stuff that doesn't really fit anywhere else |
| news | Usenet-related topics |
| rec | Entertainment, hobbies, sports, and more |
| sci | Science and technology |
| soc | Sex, culture, religion, and politics |
| talk | Debates about controversial political and cultural topics |

Most Usenet-equipped Internet service providers will give you access to all the mainstream hierarchies. There's also a huge alt (alternative) hierarchy that covers just about anything that either doesn't belong in a mainstream hierarchy or is too wacky to be included with the mainstream groups. There are also many smaller hierarchies designed for specific geographic areas. For example, the ba hierarchy includes discussion groups for the San Francisco Bay area, the can hierarchy is devoted to Canadian topics, and so on.

| | |
|---|---|
| **newsgroup** | This is the official Usenet moniker for a discussion topic. Why are they called newsgroups? Well, the original Duke University system was designed to share announcements, research findings, and commentary. In other words, people would use this system if they had some "news" to share with their |

colleagues. The name stuck, and now you'll often hear Usenet referred to as **Netnews** or simply as **the news**.

**newsreader**    The software you use to read a newsgroup's articles and to post your own articles. In Windows XP, you can use Outlook Express as a newsreader. Other Windows newsreaders include Agent (www.forteinc.com/agent/) and NewsPro (www.netwu.com/newspro/). For the Mac, you can try Microsoft Entourage, part of the Office 2004 suite, or MT-NewsWatcher (www.smfr.org/mtnw/).

> **NOTE**
>
> Instead of using a newsreader, you can access all the newsgroups through your web browser by using Google Groups (groups.google.com). This is useful if your ISP does not offer newsgroup access or if you would like to read particular newsgroups without having to subscribe to them. However, if you want to post messages to a newsgroup, you must register with Google.

**news server**
**(or NNTP server)**    A computer that stores newsgroups and handles requests to post and download newsgroup messages. There are four types of news server:

- ISP news server—Most ISPs supply you with an account on their news server in addition to your email account. Your news server username and password are almost always the same as your email username and password, but check with your ISP. You should also confirm the Internet name of the ISP's news server. This name usually takes the form news.*ispname*.com or nntp.*ispname*.com, where *ispname* is the name of your ISP.

- Commercial news server—If your ISP does not offer newsgroup access, or if your ISP offers only a limited number of groups, consider using a commercial news server, which offers newsgroup access for a fee. Two of the largest commercial news servers are Giganews (www.giganews.com) and Newscene (www.newscene.com).

- Public news server—If you are on a limited budget, try a public news server that offers free newsgroup access. Note, however, that most public servers restrict the number of users on the server, offer a limited number of groups, or place a cap on the amount you can download. For a list of public news servers, try Newzbot (www.newzbot.com) or Free Usenet News Servers (freenews.maxbaud.net).

- Semi-private news server—Some companies maintain their own news server and their own set of newsgroups. For example, Microsoft maintains a news server at msnews.microsoft.com that runs more than 2,000 groups related to Microsoft products and technologies.

**post**    To send an article to a newsgroup.

20

subscribe                In a newsreader, to add a newsgroup to the list of groups you want to read.
                         If you no longer want to read the group, you unsubscribe from the group.

thread                   A series of articles related to the same subject line. A thread always begins
                         with an original article and then progresses through one or more follow-ups.

## Figuring Out Newsgroup Names

Newsgroup names aren't too hard to understand, but we need to go through the drill to make sure that you're comfortable with them. In their basic guise, newsgroup names have three parts: the hierarchy to which they belong, followed by a dot, followed by the newsgroup's topic. For example, check out the following name:

rec.boats

Here, the hierarchy is rec (recreation), and the topic is boats. Sounds simple enough so far. But many newsgroups were too broad for some people, so they started breaking the newsgroups into subgroups. For example, the rec.boats people who were into canoeing got sick of speedboat discussions, so they created their own *paddle* newsgroup. Here's how its official name looks:

rec.boats.paddle

You'll see lots of these subgroups in your Usenet travels. (For example, there are also newsgroups named rec.boats.building and rec.boats.racing.) Occasionally, you'll see sub-subgroups, such as soc.culture.african.american, but these are still rare in most hierarchies (the exception is the comp hierarchy, in which you'll find all kinds of these sub-subgroups).

## Understanding Articles and Threads

Articles, as you can imagine, are the lifeblood of Usenet. As I mentioned earlier, every day hundreds of thousands of articles are posted to the different newsgroups. Some newsgroups might get only one or two articles a day, but many get a dozen or two, on average. (And some very popular groups—rec.humor is a good example—can get a hundred or more postings in a day.)

Happily, Usenet places no restrictions on article content. (However, a few newsgroups have **moderators** who decide whether an article is worth posting.) Unlike, say, the heavily censored America Online chat rooms, Usenet articles are the epitome of free speech. Articles can be as long or short as you like (although extremely long articles are frowned on because they take so long to retrieve), and they can contain whatever ideas, notions, and thoughts you feel like getting off your chest (within the confines of the newsgroup's subject matter). You're free to be inquiring, informative, interesting, infuriating, or even incompetent—it's entirely up to you. (Although see the section "Practicing Newsgroup Etiquette" later in this chapter.)

Earlier I told you that newsgroups were *discussion topics*, but that doesn't mean they work like a real-world discussion, where you have immediate conversational give and take.

Instead, newsgroup discussions lurch ahead in discrete chunks (articles) and unfold over a relatively long period (sometimes even weeks or months).

To get the flavor of a newsgroup discussion, think of the Letters to the Editor section of a newspaper. Someone writes an article in the paper, and later someone else sends in a letter commenting on the content of the article. A few days after that, more letters might come in, such as a rebuttal from the original author, or someone else weighing in with his two cents' worth. Eventually, the discussion dies out either because the topic has been exhausted or because everyone loses interest.

Newsgroups work in just the same way. Someone posts an article, and then the other people who read the group can, if they like, respond to the article by posting a **follow-up** article. Others can then respond to the response, and so on down the line. This entire discussion—from the original article to the last response—is called a **thread**.

## Practicing Newsgroup Etiquette

To help make Usenet a pleasant experience for all the participants, there are a few rules of newsgroup etiquette—sometimes called **netiquette**, a blend of *network* and *etiquette*—you should know. Here's a summary:

- Don't SHOUT—Use the normal rules of capitalization in your message text. In particular, AVOID LENGTHY PASSAGES OR ENTIRE MESSAGES WRITTEN IN CAPITAL LETTERS, WHICH ARE DIFFICULT TO READ AND MAKE IT APPEAR THAT YOU ARE SHOUTING.

- Write good subjects—Busy newsgroup readers often use a message's subject line to decide whether to read the message. This is particularly true if the recipient does not know you. Therefore, do not use subject lines that are either vague or overly general—for example, Info Required or A Newsgroup Post. Make your subject line descriptive enough that the reader can tell at a glance what your message is about.

---

**TIP**

When you reply to a post, the newsreader adds `Re:` to the subject line. However, it's common for the topic under discussion to change after a while. If you're changing the topic in a reply, be sure to change the subject line, too. If you think other readers of the original subject will also be interested in this reply, quote the original subject line as part of your new subject, as in this example:

```
Dog food suggestions needed (was Re: Canine nutrition)
```

---

- Quote appropriately—When posting a follow-up, you can make sure that other group readers know what you are responding to by including quotes from the original message in your reply. However, quoting the entire message is usually wasteful, especially if the message is lengthy. Just include enough of the original to put your response into context.

**20**

- Be patient—If you post an article and it doesn't show up in the newsgroup five minutes later, don't resend the article. A posted article goes on quite a journey as it wends its way through the highways and byways of the Internet. As a result, it often takes a day or two before your article appears in the newsgroup. (This is why it's also considered bad Usenet form to post articles "announcing" some current news event. By the time the article appears, the event is likely to be old news to most readers, and you'll end up looking just plain silly. If you're aching to discuss it with someone, try the misc.headlines group.)

- Don't send flames—If you receive a message with what appears to be a thoughtless or insulting remark, your immediate reaction might be to compose an emotionally charged, scathing reply. Such a message is called a **flame**, and it will probably only make matters worse. Allow yourself at least 24 hours to cool down before responding to the message.

- Ask questions—If you are just starting out with newsgroups, you may have questions about how they work or what kinds of groups are available. There is a newsgroup devoted to these kinds of questions: news.newusers.questions.

- Read the FAQ—After you've subscribed to a newsgroup and before you post your first message, read through the group's list of Frequently Asked Questions (FAQ). Some newsgroups post their own FAQs regularly, usually monthly. You can also find FAQs in the answers topic under each mainstream hierarchy: comp.answers, rec.answers, and so on. Alternatively, the news.answers group contains periodic FAQ postings from most groups that have FAQs.

- Post something—Newsgroups thrive on participation and the constant give and take of post and follow-up. Merely reading posts adds no value to a group, so every subscriber is expected to post at least occasionally.

- Post appropriately—When you want to post a message, think carefully about which newsgroup is appropriate so that you do not send a message that other people see as off-topic or even offensive. Also, unless it is absolutely necessary, do not post your message to two or more groups—a practice called **cross-posting**—even if they cover closely related topics.

- Read existing follow-ups—Before posting a reply to an existing message, check to see whether the post already has any follow-ups. If so, read them to make sure that your own follow-up will not simply repeat something that has already been said.

- Don't advertise—For the most part, Usenet is not an advertising medium, so do not post ads to newsgroups. If you really want to advertise, use the appropriate group in the biz hierarchy. For example, if you have property you want to sell, you can post an ad on biz.marketplace.real-estate.

- Use summaries—Posts that act as surveys or that ask for suggestions can often generate lots of responses, many of which are repeats. If you want to post such a message, tell the respondents to send their replies to you via email, and offer to summarize the results. Then, when all the follow-ups are in, post your own follow-up that includes a summary of the responses you received.

# Setting Up a News Account

Now that you know a bit about Usenet, it's time to get down to more practical matters. Specifically, the rest of this chapter will show you how to use Outlook Express to subscribe to, read, and post to newsgroups.

First, however, you need to know how to set up an account for the new server you want to use. Here are the steps to follow:

1. In Outlook Express, select Tools, Accounts to display the Internet Accounts dialog box.

2. Click Add, News.

3. Type your display name—this is the name that will appear in the From field when you post a message—and click Next.

4. Type an email address and click Next. The Internet News Server Name dialog box appears.

> **CAUTION**
>
> Why do you need to specify an email address for Usenet? Because people might want to respond to one of your posts privately, rather than to the newsgroup itself. Unfortunately, many spammers harvest the email addresses of Usenet participants for their nefarious ends, so it's not a good idea to use a legitimate address in your news account. I'll discuss this in more detail when I discuss spam avoidance in Chapter 21, "Implementing Windows XP's Internet Security and Privacy Features."

5. Type the name of your server in the News (NNTP) server text box. If you must log on to the server, activate the My News Server Requires Me to Log On check box. Click Next.

6. If your news server requires a logon, type your account name (your username) and your password, and then click Next.

7. Click Finish. Your new account appears in the News tab of the Internet Accounts dialog box, as shown in Figure 20.1.

8. Click Close. Outlook Express asks whether you want to download newsgroups from the news account.

9. Click Yes. Outlook Express downloads the groups (note that this might take quite a while, depending on the speed of your connection), and then displays the Newsgroup Subscriptions dialog box.

I show you how to use the Newsgroup Subscriptions dialog box in the next section, so keep it open for now.

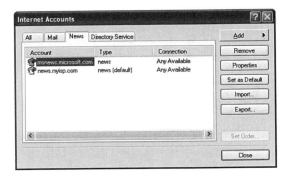

**FIGURE 20.1**    Your Internet news accounts are listed in the News tab.

# Working with Newsgroups in Outlook Express

With your news account defined, your next chore is to subscribe to one or more news-groups. If you don't have the Newsgroup Subscriptions window open from the previous section, use any of the following techniques to display it:

- Select Tools, Newsgroups
- Press Ctrl+W
- Click the news account in the Folders list and then click the Newsgroups toolbar button

If you have multiple news accounts, click the one you want to work with in the Account(s) list. (If you elected not to download the account's newsgroups from the server during the account setup, Outlook Express will automatically download the newsgroups now.) Outlook Express displays the account's newsgroups, as shown in Figure 20.2.

Newsgroups are at the heart of Usenet, so you'll need to become comfortable with basic newsgroup chores such as subscribing and unsubscribing. The next two sections take you through the basics.

## Subscribing to a Newsgroup

Before you can read or post articles, you have to add a newsgroup or two to your news server account. You have two ways of doing this: You can subscribe to a newsgroup or you can open a newsgroup without committing to a subscription.

Either way, you must first display the group you want in the Newsgroup list. You can either scroll through the groups or type all or part of the newsgroup name in the Display Newsgroups Which Contain text box. Note that Outlook Express looks for group names that contain the text you type. If you type **startrek**, for example, Outlook Express will match alt.startrek, rec.arts.startrek.fandom, and so on. This example is shown in Figure 20.3.

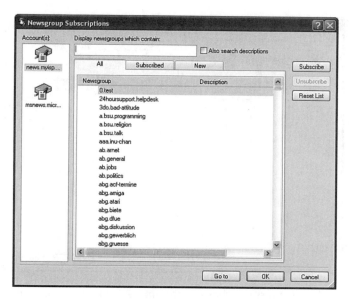

**FIGURE 20.2**    Use this dialog box to work with newsgroups in Outlook Express.

**Downloading Newsgroup Descriptions**

Some newsgroups have descriptions that give you a brief overview of what the group is about. By default, Outlook Express doesn't download these descriptions because it slows down the group retrieval process. However, if you have a fast connection, you should tell Outlook Express to download the descriptions. To do that, return to Outlook Express and select Tools, Accounts. In the News tab, click the news account you want to work with and then click Properties to open the account's property sheet. In the Advanced tab, activate the Use Newsgroup Descriptions check box and then click OK. Open the Newsgroup Subscriptions window again, click the new server, and then click Reset List. Outlook Express downloads the newsgroup names and their descriptions. To include the descriptions when searching newsgroup names, activate the Also Search Descriptions check box.

After you've selected a newsgroup, use either of the following techniques:

- If you just want to view the group without subscribing, click Go To. You'll be returned to the Outlook Express window with the newsgroup displayed. If you later want to subscribe to this group, right-click the group name in the Folders list and then click Subscribe.

- If you want to subscribe to the group, click the Subscribe button. You can repeat this process for any other newsgroup subscriptions. In each case, Outlook Express adds the name of the group to the Subscribed tab. When you're done, click OK to return to the main Outlook Express window.

20

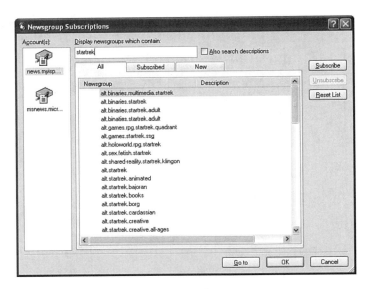

**FIGURE 20.3**    Outlook Express matches newsgroup names that contain the text you type.

## Unsubscribing from a Newsgroup

If you get tired of a newsgroup, you can unsubscribe at any time by using either of the following techniques:

- In the Newsgroup Subscriptions dialog box, display the Subscribed tab, select the newsgroup, and click Unsubscribe.

- In the Outlook Express window, right-click the group name in the Folders list and then click Unsubscribe.

# Downloading Messages

With some newsgroups selected, you're now ready to start grabbing messages to read. With Outlook Express, you have two ways to proceed:

- Online—Working online means you're connected to the news server. You can download message headers at any time, and highlighting a message downloads the message text immediately.

- Offline—Working offline means that you connect briefly to get the available headers in a group. Then, while you're not connected, you examine the subject lines of the messages and mark those that you want to retrieve. You then connect once again and tell Outlook Express to download the marked messages.

In Outlook Express, you switch between offline and online mode by activating or deactivating the File, Work Offline command.

## Downloading Message Headers

When you're in online mode, Outlook Express offers the following methods for downloading a newsgroup's message headers (this is called **synchronizing** the headers):

- Click the newsgroup in the Folders list. Outlook Express will download the headers for you automatically. For busy groups, the default download limit of 300 might not grab every header. To get more headers, select Tools, Get Next 300 Headers. (As you'll see later, you can adjust this header limit to your liking.)

- Click the newsgroup and then select the Tools, Synchronize Newsgroup command. In the Synchronize Newsgroup dialog box, activate the Get the Following Items check box, activate the Headers Only option, and then click OK.

- To synchronize multiple newsgroups at once, select the news server in the Folders list and then select all the groups that you want to work with. Click Settings and then click Headers Only. Now click Synchronize Account. Outlook Express downloads all the available headers for the newsgroups you selected.

If you're on a dial-up connection, you might want to switch to offline mode at this point so that you can review the headers.

## Downloading Messages

To view the contents of any message (the message body) while you're online, just select it in the message list. Outlook Express then downloads the message body and displays the message text in the preview pane.

### Working Offline: Marking Messages for Downloading

If you're working offline, you need to mark those messages that you want to download. Here are the techniques you can use:

- Marking a single message for download—Select the message and then select Tools, Mark for Offline, Download Message later. You can also right-click the message and then click Download Message Later.

- Marking a thread for download—Select any message in the thread and then select Tools, Mark for Offline, Download Conversation Later.

- Marking all the messages for download—Select Tools, Mark for Offline, Download All Messages Later.

In each case, Outlook Express places a small, blue arrow to the left of the marked messages.

If you change your mind about downloading a message, select it and then select Tools, Mark for Offline, Do Not Download Message. (To start over again, first choose Edit, Select All to highlight every message, and then choose the Tools, Mark for Offline, Do Not Download Message command.)

20

### Working Offline: Getting the Message Bodies

To get the message bodies, follow these steps:

1. Switch to online mode.

2. Select the Tools, Synchronize Newsgroup command to display the Synchronize Newsgroup dialog box.

3. Make sure that the Get Messages Marked for Download check box is activated, as shown in Figure 20.4.

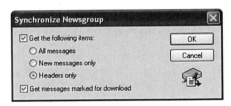

**FIGURE 20.4**   Use this dialog box to tell Outlook Express what you want to download.

4. You can also leave the Get the Following Items check box activated and then select one of the following options:

| | |
|---|---|
| All Messages | This option downloads every available header and body. |
| New Messages Only | This option looks for new messages and downloads both the headers and the bodies. |
| Headers Only | This option looks for new headers and downloads them. |

5. Click OK. Outlook Express starts downloading the messages.

6. When the download is complete, switch to offline mode.

# Notes on Working with Newsgroup Messages

You can treat newsgroup messages in much the same way that you treat email messages. That is, you can view the message text in the preview pane, open the message in its own window, save the message, copy it to another folder, and so on. I discussed all of these message techniques and quite a few others in Chapter 19, "Communicating with Internet Email." Here are a few notes on tasks that are specific to newsgroup messages:

- Dealing with threads—If you see a plus sign (+) beside a message header, it means that replies have been posted. To see the other messages in the thread, click the plus sign or highlight the message and press plus sign (+) on your numeric keypad.

- Unscrambling ROT13 messages—Some messages are encoded using a scheme called **ROT13**. This scheme encodes the message by shifting the letters of the alphabet 13 positions to the right, and wrapping around to the front of the alphabet when the end is reached. (The *ROT* part is short for *rotate*.) If you come across a message that has been encoded using ROT13, you can use Outlook Express's built-in decoder. To use it, select Message, Unscramble (ROT13).

- Canceling one of your messages—If you post a message and then have second thoughts, you can remove it from the newsgroup by highlighting it and selecting Compose, Cancel Message. (This command is available only for messages you've sent.)

- Combining and decoding multiple attachments—Some multimedia groups post large binary files that are split into multiple posts. To extract the original binary file from these posts, first select all the posts. Then select Message, Combine and Decode to display the Order for Decoding dialog box. Use the Move Up and Move Down button to order the posts (the subject lines usually tell you the proper order), and then click OK.

## Following Up a Message

Usenet is at its best when it's interactive: questions are asked and answered; the swords of conflicting opinions are crossed; debaters cut and parry to score points on contentious issues. The engine behind all this verbal jousting is, of course, the follow-up message. To post a follow-up with Outlook Express, follow these steps:

1. Select the original message in the message list.

2. Select Message, Reply to Group. (You can also press Ctrl+G or click the Reply Group toolbar button.) Outlook Express opens a message composition window and fills it with the text from the original article.

3. Cut out any unnecessary text from the original article.

4. Type your own text in the article body.

5. Select File, Send Message. (Alternatives for faster service: Alt+S or click the Send button.) Outlook Express displays a dialog box telling you that your message has been sent to the news server and that it might not appear immediately.

6. Click OK.

> **TIP**
>
> Instead of posting a follow-up message, you might prefer to reply directly to the author via email. To do this, select the message and select Message, Reply to Author (or else press Ctrl+R or click the Reply button).
>
> If you want to send a message to both the group and the author, select Compose, Reply to All.

20

# Posting a New Message

As I've said before, original messages are the lifeblood of Usenet because they get the discussions off the ground and give the rest of us something to read (as well as laugh at, sneer at, and hurl verbal abuse at). So, if you're feeling creative, you can take advantage of this section, which shows you how to post a new message from Outlook Express.

To get started, select the newsgroup to which you want to post, and then use any of the following techniques:

- Select Compose, New Message
- Press Ctrl+N
- Click the New Post button on the toolbar

Whichever method you choose, the New Message window appears. This window is almost identical to the New Message window I discussed in the previous chapter. The only difference is that the To field is replaced by a Newsgroups field.

The Newsgroups field should show the name of the current newsgroup. If you want to send the message to multiple newsgroups, separate each name with a comma (,). (Alternatively, run the Tools, Select Newsgroups command and then choose a newsgroup from the dialog box that appears.)

To post your message, select File, Send Message (or press Alt+S, or click the Send button in the toolbar).

# Filtering Newsgroup Messages

I mentioned at the top of this chapter that many newsgroups are riddled with **spam** (unsolicited commercial email) and off-topic rants and raves. Such groups are said to have a bad **signal-to-noise ratio**. To help improve this ratio, Outlook Express has a newsgroup filter feature that enables you to set up criteria for messages you don't want to see. Here are the steps to follow to set up a newsgroup filter:

1. Select the Tools, Message Rules, News command. Outlook Express displays the News Rule dialog box.

2. In the Select the Conditions for Your Rule list, activate the check box beside the rule condition you want to use to pick out a message from the herd. Outlook Express adds the condition to the Rule Description text box. Note that you're free to select multiple conditions.

3. The condition shown in the Rule Description text box will probably have some underlined text. You need to replace that underlined text with the specific criterion you want to use (such as a word or an address). To do that, click the underlined text, type the criterion in the dialog box that appears, and click Add. Most conditions support multiple criteria (such as multiple addresses or multiple words in a subject line), so repeat this step as necessary. When you're done, click OK.

4. In the Select the Actions for your rule list, activate the check box beside the action you want Outlook Express to take with messages that meet your criteria. Again, you might have to click underlined text in the Rule Description text box to complete the action. Also, you can select multiple actions.

5. If you selected multiple conditions, Outlook Express assumes that all the conditions must be true before invoking the rule (Boolean AND). To change this, click and in the Rule Description text box, activate the Messages Match Any One of the Criteria option, and click OK.

6. Use the Name of the Rule text box to type a descriptive name for the rule.

7. Click OK. Outlook Express drops you off at the News Rules tab of the Message Rules dialog box.

## Setting News Options

You saw in the last chapter that Outlook Express has all kinds of options and settings that enable you to customize many aspects of the Outlook Express email client. There are also quite a few options related to newsgroups, and this section runs through them all.

### Options for Newsgroups and Messages

The options related to newsgroups and messages are in the Options dialog box, which you can get to by selecting the Tools, Options command.

#### Setting General Options

The General tab contains just two Usenet-related settings (refer to Chapter 19 for explanations of the other options in this tab):

| | |
|---|---|
| Notify Me If There Are Any New Newsgroups | When this check box is activated, Outlook Express polls the server for the names of newsgroups added since you last connected. If there are any, Outlook Express displays a dialog box to let you know. (A list of the new groups appears in the New tab of the Newsgroup Subscriptions dialog box.) |
| This Application Is NOT the Default News Handler | The default news handler is the program that loads whenever you run your web browser's news command. (In Internet Explorer, for example, select File, New, Post to post a message to a newsgroup.) If Outlook Express is not the default news program, click the Make Default button. (This button is disabled if Outlook Express is currently the default news handler.) |

20

## Setting Read Options

The Read tab boasts the following message-related settings (refer to Chapter 19 to learn about the other options in this tab):

| | |
|---|---|
| Automatically Expand Grouped Messages | Activating this check box tells Outlook Express to expand all downloaded threads. |
| Automatically Download Message When Viewing in the Preview Pane | When this check box is activated and you're online, Outlook Express downloads and displays a message when you highlight its header. If you'd prefer not to have messages downloaded automatically, deactivate this check box. |
| Get *X* Headers at a Time | Use this spin box to specify the maximum number of newsgroup headers that Outlook Express downloads when you select the Tools, Get Next *X* Headers command. Increase this value if you read busy newsgroups with lots of messages. (The maximum value is 1,000.) |
| Mark All Messages as Read When Exiting a Newsgroup | Activate this check box to force Outlook Express to mark all the messages in the current newsgroup as read when you select a different newsgroup or folder. |

## Setting Maintenance Options

You'll find a few more message-related options in the Maintenance tab, shown in Figure 20.5. Most of these options affect the local storage that Outlook Express uses for downloaded messages. Here's a summary:

| | |
|---|---|
| Delete Read Message Bodies in Newsgroups | If you activate this check box, each time you exit Outlook Express, the program deletes from local storage the bodies of those posts that you've read. |
| Delete News Messages *X* Days After Being Downloaded | When this check box is activated, Outlook Express deletes any downloaded message a specified number of days after the download. |
| Clean Up Now | Click this button to force Outlook Express to compact its local storage space immediately. |
| News | Activate this check box to have Outlook Express maintain a log of commands sent to and from the news server. This log is stored in a file named *account*.log, where *account* is the name of the news account. The log file is saved in the server's subfolder of your Outlook Express identity's application data folder: |

```
%UserProfile%\Local Settings\Application Data\
Identities\ID\Microsoft\Outlook Express
```

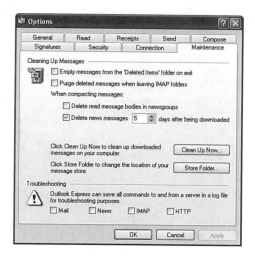

**FIGURE 20.5**   The Maintenance tab contains various options related to the local storage of downloaded messages.

## Options for Individual Newsgroups

Outlook Express also maintains a few properties related to individual newsgroups. To view these settings, right-click a newsgroup and then click Properties. The property sheet that appears contains three tabs: General, Synchronize, and Local File. The General tab tells you the name of the newsgroup, the total number of available messages, and the number of those messages that are unread.

The Synchronize tab, shown in Figure 20.6, enables you to set the default download setting for this newsgroup. These are the options that appear when you select the Tools, Synchronize this Newsgroup command, discussed earlier in this chapter.

The Local File tab, shown in Figure 20.7, contains settings that control the newsgroup's local message storage, which is a .dbx file (for example, `rec.running.dbx`) in your Outlook Express identity's folder:

`%UserProfile%\Local Settings\Application Data\Identities\`*`ID`*`\Microsoft\`
`Outlook Express`

The File Information group shows you the total size of the storage file, the size taken up by message headers, and the amount of wasted space in the file. You can adjust this storage by using the following buttons:

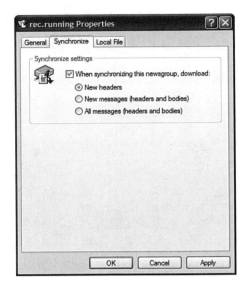

**FIGURE 20.6**    Use the Synchronize tab to set the default download option for this newsgroup.

| Compact | You saw earlier that Outlook Express deletes downloaded messages after a certain time, and it deletes read messages when you quit the program. These deletions create gaps in the local storage, which is the source of the Wasted Space value. To close these gaps and remove this wasted space, click the Compact button. |
|---|---|
| Remove Messages | Click this button to remove all the downloaded message bodies that are in the local storage file. |
| Delete | Click this button to clean out all the downloaded headers and message bodies from the local storage file. |
| Reset | Click this button to clean out all the downloaded headers and message bodies from the local storage file and to reset messages marked as *read* or *watched*. This enables you to download these headers again, which is useful if you're having trouble accessing the newsgroup or if the local storage file becomes slow or inaccessible due to its large size. |

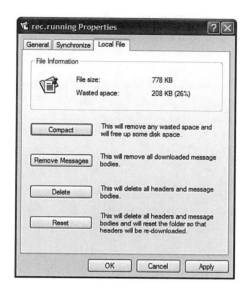

**FIGURE 20.7**    Use the Local File tab to control the local storage for the newsgroup.

# From Here

Here's a list of chapters where you'll find related information:

- To learn other ways to communicate with Windows XP, refer to Chapter 16, "Putting Your Modem to Work."

- To get the goods on TCP/IP and other Net plumbing, refer to Chapter 17, "Implementing TCP/IP for Internet Connections."

- To learn how to wield Outlook Express for Internet email, refer to Chapter 19, "Communicating with Internet Email."

- For information on Outlook Express security and privacy issues, see Chapter 21, "Implementing Windows XP's Internet Security and Privacy Features."

# Implementing Windows XP's Internet Security and Privacy Features

As more people, businesses, and organizations establish a presence online, the world becomes an increasingly connected place. And the more connected the world becomes, the more opportunities arise for communicating with others, doing research, sharing information, and collaborating on projects. The flip side to this new connectedness is the increased risk of connecting with a remote user whose intentions are less than honorable. It could be a packet sniffer who steals your password or credit card number, a cracker who breaks into your Internet account, a virus programmer who sends a Trojan horse virus attached to an email, or a website operator who uses web browser security holes to run malicious code on your machine.

Admittedly, online security threats are relatively rare and are no reason to swear off the online world. However, these threats *do* exist and people fall victim to them every day. Luckily, protecting yourself from these and other e-menaces doesn't take much effort or time, as you'll see in this chapter, in which I discuss the Internet security and privacy tools built into Windows XP.

## Working with Email Safely and Securely

Email is by far the most popular online activity, but it can also be the most frustrating in terms of security and privacy. Email viruses are legion; spam gets worse every day; and messages that should be secret are really about as secure as if they were written on the back of a postcard.

Fortunately, it doesn't take much to remedy these and other email problems, as you'll see over the next few sections.

## Protecting Yourself Against Email Viruses

Until just a few years ago, the primary method that computer viruses used to propagate themselves was the floppy disk. A user with an infected machine would copy some files to a floppy, and the virus would surreptitiously add itself to the disk. When the recipient inserted the disk, the virus copy would come to life and infect yet another computer.

When the Internet became a big deal, viruses adapted and began propagating either via malicious websites or via infected program files downloaded to users' machines.

Over the past couple of years, however, by far the most productive method for viruses to replicate has been the humble email message. Melissa; I Love You; BadTrans; Sircam; Klez. The list of email viruses and Trojan horses is a long one but they all operate more or less the same way: They arrive as a message attachment, usually from someone you know. When you open the attachment, the virus infects your computer and then, without your knowledge, uses your email client and your address book to ship out messages with more copies of itself attached. The nastier versions will also mess with your computer by deleting data or corrupting files.

You can avoid getting infected by one of these viruses by implementing a few common sense procedures:

- Never open an attachment that comes from someone you don't know.

- Even if you know the sender, if the attachment isn't something you're expecting, assume that the sender's system is infected. Write back and confirm that the sender emailed the message.

- Some viruses come packaged as scripts that are hidden within messages that use the Rich Text (HTML) format. This means that the virus can run just by viewing the message! If a message looks suspicious, don't open it, just delete it. (Note that you'll need to turn off the Outlook Express preview pane before deleting the message. Otherwise, when you highlight the message, it will appear in the preview pane and set off the virus. Select View, Layout, deactivate the Show Preview Pane check box, and click OK.)

- Install a top-of-the-line antivirus program, particularly one that checks incoming email. Also, be sure to keep your antivirus program's virus list up to date. As you read this, there are probably dozens, maybe even hundreds, of morally challenged scumnerds designing even nastier viruses. Regular updates will help you keep up.

In addition to these general procedures, Outlook Express also comes with its own set of virus protection features. Here's how to use them:

1. In Outlook Express, select Tools, Options.

2. Display the Security tab.

**3.** In the Virus Protection group, you have the following options:

| | |
|---|---|
| Select the Internet Explorer Security Zone to Use | Later in this chapter I describe the security zone model used by Internet Explorer (see "Surfing the Web Securely"). From the perspective of Outlook Express, you use the security zones to determine whether active content inside an HTML-format message is allowed to run: |

- Internet Zone—If you choose this zone, active content is allowed to run.

- Restricted Sites Zone—If you choose this option, active content is disabled. This is the default setting and it's the one I recommend.

| | |
|---|---|
| Warn Me When Other Applications Try to Send Mail as Me | As I mentioned earlier, it's possible for programs and scripts to send email messages without your knowledge. This is done using Simple MAPI (Messaging Application Programming Interface) calls, which can be used to send messages via your computer's default mail client, and it's all hidden from you. When this check box is activated, Outlook Express displays a warning dialog box (see Figure 21.1) when a program or script attempts to send a message using Simple MAPI. Click Send to allow the message; click Do Not Send to cancel the message. |

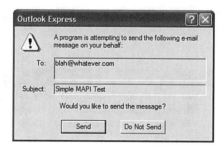

**FIGURE 21.1**    Outlook Express warns you if a program or script uses Simple MAPI to attempt to send a message.

### Sending Messages Via CDO

Activating the Warn Me When Other Applications Try to Send Mail as Me option protects you against scripts that attempt to send surreptitious messages using Simple MAPI calls. However, there's another way to send messages behind the scenes. It's called **Collaboration Data Objects** (**CDO**), and it's installed by default in Windows XP. Here's a sample script that uses CDO to send a message:

```
Dim objMessage
Set objMessage = CreateObject("CDO.Message")
```

```
With objMessage
  .To = "you@there.com"
  .From = "me@here.com"
  .Subject = "CDO Test"
  .TextBody = "Just testing..."
  .Send
End With
Set objMessage = Nothing
```

The Warn Me When Other Applications Try to Send Mail as Me option does *not* trap this kind of script, so bear in mind that your system is still vulnerable to Trojan horses that send mail via your Windows XP accounts.

| | |
|---|---|
| Do Not Allow Attachments to Be Saved or Opened That Could Potentially Be a Virus | When this check box is activated, Outlook Express monitors attachments to look for file types that could contain viruses or destructive code. If it detects such a file, it disables your ability to open or save that file, and it displays a note at the top of the message to let you know about the unsafe attachment, as shown in Figure 21.2. |

**Files Types Disabled by Outlook Express**

The file types that Outlook Express disables are defined by Internet Explorer's built-in unsafe-file list. This list includes file types associated with the following extensions: `.ad`, `.ade`, `.adp`, `.bas`, `.bat`, `.chm`, `.cmd`, `.com`, `.cpl`, `.crt`, `.exe`, `.hlp`, `.hta`, `.inf`, `.ins`, `.isp`, `.js`, `.jse`, `.lnk`, `.mdb`, `.mde`, `.msc`, `.msi`, `.msp`, `.mst`, `.pcd`, `.pif`, `.reg`, `.scr`, `.sct`, `.shb`, `.shs`, `.url`, `.vb`, `.vbe`, `.vbs`, `.vsd`, `.vss`, `.vst`, `.vsw`, `.wsc`, `.wsf`, `.wsh`.

**TIP**

What do you do if you want to send a file that's on the Outlook Express unsafe file list and you want to make sure that the recipient will be able to open it? The easiest workaround is to compress the file into a `.zip` file, which won't be blocked by Outlook Express (or Outlook or any other mail client that blocks file types).

4. Click OK to put the new settings into effect.

## Filtering Out Spam

**Spam**—unsolicited commercial messages—has become a plague upon the earth. Unless you've done a masterful job at keeping your address secret, you probably receive at least a few spam emails every day, and it's more likely that you receive a few dozen. The bad news is most experts agree that it's only going to get worse. And why not? Spam is one of the few advertising mediums where the costs are substantially borne by the users, not the advertisers.

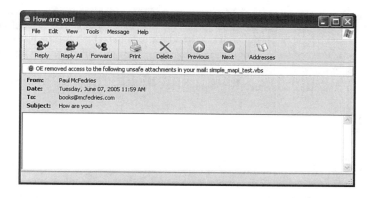

**FIGURE 21.2**    If Outlook Express detects an unsafe file attachment, it displays a notice at the top of the message to let you know that you do not have access to the file.

The best way to avoid spam is to not get on a spammer's list of addresses in the first place. That's hard to do these days, but there are some steps you can take:

- Never use your actual email address in a newsgroup account. The most common method that spammers use to gather addresses is to harvest them from newsgroup posts. One common tactic is to alter (or **munge**, in the vernacular) your email address by adding text that invalidates the address but is still obvious for other people to figure out:

    user@myisp.remove_this_to_email_me.com

- When you sign up for something online, use a fake address if possible. If you need or want to receive email from the company and so must use your real address, make sure that you deselect any options that ask if you want to receive promotional offers. Alternatively, enter the address from a free Web-based account (such as a Hotmail account), so that any spam you receive will go there instead of to your main address.

- Never open suspected spam messages because doing so can sometimes notify the spammer that you've opened the message, thus confirming that your address is legit. For the same reason, you should never display a spam message in the Outlook Express preview pane. As described earlier, shut off the preview pane before highlighting any spam messages that you want to delete.

- Never, I repeat, *never*, respond to spam, even to an address within the spam that claims to be a removal address. By responding to the spam all you're doing is proving that your address is legitimate, so you'll just end up getting *more* spam.

---

**TIP**

If you create web pages, never put your email address on a page because spammers use **crawlers** that harvest addresses from web pages. If you must put an address on a page, hide it using some simple JavaScript code:

```
<script language="JavaScript" type="text/javascript">
<!--
var add1 = "webmaster"
var add2 = "@"
var add3 = "whatever.com"
document.write(add1 + add2 + add3)
//-->
</script>
```

---

There are a host of commercial spam-killers on the market, but with a bit of work you should be able to eliminate most spam by using nothing more than the built-in tools available in Outlook Express. I'm talking specifically about using **mail rules**: conditions that look for messages with specific characteristics—for example, certain words in the subject or body—and actions that do something with the matching messages—such as delete them. I showed you how to create mail rules in Chapter 19, "Communicating with Internet Email"; refer to the section titled "Filtering Incoming Messages."

To filter spam, your rules need to look for incoming messages that meet one or more of the following criteria:

- Specific words in the Subject line—The sneakier spammers hide their messages behind innocuous subject lines such as "Here's the information you requested." But most spam comes with fairly obvious Subject lines: "Make $$$Money Now!!!" or "FREE Business Cards." Instead of creating a rule based on an entire Subject line, you only need to watch for certain keywords. Here are a few that I use (I've removed some of the more explicit terms that filter out pornographic spam):

  !!!!!!!, $, %, .name, 18+, about your site, adult, adv, advertise, ameritrade, annual reports, are you in debt, back taxes, bargain, be 18, britney, bulk, buy recommendation, cartridges, cash, casino, clients, collect your money, credit card, credit rating, creditor, debts, descrambler, dieting, diploma, don't miss, double your money, dvd movies, earning!, e-mail marketing, emarketer, erotic, excite game, f r e e, find out anything, flash alert, free cell, free credit, free pda, free phone, free trial, free vacation, free!, freee, get out of debt, giveaway, got debt, guaranteed!, hair loss, hormone, how to make money, increase your sales, incredible opportunity, interest rates, investment goals, iPod, is this a picture of you, klez, lemme, life insurance, loans, lose up to, lose weight, lose while you sleep, losing sleep, low on funds, marketing services, maximize your income, merchant, millionaire, mlm, mortgage, new car, new photos from my party, online market, online pharmacy, over 18, over 21, printer cartridge, promote your business, reach millions, reduce your debt, refinance, refinancing, s e x, satellite, saw your site, secure your future, seen on tv, sex, singles, snoring, spec sheet, steroids, stock, stock alert, systemworks, thinning hair, this one's on us, too good to be true, trading alert, trading report, uncover the truth, urgent notice, viagra, web traffic, what are your kids, work at home, work from home, xxx, years younger, you are a winner, you have to see this

- Specific words in the message body—The message body is where the spammer makes his or her pitch, so there's rarely any subterfuge here. You can filter on the same terms as you used for the subject line, but there are also a few telltale terms that appear only in spam messages. Here are some that I use:

  ///////////////, 100% satisfied, adult en, adult web, adults only, cards accepted, check or money order, dear friend, extra income, for free!, for free?, satisfaction guaranteed, money back , money-back guarantee, one-time mail, order now!, order today, removal instructions, special promotion

- Specific names in the From line—Many spammers **spoof** their From address by using a random address or, more likely, an address plucked from their distribution list. However, some use addresses that have a common theme, such as "sales@" (for example, sales@blah.com). Here are some common From line names to filter:

  @mlm, @public, @savvy, ebargains, free, hello@, link2buy, mail@, profits@, sales@, success, success@

- Specific names in the To line—The To line of spam messages usually contains either an address from the distribution list or "Undisclosed Recipients." You can't filter on the latter, however, because many legitimate mailings also use that "address." However, there are a few common To line names to watch for:

  anyone@, creditcard@, free@, friend, friend@, nobody@, opportunity@, public@, success@, winners@

If you notice that a particular address is the source of much spam, the easiest way to block the spam is to block all incoming messages from that address. You can do this using the Outlook Express Blocked Senders list, which I described in Chapter 19's "Blocking Senders" section. For other types of spam, you need to set up mail rules, as described in Chapter 19's "Creating a Mail Rule" section.

## Handling Hoaxes

It's a rare Internet user who hasn't received an email message along the following lines:

```
Subject: FW: Must Read!!!! Bill Gates (fwd)

Hello everybody, My name is Bill Gates. I have just written up an e-mail
tracing program that traces everyone to whom this message is forwarded to.
I am experimenting with this and I need your help. Forward this to everyone
```

```
you know and if it reaches 1000 people everyone on the list will receive
$1000 at my expense. Enjoy.

Your friend,
Bill Gates
```

Heeding the last sentence, less savvy users will most likely have forwarded this warning to a few dozen friends, relatives, and colleagues. There's only one problem: This message is, of course, a hoax. There is no "tracing program" and there is no $1,000 pot of gold at the end of the email rainbow.

This email hoax is part of the general category of email chain letters. Some of these messages claim to be from malicious hackers who will do something nasty to your computer if you don't forward the message to ten of your friends.

Unfortunately, bogus offers and chain letters aren't the only kind of email hoax going around. Another popular type is the virus hoax, in which the message warns you about an email that contains a virus that will wreck your hard drive (or perform some other unpleasant chore). They usually warn you to watch out for a specific subject line, such as "Good Times" (this is the oldest such hoax; it's been around since about 1994), "Win a Holiday," "Penpal Greetings," and many more.

The ironic thing about all this is that these messages end up as a kind of virus themselves. With thousands of people naively forwarding tens of thousands of copies of the message all over the Internet, they end up wasting bandwidth and wasting the time of those people who must refute their claims.

I receive many of these hoaxes forwarded to me from well-meaning readers. Fortunately, the Web offers many sources of information on these hoaxes, so people learn about them pretty fast. If you receive a virus warning or other email that seems legitimate, you can check it out using any of the following sites:

www.snopes.com/

urbanlegends.about.com/

www.vmyths.com/

www.scambusters.org/

## Maintaining Your Privacy While Reading Email

You wouldn't think that the simple act of reading an email message would have privacy implications, but you'd be surprised. There are actually two scenarios that compromise your privacy: read receipts and web bugs.

### Blocking Read Receipts

A **read receipt** is an email notification that tells the sender that you've opened the message that was sent to you. If the sender requests a read receipt and you either select the message (so that the message text appears in the preview pane) or double-click the message to open it, Outlook Express displays the dialog box shown in Figure 21.3. Click Yes to send the receipt, or click No to skip it.

**FIGURE 21.3**  You see this dialog box when you open a message for which the sender has requested a read receipt.

Many people like asking for read receipts because they offer proof of delivery. It has been my experience, however, that getting a read receipt back starts a kind of internal clock that the sender uses to measure how long it takes you to respond after reading the message. Because of this annoyance, and because I feel it's nobody's business to know when I read a message, I always click No when asked to send a read receipt. (Spammers, too, sometimes request read receipts as a way of validating email addresses.) In fact, you can go one better and tell Outlook Express to never send a read receipt:

1. Select Tools, Options to display the Options dialog box.

2. Display the Receipts tab.

3. In the Returning Read Receipts group, activate the Never Send a Read Receipt option.

4. Click OK.

### Squashing Web Bugs

A **web bug** is an image that resides on   a remote server and that is added to an HTML-formatted email message by referencing a URL on the remote server. When you open the message, Outlook Express uses the URL to download the image for display within the message. That sounds harmless enough, but if the message is junk email, it's likely that the URL will also contain either your email address or a code that points to your email address. When the remote server gets a request for this URL, it knows not only that you've opened the message, but also that your email address is legitimate.

You have three ways to combat web bugs:

- Don't open a message that you suspect to be spam, and don't preview the message in the Outlook Express preview pane. In fact, before you can delete the message, you'll need to turn off the preview pane temporarily, as described earlier in this chapter.

- Install the Internet Explorer 6 Service Pack 1 or the Windows XP Service Pack 2 (or a later service pack, if one is available by the time you read this). This service pack also updates Outlook Express. In particular, it gives you an easy way to thwart web bugs (although it also thwarts other message formatting, as well). In Outlook

Express, select Tools, Options, choose the Read tab, and then activate the Read All Messages in Plain Text check box. This prevents Outlook Express from downloading any web bugs because it displays all messages in plain text.

- Install the Windows XP Service Pack 2 (or a later service pack, if one is available). This update includes an option that is specifically designed to squash web bugs. In Outlook Express, select Tools, Options, choose the Security tab, and then activate the Block Images and Other External Content in HTML E-mail check box. This prevents Outlook Express from downloading web bugs and any other items that would otherwise come from some remote server.

## Sending and Receiving Secure Email

When you connect to a website, your browser sets up a direct connection—called a **channel**—between your machine and the web server. Because the channel is a direct link, it's relatively easy to implement security because all you have to do is secure the channel.

However, email security is entirely different and much more difficult to set up. The problem is that email messages don't have a direct link to a Simple Mail Transfer Protocol (SMTP) server. Instead, they must usually hop from server to server until the final destination is reached. Combine this with the open and well-documented email standards used on the Internet, and you end up with three email security issues:

- The privacy issue—Because messages often pass through other systems and can even end up on a remote system's hard disk, it isn't that hard for someone with the requisite know-how and access to the remote system to read a message.

- The tampering issue—Because a user can read a message passing through a remote server, it comes as no surprise that he can also change the message text.

- The authenticity issue—With the Internet email standards an open book, it isn't difficult for a savvy user to forge or *spoof* an email address.

To solve these issues, the Internet's gurus came up with the idea of **encryption**. When you encrypt a message, a complex mathematical formula scrambles the message content to make it unreadable. In particular, a **key value** is incorporated into the encryption formula. To unscramble the message, the recipient feeds the key into the decryption formula.

This **single-key encryption** works, but its major drawback is that the sender and the recipient must both have the same key. **Public-key encryption** overcomes that limitation by using two related keys: a **public key** and a **private key**. The public key is available to everyone, either by sending it to them directly or by offering it in an online key database. The private key is secret and is stored on the user's computer.

Here's how public-key cryptography solves the issues discussed earlier:

- Solving the privacy issue—When you send a message, you obtain the recipient's public key and use it to encrypt the message. The encrypted message can now only be decrypted using the recipient's private key, thus assuring privacy.

- Solving the tampering issue—An encrypted message can still be tampered with, but only randomly because the content of the message can't be seen. This thwarts the most important skill used by tamperers: making the tampered message look legitimate.

- Solving the authenticity issue—When you send a message, you use your private key to digitally sign the message. The recipient can then use your public key to examine the digital signature to ensure the message came from you.

If there's a problem with public-key encryption, it is that the recipient of a message must obtain the sender's public key from an online database. (The sender can't just send the public key because the recipient would have no way to prove that the key came from the sender.) Therefore, to make all this more convenient, a **digital ID** is used. This is a digital certificate that states the sender's public key has been authenticated by a trusted certifying authority. The sender can then include his or her public key in his or her outgoing messages.

## Setting Up an Email Account with a Digital ID

To send secure messages using Outlook Express, you first have to obtain a digital ID. Here are the steps to follow:

1. In Outlook Express, select Tools, Options and then display the Security tab.

2. Click Get Digital ID. Internet Explorer loads and takes you to the Outlook Express digital ID page on the Web.

3. Click a link to the certifying authority (such as VeriSign) you want to use.

4. Follow the authority's instructions for obtaining a digital ID. (Note that digital IDs are not free; they typically cost about $15 U.S. per year.)

With your digital ID installed, the next step is to assign it to an email account:

1. In Outlook Express, select Tools, Accounts to open the Internet Accounts dialog box.

2. Use the Mail tab to select the account you want to work with and then click Properties. The account's property sheet appears.

3. Display the Security tab.

4. In the Signing Certificate group, click Select. Outlook Express displays the Select Default Account Digital ID dialog box.

5. Make sure that the certificate you installed is selected and then click OK. Your name appears in the Security tab's first Certificate box.

6. Click OK to return to the Internet Accounts dialog box.

7. Click Close.

> **TIP**
>
> To make a backup copy of your digital ID, open Internet Explorer and select Tools, Internet Options. Display the Content tab and click Certificates to see a list of your installed certificates (be sure to use the Personal tab). Click your digital ID and then click Export.

## Obtaining Another Person's Public Key

Before you can send an encrypted message to another person, you must obtain his public key. How you do this depends on whether you have a digitally signed message from that person.

If you have a digitally signed message, open the message, as described later in this chapter in the "Receiving a Secure Message" section. Outlook Express adds the digital ID to the Address Book automatically:

- If you have one or more contacts whose email addresses match the address associated with the digital ID, the digital ID is added to each contact. (To see it, open the Address Book, open the contact, and then display the Digital IDs tab.)

- If there are no existing matches, a new contact is created.

> **TIP**
>
> If you don't want Outlook Express to add digital IDs automatically, select Tools, Options, display the Security tab, and click Advanced. In the dialog box that appears, deactivate the Add Senders' Certificates to My Address Book check box.

If you don't have a digitally signed message for the person you want to work with, you have to visit a certifying authority's website and find the person's digital ID. For example, you can go to the VeriSign site (www.verisign.com) to search for a digital ID and then download it to your computer. After that, follow these steps:

1. Open the Address Book.

2. Open the person's contact info, or create a new contact.

3. Type one or more email addresses, and fill in the other data as necessary.

4. Display the Digital IDs tab.

5. In the Select an E-Mail Address list, select the address that corresponds with the digital ID you downloaded.

6. Click the Import button to display the Select Digital ID File to Import dialog box.

7. Find and select the downloaded digital ID file, and then click Open.

8. Click OK.

## Sending a Secure Message

After your digital ID has been installed, you can start sending out secure email messages. You have two options:

- Digitally sign a message to prove that you're the sender—Start a new message and then either select the Tools, Digitally Sign command, or click the Sign toolbar button. A small, red seal icon appears to the right of the header fields.

- Encrypt a message to avoid snooping and tampering—In the New Message window, either activate the Tools, Encrypt command, or click the Encrypt toolbar button. A blue lock icon appears to the right of the header fields.

> **TIP**
>
> You can tell Outlook Express to digitally sign and/or encrypt all your outgoing messages. Select Tools, Options and display the Security tab. To encrypt all your messages, activate the Encrypt Contents and Attachments for All Outgoing Messages check box. To sign all your messages, activate the Digitally Sign All Outgoing Messages check box.

## Receiving a Secure Message

The technology and mathematics underlying the digital ID are complex, but there's nothing complex about dealing with incoming secure messages. Outlook Express handles everything behind the scenes, including the authentication of the sender (if the message was digitally signed) and the decryption of the message (if the message was encrypted). For the latter, a dialog box tells you that your private key has been used to decrypt the message.

As you can see in Figure 21.4, the preview pane gives you a few visual indications that you're dealing with a secure message:

- The message text doesn't appear in the preview pane.

- The preview pane title is Security Help and the subtitle tells you the type of security used: Digitally Signed and/or Encrypted.

- The preview pane text describes the security used in the message.

To read the message, click the Continue button at the bottom. If you don't want to see this security preview in the future, activate the Don't Show Me This Help Screen Again check box.

> **TIP**
>
> If you change your mind and decide you want to see the preview screen, you have to edit the Registry. Open the Registry Editor and head for the key named HKCU\Identities. Open your 32-character identity key and then open the Software\Microsoft\Outlook Express\5.0\Dont Show Dialogs subkey. Open the Digital Signature Help setting and change its value to 0.

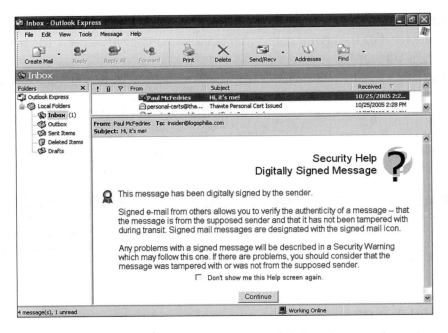

**FIGURE 21.4**    For a secure message, the preview pane describes the type of security used.

# Keeping Intruders Out of Your System

If you access the Net using a broadband—cable modem or DSL—service, chances are you have an always-on connection, which means there's a much greater chance that a malicious hacker could find your computer and have his way with it. You might think that with millions of people connected to the Internet at any given moment, there would be little chance of a "script kiddy" finding you in the herd. Unfortunately, one of the most common weapons in a black-hat hacker's arsenal is a program that runs through millions of IP addresses automatically, looking for live connections. The problem is compounded by the fact that many cable systems and some DSL systems use IP addresses in a narrow range, thus making it easier to find always-on connections. However, having a cracker locate your system isn't a big deal as long as he can't get into your system. There are three ways to prevent this:

- Turn off file and printer sharing on your Internet connection
- Turn on the Windows Firewall
- Turn off the Messenger service

## Turning Off File and Printer Sharing

File and printer sharing is used to enable network users to see and work with shared files and printers on your computer. Obviously, you don't want to share your system with strangers on the Internet! By default, Windows XP turns off file and printer sharing for Internet connections. To make sure of this, however, follow these steps:

1. Select Start, All Programs, Accessories, Communications, Network Connections. (Alternatively, open Control Panel and launch the Network Connections icon.)

2. Right-click the icon for the connection that gets you on the Internet and then click Properties.

3. Display the Networking tab. (For some types of connections, you might need to display the General tab instead.)

4. Make sure that the File and Printer Sharing for Microsoft Networks check box is deactivated.

## Turning On the Internet Connection Firewall

Although disabling file and printer sharing is a must, it's not enough. That's because when a hacker finds your address, he has many other avenues with which to access your computer. Specifically, your connection uses many different ports for sending and receiving data. For example, web data and commands typically use port 80, email uses ports 25 and 110, file transfer protocol (FTP) uses ports 20 and 21, domain name system (DNS) uses port 53, and so on. In all, there are dozens of these ports, and every one is an opening through which a clever cracker can gain access to your computer.

As if that weren't enough, hackers also can check your system to see whether some kind of Trojan horse virus is installed. (Those nasty email virus attachments you learned about earlier in this chapter sometimes install these programs on your machine.) If the hacker finds one, he can effectively take control of your machine (turning it into a **zombie computer**) and either wreak havoc on its contents or use your computer to attack other systems.

Again, if you think your computer is too obscure or worthless for someone else to bother with, think again. A typical computer connected to the Internet all day long will be probed for vulnerable ports or installed Trojan horses at least a few times a day. If you want to see just how vulnerable your computer is, several good sites on the Web will test your security:

- Gibson Research (Shields Up)—grc.com/default.htm

- DSL Reports—www.dslreports.com/secureme_go

- HackerWhacker—www.hackerwhacker.com

The good news is that Windows XP includes a personal firewall tool called Windows Firewall that can lock down your ports and prevent unauthorized access to your machine. In effect, your computer becomes invisible to the Internet (although you can still surf the web and work with email normally). Follow these steps to start Windows Firewall:

1. Launch Control Panel's Network Connections icon.

2. Right-click the icon for the connection that gets you on the Internet and then click Properties.

3. Choose the Advanced tab.

4. In the Windows Firewall group, click Settings. The Windows Firewall dialog box appears.

5. Activate the On option.

6. Click OK.

## Turning Off the Messenger Service

As a final barrier against unwelcome intrusions, you should also turn off the Windows XP Messenger Service. This service (which is not to be confused with the Windows Messenger instant messaging program) is used by network administrators to broadcast messages to users. However, some advertisers have figured out how to use this service to have ads pop up on your computer. You can block these ads by turning off the service. To do this, follow these steps:

1. Select Start, Control Panel, Performance and Maintenance, Administrative Tools, Services. Windows XP displays the Services window.

2. Double-click the Messenger service.

3. Click Stop to shut down the service.

4. To prevent the service from starting in future Windows XP sessions, use the Startup type list to choose Manual.

5. Click OK.

# Surfing the Web Securely

When implementing security for Internet Explorer, Microsoft realized that different sites have different security needs. For example, it makes sense to have fairly stringent security for Internet sites, but you can probably scale the security back a bit when browsing pages on your corporate intranet.

To handle these different types of sites, Internet Explorer defines various **security zones**, and you can customize the security requirements for each zone. The current zone is displayed in the status bar.

To work with these zones, either select Tools, Internet Options in Internet Explorer, or open the Control Panel's Internet Options icon. In the Internet Properties dialog box that appears, select the Security tab, shown in Figure 21.5.

> **TIP**
>
> Another way to get to the Security tab is to double-click the security zone shown in the Internet Explorer status bar.

**FIGURE 21.5**   Use the Security tab to set up security zones and customize the security options for each zone.

The list at the top of the dialog box shows icons for the four types of zones available:

| | |
|---|---|
| Internet | Websites that aren't in any of the other three zones. The default security level is Medium. |
| Local Intranet | Web pages on your computer and your network (intranet). The default security level is Medium-low. |
| Trusted Sites | Websites that implement secure pages and that you're sure have safe content. The default security level is Low. |
| Restricted Sites | Websites that don't implement secure pages or that you don't trust, for whatever reason. The default security level is High. |

> **TIP**
>
> You can use the Group Policy editor to hide the Security and Privacy tabs in the Internet Options dialog box. Select User Configuration, Administrative Templates, Windows Components, Internet Explorer, Internet Control Panel, and then enable the Disable the Privacy Page and Disable the Security Page policies.

## Adding and Removing Zone Sites

Three of these zones—Local Intranet, Trusted Sites, and Restricted Sites—enable you to add sites. To do this, follow these steps:

1. Select the zone you want to work with and then click Sites.

2. If you selected Trusted Sites or Restricted Sites, skip to step 4. Otherwise, if you selected the Local intranet zone, you see a dialog box with three check boxes:

| | |
|---|---|
| Include All Local (Intranet) Sites Not Listed in Other Zones | When activated, this option includes all intranet sites in the zone. If you add specific intranet sites to other zones, those sites aren't included in this zone. |
| Include All Sites That Bypass the Proxy Server | When this check box is activated, sites that you've set up to bypass your proxy server (if you have one) are included in this zone. |
| Include All Network Paths (UNCs) | When this check box is activated, all network paths that use the Universal Naming Convention are included in this zone. (UNC is a standard format used with network addresses. They usually take the form \\server\resource, where server is the name of the network server and resource is the name of a shared network resource.) |

3. To add sites to the Local Intranet zone, click Advanced.

4. Type the site's address in the Add this Web Site to the Zone text box and then click Add.

> **NOTE**
>
> When entering an address, you can include an asterisk as a wildcard character. For example, the address http://*.microsoft.com adds every microsoft.com domain, including www.microsoft.com, support.microsoft.com, windowsupdate.microsoft.com, and so on.

5. If you make a mistake and enter the wrong site, select it in the Web Sites list and then click Remove.

6. Two of these dialog boxes (Local Intranet and Trusted Sites) have a Require Server Verification (https:) for All Sites In this Zone check box. If you activate this option, each site you enter must use the secure HTTPS protocol.

7. Click OK.

## Changing a Zone's Security Level

To change the security level for a zone, first select it in the Security tab's Select a Web Content Zone to Specify Its Security Settings list. Then use the Security Level for This Zone slider to set the level. To set up your own security settings, click Custom Level. This displays the Security Settings dialog box shown in Figure 21.6.

**FIGURE 21.6**  Use this dialog box to set up customized security levels for the selected zone.

The Security Settings dialog box provides you with a long list of possible security issues, and your job is to specify how you want Internet Explorer to handle each issue. You usually have three choices:

| | |
|---|---|
| Disable | Security is turned on. For example, if the issue is whether to run an ActiveX control, the control is not run. |
| Enable | Security is turned off. For example, if the issue is whether to run an ActiveX control, the control is run automatically. |
| Prompt | You're asked how you want to handle the issue. For example, whether you want to accept or reject an ActiveX control. |

## Enhancing Online Privacy by Managing Cookies

A **cookie** is a small text file that's stored on your computer. It's used by websites to "remember" information about your session at that site: shopping cart data, page customizations, passwords, and so on. No other site can access the cookie, so they're generally safe and private under most—but definitely not all—circumstances. To understand why cookies can sometimes compromise your privacy, you need to understand the different cookie types that exist:

> **NOTE**
>
> The term **cookie** is based on the old programming term **magic cookie**, which is defined as something passed between routines or programs that enables the receiver to perform some operation. It's this idea of passing data from one thing to another (in this case, from a page to your computer) that inspired the original cookie creators.

- Temporary cookie—This type of cookie lives just as long as you have Internet Explorer running. When you shut down the program, all the temporary cookies are deleted.

- Persistent cookie—This type of cookie remains on your hard disk through multiple Internet Explorer sessions. The cookie's duration depends on how it's set up, but it can be anything from a few seconds to a few years.

- First-party cookie—This is a cookie that's set by the website that you're viewing.

- Third-party cookie—This is a cookie that's set by a site other than the one you're viewing. Most third-party cookies are created and stored by advertisers who have placed an ad on the site you're viewing.

Given these cookie types, there are two ways that your privacy can be compromised:

- A site might store **personally identifiable information**—your name, email address, home address, phone number, and so on—in a persistent first- or third-party cookie and then use that information in some way (such as filling in a form) without your consent.

- A site might store information about you in a persistent third-party cookie and then use that cookie to track your online movements and activities. They can do this because they might have (for example) an ad on dozens or hundreds of websites and that ad is the mechanism that enables the site to set and read their cookies. Such sites are supposed to come up with **privacy policies** stating that they won't engage in surreptitious monitoring of users, they won't sell user data, and so on.

To help you handle these scenarios, Windows XP implements a privacy feature that gives you extra control over whether sites can store cookies on your machine. To check out this feature, select Internet Explorer's Tools, Internet Options command, and then display the Privacy tab, shown in Figure 21.7.

You set your cookie privacy level by using the slider in the Settings group. First, let's look at the two extreme settings:

- Accept All Cookies—This setting (it's at the bottom of the slider) tells Internet Explorer to accept all requests to set and read cookies.

- Block All Cookies—This setting (it's at the top of the slider) tells Internet Explorer to reject all requests to set and read cookies.

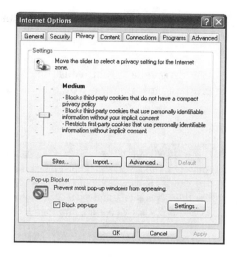

**FIGURE 21.7**   Use the Privacy tab to configure how Internet Explorer handles cookies.

> **CAUTION**
>
> Blocking all cookies might sound like the easiest way to maximize your online privacy. However, many sites rely on cookies to operate properly, so if you block all cookies you might find that your web surfing isn't as convenient or as smooth as it used to be.

In between there are four settings that offer more detailed control. Table 21.1 shows you how each setting affects the three types of privacy issues:

**TABLE 21.1**   Cookie Settings and Their Effect on Surfing Privacy

|  | Third-Party Cookies with No Compact Privacy Policy | Third-Party Cookies Using Personally Identifiable Information Without the Type of Consent | First-Party Cookies Using Personally Identifiable Information Without the Type of Consent |
|---|---|---|---|
| Low | Restricted | Restricted (implicit) | OK |
| Medium (the default) | Blocked | Blocked (implicit) | Restricted (implicit) |
| Medium High | Blocked | Blocked (explicit) | Blocked (implicit) |
| High | Blocked | Blocked (explicit) | Blocked (explicit) |

Here are some notes about the terminology in this table:

- **Restricted** means that Internet Explorer doesn't allow the site to set a persistent cookie, just a temporary one.

- A **compact** privacy policy is a shortened form of a privacy policy that can be sent along with the cookie and that can be read by the browser.

- **Implicit consent** means that on one or more pages leading up to the cookie, you were warned that your personally identifiable information would be used and you agreed that it was okay.

- **Explicit consent** means that on the page that reads the cookie, you were warned that your personally identifiable information would be used and you agreed that it was okay.

> **NOTE**
>
> If you decide to change the privacy setting, you should first delete all your cookies because the new setting won't apply to any cookies already on your computer. To delete your cookies, select Tools, Internet Options, display the General tab, and then click Delete Cookies. If you prefer to delete individual cookies, click Settings, click View Files, and then look for filenames that begin with Cookie:.

# Blocking Pop-Up Windows

Among the most annoying things on the Web arethose ubiquitous pop-up windows that infest your screen with advertisements when you visit certain sites. (A variation on the theme is the **pop under**, a window that opens under your current browser window, so you don't know it's there until you close the window.) Pop-up windows can also be dangerous because some unscrupulous software makers have figured out ways to use them to install software on your computer without your permission. They're nasty things, any way you look at them.

Fortunately, Microsoft has given us a way to stop pop-ups before they start. In the Windows XP Service Pack 2, Internet Explorer comes with a new feature called the Pop-up Blocker that looks for pop-ups and prevents them from opening. Follow these steps to use and configure the Pop-up Blocker:

1. In Internet Explorer, select Tools, Options to display the Internet Options dialog box.

2. Display the Privacy tab.

3. Activate the Pop-up Blocker check box.

4. To set options for this feature, click Settings to display the Pop-up Blocker Settings dialog box. You have the following options (click Close when you're done):

| | |
|---|---|
| Address of Web Site to Allow | Use this option when you have a site that displays pop-ups you want to see. Type the address and then click Add. |
| Play a Sound When a Pop-up Is Blocked | When this check box is activated, Internet Explorer plays a brief sound each time it blocks a pop-up. If this gets annoying after a while, deactivate this check box. |

| Show Information Bar When a Pop-up Is Blocked | When this check box is activated, Internet Explorer displays a yellow bar below the Address bar each time it blocks a pop-up so that you know it's working on your behalf. |

5.  Click OK.

With the Pop-Up Blocker on the case, it monitors your surfing and steps in front of any pop-up window that tries to disturb your peace. Figure 21.8 shows the yellow Information bar that appears under the Address bar to let you know when a pop-up was thwarted. If you want to see the pop-up anyway, click the Information bar and then click Show Blocked Pop-up in the menu that appears.

**FIGURE 21.8**    When the Pop-Up Blocker is active, it displays a yellow information bar each time it blocks a pop-up ad.

# Understanding Internet Explorer's Advanced Security Options

To close our look at Windows XP's Internet security features, this section takes you through Internet Explorer's Advanced security options. To see these options, select Tools, Internet Options, display the Advanced tab, and then scroll down to the Security section.

> **CAUTION**
>
> Don't surf the Web from an account with Administrator privileges. An account with Limited User or Power User privileges is much less susceptible to getting a virus.

- Allow Active Content from CDs to Run on My Computer (Service Pack 2)—Leave this check box deactivated to prevent active content such as scripts and controls located in CD-based web pages to execute on your computer. However, if you have a CD-based program that won't function, you might need to activate this check box to enable the program to work properly.

- Allow Active Content to Run in Files on My Computer (Service Pack 2)—Leave this check box deactivated to prevent active content such as scripts and controls located in local web pages to execute on your computer. If you're testing a web page that includes active content, activate this check box so that you can test the web pages locally.

- Allow Software to Run or Install Even If the Signature Is Invalid (Service Pack 2)—Leave this check box deactivated to avoid running or installing software that doesn't have a valid digital signature. If you can't get a program to run or install, consider activating this check box.

- Check for Publisher's Certificate Revocation—When this option is activated, Internet Explorer examines a site's digital security certificates to see whether they have been revoked.

- Check for Server Certificate Revocation (Requires Restart)—If you activate this option, Internet Explorer also checks the security certificate for the web page's server.

- Check for Signatures on Downloaded Programs—If you activate this check box, Internet Explorer checks for a digital signature on any program that you download.

- Do Not Save Encrypted Pages to Disk—If you activate this option, Internet Explorer won't store encrypted files in the Temporary Internet Files folder.

- Empty Temporary Internet Files Folder When Browser Is Closed—When this option is activated, Internet Explorer removes all files from the Temporary Internet Files folder when you exit the program.

- Enable Integrated Windows Authentication—When this check box is activated, Internet Explorer uses **Integrated Windows Authentication**—formerly known as **Windows NT Challenge/Response authentication**—to attempt to log on to a restricted site. This means the browser attempts to log on using the current credentials from the user's network domain logon. If this doesn't work, Internet Explorer displays a dialog box prompting the user for a user name and password.

- Enable Profile Assistant—This check box toggles the Profile Assistant on and off. Your **profile** is an extra entry in the Windows Address Book that stores your personal information (name, address, and so on). The Profile Assistant can work with some websites to share this data, which prevents you from having to enter this data by hand. To edit your profile, see the options in the Content tab's Personal Information group.

- Use SSL 2.0—This check box toggles support for the Secure Sockets Layer Level 2 security protocol on and off. This version of SSL is currently the Web's standard security protocol.

- Use SSL 3.0—This check box toggles support for SSL Level 3 on and off. SSL 3.0 is more secure than SSL 2.0 (it can authenticate both the client and the server), but isn't currently as popular as SSL 2.0.

- Use TLS 1.0—This check box toggles support for **Transport Layer Security** (**TLS**) on and off. This is a relatively new protocol, so few websites implement it.

- Warn About Invalid Site Certificates—When activated, this option tells Internet Explorer to display a warning dialog box if a site is using an invalid digital security certificate.

- Warn If Changing Between Secure and Not Secure Mode—When activated, this option tells Internet Explorer to display a warning dialog box whenever you enter and leave a secure site.

- Warn If Forms Submittal Is Being Redirected—When activated, this option tells Internet Explorer to display a warning dialog box if a form submission is going to be sent to a site other than the one hosting the form.

## Security and Privacy Options for Windows Media Player

You can set some options in Windows Media Player to ensure that media downloaded from or played on an Internet site is safe. You can also set options in Windows Media Player that enhance the privacy of the Internet media you play.

You'll find Windows Media Player's security and privacy settings in the Options dialog box, which you display by selecting Tools, Options.

> **TIP**
>
> You can use the Group Policy editor to hide the Security and Privacy tabs in the Options dialog box. Select User Configuration, Administrative Templates, Windows Components, Windows Media Player, User Interface, and then enable the Hide Privacy Tab and Hide Security Tab policies.

### Setting Security Options

You can play Internet media either by downloading the music or video to your computer and playing it in Windows Media Player, or by using a version of Windows Media Player that resides inside a web page. Either way, the person who created the media might have included extra commands in a script that is designed to control the playback. Unfortunately, scripts can also contain commands that can harm your computer, so preventing these scripts from running at all is the best option.

In the Security tab, there are three check boxes in the Content group that control scripting:

| | |
|---|---|
| Run Script Commands When Present | Leave this check box deactivated to avoid running scripts in downloaded media. |
| Do Not Run Script Commands and Rich Media Streams If the Player Is Running Inside a Web Page | Leave this check box deactivated to avoid running scripts in media embedded in web pages. |
| Do Not Prompt Me Before Playing Enhanced Content That Uses Web Pages | Leave this check box deactivated to have Windows Media Player ask whether you want to view a media site's **enhanced content**, or web pages that give you information related to the media. Because these pages |

can contain malicious content, it's best to have Windows Media Player ask whether you want to see the enhanced data.

## Setting Privacy Options

When you use Windows Media Player to play content from an Internet site, the program communicates certain information to the site, including the unique ID number of your copy of Windows Media Player. This allows content providers to track the media you play, and they might share this data with other sites. So, although the Player ID does not identify you personally, it might result in sites sending you targeted ads based on your media choices. If you do not want such an invasion of privacy, you can instruct Windows Media Player not to send the Player ID:

1. In the Options dialog box, display the Privacy tab.

2. Make sure that the Send Unique Player ID to Content Providers check box is deactivated.

> **CAUTION**
>
> Remember that some content sites *require* the Player ID before you can play any media. For example, a site might request the ID for billing purposes. In that case, you should read the site's privacy statement to see what uses it makes of the ID.

3. Two other privacy options are worth considering:

| | |
|---|---|
| I Want to Help Make Microsoft Software and Services Even Better | Leave this check box deactivated to avoid sending your Windows Media Player usage data to Microsoft. |
| Save File and URL History in the Player | Deactivate this check box if you don't want other people who use your computer to see the media files and sites that you play and visit. |

4. Click OK.

# From Here

Here's a list of chapters where you'll find related information:

- For the details on using the Group Policy editor, refer to the section titled "Implementing Group Policies with Windows XP, "in Chapter 7, "Using Control Panel, Group Policies, and Tweak UI."

- To find out about scripting Windows XP, refer to Chapter 9, "Programming the Windows Scripting Host."

- To learn how to block email senders, refer to the section titled "Blocking Senders" in Chapter 19, "Communicating with Internet Email."

- To learn how to create mail rules, refer to the section in Chapter 19 titled "Creating a Mail Rule."

- To learn how to secure your wireless network, see the section titled "Implementing Wireless Network Security" in Chapter 22, "Setting Up and Accessing a Small Network."

- To learn how to make secure remote connections to your network over the Internet, see the section titled "Using Virtual Private Network Connections" in Chapter 23, "Making Remote Network Connections."

21

# PART VI

# Unleashing Windows XP Networking

## IN THIS PART

# Setting Up and Accessing a Small Network

For many years, networking was the private playground of IT panjandrums. Its obscure lingo and arcane hardware were familiar to only this small coterie of computer cognoscenti. Workers who needed access to network resources had to pay obeisance to these powers-that-be, genuflecting in just the right way, tossing in the odd salaam or two.

Lately, however, we've seen a democratization of networking. Thanks to the trend away from mainframes and toward client/server setups, thanks to the migration from dumb terminals to smarter PCs, and thanks to the advent of easy peer-to-peer setups, networking is no longer the sole province of the elite. Getting connected to an existing network, or setting up your own network in a small office or home office, has never been easier.

This chapter shows you how Windows XP has helped take even more of the *work* out of networking. After going through some necessary network background, you'll learn how to set up your own simple network and access its resources.

## Understanding Networking

The chapters in Part VI, "Unleashing Windows XP Networking," are self-contained and, on a basic "how-to" level, require no further embellishment. To truly unleash Windows XP's connectivity options, however, you need a bit of network know-how, and that's what the first part of this chapter is all about. You'll learn all the necessary network nomenclature (such as the difference between *client/server* and *peer-to-peer*), hardware requirements, the ins and outs of cabling, protocol descriptions, and lots more. You can think of this section as your initiation into the black art of networking, except, as you'll see, things aren't as black as they used to be.

If you just have a single computer in your office or at home, and if you're the only person who uses that computer, your setup is inherently efficient. You can use the machine whenever you like, and everything you need—your applications, your printer, your CD-ROM drive, your modem, and so on—will be readily available.

Things become noticeably less efficient if you have to share the computer with other people. Then you might have to wait for someone else to finish a task before you can get your own work done; you might need to have separate applications for each person's requirements; and you might need to set up separate folders to hold each person's data. Windows XP's user accounts and Fast User Switching features (refer to Chapter 6, "Getting the Most Out of User Accounts") ease these problems, but they don't eliminate them. However, although this solution might ease some of the burden, it won't eliminate it entirely. For example, you might still have to twiddle a thumb or two while waiting for another person to complete his work.

A better solution is to increase the number of computers available. Now that machines with fast processors, ample RAM, and massive hard disk space can be had for less than $1,000, a multiple-machine setup is an affordable proposition for small offices. Even at home, the current trend is to buy a nice system for mom and dad to put in their office, while the kids inherit the old machine for their games and homework assignments.

Multiple machines, however, bring with them new inefficiencies:

- In many cases, it's just not economically feasible to supply each computer with its own complete set of peripherals. Printers, for example, are a crucial part of the computing equation—when you need them. If someone needs a printer only a couple of times a week, it's hard to justify shelling out hundreds of dollars so that person can have his or her own printer. The problem, then, is how to share a printer (or whatever) among several machines.

- These days, few people work in splendid isolation. Rather, the norm is that colleagues and coworkers often have to share data and work together on the same files. If everyone uses a separate computer, how are they supposed to share files?

- Most offices have standardized on particular software packages for word processing, spreadsheets, graphics, and other mainstream applications. Does this mean that you have to purchase a copy of an expensive software program or suite for each machine? As with peripherals, what do you do about a person who uses a program only sporadically?

- Everyone wants on the Internet, of course, but paying a subscription for each user seems wasteful. What's needed is a way to share a single Internet connection.

Yes, you can overcome these limitations. To share a printer, for example, you could simply lug it from machine to machine, as needed, or else get a 100-foot parallel cable that can be plugged into whichever computer needs access to the printer. This won't work if you need to share an internal CD-ROM drive, however. For data, there's always the old "sneaker net" solution: Plop the files on a floppy disk and run them back and forth between computers. As for applications, you could install some programs on a single machine and require users to share, but that brings us back to the original problem of multiple people sharing a single machine.

There has to be a better way. For example, wouldn't it be better if you could simply attach a peripheral to a single machine and make it possible for any other computer to access that peripheral whenever it is needed? Wouldn't it be better if users could easily move documents back and forth between computers, or had a common storage area for shared files? Wouldn't it be better if you installed an application in only one location and everyone could run the program on his own machine at will?

Well, I'm happy to report that there is a better way, and it's called **networking**. The underlying idea of a network is simple: You connect multiple machines by running special cables from one computer to another. These cables plug into adapter cards (called **network interface cards**; I'll talk more about them later in this chapter) that are installed inside each computer. With this basic card/cable combination—or even a wireless setup— and a network-aware operating system (such as Windows XP), you can solve all the inefficiencies just described:

- A printer (or just about any peripheral) that's attached to one machine can be used by any other machine on the network.

- Files can be transferred along the cables from one computer to another.

- Users can access disk drives and folders on network computers as though they were part of their own computer. In particular, you can set up a folder to store common data files, and each user will be able to access these files from the comfort of her machine. (For security, you can restrict access to certain folders and drives.)

- You can install an application on one machine and set things up so that other machines can run the application without having to install the entire program on their local hard drive. There's no such thing as a free lunch, however. You have to purchase a license to install the application on the other computers. However, depending on how many users you have, buying a license is usually cheaper than buying additional full-blown copies of the application.

- You can set up an Internet connection on one machine and share that connection with other machines on the network.

Not only are the problems solved, but a whole new world of connected computing becomes available. For example, you can establish an email system so that users can send messages to each other via the network. You can use **groupware** applications that enable users to collaborate on projects, schedules, and documents. As the administrator of the network, you can remotely manage other computers, such as installing new software or customizing the environment for each user.

It sounds great, but are there downsides to all of this? Yes. Unfortunately, there is no such thing as a networking nirvana just yet. In all, you have three main concerns:

Security    This is a big issue, to be sure, because you're giving users access to resources outside their own computers. You must set things up so that people can't damage files or invade other peoples' privacy, intentionally or otherwise.

Speed    Network connections are fast, but they're not as fast as a local hard drive. So, running networked applications or working with remote documents won't have quite the snap that users might prefer.

Setup    Networked computers are inherently harder to set up and maintain than standalone machines. Difficulties include the initial tribulations of installing and configuring networking cards and running cables, as well as the ongoing issues of sharing resources, setting up passwords, and so on.

The benefits of connectivity, however, greatly outweigh the disadvantages, so budding network administrators shouldn't be dissuaded by these few quibbles. Now that I've convinced you that a network is a good thing, let's turn our attention to the types of networks you can set up.

## LANs, WANs, MANs, and More

Networks come in three basic flavors: local area networks, internetworks, and wide area networks:

**Local area network (LAN)**    A LAN is a network in which all the computers occupy a relatively small geographical area, such as a department, office, home, or building. In a LAN, all the connections between computers are made via network cables.

**Internetwork**    An internetwork is a network that combines two or more LANs by means of a special device, such as a bridge or a router. (See "Hardware: NICs and Other Network Knickknacks" later in this chapter for explanations of these and other internetworking devices.) Internetworks are often called *internets* for short, but they shouldn't be confused with the Internet, the global collection of networks.

**Wide area network (WAN)**    A WAN is a network that consists of two or more LANs or internet works spaced out over a relatively large geographical area, such as a state, a country, or the world. The networks in a WAN typically are connected via high-speed, fiber-optic phone lines, microwave dishes, or satellite links.

### Intranets and Extranets

The current popularity of the Internet is spilling over into corporate networks. Management information systems (**MIS**) types all over the world have seen how Internet technology can be both cost-effective and scalable, so they've been wondering how to deliver the same benefits on the corporate level. The result is an **intranet**: The implementation of Internet technologies such as TCP/IP and World Wide Web servers for use within a corporate organization rather than for connection to the Internet as a whole.

A related network species is the **extranet**. In this case, Internet technologies are used to give external users—such as customers and employees in other offices—access to a corporate TCP/IP network. For example, many online banks use an extranet to provide web browser–based banking over a secure private connection.

### NOTE

Network resources are usually divided into two categories: local and remote. Not to be confused with the *local* in *local area network*, a **local resource** is any peripheral, file, folder, or application that is either attached directly to your computer or resides on your computer's hard disk. By contrast, a remote resource is any peripheral, file, folder, or application that exists somewhere on the network.

Other types of networks also exist. A **campus network** connects all the buildings in a school campus or an industrial park. Such networks often span large geographical areas, like WANs, but use private cabling to connect their subnetworks. A **metropolitan area network** (**MAN**) connects computers in a city or county and is usually regulated by a municipal or state utility commission. Finally, an **enterprise network** connects all the computers within an organization, no matter how geographically diverse the computers might be, and no matter what kinds of operating systems and network protocols are used in individual segments of the network.

## Client/Server Versus Peer-to-Peer

It used to be that the dominant network model revolved around a single, monolithic computer with massive amounts of storage space and processing power. Attached to this behemoth were many **dumb terminals**—essentially just a keyboard and monitor—that contained no local storage and no processing power. Instead, the central mainframe or minicomputer was used for all data storage and to run all applications.

The advent of the PC, however, has more or less sounded the death knell for the dumb terminal. Not surprisingly, users prefer having local disks so that they can keep their data close at hand and run their own applications. (This is, after all, the *personal* computer we're talking about.) To accommodate the PC revolution, two new kinds of network models have become dominant: client/server and peer-to-peer.

### Client/Server Networks

In general, the **client/server model** splits the computing workload into two separate, yet related, areas. On one hand, you have users working at intelligent front-end systems called **clients**. In turn, these client machines interact with powerful back-end systems called **servers**. The basic idea is that the clients have enough processing power to perform tasks on their own, but they rely on the servers to provide them with specialized resources or services, or access to information that would be impractical to implement on a client (such as a large database).

This client/server relationship forms the basis of many network operating systems. In this case, a server computer provides various network-related services, such as access to resources (a network printer, for example), centralized file storage, password verification and other security measures, server-based application setup, email, data backups, and access to external networks (such as the Internet).

The various client PCs, although they have their own storage and processing power, interact with the server whenever they need access to network-related resources or services, as illustrated in Figure 22.1. Client computers are also referred to as **nodes** or **workstations**.

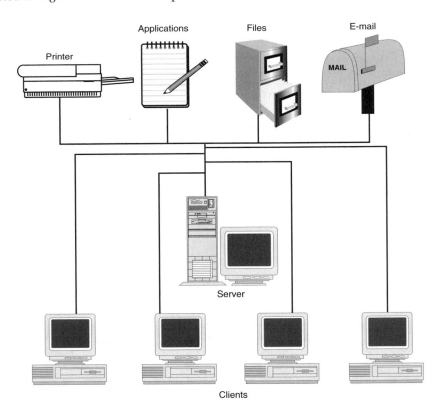

**FIGURE 22.1** In a client/server network, each client machine accesses network services and resources via a server machine.

Note that in most client/server networks, the server computer can perform only server duties. In other words, you can't use it as a client to run applications.

In this client/server networking model, two types of software are required:

| | |
|---|---|
| **Network operating system (NOS)** | This software runs on the server and provides the various network services for the clients. The range of services available depends on the NOS. NetWare, for example, provides not only file and print services, but also email, communications, and security services. Other network operating systems that use the client/server model are Windows 2003 Server and UNIX. |
| Client software | This software provides applications that run on the client machine with a way to request services and resources from the server. If an application needs a local resource, the client software forwards the request to the local operating system; if an application needs a server resource, the client software redirects the request to the network operating system. Windows XP provides clients for Microsoft networks and NetWare networks. |

For small LANs, a single server is usually sufficient for handling all client requests. As the LAN grows, however, the load on the server increases and network performance can suffer. Nothing in the client/server model restricts a network to a single server, however. So, to ease the server burden, most large LANs utilize multiple servers. In **distributed networks**, administrators are free to organize the servers' duties in any way that maximizes network performance. For example, administrators can split clients into workgroups and assign each group to a specific server. Similarly, they can split the duties performed by each server. For example, one server could handle file services, whereas another could handle print services, and so on.

### Peer-to-Peer Networks

In a **peer-to-peer network**, no computer is singled out to provide special services. Instead, all the computers attached to the network have equal status (at least as far as the network is concerned), and all the computers can act as both servers and clients, as illustrated in Figure 22.2.

On the server side, each computer can share any of its resources with the network *and* control access to these shared resources. For example, if a user shares a folder with the network, she also can set up passwords to restrict access to that folder.

On the client side, each computer can work with the resources that have been shared by the other peers on the network (assuming that it has permission to do so, of course).

### Which One Should You Choose?

If you're thinking about networking a few computers, should you go with a client/server setup or a peer-to-peer model? That's a tough question to answer because it depends on so many factors: the number of computers you want to connect, the operating system (or systems) you're using, the services you need, the amount of money you have available to spend, and so on.

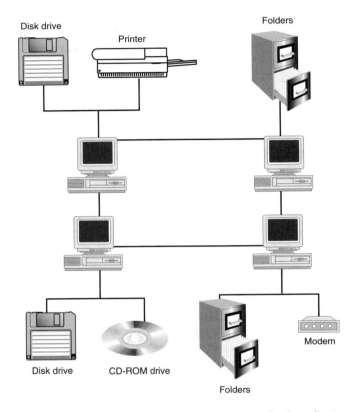

**FIGURE 22.2** In a peer-to-peer setup, every computer acts as both a client and a server and no machine has any special status in the network.

In general, the smaller the network, the more sense the peer-to-peer model makes. This is particularly true if you're running Windows XP because it's designed as a peer-to-peer NOS. After you've installed your network cards and run your cables, you're more or less ready to go. Windows XP's automatic hardware detection usually does a pretty good job of recognizing and configuring the network hardware, and the network client makes it easy to share and access network resources.

If, rather than just a few computers, you have a few dozen, you'll have to go the client/server route. Large peer-to-peer setups are just too unwieldy to maintain and administer, and performance quickly drops off as you add more nodes. A top-of-the-line client/server NOS (such as Windows 2003 Server or NetWare) comes with remote administration, scales nicely as you add more clients and servers, and is robust enough to handle large loads. The price you pay for all this power is, well, the price: These big-time operating systems are expensive and usually require an extra hardware investment beyond the standard card/cable combo. And with power comes complexity. Unlike the relative simplicity of their peer-to-peer counterparts, administration of medium-to-large client/server networks isn't for the faint of heart.

# Hardware: NICs and Other Network Knickknacks

The client and operating system software are only part of the network picture. Whether you go with a client/server or a peer-to-peer setup, you must have some kind of connection between machines. In other words, before the network of file sharing and email can become a reality, an underlying physical network must be in place. The next few sections introduce you to the various components that comprise the nuts and bolts of this physical network.

## The Network Interface Card

The **network interface card** (**NIC**) is an adapter that, usually, slips into an expansion bus slot inside a client or server computer. (External NICs that plug into USB ports or PC Card slots are also on the market.) The NIC's main purpose in life is to serve as the connection point between the PC and the network. The NIC's **backplate** (that is, the portion of the NIC you can see after the card has been installed) contains one or more ports into which you plug a network cable.

After the physical connection has been established, the NIC works with a device driver to process incoming and outgoing network data. As such, the NIC is the focal point for the computer's network connection, so it plays a big part in the overall performance of that connection. Each NIC is designed for a specific type of network architecture. The most common types are ethernet, token ring, and ARCnet, although ethernet is by far the most popular choice for small networks.

> **NOTE**
> If you have a broadband Internet connection, you'll need two NICs in your computer: one for the Internet connection and a second one for the network connection.

Ethernet works by using a carrier sense multiple access/collision detection method. This means that ethernet cards can sense a carrier signal on the network and so refrain from transmitting data. If no carrier signal is detected, the card sends data. However, if two or more cards attempt to send data simultaneously, a collision occurs. This is detected by the other cards on the network, and no data is sent until the collision has been resolved. (Specifically, the nodes involved in the collision resend their packets after waiting a random amount of time.)

There are three main types of ethernet NIC:

| | |
|---|---|
| Ethernet | This type of NIC provides 10Mbps throughput. |
| Fast Ethernet | This is a relatively new iteration of the ethernet architecture and, thanks to its support for 100Mbps throughput, is rapidly becoming the standard (if |

it isn't already). Note, too, that many NICs are 10/100 cards that support both Ethernet and Fast Ethernet.

Gigabit Ethernet    This type of card features 1Gbps throughput. This is impressive speed, to be sure, but it's probably overkill on a small network, unless you plan to transmit video or other high-bandwidth content.

---

**NOTE**

To achieve efficient and reliable data transfers, any information sent over a network is broken down into smaller pieces called **packets**. (You can think of a packet as the network equivalent of a single unit of information.) Each packet contains not only data, but also a **header**. The header contains information about which machine sent the data and which machine is supposed to receive the data. It also includes a few extra tidbits that let the network put all the original data together in the correct order and check for errors that might have cropped up during the transmission. A typical packet size is 512 bytes.

---

## The Cable Connection

To set up a communications pathway between network computers, you have to install cables that connect the various network nodes together. The starting point (figuratively speaking) for any cable is the network card. As I mentioned in the preceding section, an NIC's backplate has one or more external ports into which you insert a network cable. The key point here is that the cable you use must match the configuration of one of the NIC ports. To understand why, consider the difference between telephone cables and the coaxial wiring used by cable TV. If you examine the wall jacks for each type of cable, you'll see that the ports into which you plug the cables are completely different. There's no way, for example, to plug a coaxial cable into a telephone jack.

It's the same way with NIC ports: Each has a particular shape and pin arrangement that's designed for a specific type of cable. When buying network adapters, you need to match the ports with the type of cabling you intend to use.

This used to be a big deal a few years ago when different types of cables were used. Nowadays, however, almost all small networks use **twisted-pair** cable. It is composed of a pair of copper wires that together form a circuit that can transmit data. The wires are twisted together to reduce interference. This is similar to the cable used in telephone wiring, but network cables are usually shielded by braided metal insulation to further reduce interference problems. (You can use unshielded twisted-pair cabling, but the poorer line quality will restrict the distance between nodes and the total number of nodes.)

Twisted-pair cables use RJ-45 jacks to plug into corresponding RJ-45 connectors in an NIC or other type of network node, as shown in Figure 22.3. In ethernet circles, twisted-pair cables are also often referred to as **10Base-T cables** and RJ-45 ports are often called **10Base-T ports**.

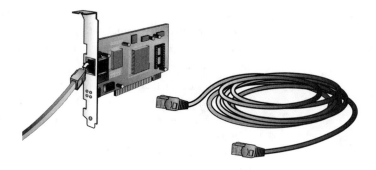

**FIGURE 22.3**    Twisted-pair cables use RJ-45 jacks to plug into the complementary RJ-45 connectors in network adapter cards.

> **NOTE**
>
> Twisted-pair cable is categorized according to the maximum transmission rates supported by various types of cable. For network data, for example, Category 3 cable supports the standard 10Mbps transmission rates available in most network installations. These days, however, few people purchase anything but Category 5 cable, which is rated at 100Mbps and can support higher-end network technologies such as Fast Ethernet.

## More Hardware Goodies

The network card/cable package is all that each PC requires to broadcast and to receive network packets, but it is by no means the only hardware you might need. Depending on the physical layout of your network, the types of services you need, and the type of card and cable you choose, you might have to spring for a few more trinkets. Just so you know what to expect, here's a list of some common network accessories:

**Hub** (also known as a **concentrator**)

A hub is a central connection point for network cables. That is, for each computer, you run a twisted-pair cable from the computer's NIC to an RJ-45 port on the hub. Hubs range in size from small boxes with six or eight RJ-45 ports to large cabinets with dozens of ports for various cable types. If you're using Fast Ethernet NICs, be sure to get a hub that also supports 100 Mbps. There are also 10/100 hubs available if you're using a mix of ethernet and Fast Ethernet.

**Router**

A router is a device that makes decisions about where to send the network packets it receives. Unlike a bridge (see the next item in this list), which merely passes along any data that comes its way, a router examines the address information in each packet and determines the most efficient route the packet must take to reach its eventual destination. For example, this is useful when the computers share a high-speed Internet connection because the router ensures that the Internet data goes to the computer that requested it. You should plug your high-speed modem directly into the router.

**Bridge**

A bridge is a device that connects two LANs, provided that the two LANs are using the same NOS. The bridge can be either a standalone device or implemented in a server by the addition of a second network card. One of the most common uses for a server bridge is to split an existing LAN into two segments. Doing so distributes the network load between the server's two NICs and thus improves overall network performance.

**Repeater**

Some cables suffer from attenuation—the degradation of the electrical signal carried over the cable is proportional to the distance the signal must travel. A repeater is a device that boosts the cable's signal so that the length of the network can be extended. Some hubs also act as repeaters (in which case they're called **active** hubs).

**Gateway**

A gateway is a computer or other device that acts as a middleman between two otherwise-incompatible systems. The gateway translates the incoming and outgoing packets so that each system can work the data. For example, you can use a gateway to connect a PC network and a Macintosh network. The gateway takes the data from one network type and translates it into a form that the other network understands. On a home network, a **residential gateway** is a computer or router that connects to the Internet.

## Understanding Wireless Network Hardware Requirements

The cabling requirements of a standard ethernet setup, and the restrictions those requirements impose on a client, have led an increasing number of network users to consider the cable-free configuration of a wireless network. Wireless devices transmit data and communicate with other devices using radio signals that are beamed from one device to another. Although these radio signals are similar to those used in commercial radio broadcasts, they operate on a different frequency. A **radio transceiver** is a device that can act as both a transmitter and a receiver of radio signals. All wireless devices that require two-way communications use a transceiver.

The most common wireless technology is **wireless fidelity**, which is also called **Wi-Fi** (rhymes with *hi-fi*) or **802.11**. There are four main types—802.11, 802.11a, 802.11b, and 802.11g—each of which has its own range and speed limits:

**Range**

All wireless devices have a maximum range beyond which they can no longer communicate with other devices. In practice, Wi-Fi networking ranges span from 75 feet for 802.11a to about 150 feet for 802.11b and 802.11g.

**Speed**

Wireless transmission speed—which is usually measured in megabits per second, or **Mbps**—is an important factor to consider when you set up a wireless network or a wireless Internet connection. Less expensive wireless networks most often use 802.11b, which has a theoretical top speed of 11Mbps. The increasingly popular 802.11g standard has a theoretical speed limit of 54Mbps.

**22**

---

**NOTE**

Another popular wireless technology is **Bluetooth**, a wireless networking standard that uses radio frequencies to set up a communications link between devices. This is called an **ad hoc network**. The Bluetooth name comes from Harald Bluetooth, a tenth-century Danish king who united the provinces of Denmark under a single crown, the same way that, theoretically, Bluetooth will unite the world of portable wireless devices under a single standard. Why name a modern technology after an obscure Danish king? Here's a clue: Two of the most important companies backing the Bluetooth standard—Ericsson and Nokia—are Scandinavian.

---

Wireless networks require two device types:

**Wireless NIC**

A wireless NIC is a special type of NIC that includes (or has built into its circuitry) a small antenna that receives and transmits data using radio frequencies. If your network consists of only computers with wireless NICs, you don't need any other equipment. (However, you will have to set up your NICs to use ad hoc mode for direct NIC-to-NIC communication; consult the operating manual that came with each wireless NIC.) There are four types of wireless NIC:

- PC Card—For notebook computers that do not have built-in wireless capabilities, you can insert a PC Card.

- Circuit board—You can insert a wireless NIC circuit board into your desktop computer.

- USB—For easier installation on a desktop computer, you can plug a USB wireless network adapter into a free USB port.

- Bluetooth adapter—To set up an ad hoc network with any Bluetooth device, your computer requires a Bluetooth adapter, most of which plug into a USB port.

**Wireless access point (AP)**

A wireless AP is a device that receives and transmits signals from wireless computers to form a wireless network. (This relatively more permanent form or network is called an infrastructure wireless network to differentiate such a network from an ad hoc network.) Many APs also accept wired connections, which enables both wired and wireless computers to form a network. If your network has a broadband modem, you can connect the modem to a type of AP called a wireless gateway, which extends Internet access to all the computers on the network.

---

**NOTE**

If you find that your wireless access point is not reaching certain areas of your home or office, you can use a **wireless range extender** to boost the signal. Depending on the device and wireless access point, the extender can more than double the normal wireless range. Bear in mind, however, that range extenders are notoriously difficult to incorporate into an existing network. For best results, use an extender from the same company that makes your wireless access point, and make sure that the extender is compatible with the access point.

---

# Walking the Walk: Topology and the Lay of the LAN

The next decision you have to make when putting together the specifications for your network is the **topology** you want to use. The network topology describes how the various nodes that the network comprises—which include not only the computers, but also devices such as hubs and bridges—are connected. Three common topologies are used in LANs: star, bus, and ring.

## The Star Topology

The **star topology**, as you can see in Figure 22.4, consists of multiple workstations connected to a hub or router. In the most common scenario, each computer has a network adapter with an RJ-45 connector running a twisted-pair cable to a port in the hub. The hub (usually) just passes along the signals, so each computer gains access to the other computers on the network.

This is an excellent topology for peer-to-peer networks because it mirrors the no-machine-is-more-equal-than-any-other-machine philosophy of peer-to-peer. It's also easy to add machines to the network because it's a simple matter of running a new cable to the hub. If the hub's ports are used up, you can connect a second hub to the first one. Another advantage of the star topology is that if one machine goes down for the count, the network access of the other machines isn't affected. On the downside, star topology networks tend to need a lot of cable because you have to connect every node directly to the hub.

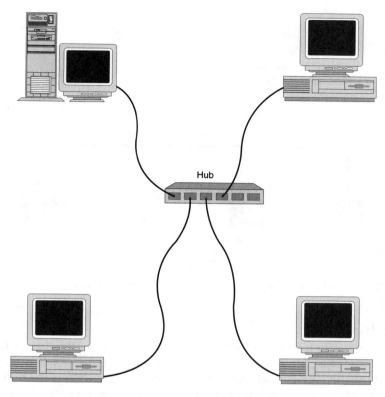

**FIGURE 22.4**   In the star topology, all the network computers are connected to a central hub.

## The Bus Topology

In a **bus topology**, shown in Figure 22.5, each node is attached to a single main cable called a bus or a backbone. For large networks, the backbone often extends throughout an entire building and is hidden behind the walls. For such lengthy cables, repeaters are often needed to boost the signal along various points of the backbone. Connections to the backbone are made via drop cables that run from network cards to wall jacks or some other junction box.

The big advantage of the bus topology is that it's relatively easy to set up (aside from the effort required to run cable through a building's walls), and its layout often mirrors the physical layout of an office or a building. The major drawback of the bus topology is that a break in the backbone brings down the entire network.

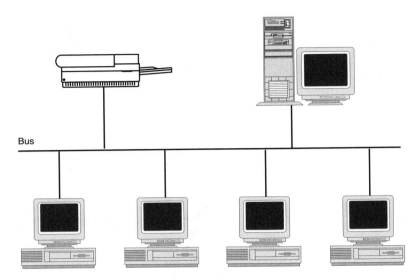

Bus

**FIGURE 22.5**    In the bus topology, each computer is connected to a backbone cable.

## The Ring Topology

At first glance, the **ring topology** sounds suspiciously like the star topology. Each network node is connected to a central device, which is a special kind of hub called a **multistation access unit (MAU)**, as shown in Figure 22.6. The difference lies in how the hub views the network. In the star topology, when the hub receives a packet, it checks the destination and then forwards the packet to the appropriate node without worrying about any other node on the network. In the ring topology, however, the circuitry of the MAU organizes the entire network as a ring, and each received packet is broadcast around the ring.

This is the topology used in token ring and ARCnet networks. This makes sense because these network architectures use a token-passing method to allocate cable access. The ring structure is a very efficient way to pass the token around to each node, so overall performance is improved.

Like star topologies, ring topologies are more stable than bus designs because one node going down doesn't affect the entire network. There is one exception, however. The ring topology requires that each node actively pass along each packet. If a node goes down before it has had a chance to pass along a packet, the entire network crashes. Such a situation, however, is relatively rare.

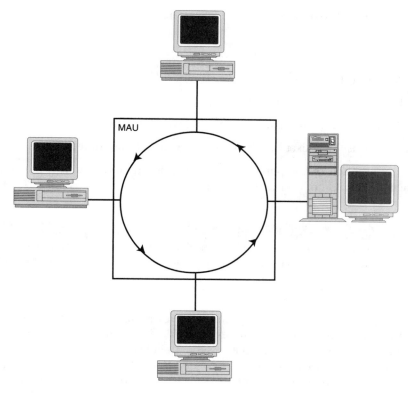

**FIGURE 22.6**   In a ring topology, the central MAU organizes the network nodes in a ring.

## Talking the Talk: Networking Protocols

In diplomacy, protocol defines the rules and formalities that ensure smooth communications between nations and cultures. A **networking protocol** performs a similar function: It's a set of standards that define how information is exchanged between two systems across a network connection.

For example, consider what appears to be a simple procedure: exchanging a file between two networked computers. I mentioned earlier that files and all other network transmissions are broken down into packets. Because a large file might consist of hundreds or even thousands of packets, there has to be some way of coordinating how all this information is sent and received. Here are just a few of the questions that must be answered for even the simplest file transfer to succeed:

- Which computer is sending the packets?

- Where are the packets supposed to go?

- What is the structure of each packet? How big is the header? How big is each data field inside the header? What order are the data fields in? What kinds of addresses are being used? What kind of error checking mechanism is being used? Where does the data start?

- How many packets are in the transfer?

- In what order should the packets be reassembled?

- What happens if a packet arrives damaged?

- How long should the destination computer wait for a packet to arrive?

- What happens if a packet hasn't arrived after the allotted time?

- How does the source computer know that the destination computer has received a particular packet and, eventually, the entire file?

> **NOTE**
>
> If you'd like to see some examples of packet structure, refer to Chapter 17, "Implementing TCP/IP for Internet Connections." That chapter shows you the structure for both IP and TCP packets.

As you can see, it takes an incredible amount of give-and-take to coordinate any kind of network interaction. The inherent complexity of this process means that if the source and destination systems are even slightly out of sync, the file either will arrive corrupted or won't arrive at all. Network protocols are designed to ensure that this doesn't happen. The protocol specifies in no uncertain terms all the details of any kind of network transfer. Generally speaking, protocols fall into two categories: transport protocols and network protocols.

With a **transport protocol** (also called a **connection-oriented protocol**), a virtual communications channel is established between two nodes, and the protocol uses this channel to send packets between the nodes. Because the source and destination are defined in advance, the packets need not contain full address information. The constant link between the two nodes provides the protocol with an efficient path for exchanging messages, so this type of communications method is useful for applications that require a long-term connection (such as a network monitoring program). However, some overhead is involved in both setting up and closing the channel, so this method isn't suitable for short-lived communications.

With a **network protocol** (also called a **connectionless protocol**), no communications channel is established between nodes. Instead, the protocol builds each packet with all the information required for the network to deliver each packet and for the destination node to reassemble the packets into the original file. These self-contained independent packets are called **datagrams**. The protocol then ships out the packets without notifying or negotiating with the destination node. All the network has to do is transmit the packets to the destination or to some intermediate stop along the way. This method requires a bit more packet overhead, but it's efficient for short bursts because there's no need to set up or shut down a channel between nodes.

Many protocols are available, but two are most common (these are the standard protocols available with Windows XP):

| | |
|---|---|
| **TCP/IP** | TCP/IP stands for **Transmission Control Protocol/Internet Protocol**; TCP is the transport protocol, and IP is the network protocol. TCP/IP is the *lingua franca* of most UNIX systems and the Internet as a whole. However, TCP/IP is also an excellent choice for other types of networks because it's routable, robust, and reliable. I talked about TCP/IP in detail in Chapter 17. |
| **IPX/SPX** | IPX/SPX stands for **Internet Packet eXchange/Sequenced Packet eXchange**. IPX is a connectionless network layer protocol. As a network layer protocol, IPX addresses and routes packets from one network to another on an IPX internetwork. SPX, on the other hand, is an extension of IPX that provides for connection-oriented transport layer functions. SPX enhances the IPX protocol by providing reliable delivery. IPX/SPX is used by NetWare networks. |

When setting up your network, you don't have to commit to a single protocol. Windows XP is happy to work with multiple protocols simultaneously, so you don't have to box yourself in. This is particularly handy in network environments that must access different types of machines. You can use IPX/SPX to access a NetWare server, and TCP/IP to access UNIX boxes, most Windows clients, and the Internet. However, most small networks operate best by using only TCP/IP.

# Setting Up a Peer-to-Peer Network

Our look at the theoretical side of networking is done, so now it's time to get down to more practical matters. I discuss peer-to-peer networks in this chapter and the subsequent networking chapters, so let's begin by looking at how to set up a peer-to-peer network with Windows XP.

> **NOTE**
>
> The procedures in this section assume that you've installed and connected all networking hardware, including NICs, cables, and topological devices (such as a router or hub).

## Running the Network Setup Wizard

In previous versions of Windows, setting up a network usually involved working with obscure settings. These are still available in Windows XP, but there's also a less perplexing route to network connectivity: the Network Setup Wizard. Even if you enjoy working with TCP/IP settings and network protocols, using the Network Setup Wizard is the best way to ensure trouble-free network operation.

Windows XP has a feature called **Internet Connection Sharing** (**ICS**) that enables you to share one computer's Internet connection with other computers on the network. How you start setting up your network depends on whether you'll be using ICS:

- If you'll be using ICS, run the Network Setup Wizard on the computer that will be sharing its connection. This machine is called the **ICS host**. Make sure that this machine's Internet connection is active before running the wizard. When you're done, you can run the Network Setup Wizard on the other clients, in any order.

- If you won't be using ICS, run the Network Setup Wizard on any computer, in any order.

### Configuring the ICS Host

Here are the steps to follow to run the Network Setup Wizard on the ICS host computer:

1. Connect to the Internet.

2. Select Start, All Programs, Accessories, Communications, Network Setup Wizard.

3. In the initial Network Setup Wizard dialog box, click Next.

4. The next wizard dialog box outlines some tasks you must have completed before continuing (such as installing NICs). You've done all that, so click Next.

5. If the wizard locates a shared Internet connection elsewhere on the network, the Do You Want to Use the Shared Connection? dialog box appears. In this case, activate the No, Let Me Choose Another Way to Connect to the Internet option, and then click Next.

6. In the Select a Connection Method dialog box, make sure that the This Computer Connects Directly to the Internet option is activated, and then click Next. The wizard displays a list of the connections defined on your system.

7. Select the Internet connection and click Next.

8. Run through the rest of the Network Setup Wizard's steps, as described later in the "Completing the Network Setup Wizard" section.

### Configuring Other ICS Machines

Here are the steps to follow to run the Network Setup Wizard on the other computers in an ICS network:

1. Select Start, All Programs, Accessories, Communications, Network Setup Wizard.

2. In the first two Network Setup Wizard dialog boxes, click Next. The Do You Want to Use the Shared Connection? dialog box appears.

3. Make sure that the Yes, Use the Existing Shared Connection for This Computer's Internet Access option is activated, and then click Next.

4. Run through the rest of the Network Setup Wizard's steps, as described later in the "Completing the Network Setup Wizard" section.

### Configuring a Network with a Residential Gateway

If your network uses a broadband Internet connection attached to a residential gateway, follow these steps to run the Network Setup Wizard to configure the network to use the gateway:

1. Select Start, All Programs, Accessories, Communications, Network Setup Wizard.

2. In the first two Network Setup Wizard dialog boxes, click Next.

3. If the wizard locates a shared Internet connection elsewhere on the network, the Do You Want to Use the Shared Connection? dialog box appears. In this case, activate the No, Let Me Choose Another Way to Connect to the Internet option, and then click Next.

4. In the Select a Connection Method dialog box, activate the This Computer Connects to the Internet Through a Residential Gateway or Through Another Computer on My Network option, and then click Next.

5. Run through the rest of the Network Setup Wizard's steps, as described later in the "Completing the Network Setup Wizard" section.

### Configuring a Network Without the Internet

If your network doesn't have Internet access, follow these steps to run the Network Setup Wizard to configure the network properly:

1. Select Start, All Programs, Accessories, Communications, Network Setup Wizard.

2. In the first two Network Setup Wizard dialog boxes, click Next.

3. If the wizard locates a shared Internet connection elsewhere on the network, the Do You Want to Use the Shared Connection? dialog box appears. In this case, activate the No, Let Me Choose Another Way to Connect to the Internet option, and then click Next.

4. In the Select a Connection Method dialog box, activate the Other option and click Next.

5. Activate the This Computer Belongs to a Network That Does Not Have an Internet Connection, and then click Next.

6. Run through the rest of the Network Setup Wizard's steps, as described in the next section, "Completing the Network Setup Wizard."

### Completing the Network Setup Wizard

The rest of the Network Setup Wizard's steps are common to all configurations:

1. If you have more than one connection on your computer, the wizard offers to bridge the connections for you. In this case, activate Let Me Choose the Connections to My Network and click Next. Now activate the check box beside the connection that you use to access the network and click Next.

2. Type a computer description and a computer name (which must be unique among the networked computers) and click Next.

3. Type a workgroup name (which must be the same for all the networked computers) and click Next.

4. Click Next to apply the network settings.

5. The wizard asks how you want to run the Network Setup Wizard on your other computers. You have four choices (click Next when you're done):

| | |
|---|---|
| Create a Network Setup Disk | Choose this option if you'll be including Windows 9x or Me computers in the network. This creates a floppy disk that includes a version of the Network Setup Wizard. You insert this disk into a Windows 9x/Me client and run the wizard on that computer. |
| Use the Network Setup Disk I Already Have | Choose this option if you've already created a network setup disk. |
| Use My Windows XP CD | Choose this option to run the Network Setup Wizard on the Windows 9x/Me computers using the Windows XP disc. In this case, you insert the disc in the other computer. When the Welcome window appears, click Perform Additional Tasks and then click Set Up a Home or Small Office Network. |
| Just Finish the Wizard | Choose this option if you don't need to run the wizard on Windows 9x/Me computers. |

6. Click Finish.

## Configuring a Wireless Gateway

A **wireless gateway** is a type of wireless access point that connects to a broadband modem to give all the computers on the network access to the Internet. This section gives you general instructions for configuring a wireless gateway.

Before beginning, make sure that your gateway is properly connected to your network:

1. Turn off the gateway and the broadband modem.

2. Run a network cable from the modem to the WAN port on the back of the gateway.

3. Run another network cable from one of your computers to any LAN port on the back of the gateway.

4. Turn on the gateway and modem.

**CAUTION**

Some broadband providers are using "smart" modems that include routing and firewall features. That's fine, but these modems almost always have a static IP address, and that address is usually either http://192.168.1.1 or http://192.168.0.1, which might conflict with your wireless gateway's IP address. If you have connection problems after you've added the wireless gateway, an IP address conflict is the likely culprit. Disconnect the broadband modem, access the gateway's configuration program, and change its IP address (to, say, http://192.168.1.2 or http://192.168.0.2).

You're now ready to access the gateway's configuration program using the computer that you connected to the gateway in step 3. Here are the general steps to follow (note that the exact procedure will vary depending on the manufacturer of the gateway):

1. On the computer connected to the gateway, start Internet Explorer, type the gateway address (usually either http://192.168.1.1 or http://192.168.0.1) and press Enter.

2. If required, type the default username and password (supplied by the gateway manufacturer). The gateway's setup page appears. Figure 22.7 shows a sample setup page.

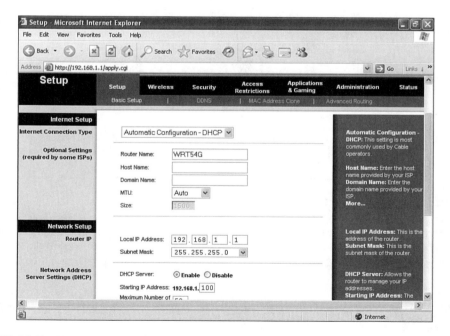

**FIGURE 22.7**    Use Internet Explorer to access the gateway's setup page and configure the device's settings.

3. Specify the type of connection used by your ISP. There are three main types:

| Dynamic IP Address | Most ISPs use **Dynamic Host Configuration Protocol** (**DHCP**) to assign IP addresses dynamically when you connect to their service. If your ISP does this, configure the gateway to obtain the address automatically. |
| --- | --- |
| Static IP Address | If your ISP provided you with a static IP address, configure the gateway with that address. You must also enter the subnet mask, gateway address, and one or more DNS addresses. Your ISP will have provided you with all of this data. |
| PPPoE | If your ISP requires a **Point-to-Point Protocol over Ethernet** (**PPPoE**) connection, type the username and password that your ISP provided to you. |

4. Each wireless network has a public name—often called a **Service Set Identifier** (or **SSID**)—that identifies the network to wireless devices. Your gateway comes with a default name, but you should change the name to something that you will remember and that uniquely identifies your network (see Figure 22.8).

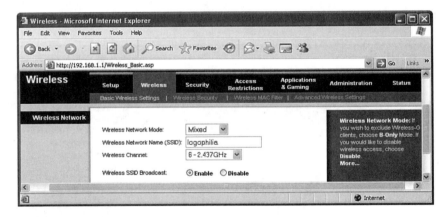

**FIGURE 22.8**    Be sure to change your gateway's default SSID.

5. Enable the gateway's DHCP Server option, as shown in Figure 22.9. Each computer on your network must also have an IP address. The easiest way to do this is to enable the gateway to generate addresses automatically using DHCP.

---

**NOTE**

Make sure that each computer is set up to use DHCP. Select Start, All Programs, Accessories, Communications, Network Connections. Right-click the Local Area Connection or the Wireless Network Connection, and then click Properties. In the connection's property sheet, double-click Internet Protocol and then make sure that the Obtain an IP address Automatically option is activated.

---

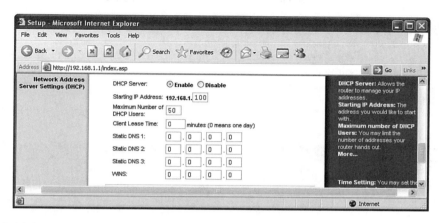

**FIGURE 22.9**    Enable DHCP on the gateway so that it can automatically provide dynamic IP addresses for each computer on your network.

## Implementing Wireless Network Security

Wireless networks are less secure than wired ones because the wireless connection that enables you to access the network from afar can also enable an intruder from outside your home or office to access the network. In particular, **wardriving** is an activity where a person drives through various neighborhoods with a portable computer or another device set up to look for available wireless networks. If the person finds a nonsecured network, he uses it for free Internet access or to cause mischief with shared network resources.

> **NOTE**
>
> If you don't believe that your wireless signals extend beyond your home or office, you can prove it to yourself. Unplug any wireless-enabled notebook and take it outside for a walk in the vicinity of your house. View the available wireless networks as you go (see "Connecting to a Wireless Network," later in this chapter), and you'll probably find that you can travel a fair distance (several houses, at least) away from your wireless access point and still see your network.

Here are a few tips and techniques you can easily implement to enhance the security of your wireless network:

- Enable encryption—First and foremost, enable encryption for wireless data so that an outside user who picks up your network packets will be unable to decipher them. Be sure to use the strongest encryption that your equipment supports. The most popular encryption method is **Wired Equivalency Privacy** (**WEP**). Older devices support only 64-bit WEP encryption, which is adequate for thwarting casual snoops. For more robust security, use 128-bit WEP encryption. Even better, use **Wi-Fi Protected Access** (**WPA**), which is even stronger than WEP, although it's a bit more complex to set up.

> **TIP**
>
> WPA isn't so complex if you use the simplest settings. For the security mode, select WPA Pre-Shared-Key, which doesn't require an authentication server. For the WPA algorithm, select **TKIP (Temporal Key Integrity Protocol)**, which works on most setups that support WPA. For the shared key, create a strong password between 8 and 63 characters long. Be sure to store this in a safe place because you'll need to adjust the wireless clients to use it.

> **NOTE**
>
> If you change your access point encryption method as described in the previous tip, you also need to update each wireless client to use the same form of encryption. In the Network Connections window, right-click your wireless network connection and then click Properties. Display the Wireless Networks tab, click your network in the list, and then click Properties. Change the following three settings and then click OK:
>
> | | |
> |---|---|
> | Network Authentication | Select WPA-PSK. |
> | Data Encryption | Select TKIP. |
> | Network Key | Type your shared key here and in the Confirm Network Key text box. |

- Disable network broadcasting—Windows XP sees your wireless network because the access point broadcasts the network's SSID. However, Windows XP remembers the wireless networks that you have successfully connected to. Therefore, after all of your computers have accessed the wireless network at least once, you no longer need to broadcast the network's SSID. Therefore, you should use your AP setup program to disable broadcasting and prevent others from seeing your network.

- Change the default SSID—Even if you disable broadcasting of your network's SSID, users can still attempt to connect to your network by guessing the SSID. All wireless access points come with a predefined name, such as linksys or default, and a would-be intruder will attempt these standard names first. Therefore, you can increase the security of your network by changing the SSID to a new name that is difficult to guess.

- Change the access point username and password—Any person within range of your wireless access point can open the device's setup page by entering **http://192.168.1.1** or **http://192.168.0.1** into a web browser. The person must log on with a username and password, but the default logon values (usually admin) are common knowledge among wardrivers. To prevent access to the setup program, be sure to change the access point's default username and password.

- Consider static IP addresses—DHCP makes it easy to manage IP addresses, but it also gives an IP address to *anyone* who accesses the network. To prevent this, turn off DHCP in the access point and assign static IP addresses to each of your computers.

- Enable **MAC (Media Access Control)** address filtering—The MAC address is the physical address of a network adapter. This is unique to each adapter, so you can enhance security by setting up your access point to allow connections from only specified MAC addresses.

> **NOTE**
>
> To find out the MAC address of your wireless network adapter, open a Command Prompt session and enter the following command:
>
> ```
> ipconfig /all
> ```
>
> Find the data for the wireless adapter and look for the Physical Address value. (Alternatively, right-click the wireless connection, click Status, display the Support tab, and click Details.)

- Avoid windows—When positioning your access point within your home or office, don't place it near a window, if possible, because otherwise the access point sends a strong signal out of the building. Try to position the access point close to the center of your house or building.

## Working with Network Settings

You can change your network settings by selecting Start, All Programs, Accessories, Communications, Network Connections (or by launching Control Panel's Network Connections icon). The configuration of the resulting Network Connections window depends on the computer's role in the network. For example, if the computer is the ICS host, you'll see a configuration similar to the one shown in Figure 22.10. There are three items here:

| | |
|---|---|
| DSL Internet Connection | This icon represents the ICS host's Internet connection—a broadband connection via a DSL modem, in this case. That is, it's the connection that runs from the DSL modem out to the Internet. |
| To Local Area Network | This icon represents the connection to the network. That is, it's the connection that runs from one NIC to the network hub. |
| To DSL Modem | This icon represents the connection to the modem. That is, it's the connection that runs from the second NIC to the DSL modem. |

Contrast this with the Network Connections window for a client machine on the same network, shown in Figure 22.11. In this case, there are only two items:

| | |
|---|---|
| DSL Internet Connection on ZEUS | This icon represents the connection to the ICS host (which Windows XP considers to be the Internet gateway). In this case, it connects this computer to the DSL Internet connection on a computer named ZEUS (the ICS host for this network). |

Local Area Connection    This icon represents the connection to the network. That is, it's the connection that runs from the computer's NIC to the network hub.

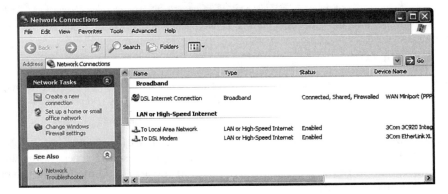

**FIGURE 22.10**    The Network Connections window for a typical ICS host.

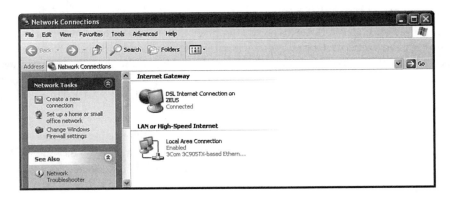

**FIGURE 22.11**    The Network Connections window for a computer that uses a shared ICS connection.

If your network uses a gateway device, the Network Connections window will look similar to the one shown in Figure 22.12, which has just two icons:

Internet Connection    This icon represents the connection to the gateway device.

Local Area Connection    This icon represents the connection to the network. That is, it's the connection that runs from the computer's NIC to the network hub.

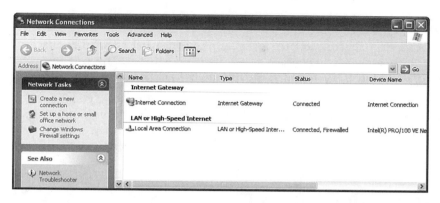

**FIGURE 22.12** The Network Connections window for a computer that accesses the Internet through a gateway device.

From the Network Connections window, you can modify your network settings in the following ways:

- Running the Network Setup Wizard—If you want to make major changes to the network configuration, these are most easily accomplished by running the Network Setup Wizard again. In the task pane, click the Set Up a Home or Small Office Network link.

> **TIP**
>
> If you want to change your computer or workgroup name, you can either run the Network Setup Wizard or you can change these values directly. To do the latter, launch Control Panel's System icon and display the Computer Name tab. Click Change, type the Computer name and/or workgroup, and then click OK.

- Renaming a connection—Windows XP supplies each connection with a generic name such as *Local Area Connection* To assign a more descriptive name to a connection, select it, press F2, type the new name, and press Enter.

- Installing a networking client, service, or protocol—You shouldn't need extra networking components in a small peer-to-peer network. Just in case you do, you can install them by right-clicking the network connection, clicking Properties, and then clicking Install.

- Disabling a connection—If you have multiple NICs and want to disable one that you don't use, right-click its connection and then click Disable. You can enable this connection in the future by right-clicking it and then clicking Enable.

# Connecting to a Wireless Network

With your wireless network adapters installed and your wireless gateway or access point configured, you are ready to connect to your wireless network. This will give you access to the network's resources, as well as to the Internet if you have a wireless gateway.

When you initially set up a computer for wireless networking, or if you move your portable computer to a hotspot or other area with new networks in range, Windows XP displays a message in the notification area to let you know that new wireless networks are in range. Click the message to display a list of the available wireless networks, as shown in Figure 22.13.

---

**TIP**

If Windows XP doesn't display the wireless network notification message, you can display the list of available wireless networks by hand. Right-click the Wireless Network Connection icon in the notification area and then click View Available Wireless Networks.

---

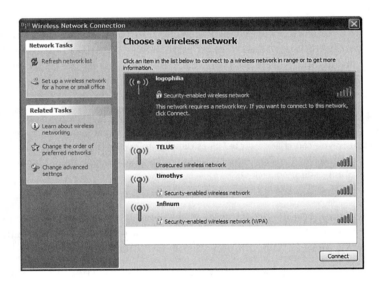

**FIGURE 22.13**    When Windows XP reports that new wireless networks are in range, click the message to see the list of available networks.

Select the network that you want to use and then click Connect.

---

**NOTE**

A **wireless hotspot** is a location that allows wireless computers to use the location's Internet connection. You can find hotspots in many airports, hotels, and even businesses such as coffee shops, restaurants, and dental offices.

---

If the network that you want to use is unsecured—as are most public hotspots—you can immediately access the network. However, most private wireless networks are (or should be) secured against unauthorized access. In this case, Windows XP will prompt you to enter the appropriate security information, such as a WEP key (see Figure 22.14). I talked about wireless network security earlier in this chapter (refer to "Implementing Wireless Network Security").

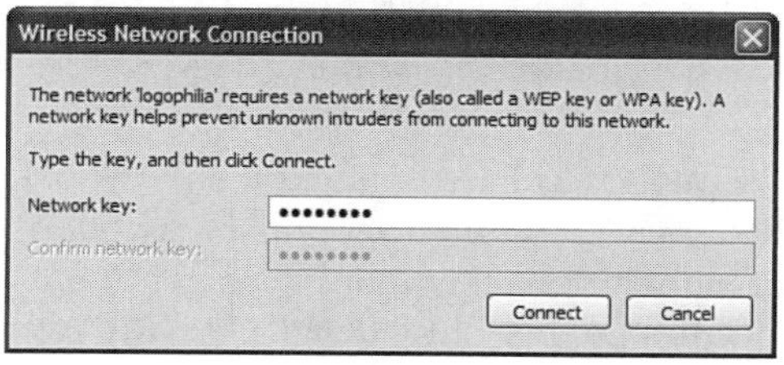

**FIGURE 22.14** To access a secured wireless network, you must enter security information, such as a WEP key.

---

**NOTE**

If you lose your wireless network connection, you must reconnect to continue using it. One way to do this is to display the list of available wireless networks and then connect to the one that you want. However, in Windows XP, you can also click Start, Connect To, Wireless Network Connection.

---

**TIP**

If you're having problems with a wireless network connection, check the signal strength. In Windows XP, place your mouse over the Wireless Network Connection icon in the taskbar. After a second or two, a banner appears and tells you the current signal strength. Alternatively, double-click the icon to display the Wireless Internet Connection Status dialog box.

---

When you no longer need a wireless network connection, or if you want to try a different available network, you should disconnect from the current network. Display the list of available wireless networks, click the network to which you are connected, and then click Disconnect.

## Accessing Network Resources

After your network has been set up, you can start using it immediately to share resources, including files, folders, programs, and peripherals. Your starting point for all of this is the My Network Places folder, discussed next.

### Using My Network Places

You can get to My Network Places using any of the following methods:

- Select Start, My Network Places. (If you don't see My Network Places on the Start menu, launch Control Panel's Taskbar and Start Menu icon, display the Start Menu tab, click Customize, select the Advanced tab, and activate the My Network Places check box.)
- In Windows Explorer, click My Network Places in the Folders list.
- In the task pane of the Network Connections window, click My Network Places.
- In most Open and Save As dialog boxes, click the My Network Places icons.

In Windows XP, a **network place** is a shared folder on a network computer (it can also be a location on a web or FTP server). When you set up a network place, you can access its files as though they reside on your own computer (subject to any restrictions that the owner of the network place has imposed). By default, the My Network Places folder shows the network places that were defined when you set up your computer for networking. The name of each network place uses the following format:

*ShareName* on *Description* (*ComputerName*)

Here, *ShareName* is the name that the owner of the network place gave to the shared resource; *Description* is the description of the computer where the network place resides; and *ComputerName* is the name of that computer (refer to step 2 in the "Completing the Network Setup Wizard" section, earlier in this chapter). Figure 22.15 shows some examples.

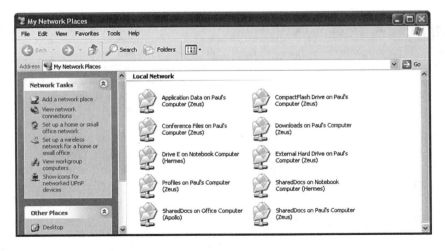

**FIGURE 22.15**    My Network Places contains icons for shared network resources.

In addition to viewing the contents of the shared resources by double-clicking a network place's icon, My Network Places also enables you to do the following:

- See the other computers in the workgroup—Click the task pane's View Workgroup Computers to see a new window that contains an icon for each computer in your workgroup (see Figure 22.16). Double-click a computer's icon to see all the resources shared by that computer. For example, Figure 22.17 shows a computer that's sharing an external hard drive, a couple of printers, and several folders. (Use the Details view to see the Comments column.)

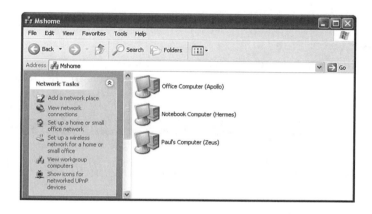

**FIGURE 22.16**    Each computer in the workgroup has its own icon.

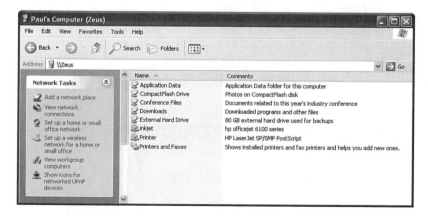

**FIGURE 22.17**    Open a workgroup computer to see the resources that computer is sharing with the network.

- See all the workgroups in your network—Click View Workgroup Computers and then click the Up button (you can also either select View, Go To, Up One Level, or press Backspace). This displays the Microsoft Windows Network folder, which contains an icon for each workgroup in your network. Double-click an icon to see that workgroup's computers.

> **TIP**
>
> If you don't have the task pane displayed, you can display workgroup computers using the Folders list. First open the following folder:
>
> ```
> My Network Places\Entire Network\Microsoft Windows Network
> ```
>
> From there, open the folder for the workgroup you want to display.

## Adding a Network Place

Whenever a workgroup computer shares a folder, Windows XP detects the new share and adds it automatically to your my Network Places folder. To add another folder (such as a subfolder of a shared resource) as a network place, follow these steps:

> **TIP**
>
> You can tell Windows XP to not add new shared resources to My Network Places automatically. To do this, launch Control Panel's Folder Options icon, display the View tab, and then deactivate the Automatically Search for Network Folders and Printers check box.

1. In the My Network Places (or any network folder) task pane, click Add a Network Place to launch the Add Network Place Wizard.

2. Click Next. If your computer has an Internet connection, the wizard will access the Internet and retrieve a list of online storage providers.

3. Click Choose Another Network Location and click Next.

4. Either use the Internet or Network Address text box to type the network address of the resource, or click Browse to select the resource using the Browse for Folder dialog box. Click Next.

> **The Universal Naming Convention**
>
> Network addresses use the **universal naming convention (UNC)**, which uses the following format:
>
> ```
> \\ComputerName\ShareName
> ```
>
> Here, *ComputerName* is the name of the computer, and *ShareName* is the name given to the shared resource. For example, the following UNC path refers to a shared resource named Downloads on a computer named ZEUS:
>
> ```
> \\ZEUS\Downloads\
> ```
>
> If the UNC refers to a drive or folder, you can use the regular path conventions to access subfolders on that resource. For example, if the resource Downloads on ZEUS is a drive and if that drive has a Device Drivers subfolder, you can refer to that subfolder as follows:
>
> ```
> \\ZEUS\Downloads\Device Drivers
> ```

5. Modify the name in the Type a Name for This Network Place, if desired, and then click Next.

6. To open the network place in a folder window, leave the Open this Network Place When I Click Finish check box activated.

7. Click Finish.

---

**TIP**

The UNC offers you several alternative methods of accessing shared network resources:

- Select Start, Run to open the Run dialog box. Type the UNC for a shared resource and then click OK to open the resource in a folder window.

- In a 32-bit application's Open or Save As dialog box, you can use a UNC name in the File Name text box.

- At the command prompt, type **START** followed by the UNC path. Here's an example:

```
START \\ZEUS\Downloads\
```

- At the command prompt, you can use a UNC name as part of a command. For example, to copy a file named `archive.zip` from `\\ZEUS\Downloads\` to the current folder, you'd use the following command:

```
COPY \\ZEUS\Downloads\archive.zip
```

---

## Mapping a Network Folder to a Local Drive Letter

Network places are useful, but they're not as convenient as they could be because you can't reference them directly (in, say, a script or command). UNC paths can be referenced directly, but they're a bit unwieldy to work with. To avoid these hassles, you can map a shared network drive or folder to your own computer. **Mapping** assigns a drive letter to the resource so that it appears to be just another disk drive on your machine.

---

**NOTE**

Another good reason to map a network folder to a local drive letter is to give certain programs access to the network folder. Some older programs aren't network-aware, so if you try to save files to a network folder, the program might display an error or tell you that the location is out of disk space. In most cases, you can solve this problem by mapping the folder to a drive letter, which fools the program into thinking it's dealing with a local folder.

---

To map a shared drive or folder, follow these steps:

1. In Windows Explorer or My Network Places, select Tools, Map Network Drive. Windows XP displays the Map Network Drive dialog box, shown in Figure 22.18.

**FIGURE 22.18**    Use the Map Network Drive dialog box to assign a drive letter to a network resource.

2. The Drive drop-down list displays the last available drive letter on your system, but you can pull down the list and select any available letter.

---

**CAUTION**

If you use a removable drive, such as a CompactFlash memory module, Windows XP assigns the first available drive letter to that drive. This can cause problems if you have a mapped network drive that uses a lower drive letter. Therefore, it's good practice to use higher drive letters (such as X, Y, and Z) for your mapped resources.

---

3. If you want Windows XP to map the resource each time you log on to the system, leave the Reconnect at Logon check box activated.

4. If you prefer to log on to the resource using a different account, click the Different User Name link, type the username and password, and click OK.

5. Click Finish. Windows XP adds the new drive letter to your system and opens the shared resource in a new folder window.

---

**TIP**

For easier network drive mapping, Windows XP enables you to add a Map Drive button to the Windows Explorer toolbar. To do so, right-click the toolbar and then click Customize. In the Available Toolbar Buttons list, double-click Map Drive. Note that there's also a Disconnect button that you can use to easily disconnect mapped resources (as described in the next section).

---

**Mapping Folders at the Command Prompt**

You can also map a shared network folder to a local drive letter by using a Command Prompt session and the NET USE command. Here's the basic syntax:

```
NET USE [drive] [share] [password] [/USER:user]
➡[/PERSISTENT:[YES ¦ NO]] ¦ /DELETE]
```

| | |
|---|---|
| *drive* | The drive letter (following by a colon) of the local drive to which you want the shared folder mapped |
| *share* | The UNC path of the shared folder |
| *password* | The password required to connect to the shared folder |
| /USER:*user* | The username you want to use to connect to the shared folder |
| /PERSISTENT: | Add YES to reconnect the mapped network drive the next time you log on |
| /DELETE | Deletes the existing shared mapped to *drive* |

For example, the following command maps the shared folder \\ZEUS\Downloads to drive Z:

```
net use z: \\zeus\downloads \persistent:yes
```

## Disconnecting a Mapped Network Folder

If you no longer need to map a network resource, you should disconnect it by following these steps:

1. Use Windows Explorer to display the drive letter of the mapped resource.

2. Right-click the drive and then click Disconnect.

3. If there are files open from the resource, Windows XP displays a warning to let you know that it's unsafe to disconnect the resource. You have two choices:

   - Click No, close all open files from the mapped resource, and then repeat steps 1 and 2.

   - If you're sure there are no open files, click Yes to disconnect the resource.

## Printing over the Network

After you've connected to a network printer, you can use it just like any local printer on your system. Windows XP offers a couple of methods for connecting to a network printer.

The easiest way is to use My Network Places to open the computer that has the shared printer, open its Printers and Faxes icon, highlight the printer, and then select File, Connect. (Right-clicking the printer and then clicking Connect also can be done.) Windows XP installs the printer using the remote machine's printer driver files.

If you like using a wizard for these kinds of things, you can do so using the Add Printer Wizard:

1. Open Control Panel's Printers and Faxes icon.

2. Click the Add a Printer link to open the Add Printer Wizard.

3. Click Next to get past the introductory dialog box.

4. In the next dialog box, activate the A Network Printer, or a Printer Attached to Another Computer option and click Next.

5. In the next dialog box, make sure that the Browse for a Printer option is activated and click Next.

6. In the Browse for Printer dialog box, use the Shared Printers list to select the network printer you want to use. (To see a computer's shared printers, double-click the computer name.)

7. Click Next and then complete the wizard normally.

# Sharing Resources with the Network

In a peer-to-peer network, each computer can act as both a client and a server. You've seen how to use a Windows XP machine as a client, so now let's turn our attention to setting up your system as a peer server. In Windows XP, that means sharing individual drives, folders, printers and other resources with the network.

## Deactivating Simple File Sharing

The first thing you need to do is deactivate Windows XP's Simple File Sharing feature. This feature is designed for novice users who, understandably, don't want or need to learn about technical topics such as maximum users and file permissions. Windows XP activates Simple File Sharing by default, even on Windows XP Professional installations. (Note, however, that you can't turn off Simple File Sharing in Windows XP Home; yet another reason to always choose Windows XP Professional.)

To help you understand the difference between simple and classic file sharing, Figure 22.19 shows the property sheet for the My Music folder on a system using Simple File Sharing. Notice the following in the Sharing tab:

- In the Local Sharing and Security group, you activate Make This Folder Private to prevent other users from accessing the folder.

- In the Network Sharing and Security group, you activate Share this Folder on the Network to share the folder, and you type a name in the Share Name text box. If you want network users to be able to modify the files, you activate the Allow Network Users to Change My Files check box.

As you can see, what this approach adds in ease of use it takes away in power and flexibility. It's an all-or-nothing, one-size-fits-all-users approach. To regain the power and flexibility to share your resources properly, you need to run off Simple File Sharing by following these steps:

1. Launch Control Panel's Folder Options icon (or, in Windows Explorer, select Tools, Folder Options).

2. Display the View tab.

3. Deactivate the Use Simple File Sharing check box.

4. Click OK.

**FIGURE 22.19**   The Sharing tab on a system using Simple File Sharing.

## Creating User Accounts

You need to set up an account for each user that you want to access a shared resource. I discussed creating user accounts in Chapter 6, so I won't repeat the details here. Here are some notes to bear in mind for creating users who will access your computer over a network:

- Windows XP does *not* allow users without passwords to access network resources. Therefore, you must set up your network user accounts with passwords.

- The usernames you create do not have to correspond with the names that users have on their local machines. You're free to set up your own usernames, if you like.

- If you create a user account that has the same name and password as an account of a user on his or her local machine, that user will be able to access your shared resource directly. Otherwise, a Connect To dialog box appears so that the user can enter the username and password that you established when setting up the account on your computer.

## Sharing a Resource

With Simple File Sharing turned off, follow these steps to share a resource:

1. In Windows Explorer, right-click the drive or folder and then click Sharing and Security. Windows XP displays the object's property sheet with the Sharing tab selected, as shown in Figure 22.20.

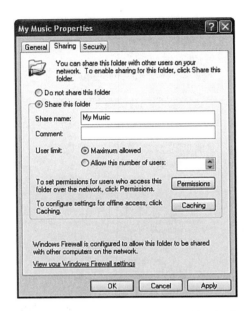

**FIGURE 22.20**     The Sharing tab on a system using classic file sharing.

2. Activate the Share This Folder option.

3. Type the share name and a comment (the latter is optional).

4. In a small network, it's unlikely you'll need to restrict the number of users who can access this resource, so leave the Maximum Allowed option activated. (The maximum number is 10.) If you'd prefer to restrict the number of users, activate Allow This Number of Users and then use the spin box to set the maximum number.

5. Click Permissions to display the Permissions dialog box (see Figure 22.21).

6. Select the Everyone group in the Group or User Names list and then click Remove.

7. Click Add to display the Select Users or Groups dialog box.

8. In the Enter the Object Names to Select text box, type the name of the user or users you want to give permission to access the shared resource. (Separate multiple user-names with semicolons.) Click OK when you're done.

9. Select a user in the Group or User Names list.

10. Using the Permissions list, you can allow or deny the following permissions:

| | |
|---|---|
| Read | Gives the group or user the ability only to read the contents of a folder or file. The user can't modify those contents in any way. |
| Change | Gives the group or user Read permission and allows the group or user to modify the contents of the shared resource. |

Full Control              Gives the group or user Change permission and allows the group or
                          user to take ownership of the shared resource.

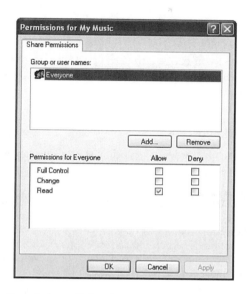

**FIGURE 22.21**    Use the Permissions dialog box to specify file permissions for the shared
resource.

11. Repeat steps 7–10 to add and configure other users.

12. Click OK to return to the Sharing tab.

13. Click OK to share the resource with the network.

> **TIP**
>
> If you want even more control over how your shared resources are used over the network, you
> should also set NTFS security permissions on the folder. (Ideally, you should do this before
> sharing the resource.) To do this, right-click the folder, click Sharing and Security, and then
> display the Security tab. This tab is similar to the Permissions dialog box shown in Figure 22.21,
> except that you get a longer list of permissions for each group or user.

## Hiding Shared Resources

Hiding your valuables is a time-honored method of securing them from prying eyes and
would-be thieves. When you share a resource on your network, however, you're displaying that resource for all to see. Sure, you can set up password-protected user accounts and
set the appropriate permissions for the resource, but others will still be able to see that
the resource is shared.

To prevent this situation, it's possible to share a resource *and* hide it at the same time. It's also extremely easy to do: When you set up the shared resource, just add a dollar sign ($) to the end of the share name. For example, if you're setting up drive D for sharing, you could use D$ as the share name. This prevents the resource from appearing in the browse list of My Network Places.

In Figure 22.22, for example, you can see that the current computer (named Apollo) is sharing drive D (which shows the hand icon to indicate that it is shared) and drive C, which according to the display property sheet, is shared with the name C$. Notice two things:

- No hand icon appears under the drive C icon.

- Drive C doesn't appear in the list of Apollo's shared resources.

---

**Hidden Administration Shares**

Hiding shares will work for the average user, but a savvy snoop will probably know about the $ trick. Therefore, you'll probably want to set up your hidden shares with nonobvious names. Note, however, that Windows XP sets up certain hidden shares for administrative purposes, including one for drive C (C$) and any other hard disk partitions you have on your system. Windows XP also sets up the following hidden shares:

| Share Name | Shared Path | Purpose |
| --- | --- | --- |
| ADMIN$ | %SystemRoot% | Remote administration |
| IPC$ | N/A | Remote interprocess communication |
| print$ | %SystemRoot%\System32\ spool\drivers | Access to printer drivers |

You cannot delete or rename these administrative shares.

---

How do you connect to a hidden share? Well, you need to know the name of the shared resource, of course. When you know that, you can use any of the following techniques:

- In the Run dialog box, type the UNC path for the hidden resource. For example, to display the hidden C$ share on ZEUS, you would enter this:

  ```
  \\zeus\c$
  ```

- In Windows Explorer, make sure that a shared resource isn't highlighted, and then select Tools, Map Network Drive. In the Map Network Drive dialog box, type the UNC path for the hidden share in the Path text box.

- For a hidden shared printer, run the Add Hardware Wizard from Control Panel, and when you're prompted, enter the UNC path to the hidden printer.

No hand icon
appears with drive C

Drive C doesn't appear in the
computer's list of shared resources

Drive D is shared normally

Drive C is set up as a hidden share

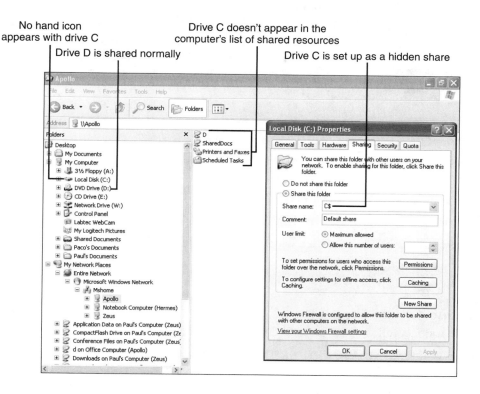

**FIGURE 22.22**    Hidden shared resources (such as drive C shown here) don't appear in the browse list.

# Working with Network Files Offline

One of the main advantages of setting up a small network in your home or office is the ease with which you can share files and folders with other users. You simply share a folder with the network, and other users can use their My Network Places folder to open the shared folder and work with the files.

However, this benefit is lost when you disconnect from the network. For example, suppose that you have a notebook computer that you use to connect to the network while you are at the office. When you take the notebook on the road, you must disconnect from the network. Fortunately, you can still get network access of a sort when you are disconnected from the network (or offline). Windows XP Professional has an Offline Files feature that enables you to preserve copies of network files on your computer. You can then view and work with these files as though you were connected to the network.

---

**NOTE**

The Offline Files feature is not available with Windows XP Home. If you have networked a note-book computer and a desktop computer, consider upgrading the notebook to Windows XP Professional. This enables you to use the desktop computer's shared files offline. You do not need to upgrade the desktop computer to Windows XP Professional for this to work.

---

## Turning Off Fast User Switching

The Offline Files feature isn't compatible with Fast User Switching, so you must first turn off the latter:

1. Open Control Panel's User Accounts icon.

2. Click Change the Way Users Log On or Off.

3. Deactivate the Use Fast User Switching check box.

4. Click Apply Options.

## Enabling Offline Files

With that done, follow these steps to enable offline files:

1. In Windows Explorer, select Tools, Folder Options. The Folder Options dialog box appears.

2. Display the Offline Files tab.

3. Activate the Enable Offline Files check box.

4. Click OK.

---

**TIP**

If you're an administrator, the Group Policy editor offers a large number of policies related to offline files. For example, you can prohibit users from configuring the Offline Files feature, set default synchronization options, prevent certain files and folders from being made available offline, and disable offline files altogether. In the Group Policy editor, open the User Configuration, Administrative Templates, Network, Offline Files branch. To work with remote policies from your computer, see "Connecting to Remote Group Policies," later in this chapter.

---

## Making Files Available Offline

With the Offline Files feature turned on, follow these steps to make network files available offline:

22

1. In Windows Explorer, open the network folder that contains the files you want to use offline.

2. Select the files you want to use offline.

3. Select File, Make Available Offline. The Offline Files Wizard appears.

**NOTE**

The Offline Files Wizard appears only the first time you make a file or folder available offline. In the future, you need perform only steps 1–3 to make a file available offline.

4. Click Next.

5. Activate the Automatically Synchronize the Offline Files When I Log On and Log Off My Computer option, and then click Next.

6. Activate the Create a Shortcut to the Offline Files Folder on My Desktop check box, and then click Finish. If the offline folder contains subfolders, the Confirm Offline Subfolders dialog box appears.

7. If you do not want to use the subfolder offline, activate the No, Make Only This Folder Available Offline option. Click OK. Windows XP synchronizes the offline files.

You can now disconnect from the network and work with the files offline.

## Working with Network Files Offline

Windows XP creates a special Offline Files Folder that contains all the shared network files that you chose to work with offline. Although you cannot delete and rename the offline files, you can open and edit the files just as though you were connected to the network. When you reconnect to the network, Windows XP automatically **synchronizes** the files. This means that Windows XP does two things: First, it updates your Offline Files Folder by creating copies of any new or changed files in the shared network folder. Second, it updates the shared network folder with the files you changed while you were offline. This synchronization occurs automatically when you log on to the network and when you log off the network.

**TIP**

When Windows XP synchronizes your offline files, it might find that a file has been changed both on the network share and on your offline computer. In that case, you see the Resolve File Conflicts dialog box, which gives you three options: Keep the Network Version of the File (you lose your offline changes); Keep the Offline Version of the File (you lose the network changes); Or Keep Both Versions (the offline version is saved under a modified filename).

You can also synchronize the offline files yourself:

1. In any folder window, click Tools, Synchronize to display the Items to Synchronize dialog box.

2. If you do not want a particular network folder synchronized, deactivate its check box.

3. Click Synchronize.

# Administering Your Network

If you're the administrator of your network fiefdom, setting up the machines on the network is only half the battle. You'll still need to spend untold amounts of time tweaking these machines, adjusting their configurations, creating and managing users and passwords, and so on. To make these chores easier, Windows XP boasts various tools that offer you **remote administration**: the ability to work with a network computer from the comfort of your own system. This section shows you how to implement these tools on your network.

Windows XP's remote administration tools are powerful features that can make a harried network administrator's life immeasurably easier. Here's a summary of just a few of capabilities you get when you use remote administration:

- Work directly with the Registry on any remote computer

- Monitor the performance of a remote system

- See which users are connected to a particular resource

- Manage various aspects of a remote computer (such as starting and stopping services)

- Send console message to a remote computer

To help you unleash all of these benefits, the next few sections take you through various techniques for remote administration.

## Connecting to a Remote Registry

The Registry Editor enables you to work with some portions of the Registry on a remote machine. First, log on as a member of the Administrators group on both machines. On the remote machine, you need to do two things:

1. Disable Simple File Sharing. To do this, launch Control Panel's Folder Options icon, display the View tab, and then deactivate the Use Simple File Sharing check box.

2. Enable remote access. To do this, launch Control Panel's System icon, display the Remote tab, and activate the Allow Users to Connect Remotely to this Computer check box.

On the local computer, follow these steps:

1. In the Registry Editor, select the File, Connect Network Registry command. The Select Computer dialog box appears.

2. In the Enter the Object Name to Select text box, type the name of the remote computer.

---

**TIP**

If you're not sure of the correct name for the remote computer, click Advanced and then click Find Now to see a list of the workgroup computers. Select the remote computer and then click OK.

---

3. Click OK. The Registry Editor adds a new branch for the remote machine's registry, although you see only the HKLM and HKU root keys, as shown in Figure 22.23.

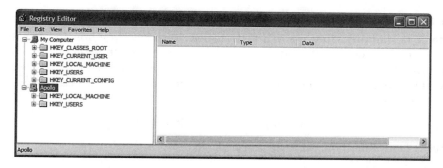

**FIGURE 22.23**   When you connect to a remote registry, the computer's HKLM and HKU root keys appear in the Registry Editor.

When you've finished working with the remote Registry, select the computer name in the Registry Editor, select File, Disconnect Network Registry, select the computer name, and click OK.

## Connecting to Remote Group Policies

You've seen in various places in this book how powerful group policies can be, particularly when you use the Group Policy editor—it has a front end for enabling, disabling, and configuring policies. How much more convenient would group policies be if you could work with them on a remote network machine?

The good news is that you *can* do this by running the gpedit.msc file with the /gpcomputer switch:

```
gpedit.msc /gpcomputer:"name"
```

   /gpcomputer:"name"          The network name or IP address of the remote computer

For example, the following command runs the Group Policy editor for the policies on a computer named APOLLO:

```
gpedit.msc /gpcomputer:"apollo"
```

The bad news is that Windows XP seems to allow the remote management of group policies only from the Administrator account. If you normally log on using a different account, create a shortcut for the gpedit.msc /gpcomputer command. Then right-click the shortcut and click Run As to display the Run As dialog box. Activate the Following User option, and specify the Administrator account and password.

> **TIP**
>
> If Windows XP fails to open the remote computer's group policies when you use the computer's name with the /pgcomputer switch, try using the computer's IP address instead.

## Monitoring Performance on a Remote Computer

In Chapter 11, "Tuning Windows XP's Performance," I showed you how to use System Monitor to keep an eye on the performance of your computer. (In particular, refer to the section "Monitoring Performance with System Monitor" in Chapter 11.) If you're also interested in monitoring the health of the remote computers on your network, System Monitor is up to the task.

To connect to a remote computer from System Monitor, follow these steps:

1. Select Start, Run, type **perfmon**, and click OK.

2. Right-click a counter and then click Add Counters. The Add Counters dialog box appears.

3. Activate the Select Counters from Computer option, and then use the text box to type the name or IP address of the remote computer.

4. Use the Performance Object list to select a counter category (such as Memory, Paging File, or Processor).

> **TIP**
>
> If you're primarily interested in monitoring network performance, choose Network Interface in the Performance Object list.

5. Activate the Select Counters from List option.

6. Select the counter you want and then click Add. (If you need more information about the item, click the Explain button.)

7. Repeat step 4 to add any other counters you want to monitor.

8. Click OK.

Figure 22.24 shows System Monitor tracking the % Processor Time value on three different computers.

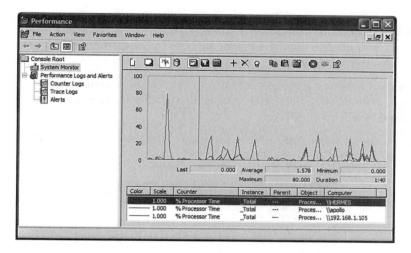

**FIGURE 22.24**   System Monitor is only too happy to monitor remote systems as well as local ones.

## Managing a Remote Computer

The Computer Management snap-in is a great tool for managing many different aspects of your system, from devices to users to services and much more. But perhaps the most incredible thing about Computer Management is that you can also use it to manage some aspects of a remote network computer, too. Here's a list of just a few of the things you can do:

- For each shared folder on any remote computer, find out the users that are connected to the folder, how long they've been connected, and the files they have open.

- Disconnect users from a shared folder or close files that have been opened on a shared folder.

- Change the properties of a remote shared folder, including its share name and the access rights to the folder. You can even stop sharing a remote folder.

- Set up a new shared folder on any remote machine.

- Add, modify, and delete user accounts and security groups on a remote computer.

- View (but not modify) a remote computer's Device Manager.

- Start, stop, and configure services.

These are powerful, not-to-be-wielded-lightly techniques. I won't describe them all here.

Instead, I'll focus on three techniques that are most useful for network administration: viewing connected users, working with remote shared folders, and working with remote open files.

### Connecting to a Remote Computer

To get started, you need to open a remote computer in the Computer Management snap-in. Here are the steps to follow:

1.  Open the Computer Management snap-in by selecting Control Panel, Administrative Tools, Computer Management. (Alternatively, select Start, Run, type `compmgmt.msc`, and click OK.)

2.  Select Action, Connect to Another Computer. The Select Computer dialog box appears, as shown in Figure 22.25.

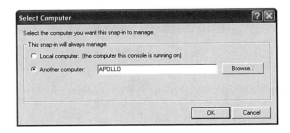

**FIGURE 22.25**    Use the Select Computer dialog box to specify the name or IP address of the remote computer you want to manage.

3.  Activate the Another Computer option.

4.  Use the text box to type the computer name or IP address of the remote computer you want to manage.

5.  Click OK. Computer Management connects to the other computer and displays the computer name or IP address in the console root, as shown in Figure 22.26.

### Viewing the Current Connections

To see a list of the users connected to any shared folder on the remote computer, select System Tools, Shared Folders, Sessions. Figure 22.27 shows an example. For each user, you get the following data:

| | |
|---|---|
| User | The name of the user |
| Computer | The name of the user's computer |
| Type | The type of network connection, such as Windows, NetWare, or Macintosh |
| Open Files | The number of open files in the shared folders |
| Connected Time | The amount of time that the user has been connected to the remote computer |

| Idle Time | The amount of time that the user has not been actively working on the open files |
| Guest | Whether the user logged on using the Guest account |

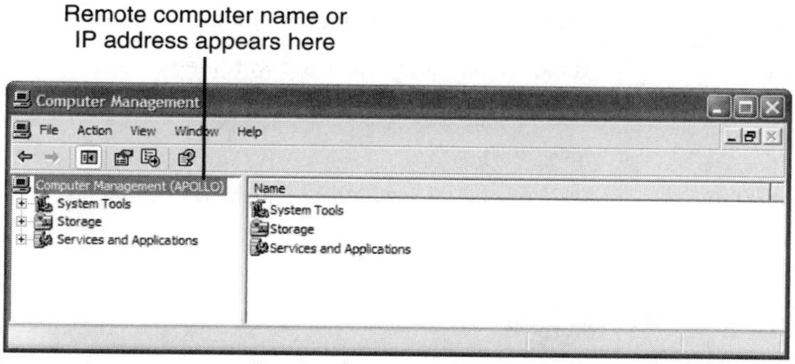

Remote computer name or
IP address appears here

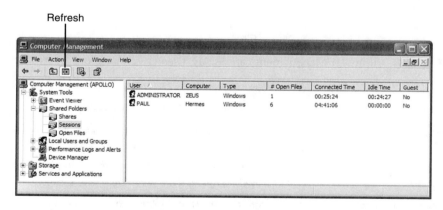

**FIGURE 22.26**    Computer Management connected to a remote computer.

To ensure that you're always viewing the most up-to-date information, regularly select the Action, Refresh command or click the Refresh toolbar button.

Refresh

**FIGURE 22.27**    The Sessions folder shows the users currently connected to shared folders on the remote computer.

Although in the interest of network harmony you'll want to let users connect and disconnect as they please, at times you might need to boot someone off a machine. For example, you might see that someone has obtained unauthorized access to a share. To disconnect that user, right-click his name in the list and then click Close Session. When Windows XP asks for confirmation, click Yes.

### Working with Shared Folders

Computer Management also makes it possible for you to view the connections to a server by its shared folders. To get this display, select System Tools, Shared Folders, Shares. As you can see in Figure 22.28, this view provides the following information:

| | |
|---|---|
| Shared Folder | The share name. Note that the list includes hidden shares. |
| Shared Path | The drive or folder associated with the share. |
| Type | The type of network connection, such as Windows, NetWare, or Macintosh. |
| # Client Connections | The number of computers connected to the share. |
| Comment | The description of the share. |

Create New File Share

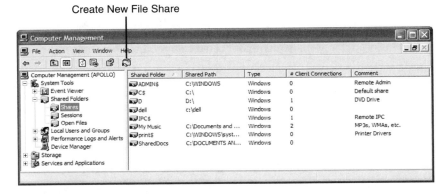

**FIGURE 22.28**   Computer Management can display a server's connections by its shared folders.

Here are the techniques you can use to work with the shared folders:

| | |
|---|---|
| To change the properties of a shared folder | Right-click the folder you want to work with, and then click Properties (or press Alt+Enter). The property sheet that appears enables you to modify various share options, including the name, comment, share permissions, and security. |
| To stop sharing a folder | Right-click the shared folder and then click Stop Sharing. When Windows XP asks whether you're sure, click Yes. |
| To add a shared folder | Click the Shares branch and then select Action, New File Share, or click the Create New File Share toolbar button (pointed out in Figure 22.28). This launches the Create a Shared Folder Wizard, which takes you step-by-step through the process of sharing a folder. |

### Working with Open Files

Computer Management can also display the files that are open on the remote computer's shares. To switch to this view, select System Tools, Shared Folders, Open Files. Figure 22.29 shows the result. Here's a summary of the columns in this view:

| | |
|---|---|
| Open File | The full pathname of the file |
| Accessed By | The name of the computer that's using the file |
| Type | The type of network connection, such as Windows, NetWare, or Macintosh |
| # Locks | The number of locks on the file |
| Open Mode | The permissions the user has over the file |

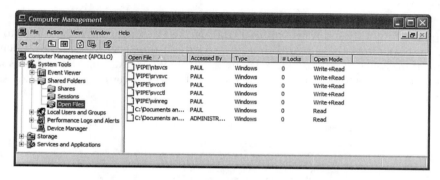

**FIGURE 22.29**    Computer Management can also display a remote computer's open files in its shared resources.

Again, you'll usually want to let users open and close files themselves so that they don't lose information. If you need to close a file, however, you can do so by right-clicking it and then clicking Close Open File. When Windows XP asks for confirmation, click Yes.

## Broadcasting Console Messages

Administering a network sometimes requires that you contact one or more users. For example, you might ask users to disconnect from the network or from a share because you need to perform some maintenance. Similarly, you might want to send an announcement to all users about a new network resource, such as a printer. To handle these and similar situations, you can send a console message from the Computer Management snap-in to one or more computers on the network.

### Starting the Messenger Service

To accomplish this, you need to activate Windows XP's Messenger service (not to be confused with the Windows Messenger instant messaging program). This service is disabled by default in most Windows XP installations (particularly Service pack 2 systems), so follow these steps to enable and start the service:

1. In the Computer Management snap-in, connect to the computer you want to manage.

2. Select the Services and Applications, Services.

3. Double-click the Messenger service.

4. In the Startup Type list, select Manual (or Automatic if you want the service available each time you start Windows XP).

5. Click Apply to enable the service.

6. Click Start to start the service.

7. Click OK.

Before proceeding, I should warn you that starting the Messenger service can lead to problems because spammers have figured out how to exploit this service to send unsolicited commercial messages to your desktop. Figure 22.30 shows an example. However, as long you you're running Windows Firewall, such spam should not get through, and so using the Messenger service is safe.

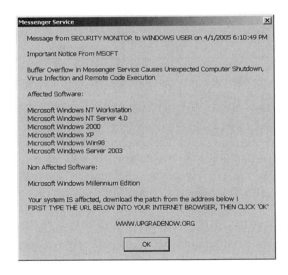

**FIGURE 22.30**    An example of Messenger service spam.

### Sending a Console Message

Here are the steps to follow to send a console message:

1. You have two choices for getting started:

   • If you want to send a console message to only the computer you're managing, select the console root.

- If you want to send a console message to all the computers that currently have open sessions in the computer you're managing, select the System Tools, Shared Folders, Sessions branch.

2. Select Action, All Tasks, Send Console Message. The Send Console Message dialog box appears.

3. Type your message in the Message text box, as shown in Figure 22.31.

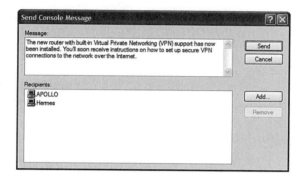

**FIGURE 22.31**   Use the Send Console Message dialog box to compose and send a message to the specified computers.

4. To add another computer as a recipient, click Add, type the computer name in the Select Computer dialog box, and click OK.

5. Click Send. Windows XP broadcasts the message to the specified computers.

Figure 22.32 shows an example of the message as it appears on the recipient computer.

**FIGURE 22.32**   An example of a legitimate Messenger service console message.

## From Here

Here's a list of other places in the book where you'll find information related to networking:

- You can use Phone Dialer and NetMeeting to communicate with network users. Refer to Chapter 16, "Putting Your Modem to Work."

- TCP/IP is quickly becoming the protocol of choice for both large and small networks. I showed you how to work with TCP/IP in Chapter 17, "Implementing TCP/IP for Internet Connections."

- Accessing your network from remote locations is often crucial, so I devote an entire chapter to this topic. See Chapter 23, "Making Remote Network Connections."

- It sometimes seems that networks are accidents waiting to happen. I cover a variety of networking woes in Chapter 24, "Troubleshooting Network Problems."

CHAPTER **23**

# Making Remote Network Connections

The networking techniques you've seen so far have assumed some kind of physical connection between machines. For standard peer-to-peer and client/server networks, the computers use a network card/cable package to connect to each other either directly or indirectly via a hub or router. What do you do, however, when a physical connection just isn't possible? For example, suppose that you're on the road with your notebook computer and need to access a file on your network server. Or suppose that you're working at home and need to send a file to your office machine. Is there any way to access a network in the absence of a physical connection? The answer is that for these remote predicaments, you *can* connect to a network and use its resources just as you can with a physical connection (albeit more slowly).

Windows XP offers three solutions: dial-up connections, Remote Desktop, and Virtual Private Networking. This chapter takes you through the details of understanding, configuring, and using these techniques.

## Creating a Dial-Up Connection

You might think that being able to dial-up a computer on your network is only the province of high-end networks configured with servers that offer remote dial-up access. Not at all. Windows XP enables you to designate any Windows XP machine as a dial-up host. That computer requires just two things:

- An installed modem
- A phone line attached to the modem

Nothing too sophisticated there! With that simple setup, you can configure the host computer to accept incoming calls on its attached phone line. A remote computer can then dial that number, enter an authorized username and password, and get complete access to the network, including My Network Places, other network shared folders, and even a shared Internet connection.

## Configuring the Dial-Up Host

You first need to choose which computer you want to use as the dial-up host. Set up the modem and phone line, if you haven't done so already, and then follow these steps to configure the host's dial-up access:

1. Select Start, All Programs, Accessories, Communications, New Connection Wizard. (Alternatively, if you have the Network Connections window open, click the task pane's Create a New Connection link.)

2. In the initial wizard dialog box, click Next. The Network Connection Type dialog box appears.

3. Activate the Set Up an Advanced Connection option, and then click Next. The Advanced Connection Options dialog box appears.

4. Activate the Accept Incoming Connections option, and then click Next. The Devices for Incoming Connections dialog box appears.

5. Activate the check box beside your modem. (You can also choose your ISDN line, if you have one, or a Direct Parallel connection over the printer port.) Click Next.

6. Leave the Do Not Allow Virtual Private Connections option activated and click Next to display the User Permissions dialog box. (If you want this to be a virtual private connection, see "Using Virtual Private Network Connections," later in this chapter.)

7. Activate the check box beside each user you want to have access to the dial-up connection. You can click Add to add new users. Click Next to display the Networking Software dialog box.

8. Leave the default networking software options as is, and then click Next.

> **NOTE**
>
> The point of this exercise is to gain access to your network with a remote dial-up. However, if you prefer that dial-up users access only the dial-up host and not the larger network, select Internet Protocol (TCP/IP) in the Networking Software dialog box and then click Properties. Deactivate the Allow Callers to Access My Local Area Network check box, and then click OK.

9. Click Finish. Windows XP adds an Incoming group to the Network Connection folder, and places an icon named Incoming Connections within that group.

## Configuring the Dial-Up Client

Now you need to configure the remote computer to act as the dial-up client. Here are the steps to follow:

1. Select Start, All Programs, Accessories, Communications, New Connection Wizard. (Alternatively, if you have the Network Connections window open, click the task pane's Create a New Connection link.)

2. In the initial wizard dialog box, click Next. The Network Connection Type dialog box appears.

3. Activate the Connect to the Network at My Workplace option, and then click Next. The Advanced Connection Options dialog box appears.

4. Activate the Dial-Up Connection option, and then click Next to display the Connection Name dialog box.

5. Type a name for the connection and click Next. The Phone Number to Dial dialog box appears.

6. Type the phone number (including, if necessary, the country code and area code) and click Next.

7. Click Finish. Windows XP adds a Dial-Up group to the Network Connection folder, and places in that group an icon with the name you specified in step 5.

> **NOTE**
>
> You can apply all the usual modem settings—such as dialing rules, modem properties, and dialing and redialing options—for the client connection. Refer to the "Installing and Configuring a Modem" section in Chapter 15, "Getting Started with Modem Communications," for more specific information.

Windows XP also displays the Connect *Name* dialog box, where *Name* is the connection name you supplied in step 5. If you don't want to connect right now, click Cancel. See the next section for instructions on making the connection.

## Making the Dial-Up Connection

With the host and client configured, you can now use the client to make the dial-up connection. First, make sure that you have a phone line attached to the client's modem. Now follow these steps:

1. On the client computer, select Start, All Programs, Accessories, Communications, Network Connections. (Alternatively, open Control Panel's Network Connection icon.)

2. Double-click the dial-up icon. The Connect dialog box appears.

3. Type your username and password.

4. If you want Windows XP to remember your logon data, activate the Save This User Name and Password for the Following Users, and then activate either Me Only or Anyone Who Uses This Computer.

5. Click Dial. Windows XP dials the number, verifies your logon data, and then registers your computer on the network.

The Network Connection windows on the client and host change as follows:

- On the client, the Status column (assuming that you're in Details view; select View, Details) changes to Connected.

- On the host, the Incoming group's Incoming Connections icon shows 1 client connected, and a second icon appears for the connected user, as shown in Figure 23.1.

**FIGURE 23.1**   When a client connects to the host, a new icon for the client appears in the Incoming group.

## Ending the Dial-Up Connection

To shut down a dial-up connection, you have two choices:

- On the client, right-click the connection (either in Network Connections or the notification area) and then click Disconnect

- On the host, right-click the client connection (again, either in Network Connections or the notification area) and then click Disconnect

# Connecting to a Remote Desktop

Windows XP's Remote Desktop feature enables you to connect to a workgroup computer's desktop and use the machine just as though you were sitting in front of it. This is handy if you can't leave your desk but need to troubleshoot a problem on the remote machine. Alternatively, if you have a network at home, you can use Remote Desktop to operate your main computer from any other computer in the house.

## Getting the Remote Computer Ready

Remote Desktop is easy to configure and use, but it does require a small amount of prep work to ensure trouble-free operation. Let's begin with the remote computer, which is also called the **host** computer. Note that this machine must be running Windows XP Professional. (XP Home can't be configured as a Remote Desktop host.)

Here are the steps to follow to prepare the remote computer for its Remote Desktop hosting duties:

1. Log on to the host as an Administrator.

2. By default, the user currently logged on to the host machine has permission to connect remotely to the host. Other users with default remote connection permissions are members of the host's Administrators and Remote Desktop Users groups. (In all cases, only users with password-protected accounts can use Remote Desktop.) If you want to connect to the host remotely, you need to set up an account for the username with which you want to connect from the client (again, you must assign a password to this account).

3. Launch Control Panel's System icon to open the System Properties dialog box. (Alternatively, click Start, right-click My Computer, and then click Properties.)

4. Display the Remote tab.

5. In the Remote Desktop group, activate the Allow Users to Connect Remotely to This Computer check box, as shown in Figure 23.2.

6. If you didn't add more users in step 2, skip to step 9. Otherwise, click Select Remote Users to display the Remote Desktop Users dialog box.

7. Click Add to display the Select Users dialog box, type the username, and click OK. (Repeat this step to add other users.)

8. Click OK to return to the System Properties dialog box.

9. Click OK.

**FIGURE 23.2** The Allow Users to Connect Remotely to This Computer check box must be activated to enable remote assistance of the computer.

## Getting the Client Computer Ready

You must install the Remote Desktop Connection software on the computer that will initiate the connection (this is called the **client**). This software is already installed in Windows XP Professional and Home. If you're running an earlier version of Windows on the client, you can install the Remote Desktop Connection software from the Windows XP CD:

1. Insert the Windows XP CD and wait for the Welcome to Microsoft Windows XP screen to appear.

2. Click Perform Additional Tasks.

3. Click Set Up Remote Desktop Connection.

---

**NOTE**

You can also download the latest client software from Microsoft:

www.microsoft.com/windowsxp/downloads/tools/rdclientdl.mspx

Note, too, that Microsoft also offers a client that operates under Mac OS X. Go to www.microsoft.com/downloads and search for *Remote Desktop Mac*.

---

## Making the Connection to the Remote Desktop

On the client computer, you can now connect to the host computer's desktop. Follow these steps:

1. Select Start, All Programs, Accessories, Communications, Remote Desktop Connection. The Remote Desktop Connection dialog box appears.

2. In the Computer text box, type the name or the IP address of the remote computer.

3. If you don't want to customize Remote Desktop, skip to step 9. Otherwise, click Options to expand the dialog box to the version shown in Figure 23.3.

**FIGURE 23.3** Clicking the Options button expands the dialog box so that you can customize Remote Desktop.

4. The General tab offers the following additional options:

User Name — Type the username of an account that has permission to connect to the remote machine.

Password — Type the password of the account you specified in the User Name text box.

Domain — Type the network domain of the remote computer, if one exists. (Small peer-to-peer networks don't use domains.)

Save My Password — Activate this check box to have Windows XP save your password so that you don't have to type it the next time you connect to this host.

Save As — Click this button to save your connection settings to a Remote Desktop (.rdp) file for later use.

Open — Click this button to open a saved .rdp file.

5. The Display tab, shown in Figure 23.4, offers three options for controlling the look of the Remote Desktop window:

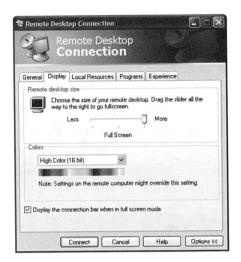

**FIGURE 23.4**    Use the Display tab to set the Remote Desktop size and colors.

| | |
|---|---|
| Remote Desktop Size | Drag this slider to set the resolution of Remote Desktop. Drag the slider all the way to the left for a 640×480 screen size; drag the slider all the way to the right to have Remote Desktop take up the entire client screen, no matter what resolution the host is currently using. |
| Colors | Use this list to set the number of colors used for the Remote Desktop display. Note that if the number of colors on either the host or the client is lower than the value you select in the Colors list, Windows XP will use the lower value. |
| Display the Connection Bar When in Full Screen Mode | When this check box is activated, the Remote Desktop Connection client displays a **connection bar** at the top of the Remote Desktop window, provided you selected Full Screen for the Remote Desktop Size setting. You use the connection bar to minimize, restore, and close the Remote Desktop window. If you find that the connection bar just gets in the way, deactivate this check box to prevent it from appearing. |

6. The Local Resources tab, shown in Figure 23.5, offers three options for controlling certain interactions between the client and the host:

**FIGURE 23.5** Use the Local Resources tab to customize how Remote Desktop handles the host's sounds, Windows key combinations, and the client's local devices.

| | |
|---|---|
| Remote Computer Sound | Use this list to determine where Windows XP plays the sounds generated by the host computer. You can play them on the client (if you want to hear what's happening on the host), on the host (if you want a user sitting at the host to hear the sounds), or not at all (if you have a slow connection). |
| Keyboard | Use this list to determine which computer is sent special Windows key combinations—such as Alt+Tab and Ctrl+Esc—that you press on the client keyboard. You can have the key combos sent to the client, to the host, or to the host only when you're running the Remote Desktop window in full-screen mode. What happens if you're sending key combos to one computer and you need to use a particular key combo on the other computer? For such situations, remote desktop offers several keyboard equivalents, outlined in the following table: |

| Windows Key Combo | Remote Desktop Equivalent |
|---|---|
| Alt+Tab | Alt+Page Up |
| Alt+Shift+Tab | Alt+Page Down |
| Alt+Esc | Alt+Insert |
| Ctrl+Esc or Windows Logo | Alt+Home |
| Print Screen | Ctrl+Alt+– (numeric keypad) |
| Alt+Print Screen | Ctrl+Alt++ (numeric keypad) |

Here are three other useful keyboard shortcuts that you can press on the client computer and have Windows XP send them to the host computer:

| | |
|---|---|
| Ctrl+Alt+End | Displays the Windows Task Manager (on a peer-to-peer computer) or Windows Security (on a domain computer). This is equivalent to pressing Ctrl+Alt+Delete, which Windows XP always applies to the client computer. |
| Alt+Delete | Displays the active window's Control menu. |
| Ctrl+Alt+Break | Toggles the Remote Desktop window between full-screen mode and a regular window. |

| | |
|---|---|
| Local Devices | Activate these check boxes to display the client computer's local devices on the host: |

- Disk Drives—Activate this check box to display the client's hard disk partitions and mapped network drives in the host's My Computer window. As shown in Figure 23.6, the client's drives appear in My Computer's Other group with the syntax *D* on *COMPUTER*, where *D* is the drive letter and *COMPUTER* is the network name of the client computer (such as HERMES in Figure 23.6).

**FIGURE 23.6**   If you elect to display the client's disk drives on the host, they appear in My Computer's Other group.

- Printers—Activate this check box to display the client's printers in the host's Printers and Faxes window. The client's printers appear with the syntax *Printer* (from *COMPUTER*), where *Printer* is the printer name and *COMPUTER* is the network name of the client computer.

- Serial Ports—Activate this check box to make any devices attached to the client's serial ports (such as a bar-code scanner) available while you're working with the host.

7. Use the Programs tab to specify a program to run on connection. Activate the Start the Following Program on Connection check box, and then use the Program Path and File Name text box to specify the program to run. After connecting, the user can work with only this program, and when he quits the program, the session also ends.

8. Use the Experience tab, shown in Figure 23.7, to set performance options for the connection. Use the Choose Your Connection Speed to Optimize Performance dropdown list to set the appropriate connection speed. Because you're connecting over a network, you should choose the LAN (10Mbps or higher) option. Depending on the connection speed you choose, one or more of the following check boxes will be activated (the faster the speed, the more check boxes Windows XP activates):

| | |
|---|---|
| Desktop Background | Deactivate this check box to improve performance by not displaying the host's desktop background image. |
| Show Contents of Window While Dragging | Deactivate this check box to improve performance by not displaying the contents of a window when you drag the window with your mouse. |
| Menu and Windows Animation | Deactivate this check box to improve performance by not displaying the animations that Windows XP normally uses when you pull down menus or minimize and maximize windows. |
| Themes | Deactivate this check box to improve performance by not displaying the host's current visual theme. |
| Bitmap Caching | Activate this check box to improve performance by not storing frequently used host images on the client computer. |

9. Click Connect.

10. If you activated the Disk Drives or Serial Ports check boxes in the Local Resources tab, a security warning dialog box appears. If you're sure that making these resources available to the remote computer is safe, activate the Don't Prompt Me Again for Connections to This Remote Computer check box. Click OK.

11. If you didn't enter a username or password in step 4, the Log On to Windows dialog box appears. Type the username and password and click OK.

12. If a person with a different username is already logged on to the remote computer, Windows XP lets you know that you'll disconnect that user:

**FIGURE 23.7**    Use the Experience tab to set performance options for the connection.

- If the remote computer has Fast User Switching enabled, disconnecting the user is the same as switching to a different user on the system. In other words, the current user's programs remain running and she will not lose any data. In this case, it's okay to click Yes to continue with the connection.

- If the remote computer has Fast User Switching disabled, disconnecting the user means forcing that user off the system, which could result in data loss. Click Yes only if you're sure that it's okay to disconnect the current user.

13. If another person was logged on to the remote computer and that computer has Fast User Switching enabled, Windows XP displays the Request for Connection dialog box shown in Figure 23.8. The user must click Yes to allow the remote user to connect. The user is then logged off and the remote user is logged on.

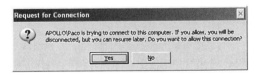

**FIGURE 23.8**    This dialog box appears if another person is logged on to the remote computer and that computer has Fast User Switching enabled.

The remote desktop then appears on your computer. If you chose to work in full-screen mode, you'll also see the connection bar at the top of the screen, as shown in Figure 23.9.

Minimize Restore

Pin            Connection bar            Close

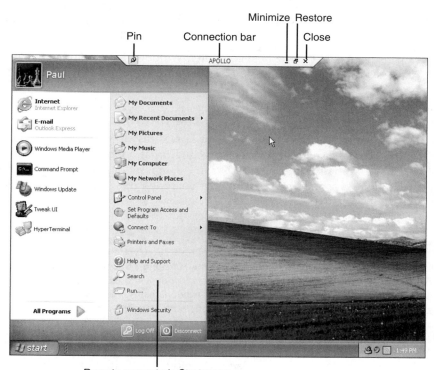

Remote computer's Start menu

**FIGURE 23.9**    After you've connected, the remote computer's desktop appears on the client screen.

If you don't want the connection bar to appear full time, click the Pin button. When you move your mouse away, the connection bar slides off the screen. To get the connection bar back, move your mouse to the top edge of the screen.

If you need to work with your own desktop, you have two choices:

- Click the connection bar's Minimize button to minimize the Remote Desktop window.

- Click the connection bar's Restore button to display the Remote Desktop window.

## Disconnecting from the Remote Desktop

When you've finished with the Remote Desktop session, you have three choices for disconnecting:

- Using the host's desktop, select Start, Disconnect. Windows XP displays a dialog box asking if you're sure. Click Disconnect.

- Click the Close button in the connection bar. Windows XP displays a dialog box to let you know that your remote session will be disconnected. Click OK.

- On the client, log on. On the host computer, Windows XP displays a dialog box to let you know that the remote session was disconnected. Click OK.

## Connecting to a Remote Desktop via the Internet

Connecting to a Remote Desktop host over your LAN is easy to set up and fast, but your LAN might not always be so local. If you're traveling, what do you do if you want to connect to your desktop or to the desktop of some computer on your network? This is possible, but it requires some care to ensure that you don't open up your computer or your network to Internet-based hackers.

---

**CAUTION**

In addition to the security precautions I present in this section, you should also set up your accounts with robust passwords, as described in the "Creating a Strong Password" section of Chapter 6, "Getting the Most Out of User Accounts." Using Remote Desktop over the Internet means that you open up a small window on your network that is at least visible to others on the Net. To ensure that this hole cannot be exploited by other Internet users, a strong password is a must.

---

Here are the steps to follow (each is explained in more detail later) to set up your system to allow Remote Desktop connections via the Internet:

1. Configure Remote Desktop to use a listening port other than the default.

2. Configure Windows Firewall to allow TCP connections through the port you specified in step 1.

3. Configure your network gateway (if you have one) to forward data sent to the port specified in step 1 to the Remote Desktop host computer.

4. Determine the IP address of the Remote Desktop host or your network's gateway.

5. Use the IP address from step 4 and the port number from step 1 to connect to the Remote Desktop host via the Internet.

### Changing the Listening Port

Your first task is to modify the Remote Desktop software on the host computer to use a listening port other than 3389, which is the default port. This is a good idea because there are hackers on the Internet who use **port scanners** to examine Internet connections (particularly broadband connections) for open ports. If the hackers see that port 3389 is open, they could assume that it's for a Remote Desktop connection, so they can then try to make a Remote Desktop connection to the host. They still have to log on with an authorized username and password, but knowing the connection type means they've cleared a very large hurdle.

To change the Remote Desktop listening port, open the Registry Editor and navigate to the following key:

```
HKLM\System\CurrentControlSet\Control\TerminalServer\WinStations\RDP-Tcp
```

Open the `PortNumber` number setting and replace the existing value—D3D hexadecimal, or 3389 decimal—with some other number between 1,024 and 65,536 (decimal). Reboot your computer to put the new port setting into effect.

### Configuring Windows Firewall

Now you need to configure Windows Firewall to allow data to pass through the port you specified in the previous section. Here are the steps to follow:

1. On the Remote Desktop host, open Control Panel's Windows Firewall icon.

2. Display the Exceptions tab.

3. Click Add Port to display the Add a Port dialog box.

4. Use the Name text box to type a name for the unblocked port (such as *Remote Desktop Alternate*).

5. In the Port Number text box, type the port number you specified in the previous section.

6. Make sure that the TCP option is activated.

7. Click OK.

### Setting Up Port Forwarding

If your network uses a router, gateway, or other hardware firewall, you need to configure it to forward data sent to the port specified in step 1 to the Remote Desktop host computer. This is called **port forwarding**, and the steps you follow depend on the device. Figure 23.10 shows the Port Forwarding screen of the router on my system. In this case, the firewall forwards data that comes in to port 1234 to the computer at the address 192.168.1.101, which is the Remote Desktop host. Consult your device documentation to learn how to set up port forwarding.

### Determining Your IP Address

To connect to a remote desktop via the Internet, you need to specify an IP address instead of a computer name. The IP address you use depends on your Internet setup:

- If the Remote Desktop host computer connects directly to the Internet and your ISP supplied you with a static IP address, connect using that address.

- If the host computer connects directly to the Internet but your ISP supplies you with a dynamic IP address each time you connect, use the IPCONFIG utility to determine your current IP address. (That is, select Start, Run, type **cmd** and click OK to get to the command line, type **ipconfig** and press Enter.) Make note of the IP

Address value returned by IPCONFIG and use that address to connect to the Remote Desktop host.

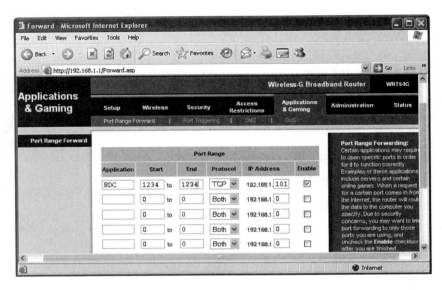

**FIGURE 23.10**    On a hardware firewall, forward the new port to the Remote Desktop host computer.

---

**TIP**

If you want to use Remote Desktop via the Internet regularly, constantly monitoring your dynamic IP address can be a pain, particularly if you forget to check it before heading out of the office. A useful solution is to sign up with a dynamic DNS service, which supplies you with a static domain name. The service also installs a program on your computer that monitors your IP address and updates the service's dynamic DNS servers to point your domain name to your IP address. Here are some dynamic DNS services to check out:

TZO (www.tzo.com)

No-IP.com (www.no-ip.com)

DynDNS (www.dyndns.org)

---

- If your network uses a gateway, determine the IP address of the gateway. You usually have to log on to the gateway's setup pages and view some sort of status page. Figure 23.11 shows an example. When you set up your Remote Desktop connection, you'll connect to the gateway, which will then forward your connection (thanks to your efforts in step 3) to the Remote Desktop host.

> **TIP**
>
> Another way to determine your gateway's IP address is to navigate to any of the free services for determining your current IP. Here are two:
>
> WhatISMyIP (www.whatismyip.com)
>
> DynDNS (checkip.dyndns.org)

**FIGURE 23.11**    Log on to your gateway device to see its current IP address.

### Connecting Using the IP Address and New Port

You're now ready to make the connection to the Remote Desktop host via the Internet. Here are the steps to follow:

1. Connect to the Internet.

2. Select Start, All Programs, Accessories, Communications, Remote Desktop Connection. The Remote Desktop Connection dialog box appears.

3. In the Computer text box, type the name or the IP address of the remote computer and the alternative port you specified in step 1, separated by a colon. Here's an example that uses the IP address 123.45.67.8 and port number 1234:

    ```
    123.45.67.8:1234
    ```

4. Set up your other Remote Desktop options as needed. For example, click Options, display the Experience tab, and then select the appropriate connection speed, such as Modem (28.8 Kbps), Modem (56 Kbps), or Broadband (128 Kbps–1.5 Mbps).

5. Click Connect.

## Making Remote Desktop Connections with a Web Browser

The steps in the previous section assumed that you'll be using your own computer to connect to and control a remote desktop. That might not always be the case, however. For example, you might borrow another person's computer, rent a computer, or use a computer in a library or Internet café. In such cases, you probably don't want to (or you

CHAPTER 23 Making Remote Network Connections

might not even be allowed to) install the Remote Desktop Connection client, much less configure and use it for the remote connection.

For situations in which you can't configure the client, you can instead configure the host. You need to do two things:

- Set up the host's network to include an **Internet Information Services** (IIS) web server

- Configure the web server to use the Remote Desktop Web Connection component

A web server running Remote Desktop Web Connection enables anyone with the proper authorization to access a computer on the network that has been configured to accept Remote Desktop connections. Most importantly, the connecting computer doesn't need the Remote Desktop Connection client. Instead, it can make the connection using any web browser that supports ActiveX controls. The next few sections take you through the process of configuring your network for Remote Desktop Web Connection.

### Installing IIS and Remote Desktop Web Connection

If your network doesn't already have an IIS web server, you can configure any Windows XP Professional machine to run IIS. This will enable you to run the Remote Desktop Web Connection component. However, after you have installed IIS , you can also use it to run a simple website and offer basic FTP access (neither of which I'll go into here).

> **NOTE**
>
> The version of IIS that ships with XP Professional is a vastly stripped-down version of the first-class web server that ships with Windows 2003 Server. If you require multiple websites, more than 10 simultaneous connections, and more robust options, consider using Windows 2003 Server.

Here are the steps to follow to install IIS and the Remote Desktop Web Connection component:

1. Open Control Panel's Add or Remove Programs icon.

2. Click Add/Remove Windows Components. The Windows Components Wizard appears.

3. Activate the Internet Information Services (IIS) check box.

4. Click Details to display the IIS components.

5. Select World Wide Web Service and then click Details.

6. Activate the Remote Desktop Web Connection check box and then click OK.

7. Click OK to return to the Windows Components Wizard.

**8.** Click Next. Windows XP installs IIS and the Remote Desktop Web Connection component.

**9.** Click Finish.

### Making the Connection

To connect to the remote host's desktop, follow these steps:

**1.** Open your web browser.

**2.** Enter the following address (where *server*) is the network name, domain name, or IP address of the IIS server:

```
http://server/tsweb
```

---

**TIP**

If you want to boost security by changing the Remote Desktop Web Connection listening port, you can do so by changing the script that runs in the default RDWC web page. Head for the following folder on the IIS machine:

```
%SystemRoot%\Web\TSWeb
```

Open the `default.htm` file in Notepad or another text editor. Scroll down to the `Device redirection options` section of the script, where you'll see several statements that all begin with the following reference:

```
MsRdpClient.AdvancedSettings2
```

Add the following statement below those statements (where *nnnn* is the new listening port number):

```
MsRdpClient.AdvancedSettings2.RdpPort = nnnn
```

When you enter the address of the IIS server in your web browser, be sure to include the new port, like so:

```
http://server:nnnn/tsweb
```

---

**3.** The first time you do this, you might see the Security warning dialog box shown in Figure 23.12. You must install the Remote Desktop ActiveX control, so click Install.

**4.** You now see the Remote Desktop Web Connection logon screen, as shown in Figure 23.13.

**5.** Use the Server text box to specify the computer name or IP address of the Remote Desktop host computer.

**6.** Use the Size list to select the screen size for the window in which the remote desktop will appear.

**7.** Click Connect.

**FIGURE 23.12**    The first time you access the web server, Windows XP asks whether you want to install the Remote Desktop ActiveX control.

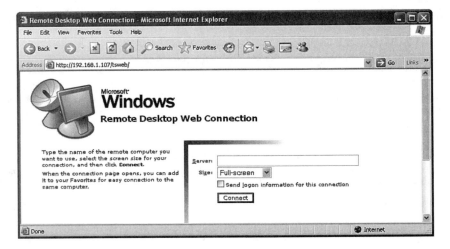

**FIGURE 23.13**    When you access the tsweb folder, the web server displays the Remote Desktop Web Connection page.

# Using Virtual Private Network Connections

In the remote connections you've seen so far, the security exists mostly at the connection point. That is, you set up usernames with strong passwords, and no one can access your dial-up or Remote Desktop connection without entering the correct logon data. This works well, but it doesn't do much for the actual data that's passed between the host and client. A malicious hacker might not be able to access your system directly, but he certainly can use a **packet sniffer** or similar technology to access your incoming and outgoing data. Because that data isn't encrypted, the hacker can easily read the contents of the packets.

What do you do, then, if you want to transfer secure data such as financial information or personnel files, but you love the simplicity of a dial-up connection? The answer is a tried-and-true technology called **virtual private networking** (**VPN**), which offers secure access to a private network over a public connection, such as the Internet or a phone line. VPN is secure because it uses a technique called **tunneling**, which establishes a connection between two computers—a **VPN server** and a **VPN client**—using a specific port (such as port 1723). Control-connection packets are sent back and forth to maintain the connection between the two computers (to, in a sense, keep the tunnel open).

When it comes to sending the actual network data—sometimes called the **payload**—each network packet is encrypted and then encapsulated within a regular IP packet, which is then routed through the tunnel. Any hacker can see this IP packet traveling across the Internet, but even if he intercepts the packet and examines it, no harm is done because the content of the packet—the actual data—is encrypted. When the IP packet arrives on the other end of the tunnel, VPN **decapsulates** the network packet and then decrypts it to reveal the payload.

Windows XP comes with VPN support built in, and it can act as either a server or a client. Windows XP uses two tunneling protocols:

23

| | |
|---|---|
| **Point-to-Point Tunneling Protocol (PPTP)** | This protocol is the most widely used in VPN setups. It was developed by Microsoft and is related to the **Point-to-Point Protocol** (**PPP**) that's commonly used to transport IP packets over the Internet. A separate protocol—**Microsoft Point-to-Point Encryption** (**MPPE**)—encrypts the network packets (IP, IPX, NetBEUI, or whatever). PPTP sets up the tunnel and encapsulates the encrypted network packets in an IP packet for transport across the tunnel. |
| **IP Security (IPSec)** | This protocol encrypts the payload (IP packets only), sets up the tunnel, and encapsulates the encrypted network packets in an IP packet for transport across the tunnel. |

**NOTE**

A third popular VPN protocol is **Layer 2 Tunneling Protocol** (**L2TP**), which goes beyond PPTP by allowing VPN connections over networks other than just the Internet (such as networks based on X.25, ATM, or Frame Relay). L2TP uses the encryption portion of IPSec to encrypt the network packets. Windows XP can use L2TP as a VPN client, but not as a VPN server.

There are two main ways to use VPN:

| | |
|---|---|
| Via the Internet | In this case, you first connect to the Internet using any PPP-based dial-up or broadband connection. Then you connect to the VPN server to establish the VPN tunnel over the Internet. |
| Via a dial-up connection | In this case, you first connect to the host computer using a regular dial-up connection. Then you connect to the VPN server to establish the VPN tunnel over the telephone network. |

## Setting Up a VPN Server

Your first chore is to set up a Windows XP computer on your network to accept incoming VPN connections.

> **NOTE**
>
> You don't need to configure a VPN server if your network uses a router or other gateway device that can act as a **VPN endpoint**, which means the router is capable of establishing the VPN tunnel itself. When you enable the tunnel, you can specify the network computers that can accept incoming VPN connections (using a subnet address, IP address range, and so on) and you can specify the addresses or the clients that can initiate VPN connections.

Here are the steps to configure a VPN server:

1. Select Start, All Programs, Accessories, Communications, New Connection Wizard. (Alternatively, if you have the Network Connections window open, click the task pane's Create a New Connection link.)

2. In the initial wizard dialog box, click Next. The Network Connection Type dialog box appears.

3. Activate the Set Up an Advanced Connection option, and then click Next. The Advanced Connection Options dialog box appears.

4. Activate the Accept Incoming Connections option, and then click Next. The Devices for Incoming Connections dialog box appears.

5. Activate the check box beside your modem. (You can also choose your ISDN line, if you have one.) Click Next.

6. Activate the Allow Virtual Private Connections option and click Next to display the User Permissions dialog box.

7. Activate the check box beside each user you want to have access to the dial-up connection. You can also click Add to add new users. Click Next to display the Networking Software dialog box.

8. Leave the default networking software options as is, and then click Next.

9. Click Finish. Windows XP adds an Incoming group to the Network Connection folder, and places an icon named Incoming Connections within that group.

## Configuring a Network Gateway for VPN

The best way to use VPN is when the client has a broadband Internet connection and the server has a public IP address or domain name. This enables you to access the server directly using your fast Internet connection. What happens, however, if the Windows XP machine you set up as the VPN server sits behind a gateway or firewall and so uses only an internal IP address (192.168.1.*)?

You can often get around this problem by setting up a network gateway to pass through VPN packets and forward them to the VPN server. (Note that some broadband routers now come with VPN capabilities built in, so they can handle incoming VPN connection automatically.)

The details depend on the device, but the usual first step is to enable the gateway's support for **VPN passthrough**, which allows network computers to communicate via one or more VPN protocols (such as PPTP and IPSec). Figure 23.14 shows a sample page in a gateway setup application that that lets you enable passthrough for the IPSec, PPTP, and L2TP protocols. In this case, I've enabled passthrough for PPTP only. (PPTP is the default VPN protocol used by Windows XP.)

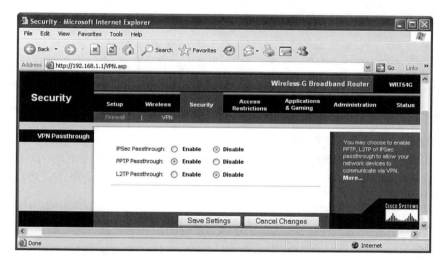

**FIGURE 23.14**    In your gateway setup application, enable VPN passthrough for the protocols you use.

In some cases, just enabling VPN passthrough is all you need to do to get VPN up and running through your gateway. If your VPN connection doesn't work or if your gateway doesn't support VPN passthrough, you have to open a port for the VPN protocol you're using and then have data to that port forwarded to the VPN server. (This is similar to the port forwarding I described earlier for Remote Desktop connections.) The forwarded ports depend on the protocol:

| | |
|---|---|
| PPTP | Forward TCP to port 1723 |
| IPSec | Forward UPD to port 500 |

Because you're using a Windows XP machine as the VPN server, you're using PPTP, so you need to configure the gateway to forward TCP packets on port 1723 to the IP address of the VPN server, as shown in Figure 23.15.

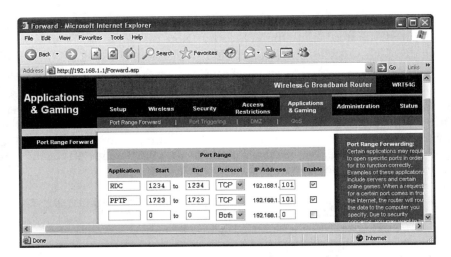

**FIGURE 23.15**    In your gateway setup application, forward TCP on port 1723 to the IP address of your network's VPN server.

## Configuring the VPN Client

Now you need to configure the remote computer as a VPN client. If you'll be connecting to the VPN server via dial-up, you first need to configure a dial-up connection to the server machine, as described earlier in this chapter (refer to the "Creating a Dial-Up Connection" section).

Here are the steps to follow to configure the VPN client:

1. Select Start, All Programs, Accessories, Communications, New Connection Wizard. (Alternatively, if you have the Network Connections window open, click the task pane's Create a New Connection link.)

2. In the initial wizard dialog box, click Next. The Network Connection Type dialog box appears.

3. Activate the Connect to the Network at My Workplace option, and then click Next. The Advanced Connection Options dialog box appears.

4. Activate the Virtual Private Network Connection option, and then click Next to display the Connection Name dialog box.

5. Type a name for the connection and click Next. The Public Network dialog box appears.

6. The wizard wants to know whether it can initiate your Internet or dial-up connection for you. You have two choices (click Next when you're done):

| Do Not Dial the Initial Connection | Choose this option if you have an always-on broadband Internet connection or if you prefer to initiate the connection yourself. |
| Automatically Dial This Initial Connection | Choose this option to have Windows XP establish the connection to the Internet or to the VPN server computer automatically. Choose the dial-up connection you want to use from the list provided. |

7. In the VPN Server Selection dialog box, you have three choices (click Next when you're done):

   - If you're using a dial-up connection, type the computer name or IP address of the VPN server.

   - If you're connecting directly to the VPN server, type its domain name or public IP address.

   - If you're using a direct connection via a network gateway, type the IP address of the gateway device.

8. Click Finish. Windows XP adds a Virtual Private Network group to the Network Connection folder, and places in that group an icon with the name you specified in step 5.

If you chose the Automatically Dial This Initial Connection option in step 6, the Initial Connection dialog box appears. Click Yes to connect the Internet or VPN server machine now, or click No if you want to connect later. See the "Making the VPN Connection" section, later in this chapter, for instructions on making the connection.

## Requiring VPN Encryption

Your VPN isn't very secure as it stands. That's because Windows XP doesn't require incoming (that is, from the client to the server) encryption by default, which seems to defeat the purpose of the whole VPN concept. To correct this problem, you need to ensure that the client uses encryption.

First, tell the server to require that all clients use encryption:

1. In the Network Connections window, right-click the Incoming Connections icon and then click Properties.

2. Display the Users tab.

3. Activate the Require All Users to Secure Their Passwords and Data check box, as shown in Figure 23.16.

4. Click OK.

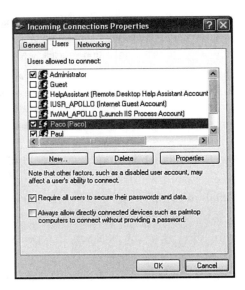

**FIGURE 23.16**   For added safety, require that VPN users encrypt their data.

To activate encryption on the VPN client, follow these steps:

1. In the Network Connections window, right-click the VPN connection in the Virtual Private Network group and then click Properties.

2. Display the Security tab.

3. Activate the Require Data Encryption (Disconnect If None) check box, as shown in Figure 23.17.

4. Click OK.

## Making the VPN Connection

With the VPN server and client configured, you can now use the client to make the VPN connection. Follow these steps on the VPN client computer:

1. If you elected to establish a dial-up connection to the Internet or to the VPN server computer by hand, make that connection now.

2. Select Start, All Programs, Accessories, Communications, Network Connections. (Alternatively, open Control Panel's Network Connection icon.)

3. Double-click the icon in the Virtual Private Network group.

4. If you asked Windows XP to make the initial connection for you, the Initial Connection dialog box appears. Click Yes to open the Connect dialog box, type your username and password, and then click Dial. Windows XP dials the number, verifies your logon data, and then registers your computer on the network.

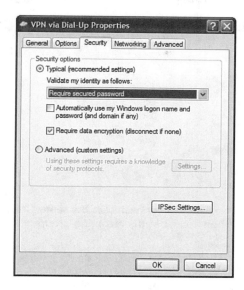

**FIGURE 23.17**   Make sure that the VPN client also requires data encryption.

5. The Connect dialog box appears for the VPN connection. Type your username and password.

6. If you want Windows XP to remember your logon data, activate the Save This User Name and Password for the Following Users, and then activate either Me Only or Anyone Who Uses This Computer.

7. Click Connect. Windows XP sets up the VPN connection.

The Network Connection windows on the client and host change as follows:

- On the client, the Status column (assuming that you're in Details view; select View, Details) changes to Connected.

- On the host, the changes depend on how you connected. If you connected via the Internet, the Incoming group's Incoming Connections icon shows 1 client connected, and a second icon appears for the connected user. If you connected by dialing up the VPN server, the Incoming group's Incoming Connections icon shows 2 clients connected, and two more icons appear for the connected user—one for the dial-up connection and one for the VPN connection—as shown in Figure 23.18.

**FIGURE 23.18**    After a VPN client has connected to the server, icons for the client's initial connection and VPN connection appear in the Incoming group.

## Ending the VPN Connection

To shut down a VPN connection, you have two choices:

- On the client, right-click the VPN connection (either in Network Connections or the notification area) and then click Disconnect

- On the host, right-click the client's VPN connection (again, either in Network Connections or the notification area) and then click Disconnect

# From Here

Here's a list of chapters where you'll find related information:

- You can use Phone Dialer and NetMeeting to communicate with network users. Refer to Chapter 16, "Putting Your Modem to Work."

- TCP/IP is quickly becoming the protocol of choice for both large and small networks. I showed you how to work with TCP/IP in Chapter 17, "Implementing TCP/IP for Internet Connections."

- To learn how to set up Windows XP for networking, see Chapter 22, "Setting Up and Accessing a Small Network."

- It sometimes seems that networks are accidents waiting to happen. I cover a variety of networking woes in Chapter 24, "Troubleshooting Network Problems."

# CHAPTER 24

# Troubleshooting Network Problems

*The greater the difficulty, the greater the glory.*

*—Cicero*

$A$s you've seen in the two previous chapters, networking is a complex, arcane topic that taxes the patience of all but the most dedicated wireheads (an affectionate pet name often applied to network hackers and gurus). There are so many hardware components to deal with (from the network adapter to the cable to the router to the hub) and so many layers of software (from the device drivers to the protocols to the redirectors to the network providers) that networks often seem like accidents looking for a place to happen.

If your network has become a notwork (some wags also refer to a downed network as a nyetwork), this chapter offers a few solutions that might help. I don't make any claim to completeness here, however. Most network ills are a combination of several factors and are therefore relatively obscure and difficult to reproduce. Instead, I'll go through a few general strategies for tracking down problems as well as offer solutions for some of the most common network afflictions.

## The First Step: Rerun the Network Connection Wizard

I mentioned in Chapter 22, "Setting Up and Accessing a Small Network," that the easiest and most reliable way to set up a network in Windows XP is to launch the Network

Connection Wizard and follow the steps it takes you through. Expert users generally hate wizards, but in this case it's worth it because the Network Connection Wizard almost always does a good job of getting the network configured right.

By the same token, the Network Connection Wizard should also be the first thing you turn to if you're having connection problems. You'll be surprised how often another run through the wizard's dialog boxes can solve connection snags. Follow the steps that I outlined in Chapter 22's "Running the Network Setup Wizard" section.

## Checking Connection Status

A good starting point for diagnosing network problems is to check the status of your network connection. This will show you things such as whether you're connected, your connection speed, your current IP address, your network's default gateway addresses, DHCP server, DNS server, and so on. Invalid entries for these and other status items could provide a hint as to where the network problem might lie.

To display the connection status, you have two choices:

- If a connection icon appears in the taskbar's notification area, double-click the icon.

> **TIP**
>
> If no connection icon appears in the taskbar's notification area, select Start, All Programs, Accessories, Communications, Network Connections. Right-click your network connection and click Properties. In the General tab of the property sheet that appears, activate the Show Icon in Notification Area When Connected check box, and then click OK.

- In the Network Connections window, double-click the connection.

Figure 24.1 shows the Status dialog box that appears. In the General tab, there are two groups to check out:

| | |
|---|---|
| Connection | This group shows the connection's current status: Connected or Disconnected. If the status value shows Connected, the Duration value shows how long the connection has been active, and the Speed value shows the connection speed in Mbps. For a wireless connection, this group also shows the network name and the current signal strength. |
| Activity | This group shows the number of network packets that the connection has sent and received. A very low number for either value gives you a hint about the direction of the problem. For example, a very low Sent value might indicate that you are not sharing your resources correctly or at all. |

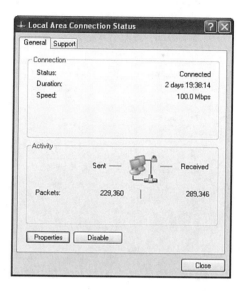

**FIGURE 24.1**    In the Status dialog box, the General tab offers basic connection details and activity metrics.

The Support tab displays basic connection data, including your IP address, subnet mask, and default gateway address, as shown in Figure 24.2. The Address Type value will be one of the following:

| | |
|---|---|
| Assigned by DHCP | A DHCP server assigns your IP address automatically. |
| Manually Configured | You entered a static IP address in the Internet Protocol (TCP/IP) Properties dialog box. |
| Automatic Private Address | Your network uses the Automatic Private Internet Protocol Addressing (APIPA). |
| Invalid IP Address | An invalid IP Address (0.0.0.0) usually indicates one of the following problems:<br>• Your network's DHCP server is down.<br>• The static IP address you entered conflicts with another IP address on the network. |

For other network connection data, click the Details button to see information such as the addresses of the DHCP server, DNS servers, and WINS server. You can also click Repair to initiate the Windows XP network connection repair utility. See "Repairing a Network Connection," later in this chapter.

24

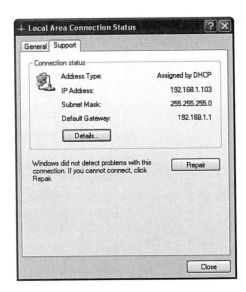

**FIGURE 24.2**    Use the Support tab to examine connection data such as your IP address, subnet mask, and default gateway address.

## Checking Network Utilization

If your network feels sluggish, it could be the server or node you're working with is sharing data slowly or that network traffic is exceptionally high. To see whether the latter situation is the cause of the problem, you can check out the current **network utilization** value, which is the percent of available bandwidth that your network adapter is currently using.

To check network utilization, follow these steps:

1. Right-click an empty section of the taskbar and then click Task Manager.

2. Display the Networking tab, shown in Figure 24.3.

3. If you have multiple adapters, click the one you want to check in the Adapter Name list.

4. Use the graph or the Network Utilization column to monitor the current network utilization value.

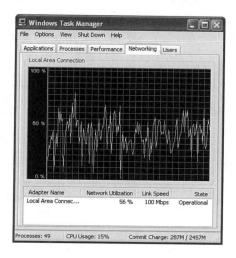

**FIGURE 24.3**   Use Task Manager's Networking tab to check the current network utilization percentage.

# Repairing a Network Connection

When a user calls Microsoft Support to resolve a networking issue, the support engineer has a list of troubleshooting steps that he takes the user through. For example, if there's a problem with a DHCP network, the engineer usually starts by telling the user to use IPCONFIG to release (`ipconfig /release`) and then renew (`ipconfig /renew`) the IP address. Other steps include running specific commands with the ARP (Address Resolution Protocol) and NBTSTAT (NetBIOS over TCP/IP Statistics) utilities.

Someone at Microsoft realized that all these steps could be automated by creating a script that runs the various `ipconfig`, `arp`, and `nbtstat` commands. The result is the network connection repair tool, which runs the following six troubleshooting steps:

- Broadcasts a request for the renewal of the computer's DHCP lease.

> **NOTE**
>
> A **DHCP lease** is a guarantee that the DHCP client computer will have the IP address supplied by the DHCP server for a specified period of time. To avoid lease expiration, the DHCP client usually sends a request—a DHCPREQUEST message—for lease renewal to the original DHCP server after 50% of the lease time has expired. If 87.5% of its lease time has expired, the DHCP client sends a lease renewal request to all available DHCP servers. This broad request for a lease renewal is what the repair tool does. Why send a DHCPREQUEST message instead of just using IPCONFIG to release and renew the IP address? Because if the current address is functioning properly, releasing that address could cause extra problems if a new address can't be obtained from a DHCP server. With a lease renewal request, the DHCP client keeps its current address.

- Flushes the ARP cache—The **ARP (Address Resolution Protocol)** handles the conversion of an IP address to a physical address of a network adapter. (To see the physical address of your adapter, open the connection's Status dialog box, display the Support tab, and click Details.) To improve performance, Windows XP stores resolved addresses in the **ARP cache** for a short time. Some networking problems are caused by ARP cache entries that are obsolete or incomplete. The cache is normally flushed regularly, but the repair tool forces a flush. This is the same as running the following command:

  ```
  arp -d
  ```

---

**TIP**

To see the contents of the ARP cache, run the following command:

```
arp -a
```

You'll see output similar to the following:

```
Interface: 192.168.1.101 --- 0x2
    Internet Address       Physical Address      Type
    192.168.1.1            00-12-17-8c-48-88     dynamic
    192.168.1.100          00-11-24-1a-7a-fc     dynamic
    192.168.1.103          00-11-11-be-c7-78     dynamic
```

---

- Flushes the NetBIOS name cache—NetBIOS handles the conversion between the network names of computers and their IP addresses. To improve performance, Windows XP stores resolved names in the **NetBIOS name cache**. To solve problems caused by NetBIOS name cache entries that are obsolete or bad, this step clears the cache. This is the same as running the following command:

  ```
  nbtstat -r
  ```

- Re-registers the computer with the network's WINS server—The repair tool asks the WINS server to release the computer's NetBIOS names that are registered with the server and then re-register them. This is useful if you're having problems connecting to other computers using their network names. This is the same as running the following command:

  ```
  nbtstat -rr
  ```

- Flushes the DNS cache—DNS handles the conversion of domain names to IP addresses. To improve performance, Windows XP stores resolved domain names in the **DNS cache**. To solve problems caused by DNS cache entries that are obsolete or bad, this step clears the cache. This is the same as running the following command:

  ```
  ipconfig /flushdns
  ```

- Re-register the computer with the DNS server. This is useful if you're having trouble resolving domain names or if you're having trouble with a dynamic DNS server. This is the same as running the following command:

```
ipconfig /registerdns
```

To launch the repair process, you have two choices:

- In the Support tab of the connection's Status dialog box, click Repair

- In the Network Connections window, right-click the connection and then click Repair

The Repair *Connection* dialog box appears (where *Connection* is the name of the connection you're repairing) and shows you the progress of the repair, as shown in Figure 24.4. When the repair is complete, click Close.

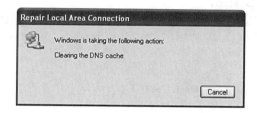

**FIGURE 24.4**   The network connection repair tool runs through six common network troubleshooting steps in an attempt to resolve the problem.

# Working with Network Diagnostics

If you suspect you're having network trouble—such as computers on the network not being able to see each other or file transfers or other network activity behaving erratically—but you aren't sure, one easy way to find out is to run the Network Diagnostics utility. This is a Help and Support Center connectivity troubleshooting tool that can help you isolate network problems.

To get started, use any one of the following techniques:

- In the Network Connections window, click the task pane's Network Troubleshooter link, and then click the Diagnose Network Configuration and Run Automated Networking Tests link.

- Select Start, Help and Support, click Fixing a Problem, click Networking Problems, and then click the Diagnose Network Configuration and Run Automated Networking Tests link.

- In the System Information utility (Start, All Programs, Accessories, System Tools, System Information), select Tools, Net Diagnostics.

- In a Command Prompt window, enter the following command:

  **`netsh diag gui`**

Network Diagnostics operates by performing three different actions:

| | |
|---|---|
| Ping | Pings various objects to check for basic connectivity. For example, Network Diagnostics pings the loopback address (127.0.0.1), your IP address, the default gateway, the DHCP and DNS servers, and more. |
| Connect | Attempts to connect to certain servers, such as your Internet mail and news servers. |
| Show | Displays information about various objects, including your network adapters, network clients, DHCP servers, IP addresses, modems, and more. |

## Setting Scanning Options

To specify which of these actions are performed on which objects, click the Set Scanning Options link in the Network Diagnostics window. You see the Network Diagnostics window shown in Figure 24.5. You have two ways to proceed:

- In the Actions section, activate the check box beside each action that you want Network Diagnostics to perform.

- In the Categories section, activate the check box beside each object that you want the actions performed on. (Note, however, that not all actions are performed on all objects. For example, the Connect action is performed only on the mail and news server and the Internet Explorer proxy server, if one exists on your network.)

When you're done, click Save Options.

## Running Network Diagnostics

To start the Network Diagnostics scan, click the Scan Your System link. Network Diagnostics displays the progress of the scan, as shown in Figure 24.6.

When the scan has finished, you'll see the results in a window similar to the one shown in Figure 24.7. Open the branches to see more detailed objects and the actions that Network Diagnostics performed on them. Look for FAILED in red type to see where possible problems occurred.

## Running Network Diagnostics from the Command Line

You can also run network diagnostics during a Command Prompt session using the NETSH (Net Shell) utility.

For the ping action, you use the following command:

```
netsh diag ping object
```

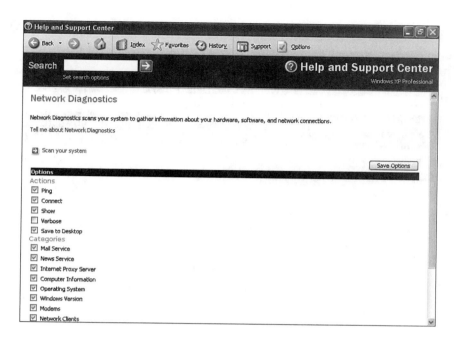

**FIGURE 24.5**   Click the Set Scanning Options link to see the list of Network Diagnostics options.

Here, *object* is a parameter that specifies the object you want to ping. You can either specify an IP address or hostname, or you can use the built-in object names listed in Table 24.1.

**TABLE 24.1**   The *object* Parameter's Built-in Names for the ping Action

| Name | Pings |
| --- | --- |
| adapter | The network adapter |
| dhcp | The DHCP server |
| dns | The DNS server |
| gateway | The default gateway |
| ieproxy | The Internet Explorer proxy server |
| ip | The computer's IP address |
| loopback | The loopback address (127.0.0.1) |
| mail | The default mail server defined by Outlook Express |
| news | The default news server defined by Outlook Express |
| wins | The WINS server |

For example, the following command pings the default gateway:

```
netsh diag ping gateway
```

For the connect action, you use the following command:

```
netsh diag connect object
```

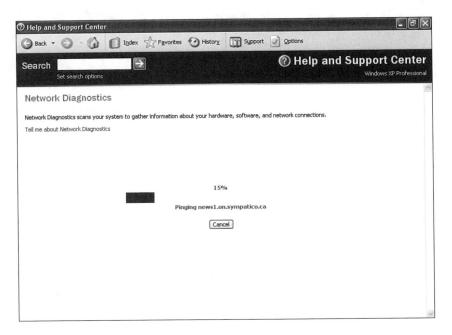

**FIGURE 24.6**    Network Diagnostics shows the progress of the scan.

Here, `object` is a parameter that specifies the object you want to connect with. You can either specify an IP address or hostname, or you can use the built-in object names listed in Table 24.2.

**TABLE 24.2**    The `object` Parameter's Built-in Names for the connect Action

| Name | Connects With |
| --- | --- |
| ieproxy | The Internet Explorer proxy server |
| mail | The default mail server defined by Outlook Express |
| news | The default news server defined by Outlook Express |

For example, the following command attempts to connect to the mail server:

```
netsh diag connect mail
```

For the show action, you use the following command:

```
netsh diag show object
```

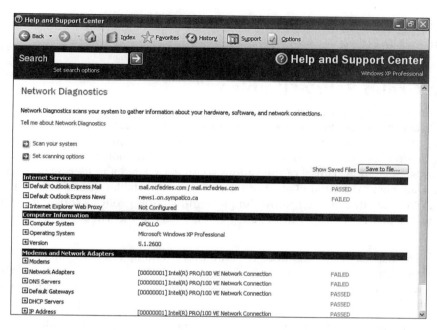

**FIGURE 24.7**    The results of a Network Diagnostics scan.

Again, `object` is a parameter that specifies the object you want to display information about. You can use the built-in object names listed in Table 24.3.

**TABLE 24.3**    The `object` Parameter's Built-in Names for the show Action

| Name | Shows Information For |
|------|----------------------|
| adapter | The network adapter |
| all | All the objects in this list |
| client | The installed network clients |
| computer | The computer |
| dhcp | The DHCP server |
| dns | The DNS server |
| gateway | The default gateway |
| ieproxy | The Internet Explorer proxy server |
| ip | The computer's IP address |
| mail | The default mail server defined by Outlook Express |
| modem | All installed modems |
| news | The default news server defined by Outlook Express |
| os | The operating system |
| test | All the objects in this list; also performs all the actions in the Ping and Connect categories |
| version | The Windows and **WMI (Windows Management Instrumentation)** versions |
| wins | The WINS server |

For example, the following command shows information for the network adapter:

```
netsh diag show adapter
```

## Some Group Policy "Problems"

If the administrator of your network has instituted group policies and hasn't done a good job of explaining them, Windows XP might seem to act strangely when it's really only honoring these policies. For example, Windows XP might complain that a password is too short or doesn't contain a number. These are almost certainly policy "problems" and not Windows woes at all. A perusal of the various computer-related and user-related network settings available in the Group Policy editor will show you the kinds of things that can be affected. (For more details, refer to the "Implementing Group Policies with Windows XP" section in Chapter 7, "Using Control Panel, Group Policies, and Tweak UI.") Here's a summary:

- You can't specify any exceptions for Windows Firewall—The Computer Configuration, Administrative Templates, Network, Network Connections, Windows Firewall, Standard Profile, Windows Firewall: Do Not Allow Exceptions policy is enabled.

- You can't activate the Offline Files feature—The Computer Configuration, Administrative Templates, Network, Offline Files, Allow or Disallow Use of the Offline File Feature policy is disabled.

- The network logon is slow—The Computer Configuration, Administrative Templates, System, Logon, Always Wait for the Network at Computer Startup and Logon policy is enabled.

- Windows XP displays the dialog box shown in Figure 24.8—The Windows XP Network, Password, Require Alphanumeric Windows password policy has been activated.

**FIGURE 24.8**    You might see this dialog box when you attempt to change your password.

- You can't access a network connection's property sheet—The User Configuration, Administrative Templates, Network, Network Connections, Prohibit Access to Properties of a LAN Connection policy is enabled.

- You can't run the New Connection Wizard—The User Configuration, Administrative Templates, Network, Network Connections, Prohibit Access to New Connection Wizard policy is enabled.

- You're not an Administrator and you can't rename a network connection—The User Configuration, Administrative Templates, Network, Network Connections, Ability to Rename LAN Connections policy is disabled.

- You're an Administrator and you can't rename a network connection—The User Configuration, Administrative Templates, Network, Network Connections, Ability to Rename LAN Connections or Remote Access Connections Available to All Users policy is disabled.

- You can't view the status of an active connection—The User Configuration, Administrative Templates, Network, Network Connections, Prohibit Viewing of Status for an Active Connection policy is enabled.

# Troubleshooting General Network Nuisances

This section takes you through a few of the most common complaints that crop up with Windows XP networking and offers some solutions.

**You receive a message telling you that A duplicate name exists on the network.**

The name you've given to your computer is the same as that of another computer on the network. Windows XP normally prevents you from changing your computer's name to a name that already exists on the network. However, if the other computer is turned off or disconnected from the network, Windows XP allows the name change. To change your computer name, follow these steps:

1. Open Control Panel's System icon (or click Start, right-click My Computer, and then click Properties).

2. Display the Computer Name tab.

3. Click Change.

4. Use the Computer Name text box to change the name.

5. Click OK. Windows XP tells you that you have to restart your computer to put the new name into effect.

6. Click OK to return to the System Properties dialog box.

7. Click OK. Windows XP asks whether you want to restart your computer.

8. Click Yes.

**No other computers appear in your workgroup.**

When you're in the My Network Places folder, you can click the task pane's View Workgroup Computers link to see the other computers in your workgroup. (Alternatively, use the Folders list to select My Network Places, Entire Network, Microsoft Windows Network, and then select your workgroup.) However, you might not see any other computers even though you know other computers exist in your workgroup.

First, make sure that you're using the same workgroup name as the other computers. To change the workgroup name, follow these steps:

1. Open Control Panel's System icon (or click Start, right-click My Computer, and then click Properties).

2. Display the Computer Name tab.

3. Click Change.

4. Use the Workgroup text box to change the workgroup name.

5. Click OK. Windows XP displays a Welcome to the *Name* Workgroup message (where *Name* is the new workgroup name).

6. Click OK. Windows XP tells you that you have to restart your computer to put the new name into effect.

7. Click OK to return to the System Properties dialog box.

8. Click OK. Windows XP asks whether you want to restart your computer.

9. Click Yes.

If the workgroup name is correct, see whether you can view the other workgroup computers via the command line. Open a Command Prompt window and enter the following command

**net view**

This displays a list of the other computers in your workgroup. Here's an example:

```
Server Name             Remark
- - - - - - - - - - - - - - - - - - - - - - - - - - - - - - - - - - - - - - - - - - - - - - - - - - - - - - - - - -
\\APOLLO                Office Computer
\\HERA                  Karen's Computer
\\HERMES                Notebook Computer
\\ZEUS                  Paul's Computer
The command completed successfully.
```

If you see the other workgroup computers now, it might mean that you simply need to wait—particularly if you've recently changed workgroups. Windows XP is sometimes a bit slow to broadcast changes, so the other workgroup machines might not show up right away. Reboot and check the workgroup folder later. In the meantime, you can work with the other computers via Command Prompt. See the section titled "Mapping a Network Folder to a Local Drive Letter" in Chapter 22.

**Other network users can't work with your shared folders or printers (or you can't work with resources shared by other users).**

As long as the other users can see your shared resources, the most likely culprit here is either that file and printer sharing has been turned off or is being blocked by the Windows Firewall. To check this out, follow these steps:

1. Open the property sheet for your network connection.

2. Display the General tab.

3. Activate the File and Printer Sharing for Microsoft Networks check box.

4. Display the Advanced tab.

5. In the Windows Firewall group, click Settings to display the Windows Firewall dialog box.

6. Display the Exceptions tab.

7. Activate the File and Printer Sharing check box.

> **TIP**
>
> It's also possible that the scope of the File and Printer Sharing exception is too limited. Select the File and Printer Sharing exception, click Edit, and then click Change Scope. Activate the My Network (Subnet) Only option, and click OK.

8. Click OK to return to the connection's property sheet.

9. Click OK.

Here are some other things to look for:

- Make sure that you've set up an account on your system for each user, and that you've given each user the correct password for the account.

- Check the type of permission you've granted each user. For example, a user given only Read access might complain because he can't modify a file or create new files.

- Make sure that your shares aren't hidden. As explained in Chapter 22, you can hide a shared resource by tacking a dollar sign ($) to the end of its name.

- The user might be attempting to access a shared folder that you've deleted, moved, or stopped sharing. You need to tell the user to either delete the share from My Network Places or set up a new Network Place.

## Cable Conundrums

If one of the software problems discussed so far isn't the cause of your networking quandary, the next logical suspect is the cabling that connects the workstations. This section discusses cabling, gives you a few pointers for preventing cable problems, and discusses some common cable kinks that can crop up.

## Some Things to Bear in Mind When Running Cable

Although most large-scale cabling operations are performed by third-party cable installers, smaller setups are usually do-it-yourself jobs. You can prevent some cable problems and simplify your troubleshooting down the road by taking a few precautions and "ounce of prevention" measures in advance:

- First and foremost, always buy the highest-quality cable you can find (for example, Category 5 for twisted-pair cable). With network cabling, you get what you pay for.

- Good-quality cable will be labeled (for example, RG-58/A-AU for coaxial). You should also add your own labels for things such as the source and destination of the cable.

- For complex installations, set up a complete wiring diagram that shows where the cables run and that indicates hubs, repeaters, wiring closets, and so on.

- To avoid electromagnetic interference, don't run cable near electronic devices, power lines, air conditioners, fluorescent lights, motors, and other electromagnetic sources.

- If you're running twisted-pair cable, try to avoid phone lines because the ringer signal can disrupt network data.

- To avoid the cable being stepped on accidentally, don't run it under carpet.

- If you plan to run cable outdoors, use conduit or another casing material to prevent moisture damage.

- Don't use excessive force to pull or push a cable into place. Rough handling can cause pinching or even breakage.

## Cable Limitations

Many cable problems are caused by exceeding the recommended limits on things such as cable length and trunk length. To help you avoid this, the following list summarizes the limitations inherent in some popular cable types:

### 10Base-T Limitations

The minimum cable length between computers is 8 feet.

Computers must be no more than 328 feet from the wiring closet.

One hub can connect up to 12 computers.

You can have up to 12 hubs to one central hub.

### 10Base-2 Limitations

The minimum cable length between computers is 20 inches.

The maximum length of a trunk segment is 607 feet.

You can connect up to 30 computers per trunk.

The maximum length of the total network trunk is 3,035 feet.

You can connect up to a maximum of 1,024 computers per network.

### 10Base-5 Limitations

The minimum cable length between taps is 8 feet.

The maximum length of a trunk segment is 1,640 feet.

The maximum length of the total network trunk is 8,200 feet.

### Token Ring Limitations

The maximum distance between Multistation Access Units (MAUs) is 100 meters for Type 1 cable, 45 meters for Type 2 cable, and 4 kilometers for fiber optic cable.

You can connect a maximum of 260 computers on Type 1 cable and on fiber optic cable at 16Mbps; you can have a maximum of 72 computers on Type 3 cable at 4Mbps.

The maximum number of MAUs on each ring is 33.

### ARCnet Limitations

The maximum distance between computers is 20,000 feet.

Computers can be no more than 600 feet from the active hub.

Passive hubs can be no more than 10 feet from the active hub.

You can connect a maximum of four computers to a passive hub, but none of these computers can be farther than 100 feet from the hub.

You can't connect one passive hub to another.

The maximum distance between two active hubs is 2,000 feet.

The maximum bus segment length for coaxial cable is 1,000 feet, with up to eight computers per segment.

The maximum bus segment length for twisted-pair cable is 400 feet with up to 10 computers per segment.

You can connect up to 255 computers per network.

## Troubleshooting Cables

If you suspect cabling might be the cause of your network problems, here's a list of a few things to check:

Watch for electromagnetic interference     If you see garbage on a workstation screen or experience random packet loss or temporarily missing nodes, the problem might be electromagnetic interference. Check your cables to make sure that they are at least 6 to 12 inches from any source of electromagnetic interference.

| | |
|---|---|
| Check your connections | Loose connections are a common source of cabling woes. Be sure to check every cable connection associated with the workstation that's experiencing network difficulty, including connections to the network adapter, wall plate, barrel connector, hub, and so on. In particular, watch the **BNC (Bayonet Neill Concelman)** cable connectors associated with thin coaxial cable because they can come loose quite easily, and it's not hard to connect them incorrectly in the first place. |
| For coaxial cable, check your terminators | If you use coaxial cable, you must terminate both ends of a network segment by installing BNC terminators. Make sure that terminators are installed at each end of the segment and that they are secured properly to the T-connector. Also, make sure that you use the proper terminator (for example, a 50-ohm impedance cable requires a 50-ohm terminator). |
| Isolate a thin coaxial cable problem by terminating the network adapter | If you're using thin coaxial cable, remove the T-connector from the network adapter of the problem workstation and replace it with a terminator. If the workstation now appears by itself in the Network Neighborhood, this probably means that you have a problem with either the cable or the connector used by the machine. |
| How's the lay of the line? | Loops of cable could be generating an electrical field that interferes with network communication. Try not to leave your excess cable lying around in coils or loops. |
| Inspect the cable for pinching or breaks | A badly pinched cable can cause a short in the wire, which could lead to intermittent connection problems. Make sure that no part of the cable is pinched, especially if the back of the computer is situated near a wall. A complete lack of connection with the network might mean that the cable's copper core has been severed completely and needs to be replaced. |
| Check your cable limitations | Double-check the limitations I outlined in the preceding section for cable length, maximum workstation numbers, and so on. |
| Check segment types | When you join two network segments, make sure that you're using the same type of cable for both segments. |

# Troubleshooting Adapter Afflictions

After cabling, network adapters are next on the list of common sources of networking headaches. Here's a list of items to check if you suspect that Windows XP and your network adapter aren't getting along:

| | |
|---|---|
| Make sure that Windows XP installed the correct adapter | Windows XP usually does a pretty good job of detecting the network card. However, a slight error (such as choosing the wrong transceiver type) can wreak havoc. Double-check that the network adapter listed in Device Manager is the same as the one installed in your computer. If it's not, click Remove to delete it, run the Add New Hardware Wizard, and choose your adapter manually. |
| Get the latest driver | Check with the manufacturer of the network adapter to see whether it has newer Windows XP drivers for the card. If so, download and install them. |
| Perform a physical check of the adapter | Open the case and make sure that the adapter is properly seated in its slot. For a PC Card adapter, make sure that the card is inserted all the way into its slot, and check the external connection (they are notorious for breaking). |
| Try a new adapter | Try swapping out the adapter for one that you know works properly. If that fixes the problem, you'll have to replace the faulty adapter. |

24

# More Sophisticated Tools

If the solutions and workarounds presented in this chapter didn't solve your problem, you might need higher-end help. Specifically, many companies now offer sophisticated software and hardware tools for detecting, analyzing, and troubleshooting networks. This section lists (in no particular order) the best of these companies, the products they offer, and contact information.

Company: Fluke

Products: OptiView, EtherScope, NetTool, and more

Address: www.fluke.com


Company: Triticom

Product: LANdecoder

Address: www.triticom.com

Company: Network General

Product: Sniffer, Netasyst

Address: www.networkgeneral.com


Company: Microtest (now owned by Fluke)

Products: OMNIScanner, ScanLink, MicroScanner, and more

Address: www.microtest.com

# From Here

Here's a list of chapters where you'll find related information:

- For the details on TCP/IP, refer to Chapter 17, "Implementing TCP/IP for Internet Connections."

- To learn how to set up Windows XP for networking, refer to Chapter 22, "Setting Up and Accessing a Small Network."

- For remote network access techniques, refer to Chapter 23, "Making Remote Network Connections."

# PART VII

# Appendices

## IN THIS PART

# APPENDIX **A**

# Windows XP Keyboard Shortcuts

Windows XP was made with the mouse in mind, so most day-to-day tasks are designed to be performed using the standard mouse moves. However, this doesn't mean your keyboard should be ignored when you're not typing. Windows XP is loaded with keyboard shortcuts and techniques that can often be used as replacements or enhancements for mouse clicks and drags. These shortcuts (as shown in Tables A.1–A.13) are often a faster way to work because you don't have to move your hand from the keyboard to the mouse and back. Also, the Windows XP keyboard techniques are useful to know just in case you have problems with your mouse and must rely on the keyboard to get your work done.

**TABLE A.1**  General Windows XP Shortcut Keys

| Press | To Do This |
| --- | --- |
| Ctrl+Esc | Open the Start menu. |
| Windows Logo | Open the Start menu. |
| Ctrl+Alt+Delete | Display the Windows Security dialog box (Windows XP Professional) or the Task Manager (Windows XP Home). |
| Print Screen | Copy the entire screen image to the Windows Clipboard. |
| Alt+Print Screen | Copy the active window's image to the Windows Clipboard. |
| Alt+Double-click | Display the Properties dialog box for the selected item. |
| Alt+Enter | Display the Properties dialog box for the selected object. |
| Shift | Prevent an inserted CD from running its AutoPlay application. (Hold down Shift while inserting the CD.) |

**TABLE A.1    Continued**

| Press | To Do This |
|---|---|
| Shift+F10 | Display the shortcut menu for the selected object. (This is the same as right-clicking the object.) |
| Shift+Right-click | Display the shortcut menu with alternative commands for the selected object. |

**TABLE A.2    Shortcut Keys for Working with Program Windows**

| Press | To Do This |
|---|---|
| Alt | Activate or deactivate the program's menu bar. |
| Alt+Esc | Cycle through the open program windows. |
| Alt+F4 | Close the active program window. |
| Alt+Spacebar | Display the system menu for the active program window. |
| Alt+Tab | Cycle through icons for each of the running programs. |
| F1 | Display context-sensitive help. |
| F10 | Activate the application's menu bar. |

**TABLE A.3    Shortcut Keys for Working with Documents**

| Press | To Do This |
|---|---|
| Alt+-(hyphen) | Display the system menu for the active document window. |
| Alt+Print Screen | Copy the active window's image to the Clipboard. |
| Ctrl+F4 | Close the active document window. |
| Ctrl+F6 | Cycle through the open documents within an application. |
| Ctrl+N | Create a new document. |
| Ctrl+O | Display the Open dialog box. |
| Ctrl+P | Display the Print dialog box. |
| Ctrl+S | Save the current file. If the file is new, display the Save As dialog box. |

**TABLE A.4    Shortcut Keys for Working with Data**

| Press | To Do This |
|---|---|
| Backspace | Delete the character to the left of the insertion point. |
| Ctrl+C | Copy the selected data to memory. |
| Ctrl+F | Display the Find dialog box. |
| Ctrl+H | Display the Replace dialog box. |
| Ctrl+X | Cut the selected data to memory. |
| Ctrl+V | Paste the most recently cut or copied data from memory. |
| Ctrl+Z | Undo the most recent action. |
| Delete | Delete the selected data. |
| F3 | Repeat the most recent Find operation. |

**TABLE A.5**    Shortcut Keys for Moving the Insertion Point

| Press | To Do This |
| --- | --- |
| Ctrl+End | Move the insertion point to the end of the document. |
| Ctrl+Home | Move the insertion point to the beginning of the document. |
| Ctrl+Left Arrow | Move the insertion point to the next word to the left. |
| Ctrl+Right Arrow | Move the insertion point to the next word to the right. |
| Ctrl+Down Arrow | Move the insertion point to the end of the paragraph. |
| Ctrl+Up Arrow | Move the insertion point to the beginning of the paragraph. |

**TABLE A.6**    Shortcut Keys for Selecting Text

| Press | To Do This |
| --- | --- |
| Ctrl+A | Select all the text in the current document. |
| Ctrl+Shift+End | Select from the insertion point to the end of the document. |
| Ctrl+Shift+Home | Select from the insertion point to the beginning of the document. |
| Ctrl+Shift+Left Arrow | Select the next word to the left. |
| Ctrl+Shift+Right Arrow | Select the next word to the right. |
| Ctrl+Shift+Down Arrow | Select from the insertion point to the end of the paragraph. |
| Ctrl+Shift+Up Arrow | Select from the insertion point to the beginning of the paragraph. |
| Shift+End | Select from the insertion point to the end of the line. |
| Shift+Home | Select from the insertion point to the beginning of the line. |
| Shift+Left Arrow | Select the next character to the left. |
| Shift+Right Arrow | Select the next character to the right. |
| Shift+Down Arrow | Select the next line down. |
| Shift+Up Arrow | Select the next line up. |

**TABLE A.7**    Shortcut Keys for Working with Dialog Boxes

| Press | To Do This |
| --- | --- |
| Alt+Down Arrow | Display the list in a drop-down list box. |
| Alt+*Underlined letter* | Select a control. |
| Ctrl+Shift+Tab | Move backward through the dialog box tabs. |
| Ctrl+Tab | Move forward through the dialog box tabs. |
| Enter | Select the default command button or the active command button. |
| Spacebar | Toggle a check box on and off; select the active option button or command button. |
| Esc | Close the dialog box without making any changes. |
| F1 | Display help text for the control that has the focus. |
| F4 | Display the list in a drop-down list box. |
| Backspace | In the Open and Save As dialog boxes, move up to the parent folder when the folder list has the focus. |
| Shift+Tab | Move backward through the dialog box controls. |
| Tab | Move forward through the dialog box controls. |

**TABLE A.8    Shortcut Keys for Drag-and-Drop Operations**

| Press | To Do This |
|-------|-----------|
| Ctrl | Copy the dragged object. |
| Ctrl+Shift | Display a shortcut menu after dropping a left-dragged object. |
| Esc | Cancel the current drag. |
| Shift | Move the dragged object. |

**TABLE A.9    Shortcut Keys for Working in a Folder Window**

| Press | To Do This |
|-------|-----------|
| Alt+Left Arrow | Navigate backward to a previously displayed folder. |
| Alt+Right Arrow | Navigate forward to a previously displayed folder. |
| Backspace | Navigate to the parent folder of the current folder. |
| Ctrl+A | Select all the objects in the current folder. |
| Ctrl+C | Copy the selected objects. |
| Ctrl+V | Paste the most recently cut or copied objects. |
| Ctrl+X | Cut the selected objects. |
| Ctrl+Z | Undo the most recent action. |
| Delete | Delete the selected objects. |
| F2 | Rename the selected object. |
| F3 | Display the Search Companion. |
| F5 | Refresh the folder contents. |
| Shift+Delete | Delete the currently selected objects without sending them to the Recycle Bin. |

**TABLE A.10    Shortcut Keys for Working with Internet Explorer**

| Press | To Do This |
|-------|-----------|
| Alt+Home | Go to the home page. |
| Alt+Left Arrow | Navigate backward to a previously displayed web page. |
| Alt+Right Arrow | Navigate forward to a previously displayed web page. |
| Ctrl+A | Select the entire web page. |
| Ctrl+B | Display the Organize Favorites dialog box. |
| Ctrl+D | Add the current page to the Favorites list. |
| Ctrl+E | Display the Search Companion Explorer bar. |
| Ctrl+F | Display the Find dialog box. |
| Ctrl+H | Display the History list Explorer bar. |
| Ctrl+I | Display the Favorites list Explorer bar. |
| Ctrl+N | Open a new window. |
| Ctrl+O | Display the Open dialog box. |
| Ctrl+P | Display the Print dialog box. |
| Ctrl+Shift+Tab | Cycle backward through the web page frames and the Address toolbar. |
| Ctrl+Tab | Cycle forward through the web page frames and the Address toolbar. |
| Esc | Stop downloading the web page. |

**TABLE A.10**   Continued

| Press | To Do This |
|-------|------------|
| F4 | Open the Address toolbar's drop-down list. |
| F5 | Refresh the web page. |
| F11 | Toggle between Full Screen mode and the regular window. |
| Spacebar | Scroll down one screen. |
| Shift+Spacebar | Scroll up one screen. |
| Shift+Tab | Cycle backward through the Address toolbar and the web page links. |
| Tab | Cycle forward through the web page links and the Address toolbar. |

**TABLE A.11**   Shortcut Keys for Working with Windows Media Player

| Press | To Do This |
|-------|------------|
| Ctrl+P | Play or pause the current media. |
| Ctrl+S | Stop the current media. |
| Ctrl+B | Go to the previous track. |
| Ctrl+Shift+B | Rewind to the beginning of the media. |
| Ctrl+F | Go to the next track. |
| Ctrl+Shift+F | Fast-forward to the end of the media. |
| Ctrl+H | Toggle Shuffle playback. |
| Ctrl+T | Toggle Repeat playback. |
| Ctrl+M | Show the menu bar. |
| Ctrl+Shift+M | Auto-hide the menu bar. |
| Ctrl+1 | Switch to Full mode. |
| Ctrl+2 | Switch to Skin mode. |
| F8 | Mute sound. |
| F9 | Decrease volume. |
| F10 | Increase volume. |

**TABLE A.12**   Shortcut Keys for DOSKEY

| Press | To Do This |
|-------|------------|
| **Command Recall Keys** | |
| Alt+F7 | Delete all the commands from the recall list. |
| Arrow keys | Cycle through the commands in the recall list. |
| F7 | Display the entire recall list. |
| F8 | Recall a command that begins with the letter or letters you've typed on the command line. |
| F9 | Display the Line number: prompt. You then enter the number of the command (as displayed by F7) that you want. |
| Page Down | Recall the newest command in the list. |
| Page Up | Recall the oldest command in the list. |
| **Command-Line Editing Keys** | |
| Backspace | Delete the character to the left of the cursor. |

A

**TABLE A.12** Continued

| Press | To Do This |
| --- | --- |
| **Command Recall Keys** | |
| Ctrl+End | Delete from the cursor to the end of the line. |
| Ctrl+Home | Delete from the cursor to the beginning of the line. |
| Ctrl+Left arrow | Move the cursor one word to the left. |
| Ctrl+Right arrow | Move the cursor one word to the right. |
| Delete | Delete the character over the cursor. |
| End | Move the cursor to the end of the line. |
| Home | Move the cursor to the beginning of the line. |
| Insert | Toggle DOSKEY between Insert mode (your typing is inserted between existing letters on the command line) and Overstrike mode (your typing replaces existing letters on the command line). |
| Left arrow | Move the cursor one character to the left. |
| Right arrow | Move the cursor one character to the right. |

**TABLE A.13** Windows Logo Key Shortcut Keys

| Press | To Do This |
| --- | --- |
| Windows Logo | Open the Start menu. |
| Windows Logo+D | Minimize all open windows. Press Windows Logo+D again to restore the windows. |
| Windows Logo+E | Open Windows Explorer. |
| Windows Logo+F | Display the Search Companion. |
| Windows Logo+Ctrl+F | Find a computer. |
| Windows Logo+L | Lock the computer. |
| Windows Logo+M | Minimize all open windows, except those with open modal windows. |
| Windows Logo+Shift+M | Undo minimize all. |
| Windows Logo+R | Display the Run dialog box. |
| Windows Logo+U | Display the Utility Manager. |
| Windows Logo+F1 | Display Windows Help. |
| Windows Logo+Break | Display the System Properties dialog box. |
| Windows Logo+Spacebar | Scroll down one page (supported only in certain applications, such as Internet Explorer). |
| Windows Logo+Shift+ Spacebar | Scroll up one page (supported only in certain applications, such as Internet Explorer). |
| Windows Logo+Tab | Cycle through the taskbar buttons. |

# Using the Windows XP Command Prompt

In Internet circles, a **holy war** is a never-ending debate on the merits of one thing versus another, in which people use the same arguments over and over, and nobody's opinion budges even the slightest bit one way or the other. Common holy war topics include liberalism versus conservatism, pro-choice versus pro-life, and neatness versus sloppiness.

Operating systems cause frequent holy war skirmishes, with most battles pitting Macintosh against Windows. Years ago, the mother of all operating system holy wars was DOS versus Windows, with correspondents devoting obscene amounts of time and energy extolling the virtues of one system and detailing the shortcomings of the other. Of course, *nobody* sings the praises of DOS any more, and its demise was mourned by few.

So, yes, DOS is dead, but **Command Prompt** is alive and well and adjusting nicely to its current role as just another Windows XP accessory. Yes, it's entirely possible that you might go your entire Windows career without having to fire up a Command Prompt session. But if you do need Command Prompt, you must know a few things in order to get the most out of your command-line sessions. This appendix shows you how to squeeze the best and most reliable performance out of them under Windows XP.

## Getting to Command Prompt

To take advantage of Command Prompt and all of its many useful commands, you need to start a Command Prompt session. Windows XP (as usual) offers a number of different ways to get to Command Prompt:

- Select Start, All Programs, Accessories, Command Prompt.

- Select Start, Run, type **cmd** in the Run dialog box, and click OK.

- Create a shortcut for `%SystemRoot%\system32\cmd.exe` on your desktop (or some other convenient location, such as the taskbar's Quick Launch toolbar) and then launch the shortcut.

- Reboot your computer, display Windows XP's Advanced Options Menu, and select the Safe Mode with Command Prompt item.

---

**NOTE**

To learn how to display the Advanced Options Menu, refer to the "Custom Startups with the Advanced Options Menu" section in Chapter 1, "Customizing and Troubleshooting the Windows XP Startup."

It's also possible to configure Windows XP's Folder file type to open Command Prompt in Windows Explorer's current folder. To see how, refer to the "Example: Opening Command Prompt in the Current Folder" section in Chapter 3, "Mastering File Types."

---

**Preventing Command Prompt Access**

To prevent a user from accessing Command Prompt, log on as that user and launch the Group Policy editor. (Depending on the user's rights on the system, you might need to create a temporary shortcut for the Group Policy editor, right-click the shortcut, and then click Run As to run the program using your credentials.) Open the User Configuration, Administrative Templates, System branch and then enable the Prevent Access to the Command Prompt policy.

---

## Using CMD.EXE Switches

For the methods that use the CMD.EXE executable, you can specify extra switches after the CMD.EXE filename. Most of these switches aren't particularly useful, so let's start with the simplest syntax that you'll use most often:

CMD [[/S] [/C ¦ /K] *command*]

| | |
|---|---|
| /S | Strips out the first and last quotation marks from the *command*, provided that the first quotation mark is the first character in *command*. |
| /C | Executes the *command* and then terminates. |
| /K | Executes the *command* and remains running. |
| *command* | The command to run. |

For example, if your ISP provides you with a dynamic IP address, you can often solve some connection problems by asking the IP for a fresh address. You do that by running the command `ipconfig /renew` in Command Prompt. In this case, you don't need the Command Prompt window to remain open, so you can specify the /C switch to shut down the Command Prompt session automatically after the IPCONFIG utility finishes:

```
cmd /c ipconfig /renew
```

On the other hand, you often either want to see the results of the command, or you want to leave the Command Prompt window open so that you can run other commands. In those cases, you use the /K switch. For example, the following command runs the SET utility (which displays the current values of the Windows XP environment variables) and then leaves the Command Prompt session running:

```
cmd /k set
```

Here's the full syntax of CMD.EXE:

```
CMD [/A ¦ /U] [/Q] [/D] [/T:fb] [/E:ON ¦ /E:OFF] [/F:ON ¦ /F:OFF]
➡[/V:ON ¦ /V:OFF] [[/S] [/C ¦ /K] command]
```

| | |
|---|---|
| /Q | Turns echo off. |
| /D | Disables the execution of AutoRun commands from the Registry. These are commands that run automatically when you start any Command Prompt session and you can find the settings here: |

HKLM\Software\Microsoft\Command Processor\AutoRun
HKCU\Software\Microsoft\Command Processor\AutoRun

---

**TIP**

The AutoRun Registry settings are handy if you always run a particular command at the beginning of each Command Prompt session. If you run multiple commands to launch a session, you can add those commands to either AutoRun setting. In that case, you must separate each command with the command separator string: &&. For example, to run the IPCONFIG and SET utilities at the start of each Command Prompt session, change the value of an AutoRun setting to the following:

```
ipconfig&&set
```

---

| | |
|---|---|
| /A | Converts the output of internal commands to a pipe or file to the ANSI character set. |
| /U | Converts the output of internal commands to a pipe or file to the Unicode character set. |
| /T:fb | Sets the foreground and background colors of the Command Prompt window, where f is the foreground color and b is the background color. Both f and b are hexadecimal digits that specify the color as follows: |

| | | | |
|---|---|---|---|
| 0 | Black | 8 | Gray |
| 1 | Blue | 9 | Light Blue |

| 2 | Green | A | Light Green |
|---|-------|---|-------------|
| 3 | Aqua | B | Light Aqua |
| 4 | Red | C | Light Red |
| 5 | Purple | D | Light Purple |
| 6 | Yellow | E | Light Yellow |
| 7 | White | F | Bright White |

**TIP**

You can also set the foreground and background colors during a Command Prompt session by using the COLOR *fb* command, where *f* and *b* are hexadecimal digits specifying the colors you want. To revert to the default Command Prompt colors, run COLOR without the *fb* parameter. For more information, see the "Specifying the Command Prompt Colors" section later in this appendix.

/E:ON    Enables **command extensions**, which are extra features added to the following commands (in Command Prompt, type the command name followed by a space and /? to see the extensions):

| | |
|---|---|
| ASSOC | IF |
| CALL | MD or MKDIR |
| CD or CHDIR | POPD |
| COLOR | PROMPT |
| DEL or ERASE | PUSHD |
| ENDLOCAL | SET |
| FOR | SETLOCAL |
| FTYPE | SHIFT |
| GOTO | START |

/E:OFF    Disables command extensions.

/F:ON    Turns on file and directory name completion, which enables you to press special key combinations to scroll through a list of files or subdirectories in the current directory that match the characters you've already typed. For example, suppose that the current directory contains files named budget2004.doc, budget2005.doc, and budget2006.doc. If you type **start budget** in a Command Prompt session started with /F:ON, pressing Ctrl+F tells Windows XP to display the first file (or subdirectory) in the current directory with a name that starts with budget. Pressing Ctrl+F again displays the next file with a name that starts with budget, and so on. You can do the same thing with just subdirectory names by pressing Ctrl+D instead.

> **TIP**
>
> You don't need to start Command Prompt with the /F:ON switch to use file and directory name completion. Command Prompt offers a similar feature called **AutoComplete** that's turned on by default. At the prompt, type the first letter or two of a file or subfolder name and then press the Tab key to see the first object that matches your text in the current folder. Keep pressing Tab to see other matching objects. If, for some reason, you prefer to turn off AutoComplete, pull down the Command Prompt window's control menu, select Defaults, and then deactivate the AutoComplete check box in the Options tab.

| | |
|---|---|
| /F:OFF | Turns off file and directory name completion. |
| /V:ON | Enables delayed environment variable expansion using ! as the delimiter: !*var*!, where *var* is an environment variable. This is useful for batch files in which you want to delay the expansion of an environment variable. Normally, Windows XP expands all environment variables to their current values when it reads the contents of a batch file. With delayed expansion enabled, Windows XP doesn't expand a particular environment variable within a batch file until it executes the statement containing that variable. |

> **NOTE**
>
> For an example of how delayed environment variable expansion works in a batch file, see the "Using Delayed Environment Variable Expansion" section in Appendix C, "Automating Windows XP with Batch Files."

| | |
|---|---|
| /V:OFF | Disables delayed environment expansion. |
| /S | Strips out the first and last quotation marks from *command*, provided the first quotation mark is the first character in *command*. |
| /C | Executes the *command* and then terminates. |
| /K | Executes the *command* and remains running. |
| *command* | The command to run. |

## Running Commands

Although many of the Windows XP accessories provide more powerful and easier-to-use replacements for nearly all commands, a few commands still have no Windows XP peer. These include the REN command, as well as the many Command Prompt–specific commands, such as CLS, DOSKEY, and PROMPT.

How you run a command depends on whether it's an internal or external command, and on what you want Windows XP to do after the command is finished.

For an internal command, you have two choices: You can either enter the command in Command Prompt or include it as a parameter with CMD.EXE. As you saw earlier, you can run internal commands with CMD.EXE by specifying either the /C switch or the /K switch.

If you use the /C switch, the command executes and then the Command Prompt session shuts down. This is fine if you're running a command for which you don't need to see the results. For example, if you want to redirect the contents of drive C's root folder in the text file root.txt, entering the following command in the Run dialog box (for example) will do the job:

```
cmd.exe /c dir c:\ > root.txt
```

On the other hand, you might want to examine the output of a command before the Command Prompt window closes. In that case, you need to use the /K switch. The following command runs DIR on drive C's root folder and then drops you off in Command Prompt:

```
cmd.exe /k dir c:\
```

For an external command, you have three choices: Enter the command in Command Prompt, enter the command by itself from within Windows XP, or include it as a parameter with CMD.EXE.

> **NOTE**
>
> When you use Command Prompt or the Run dialog box to start an external Command Prompt command, you don't need to use the command's full pathname. For example, the full pathname for mem.exe is %SystemRoot%\System32\mem.exe, but to run this command, you need only enter **mem**. The reason is that the %SystemRoot%\System32 subfolder is part of the PATH statement for each Command Prompt session.

To enter a command by itself from within Windows XP means launching the command's file in Explorer, entering the command in the Run dialog box, or creating a shortcut for the command. For the latter two methods, you can embellish the command by adding parameters and switches. The problem with this method is that Windows XP automatically closes the Command Prompt window when the command completes. To change this behavior, follow these steps:

1. Find the command's executable file in the %SystemRoot%\System32 folder.

2. Right-click the executable file and then click Properties to display the command's property sheet.

3. Display the Program tab.

4. Deactivate the Close on Exit check box.

5. Click OK.

## Adding Parameters and Switches to a Command Prompt Command

If you use Command Prompt or the Run dialog box to enter your Command Prompt commands, you can easily tack on any extra parameters or switches you want to use to modify the command. If, however, you start an external command from Explorer, the command runs without any options. To modify how an external command operates, you can add parameters and switches by following these steps:

1. Find the command's executable file in the `%SystemRoot%\System32` folder.

2. Right-click the executable file and then click Properties to display the command's property sheet.

3. Display the Program tab.

4. In the Cmd Line text box, add a space after the command and then add your parameters and switches. Figure B.1 shows an example.

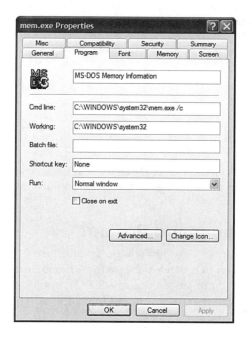

**FIGURE B.1**    Use the Cmd Line text box to append extra parameters to an external command.

5. Click OK.

**PROGRAM INFORMATION FILES**

After you've modified a command's property sheet, Windows XP creates a PIF—a **program information file**—for the command. This is a separate file that has the same name as the command, but with a `.pif` extension. Unfortunately, Explorer always hides the `.pif` extension. You can recognize the PIF, however, if you display Explorer in Details view: The PIF says `Shortcut to MS-DOS Program` in the Type column. If you prefer to display the `.pif` extension, head for the following Registry key:

```
HKCR\piffile
```

Rename the `NeverShowExt` setting to `AlwaysShowExt` (or something similar). When you next restart your computer, Windows XP will show the `.pif` extensions.

If you want to vary the parameters each time you run the command, add a space and a question mark (?) to the end of the command, like so:

```
C:\WINDOWS\system32\mem.exe ?
```

Each time you run the command (whether from Explorer or from the Run dialog box), Windows XP displays a dialog box similar to the one shown in Figure B.2. Use the text box to type your switches and options, and then click OK.

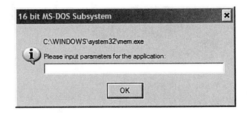

**FIGURE B.2**    If you add a question mark (?) to the end of the command, Windows XP displays a dialog box similar to this one each time you run the command.

# Working with Command Prompt

When you have your Command Prompt session up and running, you can run commands and programs, create and launch batch files, perform file maintenance, and so on. If you haven't used Command Prompt since the days of DOS, you'll find that the Windows XP Command Prompt offers a few extra command-line goodies. The next few sections highlight some of the more useful ones.

> **CAUTION**
>
> When you're working in Command Prompt, be warned that any files you delete aren't sent to the Recycle Bin, but are purged from your system.

## Working with Long Filenames

Unlike the old DOS, you can work with long filenames within a Windows XP Command Prompt session. If you want to use long filenames in a command, however, you need to be careful. If the long filename contains a space or any other character that's illegal in an 8.3 filename, you need to surround the long name with quotation marks. For example, if you run the following command, Windows XP will tell you that The syntax of the command is incorrect:

```
copy Fiscal Year 2005.doc Fiscal Year 2006.doc
```

Instead, you need to enter this command as follows:

```
copy "Fiscal Year 2005.doc" "Fiscal Year 2006.doc"
```

Long filenames are, of course, long, so they tend to be a pain to type in Command Prompt. Fortunately, Windows XP offers a few methods for knocking long names down to size:

- In Explorer, drag a folder or file and drop it inside the Command Prompt window. Windows XP pastes the full pathname of the folder or file to the end of the prompt.

- Create application-specific and document-specific paths, as described in the "Creating Application-Specific Paths" section of Chapter 5, "Installing and Running Applications."

- If you're trying to run a program that resides in a folder with a long name, add the folder to the PATH. This technique enables you to run programs from the folder without having to specify the full pathname. (I talk about this in more detail in the next section.)

- Use the SUBST command to substitute a virtual drive letter for a long pathname. For example, the following command substitutes drive Z for the current user's Start Menu\Programs\Accessories folder:

```
subst z: "%USERPROFILE%\Start Menu\Programs\Accessories"
```

## Changing Folders Faster

You probably know by now that you use the CD (change directory) command to change to a different folder on the current drive. However, Command Prompt has a few short forms you can use to save time.

You might know that both Command Prompt and Windows XP use the dot symbol (.) to represent the current folder, and the double-dot symbol (..) to represent its parent folder. You can combine the CD command and the dot notation to jump immediately to a folder's parent folder, or even higher.

To make this more concrete, suppose that the current folder is C:\ANIMAL\MAMMAL\DOLPHIN. Table B.1 demonstrates the techniques you can use to navigate to this folder's parent, grandparent (two levels up), and great grandparent (three levels up) folders.

B

**TABLE B.1**    Combining the CD Command with Dot Notation

| Current Folder | Command | New Folder |
| --- | --- | --- |
| `C:\ANIMAL\MAMMAL\DOLPHIN` | `CD..` | `C:\ANIMAL\MAMMAL` |
| `C:\ANIMAL\MAMMAL\DOLPHIN` | `CD..\..` | `C:\ANIMAL` |
| `C:\ANIMAL\MAMMAL\DOLPHIN` | `CD..\..\..` | `C:\` |
| `C:\ANIMAL\MAMMAL\DOLPHIN` | `CD..\BABOON` | `C:\ANIMAL\MAMMAL\BABOON` |

## Taking Advantage of DOSKEY

The DOSKEY utility is loaded by default when you start any Command Prompt session. This useful little program brings a number of advantages to your command-line work:

- You can recall previously entered commands with just a keystroke or two.
- You can enter multiple commands on a single line.
- You can edit commands instead of retyping them.
- You can create your own commands with DOSKEY macros.

In this section I'll focus on DOSKEY macros, but I'll begin with a quick introduction to the other DOSKEY features.

### Recalling Command Lines

The simplest DOSKEY feature is command recall. DOSKEY maintains a command history buffer that keeps a list of the commands you enter. To scroll through your previously entered commands in reverse order, press the Up Arrow key; when you've done that at least once, you can change direction and run through the commands in the order you entered them by pressing the Down Arrow key. To rerun a command, use the arrow keys to find it and then press Enter.

> **TIP**
>
> If you don't want to enter any commands from the history buffer, press Esc to get a clean command line.

Table B.2 lists all the command-recall keys you can use.

**TABLE B.2**    DOSKEY Command-Recall Keys

| Press | To |
| --- | --- |
| Up Arrow | Recall the previous command in the buffer. |
| Down Arrow | Recall the next command in the buffer. |
| Page Up | Recall the oldest command in the buffer. |
| Page Down | Recall the newest command in the buffer. |
| F7 | Display the entire command buffer. |

**TABLE B.2**   Continued

| Press | To |
|-------|-----|
| Alt+F7 | Delete all commands from the buffer. |
| F8 | Have DOSKEY recall a command that begins with the letter or letters you've typed on the command line. |
| F9 | Have DOSKEY prompt you for a command list number (you can see the numbers with the F7 key). Type the number and press Enter to recall the command. |

---

**TIP**

The command history buffer holds 50 commands, by default. If you need a larger buffer, run DOSKEY with the /LISTSIZE=*buffers* switch, where *buffers* is the number of commands you want to store. For example, to change the buffer size to 100, enter the following command:

```
doskey /listize=100 /reinstall
```

---

## Entering Multiple Commands on a Single Line

DOSKEY enables you to run multiple commands on a single line. To do this, insert the characters && between commands. For example, a common task is to change to a different drive and then run a directory listing. Normally, you'd do this with two separate commands:

```
e:
```

```
dir
```

With DOSKEY, however, you can do it on one line, like so:

```
e:&&dir
```

---

**TIP**

You can enter as many commands as you like on a single line, but just remember that the total length of the line can't be more than 8,191 characters (which should be plenty!).

---

## Editing Command Lines

Rather than simply rerunning a previously typed command, you might need to run the command again with slightly different switches or parameters. Rather than retyping the whole thing, DOSKEY enables you to edit any recalled command line. You use various keys to move the cursor to the offending letters and replace them. Table B.3 summarizes DOSKEY's command-line editing keys.

**TABLE B.3**   DOSKEY Command-Line Editing Keys

| Press | To |
|---|---|
| Left Arrow | Move the cursor one character to the left. |
| Right Arrow | Move the cursor one character to the right. |
| Ctrl+Left Arrow | Move the cursor one word to the left. |
| Ctrl+Right Arrow | Move the cursor one word to the right. |
| Home | Move the cursor to the beginning of the line. |
| End | Move the cursor to the end of the line. |
| Delete | Delete the character over the cursor. |
| Backspace | Delete the character to the left of the cursor. |
| Ctrl+Home | Delete from the cursor to the beginning of the line. |
| Ctrl+End | Delete from the cursor to the end of the line. |
| Insert | Toggle DOSKEY between Insert mode (your typing is inserted between existing letters on the command line) and Overstrike mode (your typing replaces existing letters on the command line). |

### Learning About DOSKEY Macros

Perhaps the most powerful feature you get with DOSKEY is the ability to combine one or more DOS commands into a single easy-to-use command called a **macro**. If this sounds like a batch file, you're close. DOSKEY macros and batch files are similar, but they differ in some important ways:

**Macro Pros:**

- Macros are stored in memory and batch files are stored on a disk. This means that macros execute much faster than batch files.

- Batch files must have legal filenames, but macro names can include the following symbols normally banned from regular filenames:

     * + [ ] : ; " , . ? /

- You can use macros to replace existing commands.

**Macro Cons:**

- Macros must be no longer than 8,191 characters, but batch files can be any length.

- There are no commands or symbols to suppress command echoing.

- There is no macro equivalent for the GOTO and IF batch file commands.

- You have to reenter macro definitions each time you start your computer. (However, you can automate this by using a **macro library**, a batch file that stores your macro definitions. I'll explain all this later in this section.)

In general, you should use macros as substitutes for complex commands or to combine two or more commands into a single command. You should use batch files for more sophisticated tasks.

**Creating** DOSKEY **Macros**    To create a DOSKEY macro, enter a command that has the following form:

**DOSKEY** *macroname=commands*

Here, *macroname* is the name of the macro and *commands* is the list of commands you want the macro to execute.

As an example, consider the following command:

```
dir /ogn /p
```

This displays a directory listing with the filenames in alphabetical order, with the subdirectories grouped first and a pause after every screen. Instead of typing this command every time, you could define a macro called SDIR instead. Here's the command that'll do it:

```
doskey sdir=dir /ogn /p
```

After you've defined a macro, you can use it like any other command. For this example, just type **sdir** and press Enter, and Command Prompt displays the sorted directory listing.

> **TIP**
>
> If you need to stop a running macro, press Ctrl+C.

When you're defining a macro that contains more than one command, you need to be a little careful. For example, suppose that you want to create a macro called CDD that changes to drive E and then gives you a DIR listing. Your first instinct might be to enter the command

**doskey cdd=e: && dir**

However, when Command Prompt sees the command separator symbol, it assumes that you're trying to run two commands: one to define the DOSKEY macro CDD and another to display a DIR listing. To avoid this confusion, use $T (or $t) instead of && inside your macro definition. Here's the revised command:

```
DOSKEY cdd=a: $t dir
```

> **NOTE**
>
> To make the commands easier to read, I've included spaces before and after the $T symbol. If you prefer, you can leave these spaces out when defining your own macros.

Table B.4 lists all the macro-definition symbols you can use.

**TABLE B.4**    DOSKEY Macro-Definition Symbols

| Use | To Replace |
| --- | --- |
| $B or $b | Pipe symbol (l) |
| $G or $g | Redirect output symbol (>) |
| $G$G or $g$g | Append output symbol (>>) |
| $L or $l | Redirect input symbol (<) |
| $T or $t | Command separator ( ) |
| $$ | Dollar sign ($) |

**TIP**

To delete a macro definition, use the following format:

    DOSKEY *macroname=*

**Using Replaceable Parameters in Macros**    In Appendix C's "Using Parameters for Batch File Flexibility" section, I show you how to use replaceable parameters inside batch files. Macros, too, can use replaceable parameters. Instead of the symbols %1 through %9 that are available in a batch file, use the symbols $1 through $9 for macros.

For example, the CDD macro introduced in the last section is okay, but it lacks flexibility. Instead, change the macro to the following:

```
doskey cdd=$1 $t dir
```

If you now type, say, **cdd d:**, DOSKEY replaces $1 with d: and runs the macro accordingly.

**Macro Examples**    To get you started, this section takes you through a few of my favorite DOSKEY macros.

The first example uses the fact that, as mentioned earlier, Windows XP represents the current directory's parent with the double dot symbol (..). One way this comes in handy is to use the following command to change quickly to the parent directory:

```
cd..
```

This is pretty short as it is, but I prefer to use a macro called UP, which I define as follows:

```
doskey up=cd..
```

A similar macro is UP2, which I use any time I need to move up two directory levels:

```
doskey up2=cd..\cd..
```

So, for example, if you're in the My Documents\Letters\Business subdirectory, entering the UP2 command takes you to the My Documents directory.

Suppose that you also have a subdirectory called My Documents\Letters\Personal and you want to move from the Business subdirectory over to Personal. Normally, you have to use the following command:

```
cd My Documents\Letters\Personal
```

However, both Business and Personal have the same parent directory (Letters), so you can create a macro called OVER as follows:

```
doskey over=cd..\$1
```

After you've defined this macro, you can move from Business to Personal by entering the following command:

```
over personal
```

> **TIP**
>
> To see a list of all your currently defined macros, use the command DOSKEY /MACROS.

Have you ever lost a file on your hard drive? You know it's there somewhere, but you can't remember where it is. It's happened to me more times than I've had hot dinners, so I use a macro called ? to help out. Here's the definition:

```
doskey ?=dir \$1 /s /b
```

The /S switch causes Command Prompt to search all your subdirectories, and the /B switch displays only the filename, if one is found.

My final macro definition shows that you can use macros to replace existing commands (this is called **command aliasing**). For example, the DEL command is safer if you use it with the /P switch (Command Prompt asks you to confirm each deletion). You can actually create a macro called DEL with the following definition:

```
doskey del=del $1 /p
```

Macros take precedence over commands, so whenever you use DEL, it's the macro that executes, not the command. (If you need to run the command, you can do so by preceding it with a space.)

> **TIP**
>
> If you're setting up a computer for a novice user, use macros to replace dangerous commands such as FORMAT or RECOVER. Instead of running the command, just display a message telling the user the peril they're in, like so:
>
> ```
> doskey format=ECHO Sorry, the FORMAT command is not available.
> ```

B

**Creating a Macro Library**    One of the problems with macros is that your definitions are lost whenever you turn off your computer. The solution is to create a macro library— a batch file that contains all your macro definitions. Follow these steps to create a macro library:

1. Type the following command and press Enter (if you don't have a BATCH directory, substitute the directory where you keep your batch files):

   ```
   doskey /macros > macros.bat
   ```

2. Command Prompt redirects the output of the command into a batch file called `macros.bat`. Now load `macros.bat` into your text editor.

3. For each macro definition, add DOSKEY to the beginning of the line (be sure that you leave a space between DOSKEY and the definition).

Now, whenever you need to load your DOSKEY macros, just run the `macros.bat` batch file.

---

**TIP**

You'll probably need to edit your macro library quite often to remove macros you never use and add new ones. To make this chore easier, here's another macro that loads the macro library into Notepad and then runs the batch file when you're done:

```
doskey editlib=start notepad macros.bat $t macros
```

Note that you'll likely have to include the path where you've stored `macros.bat` to ensure that Notepad can find it. Also, be sure to run the `doskey /macros > macros.bat` command again right after you define the EDITLIB macro so that EdITLIB is added to the library.

---

## Starting Applications from Command Prompt

Command Prompt isn't just for running commands. You can also use it to start applications, as described in the next two sections.

### Starting 16-Bit Applications

On the odd chance that you still use 16-bit programs, you need to either change to the drive and folder where the program resides and enter the executable file's primary name from there, or enter the executable file's full pathname from the current folder. There are two situations in which you don't have to change folders or use the full pathname:

- If the program's executable file is in the current folder
- If the folder in which the program's executable file resides is part of the PATH statement

If you enter only the primary name of an executable file, Command Prompt first searches the current folder for a file that combines your primary name with an extension of `.com`, `.exe`, `.bat`, or `.cmd`. If it doesn't find such a file, it searches the folders listed in the PATH statement. Recall that the PATH statement is a series of folder names separated by semi-colons (;). The default PATH for a Command Prompt session is this:

```
%SystemRoot%;%SystemRoot%\system32;%SystemRoot%\system32\Wbem
```

This is stored in an environment variable called PATH, so you can easily add new folders to the PATH right from the command prompt. For example, suppose that you have a DOS program that resides in the C:\Program Files\Dosapp folder. To start the program without having to change folders or specify the pathname, use the following command to add this folder to the PATH statement (%path% represents the PATH environment variable):

```
set path=%path%;"c:\program files\dosapp"
```

### Starting Windows Applications

You can also use the Command Prompt to start Windows applications, launch documents, and even open folder windows. As with DOS programs, you start a Windows application by entering the name of its executable file.

This works fine if the executable file resides in the main Windows XP folder because that folder is part of the PATH. But most Windows XP applications (and even some Windows XP accessories) store their files in a separate folder and don't modify the PATH to point to these folders. Instead, as you learned in Chapter 5, the Registry has an AppPaths key that tells Windows XP where to find an application's files. Command Prompt can't use the Registry-based application paths directly, but there's a Windows XP command that can. This command is called START, and it uses the following syntax:

```
START ["title"] [/Dpath] [/B] [/I] [/MIN] [/MAX] [/SEPARATE ¦ /SHARED]
[/LOW ¦ /NORMAL ¦ /HIGH ¦ /REALTIME ¦ /ABOVENORMAL ¦ /BELOWNORMAL]
[/WAIT] [filename] [parameters]
```

| | |
|---|---|
| "title" | Specifies the title to display in Command Prompt's window title bar. |
| Dpath | Specifies the program's startup folder. |
| /B | Starts the program without creating a new window. |
| /I | Tells Windows XP that the new Command Prompt environment will be the original environment passed to cmd.exe and not the current environment. |
| /MIN | Starts the program minimized. |
| /MAX | Starts the program maximized. |
| /SEPARATE | Starts a 16-bit Windows program in a separate memory space. |
| /SHARED | Starts a 16-bit Windows program in a shared memory space. |
| /LOW | Starts the program using the IDLE priority class. |
| /NORMAL | Starts the program using the NORMAL priority class. |
| /HIGH | Starts the program using the HIGH priority class. |
| /REALTIME | Starts the program using the REALTIME priority class. |

**B**

| | |
|---|---|
| /ABOVENORMAL | Starts the program using the ABOVENORMAL priority class. |
| /BELOWNORMAL | Starts the program using the BELOWNORMAL priority class. |
| /WAIT | Waits until the program has finished before returning to Command Prompt. |
| *filename* | Specifies the name of the executable file or document. If you enter a document name, be sure to include the extension so that Windows XP can figure out the file type. |
| *parameters* | Specifies options or switches that modify the operation of the program. |

When you use START to launch a program, Windows XP checks not only the current folder and the PATH, but also the Registry. For the Registry, Windows XP looks for an AppPaths setting or a file type (if you entered the name of a document). For example, if you type **wordpad** and press Enter at the Command Prompt, you get a Bad command or file name error (unless you happen to be in the %Program Files%\Windows NT\Accessories folder). If, however, you enter **start wordpad**, WordPad launches successfully.

> **NOTE**
>
> The START command's /WAIT switch is useful in batch files. If you launch a program from within a batch file by using START /WAIT, the batch file pauses while the program runs. This enables you, for example, to test for some condition (such as an ERRORLEVEL code) after the program has completed its work.

## Sharing Data Between 16-Bit and Windows Applications

16-bit programs don't know about the Clipboard, so they don't support the standard cut, copy, and paste techniques. However, there are methods you can use to share data between 16-bit and Windows applications. I spell them out in the next few sections.

### Copying Text from a 16-Bit Application

The best way to copy text from a 16-bit application is to place the program in a window and highlight the text you want. The following procedure takes you through the required steps:

1. Switch to the 16-bit application and place it in a window (if it isn't already) by pressing Alt+Enter.

> **NOTE**
>
> If the 16-bit application has a graphics mode, copying a section of the screen will copy a graphic image of the text, not the text itself. If you want text only, make sure that the program is running in Character mode before you continue.

2. Make sure that the text you want to copy is visible onscreen.

3. Pull down the window's control menu and select Edit, Mark to put the window into Select mode. (You can also right-click the title bar and then select Edit, Mark.)

4. Use the mouse or keyboard to select the data you want to copy.

5. Pull down the window's control menu and select Edit, Copy to copy the selected data to the Clipboard. (You can also either press Enter or right-click the title bar and then select Edit, Copy.)

6. Switch to the Windows application you want to use as the destination and position the insertion point where you want the copied data to appear.

7. Select Edit, Paste.

---

**TIP**

If you have a lot of text to copy, you might find it easier to activate Windows XP's QuickEdit option. QuickEdit mode leaves the 16-bit program's window in select mode permanently so that you can select text anytime you like. (The downside, however, is that you can no longer use the mouse to manipulate the Command Prompt program itself.) To enable QuickEdit, pull down the window's control menu and select Properties to open the property sheet for the program. In the Options tab, activate the QuickEdit Mode check box.

---

### Pasting Text to a 16-Bit Application

If you've sent some text to the Clipboard from a Windows application (or even from another 16-bit application, for that matter), it's possible to copy the text into a 16-bit program.

First, position the 16-bit program's cursor at the spot where you want the pasted text to appear. Then pull down the window's control menu and select Edit, Paste (or right-click the title bar and then select Edit, Paste).

---

**TIP**

You might encounter problems pasting text from the Clipboard to your Command Prompt program. For example, you might see garbage characters or some characters might be missing. This probably means that Windows XP is sending the characters too fast, and the Command Prompt program can't handle the onslaught. To solve this problem, find the 16-bit program's executable file, right-click the file, and then click Properties. Then display the Misc tab and deactivate the Fast Pasting check box. This tells Windows XP to hold its horses and send the characters at a slower rate.

---

### Sharing Graphics Between 16-Bit and Windows Programs

Unlike with Windows-to-Windows transfers, there's no clean way to transfer graphics between 16-bit and Windows programs.

If you have a 16-bit graphic you'd like to place on the Clipboard, display the program in a window, adjust the window so that the image is visible, and then press Alt+Print Screen.

Windows XP will copy an image of the entire window to the Clipboard. You could then paste this image into a graphics program and remove the extraneous window elements.

Unfortunately, the Clipboard can't handle graphics transfers from a Windows application to a 16-bit program. Your only choice here is to save the image in a graphics format that the 16-bit program understands and then open this file in the 16-bit program.

# Customizing the Command-Line Window

If you figure you'll be spending a reasonable amount of time using Command Prompt or 16-bit or command-line programs, you'll want to configure the windows so that you're comfortable with how they work and how they're displayed. The next few sections take you through the various options available for customizing the Command Prompt window, as well as the windows used by external command-line programs and 16-bit applications.

## Customizing the Command Prompt Window

Windows XP's Command Prompt utility has its own set of customization options and settings, so I'll discuss those first. To view these options, you have three choices:

- If you want your changes to apply to all future Command Prompt sessions, open a Command Prompt window, pull down its control menu, and then select Defaults. This displays the Console Windows Properties dialog box. Note that the changes you make in this dialog box do *not* apply to the current Command Prompt session, but Windows XP does apply them to all future sessions.

- If you want your changes to apply only to a specific Command Prompt shortcut (such as Start, All Programs, Accessories, Command Prompt), right-click the Command Prompt shortcut icon, and then click Properties. After you've made your changes and closed the property sheet, Windows XP displays the Apply Properties to Shortcut dialog box. Activate the Modify Shortcut That Started This Window option and click OK.

- If you want your changes to apply to only the current Command Prompt session, pull down the control menu and select Properties. After you've made your changes and closed the property sheet, Windows XP displays the Apply Properties to Shortcut dialog box. Activate the Apply Properties to Current Window Only option and click OK.

In the property sheet that appears, there are four tabs that offer options specific to Command Prompt: Options, Font, Layout, and Colors.

### Setting Command Prompt Options

The Options tab, shown in Figure B.3, offers a mixed-bag of settings that control various aspects of the Command Prompt window and operation:

| Cursor Size | Use these options to set the size of the cursor that Command Prompt uses to indicate where the next character that you type will appear. |
|---|---|
| Display Options | The Full Screen and Window options determine whether Command Prompt starts full screen or in a window. |
| Command History | These options control how Command Prompt stores the commands you enter: |

- Buffer Size—Use this spin box to specify the number of commands that DOSKEY stores in its command history buffer.

- Number of Buffers—Use this spin box to set the maximum number of Command Prompt processes that can maintain command history buffers.

- Discard Old Duplicates—Activate this check box to have Command Prompt automatically discard duplicate commands from the buffer. This enables you to store more unique commands in the buffer. However, if you often rerun a series of commands, activating this option could cause problems by discarding one more commands in the series.

| QuickEdit Mode | When this check box is active, you can select program text with the mouse. I explained how this works earlier in this appendix. |
|---|---|
| Insert Mode | When this check box is activated, DOSKEY starts in its Insert mode, where your typing is inserted at the cursor. If you deactivate this check box, DOSKEY switches to Overstrike mode. |
| AutoComplete (Console Windows Properties dialog box only) | When this check box is activated, Command Prompt enables you to complete file and folder names by pressing the Tab key. |

## Changing the Command Prompt Font

The font size Windows XP uses to display text in a Command Prompt window isn't set in stone. You're free to make the font size larger or smaller, depending on your tastes. The Font tab, shown in Figure B.4 offers the following options:

| Size | Use this list to select the font size you want to use (or Auto). |
|---|---|
| Font | Select either Raster Fonts or Lucida Console. If you select the latter, you can also activate the Bold Fonts check box to get bold text. |

As you make changes to the Font, the Window Preview area shows you how the new Command Prompt window will appear, and the Selected Font preview area shows you what the font looks like.

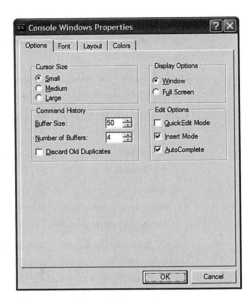

**FIGURE B.3**    Use Command Prompt's Options tab to control various aspects of the program's look and feel.

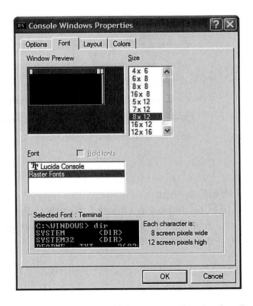

**FIGURE B.4**    Use the Font tab to select the font size to use in the Command Prompt window.

## Customizing the Command Prompt Layout

You can control the Command Prompt window's dimensions, position, and screen buffer size using the settings in the Layout tab, shown in Figure B.5:

| | |
|---|---|
| Screen Buffer Size | The **screen buffer** is a memory area that stores the lines that have appeared in the Command Prompt window and since scrolled off the screen. This is useful if you run a command that displays more lines than the Command Prompt window can hold. You can use the vertical scroll bar to scroll up and see the lines you missed. You shouldn't need to change the default Width value (80 characters), but you can set the Height value up to 9,999 lines. |
| Window Size | Use the Width and Height spin boxes to set the dimensions, in lines, of the window. Note, however, that Windows XP cannot resize the window to anything larger than what your screen can hold. |
| Window Position | Use the Left and Top spin boxes to set the location, in pixels, of the top-left corner of the Command Prompt window. You need to deactivate the Let System Position Window check box to enable these spin boxes. |

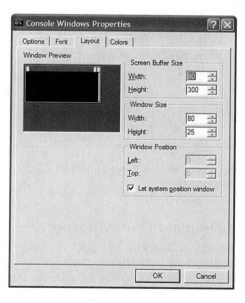

**FIGURE B.5**    Use the Layout tab to customize the Command Prompt window's dimensions, position, and screen buffer size.

## Specifying the Command Prompt Colors

You saw earlier than you can run cmd.exe with the /T:*fb* switch to control the foreground (text) and background colors of the Command Prompt window. You can also use the COLOR utility to change the colors while you're in mid-session. An alternative to these methods is the Colors tab, shown in Figure B.6. You can set colors not only for the screen, but also for the pop-up text and background. (An example of a pop-up is the window that appears when you press F7 at the command line to see a list of the commands in the DOSKEY history buffer.) Activate one of the four options—Screen Text, Screen Background, Popup Text, or Popup Background—and then use either of the following techniques to set the color:

- Click one of the preset color boxes.

- Use the Red, Green, and Blue spin boxes to set a custom color.

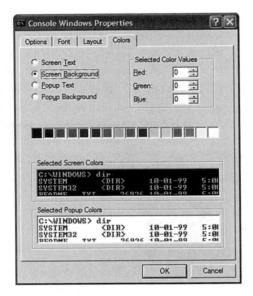

**FIGURE B.6**    Use the Colors tab to set the foreground and background colors of the Command Prompt screen and pop-ups.

## Customizing Other Command-Line Windows

A 16-bit or command-line program, like any Windows XP object, has various properties that you can manipulate to fine-tune how the program works. To display the property sheet for a 16-bit or command-line program, you have three choices:

- In Explorer, select the program's executable file and select File, Properties, or right-click the file and select Properties.

- If the program's window is open, you can get to the property sheet from the keyboard by pressing Alt+Spacebar and selecting Properties from the control menu that appears.

**NOTE**

Most of the properties I'll be talking about affect the command-line program only while it's running in a window. If your program is running full screen, press Alt+Enter to place it in a window. To change back to full-screen mode, press Alt+Enter again.

**NOTE**

To learn about the settings in the property sheet's Compatibility tab, refer to the section in Chapter 5 titled "Understanding Application Compatibility."

### Setting Program Properties

The Program tab, shown in Figure B.7, contains various settings that control the startup and shutdown of the program. The untitled text box at the top of the dialog box specifies the text that appears in the program window's title bar.

**FIGURE B.7**    Use the Program tab to set various properties for the command-line program's startup.

B

Here's a rundown of the rest of the options:

| | |
|---|---|
| Cmd Line | This text box specifies the pathname of the program's executable file. As you saw earlier, you can use this text box to add parameters and switches to modify how the program starts. |
| Working | Use this text box to set the application's default folder. |
| Batch File | This text box specifies a batch file or command to run before starting the program. This is useful for copying files, setting environment variables, changing the PATH, or loading memory-resident programs. |
| Shortcut Key | Use this text box to assign a key combination to the program. For launching the program, this key combination seems to work only if you create a shortcut for the program on the desktop. When the program is running, however, you can use the key combination to switch to the program quickly. The default key combo is Ctrl+Alt+*character*, where *character* is any keyboard character that you press while this text box has the focus. If you prefer a key combination that begins with Ctrl+Shift, hold down both Ctrl and Shift and then press a character; for a Ctrl+Alt+Shift combination, hold down all three keys and press a character. |
| Run | This drop-down list determines how the application window appears. Select Normal Window, Minimized, or Maximized. |
| Close on Exit | If you activate this check box, the window closes when the program is complete. This is useful for batch files and other programs that leave the Command Prompt window onscreen when they're done. |
| Advanced | This button displays a dialog box that enables you to specify the locations of custom Autoexec.bat and Config.sys files for the program to use. |
| Change Icon | Use this command button to assign a different icon to the program's PIF. Clicking this button displays the Change Icon dialog box. |

### Adjusting Memory Properties

The Memory tab enables you to manipulate various memory-related settings, as shown in Figure B.8.

Here's a rundown of the available controls:

| | |
|---|---|
| Conventional Memory | The Total drop-down list specifies the amount of conventional memory (in kilobytes) supplied to the program's virtual machine by Windows XP's **Virtual Memory Manager (VMM)**. (**Conventional memory** is defined as the first 640KB of memory.) If you leave this value at Auto, the VMM handles the memory requirements automatically. However, it doesn't always do a good job. For |

example, if you run a command, the VMM carves out a full 640KB of memory for the Command Prompt virtual machine. Because most commands run happily in much less, you're either wasting precious physical memory or unnecessarily paging to the swap file. You can specify a smaller value (for example, 160KB) and save memory resources. Before changing this value, check the documentation for your program to find its minimum memory requirement.

**Initial Environment**

This drop-down list specifies the size (in bytes) of the command-line environment. The environment is a small memory buffer that holds the environment variables. If you're using the Batch File text box to run SET statements or add folders to the PATH, you might want to increase the size of the environment. You shouldn't need a value any larger than 1024 bytes.

---

**TIP**

To see the contents of the environment while you're in a command-line session, run the SET command.

---

**Protected**

While your program is running, small chunks of Windows XP come along for the ride in the system memory area. If the program is ill-behaved, it might accidentally overwrite part of the system area and cause Windows XP to become unstable. To prevent this, activate the Protected check box to write-protect the system memory area.

**Expanded (EMS) Memory**

The Total drop-down list specifies the amount of expanded memory (in kilobytes) supplied to the program. If you know your program doesn't use expanded memory, you can set this value to None. If you set this value to Auto, Windows XP will supply the program with whatever it needs. If you prefer to set a limit on the amount of expanded memory the program uses, select a specific value (1024KB should be plenty for most programs).

**Extended (XMS) Memory**

If your program can make use of extended memory, use the Total drop-down list to specify the amount of extended memory (in kilo bytes) that the VMM allocates to the program. Again, use Auto to allow the VMM to allocate extended memory automatically. However, virtual memory is mapped by the VMM as extended memory, so your programs might end up grabbing all the available virtual memory for themselves! Setting a limit of, for example, 1024KB will prevent this from happening.

**Uses HMA**

This check box determines whether the program has access to the **high memory area (HMA)**. The HMA is the first 64KB of extended memory. Programs can use it to load device drivers. By default,

|                                              | Windows XP uses the HMA for MS-DOS, so it's generally unavailable to other programs. |
|---|---|
| MS-DOS Protected-Mode (DPMI) Memory | This Total drop-down list specifies the amount of DOS protected-mode memory (in kilobytes) that is supplied to the program. Use Auto to let the VMM configure this type of memory automatically. |

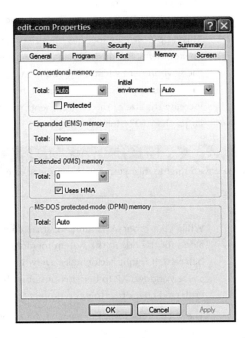

**FIGURE B.8**    Use the Memory tab to customize the memory usage for a command-line program.

### Setting Screen Properties

The property sheet for a command-line program also includes a Screen tab, shown in Figure B.9, that controls various aspects of the program's display.

Here are your options:

| Usage | The Full-Screen and Window options determine whether the program starts full screen or in a window. |
|---|---|
| Restore Settings at Startup | When this check box is activated, Windows XP remembers the last window position and size and restores them the next time you run the program. If you deactivate this check box, Windows XP just uses the original settings the next time you start the program; any adjustments you make in the current session are ignored. |

| Fast ROM Emulation | When this check box is activated, Windows XP uses the video display VxDs to reproduce (or **emulate**) the video services (that is, writing text to the screen) that are normally the province of the ROM BIOS functions. These RAM-based VxDs are faster, so the overall performance of the program's display is improved. However, if the program expects to use nonstandard ROM calls, you might see garbage characters onscreen. If so, deactivate this check box. |
| --- | --- |
| Dynamic Memory Allocation | Some command-line programs can operate in both text and graphics modes, but the latter requires more memory. If this check box is activated, Windows XP supplies memory to the program as required by the program's current mode. If you run the program in graphics mode, Windows XP allocates more memory to the program's virtual machine; if you switch the program to text mode, Windows XP reduces the memory allocated to the virtual machine, which makes more memory available to other applications. If you find that your program hangs when you switch to graphics mode, it could be that Windows XP can't allocate enough memory to handle the new mode. In this case, you should deactivate the Dynamic Memory Allocation check box to force Windows XP to always supply the program with enough memory to run in graphics mode. |

B

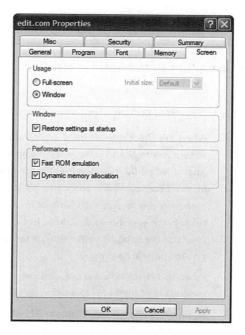

**FIGURE B.9**  Use the Screen tab to control the appearance of the Command Prompt program.

### Some Miscellaneous Properties

To complete our look at command-line program customization, let's turn our attention to the Misc tab of the program property sheet, shown in Figure B.10. This tab contains a grab bag of options that cover a whole host of otherwise unrelated properties.

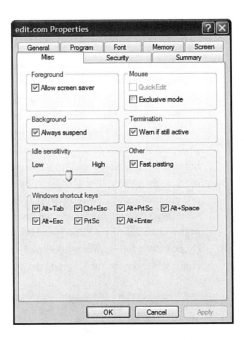

**FIGURE B.10**    The Misc tab contains an assortment of controls for customizing a Command Prompt program.

Here's a summary of what each control contributes to the Command Prompt program:

| | |
|---|---|
| Allow Screen Saver | When this check box is turned on, Windows XP allows your Windows screensaver to kick in while you're using the command-line program (that is, when the program is in the foreground). This is probably safe for most command-line programs, but if you find that the screensaver is causing your program to hang or is causing the program's graphics to go batty, you should deactivate this check box. You should definitely clear this check box if you're using a terminal emulation program or a communications program. |
| QuickEdit | When this check box is active, you can select program text with the mouse. I explained how this works earlier in this appendix. |
| Exclusive Mode | If you check this option, Windows XP offers the program exclusive use of the mouse. This means that the mouse will work only while you use the program; it won't be available in Windows XP. You should activate this check box only if the mouse won't otherwise work in the program. |

| Always Suspend | When you activate this check box, Windows XP doesn't supply any CPU time to a running command-line program that doesn't have the focus. (Such a program is said to be *in the background*.) If your program doesn't do any background processing when you switch to another window, you should activate this check box. Doing so improves the performance of your other applications. This is also a good idea if a background command-line program interferes with your foreground applications. (For example, some 16-bit games can mess up the sound in your foreground window.) If, however, you're using the 16-bit program to download files, print documents, or perform other background chores, you should leave Always Suspend unchecked. |
| Warn If Still Active | For safest operation, and to make sure that you don't lose unsaved data, you should always exit your Command Prompt program completely before trying to close the Command Prompt window. If you leave the Warn If Still Active box checked, Windows XP displays the warning dialog box shown in Figure B.11 if you attempt to shut down the program prematurely. You can force Windows XP to close the program (if it has hung, for example) by clicking End Now. |

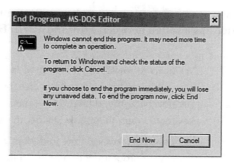

**FIGURE B.11**    If the Warn If Still Active check box is activated, Windows XP displays this warning if you try to close a command-line window before exiting the program.

| Idle Sensitivity | This slider determines how much CPU time Windows XP devotes to the command-line program when the program is idle. See "Understanding Idle Sensitivity," later in this appendix. |
| Fast Pasting | This check box controls the speed at which Windows XP pastes information from the Clipboard to the program. I discussed pasting data to Command Prompt windows earlier in this appendix. |
| Windows Shortcut Keys | These check boxes represent various Windows XP shortcut keys. For example, pressing Alt+Tab while working in a Command Prompt window takes you to another open application. Your command-line |

program, however, might use one or more of these key combinations for its own purposes. To allow the program use of any of the short cuts, deactivate the appropriate check boxes.

### Understanding Idle Sensitivity

When it's multitasking applications, Windows XP doles out to each running process fixed-sized chunks of processor cycles called **time slices**. Ideally, active applications get more time slices, and idle applications get fewer. How does Windows XP know whether an application is idle? Windows applications send a message to the scheduler that specifies their current state. For example, an application might tell the scheduler that it's just waiting for user input (a keystroke or mouse click). In this case, Windows XP will reduce the number of time slices for the application and redistribute them to other processes running in the background.

Command-line programs are a different kettle of time-slice fish. In most cases, Windows XP has no way of knowing the current state of a 16-bit program. (However, many newer command-line applications are Windows-aware and can send messages to the scheduler.) In the absence of keyboard input, Windows XP just assumes that a program is in an idle state after a predetermined amount of inactivity, and it then redirects time slices to other processes. The amount of time that Windows XP waits before declaring a Command Prompt program idle is called the **idle sensitivity**.

You can control the idle sensitivity for a command-line program by using the Idle Sensitivity slider. The slider has a range between Low and High. Here's how to work with this slider:

| | |
|---|---|
| Low Idle Sensitivity | Windows XP waits longer before declaring the program idle. Use a Low setting to improve performance for 16-bit programs that perform background tasks. This ensures that, despite the lack of keyboard input, these tasks still get the time slices they need. |
| High Idle Sensitivity | Windows XP takes less time to declare a 16-bit application idle. If you know your program does nothing in the background, using the High setting will improve the performance of your other running applications because the scheduler will reallocate its time slices sooner. |

# Automating Windows XP with Batch Files

As you saw in Appendix B, "Using the Windows XP Command Prompt," the command line is still an indispensable part of computing life, and most power users will find themselves doing at least a little work in the Command Prompt window. Part of that work might involve writing short batch file programs to automate routine chores, such as performing simple file backups and deleting unneeded files. And if you throw in any of the eight Windows XP commands that enhance batch files, you can do many other interesting and useful things. That's where this appendix comes in: You'll learn what batch files are, how they work, and what commands are available.

## Batch Files: Some Background

In Appendix B, I told you that the Command Prompt uses a program called cmd.exe to handle anything you type at the prompt. The Command Prompt has some commands—such as COPY, DIR, and DEL—built right in (these are called **internal** commands).

For most anything else, including your software applications and the **external** commands such as FORMAT, CHKDSK, and FC, Command Prompt calls a separate program. Command Prompt executes the command or program and returns to the prompt to await further orders.

If you tell Command Prompt to execute a batch file, however, things are a little different. Command Prompt goes into **Batch mode**, where it takes all its input from the individual lines of a batch file. These lines are just commands that (in most cases) you otherwise have to type in yourself. Command Prompt repeats the following four-step procedure until it has processed each line in the batch file:

1. It reads a line from the batch file.

2. It closes the batch file.

3. It executes the command.

4. It reopens the batch file and reads the next line.

The main advantage of Batch mode is that you can lump several commands together in a single batch file and tell Command Prompt to execute them all simply by typing the name of the batch file. This is great for automating routine tasks such as backing up the Registry files or deleting leftover .tmp files at startup.

## Creating Batch Files

Before getting started with some concrete batch file examples, you need to know how to create them. Here are a few things to bear in mind:

- Batch files are simple text files, so Notepad (or some other text editor) is probably your best choice.

- If you decide to use WordPad or another word processor, make sure that the file you create is a text-only file.

- Save your batch files using the .bat extension.

- When naming your batch files, don't use the same name as a Command Prompt command. For example, if you create a batch file that deletes some files, don't name it Del.bat. If you do, the batch file will never run! Here's why: When you enter something at the prompt, Cmd.exe first checks to see whether the command is an internal command. If it's not, Cmd.exe then checks for (in order) a .com, .exe, .bat, or .cmd file with a matching name. Because all external commands use a .com or .exe extension, Cmd.exe never bothers to check whether your batch file even exists!

After you've created the batch file, the rest is easy. Just enter any commands exactly as you would in Command Prompt (with a couple of exceptions, as you'll see later), and include whatever batch instructions you need.

## Making a Home for Your Batch Files

If you find yourself creating and using a number of batch files, things can get confusing if you have the files scattered all over your hard disk. To remedy this, it makes sense to create a new folder to hold all your batch files.

To make this strategy effective, however, you have to tell Command Prompt to look in the batch file folder to find these files. You do this with the PATH command, which has the following general form:

```
PATH dir1;dir2;...
```

Here, *dir1*, *dir2*, and so on are the names of folders. What this command effectively tells Command Prompt is, "Whenever I run a command, if you can't find the appropriate file in the current folder, look for it in any of the folders listed in this PATH statement." Suppose that you create a folder named batch in your My Documents folder. In this case, you want to add %USERPROFILE%\batch to the path.

Rather than doing this each time in Command Prompt, follow these steps to change the PATH variable permanently:

1. Open Control Panel's System icon. (Alternatively, select Start, right-click My Computer, and then click Properties.)

2. Display the Advanced tab.

3. Click Environment Variables to display the Environment Variables dialog box.

4. In the System Variables list, select Path.

5. Click Edit to open the Edit System Variable dialog box.

6. In the Variable Value text box, add a semicolon and the path for your batch file folder to the end of the existing value. Figure C.1 shows the Edit System Variable dialog box with %UserProfile%\batch added to the PATH value.

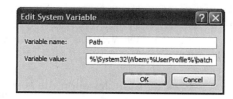

**FIGURE C.1**   Add the folder where you'll be storing your batch files to the PATH value.

7. Click OK to return to the System Properties dialog box.

8. Click OK.

## REM: **The Simplest Batch File Command**

The first of the batch-file-specific commands is REM (which stands for *remark*). This simple command tells Command Prompt to ignore everything else on the current line. It's used by batch file mavens almost exclusively to add short comments to their files:

```
REM This batch file changes to the Windows XP
REM folder and starts CHKDSK in automatic mode.
CD %SystemRoot%
CHKDSK /F
```

Why would anyone want to do this? Well, it's probably not all that necessary with short, easy-to-understand batch files, but some of the more complex programs you'll be seeing later in this appendix can appear incomprehensible at first glance. A few pithy REM statements can help clear things up (not only for other people, but even for you if you haven't looked at the file in a couple of months).

---

**CAUTION**

It's best not to go overboard with REM statements. Having too many slows a batch file to a crawl. You really need only a few REM statements at the beginning to outline the purpose of the file and one or two to explain each of your more cryptic commands.

---

# ECHO: **A Voice for Your Batch Files**

When it's processing a batch file, Windows XP normally lets you know what's going on by displaying each command before executing it. That's fine, but it's often better to include more expansive descriptions, especially if other people will be using your batch files. The ECHO batch file command makes it possible for you to do just that.

For example, here's a simple batch file that deletes all the text files in the current user's Cookies folder and My Recent Documents folder and courteously tells the user what's about to happen:

```
ECHO This batch file will now delete all your cookie text files
DEL "%UserProfile%\Cookies\*.txt"
ECHO This batch file will now delete your My Recent Documents list
DEL "%UserProfile%\Recent\*.lnk"
```

The idea here is that when Windows XP stumbles upon the ECHO command, it simply displays the rest of the line onscreen. Sounds pretty simple, right? Well, here's what the output looks like when you run the batch file:

```
C:\>ECHO This batch file will now delete all your cookie text files
This batch file will now delete all your cookie text files
C:\>DEL "%UserProfile%\Cookies\*.txt"
C:\>ECHO This batch file will now delete your My Recent Documents list
This batch file will now delete your My Recent Documents list
C:\>DEL "%UserProfile%\Recent\*.lnk"
```

What a mess! The problem is that Windows XP is displaying the command and echoing the line. Fortunately, Windows XP provides two solutions:

- To prevent Windows XP from displaying a command as it executes it, precede the command with the @ symbol:

  ```
  @ECHO This batch file will now delete all your cookie text files
  ```

- To prevent Windows XP from displaying any commands, place the following at the beginning of the batch file:

```
@ECHO OFF
```

Here's what the output looks like with the commands hidden:

```
This batch file will now delete all your cookie text files
This batch file will now delete your My Recent Documents list
```

> **TIP**
>
> You might think that you can display a blank line simply by using ECHO by itself. That would be nice, but it doesn't work (Windows XP just tells you the current state of ECHO—on or off). Instead, use ECHO. (that's ECHO followed by a dot).

## The PAUSE Command

Sometimes you want to see something that a batch file displays (such as a folder listing produced by the DIR command) before continuing. Or, you might want to alert users that something important is about to happen so that they can consider the possible ramifications (and bail out if they get cold feet). In both cases, you can use the PAUSE command to halt the execution of a batch file temporarily. When Windows XP comes across PAUSE in a batch file, it displays the following:

```
Press any key to continue . . .
```

To continue processing the rest of the batch file, press any key. If you don't want to continue, you can cancel processing by pressing Ctrl+C or Ctrl+Break. Windows XP then asks you to confirm:

```
Terminate batch job (Y/N)?
```

Either press Y to return to the prompt or N to continue the batch file.

## Using Parameters for Batch File Flexibility

Most command-line utilities require extra information such as a filename (for example, when you use COPY or DEL) or a folder path (such as when you use CD or MD). These extra pieces of information—they're called **parameters**—give you the flexibility to specify exactly how you want a command to work. You can add the same level of flexibility to your batch files. To understand how this works, first look at the following example:

```
@ECHO OFF
ECHO.
ECHO The first parameter is %1
ECHO The second parameter is %2
ECHO The third parameter is %3
```

As you can see, this batch file doesn't do much except ECHO four lines to the screen (the first of which is just a blank line). Curiously, however, each ECHO command ends with a percent sign (%) and a number. Type in and save this batch file as PARAMETERS.BAT. Then, to see what these unusual symbols mean, enter the following command at the Windows XP prompt:

```
parameters Tinkers Evers Chance
```

This produces the following output:

```
C:\>parameters Tinkers Evers Chance

The first parameter is Tinkers
The second parameter is Evers
The third parameter is Chance
```

The first line in the output (after the blank line) is produced by the following ECHO command in PARAMETERS.BAT:

```
ECHO The first parameter is %1
```

When Windows XP sees the %1 symbol in a batch file, it examines the original command, looks for the first word after the batch filename, and then replaces %1 with that word. In the example, the first word after parameters is Tinkers, so Windows XP uses that to replace %1. (This is why batch file programmers often call %1 a **replaceable parameter**.) Only when it has done this does it proceed to ECHO the line to the screen.

The replaceable parameter %2 is similar, except that, in this case, Windows XP looks for the second word after the batch filename (Evers in this example).

> **NOTE**
>
> If your batch file command has more parameters than the batch file is looking for, the extras are ignored. For example, adding a fourth parameter to the parameters command line has no effect on the file's operation. Note, too, that you can't use more than nine replaceable parameters in a batch file (%1 through %9). However, there is a tenth replaceable parameter (%0). It holds the name of the batch file itself.

Let's look at a real-world example. Consider the following slightly useful but highly inflexible batch file, called NEWFOLDER.BAT:

```
@ECHO OFF
CLS
MD \batch
CD \batch
```

This batch file simply creates a new folder called batch and then moves to it. You'll be surprised how often you need to do something like this, so it makes sense to try to automate the whole procedure.

Unfortunately, this isn't the best way to go about it. You could set up a batch file each time you need to create and move to a folder, but I assume that you want to spend your remaining years in a more fruitful enterprise. Instead, you can use replaceable parameters to add instant flexibility to NEWFOLDER.BAT:

```
@ECHO OFF
CLS
MD %1
CD %1
```

Now, if you want to create and move to a new batch folder, enter the following command:

```
newfolder \batch
```

Windows XP replaces each %1 in NEWFOLDER.BAT with \batch (the first word after newfolder), so the batch file works as it did before. The difference, of course, is that you can now use it for other folders as well. For example, to create a new scripts folder and move to it, use the following command:

```
newfolder \scripts
```

## Improving on Command-Line Utilities

Because a batch file's replaceable parameters work just like the parameters used in command-line utilities, it's not hard to create batch files that mimic—and even improve on—the standard Command Prompt fare.

### Making DEL Safer

Probably 99.9% of all accidental command-line deletions occur when you use wildcard characters to delete multiple files. A question mark in the wrong place or a *.* in the wrong folder can lead to disaster.

It would help if you could see a list of all the files that you were about to delete and then have the option of canceling the deletion if things weren't right. The easiest way to do this, of course, is to run a DIR command using the same file specification you would use with DEL. But it's usually a pain typing two commands and making sure that you get the ?s and *s in the right place each time. This situation cries out for a batch file, and here it is (it's called SAFEDEL.BAT):

```
@ECHO OFF
CLS
ECHO %0 %1
ECHO.
ECHO Here is a list of the files that will be deleted:
REM Display a wide DIR list in alphabetical order
DIR %1 /ON /W
ECHO.
```

```
ECHO To cancel the deletion, press Ctrl+C. Otherwise,
PAUSE
DEL %1
```

You use SAFEDEL.BAT just like the DEL command. For example, to delete all the .bak files in the current folder, enter the following:

**safedel \*.bak**

The following list is a quick summary of what happens:

- The command ECHO %0 %1 simply redisplays the batch filename (%0) and the file specification (%1) for reference.

- The DIR %1 /ON /W command is used to get an alphabetical listing (in wide format so that you can see more files) of everything that's about to be deleted.

- The batch file then runs PAUSE so that you can examine the files.

- If you decide to continue, the DEL %1 command takes care of the job.

---

**CAUTION**

The percent sign (%) is a perfectly good character to use in a filename, but if you try to reference a file named, for example, PERCNT%.XLS, you'll run into problems. The reason is that when Command Prompt processes batch files, it mindlessly deletes any single occurrences of % as part of its parameter replacement chores. So, PERCNT%.XLS becomes PERCNT.XLS, and things go haywire. To fix this, use double percent signs when referring to the file in a batch command (for example, PERCNT%%.XLS).

---

## Changing Folders and Drives in One Step

The CD command falls down on the job if you need to change to a folder on a different drive. You have to change to the drive first and then run CD. Use CDD.BAT to do this all in one command:

```
@ECHO OFF
%1:
CD \%2
```

For example, to change to the A drive's BACKUP folder, simply use the following command:

```
cdd a backup
```

If you hate typing backslashes, you can avoid them altogether by adding a couple of extra CD commands:

```
@ECHO OFF
%1:
CD \%2
```

```
CD %3
CD %4
```

Now, to change to the \BACKUP\123\DATA folder on drive A, enter the following:

```
cdd a backup 123 data
```

### Excluding Files from a Copy Command

The wildcard characters are used to include multiple files in a single command. But what if you want to *exclude* certain files? For example, suppose that you have a WP\DOCS folder that has files with various extensions—.doc, .txt, .wp, and so on. What do you do if you want to copy all the files to drive A except those with a .txt extension? One solution is to use separate XCOPY commands for each extension you do need, but that's too much work (and besides, you might miss some). Instead, try this batch file (it's called DONTCOPY.BAT):

```
@ECHO OFF
CLS
ATTRIB +H %1
ECHO.
ECHO Copying all files to %2 except %1:
ECHO.
XCOPY *.* %2
ATTRIB -H %1
```

To use this batch file to copy all the files in the current folder to drive D, except, for example, those with the extension .txt, use the following command:

```
dontcopy *.txt d:
```

The secret here is that DOS won't copy hidden files. So, DONTCOPY.BAT uses the ATTRIB command to hide the files that you want to ignore. The first command, ATTRIB +H %1, does just that. Now all that's needed is an XCOPY command that copies everything that's not hidden (use *.* to do this) to the target (%2). When that's done, DONTCOPY.BAT uses another ATTRIB command to unhide the files.

---

**CAUTION**

To be safe, DONTCOPY.BAT should check to make sure that a destination parameter (%2) was entered. This can be done, but you need to use the batch file commands IF and GOTO, which are discussed later in this appendix.

---

**NOTE**

You can use the same idea to exclude files with other commands. For example, Command Prompt won't delete or rename hidden files, so it wouldn't be hard to create the appropriate DONTDEL.BAT and DONTREN.BAT batch files.

---

## SHIFT: **A Different Approach to Parameters**

Although you won't be using it until later in this appendix, you should know that there's another way to handle parameters inside batch files: the SHIFT command. To see how it works, rewrite the PARAMETERS.BAT file to get PARAMETERS2.BAT:

```
@ECHO OFF
ECHO.
ECHO The first parameter is %1
SHIFT
ECHO The second parameter is %1
SHIFT
ECHO The third parameter is %1
```

If you enter the command parameters2 Tinkers Evers Chance, you get the same output as before:

```
C:\BATCH>parameters2 Tinkers Evers Chance

The first parameter is Tinkers
The second parameter is Evers
The third parameter is Chance
```

How does this work? Well, each SHIFT command shuffles the parameters down one position. In particular, %2 goes to %1, so the following command really does display the second parameter:

```
ECHO The second parameter is %1
```

All the other parameters change as well, of course: %3 goes to %2, %1 goes to %0, and %0 heads off into oblivion.

This sort of behavior is handy for two types of situations:

- Batch files that require more than 10 parameters—There aren't many times when you'll need this many parameters, but at least you know you can handle it when the need arises.

- Batch files that use a varying number of parameters—This is a much more common scenario; you'll see a couple of examples a bit later.

Note that I'm holding off on presenting SHIFT examples because to use it properly, you need an IF command to test whether there are any more parameters left to shift. I discuss the IF command later in this appendix (see "IF: Handling Batch File Conditions").

## Looping with the FOR **Command**

Pound for pound, the FOR command is easily the most underutilized and misunderstood of all Command Prompt commands. This is bad news because FOR is an extremely powerful weapon that shouldn't be left out of any command-line guru's arsenal. The problem, I think, is that FOR has a somewhat bizarre syntax that makes it wildly unappealing at first glance. So, before we look at it, I'll give you some background.

## Looping: The Basics

If you wanted to instruct someone on how to dress each day, you might begin with a simple step-by-step approach:

1. Put on underwear.

2. Put on socks.

3. Put on pants.

4. Put on shirt.

This is fine, but you can make things simpler by creating a list—underwear, socks, pants, shirt—and telling the person to put on everything in this list in the order they appear. Now, instead of a linear approach, you've got a primitive loop: The person looks at the list, puts on the first item, looks at the list again, puts on the second item, and so on.

Now you can formalize the instructions into a single, pithy statement:

```
for each item X in the set (underwear, socks, pants, shirt), put on X
```

Programmers often use loops like this to add generality to programs. Instead of writing a dozen different instructions, they can often write a single, generic instruction (something like put on X) and loop through it a dozen times, each time supplying it with a different input (underwear, socks, and so on).

## Understanding the FOR Command Syntax

The FOR command is a batch file's way of looping through an instruction:

```
FOR %%parameter IN (set) DO command
```

Looks like bad news, doesn't it? Well, see how it looks if you plug in the dressing instructions:

```
FOR %%X IN (underwear, socks, pants, shirt) DO put on %%X
```

That's a little more comprehensible, so let's break down the FOR command for a closer look:

| | |
|---|---|
| *%%parameter* | This is the parameter that changes each time through the loop (%%X in the example). You can use any single character after the two % signs (except 0 through 9). There are two % signs because, as I explained earlier, DOS deletes single ones as it processes the batch file. |

| IN (*set*) | This is the list (it's officially called the set) of choices for %%X (in the example, underwear, socks, and so on). You can use spaces, commas, or semicolons to separate the items in the set, and you must enclose them in parentheses. |
|---|---|
| DO *command* | For each item in the set, the batch file performs whatever instruction is given by *command* (such as put on %%X). The parameter %%X is normally found somewhere in *command*. |

## A Simple Batch File Example

Here's an example of the FOR command in a simple batch file that might help clear things up:

```
@ECHO OFF
FOR %%B IN (Tinkers Evers Chance) DO ECHO %%B
```

This batch file (call it PARAMETERS3.BAT) produces the following output:

```
C:\BATCH>parameters3
Tinkers
Evers
Chance
```

All this does is loop through the three items in the set (Tinkers, Evers, and Chance) and substitute each one for %%B in the command ECHO %%B. In other words, this FOR loop is equivalent to the following three ECHO commands:

```
ECHO Tinkers

ECHO Evers

ECHO Chance
```

## Different Sets for Different Folks

The set in a FOR command can hold more than simple strings such as Tinkers and Evers. The real power of FOR becomes evident when you use file specifications, command names, and even replaceable parameters as part of a set.

For example, have you ever copied a bunch of files into the wrong folder? This happens occasionally, and it's usually a mess to clean up because the files get all mixed up with whatever was already in the folder. Before smashing your monitor, check out the following batch file (called CLEANUP.BAT):

```
@ECHO OFF
FOR %%F IN (*.*) DO DEL C:\WRONGDIR\%%F
```

This batch file assumes that you copied all the files from the current folder into the WRONGDIR folder. In this case, the set is given by the *.* file specification. FOR loops through every file in the current folder and, for each one, deletes it in the WRONGDIR folder.

To see how to use command names in a set, you can redo the NEWFOLDER.BAT batch file created earlier. Here's NEWFOLDER2.BAT:

```
@ECHO OFF
CLS
FOR %%C IN (MD CD) DO %%C %1
```

As you can see, the set consists of the two commands MD and CD. These are substituted for %%C each time through the loop, so this single FOR command is equivalent to the two commands in NEWFOLDER.BAT:

```
MD %1
```

```
CD %1
```

The FOR command is very powerful if you use replaceable parameters inside the set. The most common use of this potent combination is to create your own versions of commands that accept multiple parameters. For example, here's a batch file (called SUPERDELETE.BAT) that deletes up to nine file specifications at once:

```
@ECHO OFF
ECHO.
ECHO About to delete the following files:
ECHO %1 %2 %3 %4 %5 %6 %7 %8 %9
ECHO.
ECHO Press Ctrl+C to cancel. Otherwise,
PAUSE
FOR %%F IN (%1 %2 %3 %4 %5 %6 %7 %8 %9) DO DEL %%F
```

To use this file to delete, for example, all files in the current folder that have the extensions .bak, .tmp, and .$$$, use the following command:

```
superdelete *.bak *.tmp *.$$$
```

Windows XP must do two things to process the FOR command in SUPERDEL.BAT. First, it replaces the parameters inside the set so that the command looks like this:

```
FOR %%F IN (*.bak *.tmp *.$$$) DO DEL %%F
```

Then it loops through the set to delete each file specification. In the end, this is equivalent to the following three DEL commands:

```
DEL *.bak
```

```
DEL *.tmp

DEL *.$$$
```

## Using Delayed Environment Variable Expansion

The FOR command is an excellent tool for understanding the delayed environment variable expansion that I discussed in Appendix B. To refresh your memory, if you start the cmd.exe with the /V:ON switch, you turn on delayed environment variable expansion, which means that Windows XP doesn't expand a particular environment variable within a batch file until it executes the statement containing that variable.

For example, suppose that you want to use FOR to display a list of subfolders and files in the current folder. You might think that you could loop through all the items in the folder and store each one in a custom environment variable. Here's a first pass:

```
@ECHO OFF
SET FileList=
FOR %%F IN (*.*) DO SET FileList=%FileList% %%F
ECHO %FileList%
```

This code first initializes an environment variable named FileList. Then a FOR loop runs through everything in the current folder (*.*) and appends the name of each item to %FileList%. The batch file then displays the current value of %FileList%.

Unfortunately, if you run this batch file, the final value of %FileList% is just the name of the last file in the folder. The problem is that Command Prompt expands the value of %FileList% at the beginning of the batch file. Because this variable is blank to begin with, all the FOR loop is doing is adding each subfolder or filename to a blank value.

To fix this, you must start cmd.exe with delayed environment variable expansion (/V:ON) and then change %FileList% in the FOR loop to !FileList!, as shown here:

```
@ECHO OFF
SET FileList=
FOR %%F IN (*.*) DO SET FileList=!FileList! %%F
ECHO %FileList%
```

This enables Command Prompt to retain the contents of FileList with each loop, so you get a proper listing of subfolders and files.

# GOTO: **Telling Your Batch Files Where to Go**

Your basic batch file lives a simple, linear existence. The first command gets processed, and then the second, the third, and so on to the end of the file. It's pretty boring, but that's all you need most of the time.

However, there are situations in which the batch file's usual one-command-after-the-other approach breaks down. For example, depending on a parameter or the result of a previous command, you might need to skip over a line or two. How do you do this? With the GOTO batch command:

```
...
... (the opening batch commands)
...
GOTO NEXT
...
... (the batch commands that get skipped)
...
:NEXT
...
... (the rest of the batch commands)
...
```

Here, the GOTO command is telling the batch file to look for a line that begins with a colon and the word NEXT (this is called a **label**) and to ignore any commands in between.

GOTO is useful for processing different batch commands depending on a parameter. Here's a simple example:

```
@ECHO OFF
CLS
GOTO %1
:A
ECHO This part of the batch file runs if A is the parameter.
GOTO END
:B
ECHO This part of the batch file runs if B is the parameter.
:END
```

Suppose that this file is called GOTOTEST.BAT and you enter the following command:

**gototest a**

In the batch file, the line GOTO %1 becomes GOTO A. That makes the batch file skip down to the :A label, where it then runs the commands (in this example, just an ECHO statement), and then skips to :END to avoid the rest of the batch file commands.

One handy use of the GOTO command is for those times when you need to add copious comments to a batch file. As you know, you normally use REM to add batch file remarks. Windows XP doesn't try to execute these lines, but it still has to read them, and this can really slow things down. Here's a way to use GOTO to get around this (literally!):

```
@ECHO OFF
GOTO START
You place your batch file comments here. Notice how
I'm not using the REM command at all. This not only
saves typing (a constant goal for some of us) but it
```

```
certainly looks a lot nicer, don't you think?
:START
...
... (Batch file commands)
...
```

As you can see, GOTO just leaps over the comments to end up at the :START label. Windows XP doesn't even know that the comments exist.

# IF: **Handling Batch File Conditions**

We make decisions all the time. Some are complex and require intricate levels of logic to answer (Should I get married? Should I start a chinchilla farm?). Others are simpler and depend only on existing conditions (the proverbial fork in the road):

- If it's raining, I'll stay home and work. Otherwise, I'll go to the beach.

- If this milk smells okay, I'll drink some. Otherwise, I'll throw it out.

No batch file (indeed, no software program yet developed) is sophisticated enough to tackle life's complex questions, but the simpler condition-based decisions are no problem. Here are a few examples of what a batch file might have to decide:

- If the %2 parameter equals /Q, jump to the QuickFormat section. Otherwise, do a regular format.

- If the user forgets to enter a parameter, cancel the program. Otherwise, continue processing the batch file.

- If the file that the user wants to move already exists in the new folder, display a warning. Otherwise, proceed with the move.

- If the last command failed, display an error message and cancel the program. Otherwise, continue.

For these types of decisions, you need to use the IF batch command. IF has the following general form:

IF *condition command*

|  |  |
|---|---|
| *condition* | This is a test that evaluates to a yes or no answer ("Did the user forget a parameter?"). |
| *command* | This is what is executed if the *condition* produces a positive response ("Cancel the batch file"). |

The next few sections discuss the various ways you can use IF in your batch files.

## Testing Parameters with `IF`

One of the most common uses of the `IF` command is to check the parameters that the user entered and proceed accordingly. For example, the simple batch file from the previous section that used `GOTO` can be rewritten with `IF` as follows:

```
@ECHO OFF
CLS
IF "%1"=="A" ECHO This part of the batch file runs if A is the parameter.
IF "%1"=="B" ECHO This part of the batch file runs if B is the parameter.
```

The condition part of an `IF` statement is a bit tricky. Let's look at the first one: `"%1"=="A"`. Remember that the condition is always a question with a yes or no answer. In this case, the question boils down to the following:

```
Is the first parameter (%1) equal to A?
```

The double equal sign (==) looks weird, but that's just how you compare two strings of characters in a batch file. If the answer is yes, the command is executed. If the answer is no, the batch file moves on to the next `IF`, which checks to see whether the parameter is `"B"`.

---

**NOTE**

Strictly speaking, you don't need to include the quotation marks ("). Using `%1==A` accomplishes the same thing. However, I prefer to use them for two reasons: First, it makes it clearer than the `IF` condition is comparing strings; second, as you'll see in the next section, the quotation marks enable you to check whether the user forgot to enter a parameter at all.

---

**CAUTION**

This batch file has a serious flaw that will prevent it from working under certain conditions. Specifically, if you use the lowercase `"a"` or `"b"` as a parameter, nothing happens because, to the `IF` command, `"a"` is different from `"A"`. The solution is to add extra `IF` commands to handle this situation:

```
IF "%1"=="a" ECHO This part of the batch file runs if a is the parameter
```

---

## Checking for Missing Parameters

Proper batch file techniques require you to not only check to see what a parameter is, but also whether one exists at all. This can be vital because a missing parameter can cause a batch file to crash and burn. For example, earlier I showed you a batch file called `DONTCOPY.BAT` designed to copy all files in the current folder to a new destination (given by the second parameter) except those you specified (given by the first parameter). Here's the listing to refresh your memory:

```
@ECHO OFF
CLS
ATTRIB +H %1
ECHO.
ECHO Copying all files to %2 except %1:
ECHO.
XCOPY *.* %2
ATTRIB -H %1
```

What happens if the user forgets to add the destination parameter (%2)? Well, the XCOPY command becomes XCOPY *.*, which terminates the batch file with the following error:

```
File cannot be copied onto itself
```

The solution is to add an IF command that checks to see whether %2 exists:

```
@ECHO OFF
CLS
IF "%2"=="" GOTO ERROR
ATTRIB +H %1
ECHO.
ECHO Copying all files to %2 except %1:
ECHO.
XCOPY32 *.* %2
ATTRIB -H %1
GOTO END
:ERROR
ECHO You didn't enter a destination!
ECHO Please try again...
:END
```

The condition "%2"=="" is literally comparing %2 to nothing (""). If this proves to be true, the program jumps (using GOTO) to the :ERROR label, and a message is displayed to admonish the user. Notice, too, that if everything is okay (that is, the user entered a second parameter), the batch file executes normally and jumps to the :END label to avoid displaying the error message.

## The SHIFT Command Redux

Now that you know a little about how IF works, I can show you how to use the SHIFT command introduced earlier. Recall that SHIFT operates by shuffling the batch file parameters down one position, so that %1 becomes %0, %2 becomes %1, and so on. The most common use of this apparently strange behavior is to process batch files with an unknown number of parameters. As an example, let's redo the SUPERDELETE.BAT batch file so that it can delete any number of file specifications:

```
@ECHO OFF
IF "%1"=="" GOTO NO_FILES
:START
ECHO Now deleting %1 . . .
DEL %1
SHIFT
IF "%1"=="" GOTO DONE
GOTO START
:NO_FILES
ECHO You didn't enter a file spec!
:DONE
```

The first IF is familiar—it just looks for a missing parameter and, if that proves to be the case, leaps to :NO_FILES and displays a message. Otherwise, the program deletes the first file specification and then shifts everything down. What was %2 is now %1, so you need the second IF to check the new %1. If it's blank, this means that the user didn't enter any more file specs, and the program jumps to :DONE. Otherwise, you loop back to :START and do it all again.

> **CAUTION**
>
> As you can see from the preceding example, it's okay to use GOTO to jump backward in a file and create a loop. This is often better than a FOR loop because instead of a single command, you can process any number of commands. However, you need to be careful or you might end up in the never-never land of an endless loop. Always include an IF command that will take you out of the loop after some condition has been met (such as running out of parameters).

## Using IF to Check Whether a File Exists

Another variation of IF is the IF EXIST command, which checks for the existence of a file. This is handy, for example, when you're using COPY or MOVE. You can check, first of all, whether the file you want to copy or move exists. Second, you can check whether a file with the same name already exists in the target folder. (As you probably know, a file that has been copied over by another of the same name is downright impossible to recover.) Here's a batch file called SAFEMOVE.BAT, which uses the MOVE command to move a file but first checks the file and then the target folder:

```
@ECHO OFF
CLS
IF EXIST %1 GOTO SO_FAR_SO_GOOD
ECHO The file %1 doesn't exist!
GOTO END
:SO_FAR_SO_GOOD
IF NOT EXIST %2 GOTO MOVE_IT
ECHO The file %1 exists on the target folder!
ECHO Press Ctrl+C to bail out or, to keep going,
```

```
PAUSE
:MOVE_IT
MOVE %1 %2
:END
```

To explain what's happening, I'll use a sample command:

```
safemove moveme.txt "%userprofile%\my documents\moveme.txt"
```

The first IF tests for the existence of %1 (MOVEME.TXT in the example). If there is such a file, the program skips to the :SO_FAR_SO_GOOD label. Otherwise, it tells the user that the file doesn't exist, and then jumps down to :END.

The second IF is slightly different. In this case, I want to continue only if MOVEME.TXT doesn't exist in the current user's My Documents folder, so I add NOT to the condition. (You can include NOT in any IF condition.) If this proves true (that is, the file given by %2 doesn't exist), the file skips to :MOVE_IT and performs the move. Otherwise, the user is warned and given an opportunity to cancel.

## Checking for Command Errors

Good batch files (especially those that other people will be using) always assume that if anything bad can happen, it will. So far you've seen how IF can handle missing parameters and file problems, but there's much more that can go haywire. For example, what if a batch file tries to use XCOPY, but there's not enough memory? Or what if the user presses Ctrl+C during a format or copy? It might seem impossible to check for these kinds of errors, but it is not only possible, it's really quite easy.

When certain commands finish, they always file a report on the progress of the operation. This report, or **exit code**, is a number that tells DOS how things went. For example, Table C.1 lists the exit codes used by the XCOPY command.

**TABLE C.1**    XCOPY Exit Codes

| Exit Code | What It Means |
| --- | --- |
| 0 | Everything's okay; the files were copied. |
| 1 | Nothing happened because no files were found to copy. |
| 2 | The user pressed Ctrl+C to abort the copy. |
| 4 | The command failed because there wasn't enough memory or disk space, or because there was something wrong with the command's syntax. |
| 5 | The command failed because of a disk error. |

What does all this mean for your batch files? You can use yet another variation of the IF command—IF ERRORLEVEL—to test for these exit codes. For example, here's a batch file called CHECKCOPY.BAT, which uses some of the XCOPY exit codes to check for errors:

```
@ECHO OFF
XCOPY %1 %2
IF ERRORLEVEL 4 GOTO ERROR
IF ERRORLEVEL 2 GOTO CTRL+C
IF ERRORLEVEL 1 GOTO NO_FILES
GOTO DONE
:ERROR
ECHO Bad news! The copy failed because there wasn't
ECHO enough memory or disk space or because there was
ECHO something wrong with your file specs . . .
GOTO DONE
:CTRL+C
ECHO Hey, what gives? You pressed Ctrl+C to abort . . .
GOTO DONE
:NO_FILES
ECHO Bad news! No files were found to copy . . .
:DONE
```

As you can see, the ERRORLEVEL conditions check for the individual exit codes and then use GOTO to jump to the appropriate label.

> **NOTE**
>
> How does a batch file know what a command's exit code was? When Windows XP gets an exit code from a command, it stores it in a special data area set aside for exit code information. When Windows XP sees the IF ERRORLEVEL command in a batch file, it retrieves the exit code from the data area so that it can be compared to whatever is in the IF condition.

> **NOTE**
>
> Here's a list of exit codes generated by CHKDSK:
>
> | Exit Code | What It Means |
> | --- | --- |
> | 0 | The drive was checked and no errors were found. |
> | 1 | Errors were found, and all were fixed. |
> | 2 | Disk cleanup, such as garbage collection, was performed, or cleanup was not performed because the /F switch was not specified. |
> | 3 | Could not check the disk, errors could not be fixed, or errors were not fixed because the /F switch was not specified. |

One of the most important things to know about the IF ERRORLEVEL test is how Windows XP interprets it. For example, consider the following IF command:

```
IF ERRORLEVEL 2 GOTO CTRL+C
```

Windows XP interprets this command as "If the exit code from the last command is equal to or greater than 2, jump to the :CTRL+C label." This has two important consequences for your batch files:

- The test IF ERRORLEVEL 0 doesn't tell you much because it's always true. If you simply want to find out whether the command failed, use the test IF NOT ERRORLEVEL 0.

- To get the correct results, always test the *highest* ERRORLEVEL first and then work your way down.

# Redirecting Windows XP

Windows XP is always directing things here and there. This generally falls into two categories:

- Directing data into its commands from a device called **standard input**.
- Directing data out of its commands to a device called **standard output**.

Standard input and standard output are normally handled by a device called **CON** (**console**), which is your keyboard and monitor. Windows XP assumes that all command input comes from the keyboard and that all command output (such as a DIR listing or a system message) goes to the screen. Redirection is just a way of specifying different input and output devices.

## Redirecting Command Output

To send command output to somewhere other than the screen, you use the **output redirection operator** (>). One of the most common uses for output redirection is to capture the results of a command in a text file. For example, you might want to use the report produced by the MEM command as part of a word processing document. You could use the following command to first capture the report as the file mem.txt:

```
mem /c > mem.txt
```

When you run this command, don't be alarmed when the usual MEM data doesn't appear onscreen. Remember, it has been directed away from the screen and into the mem.txt file.

You can use this technique to capture DIR listings, CHKDSK reports, and more. One caveat: If the file you specify as the output destination already exists, Windows XP overwrites it without any warning. To be safe, you can use the **double output redirection symbol** (>>). This tells Windows XP to append the output to the file if it exists. For example, if you want to add the results of the CHKDSK command to mem.txt, use the following command:

```
chkdsk >> mem.txt
```

You can also redirect output to different devices. Table C.2 lists the various devices that Windows XP installs each time you start your system.

**TABLE C.2**   Devices Installed by Windows XP When You Start Your System

| Device Name | Device |
| --- | --- |
| AUX | Auxiliary device (usually COM1) |
| CLOCK$ | Real-time clock |
| COM*n* | Serial port (COM1, COM2, COM3, or COM4) |
| CON | Console (keyboard and screen) |
| LPT*n* | Parallel port (LPT1, LPT2, or LPT3) |
| NUL | NUL device (nothing) |
| PRN | Printer (usually LPT1) |

For example, you can send a DIR listing to the printer with the following command (of course, you need to be sure that your printer is on before doing this):

```
dir > prn
```

The NUL device usually throws people for a loop when they first see it. This device (affectionately known as the **bit bucket**) is, literally, nothing. It's normally used in batch files to suppress the usual messages Windows XP displays when it completes a command. For example, Windows XP normally says 1 file(s) copied when you copy a file. However, the following command sends that message to **NUL**, so you wouldn't see it onscreen:

```
copy somefile.doc a:\ > nul
```

## Redirecting Input

Getting input to a Windows XP command from somewhere other than the keyboard is handled by the **input redirection operator** (<). Input redirection is almost always used to send the contents of a text file to a Windows XP command. The most common example is the MORE command, which displays one screen of information at a time. If you have a large text file that scrolls off the screen when you use TYPE, the following command, which sends the contents of BIGFILE.TXT to the MORE command, solves the problem:

```
more < bigfile.txt
```

When you run this command, the first screen of text appears, and the following line shows up at the bottom of the screen:

```
-- More --
```

Just press any key, and MORE displays the next screen. (Whatever you do, don't mix up < and > when using MORE. The command more > bigfile.txt erases BIGFILE.TXT!) MORE is an example of a **filter** command. Filters process whatever text is sent through them. The other Windows XP filters are SORT and FIND, discussed in a moment.

Another handy use for input redirection is to send keystrokes to Windows XP commands. For example, create a text file called ENTER.TXT that consists of a single press of the Enter key, and then try this command:

```
date < enter.txt
```

Windows XP displays the current date, and instead of waiting for you to either type in a new date or press Enter, it just reads ENTER.TXT and uses its single carriage return as input. (For an even easier way to input the Enter key to a command, check out the next section.)

> **TIP**
>
> You can send keystrokes to any Windows XP command that waits for input. You can even send multiple keystrokes. For example, a typical FORMAT command has three prompts: one to insert a disk, one for the volume label, and one to format another disk. If your normal responses to these prompts are Enter, Enter, N, and Enter, include these in a text file called, say, INFORMAT.TXT, and run FORMAT with the following command:
>
> ```
> format a: < informat.txt
> ```

One common recipient of redirected input is the SORT command. SORT, as you might guess from its name, sorts the data sent to it and displays the results onscreen. So, for example, here's how you would sort a file called JUMBLED.TXT:

```
sort < jumbled.txt
```

Instead of merely displaying the results of the sort onscreen, you can use > to redirect them to another file.

> **TIP**
>
> SORT normally starts with the first column and works across. To start with any other column, use the /+n switch, where n is the number of the column you want to use. To sort a file in reverse order, use the /R switch.

## Piping Commands

**Piping** is a technique that combines both input and output redirection. Using the pipe operator (¦), the output of one command is captured and sent as input to another command. For example, using MEM with the /C or /D switch usually results in more than one screen of data. MEM has a /P switch to pause the output, but you can also pipe it to the MORE command:

```
mem /c ¦ more
```

The pipe operator captures the MEM output and sends it as input to MORE, which then displays everything one screen at a time.

> **NOTE**
>
> Piping works by first redirecting the output of a command to a temporary file. It then takes this temporary file and redirects it as input to the second command. A command such as MEM /C ¦ MORE is approximately equivalent to the following two commands:
>
> ```
> MEM /C > tempfile
> tempfile < MORE
> ```

I showed you in the preceding section how to use input redirection to send keystrokes to a Windows XP command. But if you have to send only a single key, piping offers a much nicer solution. The secret is to use the ECHO command to echo the character you need and then pipe it to the Windows XP command.

For example, if you use the command DEL *.*, Windows XP always asks whether you're sure that you want to delete all the files in the current directory. This is a sensible precaution, but you can override it if you do things this way:

```
echo y ¦ del *.*
```

Here, the y that would normally be echoed to the screen is sent to DEL instead, which interprets it as a response to its prompt. This is a handy technique for batch files in which you want to reduce or even eliminate user interaction.

> **TIP**
>
> You can even use this technique to send an Enter to a command. The command ECHO. (that's ECHO followed by a period) is equivalent to pressing Enter. So, for example, you could use the following command in a batch file to display the time without user input:
>
> ```
> ECHO. ¦ TIME
> ```

A command that's commonly used in pipe operations is the FIND filter. FIND searches its input for a specified string and, if it finds a match, it displays the line that contains the string. For example, the last line of a DIR listing tells you the number of bytes free on the current drive. Rather than wade through the entire DIR output just to get this information, use this command instead:

```
dir ¦ find "free"
```

You'll see something like the following:

```
2 Dir(s) 28,903,331,184 bytes free
```

FIND scours the DIR listing that was piped to it and looks for the word *free*. You can use this technique to display specific lines from, say, a CHKDSK report. For example, searching for *bad* finds the number of bad sectors on the disk.

# Glossary

Throughout this book, I've introduced and defined hundreds of acronyms, abbreviations, words, and phrases related to the concepts and features of Windows XP and its associated technologies. This appendix gathers those terms—nearly 300 in all—in one place for handy reference. If you come across an unfamiliar term in the book, chances are it's defined here. And, of course, feel free to browse these pages and pick out those terms that look interesting.

**accelerator key**    The underlined letter in a menu name or menu command.

**active partition**    A disk drive's bootable *partition*. Its boot sector tells the ROM BIOS at startup that this partition contains the operating system's bootstrap code. The active partition is usually the same as the *primary partition*.

**ad hoc wireless network**    A wireless network in which each node maintains only a temporary connection to the network. See also *infrastructure wireless network*.

**ADC**    See *analog-to-digital converter*.

**Address Resolution Protocol**    A network protocol that handles the conversion of an IP address to the *MAC address* of a network adapter.

**Advanced Power Management**    A specification developed by Microsoft and Intel that lets the operating system, applications, BIOS, and system hardware work cooperatively to manage power and extend battery life.

**allocation unit**    See *cluster*.

**amplitude**    A measure of a sound's loudness (that is, the strength of the sound wave's vibration). The greater the amplitude, the greater the motion of the sound wave's molecules, and the greater the impact on your eardrum. Amplitude is measured in decibels. See also *frequency*.

**analog-to-digital converter**    A chip in a sound card that converts analog sound waves to the digital audio format. See also *digital-to-analog converter* and *sampling*.

**APM**    See *Advanced Power Management*.

**AppData**    An environment variable that stores the folder that contains the current user's application data (usually %UserProfile%\ApplicationData).

**application compatibility**    A set of concepts and technologies that enable Windows XP to adjust its settings or behavior to compensate for the shortcomings of *legacy programs*. See also *Compatibility mode*.

**application-specific path**    A path to an executable file in which the path is also associated with the *primary name* of the executable filename. This enables a user to launch the executable by entering just the primary name in the Run dialog box or Command Prompt.

**ARP**    See *Address Resolution Protocol*.

**backup job**    A backup file that includes a list of files to back up, the type of backup to use (*full*, *differential*, or *incremental*), and the backup destination.

**base priority**    A ranking that determines the relative frequency with which a program gets *processor cycles*. A program given a higher frequency gets more cycles, which improves the program's performance.

**baud rate**    The number of signal changes (which might be variations in voltage or frequency, depending on the *modulation* standard being used) per second that can be exchanged between two *modems*. In most cases, this isn't the same as *bps*.

**bit rate**    The quality of a digital audio recording, usually measured in *Kbps*.

**bitmap**    An array of bits (pixels) that contains data that describes the colors found in an image.

**blue screen of death**    A screen with white text on a blue background that displays an error message after a system crash.

**Bluetooth**    A wireless networking standard that uses radio frequencies to set up a communications link between devices to create an *ad hoc wireless network*.

**boot code**    A portion of the *master boot record* that runs the core operating system files.

**BOOT.INI**    A hidden text located in the %SystemRoot% folder that holds the startup options that appear in the Windows XP OS Choices menu.

**bps**    Bits per second. The rate at which a *modem* or other communications device transmits data.

**bridge**    A *network* device that connects two *LANs*, provided that the two LANs are using the same *NOS*. The bridge can either be a standalone device or can be implemented in a server with the addition of a second network card.

**BSOD**    See *blue screen of death*.

**character spacing**    The amount of space allotted to each character in a *font*. A font's character spacing can be either *monospaced* or *proportional*.

**checkpoint**    See *restore point*.

**client**    In a *client/server network*, a computer that uses the services and resources provided to the network by a *server*.

**client/server network**    A *network* model that splits the computing workload into two separate but related areas. On the one hand, you have users working at intelligent front-end systems called *clients*. In turn, these client machines interact with powerful back-end systems called *servers*. The basic idea is that the clients have enough processing power to perform tasks on their own, but they rely on the servers to provide them with specialized resources or services, or access to information that would be impractical to implement on a client (such as a large database). See also *peer-to-peer network*.

**Clipboard**    A memory location used to store data that has been cut or copied from an application.

**cluster**    The basic unit of storage on a hard disk or floppy disk.

**cluster chain**    The sequence of *clusters* that defines an entire file.

**codec**    A compressor/decompressor device driver. During playback of audio or video data, the codec decompresses the data before sending it to the appropriate multimedia device. During recording, the codec decompresses the raw data so that it takes up less disk space. Most codecs offer a variety of compression ratios.

**color depth**    Determines the number of colors (that is, the color palette) available to your applications and graphics. Color depth is expressed in either bits or total colors. See also *High Color* and *True Color*.

**COM**    See *Component Object Model*.

**Compatibility mode**    A Windows XP operating mode that emulates the behavior of a previous version of Windows to enhance *application compatibility*.

**Component Object Model**    The heart and soul of *OLE*. It defines not only the standards that server applications use to create objects, but also the mechanisms by which server and container applications interact when dealing with objects.

**compound document**    A *container* document that holds, along with its native data, one or more *objects* that were created using *server applications*.

**compress**    To reduce the size of a file by replacing redundant character strings with tokens.

**concentrator**   See *hub*.

**connection-oriented protocol**   See *transport layer protocol*.

**connectionless protocol**   See *network layer protocol*.

**control set**   The system's drivers and hardware configuration.

**cookie**   A small text file that's stored on your computer and is used by websites to remember information about your session at that site: shopping cart data, page customizations, passwords, and so on.

**cross-linked cluster**   A *cluster* that has somehow been assigned to two different files, or that has two *FAT* entries that refer to the same cluster.

**cycles**   See *processor cycles*.

**DAC**   See *digital-to-analog converter*.

**data bits**   In *modem* data transfer, the number of bits used to represent a character.

**datagram**   An *IP packet*. The datagram header includes information such as the address of the *host* that sent the datagram and the address of the host that is supposed to receive the datagram.

**decorative**   A specially designed *typeface* that is supposed to convey a particular effect. See also *sans serif* and *serif*.

**delay**   When you press and hold down a key, the time interval between the appearance of the first character and the second character. See also *repeat rate*.

**demodulation**   The conversion into digital data of an analog wave (a series of tones) transmitted over a telephone line. This conversion is performed by a *modem*. See also *modulation*.

**device driver**   Small software programs that serve as intermediaries between hardware devices and the operating system. Device drivers encode software instructions into signals that the device understands, and, conversely, the drivers interpret device signals and report them to the operating system. See also *virtual device drivers*.

**Device Manager**   A tab in the System properties sheet that provides a graphical outline of all the devices on your system. It can show you the current configuration of each device (including the *IRQ, I/O ports,* and *DMA channel* used by each device). It even enables you to adjust a device's configuration (assuming that the device doesn't require you to make physical adjustments to, say, a DIP switch or jumper). The Device Manager actually gets its data from, and stores modified data in, the *Registry*.

**DHCP**   See *Dynamic Host Control Protocol*.

**differential backup**   Backs up only files in the current *backup job* that have changed since the last *full backup*. See also *incremental backup*.

**digital-to-analog converter**   A sound card chip that converts digitized audio back into an analog wave so that you can hear it. See also *analog-to-digital converter*.

**directory entry**    See *file directory*.

**DLL**    See *dynamic link library*.

**DMA**    Direct Memory Access. See also *DMA channel*.

**DMA channel**    A connection that lets a device transfer data to and from memory without going through the processor. The transfer is coordinated by a DMA controller chip.

**DNS**    See *Domain Name System*.

**Domain Name System**    On the Internet, a hierarchical distributed database system that converts *hostnames* into *IP addresses*.

**dotted-decimal notation**    A format used to represent *IP addresses*. The 32 bits of the address are divided into quads of 8 bits, which are then converted into their decimal equivalent and separated by dots (for example, 205.208.113.1).

**dotted-quad notation**    See *dotted-decimal notation*.

**double-click speed**    The time interval that Windows XP uses to distinguish between two successive single clicks and a double-click. Anything faster is handled as a double-click; anything slower is handled as two single clicks.

**Dynamic Host Control Protocol**    A system that manages the dynamic allocation of *IP addresses*.

**dynamic link library**    A file that contains a library of functions and other code used by programs.

**encryption**    The use of a complex mathematical formula to scramble a text message to make it unreadable.

**environment**    A small memory buffer that holds the DOS *environment variables*.

**environment variables**    Settings used to control certain aspects of DOS and DOS programs. For example, the `PATH`, the `PROMPT`, and the values of all `SET` statements are part of the environment.

**extended partition**    The hard disk space that isn't allocated to the *primary partition*. For example, if you have a 20GB disk and you allocate 5 GB to the primary partition, the extended partition will be 15GB. You can then subdivide the extended partition into *logical drives*.

**extension**    In a filename, the part to the right of the final period. Windows XP uses extensions to determine the *file type* of a file.

**FAT**    See *File Allocation Table*.

**FIFO buffer**    A 16-byte memory buffer included with 16550 and later *UART* chips that lets a serial port handle high-speed data transfers while reducing retransmissions and dropped characters.

**File Allocation Table**    A disk filing system that contains a 16-bit entry for every disk *cluster* that specifies whether the cluster is empty or bad, or else points to the next cluster number in the current file.

**file directory**    A table of contents for the files on a disk that is maintained by the *File Allocation Table*. The entries in the file directory specify each file's name, extension, size, attributes, and more.

**file transfer protocol**    In *modem* communications, this protocol governs various aspects of the file transfer ritual, including starting and stopping, the size of the data *packets* being sent, how errors are handled, and so on. Windows XP supports seven protocols: Xmodem, 1K Xmodem, Ymodem, Ymodem-G, Zmodem, Zmodem with Crash Recovery, and Kermit.

**File Transfer Protocol**    An Internet protocol that defines file transfers between computers. Part of the *TCP/IP* suite of protocols.

**file type**    A designation that identifies certain characteristics of a file, such as the data format. In Windows XP, file types are given by the file's *extension*.

**firewall**    A software program or device that allows only authorized traffic to enter and leave a network or computer.

**font**    A unique set of design characteristics that is common to a group of letters, numbers, and symbols. Four items define the font of any character: the *typeface*, the *type size*, the *type style*, and the *character spacing*.

**frequency**    Determines the pitch of a sound. This is a measure of the rate at which the sound wave's vibrations are produced. The higher the frequency, the higher the pitch. Frequency is measured in cycles per second, or *hertz* (Hz). See also *amplitude*.

**FTP**    See *File Transfer Protocol*.

**full backup**    Backs up all the files in the current *backup job*. See also *differential backup* and *incremental backup*.

**full-screen video**    Digital video that plays back in a 720×480-pixel window.

**gateway**    A *network* computer or other device that acts as a middleman between two otherwise-incompatible systems. The gateway translates the incoming and outgoing *packets* so that each system can work with the data.

**graphics adapter**    The internal component in your system that generates the output you see on your monitor.

**hardware flow control**    A system whereby the computer and *modem* use individual wires to send signals to each other that indicate whether they're ready to receive data. To stop outgoing data, the modem turns off its CTS (Clear To Send) line. To stop incoming data, the processor turns off its RTS (Request To Send) line. See also *software flow control*.

**hardware profile**    Hardware configurations in which Windows XP loads only specified *device drivers*.

**hertz**   Cycles per second. See *frequency.*

**Hibernation mode**   A Windows XP shutdown option that saves the current contents of memory (running programs, open documents, and so on) to a file on the hard disk and then shuts down the computer. When you turn the machine back on, Windows XP bypasses the usual startup routines and just restores the memory contents from the hibernation file.

**High Color**   A *color depth* of 16 bits, or 65,536 colors.

**hive**   A subset of the *Registry* that consists of one or more Registry keys, subkeys, and settings.

**host**   A computer on the Internet.

**hostname**   The unique name of an Internet *host* expressed as an English-language equivalent of an *IP address.*

**HTTP**   See *Hypertext Transfer Protocol.*

**hub**   A central connection point for *network* cables. They range in size from small boxes with a six or eight RJ-45 connectors to large cabinets with dozens of ports for various cable types.

**hyperlink**   In the Windows XP Help system, an underlined word or phrase that takes you to another topic or runs a program.

**hypertext**   In a World Wide Web page, an underlined word or phrase that takes you to a different website.

**Hypertext Transfer Protocol**   An Internet *protocol* that defines the format of *Uniform Resource Locator* addresses and how World Wide Web data is transmitted between a server and a browser. Part of the *TCP/IP* suite of protocols.

**Hz**   See *hertz.*

**idle sensitivity**   The amount of time that Windows XP waits before declaring a DOS program idle. In the absence of keyboard input, Windows XP just assumes that a DOS program is in an idle state after this predetermined amount of inactivity, and it then redirects to other running processes the *time slices* that it would otherwise devote to the DOS program.

**Internet Message Access Protocol**   A protocol that defines how to manage received email messages on a remote server, including viewing headers, creating folders, and searching message data.

**IMAP**   See *Internet Message Access Protocol.*

**incremental backup**   Backs up only files in the current *backup job* that have changed since the last *full backup* or the last *differential backup.*

**infrastructure wireless network**   A wireless network in which each node maintains a more-or-less permanent connection to the network. See also *ad hoc wireless network.*

**Internet Protocol**    A network layer protocol that defines the Internet's basic *packet* structure and its addressing scheme, and also handles routing of packets between *hosts*. See also *TCP/IP* and *Transmission Control Protocol*.

**internetwork**    A *network* that combines two or more *LANs* by means of a special device, such as a *bridge* or *router*. Internetworks are often called internets for short, but they shouldn't be confused with *the* Internet, the global collection of networks.

**interrupt request**    An instruction to the CPU that halts processing temporarily so that another operation (such as handling input or output) can take place. Interrupts can be generated by either hardware or software.

**Intranet**    The implementation of Internet technologies such as *TCP/IP* and World Wide Web servers for use within a corporate organization rather than for connection to the Internet as a whole.

**invalid cluster**    A *cluster* that falls under one of the following three categories:

- A *FAT* entry that refers to cluster 1. This is illegal because a disk's cluster numbers start at 2.

- A FAT entry that refers to a cluster number larger than the total number of clusters on the disk.

- A FAT entry of 0 (which normally denotes an unused cluster) that is part of a *cluster chain*.

**I/O port**    A memory address that the processor uses to communicate with a device directly. After a device has used its *IRQ line* to catch the processor's attention, the actual exchange of data or commands takes place through the device's I/O port address.

**IP**    See *Internet Protocol*.

**IP address**    The unique address to assigned to every *host* and *router* on the Internet. IP addresses are 32-bit values that are usually expressed in *dotted-decimal notation*. See also *hostname*.

**IP Security**    A *virtual private networking* protocol that encrypts network data (IP packets only), sets up the *tunneling*, and encapsulates the encrypted network packets in an IP packet for transport across the tunnel.

**IPSec**    See *IP Security*.

**IPX/SPX**    Internet Packet eXchange/ Sequenced Packet eXchange. IPX is a *network layer protocol* that addresses and routes *packets* from one *network* to another on an IPX *internetwork*. SPX, on the other hand, is a *transport layer protocol* that enhances the IPX protocol by providing reliable delivery. IPX/SPX is used by NetWare networks.

**IRQ line**    A hardware line over which peripherals and software can send *interrupt requests*.

**IRQ sharing**   The management of *interrupt requests* in such a way that two or more devices can share the same *IRQ line* without conflicting with each other.

**Kbps**   One thousand bits per second (*bps*).

**LAN**   See *local area network*.

**legacy device**   A hardware device that doesn't support *Plug and Play*.

**legacy key**   A key included in the Windows XP *Registry* for backwards-compatibility with older programs.

**legacy program**   A program designed for an older operating system. See also *application compatibility*.

**local area network**   A *network* in which all the computers occupy a relatively small geographical area, such as a department, office, home, or building. All the connections between computers are made via network cables.

**local resource**   Any peripheral, file, folder, or application that is either attached directly to your computer or resides on your computer's hard disk. See also *remote resource*.

**lossy**   Describes a compression scheme that loses some data during the compression process.

**lost cluster**   A *cluster* that, according to the *FAT*, is associated with a file but has no link to any entry in the *file directory*. Lost clusters are typically caused by program crashes, power surges, or power outages.

**MAC address**   The Media Access Control address, which is the physical address of a network adapter.

**master boot record**   The first 512-byte sector on your system's *active partition* (the partition your system boots from). Most of the MBR consists of a small program that locates and runs the core operating system files.

**Master File Table**   The *file directory* used on an NTFS *partition*.

**Mbps**   One million bits per second (*bps*).

**MBR**   See *master boot record*.

**Messenger service spam**   Unsolicited commercial messages sent to a Windows machine using the Messenger service that is normally used for broadcasting messages to network users. The Windows Firewall blocks Messenger service spam.

**MFT**   See *Master File Table*.

**MIDI**   See *Musical Instrument Digital Interface*.

**modem**   A device used to transmit data between computers via telephone lines. See also *modulation* and *demodulation*.

**modulation**   The conversion, performed by a *modem,* of digital data into an analog wave (a series of tones) that can be transmitted over a telephone line. See also *demodulation*.

**monospaced**   A font that allots the same amount of space to each character. Skinny letters such as "i" and "l" take up as much space as wider letters, such as "m" and "w." See also *proportional*.

**Moore's Law**   Processing power doubles every 18 months (from Gordon Moore, cofounder of Intel).

**multimedia**   The computer-based presentation of data using multiple modes of communication, including text, graphics, sound, animation, and video.

**multitasking**   See *cooperative multitasking* and *preemptive multitasking*.

**multithreading**   A multitasking model in which multiple *threads* run simultaneously.

**munge**   To alter your email address, particularly one associated with a newsgroup account, by adding text that invalidates the address but is still obvious for other people to figure out.

**Musical Instrument Digital Interface**   A communications protocol that standardizes the exchange of data between a computer and a musical synthesizer.

**name resolution**   A process that converts a *hostname* into an *IP address*. See *Domain Name System* and *Windows Internet Name Service*.

**NetBEUI**   The NetBIOS Extended User Interface *protocol*. (NetBIOS is an API that lets network applications   such as *redirectors*—communicate with *networking* protocols.) It's a combined *transport layer protocol* and *network layer protocol*.

**NetBIOS**   A network protocol that handles the conversion between the network names of computers and their IP addresses.

**network**   A collection of computers connected via special cables or other network media (such as *Wi-Fi*) in order to share files, folders, disks, peripherals, and applications.

**network adapter**   See *network interface card*.

**network interface card**   An adapter that usually slips into an expansion bus slot inside a *client* or *server* computer. (There are also external *NICs* that plug into parallel ports or PC Card slots.) The NIC's main purpose is to serve as the connection point between the PC and the *network*. The NIC's backplate (the portion of the NIC that you can see when the card is installed) contains one or more ports into which you plug a network cable.

**network layer protocol**   A *protocol* in which no communications channel is established between nodes. Instead, the protocol builds each *packet* with all the information required for the network to deliver each packet and for the destination *node* to assemble everything. See also *transport layer protocol*.

**Network News Transport Protocol**   An Internet *protocol* that defines how Usenet newsgroups and postings are transmitted; part of the *TCP/IP* suite of protocols.

**network place**   A shared folder on a network computer.

**network operating system**   Operating system software that runs on a *network server* and provides the various network services for the network *clients*.

**New Technology File System**    See *NTFS*.

**NIC**    See *network interface card*.

**NNTP**    See *Network News Transport Protocol*.

**node**    A computer on a *network*.

**NOS**    See *network operating system*.

**notification area**    The box on the right side of the taskbar that Windows XP uses to display icons that tell you the current state of the system.

**NTFS**    An advanced file system that supports files up to 2TB in size and enables users to apply encryption and enhanced security to the folders and files on an NTFS *partition*.

**object**    A separate entity or component that is distinguished by its properties and actions. In the *OLE* world, an object is not only data—a slice of text, a graphic, a sound, a chunk of a spreadsheet, or whatever—but also one or more functions for creating, accessing, and using that data.

**packet**    The data transfer unit used in *network* and *modem* communications. Each packet contains not only data, but also a **header** that contains information about which machine sent the data, which machine is supposed to receive the data, and a few extra tidbits that let the receiving computer put all the original data together in the correct order and check for errors that might have cropped up during the transmission.

**paging file**    A special file used by the *Memory Pager* to emulate physical memory. If you open enough programs or data files that physical memory becomes exhausted, the paging file is brought into play to augment memory storage; also called a **swap file**.

**parity bit**    In *modem* data transfers that use seven *data bits,* this is an extra bit that lets the receiving system check the integrity of each character.

**Parkinson's Law of Data**    Data expands to fill the space available for storage (from the original Parkinson's Law: Work expands to fill the time available).

**partition**    A section of a hard drive that has been configured to act as a separate disk drive.

**partition table**    A portion of the *master boot record* that contains data about the various *partitions* on your system.

**PCM**    See *Pulse Code Modulation*.

**peer-to-peer network**    A *network* in which no one computer is singled out to provide special services. Instead, all the computers attached to the network have equal status (at least as far as the network is concerned), and all the computers can act as both *servers* and *clients*. See also *client/server network*.

**permissions**    For a *user account*, the *privileges* that define the user's access to system resources, such as whether the user can view, create, change, and delete objects.

**playlist**    A customized collection of digital music files defined in Windows Media Player.

**Plug and Play**    A set of technologies that enables the operating to automatically recognize and configure a device as soon as it's attached to a computer.

**Point-to-Point Tunneling Protocol**    A *virtual private networking* protocol that sets up *tunneling* and encapsulates the encrypted network packets in an IP packet for transport across the tunnel. See also *IP Security*.

**port forwarding**    Setting up a router or gateway to take data that comes in on a particular port and forward it to a specified computer on a network.

**port number**    A 16-bit number that uniquely identifies each running process on a computer. See also *socket*.

**POST**    At system startup, the POST detects and tests memory, ports, and basic devices such as the video adapter, keyboard, and disk drives. If everything passes, your system emits a single beep.

**Power-On Self Test**    See *POST*.

**PPTP**    See *Point-to-Point Tunneling Protocol*.

**prefetching**    A Windows XP performance feature that analyzes disk usage and then reads into memory the data that you or your system accesses most frequently.

**primary name**    In a filename, the part to the left of the period.

**primary partition**    The first partition (drive C) on a hard disk. See also *active partition* and *extended partition*.

**privileges**    *User account* properties that define *permissions* and *rights*.

**processor cycles**    Thin slivers of computing time that the processor doles out to each running program or process.

**property sheet**    A dialog box with controls that enable you to manipulate various properties of the underlying *object*.

**proportional**    A *font* that varies the amount of space given to each character according to the actual width of the letter. See also *monospaced*.

**protected mode**    An operating mode introduced with the 80286 microprocessor. Unlike *real mode,* which can address only up to 640KB of memory and gives a running program direct access to hardware, protected mode lets software use memory beyond 640KB. It also sets up a protection scheme so that multiple programs can share the same computer resources without stepping on each other's toes (and, usually, crashing the system).

**protocol**    A set of standards that defines how information is exchanged between two systems across a *network* connection. See also *transport layer protocol* and *network layer protocol*.

**Pulse Code Modulation**    A technique that converts analog sound into digital format by taking "snapshots" of the analog wave at discrete intervals and noting the wave's *amplitude*. These amplitude values form the basis of the digital representation of the wave; also called *sampling*.

**real mode**    The operating mode of early Intel microprocessors (the 8088 and 8086). It's a single-tasking mode in which the running program has full access to the computer's memory and peripherals. Windows XP doesn't use real mode. See also *protected mode.*

**Registry**    A central repository that Windows XP uses to store anything and everything that applies to your system's configuration. This includes hardware settings, object properties, operating system settings, and application options.

**remote resource**    Any peripheral, file, folder, or application that exists somewhere on the *network.* See also *local resource.*

**repeat rate**    When you press and hold down a key, the speed at which the characters appear. See also *delay.*

**repeater**    A device that boosts a *network* cable's signal so that the length of the network can be extended. Repeaters are needed because copper-based cables suffer from attenuation—a phenomenon in which the degradation of the electrical signal carried over the cable is proportional to the distance the signal has to travel.

**residential gateway**    On a home network, a computer or router that connects to the Internet.

**restore point**    A snapshot of the current system that includes the currently installed program files, Registry settings, and other crucial system data.

**rights**    For a *user account,* the *privileges* that define the user's ability to run system tasks, such as installing devices and updating the system.

**rip**    To transfer tracks from an audio CD to a computer.

**router**    A device that makes decisions about where to send the *network packets* it receives. Unlike a *bridge,* which merely passes along any data that comes its way, a router examines the address information in each packet and then determines the most efficient route that the packet must take to reach its eventual destination.

**routing**    The process whereby *packets* travel from *host* to host until they eventually reach their destination.

**RTS/CTS flow control**    See *hardware flow control.*

**safe mode**    A Windows XP startup mode that loads a minimal system configuration. Safe mode is useful for troubleshooting problems caused by incorrect or corrupt device drivers.

**sample depth**    The number of bits used to digitize an audio sample using *Pulse Code Modulation.*

**sampling**    See *Pulse Code Modulation* and *analog-to-digital converter.*

**sans serif**    A *typeface* that doesn't contain the cross strokes found in a *serif* typeface. See also *decorative.*

**security group**    A collection of *user accounts* defined with a specific set of *permissions* and *rights*, and any user added to a group is automatically granted that group's permissions and rights.

**serif**    A *typeface* that contains fine cross strokes (called **feet**) at the extremities of each character. See also *sans serif* and *decorative*.

**server**    In a *client/server network,* a computer that provides and manages services (such as file and print sharing and security) for the users on the network.

**service**    A program or process that performs a specific, low-level support function for the operating system or for an installed program.

**shared DLL**    A *DLL* used by two or more programs.

**shortcut**    A pointer to an executable file or a document. Double-clicking the shortcut starts the program or loads the document.

**shortcut menu**    A menu that appears when you right-click an object. The context menu gives you access to the properties and actions associated with that object.

**signature**    A few lines of text at the end of an email message that identify the sender and include his contact information (such as his company name, email address, and fax number).

**Simple Mail Transport Protocol**    An Internet protocol that describes the format of Internet email messages and how messages get delivered. Part of the *TCP/IP* suite of protocols.

**SMTP**    See *Simple Mail Transport Protocol.*

**SMTP authentication**    An ISP anti-spam feature that requires you to log on to your ISP's *SMTP server* to verify that you are the person sending the message through your account.

**SMTP server**    A server used by an ISP to process outgoing email messages.

**socket**    In the *Transmission Control Protocol,* a communications channel between two *hosts* that consists of their *IP addresses* and *port numbers.*

**software flow control**    A system whereby the computer and *modem* send signals to each other that indicate whether they're ready to receive data. To stop the transfer, a device sends an XOFF signal (ASCII 19 or Ctrl-S). To restart the transfer, a device sends an XON signal (ASCII 17 or Ctrl-Q). See also *hardware flow control.*

**start bit**    An extra bit added to the beginning of the *data bits* in a *modem* data transfer. This bit marks the beginning of each character. See also *stop bit.*

**stop bit**    An extra bit (or sometimes two) added to the end of the *data bits* in a *modem* data transfer. This bit marks the end of each character. See also *start bit.*

**subnet mask**    A 32-bit value, usually expressed in *dotted-decimal notation,* that lets *IP* separate a network ID from a full *IP address* and thus determine whether the source and destination hosts are on the same network.

**swap file**    See *paging file.*

**system cache**    A portion of memory that holds recently used data for faster access.

**system state**    The system files that Windows XP requires to operate properly, including the files used during system startup, the Windows XP protected system files, and the *Registry* files.

**SystemDrive**    An environment variable that stores the partition in which Windows XP was installed (usually C).

**SystemRoot**    An environment variable that stores the folder in which Windows XP was installed (usually C:\Windows).

**TCP**    See *Transmission Control Protocol.*

**TCP/IP**    Transmission Control Protocol/Internet Protocol. TCP/IP is the *lingua franca* of most UNIX systems and the Internet as a whole. However, TCP/IP is also an excellent choice for other types of *networks* because it's routable, robust, and reliable.

**thread**    A small chunk of executable code with a very narrow focus. In a spreadsheet, for example, you might have one thread for recalculating, another for printing, and a third for accepting keyboard input. See also *multithreading.*

**time slice**    A fixed number of *processor cycles.*

**topology**    Describes how the various *nodes* that comprise a *network*—which include not only the computers, but also devices such as *hubs* and *bridges*—are connected.

**Transmission Control Protocol**    A *transport layer protocol* that sets up a connection between two *hosts* and ensures that data is passed between them reliably. If *packets* are lost or damaged during transmission, TCP takes care of retransmitting the packets. See also *Internet Protocol* and *TCP/IP.*

**transport layer protocol**    A *protocol* in which a virtual communications channel is established between two systems. The protocol uses this channel to send *packets* between *nodes.* See also *network layer protocol.*

**True Color**    A *color depth* of 24 bits, or 16,777,216 colors.

**tunneling**    A *virtual private networking* technology that establishes a connection over a public network between two computers using a specific port.

**typeface**    A distinctive design that is common to any related set of letters, numbers, and other symbols. This design gives each character a particular shape and thickness that is unique to the typeface and difficult to categorize. However, three main typeface types serve to distinguish all typefaces: *serif, sans serif,* and *decorative.*

**type size**    A measure of the height of a *font.* Type size is measured from the highest point of a tall letter, such as "f," to the lowest point of an underhanging letter, such as "g." The standard unit of measurement is the point. There are 72 points in an inch.

**type style**    Extra attributes added to a font's *typeface,* such as **bold** and *italic.* Other type styles (often called **type effects**) include underlining and ~~strikeout~~ (sometimes called **strikethrough**).

**UART**    Universal Asynchronous Receiver/Transmitter. A special chip that resides inside every serial port (or sometimes on the computer's motherboard). (For an internal or PC Card modem, the UART chip sits on the card itself.) It's the UART's job (among other things) to take the computer's native parallel data and convert it into a series of bits that can be spit out of the serial port's Transmit Data line. On the other end, individual bits streaming into the destination serial port's Receive Data line are reassembled by the UART into the parallel format that the processor prefers.

**Uniform Resource Locator**    An Internet addressing scheme that spells out the exact location of a Net resource. Most URLs take the following form:

`protocol://host.domain/directory/file.name`

| | |
|---|---|
| `protocol` | The TCP/IP protocol to use for retrieving the resource (such as HTTP or FTP) |
| `host.domain` | The domain name of the host computer where the resource resides |
| `directory` | The host directory that contains the resource |
| `file.name` | The filename of the resource |

**URL**    See *Uniform Resource Locator.*

**user account**    A user name (and an optional password) that uniquely identifies a person who uses the system and specifies that person's *privileges.*

**user profile**    A set of customization options associated with a *user account.* Each profile includes most of Windows XP's customization options, including the colors, patterns, wallpapers, desktop icons, screen saver, and programs that appear on the Start menu.

**UserProfile**    An environment variable that stores the folder that contains the current user's documents and settings (usually `%SystemDrive%\Documents and Settings\`*Username*).

**virtual device driver**    A 32-bit *Protected-mode device driver.*

**virtual machine**    A separate section of memory that simulates the operation of an entire computer. Virtual machines were born with the release of Intel's 80386 microprocessor. Thanks to *Protected mode,* the 80386 circuitry could address up to 4 GB of memory. Using this potentially huge address space, the 80386 allowed software to carve out separate chunks of memory and use these areas to emulate the full operation of a computer. This emulation is so complete and so effective that a program running in a virtual machine thinks it's dealing with a real computer. Combined with the resource-sharing features of *Protected mode,* virtual machines can run their programs simultaneously without bumping into each other.

**virtual memory**    Memory created by allocating hard disk space and making it look to applications as though they are dealing with physical RAM.

**virtual private networking**   A system of protocols that uses *tunneling* to secure access to a private network over a public connection, such as the Internet or a phone line.

**VPN**   See *virtual private networking*.

**VxD**   See *virtual device driver*.

**WAN**   See *wide area network*.

**wardriving**   An activity where a person drives through various neighborhoods with a portable computer or other device set up to look for available wireless networks. If the person finds a nonsecured network, he uses it for free Internet access or to cause mischief with shared network resources.

**waveform audio**   A process that re-creates an audio waveform by using digital samples of the waveform. This is the standard Windows sound format.

**web bug**   An image that resides on a remote server and that is added to an HTML-formatted email message by referencing a URL on the remote server.

**wide area network**   A *network* that consists of two or more *LANs* or *internetworks* that are spaced out over a relatively large geographical area, such as a state, country, or the entire world. The networks in a WAN typically are connected via high-speed fiber-optic phone lines, microwave dishes, or satellite links.

**Wi-Fi**   A set of wireless networking standards used to create *wireless infrastructure networks*. The two most popular iterations are 802.11b, which has a theoretical top speed of 11 Mbps, and 802.11g, which has a theoretical speed limit of 54 Mbps.

**Windows Internet Name Service**   A service that maps NetBIOS names (the names you assign to computers in the Identification tab of the Network properties sheet) to the *IP addresses* assigned via *DHCP*.

**WINS**   See *Windows Internet Name Service*.

**wirehead**   An expert in the hardware aspects of computers.

**wireless access point**   A device that receives and transmits signals from wireless computers to form an *infrastructure wireless network*.

**wireless gateway**   A type of *wireless access point* that connects to a broadband modem to give all of the computers on the network access to the Internet.

**wireless hotspot**   A location that allows wireless computers to use the location's Internet connection.

**write caching**   A Windows XP performance feature in which the system doesn't flush changed data to the hard disk until the system is idle.

**XON/XOFF flow control**   See *software flow control*.

# Index

## SYMBOLS

## NUMBERS

*How can we make this index more useful? Email us at indexes@samspublishing.com*

*How can we make this index more useful? Email us at indexes@samspublishing.com*

*How can we make this index more useful? Email us at indexes@samspublishing.com*

# L

types, 356-357

voice calls, 379

   firewalls, unblocking, 381-382

   Internet/network calls, 382-383

   options, 383-384

   placing, 380

   speed dialing, 385-386

**Modems tab (Phone and Modem Options dialog box), 366**

**modulation, 352-355**

**modulator/demodulator.** *See* **modems**

**MOH (Modem On Hook), 355**

**monitoring performance, 255**

   memory-related issues, 258

   remotely, 628

   System Monitor, 259-260

   Task Manager, 256-259

**Motion Picture Experts Group (MPEG), 93**

**Motion Picture Experts Groups Audio Level 3 (MP3), 87**

**mouse**

   icon, 164

   objects, selecting, 35

**moving**

   Control Panel

      Start menu, 169

      Taskbar, 168

   email messages to folders, 504

   favorites, 467

   files/folders

      cutting and pasting, 36

      dragging and dropping, 37-39

      Send To command, 39-40

   insertion point, 689

   My Documents folder, 55

   page files, 273

**MP3 (Motion Picture Experts Groups Audio Level 3), 87**

**MPEG (Motion Picture Experts Group), 93**

**MPPE (Microsoft Point-to-Point Encryption), 657**

**MSBA (Microsoft Baseline Security Analyzer), 300**

**MT-NewsWatcher, 533**

**multibutton dialog boxes, 218-219**

**multimedia**

   backups, 294

   Internet Explorer options, 493-495

   playing, 239

   Windows Media Player

      always-on-top view, 96

      audio CDs, copying, 98-101

      codec downloads, 96

      Internet connections, 98

      keyboard shortcuts, 691

      Library, 98

      licenses, 98

      media files, 94-95, 101-103

      music files, adding, 98

      playback options, 95, 98

      playlists, 103

      privacy, 576

      screen savers, 98

      security, 575-576

      skin mode, 97

      updates, 95

**Multipurpose Internet Mail Extensions (MIME), 516**

**multistation access unit (MAU), 596**

**museum domain, 440**

**Music Album folder template, 109**

**Music Artist folder template, 109**

**Music folder template, 109**

**Musical Instrument Digital Interface (MIDI), 88**

**.mx domain, 441**

**My Documents folder, 55**

**My Music folder, 104**

# O

*How can we make this index more useful? Email us at indexes@samspublishing.com*

# Q

*How can we make this index more useful? Email us at indexes@samspublishing.com*

*How can we make this index more useful? Email us at indexes@samspublishing.com*

*How can we make this index more useful? Email us at indexes@sampspublishing.com*

# X - Y - Z